Let This Voice Be Heard

Let This Voice Be Heard

Anthony Benezet, Father of Atlantic Abolitionism

MAURICE JACKSON

PENN

University of Pennsylvania Press

Philadelphia

Published by
University of Pennsylvania Press
Philadelphia, Pennsylvania 19104–4112

Printed in the United States of America on acid-free paper
10 9 8 7 6 5 4 3 2 1

Library of Congress Cataloging-in-Publication Data

Jackson, Maurice.
    Let this voice be heard : Anthony Benezet, father of Atlantic abolitionism / Maurice Jackson.
        p.   cm.
    Includes bibliographical references and index.
    ISBN 978-0-8122-4129-7 (alk. paper)
    1. Benezet, Anthony, 1713–1784.   2. Abolitionists—United
States—Biography.   3. Quakers—United States—Biography.
4. Antislavery movements—United States—History—18th century.
I. Title.
E446.J33 2009
326′.8092—dc22
    [B]   2008040902

*To Laura, my heart, Lena, my soul,
and Miles, my inspiration*

Contents

Introduction

Three men, three black men, who wrote in three different centuries, led me to the study of the French-born, Philadelphia-based Quaker antislavery leader Anthony Benezet. Olaudah Equiano first alerted me to Benezet in his *The Interesting Narrative of the Life of Olaudah Equiano* (1789), with his references to "see Anthony Benezet throughout" to bolster his own description of the Africa of his youth before the arrival of the Europeans. In 1899 W. E. B. Du Bois, the historian, sociologist, and driving force behind the Niagara Movement, the National Association for the Advancement of Colored People, and the concept of pan-Africanism, wrote that "Anthony Benezet and the Friends of Philadelphia have the honor of first recognizing the fact that the welfare of the State demands the education of the Negro children." DuBois went on to note that "on motion of one, probably Benezet, it was decided that instruction ought to be provided for Negro children."[1]

In 1917 Carter G. Woodson, the founder of Negro History Month, wrote of the nation's debt to Benezet, who "obtained many of his facts about the suffering of slaves from the Negroes themselves, moving among them in their homes, at the places where they worked, or on the wharves where they stopped when traveling. To diffuse this knowledge where it would be most productive of the desired results, he talked with tourists and corresponded with every influential person whom he could reach."[2] Woodson later published many of the early Quaker appeals against slavery in the journal. Blacks like Equiano, Quobna Ottobah Cugoano, Ignatius Sancho, Richard Allen, Lemuel Haynes, Absalom Jones, James Forten, and subsequent generations of black leaders were deeply influenced by Benezet's contribution to the intellectual and social debates of the day.

Benezet founded the African Free School in Philadelphia, and future black leaders as Jones and Forten, who founded (in April 1787) the Free African Society at the home of Richard Allen, studied at Quaker schools. The society's articles of incorporation were written under the aura of Benezet. In January 1789 the society began to hold its meetings at what became known as the African School House, which had been founded by Benezet. The society began circulating petitions modeled in part on Benezet's earlier ones, and Forten's opposition to colonialization schemes was similar to that of Benezet, who was an early advocate of giving land to free blacks.

Benezet closely collaborated with the Quaker leader John Woolman. In 1754 they wrote the Quaker document *Epistles of Caution and Advice, Concerning the Buying and Keeping of Slaves*, which opposed slavery. The same year, Woolman published his *Some Considerations on the Keeping of Negroes*, which Benezet probably edited. In 1775 Benezet became the first president of the Society for the Relief of Free Negroes Unlawfully Held in Bondage. In 1784, a few months before Benezet's death, Benjamin Franklin and others reformed this organization into the Pennsylvania Society for Promoting the Abolition of Slavery and for the Relief of Negroes Unlawfully Held in Bondage; and for Improving the Conditions of the African Race. In 1787 Franklin took the honorary helm of this organization. Benezet had a transformative influence on Franklin, turning a former slave owner into the president of the Abolition Society.

Benezet similarly led Benjamin Rush into the struggle for black freedom. Under Benezet's tutelage Rush wrote anonymous tracts condemning slavery and followed Franklin as the head of the Society for the Abolition of Slavery in 1803. Benezet corresponded with a wide range of leading political figures, like Henry Laurens, Patrick Henry, John Jay, and other future leaders of the American Republic, on his concerns about slavery.

Benezet applied Quaker principles to his work with the enslaved Africans. Unlike most of his contemporaries, even those in the antislavery movement itself, he believed that all people were born equal in God's sight. He advocated a policy of nonviolence and disapproved of excessive material acquisitions and consumption. His observations led him to link Europeans, especially the British, with "the love of wealth" that he believed was brought on by the burgeoning Atlantic slave trade. Benezet argued that wealth drove men and nations to war; he contrasted that constant desire for wealth in his own society with an image of African societies that he derived from travel narratives and discussions with enslaved and free Africans. He believed that prior to the slave trade Africans lived in relative peace and freedom, with an abundance of the necessities of life. He asserted that the trade morally corrupted Europeans as well as some Africans, who became accomplices in the buying and selling of their fellows.

Benezet addressed his works to such men as Granville Sharp, Thomas Clarkson, and John Wesley, founders of the British abolition movement and of the Society for the Relief of the Free Negroes Unlawfully Held in Bondage. The English leaders all relied on Benezet's work, above all his writings about Africa. They frequently cited him; all spoke of him as the "father" of their movement. The correspondence between Benezet and the pioneer British abolitionist Granville Sharp proved to be one of the first links in the transnational fight against slavery and the slave trade. The two men collaborated in the famous Somerset case. Sharp had copies of

Benezet's pamphlets delivered to Lord Chief Justice Mansfield, his fellow jurists, and Somerset's legal counsel just before the trial; indeed, Somerset himself delivered the copies to his counsel.

Together Sharp and Benezet developed new methods of furthering the antislavery cause. They joined forces with Wesley, whose *Thoughts upon Slavery* (1774) is based almost entirely on Benezet's *Some Historical Account of Guinea.* Like Benezet in the colonies, Wesley conducted broad petition campaigns against slavery, collecting 229,000 signatures on one antislavery petition to Parliament. Through Wesley, Benezet's work reached the preacher's close friend William Wilberforce.

Wilberforce quoted Benezet (without attribution) at length in the great 1792 parliamentary debates on ending the slave trade. At that time a motion was forwarded in favor of abolishing that trade—the first such action taken in any parliamentary body in the world.[3] Although it did not win passage, it marked the beginning of the end of the international slave trade.

Benezet also corresponded with the founders of the Société des Amis des Noirs (Society of the Friends of the Blacks) in Paris. Among these men were Jacques-Pierre Brissot; Nicolas de Caritat, marquis de Condorcet, the leading French philosopher of the time and a defender of human rights, especially for women and blacks; Etienne Clavière; Honoré Gabriel Victor Riqueti, comte de Mirabeau, the most prominent leader of the National Assembly; Abbé Guillaume-Thomas Raynal, a Jesuit priest who left the order to devote his life to politics; and Abbé Henri Grégoire, the leading antislavery figure during the French Revolution. At the opening meeting of the Société in Paris, Brissot praised "the immortal Benezet" as the "founder" of the antislavery movement, and the Société voted to translate his antislavery writings into French. Later, when speaking of Granville Sharp, Brissot could think of no higher praise than to call him a "second Benezet."

Like many writers of the time—particularly dissenters in the English-speaking world—Benezet relied heavily on biblical citations to buttress his arguments. Unlike the early Quaker opponents of slavery, he also used Enlightenment philosophy and practical life. He followed Montesquieu's argument in *The Spirit of Laws* (1748) that slavery had a destructive effect on both the state and free men therein; Benezet noted that slavery destroyed the white soul and the black body. He was also deeply influenced by the Scottish moral philosophers. He agreed with legal theorist George Wallace, who wrote in his *System of the Principles of the Law of Scotland* (1760), "Men in their liberty are not *in comercia*, they are not either saleable or purchasable."[4] Benezet quoted from the Scottish philosopher Francis Hutcheson, who in his *System of Moral Philosophy* (published 1755) declared "no endowments natural or acquired, can give a perfect right to assume power over others, without their consent."[5] Like Adam Smith, Benezet argued that slavery diminished the productive capacity and corrupted the morals of both races.

Benezet mediated the political and social output of the *philosophes* along with the ideas of ordinary people derived from the empirical reality around them. His "good works" show the extent to which ideas moved in both directions, while his writing relied on intellectual scaffolding provided by such great thinkers as Hutcheson or Montesquieu. He disseminated his ideas through petitions, letters, and pamphlets, and his tactics—the educating of blacks and the formation of abolitionist societies in America and Europe—were the pivotal forces in igniting the Atlantic antislavery crusade in the eighteenth century.

Benezet challenged the way many early leaders viewed Africa by offering empirical evidence of Africans before the arrival of the Europeans. He analyzed early travelers' accounts (including those of Richard Jobson, André Brüe, Jean Barbot, John Atkins, and Willem Bosman) and early scientific and literary writings. He combined this research with his study of early utopian thinkers, discussions with Afro-Philadelphians, and an understanding of Quaker ideals to refute the standard proslavery depiction of Africa. His writings on Africa offered a view of many of the different peoples of Africa at work, worship, leisure, communal and community activities, and child rearing.

To refute arguments about the innate inequality of blacks, he read everything possible about African civilization. His writings were used in some of the first North American courses that discussed the positive contributions of Africa and her peoples. His command of languages allowed him to study travelers' journals in French, English, German, and Dutch and to visualize the African continent before European domination. He lived as a humanist, visualizing and trying to feel the suffering of the enslaved blacks and sensing the pain of slavery within his soul as surely as the blacks did upon their flesh. In truth, he was one of the first white intellectuals to forcefully make the argument that Africans were indeed human beings, worthy of God's and man's graces. He was not merely against slavery and the slave trade; he was for the freedom and equality of the blacks. These ideas set him apart from his fellow abolitionists, many of whom eventually came to accept his beliefs.

His most important works on Africa were *A Short Account of That Part of Africa Inhabited by the Negroes: With Respect to the Fertility of the Country, the Good Disposition of Many of the Natives, and the Manner by Which the Slave-Trade Is Carried On* (1762) and *Some Historical Account of Guinea, Its Situation, Produce, and the General Disposition of Its Inhabitants, With an Inquiry into the Rise and Progress of the Slave Trade, Its Nature and Lamentable Effects* (1771). These works were reprinted many times in Philadelphia and London and also appeared in France, Ireland, Germany, and Scotland. Seven other of his pamphlets dealt exclusively with slavery. *Some Historical Account of Guinea* became one of the first American school textbooks about Africa.

Anthony Benezet was a many-faceted figure. When kidnapped blacks were transported through Philadelphia on their way south, Benezet intervened to obtain their freedom. When Acadian prisoners of war rotted in ship holds in the Philadelphia harbor, Benezet intervened to succor them. As a Quaker educator he developed new ways to teach students to read, publishing *An Essay on Grammar* (1778) and *The Pennsylvania Spelling Book* (1778). He taught Quaker youth methods to solve complex mathematical problems and used his mathematical knowledge to gather statistics against the slave trade. Near the end of his life he renewed a study of the plight of the Native Americans and in 1784 published *Some Observations on the Situation, Disposition and Character of the Indian Natives of This Continent*. He was a genuine social reformer, who, like others who have sought to alleviate human suffering, used every possible means to achieve goals of equality and justice.

Benezet's dream was to create a transatlantic antislavery movement to free the enslaved Africans from their misery and to establish a network to support and educate blacks once freed. His dream was to educate whites both about their complicity with slavery and about their obligations to blacks, their duty to humankind. He may not have been as overtly zealous or radical in his views as the nineteenth-century abolitionist martyrs John Brown and Nat Turner, or as well known as Frederick Douglass and William Lloyd Garrison, but he exerted a transcendent influence among his contemporaries who made their voices known against slavery. Little wonder that the founders of both the British antislavery movement, Sharp and Clarkson, and of the French antislavery movement, Brissot and the Société, all regarded Benezet as the founding father of that movement in the Atlantic world.

David Brion Davis has written that Benezet "acted as a kind of middleman of ideas who was led by antislavery zeal to collect and disseminate a radical secular philosophy."[6] Yet Benezet was much more. Rush understood it better when he wrote, "If a person called upon him who was going [on] a journey, his first thoughts usually were, how would he make him an instrument in its favor; and he either gave him tracts to distribute, or sent him letters by him, or he gave him some commission on the subject, so that he was the means of employing several persons at the same time, in various parts of America, in advancing the work he had undertaken."[7]

What set Benezet apart from others of his era was his great imagination in developing new methods not just to disseminate other people's antislavery ideas but also to develop a new ideology of antislavery rhetoric to develop a powerful new rhetoric to express a radical new antislavery ideology and to organize antislavery political activities. In America, Britain, and France fellow antislavery activists adopted and refined his methods of petitioning legislatures, lobbying religious figures, and writing to men and women high and low.

The challenge of Benezet's life is the challenge of Atlantic history forged beyond the boundaries of any single nation-state. The task for the historian is to link the thoughts and actions of an individual to the multiple international contexts in which he lived. By reading Benezet's writings and correspondence and by linking his ideas and reflections to their essential contexts—to Africa and the narratives of the slave trade; to England, France, and America and the history of the antislavery movements; to Europe and philosophical debates about human rights and to scientific controversies about race and civilization; to Afro-America and the social, intellectual, and political evolution of the Atlantic slave systems—we can better understand the spread of the new antislavery ideology and the monumental tasks that confronted its proponents. Always at the very root of Benezet's thinking was the belief that black men, women, and children were indeed human beings and equal to all others.

Historians have recently returned to the serious consideration of an idea promulgated by R. R. Palmer in his 1958 classic, *The Age of the Democratic Revolution*. Palmer and the French historian Jacques Godechot argued that the revolutionary events of the Atlantic world had to be viewed collectively, as an outgrowth of intellectual, political, economic, and social developments. Palmer traced direct connections among revolutions in the English colonies, France, and the Netherlands—in short, in the entire Atlantic world. Neither Palmer nor Godechot, however, thoroughly examined the role that race, slavery, and slave revolts played in shaping the dynamics of the revolutionary-era Atlantic community. They largely ignored the obvious connections between the struggle for black emancipation in the West Indies and the evolving struggle for human rights in France and Europe.

This book intertwines the creative strands of scholarship produced by Palmer and Godechot with those of Robin Blackburn, Christopher L. Brown, Vincent Carretta, David Brion Davis, Michael Gomez, Adam Hochschild, Paul Lovejoy, Gary Nash, Sue Peabody, Cassandra Pybus, Marcus Rediker, and others. It integrates Benezet's unique approach of providing a direct personal link between the great struggles in America, Britain, and France to destroy the dehumanizing system of slavery into the larger intellectual and political currents of the eighteenth century.

Because Benezet did not leave a diary, like Benjamin Franklin, Granville Sharp, John Woolman, and John Wesley, this is not just a study about a man; it also encompasses his message and his mission. I aim to show Benezet as the leader of one of the first truly international political movements on behalf of the downtrodden, by uniting forces in France, England, and the mainland British colonies. The life and work of Benezet opens new avenues in the study of slavery, antislavery, and African American history with its Atlantic connections. While many historians focus on the nineteenth-century abolitionists as the beginning of the organized fight against slavery, this work looks at an earlier period, at the dawn of the antislavery movement, with a global focus, initiated by Benezet, and identifies the ideological, religious, and social underpinnings of the beginnings of the Atlantic world's first human-rights movement.

Benezet seldom wrote directly about his contacts with enslaved blacks, most likely because he feared it might lead to their persecution. However, the one time that he did clearly sums up his mission: "And if they seldom complain of the unjust and cruel Usage they have received, in being forced from their native Country, & c., it is not to be wondered at: as it is a considerable Time after their Arrival amongst us before they can speak our Language, and by the Time they are able to express themselves, they cannot but observe, from the Behavior of the whites, that little or no Notice would be taken of their Complaints." He aimed to change the situation. He told all who would listen that it was their duty "to seek Judgment and relieve the Oppressed, what can be expected but that the groans and Cries of these sufferers reach heaven: and what shall ye do when God riseth up, and when he visiteth, what shall we answer him."[8]

Benezet spent his life providing the answer. He was indeed, as Garry Wills has written, an "American Saint."[9]

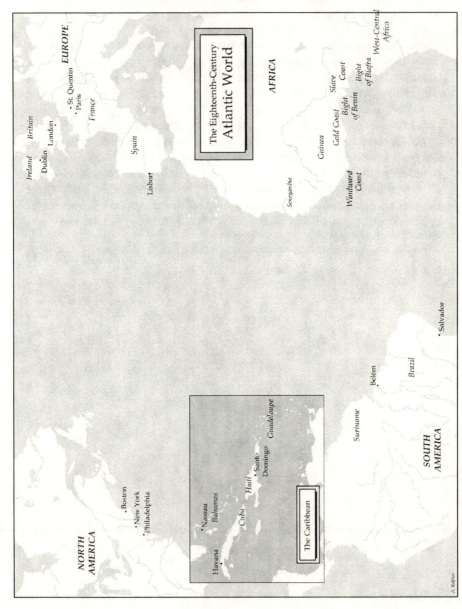

The eighteenth-century Atlantic world.

Chapter 1
A Life of Conscience

Anthony Benezet transformed early Quaker antislavery sentiment into a broad-based transatlantic movement. He translated ideas from diverse sources—Enlightenment philosophy, talks with enslaved and free Africans, Quakerism, practical life, African travel narratives, and the Bible—into concrete action, and in doing so became universally recognized by the leaders of the eighteenth-century antislavery movement as its founder.

In his first work, *Observations on Inslaving Negroes* (1760), Anthony Benezet broached the argument that slavery was contrary to the laws of man. Two years later, shifting from the economic to the social and philosophical, he wrote in his *Short Account of That Part of Africa* that slavery had trampled "under Foot all the obligations of social virtue" accorded to humankind. He argued against those who tried to separate slave owners, some of whom may have inherited their slaves, and slave traders, who were in the business for profit, asserting that such a distinction was "a plea founded more in words than supported by truth."[1]

Early in his crusade Benezet began to link the worldwide drive for profits with slavery. He wrote in a letter to his close friend Samuel Fothergill that "it is frequent to see even Friends, toiling year after year, enriching themselves, and thus gathering fuel for our children's vanity and corruption."[2] Benezet sought to reckon with this man-made corruption, the desire for profits, which wrecked the soul of the whites, as well as the bodies and the spirits of the blacks.

Even later in his life, when slavery had been greatly reduced in Philadelphia, Benezet continued his efforts, which he intended to keep up until the last enslaved African in the colonies was free. He demanded that his fellow Quakers and antislavery advocates do the same. Although he turned his primary attentions to the southern colonies and to England and the trade in slaves, he kept a steady eye on developments in Philadelphia, in Pennsylvania, and in New Jersey, even after the decline of the local slave trade.

Benezet developed strong ties to Philadelphia's most famous citizen, Benjamin Franklin. From Franklin, Benezet learned much about universal humanitarianism. From Benezet, Franklin learned much about the antislavery cause. In an April 27, 1772, letter to Franklin, then Pennsylvania's agent in London, Benezet wrote that "now as thy prospect is clear, with respect to the grievous iniquity practiced by our nation, toward the Negroes, I venture to take up a little more of thy time." Benezet asked Franklin if he would play a role in helping to "lay the iniquity & dreadful consequence of the Slave Trade before Parliament, desiring a stop be put to it."[3]

Unlike most whites of his time, Benezet sought to change the condition of the chained and the oppressed. The sight of enslaved blacks being bought and sold along the wharves and markets in Philadelphia brought his distaste for inequality to the fore, and he soon set out to do something about the subjugation he witnessed. Benjamin Rush, writing to Granville Sharp, put it best: "His soul was alive to the temporal and spiritual interests of all mankind. He seemed to possess a species of Quixotism in acts of piety and benevolence. He embraced all mankind in the circle of his love. Indians and Africans were as dear to him as the citizens of Pennsylvania."[4] Benezet summed up his ideas in a letter to the Abbé Guillaume-Thomas Reynal, one of the most prominent antislavery proponents during the French Revolution, expressing his hope that he would spend the rest of his life "earnestly desiring to the utmost of my abilities to promote the happiness of all men, even of my enemies themselves."[5] At Benezet's funeral "hundreds of Negroes [testified] by their attendance, and by their tears, [to] the grateful sense they entertained of his pious efforts on their behalf."[6] Benezet's life of conscience led him inevitably to concern for the enslaved African man, woman, and child and the struggle against the evil of slavery.

Early Years

Anthony Benezet was born to Huguenot parents, Jean-Étienne Benezet and Judith de la Méjenelle, on January 31, 1713, in St. Quentin, France. The family had been well-off: Anthony's grandfather, Jean Benezet, owned a royal office in the customs bureau; Anthony's mother, the daughter of a linen merchant in St. Quentin, brought a sufficiently large dowry that Jean-Étienne's 1750 will left her all his possessions "in compensation for the fortune she brought me upon our intermarriage."[7] Two years after Anthony's birth the family fled to Holland to escape the religious persecution of the Huguenots. A royal court hanged Jean-Étienne in effigy, subjecting him to civil death; the family thus forfeited all their possessions in France.

Jean-Étienne recorded the event in the family journal passed down from his father: "God has put it into our hearts to abandon France and to withdraw to a Protestant country in order to profess freely our holy religion; we have set out from St. Quentin with our two infants on the third of February, 1715."[8] In his later years Anthony Benezet wrote of his family's experience in letters to two French visitors to the United States: François, marquis de

Barbé-Marbois, who came to the United States in 1779 to serve as the secretary of the French legation, and François Jean, marquis de Chastellux, a professional soldier famed for the journal he wrote during his trip to the United States.

Benezet wore it as a badge of honor that his relatives had fought against religious persecution.[9] He told the Barbé-Marbois, who often visited him in Philadelphia, "I ought to be allowed to talk with eagerness about such an important subject. It was by the intolerant that one of my uncles was hanged, that an aunt was sent to a convent, that two of my cousins are dead in the galleys, and that my father, a fugitive, was ruined by the confiscation of all his goods."[10] Barbé-Marbois concluded that Benezet "tells of these persecutions as another man might talk of his titles of nobility."[11] Benezet offered a more precise account of his family's exile to Chastellux. He recounted in his journal Benezet's words to him during his visit of December 9, 1780, to Philadelphia: "Friend, this persecution is a strange thing; I can hardly believe what has happened to myself. My father was a Frenchman, and I am a native of thy country. It is not sixty years since he was obliged to seek an asylum in England, taking with him his children, the only treasure he could save in his misfortunes. Justice, or what is so called in thy country, ordered him to be hung in effigy, for explaining the gospel differently from thy priests."[12] Benezet's Huguenot background and his personal experience of injustice caused by prejudice thus played a formative role in his development into a leading eighteenth-century crusader for justice.[13]

The Benezet family came from the heartland of French Protestantism, the small town of Calvisson in the valley known as the Vaunage, west of Nîmes. Great-grandfather Étienne Benezet had been consul of Congénies in 1661; his daughter, Anne, married Pierre Mazel, a merchant and a member of the local consistory. Anne and two other siblings still lived in Calvisson in 1702, at the start of the Camisard rebellion; the final battle between royal troops and the Camisards took place in a forest named for an ancestor, Saint-Benezet. Their brother, Jean Benezet, born in Calvisson in 1645, moved north to Abbéville and then to St. Quentin; his brother Jean-Baptiste followed a similar path, becoming a deputy in the Chamber of Commerce at Dunkirk. Jean's son, Antoine, godfather of Anthony Benezet, described himself in 1713 as Benezet d'Artillon, that is, as the owner of an estate just outside Calvisson.[14] Antoine Benezet held the powerful position of Dunkirk subdelegate to the intendant of French Flanders.[15]

Possessed with substantial wealth, including expensive royal offices, the Benezet family had initially decided to stay in France and to practice Catholicism outwardly. Indeed, the fact that the Benezets of Dunkirk were buried in Catholic churches suggests that they abjured Protestantism.[16] Back in St. Quentin, Jean-Étienne took the precaution of having the Catholic curé baptize Anthony in Ste. Catherine's church on February 1, 1713. Jean-Étienne and his wife, Judith, had been married officially in the church of St. Eustache in Paris in 1709, and their children before Anthony always appeared at the baptismal font of Ste. Catherine's. Although the Benezets had not been directly touched by the persecutions at St. Quentin in the early 1680s, three related families—Bossu, Mettayer, and Testart—had been singled out in 1683–84, and Samuel Mettayer, a Huguenot minister at St. Quentin, would be forced into exile. Mettayer received special permission from the king of England to establish a French Huguenot church in London, so the Benezet family was related by marriage to the founders of the church they would join in 1715.

Although Jean-Étienne Benezet had young Anthony baptized, he was no Catholic. In England, Jean-Étienne belonged to the "Inspirés de la Vaunage." The unfortunate fate of the Camisards, who were massacred by the thousands between 1702 and 1715, convinced many of the folly of open, violent resistance to Louis XIV.[17] Centered in the Benezet family's hometown of Calvisson, the Inspirés refused to join the violent resistance; some of them fled to London, where they became known as the "French Prophets" (they called themselves the *enfants de Dieu*, the children of God).[18] Some called the Inspirés the "Congénies Quakers" because so many came from that town, in which, as we have seen, the Benezet family and their in-laws held some of the most important civil and religious positions. The Inspirés held some doctrines similar to those of the Quakers, such as nonviolence, the belief that each individual received direct inspiration from the Holy Spirit, and the admittance of women to the ministry.[19] Jean-Étienne Benezet was said to have studied at the "inner school of the French prophets," a reasonable possibility given that his father grew up in Calvisson.[20]

Benezet's Family Background

The most prominent Inspiré in England, Elie Marion, came from the Vaunage. He declared that it was by "inspiration that we forsook our Parents and Relations, and whatever was dearest to us in the World, to follow Jesus Christ, and to make War against the Devil and his Followers . . . ; this was the source of that Union, Charity, and Brotherly Love, which reign'd among us."[21] Marion was put on trial in London on July 4, 1710, for blasphemy and sedition and for publishing and distributing his ideas in both French and English. He later toured Europe seeking converts and died from an illness he acquired while serving eight months in a Polish prison. The prophets more closely resembled Quakers than Huguenots in their use of "dramatic acts like going naked or pouring ashes on themselves" to manifest "God's displeasure."[22] That the Benezet family, from Calvisson, the epicenter of the Camisards and the French Prophets, should have developed immediate ties with the Quakers when they reached England and later Philadelphia comes as little surprise.

The Benezet family reached Philadelphia by way of Rotterdam and London. The initial trip from St. Quentin to Rotterdam took thirteen days. Family legend has it that as they came upon a military outpost near the French frontier, they were approached by a sentinel. Their escort showed the guard one hand holding a gun and the other holding a purse of money, and told him, "Take your choice; this is a worthy family, flying from persecution, and they shall pass." The guard accepted the gold, and the family safely escaped.[23]

Although Rotterdam had many French Protestant refugees and the Dutch Protestants warmly welcomed them, the Benezets stayed only six months in Holland, moving to England in search of better economic prospects. Of the move Jean-Étienne wrote, on August 22, 1715, "I set out from Rotterdam with my family [and] disembarked at Greenwich, where my family remained for one month while I tr[ied] to find a house in London."[24]

Jean-Étienne's mother-in-law, Marie Madeleine Testart, was the daughter of Rachel Crommelin: the Crommelin family, one of the richest linen merchant dynasties of northern Europe, had fled St. Quentin before the Revocation. Members of the family, such as Rachel's sister, Catherine, and their relations by marriage, such as Pierre and Isaac Testart, could be found in Rotterdam and London. No direct evidence ties the Benezets to these relatives in London or Rotterdam, but this network surely played a key role in their travels. Through the Crommelins, Jean-Étienne Benezet had close family ties to some of the leading merchants of the Atlantic world (map 1). The Crommelin family, who once had a major square in St. Quentin bear their name, had rich and powerful members in virtually every major port in northern France, the Low Countries, and the British Isles. The Benezets' initial flight from St. Quentin to Rotterdam precisely mirrored that of the Crommelins.[25] Surely they helped Jean-Étienne become such a prominent merchant in London.

Jean-Étienne had achieved such success that in 1728, while staying in London, Voltaire used him as an agent, writing to Nicolas Claude Thériot that he should send all mail in care of the merchants "Simon and Étienne Benezet, of Nicolas Street [Lane], London."[26] If Anthony Benezet did attend John Kuweidt's Friends school in Wandsworth,[27] then he would have been a student alongside Voltaire, who, although older, learned both English and the elements of Quakerism there. While in Wandsworth, Voltaire read Robert Barclay's *Apology for the Quaker Religion* and desired to meet more Quakers: "Having become interested in their theories, he wished to meet a Quaker who was wealthy and powerful enough to become a man of the world if he wished." Voltaire wanted to know "what would become of Quaker principles under the temptation of worldly interest?"[28]

Voltaire's fascination with Quakerism led him to write his four famous letters "On the Quakers" between his arrival in England in 1726 and 1731.[29] Although far removed from Voltairean skepticism, Quaker doctrine "was a vindication of liberty . . . the only liberty worth having—the liberty to live and to think, as you like."[30] In Voltaire's "First Letter" he wrote, "I believed that the doctrine and the history of such an extraordinary people as the Quakers deserved the attention of a rational man."[31] Voltaire's letters mentioned Quaker simplicity of dress and manners, their aversion to theater and gambling, their unwillingness to take oaths, and their pacifism.[32] He wrote that a Quaker told him, "We never take oaths, even in the court of justice; we believe that the name of the Most High should not be prostituted in the scornful wranglings of men," adding, "We never go to war, not that we fear death; on the contrary we bless the moment which unites us with the Beings of beings."[33] In his "Second Letter" Voltaire asked, "Do you not have any priest at all, then?" "No, my friend," said the Quaker, "and we are well off without them. . . . God forbid that we should dare to ordain someone to receive on Sunday the Holy Spirit to the exclusion of all the rest of the faithful. We are the only people on earth who have no priests, thank heaven. Wouldst thou deprive us of so happy a distinction?"[34] Voltaire once wrote, "I shall tell you without repeating myself, that I love the Quakers. Yes, if I were not subject to unbearable seasickness, it would be in thy bosom, Oh Pennsylvania, that I should go to finish the rest of my life."[35] Many years later François de Barbé-Marbois saw in Anthony Benezet precisely the asceticism and simplicity that Voltaire so admired in the London Quakers, perhaps even of Jean-Étienne Benezet: "He [Anthony Benezet] is among the small number of those who profess Quakerism in all its severity. Nevertheless, Quaker seriousness has not taken away from his good refuge and any particle of his French vivacity."[36]

In London the Benezets joined the large Huguenot community, estimated at 20,000 to 25,000 in 1700.[37] Did the family join the Quakers in London? The contradictory evidence has allowed Anthony Benezet's biographers to disagree about whether he converted around 1727 in London or soon after the family came to Philadelphia, as Benezet himself implied in the preface to his *Some Historical Account of Guinea*.[38] Perhaps the best account of the Benezet family's admittance to the Society of Friends has been offered by the preeminent Quaker Historian, Henry. J. Cadbury: "Upon their arrival in America, in 1731 they brought no Quaker letters of removal, yet in a few years both Anthony and others appeared as members of the Society. We may question the usual statement that Anthony joined in England at the age of fourteen. Adhesion to the Society then required no formal action and secured no formal record. It was assumed from attendance at meetings."[39] Although the exact year of Benezet's admittance to the Society of Friends is not known, we know he was "well recommended to the Quakers of Philadelphia by divers Friends."[40]

The Family Moves to Philadelphia

The family stayed in England until 1731, when they moved to Philadelphia.[41] The Benezet family, with its likely ties to the London Quakers and with its deep personal empathy toward the sufferings of the persecuted, based on their own experience in France, was drawn to the Philadelphia Quakers. Given the principles of the Quakers, it is not difficult to see why a man like Jean-Étienne Benezet and his family would join them. We know that young Anthony had grown to detest religious ritual, as displayed by the spirit possession of the French Prophets or in the later demonstrative worship of George Whitefield's Great Awakening. Yet he may have seen in both the Quakers and the French Prophets "God's direct intervention in the lives of the oppressed."[42]

The second strand of Benezet family connections also came into play when they moved to Philadelphia. The family of Jean-Étienne Benezet's wife connected them to the great linen merchants of Europe, but Jean-Étienne's own family came from the heartland of the Camisards. Three of Jean Benezet's siblings still lived in Calvisson at the start of the Camisard war, and the family remained prominent in the region long afterward. Moving to Philadelphia, the Benezets became reconnected with the Inspiré heritage, which had reached Pennsylvania by way of London a few years before the Benezet family did. Jean-Étienne, of course, had London contacts with the Inspirés, who came from the hometown of his father and, given the small population of the Calvisson-Congénies region, almost certainly included people related to him by blood and by marriage.

Among the first converts to the French Prophets (Inspirés) in London were the Keimer family: Mary (c. 1710), her mother, and her brother Samuel (c. 1713). In 1713 Samuel married a fellow member of the French Prophets; he used her dowry to open a print shop. One of his first jobs was to print a work by Daniel Defoe.[43] In 1715 he printed a document that offended both the government and the Prophets, leading to imprisonment at the Old Bailey. He retaliated against the Prophets by writing a diatribe, *A Brand Pluck'd from the Burning*, against them in 1718. In the process he became acquainted with the Quakers, who also rejected him: they soon notified the public in print that he was not a member of the Society of Friends.

In the early 1720s Mary Keimer left for Philadelphia, still a devout French Prophet; Samuel soon followed her there. In 1724 "he became the first colonial printer to reprint *The Independent Whig*, a serial by the Englishmen John Trenchard and Thomas Gordon, authors of *Cato's Letters*, which would become of great importance in the development of a colonial political voice."[44] Keimer established the *Pennsylvania Gazette* in 1728. By now he was a rival of Anthony Bradford, Philadelphia's first printer. Some years later he took on a young Benjamin Franklin as an apprentice in his shop. Franklin later developed strong personal ties with Benezet, some of whose early works he printed in the 1750s.

Did their common connection to the French Prophets play a role in Franklin's decision? The circumstantial connection becomes all the more intriguing because Samuel Keimer early on proposed establishing a daily school for black people. This proposal gained him no favor with the Quakers or the Philadelphia elite at the time, but it surely had resonance with others tied to the Prophets. Jean-Étienne (now John Stephen) Benezet, in the 1730s, not long after Keimer's call for the school, participated in George Whitefield's unsuccessful venture to start the Nazareth training school for blacks on five thousand acres near the Delaware River.

John Stephen Benezet purchased two five-hundred-acre tracts of land from James and William Bingham. From 1735 to 1741 he resided in a large two-story house on Second Street below Race Street, in an area called Moravian Alley, which suggests he had close ties with the Moravians before he officially joined them in 1743. George Brookes cited the minutes of the Philadelphia Monthly Meeting of March 27, 1743: "Cadwallader Foulke acquainted this meeting that Stephen Benezet had been lovingly spoke to respecting his declining to attend our Religious Meetings he had joined in the Society of Moravians."[45] Early Philadelphia Moravians often had ties to the French Prophets, and members of each group joined the other.[46] Before father Benezet took the official step of announcing to the Quaker Annual Meeting of 1743 that he had joined the Moravians, two of his daughters, Susanna and Marianne, had already done so. Susanna had married John Pyraleus, one of the first Moravian missionaries sent to America, in 1742. John Stephen Benezet had sufficient standing and ties to the Moravians that Count Zinzendorf himself stayed with the Benezet family during part of his trip to Pennsylvania (1741–43). The Count had allowed Moravians to live on his estate in Saxony where under his tutelage the doctrine of "Brotherly Agreement" which outlined their tenets was developed. His associates and followers established over one hundred overseas missions and communities from the late 1720s until the mid-1740s. Pyraleus became a part of a group who began on November 14, 1740, to construct the "Charity School for the Instruction of Poor Children Gratis in Useful Literature and the knowledge of the Christian Religion." John Stephen Benezet became a trustee of the center, named simply the New Building. Among other trustees of the school were the Reverend George Whitefield, then living in Georgia; Samuel Seward of London; and Benjamin Franklin: thus Franklin would have known John Stephen Benezet from at least 1743 onward. The New Building was later deeded to the Academy, which became the College of Pennsylvania and later the University of Pennsylvania. The *Pennsylvania Gazette* of September 12, 1751, recorded that on September 16 a Free School would be opened "By Order of the Trustees of the ACADEMY . . . at the New Building for the Instruction of poor children gratis in reading, writing and arithmetic."[47]

Given young Anthony's background, his knowledge of the persecution of family members, the injustice and prejudice his family had suffered, and the close family association with the French Prophets, the Quakers, and the

Moravians, we can easily understand why he joined the Quakers and why he made the central mission of his life the defense of another persecuted minority, the enslaved Africans. He combined his mission to end slavery with his family's traditional commitment to education, particularly of the oppressed members of society; little wonder that Anthony Benezet would found both a school for girls and a school for free blacks.

The Condition of Blacks in Colonial Philadelphia

During the height of Benezet's fight against slavery Philadelphia emerged as a key industrial and maritime center. Compared with the southern colonies, Pennsylvania's slave population was relatively small. While exact numbers cannot be given prior to the 1790 Federal Census, the closest estimates reveal that in 1721 the white population in Pennsylvania totaled 60,000 and the blacks numbered 5,000.[48] The estimated population of the Pennsylvania colony in 1750 was about 150,000, with from 7,500 to 12,000 being black.[49] Between 1750 and 1770 Philadelphia's population more than doubled. By 1775 the city had a population of 19,650, and the greater Philadelphia area had 33,290 inhabitants, which ranked it as the largest city and urban area in colonial British America.

Benezet's Philadelphia was a complicated religious, racial, national, and ethnic mix: Anglicans, Catholics, Lutherans, Presbyterians, Mennonites, Moravians, and Quakers; English, Irish, German, Scotch-Irish, and French Huguenots; whites and blacks. Slaves came from nations and kingdoms in West Africa, including Benin, Senegal, Goree, Guinea, and Gambia. They had been kidnapped from the Kingdom of Fida and from Dutch forts at Delmina. They were Mandigos and Fuli, Akan, and other African ethnicities. There were enslaved Africans and some who later became free people of color. They worked next to indentured servants—bond laborers—and next to the masters of both black and white.[50]

Benezet's Philadelphia had a full and free interplay of group and individual activity, buttressed by prosperous economic activity, which fostered the development of a vigorous cultural life. The population seemed well read by colonial standards. Well-versed men like James Logan and Benjamin Franklin helped to institute libraries so that "common men" and "obscure mechanics" had the opportunity to read. Reading circles were established and sailors got the latest news in the pubs. Blacks who worked in close proximity to their white owners often picked up on the latest intellectual discourse.[51]

As Marcus Rediker vividly described Philadelphia, the city "had much to recommend it; a regular well-ordered layout; a set of sumptuous markets, allowed by many to be 'the best of its bigness in the known World, and undoubtedly the largest in America.'" Philadelphia also "featured deep-water wharves for effortless docking and a wide river of entry, the Delaware, for easy maneuvering. Philadelphia offered a number of coffee shops and taverns, but music and dancing, two of the seamen's most fancied pastimes, were not easily to be found, perhaps because Quaker merchants and city fathers preferred a sober and 'strenuous' concern for business and an austere style of life."[52]

The city depended on the efforts of hundreds of able and energetic individuals who sprang from all ranks of society and were motivated by a love of learning, a curiosity about the world around them, a belief in progress, and a desire to get ahead. Philadelphia was becoming a premier city of the New World society, enlightened and democratic, with a culture resting on a broadly popular base. Philadelphia had many tradesmen and women, artisans and craftspeople, and people who worked in many areas of commerce, agriculture, transport, and manufacturing. Among the lower ranks of laborers were the many merchant seamen who worked and lived in Philadelphia.[53] Among them were the caulkers, joiners, and riggers who worked steadily on the docks; in many cases white ships' captains preferred black labor over white sailors, as was the case of Captain Richard Jeffery who purchased blacks to serve on his ship, the *Duke of Bedford,* in 1751. In another case a master advertised the sale of his slaves who were "brought up to the sail-making trade: they have been for nine to 12 years at said trade, [and] can work well."[54] Some blacks like James Forten were trained as sail makers.[55]

Like most cities that came to prominence during the "era of the trade wars," Philadelphia had people at the top of the American colonial economic ladder and people at the bottom. Well-off Philadelphians tended to support slavery because they benefited from it and because the ownership of slaves symbolized wealth, power, influence, and comfort. As in Boston and New York, "the most prominent Philadelphians—merchants, professionals, proprietary officeholders—likewise kept retinues of black footmen, coachmen, and personal servants to help solidify their elite status."[56] Even the middling craftsmen owned slaves: in 1772 at least 10 percent of craftsmen owned slaves, and a large number of them held indentured servants. By 1775 the number of slaves, indentured servants, and apprentices equaled the number of free laborers. Most times, slavery proponents and adversaries divided along occupational lines. That is to say, those who received the most profitable returns from their business of occupational enterprises tended to support the continuation of the slave trade. There were periods during which craftsmen, merchants, and other employers promoted slavery, but that support depended largely on the amount of tax placed on a slave's head. During times of reduced import duties, employers sought to increase the production of their business by purchasing additional laborers.

Slavery's History in Philadelphia

Slavery went back to the origins of Philadelphia: in December 1684 a Bristol mercantile firm transported the first shipload of 150 African slaves aboard the slave ship *Isabella*.[57] Arriving only three years after the Quaker founders landed, these black laborers were promptly purchased and set to work clearing land and building houses. Philadelphia Quakers quickly bought the men, women, and children aboard the ship.[58] Another ship, the *Constant Alice,* sailed from Barbados to Philadelphia in 1701 with nineteen blacks among the rest of its cargo of rum, molasses, and sugar. This ship made a repeat voyage in 1702, this time with twenty-three blacks aboard.[59]

Between 1682 and 1705 approximately one in fifteen families in Philadelphia, many of them Quakers, owned slaves.[60] By 1693 the Quakers decided to place strict controls on the blacks because they feared "the tumultuous gatherings of the negroes in the town of Philadelphia, on the first days of the week."[61] The Colonial Assembly first showed their fears of unrest when, starting in 1700, they passed a series of "Black Codes," which restricted the movement and activities of blacks. Blacks could not meet in groups of more than four and could not purchase liquor. Needless to say, blacks were denied the right to trial by jury or any other judicial privileges that whites counted on.[62] Regardless of their status as slaves, indentured workers, or free people of color, blacks could not travel more than ten miles from home without the permission of their masters, and all had to be home by nine o'clock at night.

In 1700 the Assembly of Pennsylvania passed a twenty-shilling duty on imported slaves sixteen years of age or older, to raise revenues rather than as an act of antislavery defiance. Just five years later, in 1705, the duty doubled because white workers complained about their competition with black slaves as the main source of labor.[63] The English Crown eventually repealed the 1700 tax so as not to disrupt the Royal African Company's trade and to send a message to the Assembly of Pennsylvania that they had acted too independently. Pennsylvanians later showed caution when considering the further admittance of slaves after a "slave conspiracy" and attempt to burn the town erupted in New York City in 1712.[64] In the aftermath of those events, where nine whites were killed and many others injured, the New York authorities hanged thirteen enslaved Africans in retribution, burned three blacks at the stake, and broke another one on the wheel. In the same year the Quaker William Sotheby petitioned the Pennsylvania assembly to pass legislation to free all the slaves in the colony. The members of the assembly, a good many of them slave owners, decided "it is . . . just not convenient to set them at Liberty."[65] The fear of a slave revolt and the perceived need to control the influx of slaves made the Quaker-led assembly introduce a £20-per-head import duty, which was quickly disallowed by the

English Crown. The duty was in the past passed due to the fear that too large an influx of Africans into the province might possibly include some rebellious ones. In 1715 a duty was set at £5, and it too was repealed and then reimposed in 1722. By the late 1720s slave trafficking slowed as Philadelphia suffered its first economic recession.

By 1725 the assembly had outlawed interracial marriages or liaisons. These laws applied equally to all blacks, regardless of their status as slaves, servants, or free people of color.[66] If a free black and a white person married, the black could legally be re-enslaved. When whites saw blacks gathering, either in a festive mood or to worship, they protested; many times between 1693 and 1751 whites enacted legal sanctions against the blacks.[67] In 1726 the assembly required free blacks to carry a pass "if they were fit and able to work." If they were caught without a pass, they were to be charged with loitering and "bound out to service."

Philadelphia resumed slave trading with renewed vigor as it recovered from the economic recession—and the £5 duty was reduced to £2 in 1729. Early antislavery advocates like Ralph Sandiford paid strict attention to the actions of the Crown. In 1730 he wrote, "We have negroes flocking in upon us since the duty is reduced."[68] The many early duties on importation of slaves had little to do with antislavery sentiment; the Pennsylvania assembly passed some of them to raise revenues, as in 1701, and others, as in 1712, to prevent importation of blacks on security grounds. Only on March 14, 1761, when the Pennsylvania assembly passed a £10-per-head duty on enslaved Africans, did the legislators pass an act with the clear intent of stopping the slave trade in the colony.[69] The last imposition of the duty came in 1773 when it was levied at £20, a sum clearly set to prohibit the slave trade.[70]

In the absence of duties after 1731 Philadelphia's importation rates for slaves rose considerably. At this time the demand for Africans increased, and white employees used more and more skilled black laborers. During this first wave of imports men like Benjamin Franklin knew that just as time was money, so were black bodies. When a smallpox outbreak occurred in 1730 that took the lives of 288 people, Franklin noted that "64 of that Number were Negroes; If these may be valued one with another at £30 per Head, the Loss to the City in that Article is near £2000."[71]

Pennsylvania's weather and environment were not suitable for large-scale plantation agriculture, so, as in such southern cities as Charleston, many slaves obtained specialized training in skilled occupations. Mostly owned by artisans, these blacks became experts in a wide array of skilled jobs: hatters, skinners, brush makers, sugar boilers, sail makers, bakers, masons, carpenters, and even shoemakers. Slaves and free blacks in this urban setting performed a wide variety of jobs, working side by side with their masters and employers. They also worked as assistant blacksmiths, barbers, butchers, mariners, and carpenters, and in an array of shipbuilding jobs, such as riggers and caulkers. In addition to these tasks they were often called on to do household chores for their owners.[72] The harsh Pennsylvanian winters meant that the upkeep of slaves, owing to outlay for clothes and lodging, was much costlier than in southern colonies: estimates of the time suggest that food and clothing alone came annually to a sum equal to 25 percent of the slave's value.[73]

Although slavery was less profitable in the North than in the South, many northern whites made substantial profits in the slave trade. Quakers were as active as anyone in the Pennsylvania trade of black cargo. One of the best-known Quakers involved in the slave trade was Robert King, the merchant who bought Olaudah Equiano two years after the Friends barred members from owning slaves. So useful to King was Equiano, with his navigational and financial record-keeping abilities, that when Equiano sought to buy his own freedom, King initially reneged on his promise that Equiano could do so once he had the money.[74]

Like Equiano, many black men performed a variety of skilled labor tasks; slave women, however, mainly worked in the household—cooking, cleaning, washing and drying laundry, keeping fires, tending to the sick, gardening, and caring for children. Their more skilled responsibilities involved sewing, knitting, cloth making, and "housewifery or spinning."[75] Even after being freed, many black women continued working as house servants and maids. They did so because of the relative security their master's family offered them. Many children of slaves never lived under the same roof as their mothers and fathers because both parents had likely hired out since the age of ten or twelve. High mortality rates, cramped living quarters, and the large numbers of slave families displaced and separated did not allow the establishment of "stable" slave families. In part because most Philadelphia masters owned only one or two slaves, just 10 percent of the adult male and female slave partners lived under the same roof. All these negative factors aside, "some Blacks . . . manipulate[d] both their situation and their owners" and established "loving relationships with others of their own race."[76]

The decline in the slave population coincided with the drop in slave reproduction rates, which occurred simultaneously with the drop of slave importations after 1767. During this period "many female slaves passed beyond the age of fertility and were not replaced by younger slave women."[77] Anthony Benezet himself wrote to Granville Sharp on May 20, 1773, that the black population would disappear without an influx of new blacks to the city because of the alarmingly high infant mortality rate.[78] Slaves fit into broader demographic patterns. As in most of the North Atlantic world, mortality—especially infant mortality—was much higher in a city like Philadelphia than in its rural hinterlands; and among slaves, as among the overall population of colonial America, men outnumbered women.

TABLE 1. SLAVE POPULATION IN PHILADELPHIA, 1691–1770

	1691–1700	1701–1710	1711–1720	1721–1730	1731–1740	1741–1750	1751–1760	1761–1770
Calculated Slave Population	213	630	611	481	708	798	978	1,375
Percentage of Slaves in Total Population	10.4	17.4	12.4	7.5	9.1	8.5	7.6	8.2

From Gary B. Nash and Jean R. Soderlund, *Freedom by Degrees: Emancipation in Pennsylvania and Its Aftermath* (New York: Oxford University Press, 1991), 18; Gary B. Nash, "Slaves and Slaveowners in Colonial Philadelphia," *William and Mary Quarterly*, 3rd series, 30, no. 2 (April 1973): 227, 246.

From 1684 to 1730 most African arrivals came to the colony from the West Indies in lots of two and three for the personal use of wealthy Philadelphia merchants.[79] The Quakers became heavily involved in the slave trade: around 1729–30 the merchants began to trade slaves in bulk and to import them into the colony in cargoes of up to forty slaves per ship. This practice lasted until the onset of the Seven Years' War. Until then "seasoned" slaves were still being imported from the West Indies instead of directly from Africa. The period from 1755 to 1765 represented the high point of the slave trade in Philadelphia, with most slaves coming directly from Africa, perhaps because Philadelphians, looking at the example of New York, feared the rebelliousness of seasoned slaves. By 1770 the number of slaves in Philadelphia was nearly triple what it had been in 1730 (Table 1).

In 1731, 20 percent of Philadelphia Quakers owned slaves, accounting for a third of the slaves in the city. By the 1770s, however, only 7.9 percent of Quakers owned a slave, which accounted for thirty-eight slaves, or about 3 percent of the total.[80] Non-Quaker merchants steadily took over the slave trade, but some Quakers stayed in it to the end.[81] Pennsylvania residents as a whole were far more likely to own slaves: half of the estate inventories before 1750 included slaves, and six out of ten of those estates exceeding £200 did so.[82] Pennsylvania also had large numbers of German and Scotch-Irish immigrants, who often came as indentured servants. The French and Indian War drew many of these immigrants away: in 1755 the British army recruited two thousand men from among Pennsylvania's indentured servants (Tables 2 and 3).

The Pennsylvania assembly became so concerned with the shortage of their labor force that in 1756 it issued a statement professing that "if the Possession of a bought Servant . . . is . . . rendered precarious . . . the Purchase, and Of Course the Importation, of Servants will be discouraged, and the People driven to the Necessity of providing themselves with Negroe

TABLE 2. BLACKS AND WHITE UNFREE LABOR IN PHILADELPHIA CITY, 1767–1775

	1767	1769	1772	1773	1774	1775
Total Population	16,000	16,850	18,225	18,700	19,175	19,650
Number of Slaves	1,392	1,270	1,069	945	869	672
Percentage of Slaves in Total Population	8.7	7.5	5.9	5.1	4.5	3.4
Number of Indentured Servants	395	482	558	673	767	869
Percentage of Indentured Servants in Total Population	2.5	2.9	3.1	3.6	4.0	4.4

From Gary B. Nash, "Slaves and Slaveowners in Colonial Philadelphia," *William and Mary Quarterly*, 3rd series, 30, no. 2 (April 1973): Table IV, 237, and Table VI, 247.

TABLE 3. BLACKS IN GREATER PHILADELPHIA, 1767–1810

	1767	1775	1780	1790	1800	1810
Population	26,460	33,290	36,946	44,096	67,811	88,987
Slaves	1,481	728	539	301	55	2
Free Blacks	57	114	241	1,849	6,028	8,942
Total Black Population	1,538	842	780	2,150	6,083	8,944
Percentage of Blacks	5.8	2.5	2.2	5.0	9.0	10.0

From Sharon V. Salinger, "Colonial Labor in Transition: The Decline of Indentured Servitude in Late Eighteenth Century Philadelphia," *Labor History* 22 (Spring 1981), and no. 2, 175, 180; Salinger, *"To Serve Well and Faithfully": Labor and Indentured Servants in Pennsylvania, 1682–1800* (Cambridge: Cambridge University Press, 1987), 141.

Slaves, as the Property in them and their Service seems at present more secure."[83] The arrival of immigrant ships to Philadelphia almost ceased during the course of the Seven Years' War, dropping from twenty-four in 1754 to four in 1755. Given the growing unreliability of the supply of white indentured servants just as labor needs were rising, it is not surprising that Pennsylvanians shifted back to importing black slaves, as many as 500 in 1762, many of them from the Gambia.[84] Philadelphia and western New Jersey saw the importation of 1,290 enslaved Africans, brought either directly from Africa or from the West Indies, between 1757 and 1766. This pattern began to shift again in 1763, when nineteen ships with immigrant servants arrived.[85] Given the preference of employers for white indentured servants over blacks, the new influx had an impact on the importation of slaves.

The population of Philadelphia in 1767 reflected the sudden surge in slave importations in the previous decade: 590 slave owners (15 percent of the households) owned 1,400 slaves in Philadelphia, which then held 16,000 people. The return of the white immigrant flow, combined with the antislavery campaign led by Benezet and others (see below), changed these proportions dramatically by 1775: there were fewer than 700 blacks in a population of 19,175; only 376 whites still owned slaves. High mortality rates—about 87 blacks died each year—and reduced importation (about 30 slaves a year) contributed to the decline.[86] From 1767 to 1775 only 100 black newborns survived infancy, while 679 blacks were buried in Philadelphia. When combined with the increase in free blacks in or near Philadelphia, these figures suggest about 250 Philadelphia slaves were either sold to new owners outside the city or ran away to freedom between 1767 and 1775. These five factors—high mortality, reduced importation, sale to owners outside Philadelphia, escape to freedom, and manumission, probably in that order—accounted for the sharp decline in Philadelphia's black population in the decade before the American Revolution.[87]

The roughly 250 slaves who either were sold to owners elsewhere or ran away can be accounted for. Philadelphia blacks, like those throughout the Atlantic world, expressed their desire for freedom with their feet: from 1770 to 1775 around ten slaves per year ran away, or about one in ninety. The pangs of freedom's call as expressed by the white revolutionaries were echoed by the blacks, for from 1776 to 1780 the annual rate rose to twenty-four (one of every twenty-six slaves in Philadelphia).[88] Free blacks who aided a runaway slave were fined, and if they were unable to pay, they were sold into servitude; yet still the freedom train rolled on. For the period from 1767 to 1775 roughly 90 slaves achieved freedom through their own efforts, while about 160 were sold to new owners outside Philadelphia. Indeed, on February 18, 1773, Benezet wrote to Granville Sharp that "the number [of Negroes] Imported in this Province is so small, that the officer tells me, more are sent off than brought in."[89]

In Philadelphia all the blacks "lived within no more than about twenty blocks of developed urban space."[90] In other words, they lived in a densely populated urban area, where almost everything was within walking distance. Blacks, like whites, "resorted to the city's public spaces for social interaction after the day's labor was done." In addition to mingling in "the burial ground, which served as the center of festive activities on Sundays and holidays, the courthouse provided the main meeting place for after-hours socializing and conviviality."[91] Jammed together in central Philadelphia, black and white workers often socialized with each other.[92]

Manumission played a strikingly small role in Philadelphia's slave society, given that Philadelphians led the antislavery movement in the colonies. In the sixty-five-year period from 1698 to 1763, only fifty-two Philadelphia Quakers manumitted ninety slaves.[93] While eight of eleven slaveholders who released their slaves between 1741 and 1750 were Quakers, in the same years seven in ten Quakers who owned slaves refused to free them. In reality only 18 percent of Quaker slaveholders manumitted their slaves in the 1740s, and 30 percent in the 1750s. Between 1766 and 1775 only eighteen slaves were manumitted. Of those eighteen, fourteen were given their freedom by "persons not in Membership with Friends." Even the Philadelphia Meeting's decision to ban slaveholding by Quakers had a slow effect. In 1774 the meeting called on masters to free their slaves; if they refused, the meeting barred them from participating in the Society's business or even from contributing funds. Yet only seven Quakers freed their slaves in 1774 and five in 1775, so in the immediate years after the passing of the decision most Quakers remained in noncompliance.

The 1775 Yearly Meeting instituted visitation of non-complying Quakers; the visitors included Benezet. According to Jean R. Soderlund "the Philadelphia Quarterly Meeting announced in August 1776 that its members had freed 115 blacks and mulattoes and reported an additional 37 manumissions during the next year," 1777, and that "in August 1778, most of that quarter's meetings were nearly clear of slaves."[94] Of those, Gary Nash and Soderlund offer that "forty-four Quakers freed 80 slaves in 1776. Twenty-eight owners freed 56 slaves in 1777 and 1778."[95] All told, from 1763 to 1796 the Quakers manumitted only 189 slaves in Philadelphia.[96] Because clauses in the manumission certificates did not allow for immediate freedom, the periods for emancipation ran from one to twenty-one years, or from the birth of a slave to full manhood, which in some cases could be as late as the 1820s.

The Philadelphia "Query of 1776" called on members of the Society of Friends to assist blacks still enslaved and newly freed. The Philadelphia Yearly Meeting of 1778 and 1779 called for all local meetings to form committees to aid the formerly enslaved. The meeting asked Quakers who had "let the oppressed go free . . . to attend to the further openings of duty."[97] The Philadelphia Meeting for Suffering of January 1780 called for the "lively concern for the discharge of Christian duty towards the oppressed Africans." The Meeting for Suffering alerted the Quakers that the Almighty was "graciously pleased to favour such [Friends] with his paternal regard, owning them as his children, by his judgments instructing them in righteousness." The society told its members not only to free blacks but also to help with their further well-being. This act would bring spiritual benefits to the repentant slave owners. They would "know a happy dwelling place in the liberty of Truth, in which wisdom and strength is to be found to qualify to labour for the liberty of the captive, and to relieve the burden of the oppressed."[98]

In 1780 there were only 539 slaves in greater Philadelphia; the free black population had risen from 57 in 1767 to 241. The black population of 1780 was only 2 percent of the total population in Philadelphia (37,000), down from just under 6 percent in 1767, but it would rise very rapidly in the next two decades, reaching 9 percent by 1800 (see Table 3). Only 55 of the more than 6,000 blacks were still slaves, a fitting tribute to the influence of Benezet and his collaborators in the antislavery movement.

Benezet's Life in Philadelphia

Anthony Benezet spent most of his life creating and sustaining a transatlantic community of activists against slavery. He lived and worked in Philadelphia, devoting most of his energies to his activities there. In 1735 he became a naturalized British subject. He soon fell in love with Joyce Marriott of Burlington, New Jersey. She was the daughter of Samuel and Mary Marriott and granddaughter of Isaac and Joyce (Olive) Marriott. She was also the granddaughter of the prominent physician Griffith Owen, a Quaker minister. The Philadelphia Monthly Meeting minutes of "ye 29th eight mo. 1731," the year of the Benezet family arrival in Philadelphia, show that "Joyce Marriott, who for sometime appeared in publick Testimony amongst us, might be admitted to sit in the Meeting of Ministers and Elders, the Meeting consents thereto."[99] She was described as "sound, lively and edifying," and in her various roles she visited other Quaker meetings "in gospel love."[100]

Benezet and Marriott courted in accordance with Quaker norms and appeared before Public Meetings in March and April. When the necessary overseers declared that "there being nothing to obstruct their proceedings, the Meeting leaves them to the liberty to consummate their said intentions," the couple made plans to wed.[101] Family genealogy records show that "Anthony Benezet married, 3. mo. 13, 1736, at Philadelphia Friends' Meeting."[102]

Quaker women could speak in meetings and visit other meetings and Quakers for religious concerns, and generally were held by their non-Quaker contemporaries to have broader rights than other women. Quaker women were accepted into the ministry: Joyce Marriott Benezet served as a Quaker minister.[103] Indeed Henry J. Cadbury, the great Quaker historian, observed that she became an elder many years before Anthony. Cadbury writes that "he sometimes spoke in meeting, as contemporary diaries tell us. But in the ministry his wife overshadowed him."[104] Hannah Logan, the daughter of the one-time Governor James Logan, wrote of seeing Joyce Marriott Benezet preach in 1748.[105] Yet Quaker women in the main faced expectations similar to those of women in the larger society; their role was not truly equal in form and function. Sydney James writes that "there were limits to what the Women's Meeting might do." For example, the Women's Committee did not have the power to accept or reject new members or to discipline existing members. James suggests that the first role of Quaker women was to preserve "each other in virtuous conduct . . . and for clearness for marriage." They also "helped in the care of the poor, saw that the meetinghouses were cleaned, and performed other duties appropriate [in contemporary views] to their sex."[106]

Aside from the comments by Hannah Logan, little was written about Joyce Marriott Benezet except in letters by her husband. Often he would tell friends of her support or greet the family to tell them "my wife joins me in sincere Love to thy wife & family."[107] Quaker records indicate her attendance at numerous meetings. The couple had two children. Mary was born on August 21, 1737, but she died less than a year later on July 12. Anthony was born June 16, 1743, and died six days later. In his many letters Anthony never wrote about the births or the deaths of the infants, perhaps because his love of children and of his own rather large group of siblings made childlessness difficult for him. Although childless, the Benezets' home was often a center of activity. The marquis de Barbé-Marbois recalls visiting the house. "Nothing could be simpler or neater than his house," he wrote, adding that "there were a good many people there."[108] And when no other place could be found, Benezet taught in his home at least as early as 1750, when he instructed black children there. The home of Anthony Benezet stood at 115 Chestnut Street.[109] Except for a few years when he first married and later for health reasons when he moved to Burlington, New Jersey, the birthplace of his wife, he spent his adult life at this location.[110]

Benezet studied scientific treatises—he had more than a hundred books on science and medicine in his library—because he had a frail constitution most of his life. During adulthood he made detailed studies of medical journals to find ways to improve his health. He and Joyce became vegetarians like their friend Benjamin Lay, because Benezet did not want to eat anything that might have been associated with slave labor. He and his wife did not believe that any life, including that of an animal, should be taken in order to feed another living being. He would often be seen feeding rats and stray animals in his backyard, near his small vegetable garden. One of his former students, Deborah Logan, recalled in 1825 that Benezet also took daily exercises and required his students to do likewise: "And lest his pupils should be injured by too strict confinement during school hours, we were divided into three classes and suffered to go, one class at a time, into a very large apartment adjourning, where abundance of means were provided for means of recreation and exercise."[111]

His dietary habits went against the wishes of his friend of later years, Dr. Benjamin Rush, who wrote that "so great was his sympathy with every thing that was capable of feeling pain that he resolved towards the close of his life, to eat no animal food." Rush gave an example of Benezet's zealousness, recalling that "upon coming into his brother's house one day, when his family was dining upon poultry, he was asked by his brother's wife, to sit down and dine with them. 'What' (said he,) 'would you have me eat my neighbors?'" Fifty years after Benezet's death an anonymous author wrote in the Quaker journal *The Friend* that Benezet denied "himself the use of animal food, because he would avoid taking of life—how far in this he is correct, I will not inquire."[112] Of his dietary habits Rush opined that "this misapplication of moral feeling, was supposed to have brought on such a debility in his stomach and bowels, as produced a disease in those parts of which he finally died."[113]

While no portraits were ever made of Benezet, we know that he had a small frame unsuitable for the hard apprenticeships that many young men endured. One friend described Benezet "as a small man, and though his face beamed with kindly animation, it was far from being handsome." When the friend once expressed a desire to possess his portrait, Benezet replied, "Oh, no, no! my ugly face shall not go down to posterity."[114]

His passion for knowledge, his mastery of several languages, his devotion to children, and his search for the truth led Anthony Benezet to become a teacher and lifelong educator. Before starting on that career, however, he tried first a life in commerce, as befitted a merchant's son. Although we have little evidence that he was apprenticed to a merchant in London, we know from the testimony of his younger brother, Daniel, that in Philadelphia young Benezet "received an education that was deemed sufficient to qualify him for mercantile business, to acquire a knowledge of which his father placed him with one of the most respectable traders of the metropolis . . . in this situation he did not long continue, declining, from motives of a religious nature, to be occupied in the enterprises of commerce. Having chosen a mechanical business, he engaged himself with a cooper, but it proved to be an employment too laborious for his youthful and naturally delicate frame."[115] During this time Benezet told a friend, "I find being much amongst the buyers and sellers rather a snare to me, as I am of a free, open disposition. I had rather be otherwise employed, and more retired and quiet."[116] Benezet disliked the life of merchants, of bartering and deal making, and the concept of one person profiting at another person's expense. In a certain way his antimercantilist ideas were quite organic. They did not come from anything he had read at the time, only from what he had seen of the business life of his father and other Quaker and Philadelphia merchants.

Around 1739 Benezet worked as a proofreader for the printer Christopher Sower.[117] Born in Germany and originally a tailor, Sower changed his name from Saur. He later became a tool manufacturer, and imported printing equipment and a press from Germany in 1731. Later he published religious books and also the first German-language newspaper in America. Two other things stand out about Sower. First, on May 20, 1751, he and his son were witnesses to the signing of the will of Benezet's father, who signed his name as J. Stephen Benezet.[118] Second, when Anthony Benezet published his first work, *Observations on the Inslaving of Negroes* (1760), which had not been approved by the Quakers and for which he had to find funds to print, the printer was "Christopher Sower: Germantown."

Benezet and Education

Anthony Benezet, like his father, took an active part in Philadelphia's educational endeavors. Benezet first began teaching at the Quaker school in the late 1730s.[119] In 1742 "he was solicited to take charge of a school in Philadelphia, founded by and chartered for William Penn." He stayed at the Penn School for twelve years, and in 1755 he "established a school on his own account for the instruction of girls, and soon found himself entrusted with the education of the daughters of the most affluent and respectable inhabitants of the city."[120]

During his twelve years (1742–1754) at the William Penn Charter School, he earned £50 a year.[121] After retiring he took only a month's rest and began teaching at the girls' schools for £80 a year. He stayed one year and then began serving as a member of the Overseers of Public Schools and as a manager of the Pennsylvania Hospital. In 1757 he returned to the girls' school at the salary of £20, roughly the same as that paid to an inexperienced teacher. He stayed there for the next twenty years, except for a period in 1766–67, when he resigned owing to ill health.[122]

Years later, Benezet's former students told anecdotes about his concern for all creatures, even mice and rats. In one story two of his students placed a live mouse on a pillory with strings atop Benezet's desk; it bore the sign "I stand here my honest friends, For stealing cheese and candle ends." Benezet freed the mouse, proclaiming "Go, poor thing go." He pardoned the students, who got praise for "wisely and mercifully" imprisoning rather than executing the mouse, but he spent extra hours inside that afternoon to think about their injustice.[123] John F. Watson, in the collection of historical anecdotes published as *The Annals of Philadelphia*, told similar stories of Benezet's benevolence to animals. When a friend questioned him about his practice of feeding rats near his house, suggesting that the rats be killed, Benezet rejected the thought: "'Nay,' said good Anthony, 'I will not treat them so; you make them thieves by maltreating and starving them; for being so fed they never prey on any goods of mine!'"[124] Benezet also introduced reform in the realm of school discipline, preferring kindness and moral suasion to any form of corporal punishment.[125]

Known to leading Philadelphians and the humbler folk who worked on the docks alike, Benezet was a universally recognized figure in colonial Philadelphia. Benezet lived not far from the slave-trading center of Philadelphia and daily saw this activity occur. On October 3, 1751, an article in the *Pennsylvania Gazette* read: "SOLD, A Parcel of likely Negroes, very reasonable. Enquire of John Strutton, at Spencer Trotter, in Front Street. N.B. Said Negroes may be seen at a Free Negroe Woman, in Chester Street, opposite to Mr. Anthony Benezet."[126] The advertisement was a recognition that everyone knew where the Frenchman lived, for his house had been both a place for Quaker meetings and later the site of the "Free African School" also known as "The School for Black People," or in some eighteenth-century sources simply as Benezet's School. Carter G. Woodson put it best: "Let no casual reader of this story conclude that Benezet was a mere theorist or pamphleteer. He ever translated into action what he professed to believe. Knowing that the enlightenment of the black would not only benefit them directly but would also disprove the mad theories as to the impossibility of their mental improvement, Benezet became one of the most aggressive and successful workers who ever toiled among these unfortunates."[127]

The Establishment of the African Free School

As early as 1750 Benezet began to teach young black people, primarily in his own home in the evenings. This became known as Benezet's school.[128] Summing up his intentions he wrote, "having observed the many disadvantages these afflicted people labor under in point of education and otherwise, a tender care has taken place to promote their instruction in school learning, and also their religious and temporal welfare, in order to qualify them for becoming reputable members of society."[129]

At the January 1770 Monthly Meeting of Quakers in Philadelphia, a plan was presented—probably by Benezet, although the minutes do not say who did it—and a motion passed to begin a school for black students. Prominent among the Quaker men who joined in the discussions were James and Israel Pemberton, Henry Drinker, Joseph Marriott, and Daniel Stanton. The school became a division of the Penn Charter School. Because of Benezet's past as an educator and the success of the school run out of his home, he convinced the members of the Monthly Meeting that blacks were capable of being taught.[130] He initially was not a member of the formal group of overseers who maintained and monitored the school, but he nonetheless played a similar role to that of the overseers in his first months and years of operating the school. Minutes of the School Committee's meetings note Benezet's presence at meetings held primarily to evaluate the performance of the students. Overseers' minutes of the meetings of the School for Black People (African Free School) show that the school began on June 28, 1770.[131] The first class consisted of twenty-two young students, one-half boys and one-half girls. Although the exact number of students who attended the school between 1770 and 1775 is not known, at least 250 young blacks attended.[132] Several students who attended the school later became leaders of Philadelphia's black community. Among them was James Forten whose father, Thomas, had also been taught at one of the Quaker schools.[133]

Benezet especially thought highly of the black girls the schools educated. "The black girls," he wrote, "have the appearance of decency, attention and submission. It is a nursery of good servants and virtuous housekeepers."[134] The school prepared the girls to be productive members of society. He wanted the same for young white girls.[135] Indeed, attendance at the African School, according to the minutes, would give the black students "religious and literary instruction as would qualify them for the proper enjoyment of freedom, and for becoming useful and worthy citizens."[136] He wanted the same for young white men and women.In 1778 he coauthored with Isaac Zane *Some Observations Relating to the Establishment of Schools,* stressing the importance of education for young people, who required "growth of piety and virtue" as they learned the skills necessary for functioning as working adults.[137]

Benezet's opposition to slavery was based on a concept of eventual equality between blacks and whites. Through education, black students could exhibit capability in learning that would prove their intellectual equality with white contemporaries.[138] The continued success of black students bolstered Benezet's argument for black equality. He advocated teaching not only the basic courses of reading, writing, and arithmetic but also vocational education. The curriculum in Benezet's African Free School centered on those basics, as well as on sewing and knitting for girls when the school had an instructor for such skills. Benezet felt, as did most Quakers and virtually all educators of the time, especially in speaking about the education of the working classes, that education must first fit the students' practical needs. Educating blacks in a trade would assist them in continuing to serve a role in society and in providing for them after emancipation.[139]

The aging Benezet had no desire to again enter into the rigorous routine of day-to-day teaching in addition to his many other activities. However, the frequent changes of teachers over the next few years led Benezet to put forward his own name in March 1781.[140] He wrote to his close friend, the Virginia Quaker Robert Pleasants, that "the education of the poor blacks . . . had been so much the object of my consideration that I solicited to be appointed master of the School." He added that "perhaps from a fear the service would be too arduous or some other cause put me by," others did not apply to teach at the school, and "if the place be vacant I shall renew my application, for it has been indeed a matter of concern to me."[141]

Two years later, in 1783, he told Benjamin Franklin, "After teaching the youth of this city near forty years, I have solicited and obtained the office of teacher of the Black children and others of that people, and employment which though not attended with so great pecuniary advantages as others might be, yet affords me such satisfaction. I know no station in life I should prefer before it."[142] With all that he had done, Benezet considered the education of black youth his signal achievement.

Benezet seems to have been given complete oversight of the school in 1782 and ran it until his death in May 1784. He also was among those in the community of Friends who gave money to assist in the development of the school. The initial plan called for a subscription of £100 a year for three years, but the school could not make ends meet.[143] In 1784 the minutes record that "the school is indebted about 200 pounds chiefly being to the Estate of our Friend Anthony Benezet."[144] Benezet's 1784 will privileged the school "to employ a religious minded person or persons to teach a number of Negroes, Mulatto, or Indian Children to read and write, Arithmetic, plain Accounts, needlework, & c."[145]

The May 6, 1784, edition of the *Pennsylvania Packet* editorialized his contribution to black education: "For some years past he devoted his attention considerably to the education of Negro and mulatto children from a desire that they might hereafter prove useful members of Society, and worthy of that freedom to which the humane and righteous law of this commonwealth passed in 1780 has restored them, and to this we understand he has given all his property, above two thousand pounds, after providing for his ancient and feeble widow."[146]

Benezet's obituary in the *Pennsylvania Gazette* of May 12, 1784, provides more details of his bequest to educate blacks: "Anthony Benezet . . . devoted his attention considerable to the educations of Negroe and Mulattoe children, from a desire that they might thereafter prove useful members of society and worthy of that freedom to which the humane and righteous law of this commonwealth, passed in 1780, has restored them." The obituary ended with "in his last will [he] bequeathed the annual income of his whole estate, forever (after the decease of his wife), for the instruction and education of Negroe and Mulattoe children."[147] His bequest encouraged others to give to the school. Soon after he died the Overseer Committee recorded that after "our valued friend, A. Benezet having made a large bequest to the school, and several other persons having also bequeathed a sum of money for its support," the school achieved a measure of fiscal solvency.[148]

His financial contributions as well as his taking control of the administrative actions of the school effectively saved it from being shut down by the Quakers, and the school grew and flourished for many years following his death.[149] The school allowed Benezet to carry forward his ideas about the education of blacks, as set forth in *A Short Account of the People Called Quakers* (1780): "Having observed the many disadvantages these afflicted people labor under in point of education and otherwise, a tender care has taken place to promote their instruction in school learning, and also their religious and temporal welfare, in order to qualify them for becoming reputable members of society."[150]

Benezet and Philadelphia Charity

In addition to his lifelong work in education Anthony Benezet implemented his principle of defending the downtrodden and oppressed in other ways. In 1751 Benjamin Franklin began discussions with the noted Philadelphian physician Thomas Bond about the development of a community hospital. Franklin warmed to the idea and began to write articles in the *Pennsylvania Gazette* to drum up support. In his autobiography Franklin wrote with obvious pride: "In 1751, Dr. Thomas Bond, a particular Friend of mine conceiv'd the Idea of establishing a Hospital in Philadelphia for the Reception and Cure of poor sick Persons, whether Inhabitants of the Province or Strangers. . . . At length he came to me with the compliment that he found there was no such thing as carrying a public-spirited project through without my being concerned in it."[151] A petition signed by thirty-three influential Philadelphians was submitted to the assembly, but it failed to sway them. Franklin came up with an idea to incorporate the concept through a list of contributors who were to meet and elect officers and raise money. Franklin soon raised £2,751 (751 more than his goal); with a politician's glee he wrote, "I don't remember any of my political maneuvers, the success of which at the time gave me more pleasure; or wherein, after thinking of it, I more easily excused myself for having made some use of cunning."[152] On February 6, 1752, the *Pennsylvania Gazette* announced that the home of the late Judge John Kinsey on High Street (now Market Street) was ready to "receive the hospitals first patients."[153] By May 28, 1755, the cornerstone for the new hospital building was laid at 8th and Spruce streets. Franklin and Bond named a board of twelve leading men, including Samuel Rhoads, later a Pennsylvania delegate to the Continental Congress and mayor of Philadelphia, and Israel Pemberton, Jr., a leading Quaker and Benezet's lifelong friend and confidant.

Benezet was listed as one of the thirty-six voting contributors at the hospital corporation's first meetings. He had only donated £10, which was the minimum contribution required for membership. In 1757 Benezet became a full board member. Shortly after, he wrote, with his dry sense of humor, "Since I have attended the hospital as one of its managers, I am become so strong by often viewing the wounded patients when dressed by the surgeons that I think I could assist, if it were needful, in cutting off a man's leg."[154] In fact his work with the hospital prepared him to be "active in alleviating the sufferings of the prisoners" during the Revolutionary War.[155] This work also allowed him to see the effect of alcohol on some men: in 1774 he published *The Mighty Destroyer Displayed, in Some of the Dreadful Havoc Made by the Mistaken Use as Well as Abuse of Distilled Spirituous Liquors.*[156]

Benezet's work at the hospital prepared him to take the lead in another humanitarian crisis in November 1755: the arrival in Philadelphia of 454

Acadians,[157] part of between 6,300 and 7,000 Acadians whom the British forced into exile and expelled to France and the American colonies during the Grand Dérangement.[158] French in language and Roman Catholic in religion, the Acadians caused great uneasiness among the Pennsylvanians. Until the provincial authorities could decide what to do with these refugees, they were held under armed guard aboard the ships, where disease spread rapidly. Governor Robert Hunter Morris declared at a town meeting on November 19, 1755, that "I do not think it is safe in our present circumstances, to permit them to land, I have ordered these vessels that brought them to lie at a convenient distance below the Town, and have put guards upon them and ordered them provisions."[159] He also reminded the leaders that "the people here . . . are very uneasy at the thought of having a number of enemies scattered in the very bowels of the country, who may go from time to time with intelligence, and join their countrymen now employed against us, or foment some intestine commotion in connection with the Irish and German Catholics, in this province."[160]

The same town council meeting decided "that a proper person be sent on board to take account of the numbers of the Neutrals and the Provisions on Board, and how much has been expended on the voyage, and to superintend the victualling them and their guards."[161] Five days later on November 24, 1755, the council recorded that the "proper person" had been found: "Anthony Benezet, attending without was called in, and informed the House that he had, at the request of some of the members, visited the French Neutrals now on Board Sundry Vessels in the river." Benezet found, according to the records from the meeting, that those aboard ship "were in great need of blankets, shirts, stockings and other necessaries." After Benezet left the meeting, the council resolved "that this House will allow such reasonable expenses as the said Benezet may be put to in furnishing the Neutral French now in the Province with necessaries."[162]

Benezet immediately went to work, first aboard the ships and then at the "Pest House," the almshouse for the poor. Some were also taken to old military barracks, though they were not fit for human use. He also supervised the transport of some few to the newly founded Pennsylvania Hospital. So scarce were his own funds that in an uncharacteristic gesture he asked for and received recompense on December 9, 1756.[163] Ten years later he was still at his work and yet to be reimbursed for many of his efforts.[164] In March 1756 the Pennsylvania assembly appropriated funds to send the Acadians to lands the Native Americans had been run out of. Benezet refused to participate in forced removal of Native Americans or the relocation of the Acadians. Benezet continued his work for several more years and as late as November 20, 1758, petitioned the assembly on behalf of the refugees.[165] Later Benezet helped the Acadians petition for their return to Nova Scotia. They petitioned in French, with Benezet translating "we shall never freely consent to settle in this province."[166] In assessing his work, eighty years later Philadelphian Deborah Logan wrote that "he appeared almost their only friend" and "gave liberally of his own, solicited alms for others on their behalf (to which he endeavored to turn the attention of the government,) and graciously educated many of their daughters. Scarce a day passed without seeing some of these poor people applying to him as their benefactor."[167] His work established in America the Quaker tradition of "nonpartisan relief to the civilian sufferers from war."[168]

In the late 1750s he also became active in the Friendly Association for Regaining and Preserving Peace with the Indians by Pacific Measures and was elected as one of its sixteen trustees. The French and Indian War (1754–63) brought about increased struggle for westward lands occupied by Native Americans. Pennsylvania's founder, William Penn, had developed a respect and appreciation for the languages and cultures of Native Americans, something his successors did not.[169] On June 14, 1758, Benezet wrote to John Smith that the relationships between white settlers and Native Americans was "very afflicting to a sympathizing mind, and naturally leads, with deep concern, to consider the neglect which so much prevails among your politicians with respect to Indian affairs." He later told Smith that his "declaration of war against the Indians . . . may lead to some rash and cruel act." The consequences, he told Smith, "might be dreadful."[170]

The French and Indian War created an unprecedented crisis for Quaker society. Quaker pacifist principles conflicted both with the attitude of the Penn family to the war and with the reality that the fighting had started within Pennsylvania itself.[171] The concomitant offensive of Benezet and John Woolman against slavery, the arrival of the displaced Acadians, and the need to develop policies for relations with hostile Native American nations in the climate of a Franco-British war led most of the Quaker members to withdraw from the provincial assembly.[172] A good many Quakers heeded the renewed call to look inward and renew their spirituality.

During this period of relinquishing control of the assembly, a split developed within the Quaker leadership between those who wanted to retain political power and wealth and those who wanted to withdraw politically but retain wealth. Benezet and some others eschewed both wealth and political power in favor of seeking unity within the society on more universal and humanitarian themes. In April 1756 Benezet described in a letter to his friend Jonah Thompson the spiritual renewal or awakening occurring among the Quakers as the war crisis developed: "Thou wilt, have doubtless, heard of thy Troubles & Confusions which for many Months past, have surrounded us, & which, in some Respects, are likely to increase, if France should declare War." He added that "many of our friends begin to rouse from that lethargy in which they have too long been plunged, thro' a love of this world."[173]

War and Revolution

Some years later, as the American Revolution approached, Benezet and a few others with differing opinions on the independence struggle understood the obvious irony in the rhetoric of revolutionaries railing against tyranny on the one hand and the threat of their own possible "enslavement" while holding slaves themselves on the other.[174] In the wake of the Stamp Act Crisis of 1765–66 Benezet had first asked in his newly published *A Caution and a Warning to Great Britain* "how many of those who distinguish themselves as the Advocates of Liberty, remain insensible and inattentive to the treatment of thousands and ten of thousands of our fellow man," the enslaved Africans?[175]

Thinking of Benezet, Rush posed the same dilemma to Jacques Barbeu Dubourg in 1769. In a letter printed in the *Ephémérides du citoyen* he told the Frenchman, "it would be useless for us to denounce the servitude to which the Parliament of Great Britain wishes to reduce us, while we continue to keep our fellow creatures in slavery just because of their skin color."[176] He offered no further explanation, perhaps because he did not yet have the answer.

As a pacifist, Benezet did not believe in the American revolutionaries' right to use violence to resist George III's government. Surprisingly, he was able to print some pamphlets concerning war, such as *Serious Considerations on Several Important Subjects, viz on War and Its Inconsistency with the Gospel,* during the war years.[177] Woolman and Benezet, Israel and James Pemberton, Daniel Stanton, and other Quaker leaders created the twelve-man Meeting for Sufferings to act as a safeguard for religious fellowship and Quaker ideas and ideals.[178] The Quarterly Meetings nominated four men each to this committee. Benjamin Rush later wrote of Benezet's anguish during the Revolutionary War days: "During the time the British Army was in possession of the city of Philadelphia, he was indefatigable in his endeavors to render the situation of the persons who suffered from captivity as easy as possible. He knew no fear in the presence of his fellowmen."[179] Rush added that the men who commanded the British and German troops treated him with great dignity.

The Antislavery Movement and Humanitarianism

Rush summed up the centrality of Benezet to the antislavery movement in a letter to Granville Sharp: "Great events have been brought about by small beginnings. Anthony Benezet stood alone a few years ago in opposing Negro slavery in Philadelphia and now 3/4ths of the province as well as the city cry out against it. I sometimes please myself with the hopes of living to see it abolished or put upon another footing in America."[180]

Benezet began to step up his letter-writing campaign just as he and his fellow abolitionists mounted a more rigorous and concerted challenge to individual slaveholders. In the summer of 1783 two free black men were charged with being runaway slaves and were arrested and held in the Philadelphia Work House. The men reached out, as best they could, to Philadelphia leaders and citizens, but their appeals fell flat. When all else failed, in the "spirit of their ancestors," the men chose suicide over re-enslavement. They had tasted freedom. Sympathetic whites, first of all the Quakers, were angered into action. Benezet spent the last months of his life pursuing their case, writing to John Pemberton on August 10, 1783:

The case of the oppressed black people becomes rather more & more weighty with us; my situation in the Negro Schools lays me very open to frequent solicitations to assist them, almost daily & sometimes more, which is a matter of much concern to me I cannot attend to, as I could desire. Several have been brought into this City to attend great men, members of Congress &c. some of who, from circumstances or other, intitule [sic] them to claim their freedom, look to us for protection, which by the Divine Injunction [Deuteronomy 23:15] we seem bound to grant, even if they had no legal claim; others are torn children from parents & parents from children &c. to be sold in the Southward where they have reason to expect worse usage than here. The matter has been so close with some of the Black People; that redress being refused, or delayed, the poor disconsolate Creature has made away with themselves, as was the case of a sensible French Negro, who from the most clear evidence was a freeman, on whose behalf I had in vain requested a Habeas Corpus; redress thus delayed & uncertain the poor fellow hung himself to the great regret of all who knew him. Another having pressingly, on his knees, solicited a friend, without success, to prevent his being sent away to the southward, from his connections, drowned himself, as they were taking him down the river.[181]

Benezet prodded the Pennsylvania Abolition Society, which had not met during wartime, to reconvene. He urged "Thomas Harrison, James Starr, Thomas Meredith, and seventeen others to call a meeting of the Society after nine years,"[182] which set in motion a process that led to an investigation of the suicides. Benezet outlined the duties and responsibilities, as he saw them, of the abolitionists in his letter to Pemberton and appealed to all members of the "Committee appointed to treat with such members who are still in any degree concerned in the support of slavery, also affording assistance to the Black People, who we have set free, but have not yet been able to fix any effectual mode of giving them the necessary assistance, which many of their afflictive cases require." The tasks before Benezet were immense. He had daily to help provide for blacks and in the process reassure them that in him they had a friend. He had to respond to the slave suicides. He had to oversee the Quaker manumission committee, and he had to try and restart the Pennsylvania Abolition Society. Along the way he continued to organize petition campaigns to the Pennsylvanian legislative bodies that were emulated throughout the colonies and in England and eventually France. He called for a committee to be appointed made up of "Friends at large, not Monthly Meetings," for the "steady purpose of affording assistance to such Black people as may be under special suffering." He found that some slave owners rather than part with their slaves forced them on ships "to prevent the exertion of what small part of the laws might be so construed in their favor." To combat this subterfuge Benezet attempted to raise money to give directly to the blacks. In the aftermath of the war he found that the economic "difficulty of the times . . . has lessened the ability of many" to raise funds "on behalf of the Negroes, in the colonies." Appealing again to Pemberton, he "remembered the kindness of our Brethren in England & Ireland, in raising so large a sum of money for the relief of those amongst us who are brought in distress by the late war & that a great part of this fund remains unappropriated."[183]

This was a bold move. In essence, he was asking whites to spend money that had been raised to help whites displaced by the war to aid blacks displaced by that same war. He estimated that in addition to aiding blacks who preferred suicide to slavery, there were "still not less than four hundred thousand black People on this northern part of the continent, many of whom will probably be continually emigrating to the northward."[184]

Benezet told Pemberton that the proposals were "solely my own, unknown to friends," and he asked him to confer with other antislavery advocates in London, like Nicholas Waln and William Dillwyn. He concluded by asking Pemberton to reach out to people beyond the Quakers. As always, he sent to England a packet of materials. In this case he sent Pemberton a copy of David Cooper's *A Serious Address*, which was reprinted in Liverpool in 1784.[185]

Benezet's last effort, in his own final days, to eliminate the conditions that led to the suicides of the unfortunate runaway slaves in 1783 marked a fitting end to his life. The slave population of Philadelphia at his death was a third what it had been in 1767; within fifteen years of Benezet's passing, greater Philadelphia would have only 55 slaves in a black population of 6,083 people. Such was his immediate legacy to the African American community of Philadelphia. His work with the hospital, with schools for those girls who were often left out of education, with the Acadian refugees, and with Native Americans, in short, his life in service to the greater community, made Anthony Benezet, quite apart from his central role in the Atlantic world antislavery movement, "America's first great humanitarian reformer."[186]

Chapter 2

The Early Quaker Antislavery Movement

Long, long remember'd, from my earliest years,
Prophetic sounds still tingle in my ears,
Still gentle Sandiford methinks I see,
Proclaiming Blacks by God and nature free.
To wasting zeal and sympathy a prey,
Methinks I hear the venerable Lay,
Now, at distress and wrong for pity sigh,
And now, All Slave Keepers, Apostates, cry.
Columbia use had sear'd to Negro-groans,
And distant Europe heard not Afric's moans,
Until thy meeker spirit, Woolman rose,
Aiming to soften rather than oppose;
And thou, lov'd Benezet, of kindred mind,
The World thy country and the Friends mankind.

—*A Poetic Epistle to the Enslaved Africans in the Character of an*
  Ancient Negro Born a Slave in Pennsylvania

The men listed in *A Poetic Epistle*—Ralph Sandiford, Benjamin Lay, John Woolman, and Anthony Benezet—led the long Quaker battle against slavery.[1] Although Benezet transformed the Philadelphia antislavery movement into an Atlantic force in the mid- to late eighteenth century, he would have been the first to recognize the contributions of the Quaker abolitionists who had preceded him. He was fully aware of the legacy he was destined to uphold and strengthen. Following the "Epistle of 1754," Benezet started writing his sentiments and reflections first in letters and then through his tracts. Reflecting on the Quaker past and its future, he wrote to his friend Samuel Fothergill on October 17, 1757: "I may with pleasure say, there continues to be a great shaking amongst our dry bones . . . painful in many, very many respects, is our situation, particularly mine, under an uncommon sense of Poverty and desertion."[2] All through his life he questioned his own moral fortitude and worth, especially after he saw that many Quakers refused to manumit their slaves.

   The earliest Quaker antislavery actions were the protests of George Fox and William Edmundson in the mid- to late seventeenth century. Beginning with the Germantown protest of 1688 local Meetings of Friends sometimes voted for antislavery resolutions. Starting in 1710 the Pennsylvania assembly alternatively imposed and revoked tariffs on slave imports, which Britain always overruled. Then in 1729 such Quakers as Elihu Coleman, Ralph Sandiford, and Benjamin Lay took the lead, writing antislavery tracts. In the late 1740s and early 1750s John Woolman and Anthony Benezet became active in the cause and sought to motivate and unite those Quakers who opposed slavery in any form and to convince others of its sinfulness. Woolman died in 1772. Benezet continued as the leading Quaker voice against slavery; in time he became the leading crusader and theorist against the "peculiar institution" in the Western world, until his own death in 1784. Benezet and others founded in 1775 the Pennsylvania Society for the Relief of the Negroes Unlawfully Held in Bondage, and after a period of relatively quiet Quaker abolitionist activity during the Revolutionary War years the organization was reconstituted in 1784 as the broader-based Pennsylvania Abolition Society. Like its British counterpart founded in 1787, it extended beyond its Quaker base, especially after it was reorganized in 1787 when Benjamin Franklin, a former slave owner, became its president. That same year Richard Allen and Absalom Jones, free black leaders both influenced by Benezet, formed the Free African Society, founded at the site of Benezet's African Free School.

Benezet did more than provide another link in the human chain that ran from Fox and Edmundson through Sandiford and Lay and on to Franklin; he and Woolman changed the nature of the antislavery movement in the 1750s. Inheritors of a tradition of individual dissent against slavery, they forged a collective response to it. In his last decades of life Benezet brought that collective spirit across the Atlantic to Britain and France and laid the foundations for a truly pan-Atlantic antislavery movement. His writings altered the discourse on slavery. Where the activists of the early years relied almost exclusively on religious arguments, Benezet added arguments taken from Enlightenment philosophers and from his study of African history that began in the 1760s.

Quakers and Early Opposition to Slavery in the English Atlantic World

The pacifist Quakers and their principles were rejected by the English government and by other religious groups.[3] Seeking religious freedom, many Quakers emigrated to North America. Wanting a colony of their own but unable to get royal authority to support their efforts, they appealed to William Penn, the son of Sir William Penn, a high-ranking naval official and friend of King Charles II.[4]

The Quaker religion, owing to its history of struggle against oppression, had within it the seeds for the fight against slavery. Antislavery activists, from Sandiford to Benezet, built upon several tenets. First was George Fox's belief that there was "God in every man," which allowed the inner light to shine in every human being. This light allowed people to rid themselves of worldly sins and purge their souls of hurtful ideas. This tradition of equality before God endured throughout the Quaker antislavery movement. Benezet believed that all human beings came into the world "equally entitled to freedom."

The belief in equality before God, however, did not mean that all or even most Quakers thought blacks were socially equal or all forms of involuntary servitude were wrong.[5] The Quakers rejected the doctrine of "original sin," believing that every human being came into the world with no inherited wealth or debt and with no inherited sin passed on by their ancestors. Individuals would not inherit mandatory punishments or forced bondage, and the illegal slavery of their parents could not be passed down to their children. Seventeenth-century Quaker antislavery writers, like Benezet seventy-five years later, had to reject the argument of those who used biblical passages to assert that some people were born into slavery because of the sins or conditions of their ancestors. White skin was not a privilege of birth, nor black skin a lifelong burden to bear. Individuals, regardless of color or creed, had the potential to be equally blessed or equally corrupted by the wickedness of the mortal world. Each person would in time have equal responsibility to fight and struggle against individual and collective sins. The purpose of life was to do good and to leave the world, upon death, a better place.

Second, the Quaker doctrine of nonviolence rejected the concept of the "just war," which undermined a key argument in favor of slavery. John Locke most famously stated this principle, that Africans were "captives taken in a just war" and therefore legitimately slaves. These Quaker doctrines—insistence on innate equality in the eyes of God and nonviolence—attacked the two basic arguments in favor of eighteenth-century slavery. Benezet radically transformed the debate on innate equality by citing travelers' journals, written by slave traders themselves, to provide a new vision of African societies before the arrival of the slaver. With respect to nonviolent principles he also used those journals to show how Africans were violently captured, starved during the middle passage, and beaten while on the ship and on the masters' plantations.

The Quakers insisted that the holy wars of the Old Testament did not justify the right to engage in acts of war, which led them to develop the concept of the "peace testimony." Many Quakers thus opposed participation in the Revolutionary War, raising the question of whether the people of the colonies had the right to defend themselves against British colonial attempts to enslave them. How did the answer to such a question affect one's opinion of slavery itself and of the potential for violent resistance on the part of the slaves?

Quakers like Benezet made this direct correlation. If whites used their theories of the natural inferiority of blacks to justify enslavement, then what of those who believed that the slaves had the equal right to resist? The Quaker peace principle and the natural right for any oppressed person to resist could by nature clash, for if a rebellion occurred, then would it be necessary to put it down? From Fox to Edmundson in the seventeenth-century Caribbean region through Woolman and Benezet in the eighteenth-century Atlantic world, Quaker writers warned that harsh conditions would cause rebellions. In time antislavery activists would argue that the only solution was to free the slaves, not merely to better their conditions, and to find ways to ease them into "productive" society, thus ending the cause of both rebellion and war.

Third was the Quakers' belief, as interpreted by Benezet, that greed, luxury, vanity, the accumulation of wealth, and the desire for maximum profits were the "root of all the evils" and corrupted whites. Benezet summarized his thinking in one of his first pamphlets, *A Caution and a Warning to Great Britain and Her Colonies,* writing, "Thus an insatiable desire for gain hath become the principal moving cause of the most abominable and dreadful scene that was perhaps ever acted upon the face of the earth."[6]

While developing his intellectual arguments linking slavery to the profit motive, he wrote Samuel Fothergill that "it is frequent to see even Friends, toiling year after year, enriching themselves, and thus gathering fuel for our children's vanity and corruption."[7] Anyone "who is not blinded by the Desire of Gain," he argued, should recognize that "the right by which these Men hold the Negro in Bondage is no other than what is derived by those who stole them."[8]

Structure of the Quakers

Another significant aspect of Quaker views on slavery, as David L. Crosby observed, was that "as a persecuted sect, Quakers developed a system of material assistance to the persecuted, institutionalized in the Meeting for Sufferings that could be and often was, extended to non-Quakers who were also victims of persecution."[9] At the most fundamental level of the Quaker order was the meeting. Members gathered in each other's homes or, if constructed, in a meeting house, which resembled a home but was larger. In a given area, such as Philadelphia or Chester County, several of these meetings would come together as the Monthly Meeting, during which church business was conducted. The various monthly meetings of any area came together as the Quarterly Meeting and met four times a year to worship and make church transactions.[10] The meetings "had no paid clergy, and in their worship they spoke up one by one as the spirit moved them. Disregarding distinctions of gender and class, they addressed one another with the terms 'thee' and 'thou,' words commonly used in other parts of English society only in speaking to servants and social inferiors."[11]

The Yearly Meeting included the quarterly bodies within a set jurisdiction. In the American colonies yearly meetings were held for the autonomous regions of Pennsylvania, New York, New England, Virginia, North Carolina, Maryland, and New Jersey. Benezet resided within the Philadelphia Meeting, covering the Delaware River Valley, western New Jersey, Delaware, parts of Maryland, and the Pennsylvania colony.

The Philadelphia Yearly Meeting began around 1685 to function as a relatively independent body within the framework of its mother organization, the London Yearly Meeting. It directly corresponded with other Yearly meetings and issued its own epistles, which were statements that "combined religious exhortation with practical advice to sister Meetings on a wide variety of moral issues." These collective statements, along with constant letter writing, served as a way of communicating and exchanging religious ideas and preserving unity among meetings. Although "in theory all Yearly Meetings were equal," as Hugh Barbour and J. William Frost have shown, "in practice the London Yearly Meeting had the most prestige and provided answers to questions asked by Americans." The Philadelphia Meeting had a similar role in the colonies.[12] In matters concerning Parliament, the Crown, and broader colonial concerns the Philadelphia Quakers acquiesced to the London Friends. Just as the jurisdictional conflicts between political assemblies in America and Parliament Britain caused conflict, so did they also cause friction between the Philadelphia and London Quakers, especially on issues concerning publishing political, religious, and antislavery opinions.

Fox, Edmundson, and Godwyn

In 1657 the founder of Quakerism, George Fox, spoke out against the slave trade in Barbados. His epistle, called *To Friends Beyond the Sea That Have Black and Indian Slaves,* asked Quakers to think about their sins in holding people as chattel. Benezet admired Fox, who sermonized to the slaves and called on their masters to agree "that after certain years of servitude they would make them free." This call was one of the first for the gradual abolition of slavery. A century later Benezet recognized Fox as "a man of exemplary piety who was the principal instrument in gathering the religious society of people, called Quakers, expressing his concern and fellow-feeling for the bondage of the Negroes."[13]

In 1671 Fox gave a famous sermon often quoted later by Benezet and other Quakers fighting against slavery. He called on Friends to "consider with yourselves, if you were in the same condition as the Blacks are,—who came strangers to you, and were sold to you as slaves. I say if this should be the condition of you or yours, you would think it hard measure. Yea and very great bondage and cruelty. And therefore consider seriously of this, and do you for them, as you would have them, or any other, to do unto you, were you in the like slavish condition."[14] Fox did not attack slavery as an institution; rather he raised questions about its moral legitimacy while seeking better treatment for slaves. Above all he insisted that all slaveholders on Barbados follow the example he hoped to set for Quaker slaveholders by providing a religious education to their slaves. Fox had argued that proper training in Christian principles would make slaves less likely to revolt.

Governmental authorities throughout the West Indies reacted strongly against Fox's initiatives. For example, in 1671 the governor of Nevis forbade Quakers to educate blacks in their schools; four years later, in response to a slave rebellion, the colonial legislature of Barbados did the same. Mainland colonies followed suit: the Virginia House of Burgesses outlawed the education of blacks. The authorities sought to prevent the conversion of blacks to Christianity, in part because European legal traditions banned the enslavement of fellow Christians. Quakers were forbidden to bring blacks to their meetings, a stricture laid down by the governors of Barbados (1671) and Virginia (1672) and by the legislature of Barbados in 1675. The latter outlawed Quakers' bringing Negroes to their meetings, clear evidence that the governor's 1671 ban had not had the desired effect. In 1675 the Nevis governor honored the Quaker request to be relieved from patrol duty because of their religious views, but he also required them to report any signs of rebellious stirrings among the blacks and any sign of insubordination.

Fox wrote *Gospel, Family Order* in 1676, which called for all Quakers "to be kind to their slaves, to raise them in the Christian spirit and to give freed slaves the same treatment that was given to indentured servants once they were freed." He triggered the indignation of his fellow Quakers, however, when he demanded of them to "now consider, do not slight them, to wit the Ethyopians; the Blacks, now, neither any Man or Woman upon the Face of the Earth, in that Christ dyed for all, both Turks, Barbarians, Tartarians, and Ethyopians; he dyed for the Tawnies, and for the Blacks, as well as for you that are called Whites; therefore you may see in Acts 8:27 how the Lord commanded Philip to go toward the South and he arose and went and behold a Man of Ethyopia." Fox went a bit further: "Being (as the Scripture affirms) all of one Blood and of one Mind, to dwell upon the Face of the Earth: for Christ (I say) shed his Blood for them, as well as for you, and hath enlightened them, as well as he hath enlightened you and his Grace hath appeared unto them, as well as for yours and so let every Master and Governor of a Family inform them, as well as others of his family, so that they may come to know Christ."[15] Nothing could be clearer. If Christ did

not discriminate and died for all men, then whites were duty bound to follow his lead.

Fox may have been the first Quaker to use Psalm 68:31 in his work:
"There you may see Princes should come out of Egypt, and Ethyopia shall
stretch forth her hand unto God: sing unto God ye Kingdom of the Earth;
Oh! Praise the Lord." He again called for Quakers to preach to "the Ethy-
poians, the Blacks & Tawny–Moors as Philip did; I say preach, Christ Jesus
to them in your Families . . . and let not your Family of Whites and Blacks
be like Sodom and Gomorrah, like Zebulon & Zephervian." In a final statement to the Quarterly Meeting he made a request: "Friends, and all that
have Negroes to be your servants, let them have two or three Hours of the
Day once a Week . . . to meet together, to wait upon the Lord." He believed
this would "bring them Servants from under Oppression to Know the
Lord."[16]

Later in 1676 a Quaker missionary, Alice Curwen, wrote an antislavery
letter to Martha Tavernor, a slave-owning Quaker, which was subsequently
printed alongside a tract titled *A Relation of the Labour, Travail and Suffering
of That Faithful Servant of the Lord Alice Curwen.* Tavernor was "kind" to her
slaves and allowed them, as Fox had suggested, to attend religious services. Because of a slave insurrection in 1675, blacks were denied religious
privileges by the authorities. Curwen asked Tavernor to ignore the prohibition and allow her slaves to attend to their religious needs and yearn-
ings. This statement may have been one of the few known to be written by
a Quaker woman in the seventeenth or eighteenth century. She told her
friend, "I tell thee plainly, thou hast no right to reign over the Conscience
in Matters of Worship of the Living God."[17] Henry Cadbury wrote of the
letter, "It can hardly be taken as sheer abolitionism. Yet we can easily see
that the slave owners feared the results of the Quaker propaganda and
recognized perhaps before the Quakers themselves their revolutionary
implications."[18]

A few years after Fox's initial appeal he joined forces with the Irishman
William Edmundson, a recent arrival to Barbados. Edmundson was an associate of the English radical James Nayler. Nayler was a quartermaster and
Edmundson a foot soldier in Oliver Cromwell's New Model Army during
the English Civil War. Edmundson wrote in his journal, "I went into the
Parliament's army, and there continued part of the war betwixt the King
and Parliament. And when that was over, I went to Scotland under Oliver
Cromwell in the year 1650."[19] According to Christopher Hill, "as long as
the Army existed, Quakers continued to hope that it might once again
become an instrument for achieving God's purposes on earth."[20] After
1661 and the Cromwellians defeat they rethought their ideas and formulated their "peace policy."

Edmundson, the first Quaker in Ireland, became known as the "Apostle
of Irish Quakerism."[21] He was there when William Penn visited in October

1669. Penn wrote of seeing Edmundson on November 31, 1669, where "W[illiam]. E[dmundson]. Kept the meeting. & heavenly it was." Four days later "W[illiam]. E[dmundson]. Came with friends to the Citty. We were at meeting" and "pray'd and din'd & sup'd at home" with him.[22]

Edmundson soon took his missionary work to England's colony Barbados and was with Fox on his second visit there in 1671. His activities among blacks in Barbados led to harsh laws in 1676 and 1680. In an incredible passage Edmundson wrote "after one meeting priest Ramsey went to the governor, Sir Jonathan Atkins, and made a great Complaint against me, that I was a Jesuit come out of Ireland, pretending to be a Quaker, and to make the Negroes Christians; but would make them Rebels and rise and cut their throats." Edmundson added that in 1675 Governor Atkins was about to issue a warrant for his arrest, but Edmundson got wind of it and visited the governor before the warrant could be served. He told Atkins that while he wished to instruct the slaves, he was not condemning the institution of slavery: "I told him that it was good Work to bring [the slaves] . . . to the Knowledge of God and Christ Jesus, and to believe in him that died for them and all Men." He concluded that he believed religion "would keep them from rebelling, or cutting any Man's Throat." He believed colonial authorities were "keeping them in ignorance and under oppression, giving them Liberty to be in common with Women (like Beasts) and on the other Hand starve them for want of Meat and Cloths convenient." For Edmundson, as with Fox, the only alternative was to give the slave a form of the liberty that "God allowed and afforded to all Men, which was Meat and Cloaths." Edmundson wrote at the end of his session with the governor that "after some time he grew very moderate."[23]

The authorities in Barbados again struck against Edmundson in early 1676, once more accusing him of stirring up rebellion and preaching to the enslaved Africans. In denying the accusations Edmundson argued that it was the terrible treatment meted out to the slaves that caused rebellions and that religious teaching and education would prevent them from rising against slave masters. Edmundson did not go to jail but left Barbados for the mainland colonies, where he briefly continued his antislavery crusade. He traveled to Rhode Island, and at Newport's Quaker House he sent a letter of "general advice," dated September 19, 1676.[24] He went much further than any before him in condemning all forms of slavery:

It would be acceptable with God, and answer the witness in all, if you did consider their [i.e., the Negroes'] condition of perpetual slavery, and make their condition your own, and so fulfill the law of Christ. For perpetual slavery is an aggravation, and an oppression upon the mind, and hath a ground; and Truth is that which works the remedy, and breaks the yoke, and removes the ground. So it would do well to consider that they [the slaves] may feel, see, and partake of your liberty in the Gospel of Christ [that] they may see and know the difference between you and the other people, and your self-denial may be known to all.

Edmundson added words similar to those of Anglican Bishop Morgan Godwyn's: "And many of you count it unlawful to make slaves of Indians, and if so, then why not the Negroes?"[25]

Thomas Drake, the eminent Quaker historian, gave him "first place in the great succession of antislavery apostles. Compared to his unequivocal challenge to slavery and the slave trade, the tentative questioning of Godwyn or Baxter or even Fox himself, seemed very feeble." In Drake's eyes "Edmundson stands first in Britain's empire to proclaim Negro slavery a sin—but he spoke a hundred years too soon . . . neither Quakers nor other Christians would yet acknowledge the validity of his insight."[26]

Edmundson touched a sensitive nerve by asking a simple question: "Would the masters make the slaves' condition their own?"[27] His efforts did not bear immediate fruit, but in the following years there were scattered antislavery activities among the Quakers in Barbados and in Maryland, where Quaker women, not unlike Ann Curwen, called for "strict justice" in helping educate enslaved Africans.[28]

Quaker antislavery activity received a critical boost in 1682, when Penn granted the articles of the "Free Society of Traders," which contained a key provision against lifetime slavery. The articles declared "if the Society should receive Blacks for servants, they shall make them free at fourteen years end, upon Considerations that they will give into the Society's Warehouse two thirds of what they are Capable of producing on such a parcel of Land as shall be allotted them by the Society."[29]

Thus if the enslaved Africans were held in slavery at only one place and lived in servitude for at least fourteen years, and the Free Society was paid two-thirds of their potential income, the blacks would then become tenants of the company.[30] Although the measure may seem modest, it put an end to selling and transporting of "long-established" or older slaves away from their families, and it curtailed the slave owners' desire to rid themselves of unruly slaves or of slaves of a different sex than they desired. At the same time other slaves were brought in from the West Indies.[31]

The next important printed salvo against slavery, however, came not from a Quaker but from Morgan Godwyn, who had seen Fox's tract.[32] Godwyn was already opposed to the Quakers and their beliefs, and Fox's missive further angered him because it accused Anglicans of neglecting the religious training of the blacks.[33] Godwyn delved deeper into the causes of slavery than Fox had and responded with the *Negro and Indians Advocate* in 1680. He challenged Fox by paraphrasing him: "Who made you the Masters of the Gospel to white people only and not the Tawnies and Black also . . . why do you not teach your people on this point or show them by your example beginning at Home with those of your FAMILIES." He quoted "the Friend" who asks, "What should be the reason that you spend so much time in Railing against us, whom you call Quakers, and other peaceable people. But where there is Occasion have not a word to say."[34] The Quakers had issued a challenge, and Godwyn took the occasion to add a few words to show his concern for blacks. Twice he wrote that "the Negro (both Slaves and others) have naturally an equal Right with other Men to the exercise and Privilege of Religion; of which tis unjust in any part to deprive them."[35]

Godwyn realized that no matter what his differences with Fox, slavery was not the product of Quakers but rather of the West Indian planters, who argued that the blacks were not human beings. He wrote "a disingenuous and unmanly Position hath been formed; and privately (and as it were in the dark) handed to and again, which is this, That the Negro's though in Figure they carry some resemblances of Manhood, yet indeed no Men."[36] Many historians have asserted that whites never claimed that blacks were not human, only that they represented a lesser and degraded type of mankind. Godwyn shows clearly what many whites did in fact believe that blacks were closer to apes than to humans.

Godwyn was one of the first to link the oppression of the Native Americans to that of the blacks.[37] "Conceit unto which I have read," he wrote, "was some time since invented by the Spaniards, to justify their murdering the Americans."[38] He was referring to the death of Native Americans, a concern that later Quaker opponents of slavery, like Franklin and Benezet, shared with him. In Chapter 7 of *Some Historical Account of Guinea,* Benezet paid special attention to Godwyn's observations about the oppression of Indians, which were "particularly noted in a book, entitled *The Negroes and Indians Advocate* dedicated to the Archbishop of Canterbury written so long since as in the year 1680 by Morgan Godwyn, thought to be a clergyman of the Church of England."[39] Like Godwyn and later Franklin, Benezet saw the connection between the decimation of the Native Americans and the enslavement of the Africans. He, like Godwyn, cited Acts 17:26, "That God had made (of one Blood) all Nations of Men, for to dwell on all the face of the earth," and conceptualized Godwyn's preaching that "Man alone is capable and Disciplined to which our Negroes equally with other People are."[40]

Godwyn had challenged the planters: "First That naturally there is in every man, an equal right to Religion. Second, That the Negroes are men, and therefore are invested with the Same right. Thirdly, That being this qualified and invented to deprive them of this right is the highest injustice." In his most famous passage Godwyn postured, "These two words *negro* and *slave* are by custom Homogeneous and Convertible; even as Negro and Christian, and Englishman and Heathen then, are by the like corrupt Custom and Partiality made opposites." For Godwyn the blacks may not have had the right to be free, but they were human, and whites had shamed their own race by "treating their slaves with far les Humanity than they do their cattle." Never before had one placed the question so clearly as he asserted that "the consideration of the shape and figure of our

Negro's Bodies, their limbs and Members; their Voice and Countenance, in all things according with other Men's; together with their Risibility and Discourse (Man's peculiar Facilities) should be a sufficient Conviction," that they were indeed men.[41] He was one of the first to challenge the "environmentalist argument," that some humans were more suited to slavery and work in the hot sun. For Godwyn "their hair, figure, and complexion (the same with our mulattoes) be speaking no less," as they were but different physical attributes of human beings. Neither the slave's hair nor his body or skin color made him more able to work in the sun than the poor white indentured servant in the Chesapeake.

Godwyn laid the question before the colonizers and added two other observations. First, "that if the Irishman's Country had first lighted in the Englishman's way he might have gone no further to look for Negroes. That is Slaves such as the Negroes generally are." And he added words that later Benezet and the Abbé Grégoire would simulate: "It being certain, that Africa was once famous for both Arts and Arms . . . and it is also evident that, all our own people do not exceed these either for Knowledge or Piety."[42]

Godwyn asked whether slaves, if Christianized, would prove more loyal to their masters. Did Christianity establish the absolute right of the free white man to enslave the free African? Would the white man's religion help diminish the likelihood of rebellion, or would the slaves adapt this religion to seek freedom? For the slave another question arose: would baptism bring freedom? Indeed Godwyn had asked, "Lastly, if a slave seth foot upon the soil of some countries (as in France), he thereby at the very instant made a Frenchman; or else (as in the same is also customary) by receiving Baptism."[43] Once Godwyn rejected the link of baptism to black freedom, he helped allay white fears of allowing black worship. Godwyn knew that once slave owners accepted this principle, they would have "no excuse for withholding religions from their slaves."[44]

With all his pronouncements Godwyn still argued that slavery and Christianity were compatible. He simply believed that religion would quell blacks' desire for freedom and make them more obedient. The whites would be free of guilt by allowing slaves to be Christians, and they would be more secure as the likelihood of slave revolt diminished. Although slaves for generations continued to believe that baptism would bring about manumission, no such thing was true. That did not stop blacks from believing that their God would be as good to them as he was to the whites.

Godwyn's other works were less well known but still used by later activists like Benezet. In *Trade Preferr'd Before Religion,* Godwyn linked slavery with the drive for "insatiable gain" and commercialism, which undermined religious authority. The newfound powers of the commercial elite unleashed political liberties, which circumvented the church.[45] Neither Godwyn nor Fox challenged the legality of slavery, only its inhumanity, but Godwyn's view that "the Negros (both slave and others) have naturally an equal Right with other men to Exercise and Privileges of religions" had a tremendous impact on the early debates. He took two steps forward and one step back. He would go no farther. He did not fight for the slave to be free, only equal. Later abolitionists fought for the slaves' right to be free but not to be equal.[46]

A few years later in another lesser-known tract, Godwyn again unleashed another attack on Fox and the Quakers. He scornfully asked as he had some years earlier, "Who made them Masters of the Gospel, to the White People only, and not to the Tawnies and Blacks also? As is said in Fox's Pamphlet to be seen." He was quite critical of the Anglicans who accepted "all manners of Licentiousness . . . particularly allowing Polygamy to their Negroes." The blacks spent "the Sundays in Idolatrous Dance and Drunkenness's, no Time else being allowed them in Week Days." The whites were so lax because they believed "that Negroes are Creatures destitute of Souls, to be Ranked among Brute Beasts, and Treated accordingly." As far as Godwyn was concerned, the slave masters in the Islands missed out on "all Endeavors to Promote Christ among the Heathen . . . except in New England."[47]

"So vehemently," Alden Vaughn has written, "was Godwyn's condemnation of slave owner brutality that had he not insisted repeatedly on the compatibility of Christianity and human bondage, he might be labeled an early abolitionist." Vaughn surmises that "perhaps Godwyn saw no point in opposing outright a system of social control and economic exploitation that was already firmly entrenched in the colonies and that brought immense profit to the mother country."[48]

Early Antislavery Efforts

In Pennsylvania the "Germantown Protest" of 1688 provided the first major antislavery event organized by whites in colonial North America.[49] The protest came in the form of a petition dated "ye 18 of the 2nd month, 1688." It was to be delivered "to Ye Monthly Meeting Held at Richard Worrell's." It read:

These are the reasons why we are against the traffic of men . . . as followeth: Is there any [among us] that would be done or handled at this manner? viz., to be sold or made a slave for all the time of his life? How fearful and faint-hearted are many on sea, when they see a strange vessel—being afraid it should be a Turk, and they should be taken and sold for slaves into Turkey. . . . In Europe there are many oppressed for conscience sake; and here there are those oppressed who are of a Black colour. And we who protest that it is not lawful to steal, must likewise avoid to purchase such things as are stolen but rather to help to stop this robbing and stealing if possible.

The petition documented three major concerns. First, that slavery violated Christianity's "Golden Rule." They wrote, "There is a saying, that we shall doe to all men like as we will be done ourselves: making no differences of what generation, descent or colour they are." Second, the practice of slavery went against the tenets of Quakerism and caused deep embarrassment to the Friends. They admonished, "This makes an ill report in all those countries of Europe, where they hear of, that ye Quakers doe here handel men as they handel ye cattle . . . and for that reason some have no mind to come hither." Third, the Quakers feared that the inhuman conditions imposed on enslaved Africans would cause them to revolt violently. The petition put the same questions to the Pennsylvanians that the blacks had put to them and other whites: "If once the slaves (who they say are so wicked and stubborn men) should joint themselves, fight for their freedom and handle their masters and mistresses as they did handle them before, will these masters and mistresses take the sword at hand and war against those poor slaves, like we are able to believe, some will not refuse to do; or have these Negroes not as much right to fight for their freedom as you have to keep them slaves."[50] By asking if blacks had the same right to use violence to free themselves as whites claimed, the Germantown Protest provided an affirmation of black humanity. Philosophers had asked that abstractly before, but the persecuted Quakers had a more personal stake concerning violence, rebellion, injustice, and oppression.

The Germantown Friends received a response from the Dublin Monthly Meeting of February 30, 1688. The Dublin Friends replied that the matter "was so weighty that we think it not expedient for us to meddle with it here, but do rather commit it to ye consideration of ye Quarterly Meeting" to be held in Philadelphia. The Philadelphians held their meeting on April 4, 1688, and like their Dublin brethren decided that the issue was "of too great a weight for this meeting to determine."[51] They referred the issue to the Yearly Meeting held in Burlington, New Jersey. At the July 5, 1688, gathering the Quakers concluded that it would not be "proper for this meeting to give a Positive Judgment in the Case. It having so General a Relation to many other parts, and therefore at present they forbear it."[52] In an immediate sense the matter seemed to have ended there.[53] However, as the British abolitionist Thomas Clarkson would write in 1808, the "result was, advice to the members of it to guard against future importations of African slaves, and to be particularly attentive to the treatment of those who were then in their possession."[54] The Germantown meeting went farther than ever in its concern for both the image and soul of Quakerism and the actions of blacks. In 1693, George Keith, the Scottish-born convert, wrote *An Exhortation and Caution to Friends Concerning Buying and Keeping of Negroes* in Philadelphia. Using words similar to Godwyn's, he was disowned for issuing the work without formal approval.

Measures such as the Germantown Protest helped make Philadelphia the leading center of antislavery activity. In 1696 two prominent Quaker ministers, William Sotheby and Cadwalder Morgan, called for a ban on slave ownership and the end of the slave trade. Morgan was concerned about meeting the labor needs on his farm and considered using slaves. Feeling guilty, he prayed for God's guidance. He wrote on May 28, 1696, "And I was in complexity concerning it, And I could find no Satisfaction though I Enquired of men. (Some advised me to buy and others to forebear,) Then I desired of the Lord, that he would make it known to me, whether it was his will that I should buy of them or no." Morgan believed he received his answer: "It was not long before He made it known unto me That I should not be Concerned with them, And Afterwards, I had no freedom to buy or take any of them upon any account."[55] The Germantown Friends Yearly Meeting gave a reply to Sotheby and Morgan. The meeting advised, "Friends be careful not to encourage the bringing in of any more Negroes, & that such that have Negroes be Careful of them, bring them to meetings, or have Meetings with them in their Families, & Restrain them from Loose, & Lewd Living as much as in them lies, & from Rambling abroad on the First Days or other Times."[56]

These singular words again laid down the basic lines of Pennsylvania Quaker opposition to slavery and the slave trade at the start of the eighteenth century. The meeting did not speak of a legal ban on the trade but rather sought "not to encourage the bringing in of any more Negroes."[57] They further sought to bring the slaves already in the colony into Christian society, by teaching them Quaker doctrine and by admonishing slave owners to look carefully after the moral behavior of the slaves. The meeting's action provided an important step in the antislavery movement, because for a while at least it treated blacks as fellow humans whose souls needed to be saved through Quaker spirituality.

In 1700 Penn urged Quakers to allow blacks to attend the quiet meetings. In 1701 Penn wrote in his will, "I will give my blacks their freedom as is under my hand already, and to old Sam, 100 acres, to his children after he and his wife are dead forever, on common rent of one bushel of whet yearly, forever." Penn's widow asked the prominent Philadelphian James Logan to oversee the selling of her slaves and their small children to good people.

The antislavery movement received an enormous boost in 1700 from an unlikely source. Chief Justice Samuel Sewall of Massachusetts, a Puritan colonist who had persecuted Quakers, wrote a pamphlet entitled *The Selling of Joseph*. Men like Aristotle, Bodin, and Locke had over centuries argued the merits of slavery and its compatibility with human progress. As Peter Kolchin noted, they "differed from one another in many ways, but the three proponents respectively of reason, Christian theology, and liberty agreed in finding slavery an acceptable part of the social order."[58] Sewall challenged these thinkers. While his words carried great weight, they had no force of law.

Sewall wrote that "these Ethiopians, as black as they are; seeing are the Sons and Daughters of the first Adam, Brethren and Sisters of the Last ADAM, and the Offspring of GOD; They ought to be treated with a Respect agreeable."[59] Sewall wrote in his diary on June 19, 1700, "having been long and much dissatisfied with the Trade of fetching Negroes from Guinea; at last I had a strong Inclination to Write something about it; but it wore off."[60] According to Sewall biographer Mel Yazara, it was "only after reading a petition to the General Court on behalf of a black couple," whom Sewall felt were "unjustly held in bondage," and learning of a proposal to discourage the slave trade in Massachusetts by means of a forty-shilling per head tax on all slave imports that Sewall renewed his commitment to "write this Apology for them."[61]

Sewall's work resonated because of his use of a verse that Fox had used from the *Book of Psalms* (68:31) called "Ethiopia Shall Soon Stretch Her Hands unto God": "Whereas the Blackamores are not descended of Canaan, but of Cush. Psalm. 68.31, Princes shall come out of Egypt, [Mizriam] Ethiopia [Cush] shall soon stretch out her hands unto God. Under which Names, all of Africa may be comprehended; and their Promised Conversion ought to be prayed for. Jer. 13.23 Can the Ethiopian Change his Skin?" [62] This verse became the standard scriptural reference for eighteenth- and nineteenth-century antislavery writers.[63] Sewall's was one of the first to use the term *man stealers* in reference to the kidnapping and selling of Africans: "And seeing God hath said, 'He that Stealeth a Man and Selleth him, or if he be found in his hand, he shall surely be put to Death,' Exod. 21.116. This law being of Everlasting Equity, wherein Man Stealing is ranked amongst the most atrocious of Capital Crimes. What louder Cry can there be made of that Celebrated warning."[64]

The politically and economically centered tariff and duty debates of the Pennsylvania assembly coincided with discussions at individual meetings of Friends. In 1713 the Chester, Pennsylvania, Monthly Meeting became one of the first bodies to call for the elimination of slavery and requested disciplinary actions against slave-owning Friends. The 1715 Yearly Meeting, in response to the requests from local meetings, urged Friends who owned slaves to treat them with compassion and a Christian spirit. Although the Yearly Meeting urged Friends to stop buying imported slaves, it proposed only a caution and not censure. Colonial Quakers acted within the larger framework of Quakerism: they knew that any action had to be referred back to the English Quakers, who based many of their decisions on how they thought the British Privy Council would respond. The Quakers in London sought to avoid any conflict with the English authorities. Such institutional limitations notwithstanding, individual Quakers continued to agitate against slavery.

In 1715 John Hepburn, a Quaker tailor from New Jersey, published *The American Defense of the Christian Golden Rule, or an Essay to Prove the Unlawfulness of Making Slaves of Men, by Him Who Loves the Freedom of the Souls and Bodies of All Men.*[65] Hepburn was born in England and had been an indentured servant to a Scottish proprietor. He came to America "about 1683 or 1684."[66] By the time he wrote his pamphlet he had lived in

America for many years, although Hepburn did not, like some of his fellow New Jerseyans, own slaves. He publicly asserted that he would not. His work went beyond the portrayal of the horrors of slavery; it showed the hypocrisy of "God fearing Christians" who both supported the doctrine of slavery and bought and sold men, women, and children. Hepburn's ideas had a strong influence on John Woolman, another New Jersey tailor, who continued in the Quaker tradition of the religiously centered attack on slavery.

Hepburn was well-read, as his pamphlet, which reflected upon ideas of early colonial theorists like Cotton Mather, showed.[67] When Justice Sewall reprinted the *Athenian Oracle*, a collection of questions and answers on history, philosophy, mathematics, divinity, love, and poetry, Hepburn added the appendix, revealing his intellectual curiosity.[68] As Roger Bruns observed, Hepburn "catalogued, as no other antislavery piece had done, the evils of slavery: forced labor without pay, violence, cruelty and unlawful punishment, the separation of man and wife, the encouragement of adultery, murder, and war, and its inherent affront to religion."[69] The most important of Hepburn's arguments came in the section titled "Arguments Against Making SLAVES of MEN," which listed twenty arguments and a number of "objects and answers" against slavery. Citing a litany of violations against the enslaved Africans, he lists forced labor, violence, unjust punishment, making prisoners of men, forcing a man to do anything against his will, and separating husbands from wives as violations against humankind and the word of God. After each of the twenty "Arguments" he wrote, "Therefore the making of slaves is unlawful."[70]

From Sandiford to Lay

W. E. B. Du Bois wrote that after their original outburst against slavery, the Quakers "lingered thirty years for breath and courage."[71] The activism that occurred around 1690, reflective of the climate at the time of the Glorious Revolution, gave way to a period of calm and relative inactivity. In the late 1720s, however, two young activists, Elihu Coleman, a Quaker carpenter from Nantucket, and Ralph Sandiford, a Philadelphia merchant, took up the antislavery cause. Sandiford, who owned a shop overlooking the slave market, felt a profound repugnance as he witnessed the selling of slaves. Benezet would have the same reaction a generation later (see Chapter 1). In 1729 Sandiford penned an *Examination of the Practice of the Times,* perhaps because the decline in the duty on imported slaves fell to forty shillings and led to an increased traffic.[72] He paid tribute to George Fox and hoped that "there is a people the Quakers in Pennsylvania that will not own this practice in word or deed."[73]

Sandiford challenged the "curse of Cain," cited in Genesis 9:18–25, which seems the section most often used as the biblical justification for slavery. He wrote, "Neither can these Negroes be proved, by any Genealogy, the Seed of Ham, whom Noah Cursed not, but Noah's curse on Canaan, the youngest son of Ham, is thought a suitable original for the Negro Trade."[74] Frost wrote, "Friends declared that there was not a scintilla of biblical evidence linking the Blacks with either Cain or the Canaanites, but not until Sandiford did they feel it necessary to boldly challenge the doctrine."[75] In editions of the Holy Bible published in eighteenth-century Philadelphia, Verse 25 read, "And he said, Cursed be Canaan, a Servant of Servants shall be unto his brethren."[76] In some later volumes the word *servants* was changed to *slaves* and read, "And he said, Cursed be Canaan: a Slave of Slaves shall he be to his brothers."[77]

As David M. Goldenberg observed, the "curse of Ham" "in its various forms became a very powerful tool for maintaining the existing order in society. Its importance for explaining, and justifying, the enslavement of Blacks cannot be underestimated." Tracking the origins of the "curse," Goldenberg found that a "close relationship between social order and biblical justification" developed "as soon as Europe discovered black Africa and began to engage in the slave trade of its inhabitants." As slaves were transported across the Atlantic, "the Curse of Ham moved with it. . . . It was *the* ideological cornerstone for the justification of Black slavery."[78]

Through Sandiford, Benezet first came to understand the early imperialist ambitions of the Royal African Company and the international network of slave traders. The trade Sandiford believed was "introduced amongst us, as the Fruit of a corrupt tree, which was planted in . . . Time, when the African Company was Commissioned for that trade," was the "Root of all Evil."[79]

Sandiford had perhaps developed knowledge of the workings of the Royal African Company by reading *Certain Considerations Relating to the Royal African Company,* which was published anonymously in 1680 as a defense of the Royal African Company's monopoly.[80] That same year William Wilkerson wrote a document entitled *Systema Africanum: or a Treatise, Discovering the Intrigues . . .of the Guiney Company* that sounded much like the anonymously published *Certain Considerations.* He argued that "if we consider Trade of Negro Servants . . . the Royal Company manage[s], with more than an ordinary Sight for their own advantage."[81]

With the charter of 1672 the Royal African Company was granted a monopoly on the trade of five thousand miles of the western coast of Africa, from Cape Salle in the north to the Cape of Good Hope. The main goal of the company was simply to get as many Africans as possible from the Gold Coast, falling back on other regions to make up the required complements.[82] The company had the right to acquire lands and to hold them for a thousand years. The payment for the land was often as little as "two elephant's teeth." The company also had the power to make peace or war with non-Christian nations in Africa.[83]

Sandiford influenced the later debates on slavery, asking, "Shall we then undertake to remove them, whosesoever Interest shall lead us, to sell them for slaves, Husbands from Wife, and Children from both, like Beasts, with all their Increase, to the vilest of Men, and their Offspring after them, to all Eternity?"[84] He was also prompted to write his tract because in 1729 the per-capita duty on imported slaves had dropped to forty shillings, resulting in an increase in slave imports into the province.

The Overseers of the Press, the Friends' censors of members' writings, denounced Sandiford's words. He also revealed that the chief judge of the province had threatened him with "commitment" if he published the volume. He challenged both the official Quaker rules and the judge's order and had the tract printed. Although the first page reads "printed for the Author, Anno 1729," the publisher was in fact Benjamin Franklin. The Philadelphia Meeting responded by condemning Sandiford and threatened him with punishments and expulsion for publishing his volume without the approval of the Friends' Overseers of the Press.[85] In 1731 he withdrew from society and from the Society of Friends, who nonetheless to prove a point also expelled him. He died in the countryside two years later at the age of forty. Benjamin Lay, who visited his friend Sandiford in his waning days "blamed Sandiford's death on the hounding he had received from the slaveholders."[86]

In 1733 Elihu Coleman published a pamphlet he had written in 1729: *A Testimony Against That Antichristian Practice of Making Slaves of Men, Wherein It Is Shewed to Be Contrary to the Dispensation of the Law and Time of the Gospel, and Very Opposite Both Grace and Nature.* Coleman's pamphlet bore witness to the actions of his fellow Nantucket Quakers. In 1716 they had decided "that it is not agreeable to truth for Friends to purchase slaves and hold them . . . [for] life." In 1729 the Nantucket Friends, Coleman among them, sent an address to the Philadelphia Quakers against purchasing slaves. Coleman's pamphlet used the gospel of Matthew to assert that slavery was a violation of God's Golden Rules and therefore anti-Christian. He asserted that Quakers "can truly say that this practice of making slaves of men appears to be so great an evil that for all the riches and glory of this world, I would not be guilty of so great a sin as this seems to be." He called for men and women to "see the evils of slavery as he had and bring it to an end." Coleman knew well his predecessors' role in beginning the movement against slavery: he wrote that "many sober men, both in their writing and in their public [i.e.] Quaker assemblies whom I could name have condemned the practices of slavery and the slave trade."[87] His pamphlet established two important milestones: he became the first New England Quaker to publish an antislavery tract, and the Quaker Overseers of the Press made *Testimony* the first antislavery tract written by a Quaker to receive their formal support, thus allowing him to publish his work with their blessings. Jean Soderlund surmises, "Perhaps he received approval because he avoided denouncing slaveholders outright."[88]

Benjamin Lay and his wife, Sarah, came to Philadelphia by way of Barbados in 1731. Lay was born in Colchester, England, but had viewed slavery and the trade firsthand while living in Barbados. He soon became known for his eccentric and ascetic manner and for his public and radical departure from Quaker quietism and inner reflection. In 1737 Lay had published *All Slave Keepers That Keep the Innocent in Bondage, Apostates.* Lay wrote, "I know of no worse stumbling blocks the devil has to lay in the way of honest inquirers than our ministers and elders keeping slaves; and by the straining and perverting the Holy Scriptures, preach more to hell than ever they will bring to heaven by their feigned humility."[89]

He took the mostly unorganized pages of his manuscript to Benjamin Franklin, who spent long hours trying to make Lay's rambling written work coherent. Franklin was not fully committed to the antislavery cause at the time, nor was he on record as being against the slave trade. He agreed to arrange and publish the tract only on condition of anonymity. Benjamin Franklin, in retrospect, gave himself credit for coming to the slaves' cause quite early by publishing the works of the radical Quakers Sandiford and Lay. He wrote to John Wright on November 4, 1789, that "about the year 1728, or 1729, I myself printed a book for Ralph Sandiford . . .against keeping Negroes in slavery: two editions of which he distributed gratis." Franklin added that on "and about the year 1736, I printed another book on the same subject for Benjamin Lay. . . . By these instances it appears that the seed was indeed sown in the good ground of your profession."[90] Deborah Franklin said that her husband had such admiration for Lay that he kept a portrait of the eccentric Quaker in his home for many years. Lay, for his part, "seems to have visited Franklin's shop regularly when he ventured from his house in Abingdon to purchase paper, ink, legal forms, and books to give away."[91] Lay also subscribed to Franklin's *Pennsylvania Gazette.*

At the 1738 Yearly Meeting of the Philadelphia Friends the hunchbacked Lay came dressed in a military uniform with a sword hidden under his coat and a Bible that had been fitted with a bladder-like container filled with blood-colored pokeberry juice. A hush came over the meeting as they awaited Lay's next action. His warlike appearance was exhibited to his astonished audience, and he proclaimed:

Oh all you negro masters who are contentedly holding your fellow creatures in a state of slavery during life, well knowing the cruel sufferings those innocent captives undergo in their state of bondage, both in these North American colonies, in the West India islands; you must know thy are not made slaves by any direct law, but are held by an arbitrary and self-interested custom, in which you participate. And especially you who profess "to do unto men as ye would they shall do unto you"— and yet, indirect opposition to every principle of reason, humanity and religion, you are forcible retaining your fellow men from one generation to another, in a state of unconditional servitude; you might as well throw off the plain coat as I do.

Then in dramatic fashion he unloosened the buttons to his great coat and let it fall behind him as he moved forward, giving a dramatic effect to his appearance. Startling the sedate worshipers, he then proclaimed, "It would be as justifiable in the sight of the Almighty if you should thrust a sword through their hearts as I do this book!"[92] The bloodlike juice splattered all over the quiet Quaker meeting.

Sometime later, in the midst of a harsh winter snow, Lay stood in the doorway of the Quaker Meeting House, exposing one bare leg and foot. Several of the parishioners begged him to cover his limbs, as much for their shame as for his own health. Lay told them, "Ah, you pretend compassion for me, but you do not feel for the poor slaves in your fields, which go all over winter half clad." Lay lived six miles outside Philadelphia, in a cave, and was seldom seen after his stunning confrontation. While living in his cave, he befriended the child of a family that lived about a mile away. One evening he lured the child into his dwelling. He observed the worried parents looking frantically for the lad and even asked them "what is the matter"? They replied, "Oh, Benjamin, Benjamin! Our child is gone; he has been missing all day." Lay after a few moments told them, "Your child is safe in my house and you may now conceive of the sorrow you inflict upon the parents of the negro girlhood you hold in slavery, for she was torn from them by avarice."[93] Lay was later accused of kidnapping the child to show white parents and their peers the grief felt by Africans when they or their children were stolen from their African homeland.

Lay's militancy and unusual behavior shocked his fellow Quakers, who shunned him because of his beliefs and his actions. Although people like Woolman and Benezet never adopted Lay's unorthodox and confrontational methods, his ideas did affect them. Lay raised "vegetables for food and flax for clothing," and his example encouraged Woolman and Benezet, who like Lay refused to eat any food or wear any clothes thought to be produced by the labor of enslaved Africans.[94] Benezet's vegetarianism would later mark an aspect of his presentation of African societies, as well as of his personal life.

Lay was publicly disowned by the Quakers at the Yearly Meeting of 1738, but his efforts and those of other early antislavery activists eventually bore fruit: the 1758 Annual Meeting excluded slaveholders from the key Quaker leadership positions. Quakers like Sandiford and Lay made an initial appeal against slavery and then just quietly disappeared after being disowned, disgraced, or even expelled.

Lay's work was published in a climate of widespread slave revolts: rebellions on Antigua and St. Kitts in 1736; the Stono Rebellion in South Carolina in 1739; and, even closer to home, the New York slave conspiracy of

1741.[95] Moreover, Will, one of the Antiguan leaders, who had saved his own life by testifying against his fellows, ended up in New York in 1741 and played a major role in the revolt. This immediate connection further frightened slave owners and white society in general. Both in Charleston and New York, authorities resorted to the gruesome European custom of placing the heads of those executed on pikes, which they then displayed at the entrance to the city's port.

For Philadelphians the scariest revolt was the one on their doorstep, in New York. The "rumor of revolt" swept New York City in the first few months of 1741. The paranoia that overwhelmed the city lasted from May 11 until August 29. Historians are divided over whether the events that so engrossed the city constituted a real slave revolt, white hysteria, or a criminal conspiracy. The city had a population of 11,000, of which 20 percent were black. Because of the "long winter" of 1740–41, the War of Jenkins Ear (Britain against Spain), and the inability for normal trade because of the freezing of the Hudson River, tensions were high. According to the rumors a "combination of villains" (groups of enslaved and free Africans; indentured Dutch, British, and Irish servants; Irish, Spanish Black (Cuban), and West Indian sailors; and "voodoo priests" from Saint Domingue and African Obeah men) "conspired" to revolt against the New York authorities. As in other slave rebellions, the slaves knew where the center of authority and the munitions armories were, so they attacked Fort George. The conspirators set a number of fires over a ten-day period. White merchants claimed to have heard blacks scream the words "Fire, Fire, Scorch, Scorch, A LITTLE, damn it, BY-AND-BY." The New York conspirators had planned to name a king and a general just as they had in Antigua. In New York, in a reverse of positions for blacks and whites, the general was an Akan (from southern Ghana) named Caesar and the King a Dutchman named John Hughson. In the end thirty slaves were executed, thirteen blacks were quartered and burned at the stake, and seventeen others were hanged. Four whites were hanged, and their bodies, along with the blacks, were left to rot in public at the entry ports of the city so as to strike fear in other would-be conspirators. Over seventy people had been expelled from the city, and two hundred others were questioned and arrested.[96] Before the events 70 percent of the slaves in New York City had come from the West Indies, and 30 percent came directly from Africa. The authorities soon inverted the figures. This change was caused by the fear that other rebellious blacks transported from Jamaica and Antigua would again end up in the city. If goods could travel throughout the Atlantic world, so could revolutionary ideas about freedom.

Like John Brown over a century later, Lay was judged not by his actions on behalf of blacks but by how much he infuriated the whites. Like Brown and Nat Turner, he was called insane, but as David Brion Davis observed, "If Benjamin Lay was not quite sane, one should remember that the sanest minds found excuses for Negro slavery."[97] Events in New York and Lay's *All Slave Keepers* were followed in 1741 by the English Quaker John Bell's *An Epistle to Friends in Virginia, Barbados, and Other Colonies and Islands in the West Indies Where Any Friends Are.* He argued for treating slaves with compassion and with an eye for conversion, and maintained that Christians must "be as Lights to those who yet remain in Darkness."[98] Roger Anstey observed that his work "set in train amongst American Friends soul searching on the actual keeping of slaves," which helped "produce two striking figures, John Woolman and Anthony Benezet, and was to develop into a broadly based attack on slave holding by Friends and by others."[99]

The Rise of Woolman and Benezet

The development of the mid-century Enlightenment philosophy along with an internal struggle in the Quaker community coincided with the activities of John Woolman and Anthony Benezet. Robin Blackburn rightly characterized the new leadership:

In each generation there had been individual Quakers who attacked "mankeeping" as one of the worst manifestations of corruption and sin; but such prophets had quickly been isolated from their co-religionists, many of whom were bankers or merchants with a stake in the Atlantic system. The first Quakers to make a real headway in persuading the Friends to disassociate themselves from slave-trading were John Woolman, a tailor, husbandman and scribe, and Anthony Benezet, a school teacher, both of Philadelphia. They were men of modest means who argued that slaveholding and slave trafficking were incompatible with a Christian way of life and offense against that "sweetness of freedom" which should be recognized in every fellow creature.[100]

Just as Franklin began to re-examine the issue of slavery in the 1750s, so did the Quakers. Woolman took up the mantle of his predecessors, becoming the most respected of the Quakers who opposed slavery. He never publicly proclaimed the equality of blacks, as Benezet later did, but he developed a following, which was felt outside the Quaker communities as he established strong contacts with influential leaders like Franklin. Woolman's *Some Considerations on the Keeping of Negroes*, first published in 1754, had a lasting effect on the Quakers and on people outside the community who were struggling with the issue, both in the colonies and in England. Woolman began to travel extensively and take notes. In the mid-1740s he visited Quaker meetings in Pennsylvania, New England, New Jersey, Virginia, and North Carolina, and on Long Island and the eastern shore of Maryland. His three-month trip to Virginia in 1746 and his second visit there and to North Carolina in 1757 allowed him to see firsthand the harsh conditions under which the slaves lived.[101]

Woolman's saintly demeanor and sheer determination helped mold Quaker attitudes toward slavery. However, he waited almost ten years to publish his findings and his beliefs on slavery. During this period he and Benezet began to collaborate. While Benezet came to see the slaves as equal human beings in God's sight, Woolman never got that far. The "Epistle of 1754," titled *An Epistle of Caution and Advice, Concerning the Buying and Keeping of Slaves*, ushered in a new phase in the Quaker fight against slavery. The Philadelphia Yearly Meeting of 1754 "directed the Representatives to lay before this Meeting a paper relating to the Purchasing of Negroes, which hath been under their solid Consideration and that they think something of the kind published by order of this meeting may be of general Service."[102] Woolman drafted a letter formulating his basic ideas, which took the form of an epistle concerning slavery to the Philadelphia Friends in 1753. Benezet persuaded the Philadelphia Yearly Meeting of 1754 to use Woolman's letter, which he then edited into the 1754 *Epistle of Caution and Advice*, although some have asserted it was written by Benezet.[103] Benezet then presented it to the meeting.[104] Benezet's role is clearly outlined according to meeting minutes.[105]

This short document had an explosive impact on the Quakers. Quoting excerpts (without attribution) of Woolman's yet-to-be-published *Some Considerations on Keeping of Negroes*, the document declared slavery a sin. It read in part:

How then can we who have been concerned to publish the Gospel of universal Love and peace among mankind, be so inconsistent with ourselves, as to purchase such who are Prisoners of War; and thereby encourage this anti Christian practice? And more especially, as many of these poor Creatures are stolen away, Parents from Children and Children from Parents. Let us make their Case our own, and consider what we should think, and how we should feel, were we in their circumstances. Remember our Blessed Redeemer's positive command, "To do unto others, as we would have them do unto us." And that "with what measure we mete, it shall be measured to us again." And we intreat you to examine, whether the purchasing of a Negro either born here, or imported, doth not contribute to a further-Importation; and consequently to the unfolding all the Evils above mentioned, and promoting man-stealing, the only Theft that which by Mosaic Law was punished with Death, "He that stealeth a Man and selleth him, or if he be found in his Hands, he shall surely be put to death." Exodus 21:16[106]

The call of the Quakers reflected their basic beliefs: to treat everyone as one would want to be treated. They demanded that the punishment for sin be equal to the crime. Some years later Benezet outlined his beliefs in *A Short Account of the People Called Quakers*.[107]

The "Epistle of 1754" was a double blow to Aristotelian and Lockean ideas of slavery, using religious and benevolent ideas of liberty and equality and asking "how then can we who have been concerned to publish the Gospel of universal Love and peace among mankind, be so inconsistent with ourselves, so as to purchase such who are Prisoners of War; and thereby encourage this anti-Christian Practice?" They proclaimed, "Now dear Friends, if we continually bear in mind the royal Law, of doing to others as we would be done by, we shall never think of bereaving our Fellow Creatures of the valuable Blessing, Liberty." Clearly no human being was then born to be a slave or held in captivity because of a "just war," and no one had the right "to live in Ease and Plenty by the toil of those whom Violence and Cruelty have put in power." The epistle called upon Quakers to "let us make their case of own, and consider what we should think and how we should feel, were we in their circumstances?"[108] In other words, if called on, members were to imagine they were slaves.

Here we can see how the "Epistle of 1754" picked up on themes set forth by Fox, Edmundson, Sewall, and Sandiford. It took the two key principles—the denial of any "just war" and the assertion of human equality before God—and combined them into a comprehensive attack on slavery. The epistle made it clear that buying and selling of human beings for slavery, whether they were "prisoners of war," taken captive, stolen, or bought, was not a benevolent act, and could no longer be perceived as an excuse "for your private gain." They cited as evidence Exodus 21:16: "And he that stealeth a man, and selleth him, or if he be found in his hand, he shall surely be put to death."

The Bible provided a strong weapon to fortify their arguments. For if the Bible sanctioned Israel's freedom from slavery and captivity by the Egyptians as an act of the divine deliverance of God, then it could be used to do the same thing for the enslaved Africans. The epistle went on to "likewise earnestly recommend to all who have Slaves to be careful to come up in the Performance of their duty towards them, and to be particularly watchful over their own hearts." While not firmly calling for all Quakers to manumit their slaves, it asked that all Friends "seriously weigh the Cause of detaining them in Bondage." It asked, "you who by Inheritance have Slaves born in your families" to "consider them as Souls committed to your Trust." Its most powerful language called upon members of the Society of Friends "to train them up, that if you should come to behold their unhappy Situation, in the same light that many worthy Men who are at rest have done, and many of your Brethren now do; and should think it is your Duty to set them free, they may be more capable to make a proper use of their Liberty."[109]

Following the Philadelphia Yearly Meeting of 1754, Woolman published *Some Considerations on the Keeping of Negroes: Recommended to the Professors of Christianity of Every Denomination.* The pamphlet was first written in 1746 after his trip to Maryland, Virginia, and North Carolina, but he delayed publication until he felt the time was ripe. According to one of his biographers, Phillips P. Moulton, in 1750 Woolman's father on his deathbed asked John whether he would, as some Quakers had urged him, publish the manuscript. Woolman took his father's advice and "presented it for examination to some personal friends and to the Publications Committee of the Philadelphia Yearly Meeting." In 1754, after some revision and with Benezet's aid James Chattin of Church Alley in Philadelphia printed it.[110] It was reprinted at least fifteen times before the Civil War.

Other Quakers began to take up the issue. Shortly after the 1754 Philadelphia Meeting, Samuel Fothergill, a prominent Quaker minister from England, arrived in Pennsylvania; he returned to England to help initiate the London Yearly Meeting of 1758, which issued the first of a series of denunciations of the slave trade.[111] The Philadelphia Quakers took up the issue in their yearly meetings in 1757 and 1758. The 1758 meeting issued a clear condemnation of slavery.[112] Benezet wrote the minutes and drafted and wrote the "Epistle of 1758." The minutes show that Woolman, John Churchman, John Scarborough, John Sykes, and Daniel Stanton were entrusted to carry out the decree by visiting Quaker slaveholders to try to convince them to release their slaves.

Woolman then began writing *Consideration on Keeping Negroes, Part Second,* in 1761. He wrote to Pemberton that "I have looked over the piece with some care and done according to the best of my understanding" in revising the work.[113] He gave the first draft of the work to John Churchman and Israel Pemberton and to Benezet, whose imprint can be seen by Woolman's use of quotations from the journals of European travelers to Africa.[114] Until this publication in 1762 many Quakers had carefully distinguished between the slave trade and slavery. Woolman pointed out the interconnection and sinfulness of both and declared that there could no longer be a justification of slavery on the basis of helping the poor African. Woolman credited Benezet for his early understanding of slavery and the slave trade. He wrote in his journal on November 25, 1769, "that which hath so closely engaged my mind in seeking to the Lord for instruction whether, after so full information of the oppression the slaves in the West Indies lie under who raise the West India produce, as I had in reading *A Caution and Warning to Great Britain and Her Colonies,* wrote by Anthony Benezet, it is right for me take a passage in a vessel employed in the West India trade."[115]

The preliminary efforts of the late 1680s and 1690s laid a foundation for the searing attacks of Sandiford and Lay in the 1720s and 1730s. Sandiford and Lay in turn undergirded the final assault against slavery in the 1750s led by Woolman and Benezet. Where Sandiford and Lay condemned, Woolman and Benezet sought to convince. Where Sandiford and Lay chose to fight alone, Woolman and Benezet sought allies on both sides of the Atlantic. Where Sandiford and Lay condemned the slave owners, Benezet and Woolman forgave them and tried to win them over. Where Sandiford and Lay relied exclusively on religion, Woolman and especially Benezet added Enlightenment philosophy and brought empirical knowledge of Africa to the Atlantic antislavery discourse.[116]

If there is a single moment when the beginning of the new period in the fight against slavery was catalyzed, it would be the 1758 Philadelphia Meeting. The body seemed poised to defeat another motion requiring Quakers to disavow slavery and free their slaves. Benezet, who had been silent throughout the meeting, solemnly rose. Weeping profusely, he walked to the front of the meeting and recited from the Book of Psalms: "Ethiopia shall soon stretch out her hands unto God." He knew his Bible, just as he knew the words of Fox and Sewall from many years before. His message was that the children of Africa were also God's children and worthy of his grace. Benezet's message carried the day, and a new phase in the international movement against slavery had begun. That international movement would be above all constructed through writing. Benezet's contemporaries in England and France recognized unequivocally that he had founded it (see Introduction).

Chapter 3

An Antislavery Intellect Develops

In 1727 Anthony Benezet's mother sent her fourteen-year-old out to pick up a five-volume set of philosophical writings and correspondence.[1] This errand perhaps led to Benezet's lifelong pattern of reading the work of leading thinkers and authors of religious, scientific, and philosophical tracts. As an adult Benezet immersed himself in the works of the Scottish moral philosophers, who had started a learned reasoning against slavery and oppression. Because the Age of Enlightenment was also the golden age of the slave trade, people juxtaposed noble ideas and self-serving ideologies.[2] Slavery's opponents, Benezet among them, weeded through philosophical tracts and the Christian Bible to combat passages that condoned bondage and oppression and to cite those that opposed it.

Benezet knew that to extend his reach beyond the Quakers he would have to extend his grasp of new theories of freedom. He subtly tied Quaker theology to the developing philosophical ideas.[3] He found a way to use philosophy for two purposes: to combat oppression in general by helping formulate an intellectual basis for social freedom and equality without the use of violence; and to develop a philosophy of racial equality, or at least one that allowed for blacks and whites to struggle for that equality.

Benezet and the Scottish Moral Philosophers

Benezet looked to the works of Scottish philosophers James Foster, George Wallace, and Francis Hutcheson to counter the proslavery arguments of those who based their arguments on Locke, Hume, and later Lord Kames. The full titles of Benezet's *A Short Account of That Part of Africa* and of *Some Historical Account of Guinea* included specific reference to these three philosophers.[4] The Scottish thinkers had a special connection to the colonies, because such professors as William Smith and Francis Alison at the College of Philadelphia (later the University of Pennsylvania) and those teaching at King's College (later Columbia University) in New York focused heavily on Hutcheson's writings.[5]

Foster's major work, *Discourses on All the Principal Branches of Natural Religion and Social Virtue*, was published in 1749.[6] He devoted a chapter, "Of the Distinct Obligations of Masters, and Servants," to a discussion on slavery.[7] Foster found slavery as a form of commerce repulsive, believing "the practice of modern times, in order to extend their commerce . . . is much more criminal, and a more outrageous violation of natural rights" than earlier forms of bondage.[8] He made his boldest claim in a passage uniting religious and philosophical arguments: "We practice, what we should exclaim against, as the utmost excess of cruelty and tyranny, if nations of the world, differing in color, and forms of government, from ourselves, were so possessed of empire, as to be able to reduce us to a state of unmerited, and brutish, servitude."[9]

Such passages reveal a break with the past over religion and philosophy as a justification for oppression.[10] Yet Foster also found reason to accept human inequality, if it allowed for a certain stability in society. "If all men acted, as one vicious man," he wrote, and he "thinks himself at liberty to act; what would be the result upon the whole."[11] Man needed "a more universal sense of morality" that would lead him to condemn slavery as an "outrageous violation of natural rights."[12]

Francis Hutcheson, the famed University of Glasgow professor, anticipated some of the philosophical arguments of Foster when he wrote *An Inquiry into Beauty and Virtue* in 1725.[13] Hutcheson's *System of Moral Philosophy*, first published in 1755, strongly influenced Benezet.[14] Benezet cited Hutcheson to show that "man is the original Proprietor of his own liberty. The Proof of his losing it must be incumbent on those who deprive him of it by force."[15] Hutcheson reasoned that "all men have strong desires of liberty and property, have notions of right, and strong natural impulses to marriage, families, and offspring, and earnest desires of their safety."[16]

Benezet linked white liberty with black slavery when he accepted Hutcheson's logic that "he who detains another by force in slavery is always bound to prove his title. The slave sold into a distant country, must not be obliged to prove a negative, that he never forfeited his liberty."[17] Hutcheson argued against the concept of the right to enslave the captured. He quotes some authors who make such claims and writes, "This proves nothing. Conquerors have no right to murder captives in cold blood."[18] He argued that the children of any slave are all born free. For Hutcheson the plea of the captors for compensation is "not more than that of *negotium utile gestum,* to which any civilized nation is bound to humanity." If the merchant was paid for his stock, then the slaves "have a right to be free."[19]

Hutcheson argued against Aristotelian natural or "conquest" notions of slavery and accordingly sought an "ethical" or "humanitarian" attack against the institution.[20] He wrote that "the notions of slavery which obtained among the Grecians and Romans, and other nations of old . . . are horridly unjust." He argued that "the natural equality of men consists chiefly in this, that these natural rights belong equally to all. . . . Every one is a part of that great system, whose greatest interest is intended by all laws of God and nature. These laws prohibit the greatest or wisest of mankind to inflict any misery on the meanest or to deprive them of any of their natural rights."[21] Hutcheson followed that by saying "no endowments natural or acquired, can give a perfect right to assume powers over others, without their consent."[22] He believed that liberty allowed for one to acquire happiness and benevolence. Taking aim at absolutist theories, he argued that "in all governments, even the most absolute, the natural end of the trust is acknowledged on all sides to the prosperity and safety of the whole body, the subject must have the right of resistance, as the trust is broken, beside the manifest plea of necessity."[23] "Foster," as Davis observed, agreed with Hutcheson: "From a personal standpoint the freeing of a captive would give us much more 'sublime and exquisite pleasure' than in keeping him in degrading bondage."[24] When citing Hutcheson on these matters, the good Quaker Benezet unsurprisingly omitted Hutcheson's words on the right of resistance.[25]

Benezet also became familiar with the works of George Wallace, the philosopher and jurist, whose major work, *A System of the Principles of the Laws of Scotland,* was published in 1760. Wallace and Benezet took ideas from many similar authors, not just Hutcheson but also Montesquieu, Sir Thomas More, and others. In *A Short Account of That Part of Africa,* Benezet cited Wallace, who wrote "we all know that they (the Negroe's) are purchased from their Princes, who pretend to have a Right to dispose of them, and that they are, like other Commodities, transported by the Merchants, who have bought them into America in order to be exposed for sale."[26] Benezet, in *A Caution and a Warning to Great Britain,* used Wallace to show "that if this Trade admits of a moral or a rational Justification, every Crime, even the most atrocious, may be justified."[27]

Like Benezet, Wallace asserted that "the history of mankind shews, that many unexpected revolutions have happened, and that things have existed so contrary to all expectations, that he would, indeed be a rare man, who should pronounce decisively, anything, which is not naturally to be absolutely impossible." Wallace went a step further in his beliefs and wrote that "property, that bane of human felicity is too deeply rooted in Society, and is thought to be too essential to the sustenance of it, easily to be abolished. But it must necessarily be banished out of the world, before a Utopia can be established. For as long as it remains, the method of acquiring it must remain, and some people must acquire and must be entitled to hold more of it than others." In other words, the more property one acquired, the more one would seek. An unequal set of property relations would continue: the more one man acquired, the further society would be from utopia. The only way to set the wrong right would be to abolish property as an individual or private right or necessity. Wallace believed that "property and equality seemed to be absolutely incompatible. [That] it would be difficult if not impossible, to banish the former out of the world, and to bring those, who have it and are distinguished by it to part with it." Wallace was therefore led to the conclusion that utopia and even equality would be impossible to attain. Because of man's greed and disregard for other human beings, Wallace further concluded that "it may be affirmed to be hardly probable, that a perfect, absolute, and universal equality will ever be established in human Society." In a section of *A System of the Principles of the Laws of Scotland,* titled "Of Slavery," Wallace argued that "the slavery—at present exercised in America, appears to be so horrid, and so contrary to the feelings of humanity, that it cannot be agreeable to the Law of Scotland."[28]

Wallace's concepts of equality and his early antimaterialist sentiments had an impact on men and women seeking philosophical answers to issues of slavery and inequality.[29] In *A Short Account of That Part of Africa,* Benezet used a concept of Wallace's that would become a staple of antislavery activists, used by Sharp in the Somerset case (see Chapter 6) and by blacks in northern colonies to file freedom suits.[30]

Wallace's most famous words were "men and their liberty are not *in commercia*: they are not either saleable or purchasable . . . for everyone of those unfortunate men are pretended to be slaves, has a right to be declared free, for he never lost his liberty; he could not lose it; his Prince had no power to dispose of him."[31] Wallace, in an argument particularly dear to Sharp in preparing for the Somerset case and quoted by Benezet in *A Short Account of That Part of Africa,* wrote of a slave: "As soon, therefore as he comes into a country, in which judges are not forgetful of their own humanity, it is their duty to remember that he is a man, and to declare him to be free."[32]

Building on the ideas of Hutcheson and Wallace, Benezet wrote in his later major work that "it cannot be, that either war or contract can give any man such a property in another as he has in sheep and oxen; Much less is it possible, that any child of man should ever be born a slave." He added that "liberty is the right of every human creature, as soon as he breathes the vital air. And no human law can deprive him of the right, which he derives from the law of nature."[33]

In *A Short Account of That Part of Africa,* Benezet for the first time drew on the work of J. Philmore, which he attached to the end as "Extracts from a Pamphlet, entitled *Two Dialogues on the Man-Trade*—Printed in London, in the Year 1760." The dialogue was between a slave-trade sympathizer, Mr. Allcraft, and J. Philmore, a vigorous opponent of slavery. Both names were pseudonyms. Benezet carefully omitted those sections of *Two Dialogues* that gave the slaves the right to use violence to free themselves. Philmore believed that "all the Black men now in our plantations, who are by unjust force deprived of their liberty, and held in slavery, as they have none upon earth to appeal to, may lawfully repel that force with force, and to recover their liberty, destroy their oppressors." Furthermore, he argued, "it is the duty of other white as well as black, to assist those miserable creatures" in their quest for freedom.[34] As David Brion Davis observed, when "Philmore called on England to set an example to other nations by proclaiming immediate liberty to 'those captives now in our plantations,' he broke new ground by condemning England and other slave trading countries as aggressor nations that had long been 'at war and enmity with mankind in general.' "[35] The peace-loving Quaker also omitted Philmore's sections where he argued that the black has just as legitimate a right to wage war as the English or the French in the Seven Years' War. Yet he felt compelled to incorporate Philmore's ideas as to the rights of the black to liberty.

Speaking Truth to Power

With this basis in Enlightenment philosophy Benezet now felt ideologically and spiritually ready to confront slavery more openly. On October 17, 1757, he wrote his friend Samuel Fothergill in London: "Painful in many, very many respects is our situation, particularly mine, under an uncommon sense of Poverty and desertion." For the first time he expressed a loss of faith in his fellow men, telling his London friend, "Well, I hope I am cured from any more dependence & expectation from man."[36] Throughout his life he questioned his own moral fortitude and worth, especially after he saw that many of his fellow Friends refused to manumit their slaves and continued to accumulate excess worldly goods. But as always he found new sources of hope and a grain of good in a mountain of evil. Fothergill had been moved when he first visited Philadelphia and saw slaves on its shores in 1754–56. He then read John Woolman's pamphlet and the Philadelphia "Epistle of 1754." By September 1758, as he communicated with Benezet, he came to categorically denounce slavery.

In his correspondence with Fothergill, Benezet seemed dismayed about the slow progress of the antislavery movement in the 1750s. Many of his fellow Friends refused to manumit their slaves; indeed, despite the Yearly Meeting's condemnation of 1758, manumission of Quaker-owned slaves dragged on for decades. Writing on December 30, 1757, to John Smith, a Burlington, New Jersey, Quaker to whom Benezet had sent an advance copy of his first work, *Observations on the Inslaving, Importing, and Purchasing of Negroes*, Benezet lamented that "the small work which went with my last, I would particularly recommend to thy notice. Books treating of negroes are I believe not much in fashion amongst you."[37] While Benezet showed remorse about the Quaker attitude toward human bondage, he characteristically sought to reach young people whom he felt had not yet been tarnished by their elders' attitudes toward slavery and wealth. For this reason he told Smith, "Yet certain it is that all persons, but more especially the youth, ought to know by what wicked and corrupt views and methods the slave trade is carried on."[38] The letter preceded the book's publication by over a year, indicating the difficulty Benezet may have had in getting the text approved. He ended the letter with a subtle warning to all involved with slavery: "The curse will attend those who, for selfish ends, engage in it in any degree what ever."[39] In later writings he expanded on this theme; no one involved in any aspect of the trade or even those who wore the clothes made by slaves or food prepared by them was free of guilt or sin: "Without purchasers, there would be no Trade; and consequently every Purchaser as he encourages the Trade, becomes partaker in the Guilt of it; and that they may see what a deep dye the Guilt is of."[40]

Benezet appears to have at first printed the pamphlet in 1759 at his own expense; it was republished the next year. Most often he mailed it with a "circular letter, which accompanied the distribution of his books."[41] Throughout his life, in his correspondence he also included letters by other political and religious writers and excerpts from antislavery tracts, both his own and those of others.

In *Observations on the Inslaving of Negroes* he first pioneered his technique of using sources familiar with Africa, such as Willem Bosman, John (Jean) Barbot, and N. N. (André) Brüe. To give more credit to his arguments, Benezet cited anonymously "a Person of Candour and undoubted Credit now living in Philadelphia who was on a trading Voyage, on the Coast of Guinea about seven years ago" who was "an eyewitness [to] the misery and Defolation which the Purchasers of Slaves occasioned in that Country." The person also witnessed a war where "during which Time the Engagement was so bloody, that 4,500 were slain on the spot." The witness also saw "Widows weeping over their lost Husbands, and Orphans deploring the loss of the Fathers." Benezet then asked his readers, "What must we think of that cruel Wretch who occasioned such a Scene of Misery or what of those who for the sake of Gain instigated him to it?"[42]

When the Board of Press Overseers finally approved *Observations on the Inslaving of Negroes,* Benezet attached two other documents to the pamphlet. The first was *Extracts from the London Epistle of 1758.* The second was a tract titled *The Uncertainty of Death-Bed Repentance.* The latter was the story of a man known only as Penitens, "a notable tradesmen, and very prosperous in his dealings, [who] died in the thirty-fifth year of his age."[43] The reasons Benezet added the piece become clear as Penitens comes to wonder about his life, a life where he becomes rich in the pocket but poor in the soul. Penitens exclaims, "When you are as near death as I am, you will know, that all the different states of life, whether of youth or age, riches or poverty, greatness or meanness, signify no more to you, than whether you die in a poor or stately apartment."[44] Benezet believed that if Quakers waited until the end of their lives, they too would have such confessions; but he wanted them to act sooner. He asked his fellow Friends if they would be any nearer the Kingdom of God because of their wealth. Would they question their own guilt? He offered Penitens's words without any comment, just as he let the *Epistle* speak for itself. He allowed the written word to "speak truth to power."[45]

Benezet Attacks Greed and Gain

In 1762 Benezet more boldly attacked the slave trade from many angles in his initially anonymous pamphlet *A Short Account of That Part of Africa Inhabited by the Negroes . . . and the Manner by Which the Slave-Trade Is Carried On,* which went beyond religious principles. The pamphlet brings in arguments from Wallace and Hutcheson and, far more substantively than *Observations on the Inslaving of Negroes,* descriptions of Africa from the travel narratives written by explorers and slave traders (see Chapter 4).

As he widened his mission, Benezet began to question the nature of mankind. He asked himself if there was something inevitably evil in man's makeup that allowed for his use of slaves. He wondered how whites could make something so evil seem as if it were a necessary good. He looked for ways to reason with the whites, to appeal to their self-interest and desire for safety, their minds and their sense of "guilt." He reasoned that "it is a truth, as sorrowful as obvious, that mankind too generally are actuated by false motives, and substitute an imaginary interest in the room of that which is real and permanent." He added, "It must be acknowledged by every man who is sincerely desirous of becoming acquainted with himself, and impartially inspects his own heart, that Weakness and inbred corruption attend human nature."[46]

Benezet spared no individual involved in the slave trade: "Everyone who is in any respect concerned in this wicked Trafique, if not so hardened by the Love of Wealth, as to be void of Feeling, must upon a serious Recollecting, be impressed with Surprise and Terror, from a Sense there is a righteous God." He denounced the economic arguments of those who claimed that slavery was necessary to ensure the well-being of whites, asking "what Necessity does the Author mean, no other Necessity appears but that arising from the Desire of amassing Riches; a Necessity laid on worldly Men by their hard Task-master the Devil."[47]

If the inferiority of blacks was the first justification for slavery, then the need for an economic rationale became the second.[48] Time and again Benezet spoke of the drive for wealth, at one point writing that "persons whose Minds are engrossed by the Pleasures and Profits of this life, are generally so taken up with present Objects, that they are but little affected with the distant Sufferings of their Fellow Creatures, especially when their Wealth is thereby increased."

In many ways Benezet's decision not to enter into his family's commercial enterprises was reflective of his ideas and writings and his consistent fight against societal hierarchies based on gains or compound accumulation, in whatever form or by whatever name. He used language couched in moral tones to challenge the economic motives behind slavery. For Benezet the slave trade was "a lamentable and shocking instance of the influence which the love of gain has upon the minds of those who yield to its allurements." It was "a trade, which is entered upon from such sensual motives and carried on by such devilish means."[49]

Benezet soon saw the immediate effect of *A Short Account of That Part of Africa.* The Board of Overseers had not funded the second printing of his first work, and they did not approve of the publication of the first two editions of *A Short Account,* so he published it anonymously.

From this experience it had become clear to Benezet that he would have to move beyond the province of Pennsylvania, so *A Short Account* became his last work addressed only to "the inhabitants of Pennsylvania." His next volley would be shot across the Atlantic to Britain, perhaps inspired by the knowledge that his pamphlet had been published in England. Peace in 1763 allowed for the rapid expansion of the slave trade, leading Benezet to ask that his and other "pamphlets be reprinted and distributed, petitions be prepared, politicians be approached, and information be trans-mitted."[50]

Since writing to Joseph Phipps in London in 1763, he had sought to call the attention of the British public to slavery. He had told Phipps that "a proper check" to curtailing the slave trade "must come from among [the British]."[51] He demanded that the British accept responsibility for a prob-lem he believed they created. In this pamphlet he made more extensive use of the works of George Fox, the French philosopher Montesquieu, and the Scots Foster, Hutcheson, and Wallace. He also used the "Romish Mis-sionary" Labat, Richard Baxter, Sir John Templeton, the *Liverpool Memoran-dum Book,* Mosaic law, common law, and the Bible. He cited Francis Moore, N. N. Brüe, Sir Hans Sloane, George Whitefield, and the ship surgeon Thomas Jeffery.[52] He aimed to show how the slave trade had commercial and economic underpinnings as well as political ones.[53]

Benezet was elated that in October 1766 the first two thousand copies of *A Caution and a Warning* were printed.[54] The press overseers of the Meeting for Sufferings did not hesitate to issue this new work, as it had others, per-haps because of the tensions caused by the Stamp Act Crisis. In early March 1767 a second printing of two thousand came out. Shortly thereafter, on March 27, Benezet wrote to John Smith: "I have now, 2,000 of the *Caution on Negroes,* with the Extract of the Bishop's Sermon printed; and as thou wast so kind as to propose taking a number I would willingly know how many to send."[55] He asked if Smith would take a hundred copies of his work on *Christian Piety.* He bound copies of his works with other extracts and mailed them to friends and public officials in the colonies and abroad. He informed another friend, George Dillwyn, that he had sent copies "of ye Negro Trade to the Society for the Propagating the Gospels."[56] Address-ing John Smith as "a Loving Friend" on April 21, 1767, Benezet said "I herewith send 100 copies of the Caution on Negroes & 100 on Early Piety." On June 12, 1767, he wrote his friend Parmenas Horton, "I need not repeat my sentiments theron, as they are fully expressed in the piece called

'Caution and Warning &c.,' which is included in the collection; it was printed by direction of Friends, with approbation of our last Yearly Meeting." He was gratified that the plight "the poor negroes whose bondage becomes more and more an increasing concern amongst the Friends" received progressively more attention.[57]

Benezet then appealed on behalf of the Philadelphia Meeting to the London Friends to reprint his *A Caution and a Warning*. The London Meeting responded with uncharacteristic haste and "quickly republished the work in an edition of 1,500 copies." Of these, approximately eight hundred copies were delivered "to members of Parliament and Officers of the Crown," just as Benezet had sent copies to many colonial legislators.[58] *A Caution and a Warning* was the first of his pamphlets published overseas, with editions appearing in 1767 and 1768 in London.

Benezet begins the pamphlet as follows: "At a time when the general rights and liberties of mankind, and the preservation of those valuable privileges transmitted to us from our ancestors, are become so much the subject of universal consideration; . . . how many of those who distinguish themselves as the Advocates of Liberty, remain insensible and inattentive to the treatment of thousands and tens of thousands of our fellow men . . . in many parts of the British Dominions?"[59] Like Samuel Johnson he challenged the American revolutionaries who fought for their own liberty while denying the same to enslaved Africans.[60]

Benezet asked that his readers express "sympathy and sorrow" with the plight of victims of the trade in human flesh. Benezet distinguished between the "foul gain" achieved in the slave trade and "legitimate gain" by one's own hard labor. Believing honey more useful than venom, he at first took a low-key approach to those who tried to sugarcoat their relationship to slavery. He told them, "It must be allowed, there are some well minded Persons, into whose Hands some of the Negroes have fallen, either by Inheritance, Executorships or even some perhaps purely from Charitable Motives, who rather desire to manage wisely for their good than to make Gain by their own Labour." Yet he continued to try to convince them that they were just as guilty as the traders. He described the slave trade business "as detestable and shocking . . . to such, whose hearts are not yet hardened by the practice of that cruelty, which the love of wealth, by degrees, introduceth into the human mind."[61] Focusing directly on the drive for profits, he suggested that "we sacrifice our reason, our humanity, our Christianity, to an unnatural sordid gain."[62]

Borrowing more from the humanists like Montaigne than from early political economists, Benezet challenged the profit motive and linked it to human depravity. He contrasted the profits of the slave trade for the British with the cost in human lives. "Britons boast themselves," he reminded the reader, "to be a generous, human people, who have a true sense of the importance of liberty; but is this true character, whilst that barbarous, savage slave-trade, with all its attendant horrors, receives countenance and protection from the Legislature." He would later, especially in *Some Historical Account of Guinea,* repeatedly come back to the concept of "gain" and the corruption of man. Only when his contemporaries came to grips with this would antislavery forces be able to "put a stop to any progress" made by the principal proponents of slavery and the slave trade.[63]

Arguing in *A Caution and a Warning* in the language of Hutcheson, Benezet asserted that humans are "free by nature" and that the Almighty "imposed no involuntary subjections of one man to another." With this, Benezet struck a chord with the colonists, who were fighting British tax and import policy. The non-importation movement, which certainly at one time had no use for Benezet's antislavery rhetoric, soon found a place for his works. In appealing to the British, just as he would to the people of Philadelphia, he described a scene that he witnessed when the British vessels arrived in the colonies: "The poor Negroes are to be disposed of to the planter, and they are again exposed naked, without any distinction of sexes, to the brutal examination of their purchasers." He noted that this caused "deep distress, especially to the females. . . . Mothers are seen hanging over daughters, bedewing their naked breasts with tears, and daughters clinging to their parents," not knowing if "they shall ever meet again." Seeing this, "the whipper is called for, and the lash exercised upon their naked bodies, till obliged to part."[64]

Benezet understood that many Quaker merchants actually stood to lose by a weakening of the Atlantic slave trade, as they enjoyed the comforts that the profits brought them.[65] He wrote to Samuel Fothergill on November 27, 1758, that merchants would sell kidnapped Africans just so "they can add £1,000 to £1,000 or £10,000 to £10,000" in their coffers.[66] Benezet declared that such a love of wealth "snares and lust" tends to "destroy the soul" and "proves the ruin of so many thousands" of white men, women, and children.

Benezet continued throughout his life to argue against rank materialism. Sixteen years after his initial letter to Fothergill, he wrote to Samuel Allinson in New Jersey. "People," he demurred, "are afraid of being disturbed in their enjoyments, in their ease, their confidence in the world, and the things of it."[67] For the austere Benezet the comforts of life fell to the bottom while the comfort of freedom rose to the top. Unlike some reformers, however, he never lost sight of the fact that others did not share his priorities. He had to combine a moral appeal, deeply rooted in Quaker beliefs, with sound empirical knowledge of Africa and the slave trade.

Benezet on Slave Resistance

Benezet read about slave suicides.[68] In citing Captain Thomas Phillips's travel accounts he noted that "the Negroes . . . are loath to leave their own country, that they have often leaped out of the Canoe, Boat and ship, into the sea, and kept in the water until they were drowned, to avoid being taken up and saved by the boats that pursue them."[69] In his account of the slave trade Captain William Snelgrave observed that the "Blacks did not fear death but they did fear dismemberment because Blacks believed that if they were put to death and not dismembered, they would return again to their own country after they were thrown overboard," in the spirit of the transmigration of the soul.[70] After hearing about slave suicides in Philadelphia and coming to the aid of desperate slaves, Benezet understood why the enslaved Africans would seek freedom any way they could. He carefully observed the traditions of the Africans who, in the words of the old Negro spiritual, would "Steal Away," seeking freedom in this world or the next.[71]

Benezet's Quaker and nonviolent principles led him to abhor and reject violence in any form, including suicides. He rarely wrote publicly about enslaved Africans' resistance. But he also reasoned that if blacks realized their strengths, they would possibly resort to force if all other avenues to freedom were closed. He was fearful of what blacks would do to the whites if they succeeded or what the whites would do to blacks if they failed. He was "careful not to include in his writings inflammatory language which might incite literate blacks to rebellion."[72]

He did, however, in some letters to close associates write of his fear of black uprisings. On May 28, 1763, he wrote to Joseph Phipps in London, to whom he had sent a copy of A Short Account of That Part of Africa: "I herewith send thee some Treatizes lately published here, wherein is truly set forth the great Wickedness with which the Trade is carried on; whereby so many Thousands of our Fellow Creatures, equally with us the Objects of Christ's redeeming Grace, & as free as we by Nature, are yearly brought to a miserable & untimely End." He added, "I beg thou wouldst be pleased seriously to read it thro,' which I would doubt not, but thou will perceive it to be a matter which calls for the most deep consideration, of all who are most concerned for the civil, as well as religious welfare of their Country." He spoke of the "just retribution" those involved in the trade would have to bear. How would they "avert those judgments which evils of so deep a dye must necessarily sooner or later bring upon every People" who were involved with slavery?[73]

Again Benezet wrote to a personal friend what he would never have put in a pamphlet: "With respect to the Danger . . . the Southern Colonies are exposed to from the vast disproportion there is between the number of Negroes, and the whites, . . . it was too tender a point to expose to ye view of such of the blacks, as can read." In other words he feared that literate blacks would read about slave revolts and write to others to conspire. He added that a recent treatise documented that "the Proportion in South Carolina is said to be fifteen Blacks to a white, but by their own account, the difference is rather twenty to one. In Georgia and South Carolina the

Negroes are not hemmed in by the some hundreds of miles, as they are in the Islands, but have a back Country uninhabited for some hundreds of miles." The blacks, he believed, would "expect to be supported & assisted by the Indians."[74] He knew that in places like South Carolina, where blacks were in large numbers, the potential existed for mass revolts. He knew about the Stono Rebellion of 1739 and slave master retribution. Benezet may have read some of the accounts, such as one by a Captain Von Reck, who in 1734 wrote that "there are five Negroes to one white," or of another European who wrote in 1737 that "in Charleston and that neighborhood there are calculated to be always 20 blacks . . . to one white man."[75] In reality, in South Carolina in 1720 there were 11,828 slaves who accounted for 64 percent of the state's population, and in 1750 there were 39,000 slaves, who represented 61 percent of the total population.[76] While certainly not fifteen blacks to one white, the six-to-four ratio caused alarm among a jittery white population. In the rice-producing areas the proportion of blacks was even higher.

In the 1763 letter Benezet also told Phipps about an account he received from a "pious man, who is returned from a religious visit to Barbie [*sic*], a Dutch settlement near Surinam," of slave unrest.[77] He knew that with the peace of 1763 and the expansion of slavery the likelihood of slave uprisings with African and native Indian cooperation in the midst of white rule was possible.[78] In fact, that is exactly what eventually happened.[79]

Benezet wrote David Barclay about the danger of slave uprisings on April 29, 1767. He told Barclay, "I perceive by this Week's Newspaper, that the Dutch Colony of Surinam is, thought to be in imminent Danger; indeed it is what I have long expected. . . . The disproportions is said to be from 10–15 Blacks to a White." The Indians, the Black Caribs, he told his friend "are but unfavorably disposed to the English."[80]

Benezet was also aware of slave activity, maroon communities (enclaves of escaped slaves), and repression in Jamaica. The islanders had a long history, beginning in 1522, of slave rebellions. Benezet wrote to Samuel Fothergill in London on October 29, 1768, making note of the whites' peace treaties with maroon communities, a pattern that went back to the 1730s.[81] The treaties called on maroons to turn away other slaves who sought freedom.[82] In exchange, the British often vowed not to make military encroachments on established maroon communities.[83] Benezet read of these events and reported on them to his contemporaries.

Benezet then wrote to Benjamin Franklin about slave uprisings and events in Surinam in September 1772, and in his response Franklin expressed dismay.[84] He read of rebellious slave communities in Barbice and Surinam and of their traditions of being "fierce, wild and unbroken."[85] He informed Granville Sharp of a notice in "Amsterdam Dec. 19th" that included "private Letters from Surinam [that] mentions that the fugitive and Rebellious Negroes are effectually chased from their Town. But that

they are retired deeper into the Woods from whence it will be more difficult to drive them from where they were before us." Benezet noted that
slaves in the Demerara region of Guyana continued to fight openly against
their Dutch rulers. In the letter to Sharp he acknowledged, as he had done
with Phipps, the potential of blacks on account of their sheer numbers. He
asked, "What must be the strength of many thousands and Tens of thousands, who are so situate with an open back Country and assisted by the
Indians and probably such bad people as might join them?"[86]

He told Robert Pleasants, the Virginia Quaker, on April 8, 1773, "I know
it is the general opinion, that nothing ought to be published wherby the
Negroes may be made acquainted with their own strength & the apprehension of the danger the whites are from them." He continued: "For this reason in every publication I have made, I have guarded against it, but I am
persuaded this fear may be carried to[o] far, for it is certainly yet more
dangerous to withhold from the generality of people the knowledge of danger they will be in, thro a continued importation of Negro Slaves."[87] He
told Pleasants about two articles. The first was published in "our *Pennsylvania Packet* or *General Advertiser*, dated Lisbon November 17, 1772 we are told:
'that the Negroes & Slaves natives of Brazil who have already risen several
times, when rigorous methods are used to fly to the Indians, where their
number is said to be considerable encreased.'" He also sent "a dozen of a
pamphlet published here by a respectable member [Rush] of the Presbyterian Communion" to Pleasants, whom he also informed about the "resolute stand made by a few hundred Negroes in the Island St. Vincent against
so great a military force." Benezet then informed Pleasants of "another
article from the Hague Decr. 30, 1772: 'We have received the disagreeable
news here from Surinam of that settlement being in the utmost danger of
destruction by the Indians, Negroes &c who are assembled in great numbers & carry devastations wherever they go. Many plantations have been
burnt & the planters with their families have been murdered. Advice has
likewise been received of a rising of the Natives at Cayenne—In short,
Dutch & French are likely to lose their possessions in South America.'"[88]
Benezet also wrote Franklin about slave uprisings and events in Surinam.
Franklin answered simply, "The Accounts you send me relating to Surinam
are indeed terrible."[89] This was Benezet's way of both distributing Rush's
pamphlet and of warning whites of the dangers of slave rebellions.[90]

While some men's moral compasses pointed away from slavery, their
racial compasses pointed toward racial prejudices and allowed for the separation of the races and eventually servitude.[91] Benezet rejected such ideas
along with the concept that human beings should be categorized by race,
much as Linnaeus classified plants. Benezet knew that one could be profoundly against Africans being made chattel, but once enlightened philosophers allowed any basis for inequality and inferiority based on race,

climate, religion, or conquest, they gave the proponents of slavery important weapons. Benezet united the moral philosopher's ideas with his own concepts of equality and race. Denouncing slavery philosophically was one thing, but uplifting a race was another, an ideal that Benezet at first espoused alone. In creating a uniform and principled philosophical opposition to slavery, his work also created a not-so-uniform opposition to his ideas. His denunciation of racist theories and his notion that in a just society all peoples could prove equal separated his ideas and his ideals from those of most of his contemporaries.

Anthony Benezet was a man of the broad Atlantic world. He studied the works of the Scottish Enlightenment philosophers and of humanist scholars like Michel de Montaigne and Sir Thomas More. He used Quaker religious principles and developed his own ideology condemning greed and the deprivation of one group of men and women to the benefit of another. On his walks along the docks of Philadelphia he listened to the cries of African men, women, and children in their languages and dialects. He learned from some of them about Africa, combining this knowledge with what he gleaned from the many narratives of men who traveled through the vast continent to challenge the racist stereotypes that undergirded the slave trade.

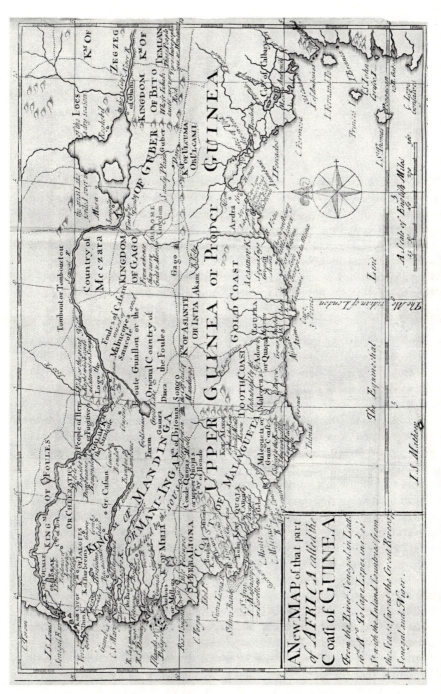

"A New Map of That Part of Africa Called the Coast of Guinea." Benezet critically studied the narratives and journals, including maps of Africa, in the narratives of men like William Snelgrave. From Snelgrave's *A New Account of Some Parts of Guinea, and the Slave Trade* (London: Knapton, 1734). Courtesy of the Library of Congress.

Chapter 4

Visions of Africa

Anthony Benezet transformed eighteenth-century discourse about slavery by using empirical knowledge of Africa to combat the existing negative image of Africans as lawless, heathen savages and even as not fully human. As the first Quaker epistles against slavery (1753–58) make clear, Benezet had by then read some of the slave traders' journals and narratives.[1] By the time he published *Some Historical Account of Guinea,* such Philadelphia collections as the Library Company of Philadelphia (where his younger brother Daniel was a member) and the Friends Library of Philadelphia and Logan's Library (Benezet worked as a librarian at both) held copies of these narratives.[2]

Using the travelers' narratives was a brilliant rhetorical strategy on his part: no one could accuse the authors of a pro-African bias or of any animosity toward slavery. Benezet took full advantage of this obvious bias: "Yet they cannot but allow the Negroes to be possessed of some good qualities, though they contrive as much as possible to cast a shade over them."[3] He did not begin using these works naively. He told his reader in the first pages of *Some Historical Account of Guinea* that he had "extracted from authors of credit; mostly such as have been principal officers in the English, French and Dutch factories, and who resided for many years in those countries."[4] Benezet combined this knowledge of Africa with both religious and philosophical attacks on slavery, thus creating a new framework for the debate on slavery. "By citing all the eyewitness accounts of the West African coast to which he had access," he could show that "what depravity and degradation appeared there was the product of slave-trader influence."[5] Far from presenting a naive utopian view of Africa, as C. Duncan Rice and others have claimed, Benezet employed a careful calculus to make his selections. Quite apart from his opposition to slavery, he wanted to use the narratives for other purposes, some part of larger campaigns, for example, promoting Quaker ideals (at least his view of them),[6] such as temperance,[7] and other intensely personal ones,[8] like vegetarianism.

Benezet discovered a discourse in which a simple dichotomy reigned: white equaled civilized; black equaled savage. Harkening back to the ideas of Montaigne (1533–1592), Benezet argued that if blacks were savages, then so were whites, and, conversely, if whites were human, then so were blacks. In the beginning of his major study on Africa, *Some Historical Account of Guinea,* he asserted that the misinformation in some of the travelers' accounts meant to show that whites were "naturally induced to look upon them [Africans] as incapable of improvement, destitute, miserable, and insensitive of the benefits of life: and permitting them to live amongst us, even on our most oppressive terms, is to them a favor." Yet he argued that "on impartial enquiry, the case will appear to be far otherwise; we shall find that there is scarce a country in the whole world afforded the necessary comforts to its inhabitants, with less solicitude and to; than Guinea."[9]

The Early Colonial Image of the African

Benezet had to combat the negative views of the African promulgated in such well-known collections as those of Richard Hakluyt. In writing to Walter Raleigh, Hakluyt called on him to "go on as you have begun, leave to prosperity an imperishable monument of your name and fame such as age will never obliterate. For to posterity no greater glory can be handed down than to conquer the barbarian, to recall the savage and the pagan to civility, to draw the ignorant with the orbit of reason."[10] Often the words *slaves, booty,* and *gold* were interchanged with *God, glory,* and *the Crown.* Authors of many of the narratives about voyages knew that their works would be used to "promote colonization, rally support for the growing naval forces, hail the achievements of great captains, and at the same time reveal the weaknesses of England's great enemy Spain."[11]

Benezet found that if the sponsor country were Spain, France, Portugal, Holland, or England, then the names of the merchant venturers might change, but the volumes served the same purpose: to solicit investors and governments and to promote the national enterprises of the European powers.[12] In America these powers built their empires on a labor force of enslaved Africans. The reasoning—even before the development of a hardened notion of racism and racial supremacy—was simple. If savages needed to be civilized and barbarians had to be saved, then slavery and the rape of Africa was, according to men like Richard Nisbet in *Slavery Not Forbidden by Scripture,* not so much a conquering mission but an act of salvation, redemption, and benevolence. It was God's will.[13] Instead of bringing joy to the enslaved Africans, Benjamin Rush responded, slavery heaped "wealth and honors on Europeans and Americans."[14]

In reading the narratives Benezet saw a way to challenge emerging proslavery arguments. He had read Richard Ligon, the Barbadian writer and historian, who argued that blacks "the most of them, are as near beast as may be, setting their souls aside" and concluded that the enslaved Africans were "Barbarous, wild and Savage Natures."[15] Benezet understood that the argument for enslavement and slavery in the New World depended on a representation of an Africa peopled by heathen savages who practiced extensive slavery in their own primitive societies.[16] The apologists for slavery thus could use the two traditional Western arguments for its legitimacy: the Aristotelian idea of "natural" slavery—that some people are born to be slaves because they have the slave's nature; and the Lockeian idea that slaves are captives taken in a "just war." Both justifications, when applied in this context, relied on the premise that Africans were godless savages, living in a brutal Hobbesian state. Enslaved Africans became chattel, mere pieces of property, and therefore were not subject to the laws of man as men: only as things to be bought, sold, and ruled.

European slave traders brought more than 11 million kidnapped Africans to the Americas between 1518 and 1850;[17] slave numbers in North America grew rapidly between 1650 and 1750.[18] By then nearly 250,000 toiled on plantations and farms and in workshops in the North American mainland.[19] Most European-Americans from Boston to Barbados knew little about the African past of this huge captive population, and they based the little they did know on racial stereotype and myth. This "knowledge" had been subtly, patiently, and profoundly shaped over the previous 150 years by slave traders and slave masters, and by many in Europe and America who had personal economic interests in perpetuating the institution of slavery.

Proponents of slavery began to construct an image of Africa that underlaid and legitimized the system of New World bondage.[20] While the words *Christian, Englishman,* and *white* came to mean "free," the words *heathen, African,* and *black* connoted "savage" and "slave." If religious leaders like Morgan Godwyn attempted to make it impossible to use religion as the single justification for slavery, then what other justifications were put forth?

Peter Fryer writes, "Although knowledge about African peoples and cultures was increasing, the pale-skinned islanders disposed to make ethnocentric generalizations about dark-skinned people from over the sea found the persistent folk myths a convenient quarry." These myths and tales of the beast-like Africans "eased English consciences about enslaving Africans and thereby encouraged the slave trade" and with it ideas that were "woven into a more or less coherent racist ideology." The Africans "were sub-human savages, not civilized human beings like us."[21] According to Winthrop Jordan, Bernard Romans, a natural philosopher, "came off second best" to Nisbet in his attack on Rush. Romans wrote in 1775 that "treachery, theft stubbornness, and idleness . . . are such consequences of their manner of life at home [in Africa] as to put it out of all doubt that these qualities are natural to them and not originated by their state of slavery."[22] Although people in Britain looked on Africans somewhat differently from those in the mainland colonies did, in part because Africans were rare in Britain, they shared this overall negative image.

The development of gradations of humankind by race coincided with new gradations by social function. The "black" skinned fell below the "white" skinned on the human scale. In the words of Winthrop Jordan "There seems to have been within the unarticulated, concern of the Negro as a different sort of person, a highly significant shift in emphasis."[23] America, unlike England, had a profound shortage of cheap labor and needed to expand its workforce. This need added an extra dimension to racial politics, because free black labor would have constituted such a threat to free white labor's bargaining position.[24] Labor scarcity and the frequent inability or unwillingness to coerce white labor in the North American colonies added to the call to enslave the darker Africans.[25]

When Benezet first became an active abolitionist in the 1740s, the colonialists in the Americas had long viewed blacks as naturally inferior. By then, as Jordan observes, slavery and racism marched together, "dynamically joining hands to hustle the Negro down the road to complete degradation." The African qualities, their "language, gestures, eating habits and so on" had for the "Englishmen added up to savagery; they were major components in that sense of difference which provided the mental margin absolutely requisite for placing the Europeans on the deck of the slave ship and the Negro in the hold."[26] European descriptions focused on differences in skin color, hair texture, and facial features, tying them to justifications for African enslavement. For whites, Philip Curtin observed in 1969, "racial views became unconsciously linked with social views, and with the common assessment of African culture. Culture prejudices slid off easily toward color prejudice, and the two were frequently blended in ways that were imprecise at the time and even harder to separate after the passage of almost two centuries."[27]

By the mid-eighteenth century the question could no longer be avoided either philosophically or socially. Did humanity guarantee equality? Were there greater or lesser individuals, degradations on the human scale based on skin color? In the words of Paul Edwards and James Walvin "It needs to be stressed moreover that arguments [about whether] blacks were things or humans were no mere abstractions, debated in the rarefied atmosphere of the courts. Blacks were after all treated as objects in everyday social practice. They were bought, sold and bartered in Britain, and advertisements for their sale can be found in British newspapers just as they were in the New World."[28] Justification of brutal treatment of slaves required that the African be a beast, a savage. Most descriptions focused on blackness because of European culture's long-standing negative attitudes and fear of black, the color of darkness, danger, and damnation.[29] The progressive Christianization of blacks took away the religious distinction, making racial characteristics ever more important. France offers the most striking example, in the Code Noir of 1685, reformed in 1716. French law had banned the holding of slaves within France, so

Louis XIV issued an edict saying the ban on slavery did not extend to blacks: skin color justified slavery.[30]

Writers who justified slavery proffered an image of Africa as a dark and forbidding place.[31] This image of Africa as a place of savagery and heathenism, in need both of Christian conversion and of European civilization, provided a necessary foundation for arguments legitimizing African slavery.[32] By presenting the "Negro nations" as barbaric, degraded, and deeply uncivilized, such writers as John Locke could argue that the whites served the interests of Africans themselves by introducing them to the benefits of Christianity and civilization. On this point Locke and the Society for the Propagation of the Gospel (SPG) could agree. Locke argued that "slavery is so vile and miserable an Estate of Man, and so directly opposite to the generous Temper and Courage of our nation; that 'tis hardly to be conceived that an Englishman, much less a Gentleman, should plead for 't."[33] Yet as an Englishman and a gentleman, he wrote, "Every freeman of Carolina shall have absolute power and authority over Negro slaves, of what opinion or Religion soever."[34]

Contradictions abounded. Just as the "more grotesque views about the blacks came from the pens of the slavery lobby," it was also true that "there were many writers markedly anti-slavery, who nonetheless conveyed highly unfavorable impressions of blacks."[35] Men like Godwyn, who did not condemn slavery outright, fought for better conditions for the slaves and even for their baptism. They had a hard time convincing their fellow whites of their sincerity regarding blacks. In reality, they had not fully convinced themselves. This dichotomy presented a dilemma, as religious and social attitudes about blacks varied even among antislavery figures.[36]

Some men held advanced views. For example, in 1730 David Humphries, the SPG missionary, held that those arguments using religion to show that blacks had no soul or human essence had "no foundations in Reason and Truth."[37] Yet John Woolman, who along with Benezet ushered in the final Quaker assault against slavery, at first believed that "the blacks seem far from being our Kinsfolk" and that they "are of a vile stock." At the same time he added that the "Negroes are our fellow creatures."[38] Arthur Lee, a Virginian, opposed slavery, yet believed that the blacks were the "most detestable and vile . . . ever the earth produced," while the whites were descended "from worthy ancestors."[39]

No less an antislavery leader than Granville Sharp was confronted with the question of the blacks' humanity on the one hand and their equality on the other, even as he pursued the freedom of the slave James Somerset. In a letter to J. Bryant in 1776 Sharp asserted, "I am far from having any particular esteem for the Negro; but as I think myself obliged to consider them as men, I am certainly obliged also to use my best endeavors to prevent their being treated as beasts by our unchristian countrymen."[40] In 1772 a writer addressed the issue by posing a question to whites in a letter to the *Virginia Gazette:* "If Negroes are to be slaves on Account of Color, the next Step will be to enslave every Mulatto in the Kingdom, then all the Portuguese, next the French, then the brown complexioned English, and so on till there be only one free Man left, which will be the Man of the palest Complexion in the three Kingdoms!"[41]

Men who opposed slavery either on philosophical grounds, like Francis Hutcheson, James Foster, and George Wallace; on economic grounds, like Adam Smith; or on religious grounds, like Richard Baxter, Morgan Godwyn, and Woolman, had a difficult time accepting blacks as equal, even if they grudgingly accepted them as human.[42] Benezet set about to change that and to correct the negative images. He seldom wrote of his personal contacts with blacks, perhaps to protect his black sources. He also wanted to use sources in print, written by whites, that he could use as documentation. Such documentation about Africa could buttress Benezet's own collection of personal testimonies from Africans in Philadelphia. He offers an example of the latter in the epilogue to *Short Observations on Slavery:*

A striking instance of this kind appeared in the case of a NEGRO, residing near Philadelphia. From his first arrival he appeared thoughtful and dejected, frequently dropping tears, when fondling his master's children; the cause of which was not known till he was able to be understood that, when he gave the following account. That he had a wife and children in his own country, that some of these being sick, he went in the night time to fetch water at a spring, where he was violently seized and carried away, by persons who lay in wait to catch men; from whence he was transported to AMERICA, that the remembrance of his family and friends that he never expected to see anymore, were the principal cause of his dejection and grief. Now can any whole mind not rendered quite obdurate by the practice of oppression, or the love of gain, hear this relation without being affected with sympathy and sorrow; and doubtless the case of many of these afflicted people will be found to be attended with circumstances equally tragic and aggravating. And if we enquire of those negroes who were brought from their native country, when children, we shall find many of them have been stolen away, when abroad from their parents on the roads, or watching their cornfields. NOW TENDER PARENTS; and all who are real friends of liberty; and you who are willing to read the book of Conscience, and those that are learned in the law, what can you say to these deplorable cases?[43]

Benezet's African informant provides us with a clear example of the corrective use of Africans' own oral history. The kidnapping scene described by Benezet bears a structural similarity to one told some years later by Olaudah Equiano, who borrowed many of his observations about Africa from Benezet's *Some Historical Account of Guinea.*[44] In effect, Equiano's tale is both oral and written history: by the time we get to his story, we are dealing with two written versions of those tales, the second written with full knowledge of (and heavy dependence on) Benezet's written text. Unfortunately, we have relatively few concrete examples like this one to enable us to determine the extent to which Benezet fused European written traditions about

African oral history to produce a more balanced narrative of African history.

After his initial study Benezet wrote and published his findings on Africa and Africans with depth and comprehension for over twenty-five years. His first major work concentrating on Africa was *Observations on the Inslaving, Importing and Purchasing of Negroes,* published in 1759.[45] Next, in 1762, came *A Short Account of That Part of Africa, Inhabited by the Negroes.* In this essay his purpose was "to invalidate the false arguments . . . frequently advanced for the palliation of this trade" and to reveal to the public the "evils attending this iniquitous practice."[46] He believed "the purpose of which is to introduce an universal and affectionate Brotherhood in the whole human Species: by removing from the Heart of every Individual, who submits to its Operations, the Darkness and Corruption of Nature and transforming the selfish, wrathful, proud Spirit, into meekness, Purity and Love."[47] By restoring humanity to the African, he would also restore it to those whites who had sought to dehumanize Africans in the first place.

Some Historical Account of Guinea was Benezet's third and most ambitious work dealing with Africa.[48] In it he used the travel narratives extensively, as well as other sources, such as John Randall's "book of Geography, printed in the year 1744."[49] In his search for additional sources Benezet found "a book, printed in Liverpool, called the Liverpool Memorandum, which contains, amongst other things, an account of the trade of that port."[50] He used publications like *Gentlemen's Magazine* as sources of reference along with other "gazetteers, which contained, in a compact form, often quite detailed information about the Negro under appropriate geographical locations."[51] The *Universal Modern History,* a sixty-five-volume compilation published between 1736 and 1765 in London, with a large section on Africa and employed for both pleasure reading and as a reference by pro- and antislavery writers, also proved useful.[52] The editor of the *Universal Modern History* even complained "in writing the history of Guiney, we labour under difficulties from too great abundance of materials, which are thrown together in one rude chaos. . . . Materials are jumbled together, without regard to method or the whole of the execution besides."[53] Nonetheless Benezet found it useful as he went through thousands of pages in the narratives and dictionaries in several languages in an attempt to create a composite picture to give the reader ample evidence of his premises.

Benezet sought to "reveal the misrepresentation spread by the vindicators of this nefarious traffic with a desire that those in authority might check its progress, and a true account of Guinea." Using the areas around Guinea as the center of West Africa and the slave trade, he argued "Guinea affords an easy living to its inhabitants, with but little toil. The climate agrees well with the natives, but [is] extremely unhealthful to the

Europeans."[54] Work was not a burden or a bore; it was a communal endeavor.

He divided the book into twenty-one chapters, each exploring different aspects of life in West Africa. The purpose was to "give some account of the different parts of Africa, from which the Negro is brought." Benezet laid out four premises that directly contradicted European notions of Africa: In *Some Historical Account* he argued:

1. "Scarce a country . . . is better calculated for affording the necessities of life to its inhabitants";
2. The inhabitants "manifest themselves to a human, sociable people, whose faculties are as capable of improvement as those of other men";
3. "Their economy and government is, in many ways commendable";
4. "It appears that they might have lived happily if not disturbed by the Europeans."[55]

These four premises lay at the heart of both Benezet's understanding of Africa and of his social and philosophical outlook on humankind.[56]

Starting with the simplest of egalitarian principles, he proposed that blacks were human beings, no different in soul and spirit from whites. They differed only in skin color, continent of birth, religion, and culture. For Benezet these differences were far smaller than they were for his fellow "countrymen." Indeed the simplicity of African life seemed more in line with Benezet's Quakerism than did the "counting house" mentality of Philadelphia's Quaker merchants. The development of his positive notions about Africa led him to wonder why a "number of innocent People are yearly destroyed, in an untimely and miserable Manner" and to ask "how miserable must be our Condition, if, for filthy Lucre, we should continue to act so contrary to the Nature of this Divine Call."[57] In other words, it was the whites' desire for gain and their racial concept of superiority to blacks that had made the social and economic conditions of blacks so miserable. By clearly stating the humanity of blacks and their inhumane treatment by whites, Benezet, as few authors or humanitarians before him, made blacks and whites equal peoples and brothers.

Benezet's moral beliefs affected his views and presentation of Africa. Because of his general distaste for commerce, trade, and the profit motive promoting individual accumulation of wealth and his belief that labor should be used solely to provide sustenance for one's family and community, he praised the African subsistence economy. He contrasted the richness of Guinean soil, owing to the "overflowing of the rivers" that kept it "regularly moist and fertile," with that of European soil. He argued that a society that has plenty of "cattle, poultry, & c." could produce the necessities of life with "much less care and toil than is necessary in our most northern climate."[58]

Benezet combined his antislavery work with his efforts for other causes, especially the temperance movement.[59] He used his writings on Africa to advance these causes. He singled out for praise those African peoples who abstained from alcohol, and he deliberately left out references to African consumption of spirits, save when it led to evil consequences. Benezet's personal habits, especially his plainness of taste in dress, food, and lodging, similarly influenced his judgment of African society. He admired Africans' simplicity in these things. As he read about the diet of some Africans, he recalled that it resembled that of his old friends Benjamin Lay and his wife, who had convinced Benezet to become a vegetarian. Benezet carefully noted that Guinea "abounds with grain and nuts . . . the earth yields all the year a fresh supply of food."[60] The climate in Africa seemed idyllic, better to his frayed, simple coats than the harsh Philadelphia winters.[61] Unlike some of the grand stone structures in which the elite merchants of Philadelphia lived, Benezet admired "the construction of [Africans'] houses, which are very simple, principally calculated to defend them from the tempestuous seasons and wild beasts." Their beds, he wrote, were made of "a few dry reeds covered with mats."[62] He contrasted this with the mansions of Quaker leaders like James Logan, the merchant, chief justice, and bibliophile, even as he did all in his power to enlist Logan and other prominent Quakers to his many causes.[63] His descriptions of the Africans' lifestyles resembled Quaker notions of a "peaceable kingdom."

The Travel Narrative as Benezet's Source for the Early Study of Africa

In reading and researching travel narratives Benezet became aware of the role of royal trading companies in the slave trade. Most of the authors were employed by these companies and were familiar with the physical capture and transportation of Africans, as well as with the traders' economic motives. He understood the contradictions of using these sources, and he employed them appropriately and critically. He told himself, "How unsafe it is to form a judgment of a distant people from the accounts given of them by travelers, who have taken but a transient view of things."[64] Some of the accounts Benezet read offered detailed scientific sketches of the abundant plant and animal life of the area. His readings allowed him to reject simplistic theories that the Europeans came upon the trade by accident or inheritance, or through missions to save a heathen race. They allowed him to explore the cold calculations and imperial natures of France, Holland, and England as he learned what nations and individuals would do to achieve maximum profits. He inverted the traditional utilization of these narratives, using their descriptions of cruel treatment meted out to natives as examples of the barbarity of the Europeans themselves.[65]

These narratives used the existence of internal slavery in Africa to describe its inhabitants first as naturally servile and then as valuable commodities to be sold to the highest bidders.[66] The existence of indigenous African slavery helped undermine moral arguments against New World slavery; in this argument European slave traders were not introducing the slave trade to Africa but merely expanding existing traffic into broader markets. Benezet explored the roles of the various trading companies and the larger structure of the international slave trade as he read these justifications. Contemporary historians like Robin Law and Philip Curtin have also, like Benezet, found these early narratives useful.[67] Unavailable to him, however, were the mostly unpublished correspondence and rare trading-company reports that would have imposed some order, organization, and chronology on events, even though they paid scant attention to the native inhabitants' socioeconomic and political structures.[68]

Few such original sources were published during the later part of the seventeenth century.[69] But as the public campaign against the finances of the Royal African Company started, the slave lobby began a propaganda campaign to defend its actions.[70] The Royal African Company's "pamphlet war" had caused a renewed interest in such earlier writers as Leo Africanus (Al-Hassan ibn Muhammad al-Wizaz al-Fasi), a Moroccan historian, who wrote in the first half of the sixteenth century.[71] A section of his work titled "Land of the Negroes" examined earlier kingdoms, such as Timbuktu, that were Muslim centers reachable from the north. However, his main areas of interest were North Africa, western Sudan, and the Sahara.[72] Benezet described Africanus as "Leo the African," noting that he wrote on "the ancient accounts of the Negroes from Nubian Geography."[73] The simplicity of African life stirred the simple Benezet. He began with Leo Africanus's description: "They lived in common, having no property in land, no tyrant or superior, but supported themselves in an equal state; upon natural produce of the country, which afforded plenty of roots, game and honey. That ambition and avarice never drove them into foreign countries to subdue or cheat their neighbors. Thus they lived without toil or superfluities."[74]

How Benezet Used Travel Narratives

In Benezet's earlier works he relied on the four-volume *A Collection of Voyages and Travels,* compiled by Awnsham and John Churchill, published in Britain in 1704 and 1732 and later published in India.[75] The four-volume *New General Collection of Voyages and Travels* by Thomas Astley was perhaps Benezet's single most important source. It was first published under the name of Thomas Green, from 1745 to 1747,[76] ushering in a new era of such narratives.[77] The Churchill brothers and Astley were among a growing group of English writers who brought the faraway world to readers.[78] Several of the works in Astley's *New General Collection* were published as separate volumes, such as those by the surgeon of the Royal Navy, John Atkins, and by the Dutch factor Willem Bosman.[79] As James Walvin informs us, although many authors "cannibalized" its passages on Africa, the narratives "kept the image of Africa before the reading public for a century and a half."[80]

Benezet made extensive use of the works of French explorer André Brüe starting in 1762.[81] He referred to him as "General Director of the French Factory at Senegal, who speaking of the Papel Negroe's (amongst whom he was then endeavoring to erect a Factory) says 'they are at continual Wars with their Neighbors, whom they invade as often as they think it for their Advantage.'"[82] In 1717 Brüe signed an important treaty with Alichandora, the emir of Trarza, giving the Senegal Company a monopoly on the gum trade along the Mauritanian coast; he then unsuccessfully mounted naval patrols against the British and Dutch to maintain the French monopoly.[83] According to the Senegalese historian Boubacar Barry, Brüe fought with the African leader Lat Sukaabe Faal over the French monopoly and the duty payments.[84] Benezet often cited Brüe's conclusion that "'excepting the vices peculiar to the Blacks, they are a good sort of people, honest, hospitable, just to their word' and industrious."[85]

Observing the wealth of the area, Brüe, revealing long-standing ties to the New World, showed that "the farther you go from the Sea, the Country on the Rivers seems more fruitful, and well improved. It abounds in Indian corn which is a never failing Commodity here." Brüe continued, "Rice . . . tobacco and indigo wheat thrives well after the second crop. Cotton-trees in plenty—Here are vast Meadows, which feed large Herds of great and small cattle—Poultry are numerous, as well as wild Fowl."[86] These crops were not indigenous to Africa, which reveals that the Africans may have been active trading partners with the Europeans and may have actively sought to improve agricultural production.

This broad experience in Senegambia made Brüe an extremely useful source of information on West Africa. Sources like Brüe's work always led Benezet to the same conclusion: men seemed to do anything for profit. Because he was such an astute reader of history, Benezet knew that the Dutch and the French fought over Senegal in 1717 and that France and England also did so in the Seven Years' War. The British captured the key French forts in 1758 and gained control of the Senegal Valley in 1763 at the Peace of Paris. They ceded Gorée back to France, which occupied Saint-Louis until 1782.[87]

Africa had become more than a source of slaves. It was now a pawn in battles and an integral part of a trade war between France and Britain.[88]

The fight for economic supremacy and territory had become international, and so had the fight against slavery. Benezet at first singled out individual Quakers and then others in the colonies. His studies led him directly to international slave traders. He did not separate individual lust for wealth from international wars and the quest for slaves. They all violated the laws of man and God.

Benezet's use of Brüe also reveals some of the ways in which he selectively took what he needed from individual sources. He was foremost an antislavery propagandist, neither more nor less than any other pro- or antislavery advocate or any advocates for any cause.[89] He cited Brüe's favorable words but left out his description of the "peculiar vices" of the blacks. Among the vices Brüe listed were that "they," meaning some Africans, "propagate the Mohammedan Religion wherever they go" and that "at present all their Knowledge consists of reading and writing the Arabic."[90] Like many of his time, Brüe saw Islam as an affront to Christianity. In what was rare for his era Benezet distinguished between the Africans of different religions and cultures who collaborated with slave traders and those who were its victims. He knew that just as not all Europeans were the same, neither were all Africans, and he refrained from attacking Africans on religious grounds. He differed with whites of other religions but did not disdain their opinions, no doubt because of his own experience with religious persecution. While he compiled and edited tracts about the Quaker religion, he attacked neither Anglicans nor Muslims solely on religious grounds, although he criticized the SPG and Anglican missionaries for not doing more to alleviate human suffering and to abolish slavery.[91]

In *A Caution and a Warning to Great Britain,* Benezet again used Brüe's narratives, rhetorically asking his readers, "upon an observation, What had been the success of The Voyage" of Brüe? He answered that Brüe "had found it a difficult matter to set the Negroes a fighting with each other, in order to procure the number he wanted; but that when he had obtained this end, and had got his vessel filled with slaves, a new difficulty arose from their refusal to take food; those desperate creatures chusing rather to die with hunger, than to be carried from their native country."[92] The pacifist Benezet used Brüe's description to document the twin evils of slavery and war. He wrote about the first form of individual and collective African resistance to slavery: refusal to eat. Africans believed in the concept of the transmigration of the soul, trusting it was better to die in captivity and have their souls return to their native lands than to live their lives in bondage.

Benezet read John Randall, who in describing the capture of slaves wrote that "in time of Peace nothing is more common, than for the Negroes of one Nation to steal those of another, and sell them to the Europeans. . . . It is thought that the English transport annually near fifty

Thousand of those unhappy Creatures, and the other European Nations together about Two Hundred Thousand more." Randall revealed contradictions, however, as he wrote "each Individual of this Number had some tender attachments which was broken by this cruel Separation; some Parent or Wife, who had not even the Opportunity of mingling Tears in a parting Embrace."[93] Benezet used similar words when he wrote about a despondent African he spoke with at the docks in Philadelphia when he gave his initial estimates of the number of slaves seized, transported, and sold yearly.

In *A Short Account of That Part of Africa,* Benezet first used the accounts of the Dutch factor Willem Bosman, whom he described as "the principal factor for the Dutch at D'Elmina."[94] Bosman was "one of the former Commanders [who] hired an Army of the Negroes, of Sasseria and Cabesteria, for a large Sum of Money, to fight the Negroes of Commany, which occasioned a battle, which was more bloody than the Wars of the Negroes usually are: And that another Commander gave at one Time, Five Hundred Pounds, and at another Time Eight hundred Pounds, to two other Negro Nations, to induce them to take up Arms against their Country people."[95]

Bosman, unlike an earlier traveler named Richard Jobson, had little sympathy for the Africans. For the Dutchman the trade in black bodies was business. He wrote his uncle, "I doubt not but this trade seems very barbarous to you but since it is followed by sheer necessity, it must go on."[96] Benezet documented Bosman's reasoning, quoting him: "When Vessels arrive, if they have no Stock of Slaves, the Factors trust the inhabitants with Goods for the Value of one or two hundred slaves, which they send into the inland of the Country in Order to buy Slaves at all Markets." Bosman indicated the role of whites in the exchange: "The Europeans furnished the Negroes with an incredible Quantity of Fire-Arms and Gunpowder, which was then the Chief vendible Merchandize there."[97]

Because of the inherent danger in kidnapping Africans and transporting them as slaves across the Atlantic, Europeans built a system of settlements along the African coast. Benezet knew of the importance of these settlements, called factories, to the royal trading companies.[98] They were established all along the western coast, from Cape Verde to the equator, by English, French, Dutch, and Portuguese traders.[99] By studying narratives and available maps Benezet understood the nature of these factories, their command structure, the role of the governor general, and the wide range of inhabitants, from soldiers to clerks to warehouseman, all of whom lived under military discipline.[100]

Benezet augmented Bosman's accounts with evidence from Jean Barbot, who like Benezet was a French Huguenot and who had also fled French Catholic persecution. Barbot was especially knowledgeable about some of the complexities of African life. His account consisted of his journal, plus the letters he wrote to acquaintances during his travels, primarily to Guinea in 1678–79 and 1681–82. He recorded his accounts of these trips in London in 1688.[101] As the agent general for the Compagnie Royale d'Afrique, Barbot had firsthand knowledge of the many vessels that left the French ports, especially at La Rochelle. When he visited the Guinea Coast, the area around the Kingdom of Benin stood at the center of the slave trade.[102] Barbot saw that the captured Africans did not submit easily.[103] He noted that "resistance and exclaiming against the Treachery" of the collaborating Africans and Europeans was common.[104] He wrote that "As slaves are, you might say, a form of money among these Africans, I consider it appropriate to say something about them here, before I finish my letter. Slaves are either those who, having no means of subsistence, sell themselves to rich men for life, or those taken in war, or children sold by their parents because they cannot keep them, or finally, those sold as slaves because they cannot pay the fines to which they have been condemned. But of all these, the largest number are those taken in war or seized in their homes and carried off."[105] In *Observations on the Inslaving of Negroes* and in other works, Benezet quoted Barbot in an attempt to show that the slaves sold by the Africans themselves "are for the most Part Prisoners of War taken either in fight or pursuit."[106] He had earlier cited Bosman: "The Booty which the Negro Soldiers aim at in their Wars, are ornaments and Prisoners of War, in Order to sell them for Slaves at Pleasure that many of the Inhabitants depend on Plunder and the Slave Trade."[107] Benezet contrasted this statement with what Barbot wrote: "The slaves they possess and sell are prisoners of war taken from among their enemies, or if from among themselves are those condemned to slavery for some crime. But there are also some who have been kidnapped by their compatriots, these being mainly children who had been stationed in the fields to guard the millet or who had been seized when traveling along the main roads."[108] Barbot's descriptions are consistent with those of other travelers.[109] For example, in *Some Historical Account of Guinea,* Benezet cites Barbot to show that "above all the Guineans are very honest and just in their dealings; and they have such an aversion for theft, that by law of the country it is punishable by death."[110] Yet in the same letter, in a passage not cited by Benezet, Barbot noted that "few or none of the Blacks are to be trusted, as being crafty and deceitful, and who will never let slip an opportunity of cheating an European nor indeed will they spare one another; Of this and their laziness, more thereafter."[111]

In *A Short Account of That Part of Africa,* Benezet again used Barbot's commentary: "The Hollanders, a People very zealous for their Commerce at the Coast, were very studious to have the War carried on amongst the Blacks, to distract, as long as possible, the Trade of the other Europeans; and to that Effect were ready to assist upon an Occasions, the Blacks, their

Allies, that they might beat their Enemies, and so the Commerce fall into their hands."[112]

William Smith, another of Benezet's sources, was sent by the English Royal African Company to conduct surveys and report on the European effect on the Africans. He stayed in Benin for nine months and published his work eighteen years later. Benezet, and those who cited his work, often employed a particularly useful quotation from Smith: "The discerning Natives account it their greatest Unhappiness, that they were ever visited by the Europeans. They say we Christians introduc'd the Traffick of Slaves, and that before our Coming they liv'd in Peace; but, say they, it is observable, that where-ever Christianity comes, there come with it a Sword, a Gun, Powder and Ball. And indeed thus far they say right, for the Christians are continually at War one with another."[113] Smith offers a good example of a source touching on a subject of personal interest to Benezet: vegetarianism. Smith wrote in his journal about Gambia, "This country is exceeding fertile, bounding with Variety of Fruits, Roots, and salads. Their Chief Fruits are Oranges, Lemons, Limes, Guava's, Bonana's, Plantanes. By some call'd Indian Figs." Benezet surely took special pleasure in Smith's claim that "there are some Reasons to believe these are the Sort of Figs mention'd in Scripture."[114]

Benezet understood the nature of slavery in Africa and elsewhere. He argued that "slavery has been a long time in practice in many parts of Africa; it was also in usage among the Romans when the empire flourished; but except in particular instances, it was rather a reasonable servitude, no ways comparable to the unreasonable and unnatural service extorted from the Negroes in our colonies."[115] He criticized both proslavery authors and self-proclaimed "friends of the blacks" who either attempted to blame the worst of the horrors of slavery on Africans themselves or reduced their own obligations by attempting to lessen the atrocities of the whites. He believed that there were no comparisons and that European slavery took millions of blacks from their birthplaces and separated mother from child. Benezet carefully used his reading to verify his documentation of white brutality toward Africans both in Africa and in the colonies. As was his custom, Benezet pointed out different opinions of writers, arguing "on inquiry why there is such a disagreement in the character given of these people, it appears, that though they are naturally inclined to be kind to strangers, with whom they are fond of trading, yet the frequent injuries, done them by Europeans, have occasioned their being suspicious and shy."He concluded that the "ill treatment they [the Europeans] have sometimes given to innocent strangers, who have attempted to trade with them" caused the Africans to have such great misgivings about whites.[116]

The English surgeon John Atkins wrote sarcastically, "We who buy slaves, say we confer a Good, removing them to a better state both of Temporals and Spirituals." Engaging in a dialogue with the reader, he asserted that "they live indeed according to our European Phrase . . . very poor and mean, destitute almost of the common Necessaries of Life but never starve, that is peculiar to trading Republicks." Atkins then resolutely asks, "Who is to judge of their Wants, themselves, or we? Or what does Poorness mean? More than a sound, to signify we have that which another does not want."[117] In short he believed that starvation may have existed among the English or the French or the colonial white poor, but not among the Africans. Sounding much like Hutcheson, Foster, and Wallace, Atkins continued, "To remove Negroes then from their Homes and Friends, where they are at ease to a strange Country, People and Language, must be highly offending against the Laws of natural Justice and Humanity; and especially when this change is to hard Labour." In a reversal of roles Atkins even paid attention to the harsh conditions in Jamaica and to the plight of the maroons. We have "subjected them to the Condition of Slaves little better in our Plantations, than that of Cattle; the Rigours of their usage, having made some hundreds of them at Jamaica run away into barren Mountains, where they chuse to trust Providence with their Substinance, rather than their Fellow-Christians (now) in the Plantations."[118]

Benezet found that Atkins, whom he described as a "Surgeon on board Admiral Ogle's squadron," offered another interesting source for information on the barbarity of the trade. He found one point of Atkins's account of slave resistance aboard a ship documenting violence insightful: "Harding, master of a vessel, in which several of the men-slaves, and a woman-slave, had attempted to rise, in order to recover their liberty; some of whom the master, of his own authority, sentenced to cruel death; making them first eat the heart and liver of one of those he killed. The woman he hoisted by the thumbs; whipped and slashed with knives before the other slaves, till she died."[119] Perhaps because he was a surgeon, Atkins paid close attention to such detail.[120] In one case he took exception to the comments of William Snelgrave, more of a proponent of slavery, who had written about cannibalism in Dahomey. Speaking of Snelgrave, Atkins observed, "Some places reported on the Coast to be Men-Eaters are by latest Accounts much doubted, if not contradicted."[121] Benezet used Atkins's rejection of black cannibalism to counter the image of black heathenism fostered by the slave trade lobby. Benezet also had read that some Africans ate monkey meat and that whites used that to add to the image of the black savage. Benezet paraphrased Barbot on whites eating apes: "They are a common diet at some places; our sailors frequently eat them." Benezet took a page from Atkins, who denounced Snelgrave for praising the "salvation mission" of the European plunderers of Africa. Atkins proved one of the better read and enlightened of the travelers.[122]

While Benezet used sections from Astley's *A New General Collection of Voy-*

ages, whenever possible he read the original versions of the narratives, as with the work of William Smith.[123] Smith wrote a long section on the sexual activities of Africans using the observations of his travel companion, a Mr. Wheeler.[124] Benezet chose not to use Smith's description—a point that one critic, Jonathan Sassi, commented on. Sassi notes that Benezet's "silence on Wheeler's commentary is deafening."[125] As a Quaker, Benezet simply would not talk or write about anyone's sexual practices, white or black.[126] Perhaps Benezet simply considered Smith too much of a fabricator.

Near the end of his work Smith came to an interesting conclusion: "And I doubted not but upon an impartial Examination of the Premises, it would be found, that we Christians have as many idle ridiculous Notions and Customs as the Natives of Guinea, have if not more."[127] While Sassi faults Benezet, one wonders why the fuss, as he admits that some of the tales recounted by Smith are so far-fetched that "whether or not his [Wheeler's] discourse is based on reality remains open to question."[128] It seems obvious why Benezet would not quote Smith on this and offer European men more ideas for abusing African women or enslaving them and their families.

Smith observed that the coasts of Guinea "which are divided into several kingdoms, have seldom any wars, which is the reason the slave trade is not too good here as on the Gold and Slave Coasts, where the Europeans have several forts and factories." This remark led Benezet to conclude that "it is the intercourse with the Europeans, and their settlements on the coast, which give life to the slave trade."[129]

The Geography of Africa

Benezet's geographic study followed the classic European voyage narrative, starting from the north and moving south, from the western coast to the southernmost tip of Africa, near the Cape of Good Hope.[130] Most of the observations in the narratives were of the natural elements—land, water, and the beauty of the flora and fauna—rather than about the many peoples and cultures of the African nations. The narratives also contained extensive descriptions of the vast riches of the area, from mineral deposits to diamond fields, followed by cold, calculating estimates of the best ways to rob and plunder native peoples of their wealth. While these accounts were essential for an understanding of how the Europeans viewed African society, remarkably few of the many thousands of written pages were devoted to the African peoples themselves. In most cases, when they did mention people, these narratives brought charges of paganism, asserting racist ideas about darker, different, and inferior peoples. Most contained purely European notions of food, clothing, sexual practices, marriage, religion, and culture. In rare instances the narratives attempted to describe rituals, feats, customs, and jewelry accurately, mainly in the western and central African regions. Barbot was one of the few to describe "the inhabitants in general;

their employments, professions, natural genius and temper; their habits, houses, cottages, hamlets, villages, and towns, with all things appertaining to them; their languages, manners, customs, religion, government, and distribution of justice, civil or criminal: the several kingdoms, principalities, or states; their power, courts, laws, wars, armies, weapons and taxes paid by the subjects."[131]

In spite of this generally negative view of Africans and other non-European peoples, the narratives offer fascinating accounts of the voyages and of the Europeans' views both of the Africans and of themselves. As the Nigerian historian Felix N. Okoye observes, "Eighteenth century travelers to Africa never tired of reminding their countrymen that 'surprising revolutions' often occurred along the coastlines of that continent."[132] Benezet's account of the geography "of that part of Africa commonly known as Guinea" closely mirrors those of modern historians as varied as Walter Rodney, J. D. Fage, and Robin Law.[133] Benezet described the area near the Cape of Good Hope as "a country settled by Caffres and Hottentots, who have never been concerned in the making or selling of slaves":

That part of Africa from which the Negroes are sold to be carried into slavery commonly known by the name of Guinea extends along the coast three or four thousands miles. Beginning at the river Senegal, situate about the 17th degree of North latitude, being the nearest part of Guinea, as well to Europe as to North America; from thence to the river Gambia, and in a southerly course to Cape Sierra Leona, comprehends a coast of about seven hundred miles; being the same tract for which Queen Elizabeth granted charters to the first traders to that coast; From Sierra Leona, the land of Guinea takes a turn to the westward, extending that course about fifteen hundred miles, including those several divisions known by the name of the Grain Coast, the Ivory Coast, the Gold Coast, and the Slave Coast, with the large Kingdom of Benin.[134]

He added that "from thence the land runs southward along the coast about twelve hundred miles, which contains the kingdoms of Congo and Angola; there the trade for slaves ends. From which to the southernmost Cape of Africa, called the Cape of Good Hope, the country is settled by Caffres and Hottentots, who have never been concerned in the making of slaves."[135]

Benezet seems to have borrowed from the description of John Atkins who wrote a chapter in his journal titled "Sierraleon," his general reference for Guinea. "By Guinea," he wrote, "here I mean all Negro-land, from about the River Senegal Northward, to within a Degrees of Cape Bon Esperance." Atkins described the area to the south and "the Hottentots at the other extremity."[136] He divided Guinea into the Windward Coast, the Gold Coast, and the Bay. The area, he suggested, benefited not only "from the warmth of the climate, but also from the overflowing of the rivers, whereby the land is regularly moistened and rendered extremely fertile; and being in many places improved by culture, abounds with grains and fruits, cattle and poultry, &C." Their agricultural methods yielded "all the year a fresh supply of food."[137]

Benezet borrowed from Smith, whom he recorded as saying that "the country about the Gambia is pleasant and fruitful; provisions of all kinds being plenty and cheap."[138] Benezet described Gambia as being between the Rivers Gambia and Senegal. He quoted Francis Moore that "they [the Fulis of the Gambia River region] were rarely angry, and that he never heard them abuse one another."[139] Gambia, he wrote, is "inhabited principally by those three Negro nations known by the name of Jalofs, Fulis, and Mandingos. The Jalofs possess the middle of the country. The Fulis principal settlement is on both sides of the Senegal, great numbers of the people are also mixed with the Mandingos: which last are most settled on both sides of the Gambia."[140]

Walter Rodney, the Guyanese historian and social activist, wrote that the Guinea Coast was distinguished by four areas: "upper Guinea with a dominating Mande presence; the Gold Coast where Akan were prominent; Yoruba/Aja territory; and Eastern Nigeria comprising mainly the Ibo and Ibibio."[141] The region extended from the present-day Cape Verde Islands, a former Portuguese colony on the west, to Cameroon, a former French colonial possession on the east. While the French concentrated on Senegal and Upper Guinea, English and Dutch companies competed for the better-established trade of the Gold Coast, with the result that the greatest concentration of European forts in West Africa was in this area. As demand for slaves increased, the needs of the slave traders as Fage outlines them were "met principally by extending the field of trading operations farther east into the Gulf Coast of Guinea and beyond."[142]

Benezet's writings on Africa focused on this region, precisely because of its centrality to the English and French slave trade. He wrote little about the Portuguese slave trade in Angola or the enslavement of blacks in Brazil. He described the area around Guinea as the "Slave Coast," a term that Jean Barbot claimed was derived from the Dutch Slave-Kust.[143] This area first became known as the Slave Coast "in reference to its role as supplier of slaves for the Atlantic slave trade, and in contrast to the Gold Coast (modern Ghana) to the west, which initially (prior to the eighteenth century) exported principally gold rather than slaves." As the trade in slaves shifted to the west and away from old Benin, the name followed the trade. In the eighteenth century the term Slave Coast took its broadest definition as most of the area along the West African coast where slaves were captured, bought, and sold. Slave Coast had a broad meaning and "as a unit of study . . . it did not represent any indigenous African political or ethnic unit . . . but was divided among large states and peoples."[144]

Benezet went on to describe "that part of Guinea known by the name of the Grain, and Ivory Coast . . . [that] extends about five hundred miles. The soil appears by account to be in general fertile, producing abundance of rice and roots; indigo and cotton thrive without cultivation, and tobacco would be excellent, if carefully manufactured; they have fish in plenty; their flocks greatly increase and their trees are loaded with fruit." He noted that some writers represented the people of the Grain or Ivory Coast as "a rude, treacherous people, while several other authors of credit gave them a very different character, representing them as sensible, courteous, and the fairest traders on the coast of Africa.[145] He then explained, "In the Collection they are said to be averse to drinking to excess. As such as they are severely punished by the King's order." Here we see Benezet using Snelgrave, a hostile source, to make a point of special interest to him.[146] Benezet found some of Snelgrave's work helpful, above all its geographical descriptions of Africa and maps. He also used Bosman's maps.[147]

The various authors had different opinions on the boundaries of the Gold Coast and the Slave Coast, which "extend together along the coast maybe about five hundred miles. And as the policy, produce, and economy of these two divisions of Guinea are much the same."[148] Adjoining the Slave Coast "is the Kingdom of Benin, which though it extends but about 170 miles on the sea, yet spreads so far inland, as to be esteemed the most potent kingdom of Guinea."[149]

Many of the people in the region around Guinea spoke dialects belonging to the Aja-Ewe language group. The early writers focused on these peoples and languages, and Benezet followed them. Olaudah Equiano, an Igbo, came from this region. To demonstrate the Africans' efficiency Benezet used Brüe, who wrote of "the Land so well cultivated, as he observed it to be scarce a Spot lay unimproved, the low Ground divided by small Canals, were all sowed with Rice." The higher ground "was planted with Indian Corn and Millet, and Peas of different sorts. . . . Beef and Mutton very cheap, as well as all other necessities of Life."[150]

Finally Brüe wrote that the "last division of Guinea from which slaves are imported, are the kingdoms of Kongo and Angola: these lie to the South of Benin, extending with the intermediate and about twelve hundred miles to the coast. Great numbers of the natives of both these kingdoms profess the Christian religion, which was long introduced by the Portuguese, who made early settlements in that country."[151] Benezet seldom wrote of the Congo region.[152] One of the few times he did, he called it the "Kingdom of Kongo" and wrote "in the government of the Kongo, the King appoints a judge . . . to hear and determine disputes and civil cases . . . but in weighty matters every one may appeal to the King."[153] John Thornton, when discussing the region's strengths, asserted that the mountainous provinces "were all more independent than those in the lowlands, for they preserved the right, even in the middle of the seventeenth century at the height of Kongo's centralization, to elect their own rulers."[154]

Benezet's knowledge of the slave trade was evident: "From the ongoing accounts, it is undoubted, that the practice of making slaves of the Negroes, its origin to the early incursions of the Portuguese on the coast of Africa, arose solely from an inordinate desire of gain."[155] Greed was international and tainted the whites' views of the Africans and of themselves. At the heart of Benezet's argument was his belief that "the desire for gain and profit" corrupted the souls of men and the core of society; he did not see *profit* and *gain* in the literal eighteenth-century usage of the words.[156]

He knew that one of the arguments used to justify slavery was that the blacks were accustomed both to harsh weather and to hard labor. Whitefield had said as much: "Hot countries cannot be cultivated without Negroes."[157] Benezet found the conditions just the opposite. He saw no proof that blacks were any more suited to hard labor in the torturous sun than were whites. The Africans in their native environments worked only when they needed to and certainly were not conditioned to the sunup-to-sundown forced labor that was imposed on them in the New World. In their work he found that the people of Guinea produced an abundance of goods combined with the "simplicity of their householdry."[158]

Africa's various regions became pawns in the economic wars of the trader nations. Gambia had first been the point of contention between England and Portugal, and it later became the center of the English and French rivalries. Senegal was at the center of French and Dutch rivalries and like Gambia was later fought over by England and France. The Gold Coast, by far the greatest prize, was intermittently the center of the struggles among most of the major powers, especially Great Britain, France, and Holland. Benezet briefly mentioned Sierra Leone as the area where the British fought Portugal, Holland, and France.[159]

The African Social Compact According to Benezet

In describing Africa at the outset of the slave trade Benezet often used excerpts from the works of the representative of the French Academy of Science, Michel Adanson, to appeal to French as well as to English colonists.[160] Adanson, a botanist, "was the first European since Richard Jobson in the early seventeenth century to describe the region from a standpoint detached from the practical difficulties and economics of the slave trade."[161] Benezet particularly appreciated Adanson's descriptions, first published in 1749, of the many different African cultures and peoples.[162] Adanson left Paris for Senegal on December 20, 1748, staying there until his return voyage on September 6, 1753.[163] Adanson was only twenty years old at the time.

Adanson, in what Benezet and his antislavery associates turned into one of the most widely quoted paragraphs from the travel narratives, showed his admiration for some aspects of African society: "Which way soever I turned my eyes on this pleasant spot, I beheld a perfect image of pure nature: an agreeable solitude, bounded on every side by a charming landscape; the rural situation of cottages in the midst of trees; the ease and indolence of the Negroes, reclined under the shade of their spreading foliage; the simplicity of their dress and manners; the whole revived in my mind, the idea of our first parents, and I seemed to contemplate the world in its primeval state."[164] Benezet used Adanson's works to buttress his own argument that even whites who thought blacks ignorant also reasoned that they could, if given opportunities, compete with Europeans. Benezet used precisely this argument to win Benjamin Franklin to the antislavery cause.

While Adanson wrote mainly about the geography and plant, animal, and insect life of Africa, he also wrote directly about the Africans he encountered, and he sought to distinguish one group from another. As Benezet studied the works of men like Jobson, who wrote in 1624, and Adanson, who wrote in 1750, he saw that Africans were indeed as varied as whites and had their own distinct paths of development. Just like Europeans they changed over time and developed new means of agricultural production and learning.

Adanson observed, as Benezet later noted in an effort to bolster his arguments, that the Africans had different languages, customs, religions, features, and even complexions. He wrote that "the people inhabiting the country along the Gambia are Mandingoes or Sofes, to express myself in their way. Their manner of life, and dress, is not preferable to that of the other blacks; but their huts are better built."[165] Benezet noted that Adanson observed both in "Negroes and Moors, great humanity and sociableness, which gave me strong hopes that I should be very safe amongst them, and meet with the success I desired with the conversation of the Negroes, their fables, dialogues, and witty stories with which they entertain each other alternately, according to their custom."[166]

Through Adanson, Benezet sought to ascertain the natural abilities of the Africans and to argue that with proper facilities, equal footing, and the good will of their fellow human beings, Africans who had been enslaved in the Americas could be free and productive members of society. Benezet adjusted Adanson's formulation somewhat and near the end of his life projected his own ideas for black progress. While he, like other authors, felt that some whites were themselves "rude and illiterate," he stood almost alone in comparing whites and blacks in this regard. For example, his words about "Hollanders" were seldom kind, because of the unwelcome treatment that his family and other refugee Huguenots received in Holland after fleeing France.

Adanson was one of the few voyagers who took the trouble to attempt to absorb any of the African languages, and he learned Wolof in Senegal.[167] Robert Norris, author of *The Memoirs of the Reign of Bossa Ahadee, King of Dahomy,* also attempted to learn a number of native languages. Norris according to Archibald Dalzel, in his *History of Dahomy,* "was well acquainted with the languages and customs of the [Dahomian] people, and was indefatigable in obtaining from both black and whites the memoirs from which his part was written."[168]

But most of the authors had little appreciation of African languages or culture. A somewhat sympathetic John Atkins believed that "the Negro Language alters a little in failing, but as they are Strangers to Arts, & c and restrained to a few Words, expressive of their Necessities."[169] This statement clearly shows his bias, as most of the narratives, as well as the writings of early Africans like Olaudah Equiano, show that Africans spoke many languages and dialects. Francis Moore seemed to agree with Atkins: "The Negroes were entirely ignorant of arts and letters and with the use of iron."[170] Although Benezet found Moore's work extremely useful, he disagreed with such an assessment. In the last paragraph of *Some Historical Account of Guinea,* Benezet summed up his belief in the natural intelligence and abilities of blacks: "For while the spirit of butchery and making slaves of each other, is promoted by the Europeans amongst the Negroes, no mutual confidence can take place; . . . to form and cement such commercial friendships and alliances, as might be necessary to introduce the arts and sciences amongst them and engage their attention to instruction in the principles of the Christian religion, which is the only sure foundations of every social virtue."[171] In other words the imposition of slavery impeded African progress across the board. Benezet cited Adanson, who thought that "it is amazing that such a rude and illiterate people, should reason so pertinently in regard to those heavenly bodies; there is no, manner of doubt, that with proper instruments, and a good will, they would become excellent astronomers."[172] At another time Benezet quoted André Brüe, who stated that the Africans were "laborious, industrious, and very ready to learn arts and sciences."[173] While Benezet seemed to agree with Moore, it must be remembered that Benezet believed that even among whites it was first necessary to learn reading, arithmetic, and life skills before studying the arts. But that did not mean that blacks were incapable of learning the arts and sciences, as Benezet sought to prove that blacks could learn just as the whites.[174]

Religion

Benezet explored some of the religious beliefs, family structures, and village patterns of the Mandingos (Malinke) in Gambia.[175] Quoting extensively from the journals of Brüe and Jobson, he offered a quite positive appraisal of what they called the "Mahometan Negroes." Benezet had specific praise for Jobson: "[He] is patently opposed to slavery, takes notice of several good qualities in these Negro priests, particularly their great sobriety. The boys are taught to read and write. They not only teach school, but rove about the country teaching and instructing, for which the whole country is open to them." Benezet then came to his own conclusion: "Some of these Mandingos, who are settled at Galem far up the river Senegal, can read and write Arabic tolerably, and are a good hospitable people, who carry on a trade with the Inland nations."[176]

In *Some Historical Account of Guinea,* Benezet paraphrased Jobson: "We are told from Jobson (11) that the Mahometan Negroes say their prayers thrice a day . . . they adored God by prostrating themselves before him."[177] Jobson's actual words were, "They do worship the same as we do, the true and only God, to whom they pray, and on his name they call, in their language, expressed by the word *Alle.*" Jobson told his readers they "do not have amongst them any Churches, nor places they dedicate to holy uses." They hold their "religious ceremonies under the shady tree."[178] Nonetheless, even though Jobson wrote at an earlier period, he, unlike Atkins, showed an appreciation of African society.

Benezet also observed the religions of "the Kingdom of Whydah," which both William Smith and Willem Bosman had written about. Bosman "speaks in commendation of the civility, kindness, and great industry of the natives of Whidah; this is confirmed by Smith, who says 'the natives here seem to be the most-gentlemen like Negroes in Guinea, abounding with good manners and ceremony to each other.'"[179] At another point Benezet wrote that "Bosman tells us the 'Whidah Negroes have a faith idea of a true God, ascribing him the attributes of almighty power and omnipresence; but God they say is too high to condescend to think of mankind; wherefore he commits the government of the world to those inferior deities which they worship.'" He then used Smith to prove the same point: "William Smith says 'that all the natives of this coast believe there is one true God, the author of them and all things; that they have apprehensions of a future state; and that almost every village has a grove, or a public place of worship, to which the principal inhabitants, on a day set, resort to make their offerings.'"[180]

Benezet also cited Jobson's *Golden Trade* because, although it was one of the earliest accounts, to Benezet it was one of the fairest. Jobson's work was included in Samuel Purchas's *Purchas His Pilgrim.*[181] Purchas's books were in his own words, written to help readers like Benezet "travel through that least knowne part of the Eldernowne world."[182] The Guinea Company employed Jobson, an Englishman, when the British first showed an interest in the Senegambia. The major commodities then were not slaves but, as Jobson wrote, "rice, waxe, hides, elephant's teeth, and golde." A line used by abolitionists came from the *Golden Trade.* Queried by a slave dealer about purchasing three female slaves, Jobson replied, "We were a people, who did not deale in any such commodities, neither did wee buy or sell one another, or any that had our shapes." Jobson wrote of "hiring Blacke-men, as I had occasioned to use them, as interpreters, likewise to send abroad, and to helpe to row." This statement is revealing. The Africans learned English, but the whites seemed unable to learn African languages. Jobson told of "hiring a young African man near the Tinba River, (the River Nièr-ico)" who "was come to speak our tongue, very handsomely, and him I used many times as an Interpreter, so all in all we had foure Blacke-men, whose help we could not misse."[183] Jobson's journal thus proved useful, as it documented Africans contentedly going about their work before the arrival of whites.

Benezet developed a special affection for the Malinke, who may have seemed to embody some values similar to those of the Quakers. Much like the Quakers, they neither drank nor cursed. Because they established schools throughout their territory much as the Quakers did, Benezet used them as an example of the development of African civilizations. Yet he also tied the Malinke king directly to the European slave trade: "The King fur-nishes the Europeans with slaves very easily. He sends a troop of Guards to some Village, which they surround; then seizing as many as they have Orders for, they bind them and send them away to the ships, where the Ship-Mark being put upon them, they are heard of no more."[184] At other times Benezet cited Brüe and others to describe African complicity in the slave trade: "Having received Goods, he wrote to the King, that if he had a sufficient Number of Slaves, he was ready to trade with him; this Prince, says that Author, as well as the other Negroe Monarch, have always sure Way of supplying his Deficiencies, by selling their own subjects. These Negroe kings, thus seeking Pretenses to cover their Crimes, shew they are not quite void of shame, not insensible that Covetousness induces them to act a Part so inconsistent with their Duty, but they may plead the Example and Solicitation of the more knowing Europeans."[185] Brüe provided a problematic legacy for an abolitionist, but the writings of Francis Moore, "factor several Years to the Royal African Company of England" in Gambia and author of *Travels into the Inland Parts of Africa*, more closely suited Benezet's purposes, much as the writings of Adanson and Jobson did.[186] Like Atkins, Moore disliked the slave trade and gave detailed accounts of the French factory at Alereda and of the English at "their settlement at Fort James, in the River Gambia, on the Coast of Guinea, in Africa." Benezet often used Moore, sometimes described as a fellow Quaker, because Moore more than other authors asserted Africans' abilities and sensibilities. Moore wrote, "Some people of a tawny Colour, called Pholeys, much like the Arabs; which language they most of them speak, being to them as the Latin is in Europe, for it is taught in schools, and their Law, the Alcoran, is in that language. They are more generally learned in the Arabick, than the People of Europe are in Latin, for they can most of them speak it."[187] Moore concluded, "In short, all the Countries hereabout (and I have seen vast Numbers of People for each) cannot come up to the Jal-loiffs for blackness of Skin, and Beauty of Features."[188] Moore borrowed Leo Africanus's descriptions of the beauty and simplicity of African life without attribution.[189] Additionally, the Frenchman Adanson used words that sounded similar to Moore's.

Moore, in a passage favored by Benezet, singled out the Malinke's dislike of liquor: "Few of them will drink brandy or anything stronger than water."[190] Benezet did not cite Jobson's rather different opinion: "One thing was remarkable, that when the King took the first cup into his Hand, if the Liquor was either uncommon, or excellent in its kind, he wetted one of his principal Gregories with it before he drank."[191] As a leader in the fight for temperance, Benezet at times coupled his writings against slavery with his campaign against alcohol. He wrote *The Mighty Destroyer Displayed, or the Potent Enemies of America Laid Open* in 1774 and a smaller pamphlet, *Remarks on the Nature and Bad Effects of Spirituous Liquors,* in 1778. That he chose to quote from Moore, who described the Moslems as nondrinkers, over Jobson simply indicates that on this matter Moore better suited his purposes. Summing up his beliefs based on reading Moore, Benezet observed, "Here it is very difficult to imagine what vices can be peculiarly attendant on a people so well disposed as the author describes them to be."[192] Moore's work was also reprinted in the *Gentleman's Magazine.*[193] He came to believe that the Malinkes of Senegambia and other Africans also shared similar beliefs with Quakers on child rearing, drink, morality, and greed.

While Benezet had read chronologically Leo Africanus, Moore, and Adanson on the Muslim presence in Africa, there is no indication that he fully comprehended how the Europeans specifically undermined Muslim culture in the eighteenth century.[194] He began by using Jobson (1623) to make his first observation of Moslems in Africa, made his way to Moore (1738), and then moved on to Adanson (1749), who wrote over a hundred years after Jobson. Benezet deliberately over time developed his argument to show continuity, just as he, conscious of the time each traveler wrote in, used the works of Bosman (1705) and Smith (1744).

The Africans held to their belief in the immortality of their souls. In his account Snelgrave observed that the Africans knew "the Kormantines to be desperate Fellows, who despised Punishment and even Death itself: For it has often happened at Barbados and other Islands, that, on their being any Ways hardly dealt with, to break them from their Stubbornness in refusing to work, twenty, or more, have hanged themselves, at a time, in one Planta-tion."[195] Benezet admired the beliefs of the Africans concerning life and death and praised their religious virtues. By demonstrating the religious devotion of the Africans, he also sought to rebut religious arguments in favor of the slave trade.

Benezet had read and written about slave suicides during the middle pas-sage and in the northern mainland. Leaving dead corpses to rot or to be eaten by vultures was a common method used to strike fear in the heart of the slaves. The slave-trading barons knew that many African religions required the body to be whole in order for the transmigration of the soul to take place. They knew that for many Africans the only thing worse than slavery and death itself was a mutilated corpse, unfit for a place in the African burial grounds or in heaven.[196] For Africans this transition was the true climax of life. Godfrey Loyer, a French monk on the Gold Coast of Africa in 1711, wonderfully described this aspect of the Africans' religious doctrines: "The doctrine of the Transformation of the Souls is believed by the Negros; . . . They believe the World to be eternal, and the Soul immortal; that after their death their Soul will go to the other World, which they place in the Centre of the Earth; that there it will animate a new Body in the Womb of a Woman; and that the Souls from thence, would do the same. So that according to this doctrine, there is a constant Intercourse or Exchange of inhabitants between these two worlds."[197] This belief kept the African alive in this world and hopeful for the next.[198]

Egalitarianism and Ethnicity

The idea that some African egalitarian ideas were similar to Benezet's seemed to resonate with and fascinate him. His notions of geographic, tribal, and religious independence led him to see that Africans had also thought out and developed their own systems of government. He often used the works of Peter Kolb (or Kolben), who has been overlooked as a source in the study of Africa. Kolb's book *The Present State of the Cape of Good-Hope* describes his visits to Southern Africa and the Hottentot, or Khoikhoin (Khoi), peoples.[199] Benezet referred to him as "Peter Holben . . . a man sent from the court of Prussia solely to take astronomical and natural observations, who had no interest in the slaving of the Africans." Kolb was born on October 10, 1675, and trained as a mathematician. Though the Russian tsar offered him a lectureship in mathematics, he instead decided to go to the Cape of Good Hope and engage in meteorological and astronomical studies. However, instead of carrying out his experiments, Kolb began to study the peoples of the region, and thus he did not have the same reasons or inducements to misrepresent the natives of Africa.[200] Although Benezet rarely wrote about Southern Africa, his use of Kolb shows that he went looking in books for passages to support his arguments.

In his earlier *Short Account of That Part of Africa*, Benezet wrote that "Peter Holben says Every Village or Kraal has a court of Justice, for civil and criminal Affairs, composed of the captain and all the Men of the Kraal, who meet for this Purpose in the open Field, fitting in the circle. Justice among the Hottentots never suffers as in Europe, either by Corruption or which is as bad, Delay." Kolb, who Benezet observed had lived eight years in "that country," added a bit of humor: "They have no lawyers thank heaven,"[201] and "the love of liberty and indolence is their All: compulsion to them is death. While necessity obliges them to work, they are very tractable, obedient and faithful, but when they have got enough to satisfy the present Want, they are deaf to all farther Entreaty."[202] Of course upper-class Europeans of the time said exactly the same thing about lower-class Europeans. They particularly made this point about peasants who lived in areas with rich land. In *Some Historical Account of Guinea,* Benezet slightly altered his early observation: "[Kolb] resided eight years at and about the Cape of Good Hope, during which time he examined with great care, into the customs, manners, and opinions of the Hottentots; whence he sets these people in a quite different light." Benezet paraphrased Kolb as saying that "the details we have in several authors are for the most part made up of inventions and hearsays, which generally prove false."[203] Benezet felt that Kolb at least tried to give a true representation.

Kolb, however, like many of his peers, had varied ideas about the Africans. On the one hand, wrote Benezet, "he sometimes faults them for their nastiness, the effect of sloth, and for their love of drink, and the practice of some unnatural customs." On the other hand, wrote Kolb, "yet some Writers have said too much upon this Point, and made them much more ravenous and uncleanly than they are." Kolb had heard accounts of the way the Khoi ate uncooked and dirty food. To find out the truth he recounted, "I have spent many whole Days among them in several Parts of the Country; and took every Opportunity to observe their Manner of preparing and eating Victuals, and never could discover any Good Ground for this."[204]

Later, according to Benezet, Kolb wrote that "they are eminently distinguished by many virtues, as their mutual benevolence, friendship, and hospitality; they breathe kindness and good will to one another, and seek all opportunities of obliging."[205] Kolb bolstered Benezet's argument that the Africans produced only what they needed to sustain themselves rather than seeking greater gains. Benezet knew that the Hottentots (Khoi) in the south of Africa were physically distinguishable from Africans on the west coast of the continent and were not immediate victims of the African slave trade.[206] He used them as an example of what could be, if Africans were left to themselves.

Using a variety of sources to examine various African societies' conceptions of justice, he made references to the Frenchman "La Maire," who appeared in Astley's *New General Collection* and wrote of the "Government of the Falofs . . . The king has under him several Ministers of State, who assist him in the Government and Exercise of Justice." Benezet noted that Barbot confirmed the above account and added "that the chief Justice inspects the Behavior of the Alkairs of the several districts."[207] Benezet cited other European witnesses to the fairness of the judicial systems of West Africa.

Brüe noted that the king listened to all parties involved, consulted with his officers, and made a decision. He "saw none here who acted either as

Counsel or Attorney, each pleaded his own Cause in very proper Terms," although he refrained from Kolb's joyous assessment of that fact.[208] Benezet added Kolb's description of the Khois' system of justice to show the widespread pattern of sound government in Africa. Kolb emphasized that a convicted criminal forfeited only his life, while his "Family, Relations and Friends are treated by everyone with the same Respect and Distinction that were paid to 'em before; and every Thing is carried as no such Misfortune had happen'd."[209]

In the end one of Benezet's greatest contributions was to foster a different view of Africa, to aid those opposed to slavery throughout the Atlantic world. He was able to encourage his British and French counterparts to alter their own views. The African was no longer a caricature, an ornament, or chattel. Africans were living, breathing human beings and, like fellow members of the human race, deserved freedom. That concept was indeed radical if not revolutionary and one that he obtained by combining the philosophical insights of the European humanist tradition, the tenets of the Quaker faith, and his knowledge of Africa and its peoples.

Already in 1759 Benezet commented, "It is these Abuses which Africans have so often suffered from the Europeans; that have given Rise to the frequent Contradictions we meet with in Authors, with respect to the Temper and Disposition of the Negroes; One Author speaking well of some Nations, whilst another Author represents the same nation as Barbarous and savage."[210] He then began to use a rich European intellectual tradition to turn the "barbarous and savage" descriptions on their heads. His writings suggest that he also knew the *Essais* of the French intellectual Michel de Montaigne, above all his "Of the Cannibals," which called into question European assumptions about Africa and the New World. Montaigne read "many accounts of the conquest of the New World."[211] He took a balanced view toward other cultures: "There is nothing savage or barbarous about those peoples, but that every man calls barbarous anything he is not accustomed to; it is indeed the case that we have no other criterion of truth or right-reason than the example and form of the opinions of our own country."[212] His perspective found little favor in the seventeenth century but became popular again in the eighteenth. Anthony Pagden and others have pointed out that Montaigne's views were no more normative in the sixteenth century than Benezet's would be in the eighteenth.[213]

Benezet rejected the traditional European notion that the culture of others was inferior, and Montaigne's ideas on Africa provided a direct underpinning for Benezet's work. Such writers as Franklin and Rousseau revived Montaigne's skepticism about the idea of the "noble savage." Franklin, who continued to share ideas with Benezet, speaking of Native Americans and Africans, once paraphrased Montaigne's writing: "Savages we call them because their manners differ from ours, which we think the Perfection of Civility; they think the same of theirs."[214]

Montaigne praised the simplicity of African peoples, as Benezet would later do: "All things, says Plato, are produced by nature, by fortune, or by art; the greatest and most beautiful by one or the other of the first two, the least and the most imperfect by the last."[215] Montaigne described his New World utopia as "a nation that hath no kind of traffic, no knowledge of letters, no intelligence of numbers, no name of magistrate nor of politic partitions, no occupation but idle, no respect of kindred but common, no apparel but natural, no manuring of lands, no use of wine, corn, or metal. The very words that import lying, falsehood, treason, dissimulations, covetousness, envy, detraction, and pardon, were never heard of amongst them. How dissonant would he find his imaginary commonwealth from this perfection."[216] Montaigne described a land of honest people where there was no "lying, cheating, avarice, envy backbiting."[217] According to Benezet, Bosman—no friend of the African—wrote, "They are generally speaking a good sort of People, honest in their Dealings. . . . Some Negroes, who have had an agreeable Education, have manifested a Brightness of Understanding equal to any of us."[218] Montaigne in "Of the Cannibals" saw a paradise where the inhabitants "spend the whole day dancing."[219] Two centuries later Olaudah Equiano described his native Africa as "a nation of dancers, musicians and poets."[220]

Francis Moore understood that the concept of the compound accumulation of goods or of land was foreign to most Africans. Most simply produced what was needed to survive and shared these things communally. He borrowed from Africanus to describe African life in similar terms as Montaigne: "They have chiefs of their own, who rule with much moderation. Few of them will drink brandy, or anything stronger than water and sugar being strict Mahometans. Their form of government goes on easy, because the people are of a good quiet disposition, and so well instructed in what is right. . . . The neighbors are not covetous of land, desiring no more than what they use, and they do not plough with horses or cattle."[221] Francis Moore understood this, observing, "In these countries the Natives are not avarious of Lands; they desire no more than what they use; and as they do not plough with Horses or Cattle."[222] He admired the Africans' early communal spirit and praised it against the growing European "love of gain." He used language couched in moral tones to challenge the economic motives behind slavery.[223]

White Brutality

Always conscious of the past, Benezet sought to link the treatment and conditions of enslaved Africans on plantations with their lives in their homelands. For this he used the work of Sir Hans Sloane (1660–1753), who wrote *Voyage to the Islands of Nieves, St. Christopher, and Jamaica, 1707–1725*.[224] His use of the learned Sloane helped him prove that Africans were not better off in British North America than they were in Africa, as some argued.[225] Benezet also referred to the Sloane work by the short title *The Natural History of Jamaica.*[226] While conducting scientific research, Sloane seems to have observed the brute force used to contain the island's slaves.[227]

Sloane described the punishment for rebellious slaves: with "Arms and legs extended, Fire is then set to his Feet and he is burnt gradually up to his Head." Others were starved to death, with a "loaf of bread dangling before them." Benezet alternated between quoting Sloane and the anonymous Philmore, who also quoted Sloane. Philmore described how "as punishment for 'less nature' than 'open rebellion they geld the Offender,' and 'chop off Half his foot with an ax.'" Such crimes as negligence required less brutal measures; the slave was "whip[ped] . . . till his Back is raw, and then scatter[ed] Pepper and Salt on his wounds, to heighten the smart." Planters then "will drop melted Wax on their skins, which puts them in intolerable pain."[228] Benezet had also read in Philmore that "Sir Hans Sloan[e], in his *History of Jamaica,* says 'that a rebellious Negroe or he that twice strikes a white Man, is condemned to the Flames; being chained flat on his Belly, at the Place of Execution, and his Arms and Legs extended." In the aftermath of a revolt, according to Philmore, "four of the principle conspirators were burnt in the same day, as were seven the next day. Six were hung alive in Chains on Giblets. . . . [F]ifty others were, at several times chained to Stakes and burnt alive."[229] Sloane wrote about the reason for the punishments: "they are three times the number of the whites in this Island, and have made frequent attempts to get the mastery." Benezet interpreted this to mean that blacks wanted "to get their Liberty, or to deliver themselves out of the miserable slavery they are in."[230] In reality, the slave-to-white ratio in Jamaica was among "the highest in the British West Indies," where it stood at ten blacks to one white.[231]

In *A Caution and a Warning,* Benezet cited "an account of the European Settlements in American, printed in London, 1757" without identifying the writer William Burke.[232] "The author," wrote Benezet, "says: 'The Negroes in our Colonies endure a slavery more compleat and attended with far worse circumstances than what any people in their condition suffer in any other part of the world, or have suffered in any other period of time; proofs of this are not wanting.'" The author explained the conditions on "the Island of Barbados," where the blacks suffered from an "unsupportable hardship . . . which wears them down in such a surprising manner; and this, I imagine, is principally the excessive labour which they undergo."[233]

Benezet also used "an account of part of North-American, published by Thomas Jeffery, printed in 1761, speaking of the usage the Negroes receive in the West India Islands." Jeffery wrote that "it's impossible for a human heart to reflect upon the servitude of these dregs of mankind, without in some measure feeling for their misery, which ends but with their lives— Nothing can be more wretched than the condition of this people." He continues that "their labour [is] almost continual, they receive no wages, but have twenty lashes for the smallest fault. . . . [The whites] whip them most unmercifully, on small occasions. They beat them with clubs, and you will see their bodies all a whaled and scarred; in short, they seem to set no other value on their lives than as they cost them so much money." Yet, as Jeffery noted, on some occasions the masters' absolute need to dominate the blacks made them forget, if only temporarily, their drive for maximum profits. In other words, if the master were not compensated for the slave that he tortured, he would lose money. Jeffery observed that if the masters were "not restrained from killing them, when angry, by a worthier consideration than that they lose so much," they would have killed the blacks. The whites, he argued, acted as though "they did not look upon them as a race of human creatures, who have reason, and remembrance of misfortunes, but as beasts, like oxen, who are stubborn, hardy and senseless; fit for burdens, and designed to bear them." At other times, speaking for those who claimed they viewed blacks as humans, albeit of a lesser nature, Jeffery argued, "They won't allow them to have any claim to human privileges, or scarce, indeed, to be regarded as the work of God." Jeffery sounded a lot like Morgan Godwyn.[234]

Proslavery Response to Benezet's Writing on Africa

The proponents of slavery, religious or not, did not have to defend their position or define their negative images of the African until opposition arose. As Lawrence Tise noted, "lacking any widespread opposition to slavery, its defense was usually sporadic and local. Throughout the 18th and 19th centuries, published defenses almost always appeared in direct response to specific antislavery tracts and for all practical purposes ended the debate." Tise added, "Impelled by the new widely circulating writings of a small coterie of Quaker emancipationists led by Anthony Benezet in Philadelphia, various colonial thinkers used proslavery ideas to counter the first major attack in the new world."[235] With this opposition came the proslavery forces' first calculated defense of slavery, racial prejudice, and their attitudes toward Africans in Africa or the Americas.

One of the most direct attacks on Benezet's vision of Africa came from Thomas Thompson, the Anglican missionary and SPG member who had traveled extensively in the West Indies. As the title *The African Trade for Negro Slaves, Shewn to Be Consistent with the Principles of Humanity, and with the Laws of Revealed Religion* implies, Thompson believed that the Bible sanctioned slavery and that slavery was consistent both with divine and natural law.[236] Thompson insisted that his views were not based on race but on religion. He mocked the religious practices of the Africans, as did other members of the SPG. He wrote about their adoption of fetishes and idols, stating that they worship "a being of *Fetisa* which inhabits there."[237] Thompson's paternalism led him to comment that there was "something very affecting, and disagreeable, in the appearance and notion of human creatures, even the lowest of such, being treated like mere beasts and cattle."[238]

In a letter to Granville Sharp on March 29, 1773, some months after he had read and dissected Thompson's pamphlet, Benezet wrote, "The answer to Parson Thompson I received and read with peculiar satisfaction; it is the most effectual plea I have met with in answer to those who pleads the Jewish practice of slavery. It will be of no such service to me if I should, as I reprint my Book of the account of Africa."[239] This assertion is about as close as Benezet would ever come to boasting. But it did show his particular pride that his life and work was having an effect.

In 1770 James Beattie wrote *An Essay on the Nature and Immutability of Truth in Opposition to Sophistry and Skeptics.* Beattie challenged the racial ideas of philosophers like Hume and Aristotle's idea that "certain groups of peoples are more suited for physical labor and therefore are through the 'intention' of nature 'destined to serve others.' "[240] Beattie quoted Hume's famous passage on the inferiority of "Negroes."[241] He noted that "these assertions are strong but I know not whether they have anything else to recommend them. For, first, though true they would not prove the point in question, except were it also proved, that the Africans and Americans, even though arts and sciences were introduced among them, would still remain unsusceptible to cultivation. The inhabitants of Great Britain and France were as savage 2,000 years ago as those of Africa and America are to this day. To civilize a nation requires a long time to accomplish."[242] Like Benezet, he wrote that the differences among the white Europeans just as among black Africans did not make one group inferior or superior to the other.[243] Part of Benezet's reasoning for human equality came from Acts 17:24–26: "God, that made the world,—hath made of one blood all nations of men, for to dwell on all the face of earth, and hath determined the—bounds of their habitation."[244] This simple formulation challenged Hume's complicated theories. Following Benezet, Beattie argued for a "one race" theory.[245] Hume responded in 1776 to Beattie's criticism, altering slightly the text of the 1754 edition "Of National Characters."[246]

On October 13, 1776, James Oglethorpe of Georgia Colony, who had read Benezet's work on Africa, wrote to Sharp. Oglethorpe had also read Leo Africanus, and he offered a fascinating example of the spread of knowledge about Africa: "You mention an argument by Hume, that the Africans were incapable of liberty, and that no man capable of government was ever produced by Africa. What a Historian! He must never have heard of Shishak, the great Sesostris, of Hannibal, nor of Tir-haka, king of Ethiopia, whose very name frightened the mighty Assyrian monarch (2 Kings 19: 9) . . . in Leo, the African's geographical description of Africa, he would have found that Africa had produced races of heroes."[247] Oglethorpe had probably also read Benezet, through the works of John Wesley. In fact Wesley wrote to Benezet in 1774 that "Mr. Oglethorp[e], you know, went so far as to begin settling a colony without Negroes; but at length the voice of those villains prevailed who sell their country and their God for gold."[248]

Benezet's descriptions of Africa do not reflect some pastoral scenario of African life; they reflect his devotion to his beliefs in the Quaker religion and in utopian equality. In order to transform the debate about slavery Benezet had to transform the debate about Africans themselves. He would have to develop a new rhetoric about Africa and her peoples if he hoped to affect the fight against slavery in the mainland colonies and in Britain and France.

Benezet's research on Africa led him to challenge two fundamental arguments in favor of the trade: that the profits of the trade enhanced and revitalized white society, and that it saved blacks from their backwardness. His reconstruction of African history proved vital for this second goal. For Benezet slavery brought the destruction of the varied nations and civilizations of Africa and of the basic family units that had long flourished there. He saw in parts of Africa some of the things that he had wanted to see in America. He admired the simple family lives of the Africans, where parents and villages loved their children, each looked out for the other, all loved and yet feared their God, and ostentation and drunkenness were taboo. In that society courage, dignity, and respect for simple hierarchical traditions added to the life of the family and village. Benezet even found the descriptions of a hardened racist like Bosman to be helpful when he offered such observations as blacks on the Gold Coast "are said to be fond of their children, whom they love with tenderness."[249]

While some men's moral compasses pointed away from slavery, their racial compasses pointed toward prejudices and allowed for the separation of the races and eventually servitude.[250] Benezet knew that one could be profoundly against the making of chattel slaves of Africans, but once enlightened philosophers allowed for any inequality and inferiority based on race, climate, religion, or conquest, they gave the proslavery forces important weapons. Benezet's ideas on Africa coupled with Scottish philosophies of freedom challenged this notion of inequality and turned his antislavery ideas into "material forces."

Keith Sandiford aptly observed that "Benezet insisted that Africans were the human equals of the Europeans: that they were honest, hardworking people whose tranquility and traditional morality were disrupted by European depredations on the Guinea Coast." Benezet showed that "European contact had a devastating effect on Africa; that the slave trade and the regimen of plantation life brutalized Africans, as they gave no incentive for the exercise of their higher faculties and sensations."[251] Benezet's studies of Africa and the Africans led him to compare the two societies and to pose questions to whites about the society they were creating. Midway through *Some Historical Account of Guinea,* Benezet made a forceful argument. Subtitled "The Conduct of the Europeans and Africans Compared," the book argued, "such is the woeful corruption of human nature that every practice, which flatters our pride and covetousness, will find its advocates. This is manifestly the case in the matter before us; the savages of the Negroes in some form of their customs and particularity their deviating so far from the feelings of humanity." Whites' "treatment of the blacks could be no excuse for the high-professing Christians; bred in a civilized country, with so many advantages unknown to the Africans, and pretending to a superior degree of gospel light." The color of the Africans could not "justify them in raising voyages for the seizure of men naturally free as themselves; and who, they know, are not otherwise to be procured than by such barbarous means."[252]

Benezet attempted to offer "abatement" to what he had read: "It is these Abuses which the Africans have so often suffered from the Europeans; that have given Rise to the frequent Contradictions we meet with in Authors with respect to the Temper and Disposition of the Negroes." He concluded, "And indeed when it is considered how often the Europeans have most grievously provoked them, by treacherously carrying away some of their Country-men, Friends or Relations. It is not to be wondered that some Negro Nations should have appear'd fired with Anger and Resentment, against those who have done them Injustice of so affecting a nature."[253]

Benezet knew, as did his fellow Frenchman Jean Bodin, that "even as we see a varietie in all sorts of beasts, in a like way we may say, there is in a manner as great difference in the nature and disposition of man."[254] Benezet understood that differences among peoples did not negate the souls of men or women, but rather they enhanced their being. Near the end of his life he put forward a program for black emancipation and enlightenment. He argued, "Let the Negroe's free, and in a few generations this vast and fertile Continent would be crowded with Inhabitants; Learning, Arts and every Thing would flourish amongst them instead of being inhabited by wild beast and Savages, it would be peopled by Philosophers and by Men."[255]

In the beginning of *Some Historical Account of Guinea* he asserted, "Too easy credit is given to the accounts we frequently hear or read of their barbarous and savage way of living in their own country."[256] Close to the end of that work Benezet quoted Adanson: "They— [the Africans] are generally speaking, very good natured, sociable and obliging. I was not a little pleased (says he) with this first Reception;—it convinced me, that there ought to be a considerable Abatement made in the Accounts I had read and heard every where of the savage Character of the Africans."[257] In his first work on Africa, Benezet wrote about "one Author speaking well of some Nations, whilst another Author represents the same nation as Barbarous and savage."[258]

Nearing the last decade of his life he again forcefully answered men like

Ligon and Nisbet and questioned his countrymen, as well as men and women throughout the Atlantic world: "Let us diligently compare, and impartially weigh, the situation of those ignorant Negroes, and these enlightened Christians; then lift up the scale and say which of the two are the greater savages."[259]

7

87 48/7

SOME

HISTORICAL ACCOUNT

OF

GUINEA,

ITS

SITUATION, PRODUCE, and the General
DISPOSITION OF ITS INHABITANTS.

WITH

An Inquiry into the RISE and PROGRESS

OF THE

SLAVE TRADE,

Its NATURE, and Lamentable EFFECTS.

By ANTHONY BENEZET.

ACTS xvii. 24. 26. GOD, *that made the world—hath made
of* one blood *all nations of men, for to dwell on all the face
of the earth, and hath determined the—bounds of their habitation.*

A NEW EDITION.

L O N D O N:
Printed and Sold by J. PHILLIPS, George Yard, Lombard-ſtreet.
M.DCC.LXXXVIII.

Title page of Anthony Benezet, *Some Historical Account of Guinea* (Philadelphia: Joseph Crukshank, 1771). The pamphlet was widely distributed to religious and political leaders and royal figures in America and Britain and translated in France. It was read by men like Benjamin Franklin, Benjamin Rush, Patrick Henry, Granville Sharp, Thomas Clarkson, and the Abbé Grégoire.

The Reverend Absalom Jones. Jones was born a slave in Sussex, Delaware, and also attended Benezet's evening school. He became the first priest of African descent in the Protestant Episcopal Church. Along with Richard Allen he was a founder of the Free African Society in 1787. The society was founded in part on the rules and organizational principles of Quaker-inspired abolition societies. Courtesy of the Historical Society of Pennsylvania, Leon Gardiner Collection.

Thomas Clarkson. Clarkson became a leader of the British campaign against slavery. In 1786 he published his *Essay on the Slavery and Commerce of the Human Species, Particularly the African,* which was his prizewinning Latin dissertation from Cambridge in 1785. Clarkson wrote that he was dismayed at the progress he was making on the essay until he stumbled upon a newspaper in a friend's house with an advertisement for Benezet's *Some Historical Account of Guinea.* He then went to a London bookstore to find the publication and later wrote that "in this precious book I found almost all I wanted." Courtesy of the Wilberforce House Museum, Hull.

Olaudah Equiano.

or

GUSTAVUS VASSA

the African.

Olaudah Equiano. In his *Interesting Narrative* Equiano wrote, "see Anthony Benezet throughout." He was referring to Benezet's *Some Historical Account of Guinea,* which he used as a reference on the history and geography of parts of West Africa. From Equiano's *The Interesting Narrative of the Life of Olaudah Equiano, or Gustavas Vassa, the African* (London, 1788). Courtesy of the Library Company of Philadelphia.

given by me   JOHN M'NEIL, executor.
TO BE SOLD,

A Parcel of likely Negroes, very reasonable. Enquire of John
   Strutton, at Spencer Trotter's, in Front-street.
   N. B. Said Negroes may be seen at a Free Negroe Woman's, in
Chestnut-street, opposite to Mr. Anthony Benezet's.   ¶

RUn away from the subscriber, on the 4th of May last, a Negroe
   man named Sampson, about 40 years of age, a short well-set
fellow, much pitted with the small-pox, has a very old look: Had.

Slave-sale advertisement. Benezet was deeply moved as he saw slaves being sold
near his home in Philadelphia. From the *Pennsylvania Gazette*, October 3, 1751.
Courtesy of the Library Company of Philadelphia.

Abbé Raynal. Abbé Guillaume-Thomas-François Raynal was the author of
L'Histoire des deux Indes. Benezet translated and extracted sections of this work
and published it with his *Short Observations on Slavery, Introductory Remarks to
Some Extracts from the Writings of the Abbé Raynal on That Important Subject* shortly
before his death in 1784. The two men exchanged letters in 1781 and 1782.
From Raynal's *Histoire philosophique et politique des établissements et du commerce
des Européens dans les deux Indes*, vol. 1 (Amsterdam, 1770). Courtesy of George
Washington University, Gelman Special Collections.

James Forten. Forten was a free-born black in Philadelphia who studied briefly at Quaker schools before he went to sea. In later years he played an active role in establishing the Negro Convention Movement, worked closely with William Lloyd Garrison against colonization, and became a leader of the American Anti-Slavery Society founded in 1833. Courtesy of the Historical Society of Pennsylvania.

Chapter 5

Building an Antislavery Consensus in North America

> The cause of African Freedom in America continues to gain ground. Our worthy friend Mr. Benezet is still indefatigable in it. His letters I presume breathe a great deal of the true spirit of Christianity.—But these, I am sure can be but a faint comment upon his life. He is not only a good man, but a great man in the full import of the words. He appears in every thing to be free from prejudices of all kinds, and talks and acts as if he believed all mankind however diversified by color—nation—or religion to be members of one grand family.
>
> —Benjamin Rush, May 13, 1774

Anthony Benezet's arguments against slavery evolved rapidly in the 1750s and early 1760s. To the existing religious arguments set forth by such men as Ralph Sandiford and Benjamin Lay, Benezet added two new dimensions: Scottish Enlightenment philosophy and empirical knowledge of Africa, drawn from accounts written by slave traders themselves. He and John Woolman drafted the key Quaker epistles of the 1750s (see Chapter 2). That work drew Benezet into contact with others, such as Samuel Fothergill in London. Fothergill's correspondence with Benezet reveals how Woolman's pamphlet and the "Epistle of 1754," in conjunction with Fothergill's visit to Philadelphia, where he saw slavery firsthand, turned Fothergill into an antislavery activist.[1] The Benezet-Fothergill link would be the beginning of a serious transatlantic correspondence network among antislavery activists.

After the "Epistle of 1758" Anthony Benezet threw himself full force into the struggle to build an antislavery consensus in North America through pamphlets, letters, and petitions. At the time, his fellow Quakers did not support the publication of his tracts or the extension of his network. He realized that to win the struggle he had to build relationships. Unlike Sharp in England, he had no Somerset case and no *Zong* affair around which to build his movement. (In this case of 1783, the captain of the ship *Zong* ordered the crew to throw 133 enslaved Africans overboard.

He claimed insufficient provisions to feed the white crewmen, let alone the blacks, and sought insurance compensation for the slaves.)[2] The colonies had no Parliament to petition, and no institutional history or organizational structure to build on, save the newfound Quaker committees. Although the Quakers in North America were a major force in Pennsylvania and parts of the mid-Atlantic, slavery and its apologists were a stronger force.

Benezet realized that to win the minds of the masses he had to win over the minds of some of the "great men" of society, and he patiently worked to do so. Through correspondence, pamphlets, and petitions he began to build an antislavery network step by step, idea by idea, and man by man. Over time Benezet convinced Benjamin Franklin and Benjamin Rush to join him; together they formed the triumvirate leading the struggle against slavery in Philadelphia and throughout the colonies in the eighteenth century. He also reached such men as Henry Laurens, Patrick Henry, John Jay, and Moses Brown, among others.

Benjamin Franklin

Though Benjamin Franklin wrote prolifically about politics, ethics, and housekeeping, among other topics in the 1740s, he virtually ignored the institution of slavery, even though it existed in Franklin's Boston and in his own household.[3]

In 1723 he ran away to Philadelphia after having served as an apprentice printer since 1718. By October 1729 the twenty-three-year-old Franklin had purchased the *Pennsylvania Gazette*. In 1737 he came to Benjamin Lay's assistance, spending long hours organizing Lay's text and trying to make his ramblings coherent. Years later, in 1789, he boasted of his earlier support for Sandiford and Lay as evidence of his antislavery stance. He saw the *Gazette* as an instrument of the ideas of an independent press and thus resistant to partisanship.[4]

While he printed antislavery literature, Franklin still had contradictions, owned slaves, and participated in the internal slave trade. In 1731 and 1732 he placed an advertisement in his own *Pennsylvania Gazette*: "To be sold: A likely Negro wench about fifteen years old and talks English. Inquire of the printer hereof. A breeding Negro woman about twenty years of age. Can do any household work."[5] The *Gazette* also profited immensely from advertisements for runaway slaves.[6] For Franklin the paper was above all a business. After owning and running it for nineteen years, he retired a rich man in 1748 at the age of forty-two.

The Swedish traveler Peter Kalm, a newly appointed member of the Swedish Academy of Sciences, visited the Philadelphia area in the late 1740s. In 1747 he wrote of Franklin, the Quakers, and their relation to slavery: "Formerly the negroes were brought over from Africa, and bought by almost everyone who could afford it, the Quakers alone being the exception." He added that there were a few "free negroes in town, who have been lucky enough to get a very zealous Quaker for their master, and who gave them liberty after they had faithfully served him for a time." But on further observation he noted after visiting with Franklin and the Quaker botanist John Barton that "these [Quakers] are no longer so particular . . . and now they have as many negroes as other people."[7] Benezet knew the contradictions with the Quakers' attitudes about wealth and slavery. He observed that "the great rock against which our society has dashed is through love of the world and the deceitfulness of riches, the desire of amassing wealth."[8]

Franklin continued to hold mixed views through the mid-1750s, when his attitude against slavery began to crystallize. Like many eighteenth-century opponents of slavery, such as Rousseau and Benezet, Franklin was influenced by the ideas of Montaigne, the sixteenth-century French skeptic whose *Essays* questioned the assumption of European cultural superiority. Montaigne's perspective found little favor in the seventeenth century, but became popular again in the eighteenth. Franklin's basic instincts were humanitarian and cosmopolitan, and with this combination he influenced Benezet. Franklin was troubled by the shabby treatment of Native Americans by whites, which had practical implications, as when such treatment provoked attacks on frontier settlements. Franklin felt, as did Benezet, that Native Americans, as members of the human race, ought to have been treated better than they often were.[9]

In 1751 Franklin wrote his first printed discussion of slavery in his essay *Observations Concerning the Increase in Mankind, Written in Pennsylvania,* on the economics of labor, population growth, and settlement of the New World. He published it anonymously in 1755. For the first time Franklin personally attacked slavery, albeit from an economic standpoint. The essay was published at least ten times in the next decade in America and England. *Observations* was a reflection of his ideas on the growing population, whose reproductive capacity at the time he believed exceeded the needs of the colonies. In many ways his ideas, which preceded those of the classical economists, ignited a transatlantic discussion on population and growth.[10]

Observations is composed of twenty-four points, or queries, on population and marriage, which in America was "more generally early, than in Europe." He noted that the colonial birth rate was twice that of the old countries and calculated how the colonial populations could double every twenty years.[11] Franklin had two views of population growth. On the one hand, it would lead to increased problems related to land, subsistence, hunting, and manufacturing. On the other hand, the colonies would thrive if the colonists proved industrious. The cost of white labor would always be high, but that did not justify slavery. He denounced the idea that "by the

Labour of Slaves, America may possibly vie in Cheapness of Manufactures with Britain."[12]

Franklin came to his objections over slavery on reverse racial grounds, believing that the introduction of slaves would decrease the white population while simultaneously racially tainting the whites. Racial bias led him to his negative assessment of the cost of slave labor: "His Pilfering from Time to Time, almost every Slave being by Nature a Thief, and compare the whole Amount with the Wages of a Manufacturer of Iron or Wool in England, you will see that labour is much cheaper there than it ever can be by Negroes here." He then asked, "Why then will Americans purchase Slaves? Because slaves may be kept as long as a Man pleases, or has Occasion for their Labour; while hired Men are continually leaving their master (often in the midst of his Business,) and setting up for themselves."[13] The changes made in the text of later editions, however, reveal a significant reversal of Franklin's thinking on a number of issues relating to slavery, especially on point 12, where he made one essential and pathbreaking change that slowly led him to object to slavery on racial grounds. The initial wording—"almost every Slave being by Nature a Thief"—suggested that thievery and dishonesty were characteristics innate in blacks, especially chattel slaves. By the time of the 1760 London edition Franklin's thinking had profoundly changed. He now argued that "almost every Slave" was "from the nature of slavery a thief."[14] Thus, it was the institution of slavery that corrupted blacks and not an inherent inclination toward thievery because of their skin color. The slaves did not produce their condition or the institution, but their condition and the institution produced the slaves. In altering just a few of his own words he acknowledged the adverse impact of slavery on the black human being.[15] He also argued the negative impact of slavery on whites, contending that "slaves also perforate the families that use them: the white Children become proud, disgusted with labour, and being educated in Idleness, are rendered unfit to get a Living by Industry."[16] He later in all of his American editions added point 24, which declared, "I am impartial to the Complexions of my Country." While it is a relatively innocuous statement, made in the spirit of Montaigne, it sums up a profoundly racist argument.[17]

By the 1750s Franklin had taken an interest in the education of blacks. His friend John Waring wrote him on January 27, 1757, that he believed the efforts of the Bray Associates would "have a good effect" on blacks and "make them more faithful and honest in their Master's service."[18] This position was principally the same one held by the SPG and by reform-minded Anglicans like Morgan Godwyn decades earlier. Franklin addressed Waring's concern a year later, on January 3, 1758, acknowledging that slaveholders believed educated blacks would be "both useless and dangerous," but in his opinion "a separate School for Blacks" would be a positive development.[19] After visiting a Bray School in 1763 he wrote of the

"Negro intellect": "I was on the whole much pleas'd" because "from what I have then saw, [I] have conceiv'd a higher Opinion of the natural capacities of the black Race than I had ever before entertained."[20] He wrote his wife that "they have since chosen me one of the Society, and I am at present chairman for the current year. I enclose you an account of their proceedings."[21] The design of the Bray Associates was not abolitionist in nature. The principal objective was to inculcate Christian behavior and make slaves more faithful to their masters. His known connections with Benezet certainly encouraged such a change of views, given Benezet's own work as a teacher of blacks.[22]

While Franklin, the deist and nonconformist, did not share the ideas of the Bray forces on religion and conversion, he did share with them and Benezet a common interest in educating blacks.[23] Franklin had acquired at least four slaves in the 1750s, and he and his wife, Deborah, held slaves for private domestic services at least until 1760, when reference to them in his papers disappeared. In 1750 he wrote his mother, Abiah, that "I still keep those Servants but the man [Peter] not in my own House." Franklin also owned Peter's wife Jemina and admitted to his mother his desire "to sell them both at first good Opportunity; for we do not like Negro Servants. We got again half what we lost."[24] He came to have misgivings about the effect slavery had on white families, especially his and Deborah's own children, as they lived with the family in a small home they rented. The former apprentice, journeyman, and printer was not afraid of hard labor, and he felt that under the institution of slavery whites at a very young age became lazy, corrupt, lacked ambition, and were unable to become productive members of society.[25] The Franklins became quite attached to their slaves and treated them generously.

When he left for his mission to London in 1757, Franklin took two slaves, Peter and King, with him, although he had talked about selling Peter as early as 1750. Franklin's will of 1757 freed all his remaining slaves upon his death.[26] His twenty-four-year-old son William also accompanied him to London. Perhaps that is why he purchased another slave, Othello, to help his wife with household duties, as she remained in Philadelphia. He also had purchased another slave, George, for her. King ran away from Franklin while in London and was taught to read, write, and play the violin by the white woman who harbored him. Franklin, ever the businessman, allowed him to stay with the woman but only after she had purchased the enslaved African. When Franklin returned to America in 1775, Peter was still with him, but since Deborah had died five months earlier, he found he had no need for George and "gave" him to his daughter Sally.[27]

During these and later years Franklin read the pamphlets of Benezet to gain knowledge of Africa and the slave trade.[28] Benezet had many other early connections to Franklin. With Benezet's job as proofreader for German-born artisan Christopher Sower, who also published one of the first

German newspapers in America, he learned invaluable lessons "in the way of accuracy of thought, expression, punctuation and writing."[29] Sower had a long-standing friendship with Franklin and surely provided one of the early contacts between Franklin and Benezet, who later worked together on education and health issues. By the early 1770s Franklin and Benezet had cemented their connection. Benezet's brother Daniel had married Deborah Franklin's cousin in 1771, which opened a family connection. The two men began in earnest to share ideas and information on a wide range of topics. Benezet used Franklin's letters as a way to search for more ammunition with which to fight slavery.

Franklin thought the British abolitionists self-seeking. He told Benezet, "I made a little extract from yours of April 27, of the number of slaves imported and perishing with some close remarks on the Hypocrisy of this country which encourages a detestable commerce by laws for promoting the Guinea trade; while it piqued itself on its virtue, love of liberty, and the equity of its courts, in setting free a single Negro."[30] Franklin had recently read Benezet's *Some Historical Account of Guinea,* which encouraged him to make a frontal assault on slavery in an article titled "The Somerset Case and the Slave Trade," published on June 20, 1772, in the *London Chronicle.* "Questioning the perception among some antislavery advocates and slaves about the extent of the case," he wrote, "it is said that some generous human persons subscribed to the expense of obtaining liberty by law for Somerset the Negro.—It is to be wished that the same humanity may extend itself among numbers if not for the procuring of liberty for those that remain in our colonies." In lines that directly paraphrased Benezet's letter Franklin wrote, "By a late compilation made in America, it appears that there are now eight hundred and fifty thousand Negroes in the English Islands and Colonies; and that the yearly importation is about one hundred thousand, of which number about one third perish by the gaol distemper on the passage, and in the sickness called the seasoning, before they are set to labour."[31]

Franklin referred to the enslaved Africans who survived the middle passage and the seasoning as "those unhappy people" who suffered from "excessive labour, bad nourishment, uncomfortable accommodations, and broken spirits." In the article he asked the British, "Can sweetening our tea, &c. with sugar, be a circumstance of such an absolute necessity? Can the petty pleasure thence arising by the taste, compensate for such misery produced among our fellow creatures and such a constant butchery of the human species by this pestilential detestable traffic in the bodies and souls of men?"[32]

Franklin wrote his Philadelphia friend on August 22, 1772, from London, in the midst of celebrations over the ruling of the famed Somerset case: he made an early and fairly accurate assessment of its meaning. By so doing he criticized "Pharisaical Britain to pride thyself in the setting free a single Slave that happens to land on thy coasts, while thy Merchants appears in all thy ports are encouraged by thy laws to continue a commerce whereby so many hundreds of thousands are dragged into a slaver that can scarce be said to end with their lives, since it is entailed to their posterity."[33] Franklin was onto something, for he realized that while Sharp and others may have claimed that the decision ended slavery in Britain, he knew that Justice Mansfield's ruling only freed one slave, James Somerset. To make sure the English abolitionists knew his thinking, Franklin told Benezet that "this was inserted in the *London Chronicle*, of the 20th of June last." Franklin further told Benezet, "I am glad to hear that the disposition against keeping negroes grows more general in North America. Several pieces have been lately printed here against the practice, and I hope in time it will be taken into considerations and suppressed by the legislature." Showing both his debt and gratitude to Benezet, he continued, "Your labours have already been attended with great effects. I hope therefore that you and your friends will be encouraged to proceed. My hearty wishes of success attend you." He signed the letter "being ever, my dear friend, yours affectionately. B. Franklin."[34] This is the first mention by Franklin of a legislative solution to the problem of slavery, although he still owned Peter at the time.

Benezet told Franklin, "When I sent the tracts on the Slave Trade to thee I also sent to some of the most weighty of our Friends in London, vizt. Doct. Fothergill, Thos Corbin, John Elliot, Mark Beaufoy &c.& now to David Barclay, Thomas Wagstaff & c. persons whom I thought might be men of interest." Benezet felt that these men would help "to lay the iniquity & dreadful consequence of the Slave Trade before Parliament, desiring a stop may be put to it."[35]

One of Franklin's most revealing letters was written on February 10, 1773, in which he told Benezet that he had just "commenced an acquaintance" with Granville Sharp and desired that together they would "act in concert in the affairs of slavery."[36] Benezet was especially happy that he had paved the way for Franklin to meet Sharp. Benezet wrote to Sharp some weeks later: "I am glad to understand from my friend Benjamin Franklin, that you have commenced an acquaintance, and that he expects in future to act in common with thee in the affair of slavery." For Benezet this relationship would be an added link in the transatlantic fight against slavery and the slave trade, which brought together two such prominent individuals, both non-Quakers, and which would be of seminal importance to his cause. Benezet, continuing his practice of constantly disseminating information, sent Sharp a packet telling him, "I send thee herewith some pamphlets; and in confidence of thy goodness of heart, which by looking to the intention, will construe the freedom I have taken in the best light."[37]

Around the same time Franklin wrote optimistically to Dean Woodward: "I have since had the Satisfaction to learn that a Disposition to abolish Slavery prevails in North America, that many of the Pennsylvanians have set their Slaves at Liberty, and that even the Virginia Assembly have petitioned the King for Permission to make a Law for preventing the Importation of more into the Colony." Franklin felt that "this Request however, will probably not be granted, as the former Laws of that Kind have always been repealed, and as the Interest of a few merchants here has more weight with Government, than that of Thousands at a Distance."[38] He had followed the Virginia debates over slavery, and his deepening misgivings are evident in a 1773 letter to Benezet. He wrote, "There is reason to hope that our colonies may in time get clear of a practice that disgraces them."[39] In 1774 he wrote to his friend Condorcet, who had asked him a series of questions about blacks: "As to Qu. 4. The Negroes who are free live among the White People, but are generally improvident and poor. I think they are not deficient in natural Understanding but they have not the Advantage of Education. They make good Musicians."[40]

During the Revolutionary War years Benezet and Franklin did not seem to correspond directly, but they later resumed their correspondence. Benezet was more than happy that a man of Franklin's intellect, humanitarian concern, and status came to accept his premise concerning the abilities of blacks. He knew that people in America and Europe would listen to such an internationally known humanitarian.

By the early 1780s Franklin's stance against slavery became stronger, although he owned slaves until 1781. His charges that Parliament intended to enslave the colonies led some to reexamine America's own conduct in enslaving Africans.[41] Benezet, who never wavered in his beliefs, wrote in 1781 that "Blacks are inferior to the whites in their capacities is a vulgar prejudice founded on the Pride of Ignorance."[42] By that time he had won over Franklin and was proud that Franklin had come to the same conclusion. On March 5, 1783, almost a year before he died, Benezet wrote to Franklin of his steadfast conviction: "After teaching of youth in this city near forty years, I have solicited & obtained the office of teacher of Black Children & others of that people, an employment which tho' not attended with so great pecuniary advantages as others might be, yet affords me much satisfaction. I know no station in life I shoed prefer before it. Indeed my kind friend the object of slavery is still an object worthy of the deepest consideration of a philosophic mind."[43]

Franklin was elected president of the newly formed Pennsylvania Abolition Society in 1787. In his last years he had a hand in the publication of several important antislavery documents.[44] In November 1789 Franklin addressed the society and submitted a document titled *A Plan for Improving the Conditions of the Free Blacks*. It built on the assumption that since "Negroes" were not responsible for what slavery had done to them, the expense of their education was society's duty.[45] Franklin called for the broader white public to come to the aid of the blacks. He said that it was the role of society "to instruct, to advise, to qualify those who have been restored to freedom, for the exercise and enjoyment of civil liberty." Giving a long list of tasks before both his fellow Philadelphians and before men and women on both sides of the Atlantic, he made a final plea: "A plan so extensive cannot be carried into execution without considerable pecuniary resources, beyond the present ordinary funds of the society." He concluded with a call to "the generosity of enlightened and benevolent free men and will gratefully receive any donations or subscriptions for this purpose."[46] Franklin listed at the end of the address the names of James Starr the treasurer of the Pennsylvania Abolition Society, and James Pemberton, the chairman of its Committee of Correspondence.

Franklin spent only three years between 1757 and 1785 in America.[47] Much of his time was spent in London as a colonial agent or in France as an American diplomatic representative. Franklin's antislavery career ended in the best possible way. The closing years of his life were devoted to a last grand attempt to do good back in America and Philadelphia. He came home in 1785 to devote himself in great part to the abolition of slavery and to work among his own people.[48] He received support from many quarters for his latest mission. From London, John Wright sent him a report in 1781 from the newly founded Society for Effecting the Abolition of the Slave Trade. Wright had credited the British with being the first to lay "seed" to the cause of the oppressed Africans. The eighty-four-year-old Franklin responded to him on November 4, 1789. It was part letter and part history lesson: "I wish you success to your endeavors for obtaining an abolition of the slave-trade." Referring to the works of John Woolman and Anthony Benezet, he continued, "The epistle from your yearly Meeting, for the year 1758, was not the first sowing of the good seed you mention." Franklin informed Wright of "an old pamphlet in my possession, that George Keith, near a hundred years since, wrote a paper against the trade . . . said to be given forth by the appointment of the meeting held by him at Philip James house, in the city of Philadelphia, about the year 1693, wherein a strict charge was given to Friends, 'that they should seek their Negroes at liberty, after some reasonable time of service, etc, etc.'"[49] Here Franklin referred to his earlier work with Benjamin Lay and Ralph Sandiford.

Franklin's last public act was a memorial to Congress, asking its members to abolish the slave trade and to restore liberty to "Negroe's," who had been "degraded into perpetual bondage." He told the Congress, "Mankind are all formed by the same Almighty Being, alike objects of his care and equally designed for the enjoyment of happiness." Later he added that "equal liberty was originally the portion, and is still the birth-right, of all men; and influenced by the strong ties of humanity." He called for the Congress to "loosen the bands of slavery; and promote a general enjoyment of the blessing of freedom." Franklin urged Congress to "promote mercy and justice toward this distressed race; and that you will step to the very verge of power vested in you for discouraging every species of traffic in the persons of our fellow men."[50]

Franklin's words caused a stir in Congress, and the debate on his comments lasted for over a month. A delegate from South Carolina took harsh exception: he told the body that his state and the other southern states "would never have entered the Confederation unless their property had been guaranteed to them." He continued, "When we entered into this Confederacy we did it for political and not for moral motives. And I don't think my constituents want to learn morals from the petitioners. If they do, they can learn it at home."[51] Franklin saw in the South Carolinian the Franklin of 1751, not the Franklin of 1790.

Between his slaveholding days and the close of his life Franklin had come a long way. Once he viewed the "Negro" as an inferior being that was justifiably held in bondage. Eventually his humanitarianism led him to understand that any black inferiority came not from a racial defect but from the institution of slavery. With that as an underlying belief, he embraced and fostered the work of Benezet. Franklin, the great humanitarian and statesman, had shown that men and women could come full circle and realize that blacks had the same qualities for goodness and for greatness that white people had. From Benezet, the teacher, he had learned his lessons well.

His closeness to Anthony Benezet had been cemented in the struggle to end slavery and the barbarous treatment of the enslaved Africans. A few years before his death Benezet had taken to writing Franklin with the endearing salutary "Mon Ami Benjamin Franklin." In a letter of July 12, 1781, sent to Franklin in Paris, Benezet wrote him that "having several times attempted to get intelligence by letter for my kindred at St. Quentin, in Picardy the place of my nativity I take the liberty to trouble thee, my kind friend, with the enclosed packet for M. Debrissac, my near kinsman."[52] Franklin also took it as a special honor that Benezet referred to him using terminology reserved for Quakers—*thee* and *thou*. It was an even greater honor that Franklin became the president of the second Pennsylvania Abolition Society, succeeding his dear friend, the president of the first one, Anthony Benezet. The voice of a man universally known as an inventor, scholar, and Renaissance man added immensely to the antislavery cause and helped it spread beyond the Quakers, beyond Philadelphia, and beyond America. Benezet harbored only admiration and good will toward Franklin. He knew that the voice and influence of one Franklin was worth the voices of hundreds, maybe thousands, of others, for Franklin's words were heard throughout the North American colonies, in Britain, in France, and in the rest of the Atlantic world.

Benjamin Rush

Benjamin Rush, who became the third president of the Pennsylvania Abolition Society in 1803, summed up the general consensus on Benezet when he wrote to Granville Sharp in 1774: "I believe he has not spent an idle hour for these forty years. In a word—he seems to have lived as if he always had in one eye, and upon his heart the words of our Savior 'wist ye not that I must be about my Father's business.'"[53] Rush was one of the most prominent early American physicians and served as a surgeon during the Revolutionary War. He founded the study of psychiatry in America at the University of Pennsylvania Medical School, the same school that grew out of the Pennsylvania Hospital, which Benezet had helped found and for which he had served as a member of its early board of directors.[54] Rush shared many of Benezet's interests: education, politics, and abolition. He founded two colleges—Dickinson and Franklin (now Franklin and Marshall)—and wrote on broad intellectual issues, as in his *Essays, Literary and Moral* (1798). He is best known to posterity as the founder of American medicine and as a signer of the Declaration of Independence.

Rush, like Franklin, was coaxed into the antislavery struggle by Benezet. Like his friends, Rush developed international networks to combat slavery. Unlike Benezet, who came to his antislavery positions because of his own persecution as a Huguenot, an experience that shaped his philosophical framework, Rush first came to his opposition to slavery through reading, above all Benezet's writings, and then developed his social and moral stance in part as a reaction to his family's and his own ownership of slaves.

Rush's father, a slave-owning blacksmith, died when Rush was six, leaving his mother, who ran a grocery store, to raise him and his six siblings. His uncle, Samuel Finley, a "New Light" Presbyterian, became president of the College of New Jersey (now Princeton University) and steered young Rush toward medicine. Rush graduated from the College of New Jersey before he was fifteen and completed medical training in Edinburgh.[55]

During his time in Edinburgh the young Rush personally met many of Europe's leading thinkers, often through his connections with Franklin, with whom he stayed in London. His new acquaintances included such painters as Benjamin West and Sir Joshua Reynolds, the lexicographer Samuel Johnson, Oliver Goldsmith, and David Hume, with whom Rush studied. While in Europe he also met with George Whitefield, whom he greatly admired, although they disagreed on slavery. Through Franklin, Rush was introduced to such leading French intellectuals as Diderot.[56]

On May 1, 1773, Rush wrote to Benjamin Franklin, thanking him for a copy of a paper of the scientist Joseph Priestley, who later preached against slavery.[57] In 1788 "Priestly [*sic*] happily found himself concurring with all of other Birmingham Christians, Anglican and Dissenters alike, in preaching a sermon on the same Sunday in opposition to the slave trade." In his sermon Priestley said that he happily joined with his fellow clergy and "to go with the multitude" on the issue of slavery. He then cited Acts 1:26: "He hath made one blood of all nations of men to dwell on all the face of the earth."[58] Using language similar to that of Benezet, Priestley asked his audience how they would feel "if we were violently seized, conveyed away from all our friends, and confined to hard labor all our lives in Africa."[59] Indeed when Priestley immigrated to America, he wrote under the pseudonym "A Quaker in Politics."[60]

Rush was not alone among medical doctors to join the antislavery crusade: the reluctant Virginia abolitionist Arthur Lee preceded him at Edinburgh. Together the two men visited John Wilkes, the radical English journalist and politician, in prison.[61] Rush knew John Fothergill, the brother of the English Quaker minister Samuel Fothergill, who became a licentiate at the Royal College of Physicians but, because he was a Quaker, was prevented from becoming a fellow at the medical school. Among other Quaker physicians were Thomas Knowles, Joseph Hooper, John Coakey Lettsom, and George Vaux.[62]

Rush was the first medical doctor to diagnose alcoholism as an illness. The issue tied him to Benezet, who years earlier had campaigned against the "evil effects of liquor" and had started one of the first temperance movements. True to his approach to life, Benezet sought to cure the problem as a societal ill through education and reform. Rush, the scientist, saw it as a personal and physical illness to be cured through confinement.[63] Rush did, however, see the importance of Benezet's approach; after reading Benezet's pamphlet *The Mighty Destroyer Displayed*, he wrote *Sermons to Gentlemen, or Temperance and Exercise* (1772).

Rush disagreed with one aspect of Benezet's lifestyle. Like Fox, Benezet refused to eat anything produced by slave labor. Rush, his personal physician, believed that Benezet's vegetarian diet was a partial cause of his health problems in middle age. According to the cataloguer of Benezet's library, the Quaker historian Henry Cadbury, "the books on medicine show that Benezet, like many other early Friends in America, had a lay interest in this subject."[64] Rush felt that those untrained in medicine should not practice it or guess at it and disagreed with Benezet's vegetarian diet. Joyce Marriot Benezet had twice miscarried, and the couple had long wanted children. Benezet thought that his diet of fruits and nuts might aid the couple in conceiving. Rush disagreed and had no sympathy with Benezet's "unscientific" beliefs. Nonetheless, years later in 1817 he wrote of Benezet's lifestyle in *A Warning Voice to the Intemperate*: "The late Anthony Benezet, one of the most laborious schoolmasters I ever knew, informed me that he had been prevented from the love of spirituous liquors by acquiring a love of tea in early life. Three or four cups, taken in an afternoon, carried off the fatigue of a whole day's labour in his school. This worthy man lived to be 71 years of age, and died of an acute disease, with the full exercise of all the faculties of his mind."[65]

Rush, like John Fothergill, became a generous contributor to Benezet's African Free School. Like Benezet, Rush was an early leader in the campaign for free public education in America. Learning from Benezet's pioneering efforts both in teaching girls and in promoting their education, Rush became the American Revolution's leading proponent of public education for both sexes. There can be little doubt that the elder Quaker influenced Rush on all counts. Some of the students, such as Absalom Jones and James Forten, at the schools founded by Benezet later collaborated with Rush in his efforts to combat the Philadelphia yellow fever epidemic of 1793.[66] Jones and Richard Allen, the black African Methodist Episcopal leader, even took instructions from Rush on when to bleed, a dubious procedure at any stage of the disease.[67] Many whites held the mistaken belief that blacks were immune to yellow fever. Jones and Allen told Rush, "Few have been the whites that paid attention to us while the blacks were engaged in the other's service. We can assure the public we have taken four and five black people in a day to be buried."[68] Thus their statement had a twofold purpose: to show the white neglect of blacks until the latter came to the aid of whites during the epidemic and to combat the false notion that blacks were immune to yellow fever.

Years later, in 1816, Rush's relative Robert S. Finley, sought to enlist the aid of Jones, Allen, and Forten in the American Colonization Society. Allen and Jones led the protest against sending freed Africans in America back to Africa.[69] Another free black, the famed sail maker Paul Cuffee, supported the concept.[70] Forten had spent a year or so in England, where he possibly associated with Granville Sharp. Sharp supported the concept of sending free blacks to colonize Sierra Leone. Forten had initially gone to England as a crew member aboard the ship *Commerce* in the summer of 1784. He stayed until late 1785 when, according to Julie Winch, his biographer, "the declining racial climate" had made "London a less attractive place than it had seemed at first glance." The paths of the tiny band of dedicated antislavery advocates and Benezet "constituents" crossed repeatedly. The London Friends had learned in 1783 that after the suspension of the slave trade during the Revolutionary War, Parliament was about to authorize its resumption. Around that time, "at the request of a committee of six appointed by London Friends, Forten's old benefactor, Anthony Benezet, sent over a manuscript copy of *The Case of Our Fellow Creatures, the Oppressed Africans,* a work Philadelphia Friends were reluctant to print because they considered it too radical." The London Committee "funded the printing of 2,000 copies, one of which they presented to Parliament with 258 signatures. The remaining copies, and a second and third printing, were sent to people who it was believed could advance the cause."[71]

Benezet encouraged Rush to write *An Address to the Inhabitants of the British Settlement in America.* Just as Rush felt that Benezet was unqualified to give medical or scientific opinions, unlike their mutual friend Franklin, Rush felt that he was unprepared to write about slavery or politics. Only twenty-seven at the time, he was just getting started in his medical practice and was fearful that abolitionist activity would hinder his burgeoning career. And there may have been another reason for Rush's hesitation: he owned a slave.

Rush succumbed to the pleas of Benezet and agreed to write the pamphlet, but only under the condition of anonymity. He issued the pamphlet under the authorship "By a Pennsylvanian." He wrote Franklin, "The Address was written at the particular request of a worthy citizen [Anthony Benezet] to accompany a Petition to the Honorable Assembly of Pennsylvania, to procure an increase of the Duty upon Negro Slaves imported into the Province."[72] Benezet wanted to lobby for the bill "to put a more complete stop to the importation of Negro slaves into the province."[73]

Rush wrote Sharp that "the pamphlet will be left at the Pennsylvania Coffeehouse in Burchin Lane. Should you incline to reprint it in London, please to make such alterations in it as you think proper, still concealing the author's name from the public." Rush ended by thanking Sharp for his "zeal in behalf of the Negro slaves in America."[74]

Because he was a scientist and a physician, Rush developed a more straightforward argument against slavery. Unlike Benezet, Rush did not see the need to work his way through all the previous arguments and justifications in favor of slavery. He wrote, "Without entering into the history of the facts which relate to the slave trade, I shall proceed immediately to combat the principal arguments which are used to support it." Rush wrote that "here I need hardly to say anything in favor of the Intellects of the Negroes, or of their capacities for virtue and happiness, although these have been supposed by some to be inferior to those of the inhabitants of Europe. The accounts which travelers give us of their ingenuity, humanity, and strong attachment to their parents, relations, friends and country, show us that they are equal to the Europeans, when we allow for the diversity of temper and genius which is occasioned by the climate."[75]

Rush had become familiar with the writings of the "travelers" through reading the works of his friend Benezet. Rush, like Benezet, was careful not to blame the enslaved Africans for their present state: "All the vices which are charged upon the Negroes in the southern colonies and the West-Indies, such as idleness, Treachery, theft, and the like are the genuine offspring of slavery, and serve as an argument to prove that they were not intended, by Providence for it."[76]

Like Benezet, Rush developed ideas regarding the plight of the blacks once they would be free. He believed that the "Negroes among us, who having acquired all the low vices of slavery, or who from age or infirmities are unfit to be set at liberty" should for the good of society "continue the property of those with whom they grow old." Rush also developed his own "affirmative action plan." He asked society to "let the young Negroes be educated in the principles of virtue and religion—let them be taught to read, and write—and afterwards instructed in some business, whereby they may be able to maintain themselves. Let laws be made to limit the time of their servitude, and entitle them to all privileges of free-born British subjects. At any rate let Retribution be done to God and to Society."[77]

Rush's support for Benezet's call for the education of blacks mattered greatly in Philadelphia society, where the doctor's prominence was such that he would soon be one of the signers of the Declaration of Independence. His call for the education and freedom of enslaved Africans was a powerful voice in the movement against slavery.

Rush admitted some time later that when it was learned that he was the author of the pamphlet, he felt it was Benezet's fault. He wrote to Jacques Barbeu Dubourg, the French physician and botanist and one of Franklin's closest friends in Paris, on April 29, 1773, that "a request has been presented to our Assembly to place a stronger restraint upon the importation of slaves in this province; and a pamphlet has been publicly circulated, a copy to which Dr. Franklin will transmit to you, which is entitled: *Address to the Inhabitants of the British Colonies upon Slavekeeping.*" Rush, it seems, could not stay angered at his friend too long, because he went on to tell Dubourg that "I am publicly credited with having written this pamphlet at the instigating of a pious Quaker of French origin, Anthony Benezet, whose name is held in veneration in these parts and deserves to be spread throughout the world."[78] In language far different from Benezet's modesty Rush wrote to the Frenchman: "This work has produced a desired effect. A law has been passed which levies a tax of from 7 to 14 pounds sterling per head upon Negro slaves; this amounts to an almost total prohibition."[79]

In the address Rush told the British that "the plant of liberty is of so tender a Nature, that it cannot thrive long in the neighborhood of slavery. Remember the eyes of all of Europe are fixed upon you, to preserve an asylum for freedom in this country, after the last pillars of it are fallen in every other quarter of the globe."[80] He believed that the North American colonists first had to deal with the contradiction of owning slaves themselves. Rush had learned the art of mass pressure from Benezet and urged various colonial congresses and assemblies in mainland America to petition the king and the Parliament. To do so they would have to act as a unified body. Benezet had recently led a petition effort in Pennsylvania calling for an end to the slave trade. He then wrote to Granville Sharp and to Samuel Fothergill and Benjamin Franklin that he thought that with sufficient time the antislavery forces might have gotten ten thousand signatures.

The campaign had proven quite successful: on February 26, 1773, the Pennsylvania Act became law, imposing a £10 duty on slave imports.[81] Following this act legislatures passed other such acts in Massachusetts, Rhode Island, Connecticut, New Jersey, and Delaware. In the following years some of the prohibitive duties and laws were nullified and overturned by legislative and gubernatorial authorities. Massachusetts and New Hampshire passed emancipation statutes based on "court interpretations of their state constitutions. The rest of the northern states followed Pennsylvania's example and freed their slaves through legislative enactment."[82] Various laws and statutes were also passed in Maryland, Virginia, and South Carolina.[83] Rush wrote to Sharp on October 29, 1773: "I am encouraged by the polite message to me thro Mr. Benezet, to trouble you with a second letter and a pamphlet on the subject of the slavery of the Negroes in America."[84] The efforts of the three men seemed to Benezet to be bearing fruit: Sharp optimistically responded to Rush that "the people, both here and in all the neighboring governments, seem to rouse from their slumbers." Four years later, on July 2, 1777, Vermont, although not one of the original thirteen colonies, passed its first Constitution and the first American constitution that declared that slavery was a violation of "natural inherent and unalienable rights."[85]

Despite some differences Rush and Benezet worked together for years to advance the antislavery cause. Perhaps the most notable example of their collaboration came in their response to the proslavery writings of Richard Nisbet. Nisbet, an "emotionally unstable" West Indian planter who had immigrated to Philadelphia, published his *Slavery Not Forbidden by Scripture* in 1773, in response to Rush's *An Address to the Inhabitants of the British Settlements in America, upon Slave-Keeping*. Nisbet's basic argument was that Africans brought to the Americas lived a much better life than they had in Africa. According to Nisbet, the enslaved African had "fewer cares, and less reason to be anxious about tomorrow, than any other individual in our species." Nisbet claimed, "It is impossible to determine, with accuracy, whether their intellects or ours are superior, as individuals no doubt, have not the same opportunities of improving that we have. However, on the whole, it seems probable, that they are a much inferior race of men to the whites, in every respect. We have no other method of judging, but by considering their genius and government in their native country. Africa, except the small part of it inhabited by those of our own colour, is totally overrun with barbarism."[86]

Following the broad lines laid down by David Hume, Nisbet provided the usual list of defects attributed to Africans: "the absence of great kingdoms, the despotism, the lack of any ideas concerning a supreme Being, the hopeless deficiency of friendship and gratitude."[87] For Nisbet the Africans were "utterly unacquainted with the arts, letters, manufactures, and everything which constitutes civilized life. A few instances may be found, of African negroes possessing virtues and becoming ingenious; but still, what I have said, with regard to their general character, I dare say, most people acquainted with them, will agree to."[88]

Nisbet's pamphlet *Slavery Not Forbidden by Scripture* outlined in detail why he felt slavery was both a justified and a necessary practice. He proclaimed that his arguments were representative of those of other slaveholding members of society. Nisbet began his defense with "evidence" that every human institution suffered from necessary faults and that human beings were by nature degenerate. Using the Old Testament validation of slavery that according to him was mandated by Moses and approved by God, Nisbet argued that slavery was the salvation of both the white and the black races. Part of Nisbet's 1773 attack was against the writings of the African-born poetess Phillis Wheatley, who in the late 1760s began a series of letters and poems to public officials.[89] Her most famous poem, "On Being Brought from Africa to America," was written in 1768 and first published in 1772.[90] Wheatley also wrote poems of record on the deaths of leading figures, many of whom were active in antislavery efforts or had made statements against slavery. Among them were "On the Death of Rev. Dr. Sewell" (the antislavery Judge Samuel Sewall, who died in 1769) and "On the Death of the Rev. Mr. George Whitefield, the leader of the Great Awakening" (1770). Her most famous letter was sent to George Washington in 1775 as a tribute to him as the leader of the revolutionary armed force.[91] However, Rush responded to Nisbet with an immediate fusillade: *A Vindication of the Address to the Inhabitants of the British Settlements, on the Slavery of the Negroes, in Answer to a Pamphlet Entitled, "Slavery Not Forbidden by Scripture; or a Defense of the West Indias Planters from the Aspersions Thrown out Against Them by the Author of the Address."* In attacking the premises of Nisbet, Rush quoted all available sources to sustain his arguments. He cited the words of "The Rev. Mr. Godwin [sic] a Clergyman of the Church of England," who wrote that the whites in Barbados "treat their Negroes with far less Humanity than they do their Cattle, for they do not starve their Horses, nor pinch the Cow by whose milk they are sustained. The more innocent and laborious are worked to Death. They are tormented and whipped almost, and sometimes quite to Death, even for slight miscarriages."[92]

Rush took many of his ideas and citations directly from Benezet. He followed Benezet's lead in using the writings of Sir Hans Sloane, "who resided many years in Jamaica." Rush cited the same passages from Sloane that Benezet had used in his *Some Historical Account of Guinea*, which referred to the brutal treatment the West Indian slave barons meted out to their slaves. Rush, like Benezet, provided his readers with the names of the key European thinkers who affected all of the antislavery writers: "In a Word, If our Author means to defend the Slave Trade, or the West-India Planters to any purpose, let him defend them from the Aspersions of Montesquieu, Franklin, Wallis, Hutchinson, Sharp, Hargrave, Warburton, and Foster, who have all employed their Talents against them." Rush perhaps had read some of the Scottish thinkers while studying in Edinburgh, but Benezet gave him a new understanding of them. Rush came to believe that "the flashes of their Eloquence have long been seen at a distance. I shall think myself happy if I have served as an Instrument of conducting to those piles of Iniquity, which slavery has raised in the British Settlements of America."[93]

Benezet sent his correspondents, like Samuel Allinson, copies of the works of both Rush and Nisbet, believing that Allinson and others would see through the proslavery argument. He told Allinson, "I herewith send thee such of the pieces relating to slavery &c., of the negroes, as I have been able to get back: people are shamefully careless in not returning borrowed books."[94]

Until the end of his life Benezet continued to circulate Rush's writings. In one of his last messages (1783) he sent a packet to William Dillwyn like the one he had also given to "Nicholas Waln with some pamphlets &c., which I shall be glad to hear come to thy hands."[95] In the packet were several of his own publications, John Wesley's *Thoughts upon Slavery,* the "Epistle of 1754," and Rush's *Address to the Inhabitants of the British Settlements.*[96] In his *Address,* Rush combined a variety of antislavery measures, including statistical data first used by Benezet and later perfected by Thomas Clarkson. He also followed Benezet's pattern of combining the philosophical outlook of Montesquieu, eyewitness accounts, and moral persuasion. In one passage he called on whites to "think of the bloody wars which are fermented by it, among the African nations . . . think of the many thousands who perish by sickness, melancholy and suicide, in their voyages to America." He wrote of the cruel punishment meted to the blacks in much the same terms as Sir Hans Sloane had used to describe the punishment given to blacks who dared resist Jamaican plantation masters. "Let us . . . see the various modes of arbitrary punishment inflicted upon them by their masters. Behold one covered with stripes, into which melted wax is poured—another tied down to a block or a stake—a third suspended in the air by the thumbs—a fourth obliged to set or stand upon red hot iron—a fifth,—I cannot relate it."[97]

The antislavery circuit ran through this handful of men: Wesley, Rush, Franklin, Sharp, and Benezet above all. Granville Sharp wrote to Rush twice on February 21, 1774. He expressed his opinion that all correspondence and "petitions against Slavery in America may be addressed to the King and not to the King and Parliament." Sharp questioned "whether the business of the proposed Petitions may not be considered as a very proper opportunity for the loyal and free Subjects of the several American Provinces to express their steady personal Attachments to the King and the Royal Family for the reasons above mentioned." He also told Rush that he had "advised in my last letter to Mr. Benezet" of January 7, 1774, the very same advice.[98] Sharp believed, unlike many British leaders, that constitutionally the colonial legislatures were completely independent bodies from the British Parliament at Westminster; therefore, the colonists had only to petition the king to express their grievances.

In the second letter Sharp wrote Rush that "I have also sent you 2 copies of Mr. Wesley's Tract ag't slavery mentioned in my last letter to Mr. Benezet" and that he could not find a publisher for his *Address to the Inhabitants.* Since Sharp had last written Rush, he had "received an answer from Mess'rs Dilly, who decline undertaking the publications of your Tract ag't slavery as they think the Sale of it would not defray the expense: and I received the same answer also from my Bookseller Mr. White."[99]

Sharp's second letter offers the most telling evidence of the great difficulties the early opponents of slavery faced in reaching the public. He told Rush that "when I reprinted Mr. Benezet's acco't. of Africa in 1768 so few copies were sold that I gave it away, by degrees." Sharp believed that people "who will not put themselves to the trouble & expense of buying" books would read books that were given to them. In a bit of humor he also told Rush that "the Person also who reprinted Mr. Benezet's Historical Acco't. of Guinea, with the Extracts from my Book & several others ag't Slavery, has been a considerable loser by it for want of Sale. I believe I was his principal Customer, for I sent Copies to all the judges, to several of the Nobility, & many others."[100] His own works fared no better at first: "And with respect to my own Tracts, I have general given away the greatest part of the several impressions even before they were advertised for sale, or published in the Booksellers' sense of the word; so that you need not wonder at the Backwardness of the Booksellers in undertaking publications of Books, which are not on entertaining Subjects, suited to the Depravity of the generality of Readers."[101] At the time Sharp did not realize that the public response to John Wesley's *Thoughts upon Slavery,* much of it taken verbatim from Benezet's writings, would soon be so great that 229,000 people signed petitions against the slave trade to be presented to Parliament.

One of Rush's greatest tributes to his teacher, coworker, and friend came in the form of an essay titled "Paradise of Negro Slaves—A Dream." "Paradise" was a utopian village very much like the one Benezet had envisioned in Africa. Of the dream Rush wrote, "I thought I was conducted to a country which, in point of cultivation and scenery, far surpassed anything I had ever heard or read in my life. This country, I found, was inhabited only by negroes. They appeared cheerful and happy." Rush dreamed, "Your apprehensions of danger from the sight of a white man said I 'are natural. But in me—you behold a friend.'" The Africans told Rush of their "paradise," a place where one told him, "We derive great pleasure from contemplating the infinite goodness of God, in allotting to us our full proportion of misery on earth. That place was to be our place of resident till the general judgment; after which time, we expect to be admitted into higher and more perfect degrees of happiness."[102] The poem became commonly known as "Anthony Benezet's Dream."

Failure: Debates on Slavery in Virginia

In 1764 Arthur Lee, the son of a Virginia planter who, like Benjamin Rush, had studied medicine in Edinburgh during the heyday of the Scottish Enlightenment, published an essay that created a stir in the debate over slavery. His education notwithstanding, Lee held his social class's views and used the essay to attack Adam Smith's *Theory of Moral Sentiments* and his view of Virginians.[103] In *An Essay on the Vindication of the Continental Colonies of America, from a Censure of Adam Smith, in his Theory of Moral Sentiments,* Lee suggested of Africans that 'we have seen that his [Smith's] nation of heroes is a race the most detestable and vile that ever the earth produced." Citing Aristotle, he added that Africans "lack any semblance of virtue."[104]

Yet Lee's racist rant concluded on a rather surprising note. He pondered "whether this proceeds from a native baseness that fits their minds for all villainy; or that they never receive the benefit of educations, I shall not presume to determine." Racist or no, Lee came to a startling conclusion, one quoted even later by Benezet: "To sum up all, it is evident, that the bondage we have imposed on the Africans is absolutely repugnant to justice. That is highly inconsistent with civil policy; first as it tends to suppress all improvements in arts and sciences . . . Secondly, as it may deprave the minds of the freemen . . . And, lastly, as it endangers the community by the destructive effects of civil commotions." Lee concluded, "Need I add to these . . . that it is shocking to humanity, violative of every generous sentiment, abhorrent utterly from the Christian religion."[105]

Three years later Lee issued an address, "Abolition of Slavery and the Retrieval of Specie in the Colony," to members of the Virginia House of Burgesses and published it in William Rind's *Virginia Gazette.*[106] According to one historian, this address would prove "one of the most significant antislavery articles of the eighteenth century." After a public outcry by Virginia slaveholders Rind refused to publish Part Two of the article, which called for the abolition of slavery. Lee wrote that "long and serious Reflection upon the nature and Consequences of Slavery, has convinced me, that it is a Violation both of justice and Religion; that it is dangerous to the safety of the Community in which it prevails: that it is destructive to the growth of arts & Sciences, and lastly that it produces a numerous & fatal train of Vices, both in the slave, and in his master."[107]

Lee argued that "slavery then, is a violation of Justice, will plainly appear when we consider what Justice is." Echoing Wallace and Benezet, he proclaimed, "Now, as freedom is unquestionably the birth-right of all mankind, of Africans as well as Europeans, to keep the former in a state of slavery is a constant violation of that right, and therefore of Justice."[108] Benezet later reprinted parts of Lee's "Address on Slavery" from the *Virginia Gazette,* albeit after deleting the sections on insurrections.[109]

Lee pointed out the hypocritical nature of the society, which had become dependent on slave labor and forced the slaves to obey the laws without the reciprocal protection of the same laws. He told his fellow Virginians, "For surely a man's own will and consent cannot be allowed to introduce so important an innovation into a society as slavery, or to make himself an outlaw, which is really the state of a slave." He continued, "Since, neither consenting to nor abiding the laws of society in which he lives, he is neither bound to obey them nor entitled to their protection." Lee believed that slavery "adds strength and experience to the slaves" and "will sink us into perfect security and indolence, which debilitating our minds, and enervating our bodies, will render us an easy conquest to the feeblest foe."[110] This argument, borrowed from Montesquieu, came up again and again in late eighteenth-century writing, from Benezet to Clarkson.

Much like the earlier Quakers, Lee cited the Golden Rule. Slavery "tramples on his [God's] reveal'd will, infringes the most Sacred rights, and violates humanity." In a passage that Benezet would somewhat alter as he castigated the slaveholders for their array of excuses, Lee argued that "it is the custom of the Country, that you found it so, that not your will but Necessity consents."[111] Other Virginians like Patrick Henry and George Mason would make precisely this defense of their own slaveholding. While Lee's words may have had less meaning to northerners whose slaves were few and far between and held in close contact, in the south, where the numbers and density of slaves were greater, it gave warning to a danger the southern slaveholders tried to ignore.

For years Lee's "Address" was debated and widely circulated among Virginia slaveholders, like Robert Pleasants, Patrick Henry, and Jonathan Boucher. The Virginia loyalist Boucher was deeply disturbed by Lee's pronouncements. In a discourse to his parishioners in 1767 (which was not published until 1797), he proclaimed that a black could never be "quite on terms of equality with a free white man because nature has placed insuperable barriers in his [the Negro's] way." Sounding like a cross between Henry and Lee, Boucher told his listeners that "some loss and inconvenience would, no doubt, arise from the general abolition of slavery in these colonies: but were it done gradually, with judgment, and with good temper, I have never yet seen it satisfactorily proved that such inconvenience would be either great or lasting."[112] For him slavery "was not one of the most intolerable evils incident to humanity, even to slaves." Despite his racist views about blacks, he believed that whites had the Christian duty to teach their slaves how to read and write and to receive as "much additional education as possible so that they may be granted at least spiritual freedom from bondage."[113] He believed that while ignorant, the slaves, "compared with any other class of people in a Christian country," were "no more so than many of the first converts to Christianity."[114]

Boucher, using the same logic later adopted by nineteenth-century proslavery leaders, maintained, "With all my abhorrence to slavery, I feel in myself no disposition to question either its lawfulness, or its humanity. Its lawfulness has again and again been clearly proved; and if it is sometimes cruel it is so only from being abused. But, if I am not much mistaken, more harm than good has been done by some late publications [Lee] on the subject of slavery."[115]

Benezet, the antislavery crusader, saw in Lee's writing the same thing that the proslavery Boucher feared—a principled and philosophical argument against slavery by one who had no sympathy for the slave. For the same reason that Benezet used the writings of men like Snelgrave and Barbot, he also used those of Arthur Lee. Lee could prove particularly useful with fellow Virginians, especially his point about the hypocrisy of those who claimed to abhor slavery yet owned large numbers of slaves themselves. Benezet did not abandon hope of converting men like Patrick Henry or Robert Pleasants, any more than he did of converting northern slave owners like Franklin, Rush, and John Jay. Benezet wrote to these men: and as we have seen, often his letters were treatises on slavery. He also sent them copies of his pamphlets and petitions. Pleasants, a Virginia Quaker whose family had become rich by owning and exploiting slaves, had become associates with both Benezet and Henry. Henry had come to Pleasants's assistance by getting him rescued from the heavy fines and penalties imposed on Quakers who refused service in the Virginia Militia during the Revolutionary War.[116]

In 1771 "Pleasants shocked his Virginia planter friends by announcing that his father and brother had chosen to emancipate all their slaves."[117] In a move that was blocked in Virginia courts for years, Pleasants tried to free his eighty slaves. In 1790 Pleasants placed several advertisements in the *Virginia Independence Chronicle* with a call for a June 15 meeting of the "Humane Society." Virginia was still Virginia, and calling the group the Virginia Abolitionist Society may not have been wise. Pleasants wrote to Patrick Henry, inviting him to join the Humane Society: "I expect thee will have seen [our notices] in the papers directed to the friends of liberty."[118] Henry and other legislators declined.[119]

Benezet often exchanged letters with Pleasants on such topics as the infeasibility of teaching Latin and Greek to schoolchildren and sent him a copy of *Some Historical Account of Guinea*, which Pleasants then sent to Patrick Henry. Henry responded with one of his longest letters to Pleasants (January 18, 1773). It is one of the most fascinating letters written by a man who proclaimed that he abhorred slavery but could not live without his slaves:

I take this opportunity to acknowledge ye receipt of Anthony Benezet's Book against the slave trade. I thank you for it. It is not a little surprising that Christianity, whose chief excellence consists in softening the Human Heart, in cherishing & improving its finer Feelings, should encourage a Practice so totally repugnant to the first Impressions of right & wrong; what adds to the wonder is, that this abominable Practice has been introduced in the most enlightened Ages. . . . Is it not amazing, that at a time when the rights of Humanity are defined & understood with precision in a Country above all others fond of Liberty; that in such an Age and such a Country, we find Men, profession a Religion the most humane, mild, meek, gentle & generous, adopting a Principle as repugnant to humanity, as it is inconsistent with the Bible & destructive to Liberty?

Henry added that "the World in general has denied your People a share of its Honors, but the Wise will ascribe to you a just Tribute of Virtuous Praise, for the Practice of a train of Virtues among which your disagreement to Slavery will be principally ranked." He concluded, "And believe me I shall; honor the Quakers for their noble Effort to abolish slavery. It is equally calculated to promote moral & political Good."

In words eerily reminiscent of Arthur Lee's, Henry then asked Pleasants: "Would any man believe that I am Master of Slaves of my own purchase! I am drawn along by ye general Inconvenience of living without them; I will not, I cannot justify it." But he kept his slaves. Henry believed that "silent meetings (the scoff of reverend doctors) have done that which learned and elaborate preaching could not effect." While his words showed his appreciation of the Quakers, in reality he knew that they did more than pray and testify in silence. Henry did not see them as traitors, as some did. He may have questioned their decisions, but he did not question their sincerity or their love of humanity. Henry did not see a solution to the issue of slavery: "I know not when to stop. I would say many things on this Subject, a serious review of which gives a gloomy perspective to future times."[120]

When the First Constitutional Congress convened in Philadelphia from September 5 to October 26, 1774, Benezet met with many of the delegates to discuss the nature of war and the situation of the Indians. Pleasants had earlier written letters of introduction to notable Philadelphia Quakers for all seven Virginia delegates (who included Henry, George Washington, Richard Henry Lee, and Edmund Pendleton, who Pleasants felt had Quaker sympathies).[121] In the letter to his friend Benezet dated August 20, 1774, Pleasants wrote, "I doubt not thou will be well pleased with an acquaintance with several of them."[122]

Benezet met with Henry in October. He wrote to Samuel Allinson, sending a copy to Pleasants, that he told Henry about his opinions on war and violence. Henry, Benezet wrote, thought "it was strange to him, to find some Quakers manifesting a disposition so different from what I had described."[123] Aware of the political tenor of the times, in 1774 Benezet wrote *The Potent Enemies of American Laid Open*. Readers, he hoped, would soon realize that the two enemies were slavery and alcohol. Throughout the Revolutionary War, Benezet sought to extend to blacks the rights that the American revolutionaries were fighting to obtain for themselves.

The Pleasants-Benezet connection had some positive effects. Pleasants wrote to Benezet on February 2, 1781, thanking him for a recent supply of pamphlets. He told Benezet of some success he had in the Virginia Assembly "at their late session, in behalf of Negroes, who have been manumitted under hand & seal of left free by will & detained or sold by Heirs or Exectrs."[124] One of the active Quakers in Virginia was Isaac Zane, who had been a student of Benezet. He was elected to the Virginia House of Burgesses at age thirty-one and later expelled for his support of the Committee of

Correspondence. In the end the economic interests of men like Henry and George Mason overpowered their humanitarian sentiments: the antislavery movement failed in Virginia.[125]

Benezet had first published *Thoughts on the Nature of War* in 1766 and then twice during the Revolutionary War years.[126] On April 12, 1776, he sent the pamphlet to many colonial leaders, among them the South Carolina revolutionary leader Henry Laurens, who became president of the Continental Congress in 1777–78. (Benezet also sent copies of the pamphlet to Frederick the Great around the same time.) Benezet apologized to Laurens, a fellow Huguenot, for "intruding upon thy engagements" but nonetheless asked him to "seriously peruse" the pamphlet *Thoughts on the Nature of War* that he was sending him. Benezet, knowing that Laurens had fundamental disagreements with the Quakers, told him that the pamphlet "will, I trust lessen, if not remove any prejudice which our Friends' refusal to join in any military operations may have occasioned."[127]

Laurens had been one of the leading slave traders in North America in the middle of the eighteenth century, as over half the slaves that came to the mainland colonies came through the port of Charleston and were sold throughout the south.[128] Then in 1762 his firm Austin, Laurens and Appleby was dissolved. Around that time "Lauren reduced his mercantile activities, in large part because he needed to free himself to take a greater role" in his son's John education and allow "his oldest son to have advantages he had lacked."[129] Deciding to shift most of his primary economic interests, he nonetheless kept some involvement in the trade. Laurens's earliest biographer, the historian and fellow South Carolinian David Duncan Wallace, described Laurens as kind to his slaves and as "an opponent of the system and a prophet of its overthrow; but the temptations of the extraordinary profits to be derived from the slave trade closed Henry Laurens' heart against the precepts of that."[130]

Laurens's son John became a lieutenant-colonel in the Revolutionary Army and a vocal advocate of immediate manumission. He even wrote his father about his idea for raising a black regiment, an idea that his father categorically opposed.[131] Henry wrote John on August 14, 1776: "You know my dear son, I abhor slavery. . . . I am not the man who enslaved them; they are indebted to the Englishmen for that favor. . . . I am devising means for manumitting many of them and for the cutting of the entails of slavery . . . great powers oppose me: the laws and customs of my country and the avarice of my country oppose me."[132] Laurens asked, in words remarkably similar to those written by Henry to Pleasants three years earlier, "What will my children say if I deprive them of so much estate? These are the difficulties, but not insuperable. I hope to receive your advice and assistance in this affair in good time."[133] The son answered, reminding his father that the West Indian and Carolina planters gave the same reasoning. He told him, "When driven from everything else, they generally exclaimed; Without slaves how is it possible for us to be rich?"[134] Young Laurens was killed in battle in August 1782, as he led his command against the British, at the age of twenty-seven.[135]

Benezet sent Laurens his *A Caution and a Warning to Great Britain*. He told Laurens that he thought it would "in general . . . meet with thy approbation" and informed the South Carolinian that "it was reprinted in London and [given out to] about eight hundred members of parliament, and officers of the crown."[136] Southerners as far away as Arthur Lee, then living in London, had written to Laurens about potential slave revolts or slaves possibly running away to the British side.[137] Laurens replied to Lee, but there is no evidence that he also replied to Benezet. Benezet soon published *Serious Reflections Affectionately Recommended to the Well-Disposed of Every Religious Denomination*.[138] The work was also sent in 1778 to every member of the Continental Congress, to state legislators, and to such leaders as Governor Livingston of New Jersey.

Success: Antislavery Campaigns in the North

On July 21, 1773, the antislavery debate reached Harvard University. Two candidates for the bachelor's degree, Theodore Parsons and Eliphalet Pearson, entered into a debate, *A Forensic Dispute on the Legality of Enslaving the Africans Held at the Public Commencement*.[139] Parsons defended slavery while Pearson borrowed extensively from Benezet's *Some Historical Account of Guinea* to attack the institution.[140] Benezet's influence can also be seen in other northern antislavery activities of the 1770s.[141]

That same year an itinerant Baptist preacher, John Allen, wrote *The Watchman's Alarm to Lord N—th* [North]. He stated, "Ye trifling patriots who are making a vain parade of being the advocates for the liberties of mankind, who are thus making a mockery of your profession, by trampling on the sacred natural rights and privileges of the *Africans*."[142] Allen thus picked up the argument from Benezet that Africans held the same natural rights as Americans. He called attention to the commonality of the colonialists' struggle with that of the enslaved Africans. Allen also emphasized the contradiction between demanding freedom for oneself while enslaving others.[143]

In 1773 Stephen Hopkins, who had nine times been elected governor of Rhode Island and become one of two Quakers to sign the Declaration of Independence, was disowned from his Meeting for refusing to manumit his slaves. In 1774 the New York Quakers voted to make the prohibition of buying or selling slaves mandatory. That same year, in the midst of revolutionary ferment the Quaker meetings in New Jersey and Pennsylvania asked for the 1758 *Epistle* to be revised and strengthened. In Quaker assemblies where abolitionists were in control, they voted for disownment if any members were found to be selling or transferring slaves for any other reason than to free them. The Monthly Meetings demanded that any one "in the service of Truth" who refused to release their slaves who were "suitable for liberty" would also be disowned. During the war years, when white labor became scarce, Friends were advised by their Meeting against hiring slaves for wages. They were also forbidden to act as executioners and administers of estates that included slaves.

Rhode Island's Moses Brown also corresponded with Benezet and Pemberton in Philadelphia. Brown's friend Thomas Arnold told him that Benezet was a person "whose first appearance by no means does him justice" and who "perfectly despises or neglects the goods of this world, any further than they contribute to a comfortable existence." He was above all "a man of sense and reading."[144] Brown's grandfather James was a Baptist minister and his father, also James, became a prosperous merchant.[145] Like his brothers, he owned slaves, but on conversion to Quakerism he freed his. On May 9, 1774, Benezet wrote to Brown, telling him of his work and correspondence with Sharp, Pleasants, and Henry. He wrote of his concern about the spread of slavery in the south. He then urged his northern friends to lobby their assemblies to pass "a law to prevent any farther import and also to make the manu[mission] of slaves more easy."[146] He also sent Brown copies of one of the letters he had sent to Patrick Henry. Brown observed the methods of Benezet and, as his newest biographer Charles Rappleye writes, "adopted the tactics of Anthony Benezet, drawing on a variety of sources to illuminate the cruelty and inhumanity that attended the slave system in Africa and the West Indies." If his appeal to his peers on moral grounds did not work, "then perhaps Moses could shame the deputies at the general Assembly into submission."[147]

Benezet also had ties to other northern antislavery leaders like John Jay, the president of the Continental Congress who, like Laurens and Benezet, was of Huguenot background.[148] On February 7, 1779, Benezet sent Jay copies of "some thoughts on war, slavery, c."[149] The pacifist Quaker asked Jay, the Episcopalian, to try "to soften if not remove, any offense which the Friends' refusal to take part in matters of a military nature may have raised in thy mind, and induce thee to distinguish between such who are active in opposition, and those who have been restrained from an apprehension of duty, and a persuasion that our common beneficent Father, who has the hearts of all men in his power."[150]

Unlike Laurens, the past president of the Congress, Jay sent Benezet a response. "Sir," he wrote, "I have perused the pamphlets you [are] so obliging as to send me. The benevolence by which the author appears to have been influenced does him credit—and though I cannot subscribe to all his opinions, many of his sentiments are liberal, and merit consideration." He added, "I sincerely wish to all mankind; and I hope it will ever be the policy of these states so as to extend and secure it to all their citizens, as that none may have reason to complain of partiality of oppression."[151]

The letters were exchanged after the British forces laid siege to and occupied Philadelphia from the fall of 1777 until the summer of 1778. Surprisingly, Benezet was able to reprint some pamphlets concerning war in Philadelphia, although few new ones were written during the war. Benezet was so enthusiastic about receiving a reply from Jay that he again wrote him in the spring of 1779, sending him copies of William Law's *The Spirit of Prayer,* "sent for JJ's 'wisdom and comfort'" and a copy of Daniel Defoe's *The Dreadful Visitation.*[152] The letters from Pennsylvania must have had an impact on Jay, as he wrote his friend Edgar Benson, "an excellent law might be made out of the Pennsylvania one [passed March 1, 1780] for the gradual Abolition of Slavery." Jay added, "Till America comes into this measure her Prayers to heaven for Liberty will be impious."[153]

Yet Jay, like so many other antislavery advocates, owned slaves.[154] A September 1, 1779, letter from his father, Peter, made it clear that Jay and his brother Frederick (Fady) still owned slaves at that time.[155] Letters from 1782 to 1810 show that Jay continued to hold blacks in bondage; even in 1820 the "two black females in the household" included "Clarinda" (not called a slave in 1820 but so described in 1810) and "her daughter Zilpah."[156] Yet in 1785 Jay, then the governor of New York, wrote, "I wish. . . . the time may soon come when all our inhabitants of every color and denominations shall be free and equal partners of political liberty."[157]

Bound by the contradictions of his time, which he fought to outgrow, Jay helped found the Society for the Promoting the Manumission of Slaves and Protecting Such of Them as Have or May Be Liberated in 1785 and became its first president. In 1787 Jay, similar to Benezet's actions many years before, helped found the African Free School in New York. As the governor of New York, he later oversaw the enactment of the state's gradual abolition law, which would end all slavery in 1827. The law stated that any slave born after July 4, 1799, to slave parents would be freed after the age of twenty-five for a woman or twenty-eight for a man.

Transcending America

Benezet above all had laid the foundation for the debate over slavery. He came to believe that with slavery "an insatiable desire for gain hath become the principal and moving cause of the most abominable and dreadful scene that was perhaps ever acted upon the face of the earth."[158] He first argued that slavery was contrary to the laws of man.[159] Going from the economic to the social and philosophical, Benezet forcefully argued that slavery had trampled "under Foot all the obligations of social virtue" accorded to humankind. He argued against those who tried to separate slave owners, some who claimed they simply inherited their slaves, and slave traders, asserting that their distinction was "a plea founded more in words than supported by truth."[160]

At first Benezet had been alone in his mission, but gradually, through reason and determination and by linking slavery to moral decay and excess wealth, he convinced many others to listen to his pleas. He and his colleagues, such as Wesley in England, perfected the art of mass petitioning: he and collaborators like Brown and Pleasants created through their letters and sharing of antislavery writings an antislavery network that transcended the boundaries of the thirteen colonies.

The flow of ideas back and forth across the Atlantic proved essential to activists both as an organizational weapon and an ideological arsenal. No one better illustrated this transatlantic dimension than the great political pamphleteer Thomas Paine. More than a year before arriving in Philadelphia, Paine had met in England with none other than Benezet's friend and collaborator Benjamin Rush. One of the first essays Paine penned on coming to America was "African Slavery in America." "To Americans," he wrote, "that some desperate wretches should be willing to steal and enslave men by violence and murder for gain, is rather lamentable than strange . . . though it has been so often proved contrary to the light of nature, to every principle of Justice and Humanity, and even good policy, by a succession of eminent men, and several late publications."[161] More than a year earlier in England, Paine had written another essay against slavery and signed it "Justice and Humanity." Paine, reprising the words of Benezet, was just another in a long list of individuals Benezet had influenced. Paine used the term *Man-stealing* that naturally reminds us of Philmore and Benezet who popularized it.[162]

At war's end, sensing the opportunity to push for human rights, Benezet reignited his campaign, "reviving his publishing campaign and pressing the Pennsylvania–New Jersey yearly Meeting in 1783 to lodge a formal petition with the Constitutional Congress calling for a ban on the slave trade." He also traveled with fellow Quakers James Pemberton and Warner Mifflin to Princeton, New Jersey, where the Congress was sitting, to present their petitions.[163]

In an ironic way David Cooper in 1783 praised the ideas that helped spark the antislavery fire. In his pamphlet *A Serious Address to the Rulers of America, on the Inconsistency of Their Conduct Respecting Slavery* he wrote, "We need not now turn over the libraries of Europe for authorities to prove that blacks are born free and equally with whites; it is declared and recorded as the sense of America." Yet the ideas of the Enlightenment affected Cooper, whether he admitted it or not. He argued that "now it is time to demonstrate to Europe, to the whole world, that America was in earnest, and meant what she said, when with peculiar energy, and unanswerable reasoning, she pleads the cause of human nature, and with undaunted firmness insisted, that all mankind came from the hand of their Creator, equally free."[164]

Cooper argued that the "unenlightened Africans, in their own native land, enjoyed freedom, which was their birthright, until the more savage Christians transported them by the thousands, and sold them for slaves in the wilds of America, to cultivate it for their lordly oppressors." He stated mockingly, "Unless we can shew that the African race are not men, words can hardly express the amazement which naturally arises on reflecting, that the very people who make these pompous declarations are slave-holders, and, by their legislative, tell us, that these blessings were only meant to be the rights of white men." He then proclaimed, "When men talk of liberty, they mean their own liberty, and seldom suffer their thoughts on that point to stray to their neighbors."[165]

Benezet thought so much of Cooper's pamphlet that he sent a copy to his friend John Pemberton in London on September 10, 1783. In a postscript he wrote, "I also inclose a piece lately published on Slavery & c. viz. *A Serious Address*."[166] Cooper, like Rush, had written his pamphlet anonymously and, like Rush, was not happy that Benezet publicized his authorship. Benezet wrote Cooper asking if their pamphlets could be "stitched together." Benezet's request did not sit well with Cooper, "as he [Benezet] knows how careful I was of having the author suspected." Cooper went on, "I regret he saw it, concluding I might near as well have put my name to it. He has sent one to each member of Congress, and to our own Assembly at Burlington, and is about writing to our Governor."[167] Benezet also sent a copy to George Washington.[168] Not long after, in 1788, the attorney general of Maryland, Luther Martin expressed similar sentiments as Cooper. He too sought to crop the sentiment in homegrown ideas, proclaiming that slavery was "inconsistent with the genius of republicanism and has a tendency to destroy those principles on which it is supported, as it lessens the sense of the equal rights of mankind, and habituates us to tyranny and oppression."[169]

Gary Nash surmised that "none of the many leaders of the revolutionary generation found the idea of abolition fanatical." He argued that "in fact a great many of them regarded it as unthinkable that a republic based on natural rights theory could survive without the emancipation of the enslaved fifth of the population."[170] Yet many revolutionaries claimed not to see the contradictions, while others feared that the British would enslave them just as they had the Africans.[171]

The British writer Samuel Johnson noted their seeming hypocrisy, asking in 1775 in his *Taxation No Tyranny*, "How is it that we hear the loudest yelps for liberty among the drivers of Negroes?"[172] Paine, the son of a Quaker, also asked "with what consistently, or decency" did the American have the right to "complain so loudly of attempts to enslave them while they hold so many hundred thousands in slavery?" He wrote that "we have enslaved multitudes, and shed much innocent blood, and now are threatened with the same."[173] Even George Washington voiced his concerns in 1776: "The time is now near at hand which must probably determine, whether Americans are to be, Freemen, or slaves."[174]

As it turned out, the revolution and its republic did survive and thrive with slavery intact.[175] Benezet worked hard with such men as Franklin, Rush, and leaders of "the revolutionary generation" and America's fighters for independence, who saw the revolution as being foremost about freedom from England. For Benezet independence without equality meant little, if anything. He issued an appeal: "It cannot be, that either war or contract can give any man such property in another as he has in sheep and oxen; Much less is it possible, that any child of man should ever be born a slave. . . . Liberty is the right of every human creature, as soon as he breathes the vital air. And no human law can deprive him of the right, which he derives from the law of nature."[176]

The ideas about liberty were for Benezet as much about the rights and freedoms of the enslaved Africans as they were about the white fear of their own enslavement by the British. If it is true that an idea is nothing until it reaches the masses, then it was Benezet, above all others, who took the ideas of freedom, liberty, and democracy, coupled with new concepts on the humanity and rights of black people, to his fellow colonialists. And it was here that these ideas took on a life of their own, a life where they were put to use regarding free men and women with black skin.

Chapter 6

Transatlantic Beginnings and the British Antislavery Movement

Anthony Benezet knew that the fight to end slavery and the slave trade had to be a transatlantic battle. Although he realized that slavery did not exist in the pure chattel form in Britain, he knew that British vessels, with British owners, transported blacks across the Atlantic. As he corresponded with men in England, he also learned about the conditions of the roughly fourteen thousand blacks there who came to be known as "body servants."[1]

Benezet began his campaign in England with a 1758 letter to Thomas Seeker, archbishop of Canterbury, boldly referring to the enslaved Africans as "our deeply oppressed fellow creatures." He wondered, "How an evil so deep a dye has so long, not only passed unnoticed, but has even had the countenance of the government, and has been supported by law is surprising." Benezet answered his own rhetorical question with an unambiguous response declaring that "it must be because many worthy men in power, both of the laity and clergy, have been unacquainted with the horrible wickedness with which the trade is carried on and to the groans, the numberless dying groans [of the slaves], which daily ascent to God, the common father of mankind."[2] Clearly Benezet did not accept the arguments of white ignorance of the plight of the enslaved Africans, as he argued that all men and women were sisters and brothers under God.

Benezet affected the antislavery debate in England in countless ways; however, his influence can best be understood through his relationships, personal and intellectual, with four men: Granville Sharp, John Wesley, Thomas Clarkson, and William Wilberforce. In 1766 he issued from Philadelphia a challenge to the government and people of Britain and her role in the trade in *A Caution and a Warning to Great Britain*. A London edition was published the very next year. He began with a simple statement: "How the British nation first came to be concerned in a practice, by which the rights and liberties of mankind are so violently infringed, and which is so opposite to the apprehensions Englishmen have always had of what natural justice requires, is indeed surprising."[3]

Benezet wrote to several individuals and groups in England during the 1760s. In 1767 he first wrote to the Society for the Propagation of the Gospel, who did not appreciate his gently nudging them to do more than bring the Christian religion to enslaved Africans.[4] He had greater success with Granville Sharp, whom Clarkson, in his account of the founding of the Society for Effecting the Abolition of the Slave Trade, called "the father of the cause in England."[5] Benezet's correspondence with Sharp saw his transatlantic connections bring results. Sharp and Clarkson, like the founders of the French Société des Amis des Noirs, regarded Benezet as the founder of the transatlantic antislavery movement. Through letters and exchanges of publications—sections of which authors on each side of the Atlantic liberally copied into their own works with the full blessing of their colleagues—the founding generation of the movement, Benezet and Sharp above all, laid out the designs others would soon follow.[6] Through the blowing of a transatlantic common wind, antislavery communication sailed back and forth across the waters creating an ideological and activist current.[7]

Benezet and Granville Sharp: Laying the Foundations

Nowhere was this more evident than in the joint efforts of Benezet and Sharp. Sharp, a minor civil servant in London employed by the Ordnance Office, played a central role in two critical legal cases that had a profound impact on the history of slavery. He described his job in a letter to Benezet on July 7, 1773. Apologizing for his delay in answering a Benezet letter and query, he told his new Philadelphia friend, "I am really sort of a slave myself being obliged to employ every day in the week, constantly, in the ordinary business of my office, and having no holidays but Sundays, as the prance I am in requires more attendance than any in the whole office."[8] Sharp was born on November 10, 1735, in Durham, the twelfth of fourteen children of Thomas Sharp and Judith Sharp. Thomas Sharp was appointed the archdeacon of Northumberland in 1722 and later prebendary of cathedrals; he was also a prominent religious writer. Granville Sharp's grandfather, John Sharp, had been the dean of Canterbury from 1689 to 1691 and was later the archbishop of York, the second highest-ranking official in the Church of England.[9] In early 1750 Granville left Durham and became a bound apprentice in London to a Quaker linen draper named Haley. He was later "turned over to Presbyterian, or rather as he was more properly called, an Independent. . . . I afterward lived some time with an Irish papist." In an August 1770 letter to John Fothergill (a key interlocutor between Sharp and Benezet) Sharp wrote, "Though my father was a dignified clergyman of the Church of England, and brought me up in the public profession of that church, yet he was so far from being prejudiced against any man for being of a different persuasion from himself, that he did not scruple to bind me as an apprentice to a Quaker." Sharp later proclaimed, "This extraordinary experience has taught me to make a proper distinction between the opinions of men and their persons."[10]

Sharp's exposure to different creeds bore similarities to the lives of the Huguenot-born Benezet and of another antislavery leader, Olaudah Equiano; however, unlike Benezet and Equiano, Sharp did not suffer from religious or racial persecution. Like Benezet and Equiano, he taught himself several languages, including French, Latin, and the so-called sacred languages, Greek and Hebrew. In fact he learned Greek from an "inmate" at one of his master's houses and Hebrew from another with whom he engaged in religious dialogues. When told by his discussants that he had misinterpreted certain religious passages, he decided to learn Greek and Hebrew texts to further the dialogue with them. Like Benjamin Lay and Benezet before him and John Brown, David Walker, and Nat Turner after, Sharp has been called "obscure and slightly eccentric."[11]

In 1765, "as he was leaving his brother's house, Sharp noticed a black youth about 16 or 17 years old, queuing up with the other sick people. His head was badly swollen, he was almost blind, and he was so weak and lame that he could hardly walk." The lad identified himself as Jonathan Strong and told them, "A lawyer and planter called David Lisle had brought him from Barbados as a slave. Strong told Sharp that he had been beaten 'upon his Head with a Pistol till the Barrel and the Lock were separated from the Stock.'"[12] Lisle had brutally beaten and then abandoned the slave, figuring that it would be more costly to rehabilitate him than to replace him, a common slaveholder's sentiment until the international slave trade ended and "new" slaves were not so easily purchased. At Granville's request his brother, William Sharp, a surgeon based in East London, cared for Strong and placed him at St. Bart's hospital where he stayed for four months. Granville helped young Strong find employment at a local apothecary shop, where he worked for wages and board. Two years later, by chance seeing a healthy Strong, Lisle sought to reclaim him. After following him home one evening Lisle then hired two professional "slave-hunters" to capture Strong. Lisle had originally paid £70 for Strong but advertised him for £30 and sold him to James Kerr, a Jamaican planter, to be paid only after Strong boarded a ship sailing to Jamaica.[13]

Having been baptized, Strong wrongly believed that his conversion ensured his freedom. He was not allowed to see his "godfather" and so sent a letter to Sharp, who after getting the runaround from the prison guards was allowed to visit him. Sharp then sprang into action, visiting the town's lord mayor, who said, "The lad had not stolen anything, and was not guilty of any offense, and was therefore at liberty to go away."[14]

Kerr protested the lord mayor's decision, and all involved went to court. Kerr had hired Captain David Laird, the skipper of the ship *Thames,* to transport Strong back to the West Indies. Soon afterward Laird physically assaulted Sharp; Thomas Beech, the coroner of London, advised Sharp to bring assault charges. In his *Memoirs,* Sharp wrote that, "G.S. was charged, by a writ, with having robbed the original owner master, David Lisle, the lawyer, of a Negro slave and also of another slave, & c. & c."[15] Lisle accused Sharp of kidnapping, trespassing, and deprivation of property to the tune of £200 and challenged Sharp to a duel. He also filed suit against Jonathan Strong. Sharp, who began to spend considerable time studying British law, told the magistrate that Lisle "should want no satisfaction that the law could not give him." He also hired a lawyer. Sharp had by then also found favor with the famed jurist Lord Mansfield, who advised his counsel.[16]

The magistrate ruled that legal precedent would prevail in this case, meaning the Yorke and Talbot opinion of 1729.[17] The thirty-eight-year-old law had been fostered by Attorney General Sir Philip Yorke, later the earl of Hardwicke, and by Charles Talbot, the solicitor general.[18] Both men would later become lord chancellors. Their opinion, issued January 14, 1729, asserted that "a Slave coming from the West Indies to Great Britain or Ireland does not become free."[19] The ruling read: "We are of the opinion that a slave by coming from the West Indies to Great Britain or Ireland, either with or without his master, doth not become free, and that his master's property or right in him is not therefore determined or varied, and that Baptism doth not bestow freedom on him nor make any alteration in his temporal condition in these Kingdom's; we are also of opinion that the Master may legally compel him to return again to the plantations.—P. Yorke; L. Talbot."[20] Steven M. Wise relates that Yorke and Talbot had been invited to a London evening of food and drink by West Indian planters, who sought to "negate the two principle arguments against black chattel slavery, baptism and the breathing of fresh air." Wise, an attorney, claims that Yorke and Talbot based their decision on "mere opinion" unjustified by any law, although their ruling took on the force of precedent and was duly cited in later cases by Mansfield.[21]

During the Strong trial Sharp came upon a copy of Benezet's *A Short Account of That Part of Africa* while browsing in a London bookstore. Sharp reprinted it, without consulting Benezet, adding his own conclusion, "calculated to increase the public interest in the cause which he had undertaken."[22] The Anglican Sharp republished and distributed the tract before the Quaker London Meeting for Sufferings approved, published, or distributed it. He rushed it to print, just before Jonathan Strong's case went to trial. Sharp later wrote that the pamphlet did not sell well.[23] As later letters show, Benezet never had a problem with those who reprinted his works or borrowed freely from them. He encouraged them to do so. The tract helped Sharp form his arguments, especially about the humanity of the Africans, because *A Short Account* gave Sharp vital empirical information about Africa and tied the antislavery cause to the ideas of some of the philosophers of the Scottish Enlightenment.

Sharp's efforts eventually wore down Strong's new owner, Kerr. The courts later exonerated Sharp of kidnapping and other charges, and the courts released Strong. The young man died five years later from complications from the initial beating; he was only twenty-five years old.

Sharp continued his work through pamphlets and sermons, all the while waiting for just the right court case to test and perhaps change the law. In 1768 Sharp published *A Representation of the Injustice and Dangerous Tendency of Tolerating Slavery in England.* He had written the pamphlet, which summarized his legal arguments, shortly after the two-year struggle over Strong's freedom had finally been won. The tract had also been written to counter the opinion of the York and Talbot ruling.

Sharp immediately took on several cases seeking the court's clarity. He took up the case of Thomas Lewis and helped win his freedom. Lewis then petitioned the court to get a clear statement. Did a black person have a right to freedom in England or could they at any time be forcibly expelled? Lord Chief Justice Mansfield wrote in the Lewis ruling, "I don't know what the consequences may be, if the masters were to lose their property by accidentally bringing their slaves to England. I hope it will never be finally discussed; for I would have all masters think them free, and all Negroes think they were not, because then they would both behave better."[24] At one point Sir William Blackstone, author of *Commentaries on the Laws of England* (1765–69), warned Sharp that it would be "up-hill work" to win a ruling making all slaves free in England.[25]

Later in 1772 Sharp published *An Appendix to the "Representation."* Relying on the legal arguments of George Wallace, he wondered whether the British Parliament would "become so miserably degenerate as to repeal, or annul, the Habeas Corpus Act, and adopt, instead of it, the most horrid and diabolical of the West Indian Laws." Sharp's use of Wallace mirrored Benezet's reliance on Wallace and Hutcheson.

Benezet, Sharp, and the First Fruits of the Antislavery Movement

Shortly after publishing these works, Sharp became the principal proponent for James Somerset, whose case became the landmark ruling concerning slavery in Great Britain, with repercussions in her colonies. Somerset, the slave of a Boston customs official, Charles Stewart, had escaped from his owner in London. He was later captured and returned to his owner, who imprisoned him on a ship that was owned by Captain James Knowles and bound for Jamaica. Lord Chief Justice Mansfield ordered under a writ of habeas corpus that the slave be produced. Sharp, who had been looking for a test case, undertook Somerset's case with vigor, proclaiming, "Slavery was so odious that nothing can be suffered to support it"; Sharp legally challenged Knowles over Somerset's freedom.

The issue, however, went beyond Somerset's freedom: Sharp wanted the court to rule whether according to English law one human being could be the property of another human. His argument was simple: a slave coming to a land that did not have slavery could not remain a slave in that territory. Sharp, who saw the international significance of the matter, proposed a simple legal question: "Whether a Slave, by coming into England, becomes free?"[26]

Sharp had already made up his mind on the matter. He wrote to a friend shortly before the trial commenced: "I have long formed my Opinion upon the subject, and am thoroughly convinced that the State of Slavery, in which a Negro may be before his arrival in England, gives no title whatever to Service here, either on the ground of property, or on the presumption of a Contract."[27] His argument extended slavery into the realm not just of the fundamental rights of man but also of the fundamental rights of black men and women. Indeed a few years after the case had been settled, Sharp wrote an essay titled *The Law of Liberty or Royal Law* that appealed especially to Christians and questioned the legality of slavery among his brethren.[28]

Sharp's early biographer, Prince Hoare, wrote, "It is feelingly remarked, by an eminent and intimate friend of Mr. Sharp, that his extraordinary action in behalf of the African race did not take its rise in theory, but was elicited by the occurrence of natural circumstances."[29] Sharp thus took the reverse of the path of Benjamin Rush, starting with the social and practical and moving to the intellectual opposition to slavery. However much Sharp put deeds ahead of words, ideas were clearly very important in forming his plan of action. These ideas developed with his correspondence and contact with Rush, Franklin, Wesley, Fothergill, and Benezet.

In a letter to Sharp, Benezet wrote, "I have sent some of the last and former Treatises to our Agent Benjamin Franklin who, I know, has a due sense of its iniquity and evil consequences; I published in the year 1767 a smaller Treatise on the Head, entitled *A Caution and A Warning to Great Britain & Colonies & c* . . . requesting that they [the London Quakers] would cause it to be Reprinted and put into the Hands of several Members of Parliament." Benezet later told Sharp that "Six Hundred Copies had been actually delivered to, or left at the Lodgings of so many Members of both Houses of Parliament." Benezet also informed Sharp that people in Maryland and Virginia were against the further importation of slaves because of fear of an uprising. Benezet then wrote about "a person who spent some time in these provinces" . . . who "thinks ten or twenty thousand people would freely join in a petition to Parliament against further import" and were willing to sign a petition to prohibit the trade.[30]

In his manuscript notes of February 18, 1772, Sharp offered a fine example of the circulation of ideas, letters, and pamphlets: "[I] wrote to Lord North [the prime minister] with my tract against tolerating slavery in England, and a paper of references to a law in Barbados, whereby a man may wantonly or bloody-mindedly, or with cruel intention, kill his Negro servant, and be liable to no penalty except £15 to be paid to the public treasury."[31]

Sharp's letter provides clear evidence of Benezet's influence even before they began correspondence. He told Lord North, "I have also sent another book, on the same subject, lately printed at Philadelphia, which amongst other things worthy of notice, contains some sensible propositions for abolishing Slavery in the Colonies."[32] The book was Benezet's *Some Historical Account of Guinea*. At the time the conduit between Sharp and Benezet was John Fothergill, a close friend to both men.

Benezet corresponded with Sharp in the spring of 1772. He had read Sharp's pamphlet *A Representation of the Injustice and Dangerous Tendency of Admitting the Least Claim of Private Property in Men* (1769). In Benezet's first letter to the "Esteemed Friend Granville Sharp" he wrote, "I have long been desirous of having an opportunity to communicate & advice with such well minded Persons in England who have a Prospect of the Iniquity of the Slave Trade and are concerned to prevent its Continuation." Those like-minded persons included Fothergill, John Wesley, and Benjamin Franklin, the first two of whom had provided Sharp and Benezet with copies of each other's writings. The exchange of letters and pamphlets and the development of antislavery networks beyond the Quakers began to give structure to the antislavery movement in Great Britain and in the American colonies.[33] Unlike some of his fellow Americans, Benezet spent a good deal of time assessing how to win over public opinion in Britain as well as in America. In the 1760s and early 1770s Parliament remained the supreme lawmaking authority for the American colonies (and Benezet believed it should be petitioned while Sharp philosophically disagreed), just as George III remained their king, with jurisdiction over whether or not slavery lawfully existed in a Crown colony. Fundamental change in laws about the slave trade (especially) and slaveholding, Benezet believed, had to be enacted by Parliament, not simply by local legislatures. Sharp differed in opinion. In his February 18 letter to the British prime minister, Lord North, Sharp asked him to use his authority to help end the international slave trade but made clear his own views as to the limitations of parliamentary action. Sharp told Lord North that he knew of no matter "which requires more immediate redress than the present miserable and deplorable slavery of Negroes and Indians, as well as white English servants in our colonies." He added, "I don't mention this as a subject proper for Parliamentary consideration; for the laws of England (God be thanked) are sufficiently clear with respect to slavery in this island." Sharp repeated his opinion that "with respect to the Colonies, the pernicious practice of slave-holding . . . cannot with propriety, fall under the consideration of the British Parliament." He concluded that "no Parliament can have a just right to enact laws for places which it does not represent."[34] Even after 1776 an attack on the slave trade caused agitation in England because of England's dominant role in the trade.

Benezet soon wrote to Sharp to apologize for excerpting some of Sharp's work without permission. He wrote, "I trust thou wilt excuse the freedom we have taken in so much curtailing thy *Treatise*. I trust the generosity of thy heart will excuse the freedom we have taken, even tho' thou should not quite approve of our Reasons for doing so."[35] Sharp responded, "You need not have made an apology for having abridged my book. It is sufficient satisfaction to me to find that you thought it capable of doing some service in a cause which we have both of us much at heart." Sharp added, "I not only approve, sir, of the abridgment you have made of my arguments in particular, but of your whole performance."[36] The exchanges between Sharp and Benezet were notable not only for the information that they exchanged but also for the delight each man showed that the other held their work so highly and used it at will.

In 1773 Benezet had written to John Fothergill in Britain, asking that he join his cause by "using the best endeavors in our power to draw the notice of the government upon the grievous iniquity and great danger attendant on a farther prosecution of the Slave Trade."[37] The beginnings of the transatlantic exchange went far beyond their letters, although they alone would powerfully help spur many men and women to action. As Christopher L. Brown has observed, "Their correspondence established the transatlantic networks critical to the success of the subsequent campaigns in both Britain and British America."[38] Their correspondence led to the signing of tens of thousands of petitions and to the circulation of thousands of pamphlets. Nowhere was this more evident than in the Somerset case.

The original exchange of letters between Sharp and Benezet had in fact begun during the Somerset case.[39] Although Benezet's first letter to Sharp did not arrive until the very day Mansfield announced his decision, Benezet's writings had played a fundamental role in Sharp's appeal to the judges and in Somerset's counsel.[40]

Shortly before the case came to docket at the Court of King's Bench, as Sharp told Benezet in a letter of August 1772, he had received copies of Benezet's *Some Historical Account of Guinea*: "Delivered by Dr. Fothergill's kindness, I was enabled immediately to dispose of six; one to Lord Mansfield, the Chief Justice, one to Lord North, first Commissioner of the Treasury; and four to the learned Counsel who had generously undertaken to plead gratis for Somerset."[41] Sharp offered greater details about the process in two letters to Fothergill, in February and April 1772. The first gave Sharp's positive reaction to Benezet's *Some Historical Account of Guinea*. Just as Sharp had republished on his own initiative Benezet's *A Caution and a Warning to Great Britain*, adding his own conclusion, so Benezet had added some of Sharp's 1768 *Representation of the Injustice* to his new work. Sharp asked Fothergill to procure copies and to send them to counsel via Somerset himself: "The bearer, James Somerset, is the Negro whose cause comes on next Friday, and will be the proper person to present to his Counsel what copies you may be able to procure."[42]

Two months later, on April 18, 1772, Sharp again wrote Fothergill and sent him a copy of the pleadings from the last term of James Somerset: "[I] have great satisfaction in finding Mr. Benezet's book, for which you favored me with so many copies, is now republished [Sharp here neglects to mention that he was responsible]. . . . The copies which you were so obliging to send me, were given to four Counsels for James Somerset, and to Lord Mansfield; and if I were not sure that the Editor had not sent copies to the other Judges, I would have bound neatly for that purpose immediately. The 7th of next month is fixed for the continuance of the argument."[43] Lord Chief Justice Mansfield soon issued his Somerset decision.[44]

In short, Mansfield ruled that a slave could not be forced to leave Britain for a life of slavery elsewhere.[45] He ruled that the law of England did not specifically allow slavery; lacking positive law to the contrary, men were free. He thus did not attack slavery in the colonies, where positive laws about slavery were in fact on the books, but only in England, where no such law existed. Mansfield thus had three elements to his ruling, two that touched on Benezet's philosophy: the first was that Africans are humans (clearly taken from Benezet); the second was that all humans have the right to liberty, which Mansfield may have read in Hutcheson or from the works of Sharp or Benezet. Mansfield ruled that the positive law (i.e., man-made law) of England did not legalize slavery.

Mansfield's reasoning, particularly with respect to the idea that slavery violated the law of nature, has obvious roots in precisely those passages of the writings of George Wallace, emphasized in the works of Sharp and Benezet. Moreover, as Sharp's letter to Fothergill of February 1772 makes clear, Sharp considered Benezet's *Some Historical Account* to have made a particularly concise "extraction of the marrow" of his own comments about Wallace. Wallace's *A System of the Principles of the Laws of Scotland* (1760) had asserted of a slave, "as soon as therefore he comes into a country in which the judges are not forgetful of their own humanity, it is their duty to remember that he is a man and to declare him to be free."[46]

Sharp was the one who informed Benezet of the outcome of the case. On August 21, 1772, he wrote to Benezet: "I have likewise sent a copy of the judgment given by Lord Mansfield in the case of Somerset. This judgment would have done Lord Mansfield honor, had he not all along seemed inclined to offer the other side of the question."[47] The ruling immediately became subject to various interpretations. Although pleased with the outcome, Sharp had misgivings about the ruling because he understood the power of the proslavery lobby. A few days after his letter to Benezet he wrote to Fothergill, "The West-India merchants, traders, and other interested persons, have formed a considerable association to promote a Bill at the next meeting of Parliament for the Toleration of slavery in this kingdom, in order to counteract the late clear decision of the Court of King's Bench in favor of James Somerset and of the Negroes in general." Sharp

concluded by telling Fothergill that "Mr. Benezet is endeavoring to procure signatures in Pennsylvania and Maryland, to a petition against
slavery."[48]

Four years after the Somerset decision, in 1776, Sharp presented the
Mansfield ruling as a clear victory. He wrote, "The opinion of the lords
Hardwick [Yorke] and Talbot, which I laboured to refute in my Tract
against *Slavery in England* (printed in 1769,) has since been effectually set
aside by a clear determinations, in the Court of King's Bench, in favor of
James Somersett, a Negro, against his former Master . . . in the year 1772."[49]
The chief justice did not declare, as was wishfully thought, even by Thomas
Clarkson, "that as soon as any slave sets foot upon English territory he is
free."[50] Slaves in North America, as in England, gave the Somerset decision
their own positive interpretations. In Britain "slaves bowed with profound
respect to the Judges and shaking each other by the hand congratulated
themselves upon the recovery of the rights of human nature."[51] In another
case an advertisement was placed for a runaway couple on their way to
Great Britain "where they imagine they will be free (a Notion now too prevalent among the Negroes, greatly to the vexation and Prejudice of their
Masters)."[52]

In Boston, on April 20, 1773, four enslaved Africans presented a "Petition for Freedom by Massachusetts Slaves" on "behalf of our fellow slaves
in this province, and by the order of their committee."[53] Influenced by the
Somerset ruling, the petition read, "We expect great things from great
men who have made such a noble stand against the designs of their fellow
men to enslave them."[54] In this case "their demands," as James Oliver Horton and Lois Horton argue, "were not revolutionary, simply that slaves be
allowed one day a week to labor for their own benefits, so they might accumulate funds to purchase their own freedom." Although the white colonists did not accept this petition, the blacks continued their efforts,
"carefully worded to highlight the parallels between their cause and the
colonists' desires for a 'free and Christian Country.' "[55]

In spite of the hope that the Somerset case engendered in black slaves
in England and America, Benezet took a more sobering view of the ruling.
Relying on Sharp's letter of August 21, he wrote to his friend Samuel Allinson in Burlington that "it seems Lord Mansfield, notwithstanding truth
forced him to give such a judgment, and was rather disposed to favour the
cause of the master than that of the slave." Seeking more information
about the decision and future actions in Parliament, Benezet concluded,
"I have also to communicate an interesting letter to Benjamin Franklin on
the same subject."[56] Franklin understood the meaning of the ruling. He
would later write that Britain "piqued itself on its virtue, love of liberty,
and the equity of its courts, in setting free a single negro." At another time
Franklin called the English "Pharisaical" for "setting free a single Slave
that happens to land on thy coasts, while thy Merchants in all ports are

encouraged by thy laws to continue a commerce whereby so many hundreds of thousands are dragged into slavery than can scarce be said to end with their lives, since it is entailed on their posterity."[57]

Black perceptions of the Somerset case came about precisely when white colonialists were proclaiming their natural rights and petitioning for their own grievances. Whites "concerned about the loss of their own freedom used the word 'slavery' to describe the relationship with Britain they wished to avoid. African Americans pointed out the hypocrisy inherent in the use by slaveholders of the rhetoric of slavery and freedom."[58] One black wrote, "We have in common with all other men, a natural right to our freedoms without Being depriv'sd of them by our fellow men as we are a freeborn Pepel and have never forfeited this Blessing by any compact or agreement whatever."[59] Some blacks tried to file "freedom suits" in the northern courts in North America. However, most of the time they were denied the right to submit their petitions. In the end, many colonial blacks who may have considered filing suits did not, as they realized that laws there legalized slavery.

Like Sharp himself, social and legal historians have grappled with the true meaning of the Somerset ruling. The late prime minister of Trinidad, the historian Eric Williams, asserted in *Capitalism and Slavery,* "the assiduous zeal of Granville Sharp brought Chief Justice Mansfield in 1772 the case of the Negro James Somerset who was about to be returned by his owner to Jamaica, there was abundant precedents to prove the impurity of the English air." Williams believed that Mansfield "tried hard to evade the issue" and focused narrowly on the issue that English law did not allow the forcible removal of slaves from England.[60] Nonetheless, some blacks continued to attempt to file countless "freedom suits" in the northern courts and like Benezet secured more petitions. Most of the time, they were denied the right to file their petitions or to be heard in court.

Mansfield avoided the complicated property issues, and, because the writ of habeas corpus applied so narrowly to England itself, never considered the legal situation in the colonies. Somerset case or no, black slaves remained the property of their owners.[61] In reality, as Sharp and Clarkson would later see, Justice Mansfield did not declare that all slaves brought into a non-slaveholding territory be declared free, only that James Somerset was free. As Eric Metaxas observed, "Mansfield was no fool, however. His ruling was fussily careful to declare that only the one African, Somerset, was freed. But somehow, in the public mind, this detail was lost, or didn't matter. For all intents and purposes, slavery had been abolished in England! And to some very real extent, because of the public perception, it had."[62] James Oldham, a legal scholar, sums up the current historiographical consensus by saying that Somerset did not free slaves in England, yet the extent to which that opinion of "popular history" and of contemporaneous blacks "should be revised has been debated."[63]

Benezet and Sharp quickly understood that the Somerset ruling, although a positive step, was not in its immediate legal ramifications one of the "triumphs for humanitarianism."[64] Mansfield said at the conclusion of the Somerset case, "The setting 14,000 or 15,000 men at once loose by a solemn opinion, is very disagreeable in the effects it threatens."[65] Mansfield, with his deep respect for property rights, carefully avoided the bigger issues related to them.[66] As James Walvin noted, "Mansfield was an expert on commercial law and was loath to make a decision which might disturb the property-basis of black slavery. So much commercial wealth flowed to Britain from its slave empire that any judgment which ran counter to that economic interest, even in so minor a fashion as slavery in England, was to be resisted."[67] And resist the slave owners did, in Britain, in the mainland colonies, and especially in the West Indies, as Sharp's letter to Fothergill documents.

The Somerset case firmly initiated the Sharp-Benezet cooperation. In the same August 1772 letter in which he informed Benezet of the Somerset decision, Sharp told Benezet he had "thought indeed of reprinting it [*Some Historical Account*], as I did your former tract in 1768 [*Short Account of That Part of Africa*], but Mr. Clark, the printer, was luckily beforehand with me; so that I had an opportunity of purchasing more copies to distribute." Sharp did indeed reprint *Some Historical Account,* as the letter informed Benezet; he sent a copy of the new edition, as well as "some other pamphlets lately published on the subject; with a few little tracts of my own of which I beg your acceptance as a token of my esteem"[68] Clarkson later noted that Benezet "availed himself of every circumstance, as far as he could, to the same end . . . to spread the antislavery word."[69] Sharp, Wesley, Benezet, and later Clarkson saw the importance of transatlantic communication; all of them borrowed heavily from each other's writings, without seeking prior consent, knowing that the devotion of each to the cause of liberty was grounds for assuming, as Sharp had written to Benezet, that the colleagues would approve the appropriation of their words.

After the Somerset ruling West Indian slave traders and plantation owners claimed partial victory through both the Parliament and the courts. They further clamped down on blacks and sought to regain any lost property and to end the anxiety of whites and the hopes of the blacks. Sharp believed that the harsh measures in the West Indies would have the reverse of the intended effect and lead to greater danger for the whites in the Islands because the increased brutality would lead to black uprisings, as the slaves would have no other redress. In the very letter that informed Benezet of the Somerset decision, he wrote that "it is on this account that I have now undertaken to write once more upon the subjects, in order to apprise disinterested people of the dangerous tendency of such a measure."[70]

Benezet had written Sharp about his concern relating to slave uprisings in St. Vincent's and other islands in the West Indies. Based on information from Benezet, Sharp wrote a letter on October 10, 1772, "To the Right Hon. The Earl of Dartmouth his Majesty's Secretary of State" about the conditions in the British Islands. Because of the impending crisis with the colonies and his increasing lack of faith in parliamentary or judiciary action against slavery, Sharp wrote Benezet that "my former tracts were built chiefly on the laws of England; but my present work is for the most part founded on Scripture, to obviate the doctrines of some late writers and disputers, who have ventured to assert that slavery is not inconsistent with the Word of God."[71] Sharp, who had once earlier written, "Mr. B. is obliged to earn his bread in the laborious office as a schoolmaster, and is unhappily involved in the errors of Quakerism," seemed to turn inward in a reflective moment.[72] Citing Deuteronomy 23:15—"Thou shall not deliver unto his master the servant which is escaped from his master unto thee"—Sharp discreetly supported runaway slaves. He later wrote to Rush, "No Man can lawfully be prosecuted for protecting a Negro, or ANY OTHER SLAVE, whatever, that has escaped from his Master, because that would be punishing a Man for doing his indispensable Duty, according to the Laws of God." Sharp later wrote *The Just Limitation of Slavery* (1776), which was published "as an answer to Rev. Mr. Thompson's Tract in favour of the African Slave Trade," and other pamphlets, including *The Law of Obedience* (1776).[73]

Sharp's August 21 letter also reveals his collaboration with Benezet on the petition campaign against slavery. He advised Benezet, "Your proposal of petitioning Parliament is certainly very proper, if the subject of the petition be confined to the African slave trade (which is protected and encouraged by Parliament), but with respect to the toleration of slavery in the colonies, I apprehend the British Parliament has no right to interfere, and that your Petition on this head shou'd be addressed only to the King, or the King in Council."[74] Sharp expressed the same concern to Rush two years later. Again maintaining that the colonial legislatures were completely independent of the British Parliament, he told Rush of his "present differences with the Colonies." He wrote that "the Petitions against Slavery in American may be addressed to the King; and not to the King and Parliament."[75]

Sharp later wrote Benezet:

You mention the information you have received from a person who has spent some time in Maryland and Virginia that he thinks 10 or 20 thousand people would freely join in a Petition to Parliament against the further importation of Negroes. Such a petition would retrieve in some respects the honor of those colonies. Yet as I have mentioned above, respect must be had to the rights of the Colonies, and a Petition from thence if addressed to the Parliament ought to relate to the Slave trade in general, with its bad effects and dangerous Consequences, but with respect to the Petition to Parliament against the iniquity of the Slave trade in general and its bad effects in the Colonies, if you could procure even less than a thousand hands I should think it a very considerable point.[76]

Here Sharp showed the importance that he placed on the multifaceted aspects of Benezet's efforts to get petitions against the slave trade before the Parliament of Britain. The petitions were to be a two-edged sword. They mobilized hundreds of thousands of people and raised public opinion against the trade, thus letting parliamentary leaders know that the tide against slavery was turning. Benezet ensured that Granville Sharp and his London neighbor Benjamin Franklin would cross paths. On April 4, 1773, he wrote to Sharp: "I am glad to understand from my friend Benjamin Franklin, that you have commenced an acquaintance, and that he expects in future to act in concert with thee in the affair of slavery." As usual, he made the best use of his letters, adding, "I send thee herewith some pamphlets; and in confidence of thy goodness of heart, which by looking to the intention, will construe the Freedom I have taken in the best light."[77] Sharp's memoirs contain several other letters sent to him by Benezet. They include a November 8, 1772, letter, which included extracts from the minutes of the Virginia Assembly concerning the slave trade and copies of letters that antislavery advocates sent to the assembly. Benezet's third letter, dated February 18, 1773 (n.s.), brought Sharp up to date on several developments: "We have pushed the point among ourselves [the people of Pennsylvania] by handing about extracts of thy letter of the Virginia Petition, & c., to some weighty members of three different counties in New York government, and the same two counties in New Jersey, &c. . . . If time would have allowed we might have had ten thousand signers."[78]

A month later Benezet told Sharp about the success of the Pennsylvania petition campaign, which led to the assembly levying "a further duty of slaves (and made it perpetual) at £20 per head: and that they apprehended that the passing or refusal of this law by the King and Council, will better enable them to judge what further steps to take, with respect to making head with the King and Parliament that the Slave Trade may be put to an end."[79] Sharp received Benezet's fifth letter of April 5 on June 7, 1773. Benezet told him "that an opposition to any further importation of slaves appears to be an increasing concern; and even the putting an end to slavery itself is endeavored for in New England." Benezet also informed Sharp that "the Assembly [Massachusetts] has proposed, or intends to propose a law for setting all Negroes free at a certain age, and declaring those to be imported in the future, free, either at their landing, or after some time of service, & c."[80] In fact, the 1780 Massachusetts Constitution would proclaim "that all men are born free and equal; and that every subject is entitled to liberty"; three years later the Massachusetts Supreme Court ruled that "slavery is . . . as effectively abolished as it can be by the granting of rights and privileges wholly incompatible and repugnant to its existence."[81] In a packet Sharp received from Benezet in January 1774, he also found a copy of the Pennsylvania petition "and of the Act of Assembly which passed in consequence of it." Sharp recorded that Benezet asked to be alerted "by the return of the same ship, whether any notice had been taken by the British Government of the Virginia Petition, and the acts of the Pennsylvania Assembly for laying a duty on Negroes."[82] Commenting on the previous Benezet letter, Sharp wrote of his opinions "against the iniquity of attending to political or mercenary pleas for tolerating slavery and the Slave Trade." Sharing his fears with Benezet, he wrote of "notorious instances of doing evil that good may come and that we have therefore the greatest reason to expect some dreadful judgment on the kingdom, for tolerating such monstrous wickedness."[83]

Benezet's next letter was not as positive as others had been, perhaps in part because of Sharp's own pessimism. Written in May 1774, it was, according to Sharp, Benezet's seventh letter to him. As was often the case, William Dillwyn personally delivered it. Benezet informed Sharp that the "importation of Negroes, and indeed slavery itself, receives all the discouragement that can be expected in these northern colonies; and some in the more southern are also sensible of the danger and destructive tendency of the increase of slaves among them." He then made a plea to Sharp: "Except some check can be put with you to the importation of slaves from Guinea, I fear little will be done." Benezet then told Sharp of a few setbacks, including in the north where the "Assembly at New York had lately passed a law declaring the children of slaves to be born free, but it was not confirmed by the Governor." Benezet made clear, as he had in other letters, that pressure from the British government led to the defeat of such proposals, and he felt that only his friends in Britain could change that.[84]

In 1774 Sharp published *A Declaration of the People's Natural Rights to a Share in the Legislature, Which Is the Fundamental Principle to the British Constitution.* He gave 250 copies of the tract to Benjamin Franklin, who sent them to America the same day he received them. The work was so well accepted that seven thousand copies were reprinted in Boston, New York, and Philadelphia. The tract was also excerpted in many "public journals."[85] Sharp called on the British to show their true love for the rights of humankind by ending slavery. If they did this then their American colony, instead of being "the land of the brave and the home of the slave," would be known as "the land of the brave and the home of the free."[86] Through mutual friends, such as Rush and Franklin, Sharp and Benezet also exchanged ideas. Each continued to write to prominent figures of the time in hopes of eliciting their support: Sharp also took up correspondence with Lord Dunmore, which lasted from 1776 to 1782, and with Henry Laurens, in 1781–82. The Revolutionary War had interrupted the correspondence between Sharp and Benezet.[87] However, during the war they had continued to read and distribute each other's tracts, as we know from a March 1779 letter from James St. David to Sharp, with which St. David returned a book by Benezet that he had borrowed from Sharp. He told Sharp that "Mr. Benezet's book . . . replete with religious benevolence and humanity, and both in acts and reasoning, carry conviction on a subject which natural sensibility and common sense alone must reprobate."[88] Sharp would receive many such references to the work and deeds of Benezet. The two men resumed correspondence briefly at the war's end, but Benezet died soon after the 1783 Treaty of Paris. Hoare relates that Benezet's failing health meant that Sharp's final letter to the elderly Quaker could not even be read to him.

In 1783 Sharp took up the notorious *Zong* case, after Olaudah Equiano had alerted him to the atrocities. Sharp immediately began to publicize the facts surrounding the ship *Zong*, in which 133 blacks had been thrown overboard at sea. The ship's captain had claimed there were insufficient provisions to feed the white crewmen, let alone the blacks; so he threw the blacks overboard and then sought insurance compensation for the slaves. Sharp noted that on March 19, "Gustavus Vasa, a Negro called on me, with an account of one hundred and thirty Negroes being thrown alive into the sea, from on board an English ship." On March 21 Sharp met with General James Oglethorpe, the aged philanthropist, founder of Georgia Province in the 1730s, and contemporary of John Wesley. That same day he made notes of his meeting with the Anglican bishops of Chester and Peterborough and earlier attended the proceedings at the Court of King's Bench. On May 22 he documented that the "insurers and owners of the slave ship, from on board of which the one hundred and thirty poor Negroes were cast into the sea. A new trial is granted to the insurers."[89] Judge Mansfield ruled in favor of the ship owners, who, claiming the lost blacks as private property, were compensated for their loss. He also ruled that the presence on board of over four hundred gallons of water when the ship docked at Jamaica showed that the pretext of the captain was false, so he denied him compensation.

By the time of Benezet's death in 1784 he and Sharp together had done much to change opinions about slavery in the mainland colonies and in Britain. Long after Benezet's death Sharp continued to extol his friend's merits. In 1795 Sharp wrote to the Anglican bishop of London, summing up the origins of his work in the antislavery movement: "The tract which I had drawn up and printed in 1769, was soon afterwards reprinted in America by Mr. Anthony Benezet, a worthy old Quaker at Philadelphia, whose other publications had already begun to awaken the attention of the Americans to the injustice and danger of tolerating slavery."[90] Going further, Prince Hoare wrote that "although his [Benezet's] zealous labours failed to eradicate from his native soil the evil which he deplored, they contributed to strengthen the arm of the great champions of his favorite cause, and finally to wipe away no small portion of human disgrace."[91]

Generating a Mass Movement: Benezet and John Wesley

John Wesley, the founder of British Methodism, proved to be a vital link between the British and the Americans. Like Sharp, Wesley came from a family of ministers, in his case going back four generations. He was one of nineteen children, ten of whom survived infancy. The young Wesley was ordained in 1728.[92] Persecuted because his religious zeal and views differed from those of the Church of England, he formed the first Methodist Chapel in 1739.

Benezet reached out to Wesley as part of his effort to expand the antislavery movement among non-Quakers. His approach to Wesley proved far more positive than Benezet's ill-fated overtures to the Society for the Propagation of the Gospel.[93] In late 1771 Benezet sent Wesley a copy of his *Some Historical Account of Guinea*. On its receipt Wesley wrote in his journal (February 12, 1772), "I read a very different book, published by an honest Quaker, on that execrable sum of all villainies, commonly called the Slave trade. I read of nothing like it in the heathen world, whether ancient or modern; and it infinitely exceeds, in every instance of barbarity, whatever Christian slaves suffer in Mahometan countries."[94] Wesley wrote back to Benezet to inform him that he would work with Granville Sharp to seek the "expediency of some weekly publications in the newspapers, on the origin, nature, and dreadful effects of the slave-trade."[95]

Wesley next wrote his own attack on human bondage, *Thoughts upon Slavery*, lifting entire sections from Benezet's pamphlets, without attribution; when he learned of it, Benezet wrote his effusive praise and thanks to Wesley and had *Thoughts* published in Philadelphia. Works by these antislavery writers cannot be thought of as freestanding texts; they need to be understood in the same way the writers themselves understood them: as protean and collective works in progress. Benezet, Sharp, Wesley, and other antislavery writers had no qualms about using any text created or found by their colleagues. Modern societies tend to think of each pamphlet, book, or essay as the creation of a single author, as a work worthy of copyright protection; these antislavery writers had no such thoughts.

No better example of this process exists than the collaborative text of Benezet and Wesley (1771–74), which began with *Some Historical Account of Guinea*; took somewhat different shape with the London edition of Wesley's *Thoughts*, about a third of which comes virtually verbatim from Benezet; and metamorphosed into the 1774 Philadelphia edition of *Thoughts upon Slavery*, "reprinted with considerable additions by Anthony Benezet."[96] In the transatlantic exchange of ideas and strategies, for Benezet, Wesley, Sharp, Equiano, and other antislavery writers, what mattered was the message, not the messenger. A brief look at the process at work from 1771 to 1774 shows precisely how it functioned.

Here are Benezet's and Wesley's respective initial descriptions of the Guinea coast:

Some Historical Account of Guinea, 1771
   That part of Africa from which the Negroes are sold in slavery, commonly known by the name of Guinea, extends along the coast three or four thousand miles.

Beginning at the River Senegal, situated about the 17th degree of North latitude, being the nearest part of Guinea, as well to Europe as to North America; from thence to the river Gambia, and in a northerly course to Cape Sierra Leona, comprehends a coast of about seven hundred miles; being the same tract for which Queen Elizabeth granted charters to the firsttraders of that coast. From Sierra Leona, the Land of Guinea takes a turn to the eastward, extending that course about fifteen hundred miles, including those several divisions known by the name of the Grain Coast, the Ivory Coast, the Gold Coast and the Slave Coast with the large kingdom of Benin. From then the land runs southward along the coast about twelve hundred miles, which contains the kingdoms of Congo and Angola.[97]

Thoughts upon Slavery, 1774
    That part of Africa whence the negroes are brought commonly known by the name of Guinea, extends along the coast, in the whole between three and four thousand miles. From the river Senegal (seventeen degrees north of the line) to Cape Sierra Leona, it contains seven hundred miles. Thence it runs eastward about fifteen hundred miles, including the Grain Coast, the Ivory Coast, the Gold Coast, and the Slave Coast, with the large kingdom of Benin. From thence it runs southward about twelve hundred miles, and contains the kingdoms of Congo and Angola.[98]

Fifteen years after Wesley wrote his book, Olaudah Equiano paraphrased Benezet this way: "That part of Africa, known by the name of Guinea, to which the trade along for slaves is carried on, extends along the coast above 3400 miles, from the Senegal to Angola, and includes a variety of kingdoms. Of these, the most considerable is the kingdom of Benin." As Werner Sollors has noted, Benezet allowed Equiano access to some of the first positive written assessments of Africa, provided by such slavers as André Brüe and Michel Adanson.[99] Equiano leaned so heavily on Benezet's text that he even emphasized those elements of African life that the Quaker had singled out for his own reasons, such as the abundance and variety of vegetables (after noting a few pages earlier the African preference for simple meat stews). Wesley, by way of Benezet, also quoted long passages from Adanson, Brüe, and other travelers.[100]
    Wesley also borrowed liberally from Benezet's *A Caution and a Warning to Great Britain*, first published in London in 1767. Benezet used "the original manuscript of the Surgeon's journal . . . in a vessel from New-York to the coast of Guiney, about nineteen years past." Benezet then cited the surgeon's journal for the days December 29–31, 1724, and January 2, 1725. Wesley cited the same pages. On December 29 the surgeon observed, "No trade to-day. Though many Traders come on board; they inform us, that the people are gone to war with in land, and will bring prisoners enough in two or three days." On December 30 the surgeon wrote, "No trade yet, but our Trades come on board to-day and informed us, the people had burnt four towns of her enemies, so that to-morrow we expect slaves." He observed on December 31, "Fair weather, but no trade yet: We see each night towns burning, but we hear the Sestro men are many of them killed

by the inland Negroes, so that we fear this war will be unsuccessful." His last entry came on January 2 of the following year: "Last night we saw a prodigious fire break out about eleven o'clock, and this morning we see the town of Sestro burnt down to the ground, (it contained some hundreds of houses) so that we find their enemies are too hard for them at present, and consequently our trade spoiled here." Frustrated that no Africans had been captured, " 'About seven o'clock' the vessel pulled up its anchor 'as did likewise the three other vessels to proceed lower down' to attempt kidnapping other Africans."[101] These graphic scenes of the cold calculations of the English slave traders had convinced Benezet, as they did Wesley, and the two men hoped, their readers, of the barbarity of the slave trade.

Benezet, in fact, knew of Wesley's work while it was still in progress because of a letter Granville Sharp wrote to him on January 7, 1774: "Sometime ago the Rev. Wesley signified to me by letter, that he had a desire to write against the Slave Trade; in consequence of which I furnished him with a large bundle of Books and Papers on the subject; and a few days ago he [John Wesley] sent me his manuscript to peruse; which is well drawn up, and he has reduced the substance of the argument respecting the gross iniquity of that trade into a very small compass; his evidence, however, seems chiefly extracted from the authors quoted in several publications."[102] By "his evidence" Sharp meant the original sources, such as Adanson, Brüe, and others, which had come not from "several publications" but from Benezet himself, as Wesley openly admitted to others. Sharp was never as effusive in his praise as were Clarkson, Wesley, Rush, Brissot, or others.

On receiving a copy of the work from Wesley, Benezet sent him a letter via his former student William Dillwyn. He told Wesley, "The tract thou has lately published entitled, *Thoughts on Slavery,* afforded me much satisfaction. I was more especially glad to see it, as the circumstances of the times made it necessary that something on that most weighty subject, not large, but striking and pathetic, should now be published. Therefore I immediately agreed with the Printer to have it republished here."[103] Neither Benezet nor Wesley minded in the slightest when the one borrowed literally from the other. They, in fact, felt honored.[104]

Benezet went straight to his own publishing agent, Joseph Crukshank, and in a short time the work was published in Philadelphia.[105] Wesley's original came to fifty-seven pages, but Benezet added some of his works along with a document written by an English physician, Edward Bancroft, who had lived in "Dutch Guiana." Benezet also added another document: an "Extract from a Sermon preached by the Bishop of Gloucester, before the Society for the Propogation [*sic*] of the Gospel at their anniversary meeting, on the 21st of February, 1766."

After the publication of *Thoughts,* a public petition campaign among Methodists led to the gathering of 229,000 signatures against the slave trade being presented to the Parliament. That kind of success naturally elicited a quick response from the proslavery forces; soon after Wesley's work came out, an anonymous author wrote *A Supplement to Mr. Wesley's Pamphlet Entitled Thoughts upon Slavery,* which was twice the size of Wesley's text. The author challenged many of Wesley's theories and attributed his errors to "the same source of Human Imperfections, and admire some of his conclusions, though we assent not to the Premises." Although veiled in words meant to soften its defense of slavery, it concluded, "Let us therefore proceed in the glorious Cause of Humanity, and, by increasing and cherishing our Colonization in American, prevent those atrocious Villains of Mercy, Truth and Justice,—the avowed Intentions of Mr. Wesley's Pamphlet."[106]

Benezet's letters urged Wesley to amend his tract "in case of further publication; as it might give an advantage to the advocate for the trade, to lessen the strength of what is strictly true." Benezet worried about a section of Wesley's tract that he felt did not show the true strength of the Africans. He told Wesley that the "Treatise upon the Trade was better calculated to show the iniquity, and dishonesty of the African Traders, even to one another, than to give any grounded answer to what has been written against the Slave-Trade."[107] Benezet knew that he, Wesley, and all other antislavery writers had to be extremely careful in their writings because of the need to overcome a long-standing climate of opinion about Africa. He realized that the new tactics of the slave traders were to try to show African complicity in the trade and to show that slavery had always existed, would always exist, and was necessary for the survival of European society.

Wesley, a subscriber to the first edition of Equiano's *Narrative,* understood Equiano's words that black freedom was "nominal for they are universally insulted and plundered without the possibility of redress."[108] Wesley had been moved by Equiano's account of his friend John Annis, a black man kidnapped on the island of St. Kitts. Like Sharp, Equiano came to Annis's defense, but to no avail. Annis was "according to custom, staked to the ground with four pins, through a cord, two on his wrist, and two on his ankles, was cut and flogged most unmercifully and afterwards leaded cruelly with irons about his neck."[109]

Benezet wrote to Wesley about those who attacked his antislavery work, above all "a certain author, who called himself an African-Merchant, in a *Treatise upon the Trade from Great Britain to Africa.*" He informed Wesley that the *Treatise* "has endeavored though without real ground, to make me appear inconsistent in the account I give of those and other Negro-nations, in my *Historical Account of Guinea.*"[110] Benezet was referring to Thomas Thompson. Additionally, Benezet wrote Wesley on his concerns about slave revolts. He and Wesley also exchanged information they had received by way of Nathaniel Gilbert in Antigua on the treatment of slaves and their fear of slave rebellion. Gilbert was a wealthy Antiguan who had resigned from the assembly and begun preaching to his slaves.[111]

Benezet went on to explain to Wesley that the laws in Virginia and North and South Carolina served the same purpose as those in the Islands, "tending rather to promote a murderous disposition in the Master towards their poor Slaves." He called the legally sanctioned treatment of the blacks in the southern colonies and the Islands "worse than Savage laws," which the "slaveholders apprehend necessary for their safety." They were "laws, at which the darkest ages would have repugned!" Benezet then alerted Wesley of advisements in the "Public Prints of the province of Virginia and North-Carolina" about a runaway slave, "a lusty Negro named Bob, & c.& c. . . . The said fellow is outlawed, and I will give £10 reward for his head severed for his body, and forty shillings if brought home alive [*Williamsburg Gazette*]."[112]

While Benezet continued to make a study of recent events and uprisings among the blacks and of the uncompromising positions of the whites in the West Indies, the Methodists were spreading his ideas and his work, even before they were fully spread among the Quakers. In an interesting bit of irony, just as Sharp had misgivings about the ways of the Quakers, Benezet also had his own sectarian ideas about the Methodists. On one occasion Benezet wrote to Dillwyn that there were "things the Methodist & Moravians don't seem to understand. . . . They use care in certain prospect & mode of expression which may be good for beginners but cannot impart teaching to those who have all their hopes from Christ the spring, whose name Jesus implied his office to deliver his people from their sins & sanctify unto himself an (humble) people zealous of good works."[113]

Benezet, in his 1778 *Observations on Slavery* and 1783 *Notes on the Slave Trade,* also borrowed from the last section of Wesley's *Thoughts upon Slavery.* In the introduction to *Observations* and repeated in *Notes* Benezet wrote,

[Here] It may not be necessary to repeat what has been so fully declared in several modern publications, of the inconsistence of slavery with every right of mankind. With every feeling of humanity, and every precept of Christianity; nor to point out its inconsistency with the welfare, peace, and prosperity of every country, in proportion as it prevails; what grievous sufferings it brings on the poor Negroes; but more especially what a train of fatal vices it produces in their lordly oppressors and their unhappy offerings. Nevertheless for the sake of some who have not met with, or fully considered those former publications, and in hopes that some who are still active in support of slavery, may be induced to consider their ways, and become more wise, the following substance of an address or expostulation made by a sensible Author, to the several ranks of persons most immediately concerned in the trade is now republished.[114]

Here Benezet followed the line of Wesley and Woolman, making a plea to white self-interest. All three men consistently used the two-pronged approach: 1) appeal to the physical well-being of whites in terms of fears of potential slave uprisings; and 2) appeal to the whites' sense of moral worth—to the protection of their souls. Benezet never mentioned the name of "the sensible Author" whose words he reprinted above, but the text makes it clear that it was Wesley.

Benezet used Wesley's words to fortify his argument to those who made excuses for having slaves: the merchants, the traders, the plantation owners, and those who exclaimed that they came by their slaves "honestly" or by inheritance. To men who told of their humane treatment of the Africans, he asked, in the rolling cadence of the preacher, "Are you a man? Then you should have a human heart. . . . Do you never feel another's pain? Have you no sympathy? No sense of human woe? No pity for the miserable?"[115] He continued, "When you saw the flowing eyes, the heaving breasts, of the bleeding sides of tortured limbs of your fellow creatures, was you a stone, or a brute? . . . Did not one tear drop from your eyes?"[116] The cadence, in fact, came from the consummate preacher Wesley, whose *Thoughts upon Slavery* Benezet quoted here.

Wesley described the sufferings the trade brought to the blacks and addressed the "Captains employed in the trade." He told them of the beauty of Guinea (West Africa) and of the kindness of the people who had been separated from their loved ones. Wesley told the captains, "Most of You know the country of Guinea, between the River Senegal and the kingdom of Angola."[117] Benezet, knowing more about Africa, changed the wording in this section to add more about the people and geography of Africa and left out the section on the River Senegal and the kingdom of Angola. The slave traders, Wesley argued, separated "brethren and sisters, from each other," and herded "them into ships like swine." They were "stewed together, as close as they ever could lie, without any regard to decency. Such slavery is not found among the Turks at Algiers, or among the heathens in America." Wesley begged the captain to "immediately quit the horrid trade. At all events be an honest man."

He then turned his attention to the merchant, telling him that "it is your money that is the spring of all that powers him to go on." He told of the need to challenge the morality of the slave owners and urged them to promise, "I will never buy a slave more while I live." Moving on to the conscience of the merchants, Wesley asserted, "Oh let his resolution be yours! Have no more of any part in this detestable business."[118]

Wesley then appealed to the plantation owner, who asserted that he "pays honestly for my goods, and am not concerned to know how they are come by." The goods were, of course, chattel slaves, whom the plantation owners viewed as property, always replaceable for a fee and profit. Wesley accused the planters of not being as honest as "pickpockets . . . housekeepers" and those who committed "robbery upon the highway." Indicting them for fraud, robbery, and murder, he told the plantation owners that it was their "money that pays the merchant, and through him the captain and the African butchers." Wesley concluded that they were the "spring that puts the rest in motion."[119] Benezet reproduced all of these comments virtually verbatim in the opening pages of *Notes on the Slave Trade.*

Of course, Benezet and Lay had influenced Wesley, as they had long ago sworn never to wear or eat anything produced with slave labor. "Thy hands, thy bed, thy furniture, thy house, thy lands are at present stained with blood," Wesley proclaimed. Sensing that he had won a convert, Wesley declared, "Surely it is enough: accumulate no more guilt: spill no more blood of the innocent! Do not hire another to shed blood: Do not pay another for doing it! Whether you are a Christian or no, shew yourself a man! Be not more savage than a lion or a bear!"[120]

No person who had any part in slavery could claim innocence: not the "man-stealer," or the ship captain, the merchant, the plantation owner, or even the person who proclaimed innocence by inheriting slaves. For Benezet and Wesley not even those who sat idly by and did nothing either to eliminate slavery or to improve the conditions of the slaves were innocent. They too had committed a sin and would be consumed with guilt if they looked inward.[121]

Even the person who had inherited slaves, as did the children of Patrick Henry and Henry Laurens, bore the wrath of the Methodist leader. "Perhaps you will say," he asked, "'I do not buy any Negroes: I only use those left by my Father.'" Wesley wrote that neither they nor their fathers "has any right to use another as a slave." Wesley then resorted, like Benezet, to the philosophy of Wallace and Hutcheson: "Liberty is the right of every human creature, as soon as he breathes the vital air. And no human law can deprive him of that right, which he derives from the law of nature." Wesley concluded, "Give liberty to whom Liberty is due, that is to every child of man. . . . Away with all whips and chains, all compulsion! Be gentle toward all men. And see that you invariable do unto everyone, as you would he should do unto you."[122]

The Second Generation: Thomas Clarkson and William Wilberforce

Seeking to learn about the economic impact of the slave trade, Benezet studied commercial records, something that Thomas Clarkson later perfected. He wrote of "a book printed in Liverpool called the *Liverpool Memorandum-book,* which contain amongst other things, and account, of the trade of that port." For him it was "an exact list of the number of vessels employed in the Guinea trade" and "the number of vessels employed by the African Company in London and Bristol." He stated that from the book "we may with some degree of certainty, conclude, there are one-hundred thousand Negroes purchased and brought on board our ships yearly from the coast of Africa."[123]

The *Liverpool Memorandum Book* provided the list of names and activities of 135 merchants in London and 157 in Bristol, "whereas Their Trade to Africa is not so extensive as the Merchants of Liverpool." The *Liverpool Memorandum Book* also listed 12 men involved in the slave trade who had been mayor of Liverpool from 1754 to 1788.[124] Benezet's great achievement in using the *Liverpool Memorandum Book* was that existing estimates of the numbers of ships involved underestimated the extent of the trade.[125] Although he had no access to the minutes of the Company of Merchants or commercial records later used by Clarkson with details on merchants trading to Africa, Benezet did read commercial records on the Liverpool trade.[126] In 1750 there was also published *A List of the Company of Merchants* trading to Africa, as well as "An Act for extending and improving the trade to Africa belonging to Liverpool."[127] By the time the list was published, the port city had for the previous ten years overtaken both London and Bristol as the country's most important slave-trading port.[128] If Benezet had seen this list, it would only have confirmed his belief that Liverpool was indeed a central point of the international slave trade.[129]

Benezet confirmed the figures he obtained from the *Liverpool Memorandum Book* and in Anderson's *History of Trade and Commerce* "that England supplies her American colonies with Negro slaves, amounting in number to about one hundred thousand every year."[130] In *Two Dialogues in the Man Trade,* James Philmore gave even higher yearly figures for an earlier period. In his debate with a Mr. Allcraft, Philmore cited William Snelgrave, who wrote that it was "proved before the commissioners of trade" that in 1725 "200 slave trade ships went to the coast of Guinea" with what he estimated were "50,000 slaves traded yearly, of whom a tenth of them die upon the voyage." Comparing Benezet's, Cugoano's, Snelgrave's, and Philmore's figures with those of Philip Curtin and earlier ones of Elizabeth Donnan, we find a quite similar estimation.[131]

The highest honor paid to Benezet was the continued use by others of the many materials that he published and circulated. Thomas Clarkson entered Cambridge University in 1779 intending to become a clergyman. Although his antislavery activities began after Benezet's death, he was in many ways his closest intellectual descendant, just as it might be said that Wesley was Benezet's principal spiritual heir. Clarkson said that "[Anthony Benezet] did not write for America only, but for Europe also, and endeavored to spread a knowledge and hatred of the traffic through the great society of the world." He described his debt to Benezet in his *History of the Abolition of the Slave Trade*: "Anthony Benezet may be considered as one of the most zealous, vigilant, and active advocates, which the cause of the oppressed Africans ever had."[132]

Clarkson's antislavery work began while he was a student at Cambridge, in 1785, when he entered an essay contest sponsored by the university. Richard Roberts, the school vice chancellor, proposed the question *Anne liceat invitos in servitutem dare?* Is it lawful to make slaves of others against their will? Roberts had been moved by the *Zong* case, which Clarkson described in his essay as "that cruel and disgraceful case, in the summer of 1781, when 132 negroes, in their passage to the colonies, were thrown into the sea alive, to defraud the underwriters."[133] Clarkson won the essay prize. A few years later Clarkson wrote *An Essay on the Impolicy of the Slave Trade.*[134]

Clarkson had read that Lord Chief Justice Mansfield ruled in favor of the insurance company, stating that a "higher law applies to this very shocking case" and that "the slaves could not be treated simply as merchandise." In preparing for the essay Clarkson collected a voluminous amount of information about the slave trade. Dismayed and overwhelmed by his slow progress, Clarkson later wrote in his *History of Abolition* that he was "determined, however to make the best use of my time [he was wholly ignorant of the subject]. I got access to the manuscript papers of a deceased friend, who had been in the trade. I was acquainted also with several officers who had been in the West Indies, and from these I gained something." Still it was not until he discovered the works of Anthony Benezet that he found his bearings. Like Sharp, Equiano, Cugoano, Wesley, and countless others, Clarkson remembered the exact time and place he first discovered Benezet. Reflecting in wonder and awe, he wrote, "But I still felt myself at a loss for materials, and I did not know where to get them; when going by accident into a friend's house, I took up a newspaper then lying on his table. One of the articles which attracted my notice, an advertisement of Anthony Benezet's *Historical Account of Guinea.*" He added, "I soon left my friend and his paper, and to lose no time hastened to London to buy it. In this precious book I found almost all I wanted. I obtained by means of it, knowledge of, and gained access to, the great authorities of Adanson, Moore, Barbot and others."[135]

Clarkson made it a point to follow Benezet's practice of citing the works of such philosophers as David Hume and Adam Smith. In *An Essay on the Impolicy of the African Slave Trade, in Two Parts*, he also employed the methods of Benezet, Woolman, and Wesley in showing the effects of slavery on whites. And following the example of the leaders of the first generation, Clarkson adopted the tactic of petitioning leading civic authorities. As James Walvin has noted, "The abolitionist cause not only transformed petitioning into a major and qualitatively new political phenomenon, but it established petitioning and local activity needed to raise a petition, as the central tactic to extra-parliamentary politics in subsequent decades."[136] Benezet and Wesley certainly did not invent petitioning, but they revolutionized its use through the antislavery movement.

Clarkson visited the docks in Liverpool and Bristol, speaking with the slaves and the whites who worked aboard the slave-trading vessels. He also helped create what Benezet had dreamed about: a network that was to extend the organizational center beyond the Quakers and to include other religious bodies, as well as statesmen and "reformed" slave dealers like

TABLE 4. COMPARATIVE MORTALITY OF SAILORS AND SLAVES, 1766–1780

	Year	Number of Sailors	Number of Sailors Who Died	Number of Slaves	Number of Slaves Who Died
Royal Charlotte	1766	17	0	120	3
Royal Charlotte	1767	18	0	455	10
Molly	1769	13	7	105	50
Ferret	1770	13	3	105	5
Surrey	1771	25	4	255	10
Three Friends	1773	12	2	144	8
Venus	1775	22	2	321	10
Harriet	1776	18	0	277	7
Camden	1780	65	4	580	51
TOTAL		203	22	2,362	154

Based on statistics in Thomas Clarkson, *An Essay on the Impolicy of the African Slave Trade, in Two Parts* (London, 1798). Clarkson took figures from muster rolls and ship inventory at Crestar House.

TABLE 5. DEATHS AMONG GUINEA SEAMEN BOUND FROM PORTS AT LIVERPOOL AND BRISTOL, SEPTEMBER 1784–JANUARY 5, 1790

	Number of Vessels	Number of Sailors in Original Crews	Number Who Died	Number Brought Home
1784–85	74	2,915	615	1,279
1785–86	62	2,163	436	944
1786–87	66	2,136	433	1,073
1787–88	68	2,422	623	1,114
1788–January 5, 1790	80	26,627	536	1,350
TOTAL	350	12,263	2,643	5,760

Based on statistics in Thomas Clarkson, *An Essay on the Impolicy of the African Slave Trade, in Two Parts* (London, 1798). Clarkson took figures from muster rolls and ship inventory at Crestar House.

John Newton. Organizationally more like John Woolman than Benezet, between 1787 and 1794 Clarkson logged some 35,000 miles throughout Britain (and France) helping establish abolition committees.

He dramatically expanded Benezet's use of statistics in showing the rising death rate among white sailors working in the slave trade. In doing so, he went one step further by using commercial records to show its horrors. He estimated that between September 1784 and January 1790, 1,950 of the 5,000 white seamen (39 percent) who went to sea in the slave trade were lost (Tables 4 and 5). Clarkson summarized his findings quite simply. He wrote, " First: Every vessel that sails from the port of Liverpool to the coast of Africa, loses on an average more than seven of her crew, or a fifth of the whole number employed. Secondly: Every vessel from the port of Bristol loses on the average nearly nine, or almost a fourth of the whole crew. Thirdly: Every vessel from the port of London loses more than eight, and between a fourth and a fifth of the whole complement of her men." He calculated that each ship "may be said to lose more than eight of her crew," and all told "between a forth and a fifth, may be said to perish." He then concluded "that in 1786, eleven hundred and twenty-five seamen will be found upon the dead list, in consequence of this execrable trade."[137]

Just as Benezet appealed to fears of the moral decay of whites caused by slavery, Clarkson put the debate in terms of the loss of white lives (as Adam Smith did when relating the loss of income for those at the lower rungs of the British economic ladder), which was a powerful force in the hands of the abolitionists.[138] Here again the triangular route of antislavery thought was developed and transmitted throughout the Atlantic. Clarkson took Benezet's moral appeal and put the debate in cold, hard numbers based on dead white bodies. His appeal had a tremendous effect on the minds of whites in America and Europe.

In 1782, the year before the signing of the peace between the Americans and the British, the American Quakers began writing to those in Britain to step up their campaign against slavery. Just as the Philadelphia Quakers were making plans to revise their abolition society, their British counterparts in June 1783 appointed a committee of twenty-three to study and make recommendations regarding the slave trade and their work.[139] In the ensuing years the committee and Quaker abolitionists spent most of their time publishing and distributing anti–slave trade tracts. In 1783 two British Quakers, Joseph Woods, who had written opposing Hume's ideas on slavery and blacks, and John Lloyd, who penned an essay using Adam Smith's arguments against slavery, began drafting an essay titled *The Case of Our Fellow Creatures, the Oppressed Africans, Respectfully Recommended to the Serious Consideration of the Legislature of Great Britain by the People Called Quakers,* which was published in 1784. Although published anonymously, the Friends' Overseers of the Press Committee approved it, and two thousand copies were immediately printed. In May of the following year, the same month that Benezet died, parliamentary elections were held in Britain. Eleven thousand copies of *The Case of Our Fellow Creatures* were printed and distributed to the royal family, cabinet ministers, and members of the new Parliament and throughout British society.[140] At the urging of Sharp and others, two thousand copies of *The Case of Our Fellow Creatures* were printed in November 1783 and another ten thousand in June 1784. Because the tract was written in tones similar to Benezet's, it was erroneously attributed to him, although the last page in the publication reads "signed by the order of the meeting for sufferings, London, the 28th day of the 11th month, 1783, by

John Ady, V Clerk of the Meeting." The end page contained an advertisement for Benezet's *A Caution and a Warning to Great Britain,* at a cost of
sixpence.[141] Benezet next urged the British Friends to publish a London
edition of the New Jersey Quaker David Cooper's *A Serious Address to the
Rulers of America* (1783). The next year they published John Woods's
Thoughts on the Slavery of Negroes and the second London edition of Benezet's *A Caution and a Warning* along with James Ramsay's *Essays on the Treatment and Conversion of African Slaves in the Sugar Colonies.* These pamphlets
marked a new stage in Quaker and British antislavery efforts.[142] The situation, however, changed dramatically when Clarkson published his works.

The transatlantic exchange of letters and ideas set the stage for the development of a transatlantic antislavery network. This exchange first united
Benezet and Sharp but soon also brought in Rush, Wesley, and Clarkson.
Their correspondence led to the signings of hundreds of thousands of petitions and to the circulation of thousands of pamphlets. The efforts led
these men to create abolition societies first in Philadelphia, then throughout Britain, the mainland colonies of America, and later France.

Over time these activities had a direct, personal impact on the political
process. The political leader William Wilberforce first made his stand
against slavery unequivocal at a dinner party attended by Clarkson and others.[143] Then on May 22, 1787, a group of twelve men, including William
Dillwyn and the non-Quakers Clarkson and Sharp, formed the Society
(Committee) for Effecting the Abolition of the Slave Trade, commonly
called the London Abolition Committee. Clarkson wrote of their choice of
the first leader of the committee: Granville Sharp "stands at the head of
the list and who, as the father of the cause in England, was called to chair
[and] may be considered as representing the first class of forerunners and
coadjutors."[144] Wilberforce, like Clarkson a former Cambridge student,
later became its honorific leader. Clarkson later wrote with pride, "I was
particularly attentive to Mr. Wilberforce, whom I found daily becoming
more interested in the fate of Africa."[145] One of the committee's initial acts
was to republish and to distribute 1,500 copies of Benezet's *Some Historical
Account of Guinea,* edited by George Harrison and William Dillwyn. In 1788
alone the committee sent thousands of antislavery petitions to the House
of Commons.[146]

Shortly before the parliamentary debates on slavery Wesley had concluded a letter to Wilberforce with a prayer for the parliamentary leader
and in all likelihood copies of his works and those of Benezet.[147] Although
Wilberforce's motion to abolish the slave trade was defeated, he would
again raise the question the next year. Wesley died soon after he addressed
the letter to Wilberforce.[148]

Perhaps the most enduring tribute to the legacy of Benezet occurred in
the House of Commons in "The Debate on a Motion for the Abolition of

the Slave Trade, 2nd April 1792, Wilberforce and Pitt Present." Wilberforce, the British politician and philanthropist, had close ties to the parliamentary leader William Pitt the Younger (1759–1806). In addition to an
association with Clarkson, Wilberforce had visited with John Wesley in 1789
and referred to him as a "fine old fellow." Wesley wrote of the meeting,
"We had an agreeable and useful conversation. What a blessing it is to Mr.
Pitt to have such a friend as this."[149] The House of Commons had had
extensive debates in 1791, in which Wilberforce took the lead and proposed a motion to introduce an abolition bill. The Parliamentary records
show that "Mr. Wilberforce's motion, after a debate of two days, was nega-
tived by a majority of 163 to 88."[150]

The 1792 parliamentary records show "a great number of Petitions were
presented praying for the Abolition of the slave trade." Addressing the
members, Wilberforce said,

It is not only that I make this remark, or the friends of the Abolition of the Slave
Trade; it was Mr. Long, the historian of Jamaica; he pointed out the abuse, he specified the many evils which flowed from it; he stated that the insurrections had chiefly
been found to break out among the slaves of Absentee proprietors; he regretted
that after the Manager had an interest altogether distinct from that of the Owner;
that it was frequently his object to make large crops of sugar, regardless of the cruelties to be exercised on the Slaves, or the ruinous load of expense to be incurred, in
purchasing new Slaves, to replace such as should be worn out by excessive labor.[151]

Wilberforce quoted from Clarkson's *An Essay on the Impolicy of the African
Slave Trade.* "He asserted as a result of a long and laborious inquiry, that of
the sailors employed in the African trade between a fifth and a sixth actually died, and that they seldom brought more than one half of their crews
home from slaver voyages." Wilberforce, still quoting from Clarkson, told
the Parliament that it "appeared that of 12,263 persons, the number of the
original crews, there had died, 2,643."[152]

Wilberforce next quoted "Mr. Moore, an author of credit, and himself
seven years factor to the African Company." Wilberforce took the quotation not from Moore directly but indirectly from Anthony Benezet's *Some
Historical Account of Guinea.*[153] He then said, "Since the trade had been
used, all punishments are changed into slavery." Later, he came back to
the words of Benezet, "Never before was another system so big with wickedness." The speech turned to the Dutch factor Bosman, again by way of
Benezet, noting "that the discerning natives account it their greatest
unhappiness that they were ever visited by the Europeans."[154] Wilberforce,
moving to *A Caution and a Warning to Great Britain,* shifted from Bosman to
Brüe: "Wherever Christians come, they come with a sword, a gun, powder
and a ball."[155]

Later in his speech Wilberforce revisited Brüe by way of Wesley and
Benezet. Wilberforce declared, "The European settlers according to Brüe

are far from desiring to act as Peacemakers among them. It would be too costly to their interest: for the only object of their wars is to carry off slaves." Wilberforce summed up his argument in words that have the ring of Benezet: "Oh! Sir, for their own happiness it were to have been wished, that these poor creatures had not been possessed of human feelings! But they have shown the contrary, by their thousand different proofs."[156] Wilberforce ended forcefully: "Thus, Sir, it appears that, leaving Africa wholly out of the question, Justice and Humanity would dictate to us Abolition of the Slave Trade in the shortest terms, as the only sure expedient for bringing the slaves into that state of comfort wherein it must be our common wish to see them placed; that in the Abolition alone can the Islands find security, and that this measure is enforced on us by the principals of sound policy, and a regard to the political interests of the British empire."[157] Pitt closed the proceedings, and Wilberforce offered a motion that proved to be one of the greatest moments in the history of the fight against slavery and the slave trade: "That it is the opinion of this committee, that the trade carried on by British Subjects, for the purpose of obtaining Slaves on the coast of Africa, ought to be abolished."[158]

The proceedings then show that "were this motion carried, Mr. Wilberforce gave notice that he intended to follow up by another." And with this Wilberforce proclaimed, "That the Chairman be directed to move the House for leave to bringing in a bill for the Abolition of the Slave Trade."[159] Pitt closed the debates. So began the end of the English slave trade.[160] This movement led next to the abolition of slavery in England in 1807–1808. In 1833 five thousand petitions were handed to Parliament containing one-and-a-half million signatures. This campaign was led by the Society for the Mitigation and Gradual Abolition of Slavery, which was formed in 1823 with Wilberforce, Clarkson, and others at its head. Wilberforce's poor health caused him to retire from the Parliament in 1825, one month before Parliament passed the Slavery Abolition Act.[161] Their efforts and petitions led to the final passage of the British Emancipation Act, which provided that as of August 1, 1834, slavery would cease to exist in the British colonies.

Chapter 7

Benezet and the Development of the Antislavery Movement in France

Anthony Benezet had a powerful influence on the leaders of the French antislavery movement. Following the lead of Abbé Henri-Baptiste Grégoire, French writers considered Benezet to be one of their own. Grégoire dedicated his *Enquiry Concerning the Intellectual and Moral Facilities, and Literature of Negroes* "to all those men who have had the courage to lead the cause of the unhappy blacks and mulattoes, whether by the publication of their works, or by discussion in the national assemblies, &c."[1] Grégoire did not list Benezet among the dozen Americans—such as Franklin and Rush—but with the roughly fifty Frenchmen. Here Benezet's name is placed alongside those of the founders of the Société des Amis des Noirs, like Brissot, Condorcet, Lafayette, and the Abbé Raynal.

In the text itself Grégoire argued that great men, such as Samuel Pufendorf, are often omitted by history. He added his own choice to the list: "And the good Quaker Benezet, born at St. Quentin, the friend of all men, the defender of the oppressed, who during his whole life, combated slavery by reason, religion and example." He added, "His name is not mentioned by our compilers of dictionaries, but Benjamin Rush and a number of English and Americans, have at least repaired this omission."[2]

From the French perspective Benezet's writings belonged to a growing body of *littérature négrophile,* literature written about Africa or the black presence in Europe. Among those works were Abbé Prévost's *Le Pour et contre* (1733), Gabriel Mailhol's *Le Philosophe nègre* (1764), Jean-François Saint-Lambert's *Ziméo* (1769), and Jean-François Butini's *Lettres africaines, ou Histoire de Phédima et d'Abensur* (1771). In addition, French translations of such works as Aphra Behn's *Oroonoko* came out between 1745 and 1799.[3] Benezet's work thus fit into a larger pattern. A French edition of *A Caution and a Warning to Great Britain* appeared as early as 1767; a later work, *A Short Account of That Part of Africa, Inhabited by the Negroes,* was also published in Paris in 1767 and republished in 1788, the year of the founding of the Société des Amis des Noirs.[4] The extent to which these works were read in France in their first years of publication remains unclear, but the textual evidence strongly suggests that such French authors as Raynal, Grégoire, and the *encyclopédistes* read them.[5]

The intellectual connection between Benezet and France began with Guillaume-Thomas Raynal's *Histoire philosophique et politique, des établissements et du commerce des Européens dans les deux Indes.* Known as *L'Histoire des deux Indes* and initially published in 1770, the book gained Raynal a reputation both in France and abroad as a leading voice among antislavery intellectuals.[6] Raynal's comments on Quakers followed earlier French writings about them. Sue Peabody, a historian of France, tells us that the first French abolitionist, Henrion de Pansy, spoke of the role of some Pennsylvania Quakers in freeing their slaves.[7] Voltaire, in his *Letters on the Quakers* (1733), *Lettres philosophiques* (1734), and *Traité sur la tolérance* (1763), praised the virtue and tolerance that guided Quaker attitudes against slavery.[8] As we know, Voltaire had been an associate of Benezet's father when they both lived in exile in England; he took English lessons at the same school that Anthony Benezet attended. Like Voltaire, in *L'Histoire des deux Indes* Raynal praised the Quakers for setting an example that he considered extraordinary in "the epoch of the history of the religions of humanity." Raynal included the story of a Quaker, no doubt Benjamin Lay, who rose in meeting to deliver a powerful speech condemning slavery. Raynal most likely acquired this anecdote from a letter written by Benjamin Rush (August 30, 1769), later published in *Ephémérides du citoyen.*[9]

As Sue Peabody has demonstrated, African slavery created many ambiguities and uncertainties in France because of the "freedom principle," which proclaimed that "there are no slaves in France" and that "a slave who sets foot on French soil becomes free."[10] The legal situation of a slave in France itself was as confused as it would be in Britain after the Somerset case. Raynal illustrated the ambiguities: on the one hand he made a cry for slave insurrection; on the other hand he advocated the strengthening of colonial power.

The relationship between Raynal and Benezet offers an excellent look into the exchange of ideas across the Atlantic.[11] Both found ways to incorporate the competing ideas of the day with empirical data collected from a large array of sources. Some, like Thomas Paine and Benjamin Franklin, regarded Raynal's work as encyclopedic, while others, like Thomas Jefferson, thought his ideas arrogant and ignorant and expressed extreme reservations. Jefferson wrote *Notes on the State of Virginia* (1781) partially in response to men like Raynal. As Grégoire stated, "Jefferson furnishes arms against himself in his answer to Raynal, who reproaches America for not having produced one celebrated man. When we shall have existed, says this learned American as a nation, as long as the Greeks before they had a Homer, the Romans a Virgil, or the French a Racine, there will be room for astonishment. We may in like manner say, that when the negroes shall have existed in a state of civilization as long as the inhabitants of the United States, without having introduced such men as Franklin, Washington, Rush

. . . there will be reason for believing that among them there is a total absence of genius."[12]

Raynal and Benezet

Raynal found a great American admirer in Benezet.[13] Conversely, Benezet saw in Raynal's oppositional stance to slavery many ideas that reflected his own.[14] He found intellectual support in *L'Histoire*'s critique of the idea that the supposed intellectual inferiority of blacks justified slavery; Raynal's philosophical ideas—and they were purely philosophical because, unlike Benezet, Raynal had no real experience with blacks—thus buttressed Benezet's own experience teaching black children and speaking with their parents and in many cases teaching these parents and other adults at his night school.[15] In 1781 and 1782 Benezet translated an extract from *L'Histoire* and published it with his introduction to *Short Observations on Slavery, Introductory Remarks to Some Extracts from the Writing of the Abbé Raynal on That Important Subject,* his last major work before his death in 1784.[16] Here he reiterated the principles of the Declaration of Independence, then proceeded to argue that slavery violated these very principles. In his effort "to assist in eradicating the deep rooted prejudice which an education amongst Slaves have planted in many minds," he used excerpts from "that celebrated Philosopher and friend to Mankind," Raynal.[17] Over time *L'Histoire* became a classic in both private and semipublic libraries.[18] Although Voltaire remained the most widely read *philosophe* in North America, Raynal also grew to prominent stature.

L'Histoire offered an extensive historical and philosophical analysis of European expansion overseas. Raynal drew on a vast network of social relations and personal contacts to gather adequate information for this expansive work.[19] These contacts allowed him access to unedited administrative documents concerning slavery.[20] He also employed questionnaires—something that Condorcet also did—and sent them to important figures. One questionnaire was delivered, via Benjamin Franklin, to the American Philosophical Society of Philadelphia and another to Edmund Burke.

Raynal, like Benezet, relied on a variety of sources, including his contemporaries, for his factual information, which underlined the philosophical underpinning of *L'Histoire*.[21] As collaborative works, many eighteenth-century pieces took the liberty of reproducing the original thoughts, if not the exact wording, of other writers without giving credit. (See Chapter 6 concerning John Wesley's use of the works of Benezet.) In the case of *L'Histoire des deux Indes* this stylistic peculiarity coupled with a reasonable fear of arrest initially caused Raynal to identify himself only as an editor.[22]

Denis Diderot is consistently named as one of Raynal's most influential collaborators.[23] Notably some attribute the more controversial passages of

L'Histoire to the influence, if not the direct authorship, of Diderot. Specifically Diderot is believed to have worked on the passages dealing with slavery. E. D. Seeber offers an example of an extract that Diderot published independently of Raynal in 1772 but which also appeared in *L'Histoire*: "The true notion of property entails the law of customs and of abuse, never may a man be the property of a sovereign, a child the property of a father, the woman the property of a husband, a domestic the property of a master, a negro the property of a colonist. There cannot exist, therefore, a slave, not even by the right of conquest, even less so by way of sale and purchase."[24] Raynal's inconsistencies would lead to a controversial aspect of his philosophy. How could he simultaneously support slave insurrections and French colonialism? Just as *L'Histoire* condemned slavery on the basis of common humanity, it lamented the missed opportunities of Europeans in Africa. In a chapter describing the move of the French into Madagascar, Raynal offers these words: "What glory it would be for France to raise a numerous people from the horrors of barbarism; to give them decent manners, a well regulated policy; wife laws, a beneficent religion; to introduce them to the agreeable as well as the useful arts, and to raise them to the rank of civilized and enlightened nations."[25] Here Raynal upheld his ideas; he called for both the emancipation of slaves and the imposition of European civilization on African societies.

Although Raynal published these indictments of slavery under his own name, Seeber doubts that Raynal would have whole-heartedly condemned slavery. The revolutionary content of the passages on slavery in *L'Histoire* have drawn a particularly close examination of Raynal's sources.[26] After the outbreak of the French Revolution critics of Raynal began to name and investigate possible collaborators, such as Diderot, Jean de Pechméja, Saint-Lambert, Tronchin Dubreuil, Naigeon, and d'Holbach.[27]

That is not to say that *L'Histoire* lost its radical stance through revision. The following passage remained in the third edition as testimony to a resolute antislavery position: "These enterprises are so many indicators of the impending storm, and the Negroes only want a chief, sufficiently courageous to lead them to vengeance and slaughter. Where is this great man to be found, whom nature perhaps, owes to the honor of the human species? Where is the new Spartacus, who will not find a Crassus?"[28]

Raynal clearly believed that a black man was capable to lead, either through violence or through reason.[29] Because "French abolitionists did not make French participation in the slave trade a matter of intense investigation," they were, as Daniel Resnick believes, "unable to develop cutting arguments that only knowledge of that trade could produce."[30] Unlike Adam Smith, who made economic calculations about the loss of actual profits in his arguments against slavery, or Thomas Clarkson, who used the loss of white British sailors aboard slave-trading vessels as a rallying cry for abolitionists, the French did not employ such methods. Yet the records reveal that on slaving ships leaving the port of Nantes between 1748 and 1792, one of six crewmen were lost during the voyages, the same percentage Clarkson found among the English. French abolitionists also reprinted representations of the slave ship, the *Brooks*, which had been presented by Thomas Clarkson at the hearings of the British Privy Council in 1788.[31]

Before American independence only the intellectual elite in North America were aware of Raynal.[32] Raynal's work had first appeared in English as an extract published in 1775. One of the first full English translations of the volume appeared in Edinburgh in 1776; knowledge of his book spread in America starting in roughly 1780–81.

David Brion Davis acknowledges the debt owed to the Scotsman George Wallace by the French *Enyclopédistes,* most notably Chevalier Louis de Jaucourt. His article "Traite des Nègres" in the 1765 *Encyclopédie* borrowed heavily from Wallace's *Systems of the Principles of the Laws of Scotland.* Davis observed, "Given the obscurity of Wallace's tome, one is tempted to ask whether de Jaucourt lifted the antislavery arguments from Benezet's *A Short Account of Africa* . . . a pamphlet published in Philadelphia in 1762." De Jaucourt translated passages from Wallace for *L'Encyclopédie* and seems to have also translated passages from Benezet. "It would be a nice irony of international communication," Davis muses, "if Montesquieu's influence, radicalized by George Wallace, returned to the *Encyclopédie* by way of an American publication." He concluded, "Unfortunately, textual discrepancies rule out this possibility."[33]

Davis reached this conclusion because "Benezet omitted a few lines from Wallace which de Jaucourt translated,"[34] but that fact hardly excludes the likely possibility that de Jaucourt reached Wallace through Benezet. Moreover, de Jaucourt's other articles, such as the one on Guinea, indicate that he knew Benezet's descriptions of Africa. Davis does admit that "Benezet unlike de Jaucourt, identified Wallace as the author of the doctrine that 'everyone of those unfortunate men, who are pretended to be slaves, has a right to be declared free, for he never lost his liberty.'"[35]

However else Wallace's work may have reached France, it did travel via Benezet. Throughout the eighteenth century antislavery ideas crossed the Atlantic with a rapid fluidity, augmented by the fact that authors rarely cited those whose ideas they borrowed; moreover, virtually all of those involved in the antislavery cause encouraged their peers to borrow in this way. Davis and other historians recognize that Benezet served as an indirect source for the *Ephémérides du citoyen, ou Bibliothèque raisonnée des sciences morales et politiques* (1765–72), the publication that helped spread awareness in France of Quaker antislavery activity.[36] The *Ephémérides du citoyen* was described by its founders as "a critical and moral periodical work by and large in the taste of the English Spectator."[37] It was the official organ of the Physiocrats, French economic and poltical theorists, and works printed in the *London Chronicle* often appeared in the journal. It was a favorite of Benjamin Franklin during his Paris years.[38]

Benezet tried many times to contact Raynal, first by sending letters through Benjamin Franklin.[39] Finally through Samuel Powell Griffiths a letter that Benezet had written on July 16, 1781, reached Raynal. In the letter Benezet asserted to "My Friend Abbé Raynal,"

From the idea which I conceived of the justice, and generosity of thy sentiments, I took the liberty of writing to thee about seven or eight months past under cover of my friend Benjamin Franklin. . . . Above all, my dear friend, let us represent to our compatriots the abominable iniquity of the Guinea trade. Let us put to the blush the pretended disciples of the benign Savior of the World, for the encouragement given to the unhappy Africans in invading the liberty of their own brethren. Let us rise, and rise with energy against the corruption introduced into the principles and manners of the buyers and owners of slaves, by a conduct so contrary to humanity, reason and religion.[40]

While expressing his sense of solidarity with the cause he believed he shared with Raynal, Benezet took an unusually distinct political stance: "How desirable is it that Louis XVI, whose virtues and good dispositions have been nobly praised, would set an example to the other potentates of Europe, by forbidding his subjects to be concerned in a traffick so evil in itself, and so corrupt in its consequences, and that he would also issue out ordinances, in favour of such of the Negroes who now are slaves in his dominions."[41]

Raynal wrote to Benezet from Brussels six months later, but Benezet did not receive the letter until June 1782. Raynal thanked the Quaker for the letters and pamphlets. He told him, "All your letters have miscarried; happily, I received that of the sixteenth of July, 1781, with the pamphlets filled with light and sensibility, which accompany it. Never was any present more agreeable to me. My satisfaction was equal to the respect I have always had for the society of the Quakers." He did not respond to Benezet's political overtones and concluded, "May it please Heaven to cause all nations to adopt their principles; men would then be happy, and the globe not stained with blood. Let us join in our supplications to the Supreme Being, that He may unite us in the bonds of a tender and unalterable charity."[42]

Despite Benezet's correspondence with Raynal in 1781 and the French editions of Benezet's works, historian David Brion Davis concludes that the Quaker was not well-known in France until the late 1780s.[43] Yet his pamphlets had been translated in 1767, and he was sufficiently well-known that an author like J. Hector St. John de Crèvecoeur wrote specifically about Benezet in his section on the role of the Quakers in the fight against slavery. Other Frenchmen followed Crèvecoeur's lead.

Brissot, Chastellux, and Crèvecoeur

In 1787 Jacques-Pierre Brissot de Warville and Etienne Clavière, who were to become leading members of the Société des Amis des Noirs, expressed hope that the work done by Anthony Benezet, would aid their cause in Europe. They jointly wrote, "Benezet, that distinguished Quaker, that apostle of humanity, traverses all of the United States, preaching everywhere for the liberty of Negros. He first converted his brothers. His brothers will in turn convert all the other sects, all the states. Those who are backward will be ashamed by their barbarity and perhaps the day is not far when all Europeans, ashamed of their scandalous trade, will renounce it. That is what the example of a single American will produce!"[44] The Société des Amis des Noirs was founded a year later in 1788 in Paris. Its charter members, along with Brissot and Clavière, were "Mirabeau, Cerisier, Carra, and Duchesnay. They were a part of a larger group of 141 enrolled by the beginning of 1789, the better known of whom included Lafayette, Condorcet, the Duke de la Rochefoucauld, Pétion and Abbé Grégoire."[45]

Brissot served as the president of the Société in 1790–91. His *Nouveau Voyage dans les Etats-Unis de l'Amérique septentrionale* (*New Travels in the United States;* 3 volumes) was first published in 1791. Brissot's outlook on America was much too optimistic for the realities of the time, concerning not just the fate of blacks but also the ability of the American revolutionaries to see blacks as equal human beings. In his *An Oration upon the Necessity of Establishing at Paris, a Society to Promote the Abolition of the Slave Trade and Slavery of the Negroes,* published in Philadelphia in 1788, he wrote, "Such is the empire of reason, when it unfolds itself under the auspices of liberty; that scarcely was the independence of the United States confirmed, than the question concerning slavery of the blacks was agitated in the southern states, than their cause was embraced there, defended with warmth by the best geniuses, by the most respected personages."[46] In his *New Travels,* Brissot wrote of the Philadelphia abolitionists, "How great was their joy when they learned that a society similar to theirs was being formed in Paris," a city known for "its influence over a vast kingdom and over almost all the states of Europe!" He continued, "How quickly did they publish this news in all their gazettes and circulate everywhere the translation of the first speech read before the Paris society." In speaking of Lafayette he added, "How great was their joy when they saw on a list of members of that society a name dear to their hearts, one which they pronounce only with affection." Brissot added that the antislavery proponents in America felt that "if it united with the London society, then the information spread by these two groups on the slave trade and its unprofitable infamy would enlighten governments and persuade them to suppress the traffic."[47] Taking another cue from Benezet, Brissot wrote of actually visiting with blacks, in this case in a house of correction.[48] Brissot noted the contradictions among Americans, just as with the French who loved the by-products of slavery—"sugar and coffee." And he praised American antislavery forces who showed support not only with "words and gestures" but also "appointed committees to assist me in my work and opened their archives to me."[49]

Brissot dedicated his Letter 21 to the "Schools for Negroes in Philadelphia—American Authors who have written in defense of slavery." He described Benezet's early life, his exile from France, his conversion to Quakerism, and his role as a teacher of blacks: "All of his time was devoted to public education, to the relief of the poor, and to the defense of the Negro slaves." Brissot added, "Benezet's philanthropy was of a universal sort not very common at that time."[50] Of Benezet he wrote to his fellow Frenchmen, "Whatever time he did not devote to teaching he spent gathering all the passages he could find that could be used against slavery and the slave trade." He informed them of Benezet's treatises, which "were instrumental in converting his brethren to his view and winning them over to the abolition of slavery."[51] He also wrote of Benezet's generosity and his leaving a "small fortune" to the establishment of the school, which received the financial support of Friends in London as well as those in Philadelphia. He took special pleasure in the fact that "while at General Mifflin's place I met an old Quaker who said that he took particular pleasure in shaking my hand because I resembled Anthony Benezet," adding "this resemblance was later confirmed by other Quakers. I mention this without vanity for you will recall Chastellux's description of Benezet. But Benezet's eyes were kind and full of humanity."[52] Quaker Warner Mifflin of Delaware observed of Brissot that "like Benezet, he devotes all of his efforts to propagate the ideas of the Quakers on the necessity of a society [in Delaware] for the abolition of the slave trade and of slavery, organized on the model of the Pennsylvania Society."[53] Here he was referring to a meeting held at the Delaware Society for Promoting the Abolition of Slavery and the Relief of Free Blacks and People of Colour Unlawfully Held in Bondage, which was first organized in 1788.[54]

Brissot had two purposes in his praise of Benezet, who had written "how inconsistent is this abhorrent practice, with every idea of Liberty, every principle of humanity."[55] First, he wanted to relate to the French audience the nature of the fight against slavery in America and to show that their countryman was the leader of that fight. Second, he wanted to counter the negative views of the Quakers that Chastellux had given. In combating Chastellux's ideas Brissot wrote, "America owes this useful establishment to Benezet, that same Benezet whom M. Chastellux was not ashamed to ridicule to the imperious applause of those vile sycophants that are spawned by despotism and aristocracy. The life of this extraordinary man should be known to thinking men, that is, to those who respect more the benefactors of humanity than they do the flattered and basely idolized oppressors of mankind." Brissot also visited Benezet's school in Philadelphia. He duly observed that "there appears to be no difference between the powers of memory of a curly head and those with straight hair, and today I have proof of this. I have seen, questioned, and listened to Negro children, some read well, others recited from memory, others did sums quite rapidly." Brissot concluded that it was to Benezet that humanity "owes this useful establishment."[56] Brissot also spent time in England in 1783–84 and had close ties with Quakers. When he returned to France, he ran afoul of the authorities and received letters from Priestley and Wilberforce on his behalf. While back in London for two months, Clarkson and Sharp arranged for him to be inducted into the British antislavery society.

The marquis de Chastellux first published his *Voyages dans l'Amérique Septentrionale* in 1786: an English translation, *Travels in North America in the Years 1780, 1781 and 1782*, came out the same year. Chastellux had great praise for men like George Washington and Thomas Jefferson. But he had harsh words for the Quakers, who he accused of being "smooth tongued, mealy mouthed, Jesuitical and . . . indifferent to the public good," because of their neutralism during the Revolutionary War.[57] Chastellux had also spoken negatively of the American abolitionists and especially so of blacks.

Chastellux, however, did not, as Brissot suggested, ridicule Benezet and on December 9, 1780, he wrote that "this Mr. Benezet rather may be regarded as the model, than as a specimen of the sect of Quakers; wholly occupied with the welfare of mankind." Benezet answered Chastellux: "Friend, I know thou art a man of letters, and a member of the French Academy. The men of letters have written a great many things of late; they have attacked errors and prejudices and, above all intolerance."[58] Benezet apparently had given Chastellux a copy of his *A Short Account of the People Called Quakers*.[59] Still Chastellux was not convinced of the righteousness of the Quakers and concluded that "to whatever sect he belongs, a man burning with zeal and love of humanity is, let there be no doubt to it, a being worthy of respect; but I must confess that it is difficult to bestow upon this sect in general that esteem which cannot be refused to some individuals."[60] Chastellux certainly admired Benezet, but he did not adhere to the Quakers' denunciation of untold individual wealth and pretentiousness. He also felt that some Quakers violated their own rules. While he and Brissot would have deep differences over the Quakers, Benezet was able to unify these two Frenchmen, who took his name to France, just as they did his antislavery appeal.[61]

Brissot was also close to Crèvecoeur, author of *Letters from an American Farmer*. In his "Letter IX, Description of Charles-Town: Thoughts on Slavery; on Physical Evil; A Melancholy Scene," Crèvecoeur described slavery in the colonies. In describing a kidnapping scene, much like one Benezet had written about some years earlier, Crèvecoeur wrote of "the daughter torn from her weeping mother, the child from the wretched parents, the wife from the loving husband; whole families swept away, and brought through storms and tempests, to this rich metropolis! There arranged like horses at a fair, they are branded like cattle and then driven to toil, to starve, and to languish. And for whom must they work? For persons they know not."[62] Crèvecoeur depicted the work of the Quakers in fighting for the abolishment of slavery, praising their efforts to educate blacks, although it is not clear how many blacks he visited. Using a wealth of details he described black slaves among Quakers in Nantucket, who "enjoy their liberty as their masters, they are as well clad and as well fed, in health and sickness, they are tenderly taken care of, they live under the same roof, and are, truly speaking, a part of our families. Many of them are taught to read and write, and are well instructed in the principles of religion."[63] Of course the pictures that Woolman and Benezet had given, and Sandiford before them, were quite different.

Men and women in America and Europe were moved as Crèvecoeur asked, "Is it really true, as I have heard it asserted here, that those blacks are incapable of feeling the spurs of emulation and the cheerful sound of encouragement? By no means; there are a thousand proofs existing of their gratitude and fidelity." The blacks, he told them, had "hearts, in which such noble dispositions can grow, are then like ours, they are susceptible of every generous sentiment, of every useful motive of action, they are capable of receiving lights, of imbibing ideas that would greatly alleviate the weight of their miseries." He asked, "But what methods have in general been made use of to obtain so desirable an end?" He then answered his own question with one word: "none."[64]

In the 1787 French edition Crèvecoeur added a small chapter entitled "Thoughts on the Slavery of the Negroes." In subsequent French editions he inserted a long and endearing eulogy to Benezet, who had died in 1784. Crèvecoeur surely helped substantiate Seeber's observation that Benezet's name "was slow in reaching France, but he was soon to be revered as a second Las Casas" in the late 1780s.[65] No doubt the publication of the French editions of Crèvecoeur's *Letters* in 1783 and the publication of Benezet's *Short Account of the People Called Quakers* in Paris in 1780 and 1783 helped add to the growing knowledge of Benezet among French readers. Benezet's *Some Historical Account of Guinea* (1771) was published in France in 1788 as *Relations historique de la Guinée,* a parallel to the emerging work of the Société des Amis de Noirs. Like Brissot and Benezet, Crèvecoeur expressed optimism that the abolition of slavery was not far off in North America. And similar to the optimism of both Brissot and Benezet, his faith at times proved unfounded. The men who created revolutions in America and in France still wrote beside the slogans "all men are created equal" and "liberté, equalité, fraternité," for whites only.

Condorcet and Grégoire

Marie-Jean-Antoine-Nicolas de Caritat, marquis de Condorcet, was born into an ancient family and originally became known for his brilliance in philosophy and especially mathematics in the 1760s. He wrote one of his first correspondences about slavery in America in a letter to Benjamin Franklin on December 2, 1773. Franklin answered on March 20, 1774. He wrote, "I transmitted your Queries to our Society in Philadelphia where they will be well considered, and full answers will be sent to you." He continued, "As to Qu. 4. The Negroes who are free live among the White People, but are generally improvident and poor. I think they are not deficient in natural Understanding but they have not the Advantage of Education. They make good Musicians."[66]

Condorcet's main contribution to the fight against slavery came in two forms. First, he wrote in 1781 "Reflections on Negro Slavery." He published this under his adopted pseudonym, Dr. Swartz, much as other antislavery writers, such as Benjamin Rush, had done with their early contributions. In this essay Condorcet wrote, "Nature formed you to have the same minds, the same reason, the same virtues as Whites," adding in reference to the French colonies, "I will not do to you [the slaves] the injury of comparing them with you."[67]

Writing the preamble to the *Rules for the Society of the Friends of Negroes* (1788), he asked the public "to understand the reasons for the formation of the Society for the Friends of Negroes[;] we simply think for a moment about the negro slave trade and trace its development through to the present, when its victims are groaning under the yoke of slavery."[68] Internationalizing the struggle as Benezet had done before him, he argued that "the combination of mankind suffering in one corner of the world while greed and cruelty are encouraged in the other is bound to produce horrific scenes, since the laws of justice are infringed by all nations which are engaged in the Negro slave trade or who benefit from their slavery."[69] In praise of the Quakers in America, the preamble paid tribute to abolition societies that the Quakers helped start and their efforts in getting certain states to end the importation of slaves.[70]

Condorcet's antislavery positions helped him develop part two of the Declaration of Rights, in which he wrote the sections delineating personal freedoms. In the most important section on "Equality" he argued that "men have joined together in society in order to preserve their natural rights, and these rights are the same for all. Society must therefore ensure that everyone has an equal enjoyment of all these rights. Any social institution which gives an individual or a body of men an advantage of which others are deprived therefore violates the rights of natural equality."[71] One of Condorcet's key allies in the quest for equality across races was Abbé Henri-Baptiste Grégoire. Born to a noble family, he entered the cavalry as a youth.

Later he entered the priesthood. Like Benezet, who first championed the rights of his own Huguenot people and later those of the enslaved Africans, Acadians, and Native Americans, Grégoire championed the cause of the oppressed. His earliest writings were in favor of the oppressed Jewish people in France. According to the historian Graham Hodges, Grégoire "wrote more essays arguing for assimilating and noted the moral, intellectual and social progress made by acculturated Jews. Similar arguments appeared later in his work on Africans."[72]

Grégoire made his most enduring contribution against both slavery and the treatment of blacks with the publication of *An Enquiry Concerning the Intellectual and Moral Facilities, and Literature of Negroes.* In the dedication to those who had fought for the "cause of the unhappy blacks and mulattoes," as noted above, he singled out members of ten different national groups. The list reads likes a who's who of the antislavery movement: Frenchmen like Etienne Clavière, the marquis de Condorcet, Brissot, abbé de Sieyès, Léger-Félicité Sonthonax, Jacques Necker, Alexandre Pétion, and the marquis de Lafayette; Englishmen, such as John Newton, Mungo Park, Granville Sharp, and John Wesley, as well as the Scots Frances Hutcheson, George Wallace, and James Foster; and the Americans Franklin, David Humphreys, William Pinkney, and Rush. He listed Benjamin Lay and John Woolman as Englishmen and Benezet as a Frenchman. Grégoire also cited six "Negroes and Mulattoes": "Cugoano, Othello, Phillis Wheatley, Julien Raymond, Ignatius Sancho, Gustavus Vasa."[73]

Grégoire's list also reads like a roster of those influenced by Benezet, who significantly affected Sharp and Wesley, to say nothing of Rush (see Chapter 6); among the Americans few had greater influence over Franklin with respect to the rights of blacks, and Benezet and Woolman collaborated on some key Quaker antislavery documents. As for the French, Brissot and the members of the Société des Amis des Noirs held Benezet in very high regard. Finally, Benezet had a fundamental influence on several black writers: most important was Olaudah Equiano (Gustavus Vasa above), who took virtually everything he said about Africa from Benezet.

Grégoire himself borrowed directly from Benezet, both from the Quaker's own texts and in his use of travel narratives. In *A Short Account of That Part of Africa* (1762) Benezet cited Adanson: "The Simplicity of the Natives, their Dress and manners, revived in my mind, the idea of our first Parents, and I seemed to contemplate the World in its primitive State. . . . they (the Negroes) are generally speaking, very good nature, sociable and obliging."[74] Grégoire changed the sentence structure slightly to write that Adanson "found the Negroe's, very sociable, obliging, humane and hospitable; their amiable simplicity, says he, in this enchanting country, recalled to me the idea of the primitive race of man; I thought I saw the world in its infancy."[75]

Perhaps more than any other Frenchman save Benezet, Grégoire saw the possibilities of the black race once freed. He saw the ability of black people to reason, to think, and to act just as white people did. Just as Benezet read Ukawsaw Gronniosaw's account before composing his final works, Grégoire read both Cugoano and Equiano.[76] In the conclusion of his *An Enquiry* he wrote, "We need not therefore be surprised that no mention is made of negro authors, in our historical dictionaries, which are little else than financing speculations. They contain a pompous list of ephemeral romances, and theatrical pieces long forgotten."[77] He admired both the astronomer Benjamin Banneker and the poet Phillis Wheatley, and quoted the English writer Joseph Nicholls, stating that "among the defenders of slavery, we do not find [says he] one half of the literary merit of Phyllis [*sic*] Wheatley and Francis Williams."[78]

Grégoire had read what François de Barbé-Marbois had written about Wheatley. Barbé-Marbois had asked Jefferson for information on various states of the new nation.[79] Jefferson's response became the *Notes on the State of Virginia*. Barbé-Marbois had read Wheatley's *Poems* in 1779, and one of his queries concerned her. He wrote to his fiancée in Paris on August 28, 1779, that Wheatley was "a negress, born in Africa, brought to Boston at the age of ten, and sold to a citizen of that city." He later added, "At the age of seventeen, [she] published a number of poems in which there is imagination, poetry, and zeal, though no correctness nor order nor interest. I read them with some surprise and zeal." He thought that Wheatley "reminds us that Terrance was her compatriot," adding "almost all of her poetical productions have a religious or moral cast—all breathe a soft and sentimental melancholy."[80]

Jefferson differed with Barbé-Marbois point by point, writing in his famous response, "Comparing them by their faculties of memory, reason, and imagination, it appears to me that they are equal to white, in reason much inferior . . . in imagination they are dull and tasteless and anomalous." Speaking of Wheatley, Jefferson wrote, "Misery is often the parent of the most affecting touches in poetry. Among the Blacks is misery enough, God knows, but not poetry." He saw that "their love is ardent, but it kindles the senses only, not the imagination. Religion, indeed, has produced a Phillis Whatley [*sic*] but it could not produce a poet," as "the compositions published under her name are below the dignity of criticism."[81]

Grégoire sent a copy of his book *De la littérature des Nègres* to Jefferson. Jefferson responded that with his *Notes* he wished for "a complete refutation of the doubts I have myself entertained and expressed on the grade of understanding allotted to [African Americans] by nature." But as Graham Hodges wrote in his introduction to Grégoire's *Enquiry*, in reality "Jefferson derided Grégoire's study as a collection of fantastic tales and raised suspicions about the quality of the talented Blacks."[82] Grégoire also responded to Jefferson's comments on the blacks Ignatius Sancho and Benjamin Banneker.[83]

The Société des Amis des Noirs

As Dorigny and Gainot recounted, "The Société des Amis came into being with an already well delineated foundation."[84] The authors described the Société as *une machine de guerre*, just as Hans Wolpe described Raynal's *L' Histoire* as *une machine de guerre* in its efforts to destroy the legal, moral, and religious foundations of slavery in France.[85] Although Benezet had died in 1784, others continued the international campaign. Sharp wrote to Brissot and Clavière that he had heard of the effort "to establish a committee on the same principles as our [Society for the Effecting the Abolition of the Slave Trade]."[86] By then the British organization patterned after the Americans had among its members Clarkson, Wilberforce, Sharp, and others who would become regular correspondents with the members of the Société.

On March 4, 1788, Brissot announced to members of the Société that he planned to travel to North America, where he would consult with political leaders and abolitionists. He also planned to look for land to purchase for French settlements. At the initial gathering of the Société the argument set forth most forcefully in *Some Observations* carried enormous weight in the emerging antislavery movement. At the March 13, 1788, meeting Brissot gave a presentation to the group about Benezet's work, which he referred to as *Détails historiques de M. Bénézet, sur la Guinée, et sur le commerce des esclaves.*

The projected French translation of this work never appeared, although a meeting held two months later specified that the first two English works on the slave trade that the Société wanted to translate into English were those of Benezet and Clarkson. (The latter's work did, in fact, appear in 1789). Brissot wrote that "the historical details of M. Benezet on Guinea, relative to the trade in Negroes, seem to me even more interesting because they demonstrate in a positive manner that the slavery of these unfortunate beings is not the effect of the arid and harsh nature of their countries, nor of the ferocious character of the inhabitants, but that of a vertiginous accident, and of a foreign corruption introduced in their country by the avarice and cupidity of Europeans." He concluded that "it is the thirst for gold that, having pushed the most advanced nations of our continent to depopulate America, to remain its sole masters, pushes them ceaselessly to depopulate Africa, not to repopulate the New World, but to exploit the treasures it holds."[87]

As Dorigny and Gainot have emphasized, the Société was not a philanthropic society in the sense of the Quaker abolition groups, which ministered to the blacks, or the Paris societies that administered to the needs of the Paris poor. The members of the Société were products of the upper classes in the main, unlike Benezet in America or Sharp in England. Unlike

Benezet or Woolman, Sharp or Clarkson, the members had no firsthand knowledge or contact with blacks either in France or in French colonies. Clarkson went to Paris in 1789 to work with the Société; later in comparing them with the Quaker-led organizations, he recalled, "It is a remarkable circumstance that when the lists [for local correspondence and action] were arranged, the committee, few as they were, found they had friends in no less than 39 counties."[88] No such organizational outreach occurred with the French, and in fact the Société did little to extend its reach beyond intellectuals in France, although its members included several of the leading politicians of 1789–91 (Brissot, Mirabeau, Sieyès, and Lafayette).[89] Its membership fee was set at two louis, equivalent to two months of a laborer's salary, which in itself limited its membership to a very few.

While the Quaker-led abolitionists in North America and the forces around Clarkson and Sharp in England had developed extensive networks, the Société was an organization made up primarily of Parisians and did not have affiliates throughout the country. In fact, Clarkson publicly complained about the low attendance of the Société's meetings and that they would go for five or six weeks without meeting. He compared this with the frequency of the meetings held in England. Of course France, or for that matter England, had no counterparts to Benezet, who not only taught black students but spent portions of each night writing copious letters and petitions, and reading notes or planning for his next projects. And France did not have a Sharp or a Clarkson, who took charge of gatherings and mobilized men. What France did have were men of intellect and letters who relied more on the written word and on their direct influence in politics.

Unlike Woolman in America and Sharp in England, the French antislavery advocates did not seem to visit the French provinces, much less the colonies of the Antilles. In short, their activities to end slavery were not as widespread as were those of their allies in England and the North American colonies; neither were their commitments as deep. The main goal of the Société was not the ending of slavery in itself but the abolition of the slave trade. Slaves would become *serfs de la glèbe*, tied to the land before they would be freed under their gradual emancipation plan. The Société would function as a sort of pressure group, something new in France, operating within the mainstream of French society, hoping that once they explained to the French people their goals, the people would respond favorably.[90] The Société organized itself around committees, one of the most important dealing with research and the dissemination of ideas. They used two methods to get their information. First, they used documents already published in French to avoid translations. Second, by using Raynal's methods of establishing contacts with government officials of all ranks to collect data, they would see whether the government had existing materials.[91]

The Société published through newspapers, with Brissot relying on *Le*

Patriote français. Mirabeau moved from *L'Analyse des papiers anglais* to the *Courier de Provence,* and Condorcet used the *Chronique de Paris* and the *Journal de Paris.*[92] The Société also published their parliamentary rules and articles. Louis XVI refused to sign a *lettre de cachet* against them, giving them a sort of informal approval. And while they spoke about the need to publish articles and a book in the name of the Société, that was never done. They were careful to immediately let the public know that they were against slave rebellions in the colonies. On this Raynal would disagree. As David Brion Davis wrote, "This philanthropic organization, formed in 1788 upon the urging of the British Quakers and based on a literary idealization of the Quakers of Pennsylvania" in addition to a lack of funds "lacked the perseverance, the organizational ability and the communications network of the British and American Society of Friends." These reasons led to its failure to materialize as a potent force.[93] The Société did eventually collapse, but its members (and others) achieved far more for blacks between 1789 and 1794 than did people in England or America. And men like Mirabeau acted strongly in the National Assembly of 1790–91 for the rights of blacks.[94]

From the beginning the restrictions placed on the Société were harsher than those their American and British counterparts faced in their countries. In Britain and the United States there was some freedom of the press and of public meetings. The Parliament in England and the new legislative bodies in America made the laws of society. While in America those antislavery advocates did not represent a powerful force in the legislative bodies, they did in Britain. The English Quakers "had achieved a pragmatic accommodation with the British political order and were acutely sensitive to any public actions which might rekindle prejudice or jeopardize their informal mechanisms of influence."[95] However, in France the press was still controlled by the government ministries that in turn controlled political decisions and freedom of association until the beginning of the revolutionary activities in April 1789. The relaxation of censorship that spring led to an explosion of daily newspapers. By 1790 one could say virtually anything.[96]

The Société printed English antislavery materials and some of the latest parliamentary debates concerning slavery. Gabriel Vaugeois wrote to Brissot that he had recently translated John Wesley's *Thoughts upon Slavery* and would send him a copy.[97] This work was copied verbatim from Benezet's *Some Historical Account.* It is possible that they read the parliamentary sessions led by Wilberforce of April 2, 1792, which were the first in the western world to call for an end to the slave trade. These tracts would have a tremendous impact on the decision of the revolutionaries to abolish slavery in the colonies on February 4, 1794.[98] The Société, however, did not develop a lot of materials solely for the French audiences, which led again to charges that the Société was unpatriotic and a pawn of the British. Clarkson's presence in France only rekindled that accusation as the internationalization of antislavery efforts would also be used against them.

Thus, according to Dorigny and Gainot, M. Magol addressed the Commune of Paris and accused the Société of seeking to cause slave rebellion in the French Antilles and of being paid agents of the English.[99] Many elites enjoyed the benefits that went along with their status, and although intellectually and politically antislavery and anti–Ancien Régime, would not join the Société. Marie-Jean Hérault de Séchelles wrote to the Société that while he appreciated their invitation to join and would pay close attention to their work, he could not be a part of the government and simultaneously be a member of an organization that his government did not sanction. Thanking the Société for its invitation to join, Thomas Jefferson, the U.S. ambassador to France, wrote, "You know that no one desires more ardently than me to see the abolition of this traffic in slavery. And certainly no one would be more disposed to make all possible sacrifices to make that happen."[100] Jefferson, the slaveholder, also declined membership, citing his role as a public servant of his country. Yet others like the marquis de Lafayette, who owned slaves in Guyana, did in fact join the Société. The Société had 140 known members, among whom were 11 judges, 26 *fermiers généraux*, as well as *financiers*, abbots, and wives of members of Freemason societies. Many of these members had a financial interest in the slave trade, even if they did not own slaves. And many owned slaves outright.[101]

Despite the obvious connection between his publications and the work of the Société, Raynal seemed to view himself as separate from the realm of their work.[102] Returning to France, Brissot delivered to Raynal an honorary membership on behalf of the Philadelphia Society for the Abolition of the Slave Trade. Raynal wrote to Brissot: "The Friends of the Blacks have the approval of all enlightened men, and with time will win the approbation of the multitudes. Good will be brought about and it will be owed to you and your virtuous colleagues."[103] Although Raynal also bestowed praise upon the Société, he never joined.

Events in France took a sweeping turn in the aftermath of the founding of the Société. It came under assault by the Club Massiac, which was founded on August 20, 1789, as an organization of colonists in defense of slavery and its interests. The Société accused the Club Massiac of "scandalous libel" for publishing the names of its members, which it feared would subject them to violent attacks. In the footnotes attached to the September 1, 1789, minutes of the Société, Mirabeau who had just published his *Courier de Provence* offered support that Article 1 of the Declaration of the Rights of Man should include a mention of slaves and was subsequently attacked verbally by colonists.[104] The last recorded meeting of the Société was on June 11, 1790, although there is some evidence that the organization lasted until September 1791. Slavery in the French Antilles would be first banned in 1794. By then Brissot, Clavière, and Condorcet had died during the Terror, and the Société no longer existed. The rest of the members had been forced into hiding, imprisoned, or killed or had committed suicide.[105]

In 1796 a new organization, the Société des Amis des Noirs et des Colonies, was formed. Its goal was the abolition of slavery in the French colonies, a goal that would not be accomplished until 1838. As Alyssa Sepinwall noted, in the newly formed Société, "which met frequently from 1796 to 1799, Grégoire joined other old time-Amis des Noirs, prominent legislators, and white and mixed-race *colons*, in making a case for colonialism to continue, although in reformulated terms." Men like Grégoire chose to abandon their initial goals and as Sepinwall relates, "At a moment when France could have given up its empire, Grégoire and the other members urged that regenerated colonies remain at the heart of the Republic. Abolishing colonialism was impractical and unwise and would harm France's interests as well as those of the colonies."[106] Grégoire also offered a link between the Société des Amis des Noirs, which became known as the First Société, and the Société des Amis des Noirs et des Colonies, the second Société, which as Dorigny and Gainot believe "was probably organized by February 1796 out of the debris of the first group, which had been torn apart between 1792 and 1793." The final acts of the Société were much like those of their counterparts in America and England: they were spent debating plans not for the total or immediate abolition of slavery but for the gradual emancipation of the slaves.

The influence and work of Benezet had a tremendous impact on the French antislavery movement, as shown by the depth of appreciation shown for him. Brissot distinguished between "exalted heads" the men of official France, and those afraid of reforms and "exalted souls a name he saved for men like Benezet. He wrote that exalted heads were "afraid that reforms will take away privileges. Nothing good will come as long as the designation of exalted head will not be outlawed."

Brissot added that there were few exalted souls in France. He wrote that "Exalted souls believe that the most honorable occupation is to fight for justice. . . . The Quaker [Anthony] Benezet during the last war used his fortune to help his brothers, deploring the ignorance in which the negroes were left, insisting that we cannot simply be content with giving them freedom, without giving them something to better themselves. He opened schools and taught, himself, in those schools. No one has ever called that good Quaker an exalted head, but that is whet he would have been called in our country. . . . In the early days in American they were called 'new lights' or visionaries." Brissot added Benezet to the list of Franklin, the Marquis de Lafayette and George Washington. They were exalted souls he reasoned because "they believed in virtue, searched for liberty and did not sell their souls."[107]

When Benezet died, Brissot gave the prevailing opinion of that time:

"What author, what great man, will ever be followed to his grave by four hundred Negroes, snatched by his own assiduity, his own generosity, from ignorance, wretchedness, and slavery? Who then has a right to speak of haughtily of this benefactor of men?"[108] Brissot ended, "Where is the man in all of Europe, of whatever rank or birth, who is equal to Benezet? Who is not obliged to respect him? How long will authors suffer themselves to be shackled by the prejudices of society? Will they never perceive that nature has created all men equal, that is wisdom and virtue are the only criteria of superiority? Who was more virtuous than Benezet? Who was more useful to society, to mankind?"[109]

Brissot highlighted the fundamental way in which Benezet transformed the debate on slavery in the Atlantic world. Proslavery writers had long presented Africans as having a "ferocious character" and of living in an "arid and harsh" country. Using the accounts of slavers themselves, Benezet was able to demonstrate that Africans had variety, just like Europeans, that they were not "ferocious," and that their environment was hardly a harsh and arid place. His work and legacy helped convince the French of the need for an organized structure and literature to combat slavery.[110] The French and the American antislavery societies continued to stay in touch with each other. On May 9, 1797, Joseph Bloomfield, the president of the Convention of Pennsylvania Abolition Society, sent a letter from its convention meeting in Philadelphia to the Society for the Friends of the Blacks in its reconstituted form. The letter said that Philadelphians "have with pleasure received the Intelligence that the Society of the fried of the Blacks has again resumed their labors." It also asked the Frenchmen to keep them posted via letters to the society's president, James Pemberton, on the steps they are "taking to enlighten the minds of the emancipated blacks" in the colonies.[111] On March 2, 1802, Grégoire, then referred to as Senator Grégoire, formerly bishop of Blois, member of the National Institute, also wrote to Pemberton acknowledging his letter of December 14, 1801. Much like Benezet, Grégoire sent Pemberton a tract he had recently written "closely connected with the cause of the Negroes" and "a packet containing several other pamphlets." Grégoire then informed Pemberton that "the Society instituted at Paris for the liberty and Instruction of the Negroes was dissolved." Yet Grégoire remained optimistic: "Let us continue, my respectable friends, to do good and we shall have our efforts as a legacy to those who follow us in the path of life. Let me hear from you soon."[112]

Chapter 8
African Voices

My bosom, at the same time, glowed with gratitude—and praise toward the humane—the Christian—the friendly and learned Author of that most valuable book.—Blest be your sect, and heaven's peace be ever upon them!
—*Ignatius Sancho,* Letters *(1782)*

The writings and deeds of Anthony Benezet had a profound influence on men and women of African descent. Although only a few Africans who were transported to Europe or the Americas had learned to read and write, by the mid- to late eighteenth century Ignatius Sancho, Quobna Ottobah Cugoano, Olaudah Equiano, and James Albert Ukawsaw Gronniosaw wrote about their experiences and about the injustice of slavery. Equiano, Cugoano, and Sancho were all influenced by the work of Benezet. These African-born men in turn influenced the thinking of others, both black and white, in Britain, France, the American mainland, and the Caribbean, although their work was more appreciated and had more influence in Europe than in the British colonies. Equiano, Cugoano, Sancho, and Gronniosaw went through many stages in their search for identity. They were first Africans, then enslaved Africans, or mere chattel slaves. Next they had to prove themselves to the whites to be God-fearing and worthy human beings. But to be considered as such, they had to become British. As they became British, they "rediscovered" in part their African identities and became Afro-Brits. They then moved between two worlds, perhaps more, as they came to accept and to proclaim their African past openly. Thus Gronniosaw became "An African Prince," Sancho, "An African," Cugoano, "A Native of Africa," and Equiano, "The African."

Yet most whites still considered these men to be beneath them, and in reality they were often just one step above slavery. They experienced the "half-freedom" that Frederick Douglass would later write about—a freedom that brought with it the constant fear of reenslavement and transportation. Douglass wrote that "our path was beset with the greatest obstacles; and if we succeeded in gaining the end of it, our right to be free was yet questionable—we were yet liable to be returned to bondage."[1] In many ways these men experienced what W. E. B Du Bois labeled "double consciousness" long before Du Bois had written about the phenomenon. In his *Souls of Black Folk*, Du Bois wrote, "One ever feels his two-ness—an American, a Negro; two souls, two thoughts, two unrecognized strivings; two warring ideals in one dark body, whose dogged strength alone keeps it from being torn asunder."[2]

James Albert Ukawsaw Gronniosaw

Gronniosaw's *A Narrative of the Most Remarkable Particulars in the Life of James Albert Ukawsaw Gronniosaw, an African Prince, As Related by Himself* underwent twelve editions between its initial publication in 1771 and 1800.[3] "By representing himself as 'an African Prince,'" in the words of Henry Louis Gates, Jr., "Gronniosaw implicitly ties his narrative to the literary tradition of the 'Noble Savage.'"[4] Being a "prince" also negates the classic Aristotelian definition of the legitimate slave, born to slavery. Cugoano and Equiano also claimed descent from "nobles," in part rhetorically, for the same reason. This is not to say that they did not descend from men of high status, but it is an interesting coincidence.

Gronniosaw's work was first published when the author, who was born in what was then called Guinea but is now Nigeria, was sixty years old.[5] Like Cugoano and Equiano, he married a white woman. Like Phillis Wheatley, he had come to the attention of the countess of Huntingdon, a philanthropist and an associate of George Whitefield and John Wesley. He dedicated his book to "To the Right Honorable The Countess of Huntingdon" and signs it "An obedient Servant, James Albert." The Gronniosaw *Narrative* appeared first in 1772, the year after Benezet's 1771 work on Guinea but ten years after his *Short Account of That Part of Africa*, first published in 1762.[6] Benezet, in fact, owned a copy of Gronniosaw's narrative.[7] Both Benezet and Gronniosaw cited the work of the minister Richard Baxter (*A Call to the Unconverted to Turn and Live* [1658]), who in the seventeenth century was an early opponent of slavery and the slave trade. Gronniosaw wrote that his master had given him a copy of Baxter's work and that "he began to relish the book" and "took great delight in it."[8] His mistress had given him a copy of John Bunyan's *Pilgrim's Progress*, and, like Benezet, he had read Michel Adanson's *Voyage to Senegal* and Willem Bosman's *New Description of the Guinea Coast*.[9] Gronniosaw had been the slave of Dutch masters in New York.[10] He "may have encountered Bosman at the Fort of Elmina" where a Dutch slave ship brought the African to the mainland colonies. He "knew Bosman's work in the Dutch Language" as he spoke that language.[11]

Benezet and Quobna Ottobah Cugoano

Cugoano was perhaps the second most influential African writer of the day, after Equiano. Cugoano arrived in England around the time of the Somerset decision, in June 1772, and learned of the debates surrounding the case. Cugoano's narrative, *Thoughts and Sentiments on the Evil and Wicked Traffic of Slavery and Commerce of the Human Species, . . . by Ottobah Cugoano, a Native of Africa,* was first published in 1787 and again in 1791.

As an African, Cugoano wrote, "And we that are particularly concerned would humbly join with all the rest of our brethren and countrymen in complexion [in] imploring and earnestly entreating the most respectful and generous people of Great Britain." As an Englishman or an Afro-Brit, Cugoano denounced the Christian theory of the great chain of being and challenged those who argued "that an African is not entitled to any competent degree of knowledge, or capable of imbibing handy sentiments of probity; and that nature designed him for some inferior link in the chain fitted only to be a slave." He added a biblical phrase that had been used by men like George Fox: "An instructive question, by the prophet could not have been proposed as this, Can the Ethiopian change his skin, or the leopard his spots? Then, may ye also do good that are accustomed to do evil. Jer[emiah] xiii."[12]

Like Equiano, Sancho, and Gronniosaw, Cugoano made sure that his African heritage was mentioned prominently in the title. He wrote that "the worthy and judicious author of *Historical Account of Guinea,* [Anthony Benezet] and others, have given some striking estimations of the exceeding evil occasioned by that wicked diabolical traffic of the African slave trade; wherein it seems, of late years, the English have taken the lead, or the greatest part of it, in carrying it on."[13] Cugoano was in many ways the more radical of the African writers and the most philosophical. Henry Louis Gates, Jr., argued that Cugoano "tends toward the polemic" and that "his text wrestles with several other eighteenth-century works on slavery." Among those were Hume's 1754 essay *Of National Characters,* James Ramsay's *Essay on the Treatment and Conversion of the African Slaves in the British Sugar Colonies* (1784), and Benezet's *Some Historical Account of Guinea.*[14] As the historian Christopher L. Brown put it, "Cugoano took an unusually broad view of the problem of slavery. Most British antislavery writers avoided sweeping critiques of the imperial project when trying to win support for slave abolition . . . . Cugoano, by contrast, described the exploitation of Africans as symptomatic of the larger crimes attending European expansion."[15]

Cugoano also used Benezet's figures to calculate the number of slaves in and passing through Barbados and gave the Quaker credit for having "computed that the ships from Liverpool, Briton and London have exported from the coast of Africa upwards of one hundred thousand slaves annually." Benezet added that "among other evils attending this barbarous inhuman traffic, it is also computed that the numbers which are killed by the treacherous and barbarous methods of procuring them, together with those that perish in the voyage, and die in the seasoning, amount to at least an hundred thousand, which perish in every yearly attempt to supply the colonies."[16]

The Liverpool source that Cugoano referred to was the *Liverpool Memorandum Book,* which provided Benezet with precise figures on ships and slaves.[17] Cugoano, like Equiano, was moved by a long passage that Benezet first wrote in *A Caution and a Warning* and amplified in *Some Historical Account of Guinea,* which was devoted exclusively to the "usage of the Negroes, when they arrive in the West Indies." The passage began, "When the vessels are full freighted with slaves, they sail for our plantations in America, . . . during which time, from the filth and stench that is among them, distempers frequently break out, which carry off commonly a fifth, a fourth, yea sometimes a third or more of them. . . . One may reasonably suppose that at least ten thousand of them die on the voyage." Benezet concluded, "Injustice may be methodized and established by law, but still it will be injustice, as it was before; more insensible of the guilt, and more bold and secure in the perpetuation of it."[18]

Cugoano wrote very eloquently about what few before him—black or white—had been able or willing to conceptualize. Paraphrasing the biblical story of Adam and Eve, he wrote "that all mankind did spring from one original, and that there are no different species among men. For God who made the world, hath made of one blood all the nations of men that dwell on all the face of the earth." He continued that there "are no inferior species, but all of one blood and of one nature, that there does not an inferiority subsist, or depend, on their colour, features or form, whereby some men make a pretence to enslave others." Using the language of the Scottish moral philosopher George Wallace, whom he had read about in Benezet's works, he concluded, "It never could be lawful and just for any nation, or people, to oppress and enslave another."[19] In short, as Christopher Brown asserts, "his *Thoughts and Sentiments* represented the most radical antislavery publication printed in Britain before 1788."[20]

Cugoano confronted color in religious and philosophical terms. "I must again observe," he told his readers, "that the external blackness of the Ethiopians, is as innocent and natural, as the spots in the leopards; and that the difference of color and complexions, which it hath pleased God to appoint among men, are no more unbecoming unto either of them as the different shades of the rainbow are unseemly to the whole." He accepted Africans, Afro-Brits, and later, Englishmen as his "countrymen." For Cugoano "colour does not alter the nature and quality of a man . . . whether he was black or white. Whether he was male or female, whether he was great or small or whether he was old."[21] Cugoano therefore was able to reconcile his past heritage and African identity with his current condition and status. Roxann Wheeler has understood his duality, precisely writing that "Although Cugoano's references to skin color often try to reconcile the apparently intractable differences embodied in the black/white binary, he also intimates that complexion should function as a visible reminder of shared origins, despite language and other cultural variations."[22]

Cugoano's work offers a more critical and polemical argument against slavery than Equiano's.[23] He seems to have read the tracts of Granville Sharp and other British antislavery and radical publications.[24] It does not seem coincidental that the title of his work, *Thoughts and Sentiments of the Evil and Wicked Traffic of the Slavery and Human Commerce of the Human Species*, should so closely resemble Thomas Clarkson's *An Essay on the Slavery and Commerce of the Human Species, Particularly the African*, which was published in London one year earlier. Nor should it be ignored that the title coincided with Benezet's *A Caution and a Warning to Great Britain and Her Colonies*.[25]

In *Thoughts and Sentiments*, Cugoano borrowed from Benezet in *A Caution and a Warning* the technique of posing questions to the British. He lamented, paraphrasing Benezet: "Were the inhabitants of Great Britain to hear tell of any other nation that murdered one hundred thousand innocent people annually, they would think them an exceedingly inhuman, barbarous, and wicked people." Cugoano praised Benezet, writing that "the worthy and judicious author of the Historical Account of Guinea and others, have given some very striking estimates of the exceeding occasioned by that wicked diabolical traffic of the African slave trade; wherein, it seems of late years, the English have taken the lead."[26]

Like Gronniosaw and later Equiano, Cugoano sought to give a positive portrayal of Africa as it existed before the arrival of the Europeans. He told his readers, "As to the Africans selling their own wives and children nothing could be more opposite to every thing they hold dear and valuable; and nothing can distress them more, than to part with any of their relations and friends. Such are the tender feelings of parents for their children." Those "brought away from Guinea," he asserted, "are born as free, and are brought up with as great a predilection for their own country, freedom and liberty, as the sons and daughters of fair Britain."[27] Benezet had used similar language in *A Caution and a Warning to Great Britain, Some Historical Account of Guinea,* and in one of his last works, *Short Observations on Slavery*.

Cugoano combined the ideas of Clarkson, Benezet, James Ramsay, and William Robertson's *History of America* in his work.[28] He went further than most early abolitionists in his demands for justice. He wrote "that there is an absolute necessity to abolish the slave trade, and the West India slavery; and that to be in power, and to neglect even a day in endeavoring to put a stop to such monstrous iniquity and abandoned wickedness . . . endangers a man's own eternal welfare" and his "temporal dignity." He warned the British, "It is therefore necessary" that the inhabitants of the British nation "should seriously consider" the ending of slavery and the freeing of the slaves "for their own good and safety, as well as for our benefit and deliverance."[29]

He outlined an abolition plan where blacks would, like whites, work as indentured servants and "at the end of seven years to let every honest man and women become free" after "they sufficiently paid their owners by their labor." "Secondly," he declared "that a total abolition of slavery should be made and proclaimed; and that an universal emancipation of slaves should begin from the date thereof to be carried on in the following manner," which he delineated in detail. If there were "intelligent people amongst them to give them as good education as they could, . . . that as soon as they have made any progress in useful learning and the knowledge of the Christian religion, they might be sent back to Africa, to be made useful" . . . and "fit for instructing others." Guarantees would be given to those remaining "in the colonies" where "employment enough [would be] given to all free people, with suitable wages according to their usefulness, in the improvement of land."[30] Later black leaders, such as Richard Allen and Absalom Jones, would no doubt have disagreed with him about blacks returning to Africa, but others like Paul Cuffee would have agreed.

Cugoano corresponded with Equiano, Granville Sharp, and Edmund Burke. Like Equiano and Benezet, he made a practice of writing letters to newspapers and to notable people, such as parliamentarians and European nobility. Like Benezet, he authored letters to Queen Maria of Portugal, as well as to the prince of Wales and to Sir Charles Middleton, the comptroller of the British Navy from 1778 to 1790. Cugoano and Equiano cowrote a letter dated April 25, 1789, to William Dickson, the former private secretary to the Hon. Edward Hay, governor of the Island of Barbados. They wrote,

We who have perused your well authenticated Book, entitled, *Letters on Slavery*, think it is a duty incumbent on us to confess, that in our opinion such a work cannot be too much esteemed; you have given but too just a picture of the Slave Trade, and the horrid cruelties practiced on the poor sable people in the West Indies, to the disgrace of Christianity. Their injury calls aloud for redress, and the day we hope is not far distant, which may record one of the most glorious acts ever passed the British Senate—we mean an Act for the total Abolition of the Slave Trade.[31]

Cugoano became, in Vincent Carretta's words, the "first Anglophone-African historian of slavery and the slave trade, and the first African to criticize European imperialism in the Americas" in print.[32] Much like Benezet, Cugoano documented the duty and obligation of the whites themselves to abolish slavery and the trade in human beings. Like Benezet, he dreamed of opening a school for blacks. In the epilogue to his work he wrote in the third person: "He further proposes to open a School, for all such of his

Complexion as are desirous of being acquainted with Knowledge of the Christian Religion and the Laws of Civilizations."[33] He used his writings to show both the horrors of the trade and the beauty and resources of Africa and her peoples. Having spent the greater part of his life working to prove his humanity and his worth to whites, he no longer felt the need to do so. In calling for the passage of the Abolition Act, he now called on whites to prove their own humanity. It was their Christian duty to abolish the slave trade. Yet he knew he had to do more. He, like Benezet and the men of the Enlightenment, equated knowledge with freedom. To free his people he would have to educate them, and in so doing he would also educate the whites, to the full meaning of liberty.

Olaudah Equiano

The most famous of the Africans' narratives was that of Olaudah Equiano. His *Interesting Narrative of the Life of Olaudah Equiano or Gustavas Vasa, the African,* was widely read in the early Atlantic antislavery community. Equiano was a worldly, self-educated man who visited countless countries in Africa, Asia, Europe, North and South America, and the Arctic. He was a musician, linguist, navigator, hairdresser, accountant, astronomer, sailor, and author. He studied Islam, Methodism, Quakerism, Catholicism, and several religions of Asia. He was the chattel slave of Quakers, Anglicans, and Catholics at one time or another. Few people of his time, especially among blacks enslaved or free, regardless of wealth or background, had led such a rich and varied life.

By adding "The African" to the book title just after his "slave name," he asserted his pride in his African past, a pride that his kidnappers and his many masters had tried but failed to destroy: "When I came to Kingston, I was surprised to see the number of Africans who were assembled together on Sundays, particularly at a large commodious place, called Spring Path. Here each different nation of Africa meet and dance after the manner of their own country. They still retain most of their native customs; they bury their dead, and put victuals, pipes and tobacco, and other things, in the grave with the corpse, in the same manner as in Africa."[34] Equiano, like most other antislavery writers, came to use European sources, such as Michel Adanson, Willem Bosman, and Jean Barbot, as resource guides on Africa.[35] Equiano learned of these sources from Benezet's *Some Historical Account of Guinea,* his initial source for information about Africa, as he openly asserted in his notes. Where Benezet had written, "That part of Africa, from which the Negroes are sold to be carried into slavery, commonly known by the name of Guinea, extends along the coasts for three or four thousand miles,"[36] Equiano would write, "That part of Africa known by the name of Guinea, to which the trade for slaves is carried on, extends along the coast above 3,400 miles."[37] In the literature of the period the word *Guinea* was often used as a description for the entire west coast of Africa. It referred to the "vast stretch of West African coast from the river Senegal down to the kingdom of Angola."[38]

Robert Allison pointed out in the introduction to Equiano's book that "it is important to note that Equiano copied Benezet's general geographical survey of West Africa and Benezet's account of West African governments. An 11-year-old boy would not know these facts." Equiano relied on personal memory for other details, as "Benezet did not know the details of Isseke that Equiano knew. Equiano remembered the *igbu ichi* ceremony, the facial scarring he would have undergone had he stayed in Isseke; he remembered the perfumes and dances, the cultural significance of snakes, the folktales and proverbs, local details unknown to Benezet or any writer outside of Ibo society. A boy would know these things and would remember them long after he became a man."[39]

The question that has been raised concerning Equiano's birthplace—Africa or North America (South Carolina)—has a direct bearing on the connection between Equiano and Benezet.[40] If he was born in Africa, Equiano used Benezet's account to refresh the memory of his long ago past.[41] If he was born in North America, then he also used Benezet to learn about the Africa of his ancestors. There simply was no other such positive written source for the history of his people. Either way, Benezet's importance to Equiano's understanding of Africa remains intact. Either way, Equiano added what he knew to what Benezet offered.[42]

Carretta observed that Equiano "conflates passages he adapts from Acts 17:26 and Isaiah 55:8 to close his opening chapter: 'If, when they look a round the world, they feel exultation, let it be tempered with benevolence to others, and gratitude to God, who hath made of one blood all nations of men for to dwell on all the face of the earth; and whose wisdom is not our wisdom, neither are our ways his ways.'" Carretta believed that Equiano was subtly acknowledging his debt to Benezet by quoting the same words of St. Paul he used the year before as the epigraph to *Some Historical Account of Guinea.*[43] Just as Benezet had no qualms about John Wesley, Granville Sharp, or William Wilberforce using his words on the humanity of the Africans without attribution, he would certainly have had no qualms about Equiano, "the African," doing the same.

Equiano's text went through nine English-language editions in his lifetime and soon appeared in several other European languages. It allowed readers to trace precisely how "the African" came to understand African history and its inclusion in the ongoing debates about slavery.[44] Benezet's description of Africa and his Quaker concepts of morality deeply influenced Equiano. In the first chapter of the *Narrative,* Equiano wrote, "Adultery, however, was sometimes punished with slavery or death; a punishment which I believe is inflicted on it throughout most of the nations of Africa." He concluded that these punishments existed because "so sacred among them is the honor of the marriage bed, and so jealous are they of the fidelity of their wives." The men, he added, "do not preserve the same so constancy to their wives which they expect from them; for they indulge in a plurality, though seldom in more than two." At the bottom of the page (next to the asterisk) Equiano wrote simply, "See Benezet's *Account of Africa* Throughout."[45]

Equiano referred to chapter 2 of *Some Historical Account,* in which Benezet wrote "that murder, adultery and theft were severely punished" in "that part of Guinea known by the Grain, and Ivory Coast." In chapter 3 Benezet added some specifics: "There is in Benin a considerable order in government. Theft, murder, and adultery being severely punished." Benezet wrote that Jean "Barbot says, 'if a man and a woman of any quality be surprised in adultery, they are both put to death, and their bodies are thrown on a dunghill, and left there a prey to wild beasts.'" He added, using words taken from Bosman, "The severity of the laws in Benin against adultery, amongst all orders of people, deters them from venturing, so that it is but very seldom any persons are punished for that crime."[46]

The second citation alerts us to the fact that it was Bosman, not Barbot (as Benezet had written), who wrote, "Here are very few Capital Crimes, which are only Murders and committing Adultery with the King's or his great Men's Wives: But the Negroes, as I have already hinted, being very fearful of Death, are the most careful People in the World how they incur that Penalty." Bosman concluded that "notwithstanding which, from time to time, several venture so far as to deserve that Punishment," meaning death.[47] Barbot, it seemed, believed otherwise.[48]

Equiano continued to paraphrase Benezet in his description of family life in Africa. The latter saw a correlation between the beliefs and lifestyles of the Africans and his own utopian vision of humankind. Just as Benezet had written that the Africans lived in relative peace and abundance before contact with the Europeans, so did Equiano. In one passage he paraphrased Benezet: there were "eruptions of one little state or district on the other, to obtain prisoners or booty. Perhaps they were incited to this by those traders who brought the European goods, I mentioned amongst us." He concluded that "such a mode of obtaining slaves in Africa is common; and I believe more are procured this way, and by kidnapping, than any other." Again he wrote at the bottom of the page, "See Benezet's '*Account of Guinea,*' throughout."[49] Equiano here summarizes Benezet's passage: "The practice of making slaves of the Negroes, owes its origins to the early incursions of the Portuguese on the coast of Africa, solely for an inordinate desire of gain." Benezet later added that "an inordinate desire of gain in the Europeans, [was] the true occasion of the slave trade."[50] "Earlier," Equiano paraphrased Benezet in saying that the Africans "use no beasts or husbandry; and their only instruments are hoes, axes, shovels and beaks, or pointed iron to dig with."[51]

Equiano described the treatment of slaves in Barbados again using Benezet's writings: "This island requires 1,000 Negroes annually to keep up the original stock, which is only 80,000. So that the whole term of a Negro's life may be said to be there but 16 years."[52] At the bottom of the page Equiano made a note: "Benezet's 'Account of Guinea,' p. 16." In his work Benezet had written that in Jamaica and "Barbados, it is reckoned that a fourth Part die in Seasoning; and . . . there are twice as many imported into these two islands, as into all our other Islands in the West Indies, and all our colonies in North America."[53] Both men's antislavery arguments were based on quantification, documenting the sheer numbers of Africans, not only those who reached the west but also those who died of hunger and maltreatment and in resistance during the Middle Passage. After all, the figures cited represent only those who actually arrived in the Americas. Large numbers of enslaved Africans committed suicide by jumping overboard; sick and severely malnourished slaves were thrown to the sharks.

Like Benezet, Equiano believed that once Europeans changed their views of Africa they would see the benefits of "fair" trade with the region. James Walvin believes that "the argument that the slave trade might be replaced by an even more profitable trade was later advanced by the Quaker Anthony Benezet." He added that "thanks to Benezet this simple economic proposition—that Africa beckoned with its incalculable and yet undoubted bounty—quickly embedded itself in early abolitionist thought, and thence moved even further a field."[54]

Arguing that slavery was unprofitable, Benezet wrote that "a competent number of labouring people might be procured from Europe, which affords numbers of poor distressed objects, who if not overlooked, with proper usage, might in several respects, better answer every good purpose in performing necessary labour in the islands, than slaves now do." Equiano and Benezet rejected the notion that whites were any more unsuitable for labor in the West Indies or mainland southern colonies than they were in Europe. Both developed a simple economic proposition to improve slave conditions, quell slave rebellions, and eventually foster fair trade between free peoples. Benezet believed that "a considerable advantage might accrue to the British nation in general if the slave trade was laid aside, by the cultivation of a fair, friendly, and humane commerce with the Africans." He added that "without which, it is not possible the inland trade of that country should ever be extended to the degree it is capable of." Going farther, Benezet saw that fair trade would be even more beneficial to the Europeans as it would "allow them to travel safely in the heart of the country, to form and cement commercial friendships and alliances as might be necessary to introduce the arts and sciences amongst them."[55] Equiano, like Benezet and Thomas Clarkson, also saw trade with Africans as the logical outcome of the ending of the slave trade and of great benefits to the whites. Near the very end of his narrative Equiano concluded, "It is trading upon safe grounds. A commercial intercourse with Africa opens an inexhaustible source of wealth to the manufacturing interest of Great Britain; and to all which the slave trade is an objection."[56]

Carretta observed that "like many other opponents of the trade, Equiano attributed much of the brutal treatment meted out to slaves and the consequential decline in population to the use of 'overseers,' who did not share the owners' vested interest in the well-being of the slaves."[57]

Like John Wesley, the Africans first read the words of Sir Hans Sloane describing slave-master brutality in Benezet's works.[58] Sloane had written "the Punishment for crimes of Slaves are usually for Rebellions, burning them, by nailing them down on the ground with crooked Sticks on every Limb, and then . . . burning them gradually up to the Head." He added, "For Crimes of a lesser nature, Gelding or chopping off half of the Foot with an Ax. These punishments are suffered by them with great constancy."[59] Benezet came back to the cruel treatment of slaves in the Islands and the laws that allowed this treatment: "But bad as these laws are, . . . I must acknowledge, that their laws are not near so cruel and inhuman as the laws in Barbadoes and Virginia."[60] Benezet quoted a Barbadian statute known "by the 329th act. p. 125" that outlined details for whether or not slave masters were to be compensated if their slaves were killed when seeking to escape. Equiano cited the same passage using Benezet.[61]

Equiano wrote, "I doubt not if a system of commerce was established in Africa, the demand for manufactures would most rapidly augment, as the native inhabitants would insensibly adopt the British fashions, manners, customs, & c. In proportion to the civilizations, so will be the consumption of British manufactures." He further added, "A commercial intercourse with Africa opens up an inexhaustible source of wealth to the manufacturing interest of Great Britain, and to all which the slave-trade is an objection."[62]

Equiano appreciated Benezet's observations that "Guinea affords an easy living to its inhabitants with but little toil."[63] Benezet would have been uncomfortable with the full-scale export of western values, "manners and customs" to Africa. He would have thought that unfettered production and manufacturing would increasingly take away the value of individual and collective labor. He had doubts about what such a system was doing to the whites in Britain and the Americas, where the labor of human beings, white or black, was so callously manipulated for profits. Benezet understood the structural roots of slavery and the profit motive that drove the capitalist economic system a bit better than Equiano, who seems to have adopted Adam Smith's reasoning that the self-interest of capitalists would lead them to seek maximum profits, which would come from a free Africa (and Africans), not from slaves.

Equiano, the former slave, had perhaps more faith in the whites than did

Benezet. Equiano seemed to appeal to their greed, arguing like Adam Smith that they could maximize profits by freeing the slaves and trading with Africa. Smith makes an excellent case that higher wages work to the advantage of manufacturers as a whole by increasing demand for goods. Slaves by definition minimize such demands.[64] Smith argued that "it appears . . . from the experience of all ages and nations, I believe, that the work done by freemen comes cheaper in the end than that performed by slaves."[65]

Equiano, who dressed in European fineries, had in many ways become more of a western modern man than the poorly clad Benezet. While he knew the dangers of full-scale westernization, he also believed that "industry, enterprise, and mining, will have their full scope, proportionally as they civilize. In a word, it lays open an endless field of commerce to the British manufacturers and merchant adventurers."[66]

Benezet died before the advent of the modern industrial age. Equiano lived during the beginning of the period. He saw some contradictions when he wrote that "if I am not misunderstood, the manufacturing interest is equal, if not superior, to the landed interest. . . . The abolition of slavery, so diabolical, will give a most rapid extension to manufacturers, which is totally and diametrically opposite what some interested people assert." He believed that "the manufacturing interest and the general interest are synonymous. The abolition of slavery would be in reality universal good" to these classes of men. That day was a long way off.[67]

Equiano hoped that modern machinery would free individual labor and the need for slavery. Equiano had a vision for Africa: "If the blacks were permitted to remain in their own country, they would double themselves every 15 years. In proportion to such increase will be the demand for manufacturers." Trade with Africa "opens a most immense, glorious and happy prospect—the clothing, &c., of a continent then ten thousand miles in circumference, and immensely rich in productions of every denomination in return for manufactures."[68] Perhaps without fully realizing it, he accurately described imperialism and the unequal exchange of raw materials, labor, and manufactured goods. The drive for profits, the creation of the cotton gin, and continued brutal racism dashed Equiano's hopes for Africa.

In the last chapter of his narrative Equiano wrote on his thoughts about the Quakers and especially about Benezet. Equiano left London on a ship for Philadelphia on April 5, 1785. As he completed the long and arduous trip, he "was glad to see this favorite old town once more and my pleasure was much increased in seeing the worthy Quakers freeing and easing the burdens of many of my oppressed African brethren."[69] Equiano later said, "It rejoiced my heart when one of these friendly people took me to see a free school they had erected for every denomination of black people, whose minds are cultivated here, and forwarded to virtue; and thus they are made useful members of the community."[70] The school that he visited was Benezet's African Free School.

Equiano wrote an astonishing passage, dated October 1785. He, "accompanied by some Africans," visited the Quakers "in Grace Church Court, Lombard Street." He wrote, "Gentlemen: By reading your book, entitled, *A Caution and a Warning to Great Britain . . .* We part of the poor, oppressed, needy, and much degraded Negroes, desire to approach you with this address of thanks, with our inmost love and warmest acknowledgment; and with the deepest sense of your benevolence, unwearied labor, and kind interposition, toward breaking the yoke of slavery, and to administer a little comfort and ease to thousands and tens of thousands of very grievously afflicted, and too heavy burthened Negroes."[71] His letter was "a hymn of praise for Quaker efforts on their behalf."[72] He equated the totality of the Quakers with Benezet and Benezet as the embodiment of the good Quaker. He believed in the old proverb "evil flourishes when good men do nothing." The good of men like Benezet would always trump the evil of men like Robert King, the Quaker who had once owned him.

Such blacks as Equiano believed in the merits of the Somerset case: like many blacks in mainland North America, he took it to be more than it was. Equiano had taken up the case of his friend John Annis, a black man kidnapped on the island of St. Kitts. Following the path set by Granville Sharp, Equiano came to Annis's defense in 1774 to no avail. Annis was "according to custom, staked to the ground with four pins, through a cord, two on his wrist, and two on his ankles, was cut and flogged most unmercifully and afterwards leaded cruelly with irons about his neck." Equiano's account of the Annis case so moved Wesley that he wrote about it to William Wilberforce: "Reading this morning a tract written by a poor African, I was particularly struck by that circumstance, that a man who has a black skin, being wronged or outraged by a white man, can have no redress; it being a law in all our Colonies that the oath of a Black against a white goes for nothing. What villainy is this!"[73]

Equiano's narrative motivated such British antislavery activists as John Wesley, who worked with him. It was Equiano who, after reading about the *Zong* case in a London newspaper, took the news to Granville Sharp. A letter had been published in the *Morning Chronicle and London Advertiser* on March 18, 1783, describing the case. The author of the letter had been a witness in the case between the ship owner and the insurance underwriters. The pretense that there was a shortage of water aboard the vessel, they said, led to the need to dump enslaved Africans overboard in order to save white sailors.[74]

Sharp wrote in his diary on March 19, 1783, that "Gustavus Vasa Negro called on me with an account of one hundred and thirty Negroes being thrown alive into the sea, from on board an English slave" and asked him "to avenge the blood of his murdered countrymen."[75] The next day, March

20, Sharp visited Thomas Brever, a barrister and professor of law at Oxford, "to consult about the prosecuting the murders" of the kidnapped and enslaved Africans.[76] Sharp jumped on the case, and soon the *Gentleman's Magazine* editorialized on the matter. However, as F. O. Shyllon observed, the legal "action did not get off the ground. Blacks were property. And that was that."[77] Nothing else came of the case in a legal sense. Yet it did galvanize public opinion, especially in 1783, and helped move men like Ramsay, Wesley, Clarkson, and Wilberforce to act.[78]

Charles Ignatius Sancho

Charles Ignatius Sancho was born aboard a slave ship during the middle passage "a few days after it quitted the coast of Guinea for the Spanish West Indies."[79] Consequently, he had no immediate memories of Africa, even though he was born to an African mother and father.[80] His father committed suicide rather than live the life of a slave; his mother died when he was two. Baptized by a Catholic bishop as Ignatius, he was given to three maiden sisters in Greenwich, England, who then gave him the surname Sancho purportedly because he resembled the antihero squire in Cervantes's *Don Quixote*. Unlike the Guerin sisters, who helped educate Equiano, they denied Sancho education, thinking it would make him indolent. Sancho's earliest biographer, Joseph Jekyll, wrote that the sisters' "prejudices had unhappily taught them that African ignorance was the only security for his obedience."[81] Such attitudes extended beyond race to class, and the literature of the period is replete with citations from upper- and middle-class writers about the unfortunate effects of education on those who worked with their hands, whether peasant, day laborer, artisan, or black, enslaved or free. Fortunately for Sancho, he came to the attention of John, the second duke of Montagu, who lived nearby in Blackhearth, took a liking to the lad, and taught him to read and write. Jekyll wrote that the duke "accidentally saw the little Negro, and admired in him a native frankness of manner yet unbroken by servitude, and unrefined by education." He admired the young boy so much that "he brought him frequently home to the Duchess, indulged his turn for reading with presents of books, and strongly recommended to his mistress the duty of cultivating a genius of such apparent fertility."[82]

When the duke died in 1749, Sancho ran away from the sisters "and sought refuge in the household of the duke's widow, eventually becoming the valet of the duchess's son-in-law, the next duke of Montagu." As Carretta noted, "Black men were especially desired as servants in wealthy households—and particularly in the public roles of butler and valet—because they were associated with the exotic riches of the empire and thus served as the most obvious indicators of the status of their owners and employers."[83] Sancho in turn reaped some benefits. When Mary, the duchess, died in 1751, she left him £70 and an annuity of £30, a rare gesture of white magnanimity toward a person of African descent.[84] (Then £30 a year was enough money to live a comfortable, if simple life; the poverty line was £10 a year.) In addition to being a place to learn about literature, art, and music, the duke's home was also a magnet for artists, writers, and other people of ideas and influence. Sancho lost his inheritance, according to Sukhdev Sandhu and David Dabydeen, because he was "forever, wenching, boozing and gambling," and his health deteriorated to the extent that he was physically unable to continue the strenuous work of valet and butler. But the duke helped Sancho and his West Indian wife become the first non-white "corner proprietors," or modern-day grocery-store owners, in Britain. As he lost his mobility because of ill health, Sancho became a vociferous letter writer and also published his musical compositions. His friends and correspondents included a "who's who" of English enlightened society, especially booksellers, artists, writers, and painters. Sancho died on December 14, 1780, and was the first African person with an obituary in the British press.

Two years after his death, in 1782, Frances Crewe, one of Sancho's correspondents, drew together many of his letters.[85] The full title of the work was *Letters of the Late Ignatius Sancho, An African, to Which Are Prefixed, Memoirs of His Life.*[86] To afford the printing, Crewe, like Equiano, developed a list of subscribers. Such men as the Abbé Grégoire praised the *Letters,* which were widely read in England. Some reviewers praised the abilities of the black man, and some demurred them in journals like the *Critical Review, Town and Country Magazine,* the *Monthly Review,* and the *Gentleman's Magazine.* One of Sancho's first letters was to Laurence Sterne, the author of the extremely popular novel *Tristram Shandy.*

Sancho wrote from "Charles Street, January 27, 1778," in praise of Benezet, "the Christian, the learned author of that most valuable book" *Some Historical Account of Guinea.* The letter was addressed to Jabez Fisher, a Philadelphian who had sent Sancho the works of Benezet and the poems of Phillis Wheatley. Sancho wrote, "Blest be your sect—and heaven's peace be ever upon them! . . . I with these notions (which, perhaps, some may style absurd) look upon the friendly Author—as a being far more superior to any great name upon your continent.—I could wish that every member of each house of parliament had one of these books."[87]

Sancho dotted his letters with references to Shakespeare, Pope, and Voltaire and occasionally used the French salutation "Ma chere amie." Like Equiano, he had come to see himself as both African and British. As Carretta observed, "The choice of identities was possible because both British and American identities were recent political constructions invented in the eighteenth century, rather than the traditional ethnic or religious categories, which they subsumed."[88] In another letter to a Mr. M. dated November

8, 1772, he called on his fellow men to "scourge them [the slave keepers] into shame."[89]

In a letter to a Mr. J(ack) W(ingrav)e, Sancho found ways to attack slavery and admonished the whites in his new country for the treatment of blacks in his old one: "I am sorry to observe that the practice of *your* country (which I as a resident love—and for its freedom, and for the blessings I enjoy in it, shall ever have my warmest wishes, prayers, and blessings)." He continued, "I say in reluctance that I must observe your country's conduct has been uniformly wicked in the East—West Indies—and even on the coast of Guinea.—The grand object of English navigators—indeed of all Christian navigators—is money—money—money." Sancho came to see greed as part of the international chain of domination and in this he was careful to call Britain "your country" instead of "mine."[90]

Like other British writers such as Wilberforce, Sancho paraphrased the words of Benezet without attribution. "In Africa," he wrote, "the poor wretched natives—blessed with the most fertile and luxuriant soil—are rendered so much miserable for what Providence meant as blessing—the Christian's abominable Traffic for slaves—and the horrid cruelty and treachery of the petty Kings—encouraged by their Christian customers—who carry them strong liquors, enflame their natural madness." Just as Benezet wrote that the Europeans came "with powder and a ball," Sancho concluded that they came with "powder and bad fire-arms, to furnish them with the hellish means of killing and kidnapping."[91]

In 1803 Joseph Jekyll, a young attorney, republished the collection of letters along with a memoir of Ignatius Sancho. Jekyll went on to become a member of Parliament and later solicitor general. His brief biography has served as the preface to every edition of *The Letters of the Late Ignatius Sancho.* In his work Jekyll "drew attention to the efforts of benevolent political economists, by way of trade on virtuous commercial principles."[92] Jekyll, in language like that of Grégoire, added Sancho's name to the list of those who, like Benezet, were early opponents of slavery. Jekyll wrote of Sancho, "Such was a man whose species philosophers and anatomists have endeavored to degrade as a deterioration of the human; and such was the man whom Fuller, with a benevolence and quaintness of phrase peculiarly his own accounted 'God's Image, though cut in Ebony.' To the harsh definition of the naturalist, oppressions political and legislative have been added: and such are hourly aggravated towards this unhappy race of men by vulgar prejudice and popular insult. To combat these on commercial principles has been the labour of Labat, Ferman, and Benezet."[93] The works of men like Equiano, Sancho, Cugoano, and Gronniosaw, as well as Lemuel Haynes, combined what they witnessed, experienced, and read. These men offered a unique view of the African and indeed the European past. The African informants provide us with a clear example of the corrective use of the Africans' own oral history. We have relatively few concrete examples like these to enable us to determine the extent to which the Africans fused European written traditions about Africa with African oral history in order to produce a more balanced narrative of African history. The triangular slave trade had brought about an unexpected consequence as it fostered a many-sided exchange of ideas and values. From Equiano and Cugoano to Sancho, the light added by eighteenth-century Africans to their own history was refracted through the prism of Benezet's works and via Benezet through the works of such European eyewitnesses as Bosman and Adanson.[94] There were black voices on the American side of the Atlantic, but in the main they were treated with much less dignity than they were even in England at the end of the eighteenth century. Even as Allen and Jones fought to save white lives in the 1790s, their motives were impugned. Yet these men held to their dignity and to their mission to free and to educate their enslaved brethren. Like Benezet and Equiano, Allen, Jones, Haynes, and their peers "took their cases to the public," and they were heard.

The Black American Intellectual Tradition

LEMUEL HAYNES

Lemuel Haynes was born in 1753 to an enslaved black father and a white mother. Abandoned by his mother at five months, he was raised by a white Congregationalist family headed by David Rose, a church deacon.[95] He was given the name Lemuel, meaning "belonging to God."[96] On April 19, 1775, while serving as a militiaman at Lexington, he wrote his poem "The Battle of Lexington." The final lines read,

> This Motto may adorn their Tombs
> (Let tyrants come and view)
> 'We rather seek these silent Rooms
> Than live as Slaves to You.[97]

Of course he was speaking not of chattel slavery but of the white's belief that Britain meant to enslave them.[98]

Haynes became the first black minister in the Congregational Church, pastoring as the minister of a church in Rutland, Vermont, for thirty years.[99] In July 1801 Haynes gave an oration (later published) titled *The Nature and Importance of True Republicanism*; it called for liberty based on the theory of natural rights.[100] Many years later, when on July 5, 1852, Frederick Douglass gave his immortal speech to the Rochester Ladies Anti-Slavery Society ("The Meaning of the Fourth of July for the Negro"), he used a variation of Haynes's theme, asking whites, "What to the American slave is your 4th of July? I answer a day that reveals to him, more than any other days in the year, the gross injustice and cruelty to which he is the constant victim." Douglass added, "To him your celebration is a sham: your boasted liberty, an unholy license; your nations greatness, swelling vanity, your sounds of rejoicing are empty and heartless; your denunciation of tyrants, brass fronted impudence; your shouts of liberty and equality hollow mockery."[101]

Haynes's first and perhaps most important work, *Liberty Further Extended*, was written in 1776.[102] He argued that "he that would infringe upon a man's Liberty may reasonably Expect to meet with opposition, seeing the Defendant cannot Comply to Non-resistance, unless he Counter-acts the very Laws of nature."[103] For him freedom was a gift from God granted to every man, thus for any man to take another's liberty from him was to go against God. Much like the Quakers, he argued, "If we strictly adhere to the [Golden] rule, we shall not impose anything upon Others, But what we should Be willing should Be imposed upon us were we in their Condition."[104] Haynes refuted the belief that blacks were resigned to servitude as the descendants of Ham, stating that the arrival of Christ on Earth negated such earlier curses. "It is plain Beyond all Doubt, that at the coming of Christ, this curse that was upon Canaan, was taken off; and I think there is not the Least force in this argument than there would Be to argue that an imperfect Contexture of parts, or Base Birth, Should Deprive any from Gospel privileges; or Bring up any of those antiquated Ceremonies from oblivion, and reduse them into practise."[105]

Haynes disputed the popular notion that superiority and inferiority could be assigned to color and the assumption that they were inherent. Haynes recognized his separate status (as a mixed-race black) from the racial dichotomy as evidence of failed expectations assigned to color. "God has been pleas'd to distiungs [distinguish] some men from others, as to natural abilities, But not as to natural *right*, as they came out of his hands."[106] Differences in skill and capability were natural, but the dramatically disparate racial power structure had nothing to do with the gifts endowed to humans by God.

Haynes was influenced by Benezet's *Some Historical Account of Guinea* and *A Short Account of That Part of Africa*. Like Equiano, Cugoano, and Sancho, the Afro-Brits, he quoted directly from Benezet and his use of the travel narratives.[107] In *Liberty Further Extended*, Haynes, like Benezet, also asserted that the repressive nature of slavery meant that any perceived intellectual deficiencies in blacks could not be assumed to be inherent.[108] He wrote, "Those Slaves in these Colonies are generally kept under the greatest ignorance, and Blindness, and they are scersly [scarcely] Ever told by their white masters whether there is a Supreme Being that governs the univers; or wheather there is any reward, or punishments Beyond the grave. Nay such are those restrictions that they are kept under that they Scersly [scarcely] know that they have a right to Be free."[109] Haynes obviously had read Benezet, who made the same point in quoting the Barbadian priest Griffith Hughes in 1750.[110]

Haynes, like Benezet, argued that whites who participated in the institution of slavery at any level would suffer God's retribution. He wrote, "If you have any Love to yourselves, or any Love to this Land, if you have any Love to your fellow-men, Break these intollerable yoaks, and Let their names Be remembered no more, Least they Be retorted on your own necks, and you Sink under them: for god will not hold you guiltless."[111] Benezet had written,"Let the hardiest slave-holder look forward to that day, when he must give an account to God of his stewardship; and let him seriously consider, whether, at such a time, he thinks he shall be able to satisfy himself, that any act of buying and selling, or the fate of war, or the birth of children in his house, plantation, or territories, or any other circumstance whatever, can give him such an absolute property in the persons of men, as will justify his retaining them as slaves, and treating them as beasts?"[112] Haynes, like Benezet, challenged common misconceptions about the "uncivilized" nature of Africans in their homeland. Whether or to what extent others read Haynes's work before it was "discovered" is not known, but the possibility cannot be ruled out. And how many people heard about his talks or whether he made speeches similar to *Liberty Further Extended* that were not published is also unknown.

Dickson Bruce argued that Haynes was never a sustained vocal opponent against slavery or prolonged advocate for black rights. He wrote that Haynes "rarely spoke out on issues of slavery and color" but instead "made his mark more for his theological rigidity—and staunch Federalism—than for anything having to do with his African background."[113] Yet racial tensions and his "outspoken pro-Federalist statements" caused Haynes to leave his church in 1818. And Haynes's later actions show him to be an eloquent opponent of slavery and racism. Haynes's sermons and talks go to the heart of the proslavery arguments and provide abundant evidence that he thought Scripture supported human equality. He may not have talked directly about slavery, but his discussion of equality undermines the foundations of slavery as thoroughly as anything he could do. While he has been criticized for not being more vocal, he did in fact minister to an all-white congregation that at the time was not vocally against the institution of slavery. When he wrote that "Liberty is Equally as precious to a black man, as it is to a white one and Bondage as equally as intollarable to the one as it is to the other,"[114] he could not have been more forceful or direct. In the words of John Saillant, "Haynes drew out the abolitionism with republican thought more fully than did any of his contemporaries, and he made the test of nationhood—the proof of whether American had really freed themselves for England—the abolition of slavery and the incorporation of African-Americans into the new republic."[115]

There can be little doubt that Haynes's few remarks against slavery, like the messages of those in the Underground Railroad many years later, often traveled where the white man could not hear. That as a minister Haynes might have been able to do more may be true; that his work shows his clear opinions and his ties to Anthony Benezet is without a doubt true.

RICHARD ALLEN, ABSALOM JONES, AND THE FREE AFRICAN SOCIETY

In 1787 former slaves Richard Allen (1760–1831), the African Methodist Episcopal Church leader, and Absalom Jones (1746–1818), the Protestant Episcopal Church leader, founded the Free African Society (FAS) to aid Philadelphia's free black population. The society had originally branched off from a predominantly Methodist group that often gathered to hear Allen preach. They at first planned to form a religious group, but the initial gatherings were deemed too small to sustain an independent church. They met at Richard Allen's home until May 1788, but "his room being too small for the accommodation of the increased number of members," they moved first to Sarah Dougherdy's home and then from "December 28th . . . up to 1791, the monthly meetings were held in Friends Free African School House."[116] Jones had attended Benezet's night school for a while, and disciples of Allen and Jones had attended "Benezet's School." The FAS also held religious services at the school. Among those present at the founding meeting, in addition to Jones and Allen, were Moses Johnson, Cato Freeman, Caesar Cranchell, James Porter, William White, and Samuel Boston. In thinking of that first meeting and the role of the society W. E. B Du Bois wrote, "How great this was, we of to-day scarcely realize; we must remind ourselves that it was the first wavering step of people toward organized social life."[117]

The FAS soon developed into a nondenominational service organization. It provided a response by free people of color to whites, who ever more divided society and their own congregations by race.[118] They kept records of black Philadelphians; provided funeral services; assisted widows, orphans, and other needy blacks in the area; and "visited members . . . to give advice as may appear necessary."[119] As pointed out earlier, they assisted Benjamin Rush during the yellow fever epidemic in 1793. Allen and Jones documented their efforts in *A Narrative of the Proceedings of the Black People.*[120]

Though the FAS did not explicitly belong to one religion or another, it formed an alliance with the Quakers, who had by then forbidden slave ownership among their members. Holding themselves to high principles, the members set the dues at a silver shilling a month: the money went to aid needy members, but only if they could prove that their "necessity is not brought on them by imprudence. . . . No drunkard or disfit person" could be a member. Their organizational structure was based on one established by the Quakers: in the early years of the FAS those in charge included a Quaker acting as the group's clerk-treasurer.[121] Du Bois noted, "For a time they leaned toward Quakerism . . . a fifteen-minute pause for silent prayer opened the meetings."[122] Nash observed, "In fact, the society's articles of incorporation, written when the aura of the influential Anthony Benezet still prevailed, specified that 'it is always understood that one of the people called Quakers . . . is to be chosen to act as Clerk and Treasurer of this useful institution.'"[123]

Allen and other blacks believed that the quiet, staid manner of Quaker worship was antithetical to the more active, vocal practices of black worshipers. Allen came to believe that Methodism was the "perfect system for lifting up an oppressed people and healing the suffering experienced under slavery."[124] He also came to believe that the Quaker presence influenced the way the FAS conducted their meetings, and in 1789 he left the society as his commitment to Methodism grew. He later became the founder of the African Methodist Episcopal Church and its first bishop. Records of the Free African Society reveal that the members found it their "duty to declare that he disunited himself from membership with us by refusing to submit himself to the rules of the Society, and to attend our meetings."[125]

Simultaneously, racism was still very much a force within the Society of Friends. Blacks in the main could not join the Friends, and the few who did could not be buried in Quaker cemeteries. For example, in Sandwich, Massachusetts, according to Thomas Drake, as far back as 1674 Quakers decided to "set aside for Negroes a portion" of the burying place, next to the swamp, . . . which "is as quiet and peaceful as it was two centuries and a half ago, unchanged except for the swamp which is now a cranberry bog."[126] The eminent Quaker historian Henry Cadbury documented Quaker feeling about blacks and wrote, "In Philadelphia, Christ Church (Episcopal) made many more baptisms of Negroes, probably far outnumbering the colored adherents of the entire Friends' meetings in the city."[127] Of other denominations "the first Negro Methodist was baptized by John Wesley in 1748 and from that time on there grew a large following. The Methodist and Baptist soon developed special Negro congregations with Negro preachers." But not the Quakers. Cadbury argues that one reason blacks may not have been more involved with the Quakers was because of the "quietness of worship," although he allows that there were more black "attenders than members" within the church. When blacks attended Quaker gatherings in the eighteenth century, "they usually sat in a special place, against the wall, under the stairs or in the gallery."[128] It was not until 1796, when the "Quaker Rebecca Griscomb published an essay chiding the Society of Friends for excluding blacks from regular meeting, the Friends finally dropped the formal exclusion of blacks from their worship."[129] Few blacks joined the society. The blacks found that in life as in death they could not evade discrimination, even among their friends, the Friends.

Tensions continued at St. George's Methodist Episcopal Church as blacks continued to join and to fill the pews. In the past they had worshiped side by side with the whites, but now they were in Allen's words "placed . . . around the wall."[130] To accommodate the growing church, a building campaign was undertaken, and blacks contributed money and might. Expecting to be seated on a first-come first-seat basis, the blacks were surprised to find that the white elders had relegated them to the newly built balconies.

By 1791 Jones, who had attended Benezet's night school as a young man, had identified with some of the Quaker sensibilities, and Allen began thinking about the formation of black churches in Philadelphia.[131] Events came to a head when one Sunday in late 1792, five years after the FAS was founded, Absalom Jones was on his knees in prayer. A white trustee grabbed him by the arm and began to pull him.[132] The normally even-tempered Jones asked the white man to wait until he finished his prayers, but the abusive trustee had his marching orders and told Jones, "No, you must get up now, or I will call for aid and force you away." The blacks had had enough, and as soon as the prayer ended, they left the church: for good and en masse. As Allen would later recall, in a play on words (as the blacks had worked with whites to rid the city of the yellow fever), "They were no more plagued with us in the church."[133]

Within a twelve-day span in 1794 Jones founded the St. Thomas African Church (Episcopal), and Allen opened the Bethel African Methodist Episcopal Church (Methodist). Through the development of a network of black churches and free African societies, Allen and Jones became formidable leaders of the free black community in Philadelphia and to some degree in other urban centers in the northeastern United States. Members of the FAS extended their services beyond Philadelphia's black community. During the yellow fever epidemic in 1793 Benjamin Rush, a prominent member of the Pennsylvania Abolition Society, appealed to Jones and Allen for help, believing that those of African descent were immune to the deadly disease.[134] "[Black Philadelphians] nursed the sick, carried away the dead, dug graves, and transported the afflicted to an emergency lazaretto set up outside the city."[135] Rush had accepted the notion of such men as Sir Hans Sloane that blacks were immune to the disease, while in fact approximately the same proportion of blacks as whites died from yellow fever in Philadelphia. Even so, despite the hard work of members of the black community, the Irish immigrant publisher Mathew Carey accused them of being opportunistic by charging for nursing services, even though it was he who reaped profits by publishing a pamphlet *A Short Account of the Malignant Fever*. Allen and Jones disputed Carey's claims, and their work ultimately lifted most white opposition to the formation of black churches in Philadelphia.[136] Along with other leaders of the free black community, such as the wealthy sail maker James Forten, the blacks petitioned the federal government and fought the 1793 Fugitive Slave Act, which among other things made it easier for those in search of fugitive slaves to take free blacks into captivity, an issue that was also a concern of the Pennsylvania Abolition Society.[137] On November 25, 1793, the Acting Officers of the newly formed African Church of Philadelphia—Absalom Jones, William Grey, and William Gardner—addressed a letter of thanks and appreciation to Granville Sharp. The letter read in part: "We want to express our gratitude to you for all your labours of love to our afflicted nations. You were our advocate when we had but few friends on the other side of the water. We request you to accept of our thanks for all your kind and benevolent exertions in behalf of the people of our colour, and in particular for your late humane donation to our church."[138]

The development of the FAS was instrumental in the later birth of the official black church: "The historic decision of Richard Allen and Absalom Jones to transcend white denominationalism by organizing a nonsectarian society that could solidify the community for morality and mutual welfare led directly to the founding of the first black churches in the North."[139] The birth of the society represented one of the first times that free blacks united to provide for their community as a whole, and its activities became a lodestar for later work that would become a keystone for black churches.[140] The FAS "was a fellowship of black citizens who craved independence and social progress without reference to the creeds and confessions used in most of the mainline white churches . . . [Free African societies] created, therefore, the classic pattern of religious commitment that has a double focus: free and autonomous worship in the African American tradition and the solidarity and social welfare of the black community."[141] It established practices in the free black community of Philadelphia that would over time become a way of life for America's increasing free black population.

Du Bois attributed the "rise of the Free African Society" to the "beginning of the Negro Church in the North." But he went further in exploring its role in linking the FAS to the African past. He wrote, "The church really represented all that was left of African tribal life, and was the sole expression of the organized efforts of the slaves. It was natural that any movement among freedmen should center about their religious life, the sole remaining element of their former tribal system."[142] Many similar benevolent societies followed in the mold of the FAS. In 1795 St. Thomas's Church launched the African Friendly Society and the following year the Female Benevolent Society of St. Thomas. In 1795 Richard Allen opened a day school for sixty black youth, and in 1804 he helped form the Society of Free People of Color for Promoting the Instruction and School Education of Children. Like white abolition societies, organizations similar to the FAS grew up in Boston and in Newport, Rhode Island.[143] The FAS existed until 1799, and in 1809 many of its leaders joined to form the Society for Suppressing Vice and Immorality, with Allen as its spokesman.[144] Using the experiences and the organizational methods they had first learned at Benezet's schools, a generation of black leaders would continue to train the generations to come to educate and fight for the rights of black people.[145]

Benezet's Dream

"What Shall Be Done with Those Negroes"

In Thomas Paine's 1775 essay "African Slavery in America" he proclaimed, "The great Question may be—What should be done with those who are enslaved already?" He then wrote that "to turn the old an[d] infirm free, would be an injustice and cruelty." He proposed to keep them in slavery "and treat them humanly." The plight of the able bodied would be left up to the legislatures to determine what was practicable for master, and best for them. He proposed to rent land to some blacks who may "form useful barrier settlements on the frontiers." They might "become interested in public welfare."[1] Paine did not develop these ideas. He probed the concept by reading the works of men like Benezet. However, he fell short of creating workable proposals.

That same year Granville Sharp, in a letter to Rush, offered his own ideas for black emancipation. His plan called for the value of every slave to be "fairly estimated by juries appointed for that purpose." Then white landlords who did not use all of their arable land would divide the acreage "they could spare into compact little Farms, with a small wooden cottage" for the blacks, who would lease the land and cottage for a set number of years." Above all, the plan would "yield the landlords a due profit from each portion of their estates." The whites would also receive an "adequate annual allowance" and be reimbursed for whatever advance they made to the slaves for the "expenses of Buildings, of Implements, of Livestock; of Seed & Tea." He added, "other Negroes that are not capable of managing and shifting or themselves, nor are fit to be trusted, all at one with liberty" would become wards of a county committee and hired out at will. Sharp hoped that, over time, the status of slaves would "be changed into a condition more nearly resembling 'Hired Servants,' who would become a "hardy Body of Free Peasants, serving as trusty tenants." In the end the landlords would have their "Estates better peopled and improved, and yet avoid the Guilt and danger of oppression." He thought that "American Liberty cannot be firmly established till this is done."[2] Some years later, in 1787, he became a leading advocate of resettling blacks in England to Sierra Leone. On May 14, 1787, the first blacks arrived and the settlement was named Granville Town, after Sharp. Another supporter of resettlement was Olaudah Equiano.[3] Sharp's ideas for blacks in North America, of course, would have led to debt peonage and a system of tenant farming and land leasing that would have exchanged one form of exploitation for another. And the whites would live guilt free. By 1791 more than 1,000 black Loyalists had left Nova Scotia en route to Sierra Leone to join the blacks who had left England.[4]

Nowhere in his plan did Sharp advocate the immediate and complete freedom of the slaves. Richard Allen and Absalom Jones, like Benezet, rejected colonization attempts. They wrote and spoke out against on many occasions, espeically against efforts led by the American Colonization Society's efforts to rid Pennsylvania in particular and North America in general of free blacks.

On four separate occasions Benezet offered his own different emancipation plans, each a bit more developed than the last, and "more elaborate, and are exceptional in having recourse to law."[5] In the first 1762 edition of *A Short Account of That Part of Africa,* Benezet called for both manumission and education for enslaved Africans and for whites to "use all reasonable endeavors, to enable them to procure a comfortable living, not only as an act of justice to individuals, but as a debt due to them, on account of the oppression and injustice perpetuated on them, or their ancestors."[6] Later in 1762 Benezet issued a revised and expanded edition of the work, adding a more detailed plan for both emancipation and freedom and listed his recommendations. Why Benezet further developed his plans in the new edition is not known, but it is obvious that he was responding to those who were advocating some form of colonization. Nine years later, in *Some Historical Account of Guinea*, he made a few minor changes. He first asked, "What shall be done with those Negroes already imported and born in our Families? Must they be sent to Africa? That would be to expose them in a strange land, to greater difficulties than many of them labor under at present."[7] Benezet had heard some argue that freeing the slaves into society would create too many difficulties. He answered, "Indeed, it must be granted there are difficulties in the way," but there was "not any general change . . . made, or reformation . . . effected, without some" difficulties. The ever-optimistic Benezet argued that "the difficulties are not so great but that they may be surmounted."[8]

In his first program he demanded that "in the first Place, that all further Importation be absolutely prohibited." Second, "as to those already purchased, or born among us, after serving so long as shall be adequate to the Money paid, or the Charge of bringing them up (which may be decided by the Courts of Justice) let them by Law be declared free."[9] In *Some Historical Account of Guinea* he made a slight but important change, rewriting "adequate" as "so long as may appear equitable" in an attempt to satisfy those who believed their slaves' value had risen or those whose slaves had been left or given to them.[10] Of course, he realized that those who inherited slaves denied any sin in owning them since they did not buy the slave. The new reasoning would answer those who claimed hardship on the basis of the loss of property. Third, each "slave thus set free be enrolled in the County Court, and be Obliged to be a Resident during a certain Number of Years" and under "the inspection of the Overseers of the Poor." While such a provision could be seen as benefiting the whites, Benezet saw it as more helpful to the blacks, who he felt needed a transition period for the "proper Use of their liberty."[11] He believed his plan would prevent vengeful whites from abusing blacks. Fourth, the freed slaves' children should "have an Opportunity of such Instruction, as might be provided for them, under the Tuition of proper Instruction." Fifth, "where the Nature of the Country would permit as certainly the uncultivated Condition of our southern Colonies easily would; suppose a small Tract of Land, for Instance, five and twenty acres were assigned to every Negro Family."[12] In *Some Historical Account of Guinea*, Benezet did not give an acreage number, but instead he proposed a question: "Suppose a small tract of land were assigned to every Negro family, and they obliged to live upon and improve it."[13] He may have changed the proposed acreage allotment because of westward expansion into Native American lands and of tensions surrounding the conflict with the British. Booker T. Washington and other blacks and whites developed multiple variations on this theme generations later. For Benezet the blacks were not to substitute chattel slavery for another form of peonage but should be gradually introduced to freedom among the whites, many of whom would have the responsibility of giving them day-to-day assistance. Benezet hoped that enlightened whites would heed his call. How Benezet expected this to happen in the southern colonies may never be known, although in *Some Historical Account of Guinea* he added western colonies in addition to those in the south. Benezet believed that his plan would encourage blacks "to exert their abilities, and become industrious subjects. Both planters and tradesmen would be plentifully supplied with cheerful and willing minded labourers; much vacant land would be cultivated, the produce of the country greatly increased. Arts and manufacturers advanced; the taxes for the support of government lessened to individuals by the increase of taxables."[14] Finally, he believed that the "Negroes instead of giving just cause of fearful apprehensions, and weakening the internal Strength of the Government where they reside, as they certainly must in their present conditions," would become interested in the country's "Security and Welfare."[15] In both works he added a footnote, arguing that the harsh treatment of the slaves will always be a "just cause of terror." He was warning whites about the large discrepancies in slave-to-white ratios in some southern colonies and the Caribbean.[16] However, he made a radical change in the later work. He wrote that "Negro instead of being an object of terror, as they certainly must be to the governments where their numbers are great, would become interested in their safety and welfare."[17] By substituting the word *safety* for *security*, he clearly warned the whites that it was in their self-interest to free the enslaved Africans.

Benezet addressed an imaginary manumission question: "To let them suddenly free here, would be perhaps attended with no less difficulty; for, undisciplined as they are in religions and virtue, they might give a loose to their evil habits, which the fear of a master would have restrained." He answered this question, asserting that "these are difficulties in the way" and no "general change can be made, or reformation erected, without some" fundamental changes in the status of the blacks. Optimistic as always, he argued that "the difficulties are not so great but they may not be surmounted."[18] In other words, he believed that where there was a will, there was a way. If the government was so concerned about the perceived problems emblematic with manumission and sought a solution, then "the Almighty would bless this good intention" and would "enable them [blacks] to become profitable members of society."[19]

He wrote Joseph Phipps that "in Georgia and South Carolina the Negroes are not hemmed in by the some hundreds of miles, as they are in the Islands, but have a back Country uninhibited for some hundreds of miles, where the Negroes might not only retire, but who expect to be supported & assisted by the Indians."[20] Benezet called for a sort of reparation to the freed blacks in the form of communally shared acres of land. Although he did not say so directly in his proposals, the land-sharing plan came close to what he had learned about African forms of communalism existent before European conquest. He said as much: "The mistaken Opinion, which most People entertained, that the Negroe's in Africa" live in a "wild unsettled manner . . . has led many to think it impossible to bring them in to that civilized Order which is required for their becoming good Members of Society."[21] Africans, he had long written, were capable of sustaining themselves if allowed to do so. His idea of giving land to the newly freed blacks preceded the Reconstruction dream of "forty acres and a mule" by almost a century.

Benezet went back and forth with his ideas about manumission. Ten years after his initial discussion with Phipps he wrote to John Fothergill on April 28, 1773: "I am like minded with thee, with respect to the danger which would attend a sudden manumission of those negroes now in the southern colonies, as well as to themselves, as to the whites." He wrote in support of colonization to western lands that the area "from the west side of the Allegheny Mountains to the Mississippi on a breath of four or five hundred miles, would afford a suitable and beneficial means of settlement for many of them among the white people, which in all probability be as profitable to the negroes as to the new settlers."[22]

In short, while Benezet thought that the slaves should be freed, he also thought, like others of his day, that they would need assistance in their quest for full-fledged freedom. W. E. B. Du Bois asked of the American people something that Benezet had pondered over a hundred years earlier: "A people thus handicapped ought not to be asked to race with the world but rather allowed to give all its time and thought to its own social problems."[23] Society would still have a responsibility to aid the newly free.

Benezet called on whites to go beyond manumission, to educate blacks and "use all reasonable endeavors, to enable them to procure a comfortable living, not only as an act of justice to individuals, but as a debt due to them, on account of the oppressions and injustice perpetrated on them, or their ancestors."[24] He did not want the newly free to face the world alone.

Du Bois rephrased the question 141 years later. He wrote, "No sooner had Northern armies touched Southern soil than this old question, newly guised, sprang from the earth,—What shall be done with the Negroes?"[25] Until his death Benezet asked the same question. And most of his life he did his part, philosophically and practically, to end slavery and to elevate the condition of black people.

The Society for the Relief of Free Negroes Unlawfully Held in Bondage

Realizing the tenor of the times, the impatience of the blacks, and the urgent situation among the whites, Benezet solicited a group of ten men, mostly Quakers, on April 14, 1775, to convene at the Rising Sun Tavern on Second Street in Philadelphia.[26] Since November 1774 Benezet had spent considerable time preparing and organizing for the meeting.

Giving itself the name the Society for the Relief of Free Negroes Unlawfully Held in Bondage, the men were in part motivated by the 1773 case of Dinah Nevil, a Native American, who, with her children, was captured and all held as slaves despite her protests that they were free.[27] The Quaker members, while advocating abolition and overseeing the manumission of slaves, had as one of their first concerns the assistance of free people of color. The new society was formed on the same day that Great Britain ordered the new Massachusetts governor, General Thomas Gage, to enforce the Coercive Acts to use any measure to suppress revolutionary activities. On April 19, 1775, seventy "minutemen" repelled the British at Lexington and Concord. One of the minutemen was Lemuel Haynes.[28]

Prince Hoare was one of the first to document the efforts of the first society. Inadvertently omitting Benezet, he wrote, "In 1774, Dr. Rush, in conjunction with James Pemberton, and others of the most conspicuous among the Quakers in Pennsylvania, undertook to unite in one body all those of different religious persuasions who were zealous in behalf of Africans sufferers; and hence arose a society, which was confined to Pennsylvania, and was the first of that nature ever formed in America."[29] Hoare got the year wrong, but he got the mission right. At the initial gathering, the first of four that year, they formed the first antislavery society in America, and they elected John Baldwin as president, Samuel Davis as treasurer, and Thomas Harrison as secretary.[30] The first meeting gave the steering or standing committee the duty to "take charge of the several reports of slavery as they come to their knowledge and are requested to use the utmost of their endeavors to obtain justice to those people according to their several solicitations and make a report of the same to our next meeting."[31] The standing committee also worked among illegally captured freedmen by paying expenditures to help them reestablish their freedom. Committee members set out on horseback to gather evidence in order to write memorials and "statements of facts written to the government or some branch within it."[32]

The Pennsylvania Abolition Society (PAS) meetings were largely informal to avoid comparison with the more structured meeting schedule of the Quakers, whose pacifism was increasingly looked down upon during the Revolutionary War years. Those years interrupted the work of the society, and in November 1775 formal meetings ceased: "because sixteen of the original twenty-four members were Quakers, the Society decided that Quaker pacifism might discredit or render ineffectual the Society's antislavery testimony."[33] Because Quaker pacifism was unpopular during wartime, the society did not meet again until 1784.[34]

Just as the first Abolition Society was being established, Benezet wrote to Selina Hastings, countess dowager of Huntingdon, on March 10, 1775. Lady Selina, as Brookes notes, "at the importunity of Whitefield, had established a 'college' known as the Orphan House, to promote the enlightenment of the poor, and to prepare students for the clerical profession."[35] She called the home for orphaned white girls, located near Savannah, Georgia, Bethesda and made George Whitefield its keeper. The home covered 640 acres, including fields of rice and flax worked by enslaved Africans. As has been noted, Whitefield, an old friend of Benezet's and his father's, had a conflicted approach to slavery. At one time Whitefield admonished slave keepers in North Carolina, Maryland, and South Carolina about their misdeeds. He told them in 1740 "your dogs are caressed and fondled at your tables; but your slaves, who are frequently styled dogs or best, have not an equal privilege. I think God has a quarrel with you, for your cruelty to the poor Negroes."[36] Later in life Whitefield became more ambivalent about the treatment of blacks and about slavery as he urged the countess to use them on the plantation.

Although Benezet had known Whitefield since 1749, he parted ways with the elder on this subject. Whitefield died in 1770, but the slaves still remained at the Savannah plantation near the orphanage. After introducing himself to the countess, Benezet gave her a brief description of the state of slavery in the colonies, especially in the south. Benezet at first told the countess that "persons concerned in the management of the Orphan House at Georgia should be particularly guarded against giving any support to this abominable practice." He added that he had "more than once conversed on this interesting subject with my esteemed friend George Whitefield now deceased. He at first clearly saw the iniquity of the horrible abuse of the human race." Whitefield he believed had faltered "after residing in Georgia & being habituated to the sight & use of Slaves, his judgment became so much influenced as to paliate, & in some measure defend the use of slaves," adding that "this was a matter of much concern to me." Urging her to read sections of John Wesley's work, he sent her page forty-one of *Thoughts on Slavery* as well as other materials. After signing the letter

Benezet decided to add one more comment where he had unusually harsh words for Whitefield, writing, "I cannot with satisfaction . . . upon the Slave trade." Benezet went on to present his views on slavery and to urge the countess to release her slaves. He concluded, "nevertheless, where the lives & natural as well as religious welfare of so vast a number of our Fellow Creatures is concerned, to be Silent, where we apprehend it a duty to speak our sense of that which causes us to go mourning on our way, would be criminal." Her deeds did not match her words, and she did not immediately manumit her slaves.[37]

As Hoare explains, "The society had barely begun to act, when war broke out with England and materially checked its operations. The cause however, did not languish in the minds of good men, although, from the calamitous circumstances that followed the commencement of an unnatural contest, it was unfortunately confined to those alone."[38] Nonetheless, just as the PAS was being established, the Philadelphia Yearly Meeting adopted the Philadelphia Query of 1776, which declared that "many there are in membership with us who notwithstanding the labor bestowed, still continue to hold these people [our fellow men of the African race] as slaves."[39]

The 1776 Yearly Meeting accepted a "Report of committee to visit slaveholders in Philadelphia Quarterly Meeting." The committee reported "that in the Course of our several Visits on this Occasion, we have found many who are possess'd of these poor Captives." As it would often do, the meeting once again instructed all slave-owning Quakers to make plans to manumit their slaves, and it "endeavour'd to obtain the best Accounts we could of the number of Persons who are still detained in Bondage, within several Monthly Meetings" in the Philadelphia area. Nonetheless, the committee knew that many Quakers violated their decree.[40] The committee reported that from the time of its decree of August 1776 until the first accounting on September 21, 1776, nine more slaves "have obtained freedom" that were left under the care of the committee.

Thirty-eight years after Lay's 1738 "bloody" outburst and twelve years short of the hundredth anniversary of the Germantown Protest of 1688, many Quakers were still ambivalent toward slavery. Over the decades of the debate some Quaker slaveholders manumitted their slaves, others replaced slaves who died in captivity, and some saw no need for slave labor owing to the influx of German and other European immigrants who provided cheap labor.

The Quaker decision to move from a ban on the buying and selling of slaves to prohibiting slave ownership took nearly twenty years, from 1755 to 1774. In 1775 the Quakers made a decision to start "a speedy & close Labour" within the society and voted to begin visiting Quaker slaveholders. Du Bois noted with a hint of criticism that the Quakers had initially made strides against slavery, but they stalled. "Here," he wrote, "they rested until 1775, when after a struggle of 87 years, they decreed the exclusion of slaveholders from fellowship in the Society."[41] Du Bois was one year off, but he was otherwise correct.

Benezet served on the manumission committee and added to his already enormous tasks of teaching, writing, petitioning, and lobbying. His name appears often in the Monthly Meetings' "Manumission Book" as one of several members who visited Quaker slave keepers. Often it was in his handwriting that the minutes were recorded. For example on April 15, 1776, Esther House's manumission of her slave is recorded: "Esther House widow of George House deceased do hereby set free from bondage" her slave. The statement was "Sealed and Delivered . . . In the Presence of Esther House" and signed by Hugh Roberts and Benezet.[42]

In October 1779 the records showed "a testimony against John Lewis [has] been brought in and the contents of it approved by the Meeting . . . to be delivered to him by Anthony Benezet, Hugh Roberts and Isaac Lane." The records indicate "our friend Anthony Benezet reports that he hath taken an Opportunity of treating further with John Lewis, wherin he manifested his fixed resolution of holding the Negro in Bondage, but as the Testimony directed is not yet prepared; it is desired that past Services may be attended to the ensuing month."[43]

At a March 5, 1780, meeting the minutes of a visit to a Quaker slave owner, Richard Wistar, were recorded in Benezet's hand. He and Owen Jones visited Wistar, who owned "a Negro girl named Jane said to be Eleven years of age" and "a Negro boy named Richard, said to be twelve years of age." Benezet wrote that "some further labour appears to have been extended Richard Wistar, but as yet an unwillingness to comply with the advice of his Friends." Wistar appears to have asked for another extension and offered an excuse as to why he had not manumitted the slaves. Benezet recorded that "upon solid Consideration of his case . . . it may be best to discontinue the case" until the next meeting.[44] In this manner Quaker slaveholders could put off the manumission of their slaves for many years.

It seems that in the case of Wistar the committee prevailed some days later, for on May 10, 1780, Benezet signed a statement entered into the record: "a Negro boy name Richard said to be twelve years old" was given his freedom. Benezet added a caveat: "His setting them free in a mode differing from that advised by Friends of declining to suffer the manumissions to be Recorded in a Book kept by them for that purpose does not appear becoming of a Member of our religious Society and has given much pain to this meeting." At the same meeting testimony "against the misconduct of Abraham Shoemaker and Joseph Carr," also slave owners, was heard.[45]

The process of disciplining slave-owning Quakers could go on for years. Benezet's efforts are listed no less than fifty-five times from the time the manumission records were first kept until the time of his death. No other Quaker's involvement came close in the number of entries in the manumission ledgers. This work had long-term effects, as the number of slaveholding Friends in Philadelphia drastically dropped in the years before the Philadelphia Annual Meeting voted to expel them.

The Philadelphian Yearly Meetings of 1778 and 1779 called for all local meetings to form committees to aid former slaves. The meeting called on Quakers not just to free their own slaves but also to pressure others who refused to do so. The meeting called on the Friends to "let the oppressed go free" and "to attend to the further openings of duty."[46] The Philadelphia Meeting for Suffering of January 1780 called for the "lively concern for the discharge of Christian duty towards the oppressed Africans." The meeting went on to alert the Quakers that the Almighty was "graciously pleased to favour such [Friends] with his paternal regard, owning them as his children, by his judgments instructing them in righteousness." In other words, they not only had to fight to free blacks but they also had to ensure their well-being once freed. These actions would bring about spiritual benefits to the repentant slave owners, who would "know a happy dwelling place in the liberty of Truth . . . and to relieve the burden of the oppressed."[47]

Benezet and other leading Quakers also supported the efforts of Quaker wives to establish in 1781 the Committee to Inquire into the Condition of Freed Slaves.[48] The Quaker women met regularly from 1781 until 1785, when it was decided that "the business for which the committee was nominated is now nearly gone threw."[49] At one general meeting the women testified against "the misconduct" of Margaret Cummings and Gainer Luckens, both slaveholders.

The Pennsylvania Emancipation Act of 1780 provided for gradual emancipation, which substituted a form of indentured servitude to aid formerly enslaved Africans. In other words, like former white indentured servants they would be freed in a set number of years. The law stated that no enslaved African born after 1780 in Pennsylvania could be kept in slavery past the age of twenty-eight; additionally, a slave born in 1780 also had no guarantee of freedom until January 1, 1808, the date that a law banning the import of slaves in the United States came into effect. In the words of Nash and Soderlund, "Not only did the act prevent further growth of slavery in the state, but it undercut the legitimacy of the institution and this spurred slaves to free themselves, and owners to release their bondsmen and women."[50] The law was not retroactive and did not affect slaves born before March 1, 1780, "so that as late as 1840, Pennsylvania's census still listed a few aging slaves."[51] Some Pennsylvania slave owners still resisted the law, and slave owners in "western Chester, Lancaster, York, Cumberland, Westmoreland, and Washington counties—all located along the border with Maryland and Virginia—held on to slaves most persistently."[52] Slavery continued and expanded in the southern colonies.

Benezet, ever the optimist, kept up his relentless work as he neared his final hour. In 1783 he continued his prolific letter-writing campaign. Early in the year he wrote his friend George Dillwyn in London, saying, "I received thine [letter] by Johnny Morris, so late in ye evening, that I have not time to write Brother William."

Sometime in 1783 Benezet had written a pamphlet that was, according to Henry Cadbury, "rejected from publication by the Meeting for Sufferings." Benezet did publish *Notes on the Slave Trade* that year, but it did not offer any emancipation plan. In his packet to George Dillwyn he included his *Short Observations on Slavery,* which included extracts from the writing of Raynal on slavery. He told Dillwyn that he had placed "I think more than six months before ye committee of ye Meeting of Suffering an Essay a short representation of ye state & grievous Effect of Slavery." But it seems that he had difficultly in getting the press overseers to approve publication of the work "arising from a contradicting of Ideas." He told Dillwyn, "I hence several times intended to lay aside ye design but cannot with ease of mind." Cadbury believes that Benezet's ever developing ideas and his "suggestion of universal immediate emancipation seemed too radical and a pamphlet which he wrote upon the subject in 1783 was rejected form publication by the Meeting for suffering." As Cadbury concluded, "unfortunately we shall never know just what this paper contained."[53]

Benezet proceeded nonetheless to ignore his own pronouncements and immediately wrote William Dillwyn a lengthy letter, telling him of the necessity for "Friends, by themselves or in conjunction with others laying before Parliament that if they expect the Divine Blessing on their labour, they must endeavor to put an end to the Slave Trade." The letter revealed two important points about Benezet: first that he had no intent of slowing down his relentless attack on slavery, and second that, while he wrote Dillwyn of his desire to work in conjunction with "Granville Sharp, Parson Duche, David Barclay and Thoms. Wagstaf," he was prepared to go it alone if necessary to approach the Parliament. He praised Sharp, who "has taken a great deal of pains, by personal application to most of ye Bishops, to interest them in promoting the cause of freedom of the Negroes" and to end "ye iniquitous traffick."[54] Benezet was impressed by the work of the London Yearly Meeting in lobbying Parliament and its use of methods learned from him.

Pennsylvania Society for Promoting the Abolition of Slavery and for the Relief of Free Negroes Unlawfully Held in Bondage

In 1784, the year of Benezet's death and four years after Pennsylvania's gradual emancipation act, Connecticut and Rhode Island adopted gradual abolition plans, and the Pennsylvania Abolition Society was reestablished. The year after the gentle Quaker passed away, New York and New Jersey legislatures defeated gradual abolition plans. New York finally passed a gradual abolition act in 1799, and New Jersey became the last northern state to do so in 1804, four years before the ban on the international slave trade. No such act was passed in Virginia, but the Virginia Abolition Society was founded in 1790. For an organization in Virginia to include the word *abolition* in its name was imprudent at the time, so it took the name the Virginia Humane Society.[55] Slave imports began anew in Georgia and South Carolina, two of the states that had lost the most slaves.

In 1784 an effort was made to revise the old society. Regular meetings began for the first time since 1775. The standing "Negro Committee" of the Pennsylvania Monthly Meeting in 1784 reprinted the London Quakers' appeal to the British Parliament, "The Case of Our Fellow Creatures, the Oppressed Africans," and sent it to all members of Congress in Pennsylvania and New Jersey.

Benezet had only a few months to live, but his work in publicizing recent black suicides led in the effort to renew the society. Only a few weeks before he died, twenty men met, and the Pennsylvania Abolition Society was revived. Among the twenty, Thomas Meredith became its president, John Todd its secretary, and James Starr its treasurer. Meredith soon resigned, and Samuel Richards was elected president. A year later James Whiteall was elected president, and Todd and Starr were reelected.[56]

Early in 1787 six members from the original society joined with thirty-six new members, and the society was reorganized as the Pennsylvania Society for Promoting the Abolition of Slavery and for the Relief of Free Negroes Unlawfully Held in Bondage; and for Improving the Condition of the African Race, still known as the PAS. Benjamin Rush joined with Tench Coxe, Thomas Harrison, William Jackson, and the shipbuilder Jonathan Penrose to help write its new constitution, and the secretaries were "directed to have one thousand copies of the Constitution printed, together with the names of the officers of the Society, and the acts of the Legislature of Pennsylvania for the gradual abolition of slavery."[57]

The first official meeting was held on April 23, three weeks before the first meeting of the Constitutional Convention. Among its new members, along with Coxe, were the wealthy entrepreneur James Pemberton; the Quaker merchant and revolutionary leader Thomas Paine; Hilary Baker, who would soon become the mayor of Philadelphia; and other wealthy men such as Casper Wistar, John Keighn, and Casper Haines.[58]

Franklin, who had recently returned from Paris, became the honorary president in 1787, although "he was so crippled with gout that he had to be carried in a sedan chair to the opening of the Constitutional Convention."[59] James Pemberton and Jonathan Penrose were the vice presidents, although Penrose, as the first vice president, presided at the meetings.[60] The PAS was multidenominational. Rush was a Presbyterian, Franklin an agnostic, and Coxe was also not a Quaker.[61] In the words of Thomas Drake, "Liberals of every kind joined in the work."[62] In this disciplined manner they were also instructed to "prepare letters to be sent to each of the Governors of the United States, with a copy of the Constitution and Laws, and a copy of Clarkson's Essay on the Commerce and Slavery of the Africans."[63]

Franklin gave the newly reconstituted organization national and international respect because of the enormous prestige of his name. During his presidency Franklin, as a delegate to the Constitutional Convention, enabled the group to pass along their petitions regarding the slave trade to the men determining the future of American government. His membership also kept the group's petitions and memorials from being dismissed outright by the new Congress, as even the staunchest supporters of the institution of slavery held him in high esteem. Shortly after he had taken the position of society president, he received a congratulatory letter from a Dr. Price, a friend in London and the author of a tract titled "Observations on the Importance of American Liberty." Dated September 26, 1787, Price's letter read, "A similar institution to yours, for abolishing Negro slavery, is just formed in London. . . . I need not say how earnestly I wish success to such institutions." Writing of the Constitutional Convention, he remarked, "God guide their deliberations. The happiness of the world depends, in some degree, on the result." Clearly optimistic about both the Constitutional Convention and the Abolition Society, Price told Franklin that "the minds of men are becoming more enlightened; and the silly despots of the world are likely to be forced to respect human rights, and to take care not to govern too much, lest they should not govern at all."[64]

The society members wrote "letters to the Society in New York for the relief of the free Negroes, & c—to Thomas Clarkson and Dr. Price, of London, and to the Abbé Raynal, in France."[65] Indeed, the international links of the fight against slavery began to be forged. Samuel Hoare, Jr., the secretary of the British Antislavery Society that had just been formed on July 17, 1787, sent a letter to his Philadelphia cohorts that was well received. He requested information on the treatment of newly manumitted slaves. The Philadelphia society in reply told him, "Respecting the treatment of slaves, we can say but little from our own personal observations, inasmuch as the progress of truth and humanity has in some degree extirpated Negro slavery from amongst us: but we have no doubt of the truth of the numerous histories which have been published of the cruel treatment and sufferings of slaves in the Southern States and in the West Indies." Of those slaves that had been set free, the Philadelphians told the Londoners, "Their behavior in general has been more orderly than that of the same class of white people."[66] In a remarkable exchange the members of the Philadelphia society wrote lauding the Londoners and shared with them their joy at how far the abolitionist movement had come on both sides of the Atlantic: "About thirty years ago, a few well-disposed men published several tracts upon this subject. These tracts met with great and general opposition. The controversies produced by them contributed to excite the attention of the public to the claims of the Africans, and thereby increase the number of their advocates in the Middle and eastern Provinces of America."[67] The Philadelphia authors were referring to the "Epistle of 1754" and Woolman's and Benezet's tracts and more directly to Benezet's letter to the SPG. Rush was so taken up with the activities that he even promised to release his own slave William Grubber. Franklin wrote to Sharp on June 9, 1787, and sent him in the name of the PAS copies of its new constitution and by-laws. He then told Sharp that "from a most grateful sense of the zeal and abilities with which you have long and successfully defended the claims of the oppressed Africans, the Society have done themselves the honor of enrolling your name in the number of their corresponding members and earnestly request the continuance of your labors in the great object of the institution." Sharp replied on January 10, 1788, from London: "I ought long ago to have acknowledged the deep sense which I entertain of my obligation to the Pennsylvania Society for Promoting the Abolition of Slavery, for the honour they have been please to confer upon me." On September 1788, John Jay the President of the New York Anti-Slavery Society, conferred honorary membership on Sharp.[68]

Rush wrote to Jeremy Belknap, the Congregationalist and reform-minded minister of Boston's Federated Street Church, on August 19, 1788. He told Belknap, "I love even the name Africa, and never see a Negro slave or freeman without emotions which I seldom feel in the same degree towards my unfortunate fellow creatures of a fairer complexion . . . let us continue to love and serve them, for they are our brethren not only by creation, but by redemption." He asked as Benezet did many years before, "When shall Ethiopia stretch forth her hand to embark the olive branch of the Gospel?"[69] With thoughts of Benezet always close to his heart, Rush rekindled his abolitionist fire.

Benezet was elated as others began to play the role that he at first had handled almost alone. This was achieved by petitions and memorials to the state and national legislatures, printed appeals to the public, and speeches and letters by political and religious leaders. Much of the work was initiated by the emerging abolition societies, which "accomplished a vast amount of work, intensifying, extending, and perpetuating the antislavery sentiment which without their aid might have died out after the influence of the Revolution had spent its strength, or would have lingered only in the hearts of a few individuals."[70] Benezet's purposefulness as an individual and as a mass organizer served as the lodestar.

The PAS soon petitioned the Constitutional Convention, calling for a ban on slaveholding. By war's end the discussion and reasoning behind abolitionism changed from religious, philosophical, and humanitarian concerns to cold politics.[71] After the Quaker persecution during the Revolutionary War years had ended, abolitionism to some was not seen as radical or dangerous, as it once was, and a broader array of men joined the ranks. Yet some whites who had called for abolition, once they achieved their own unqualified freedom, abandoned the plight of the enslaved Africans.[72]

As the Constitutional Convention convened on May 28, 1787, one of its first orders of business was slavery. As Adam Rothman has observed, "The new Union could not survive without the participation of the southern states, and the price of the southern states' participation was a guarantee that the national government would refrain from trampling on the rights of shareowners." Thus the "three-fifths clause" came into being.[73] The Constitution did not mention the words *slave* or *slavery*, but at the insistence of the southern delegates it was agreed that the international slave trade would last for another twenty years. The carefully formulated words of the Constitution allowed for the "migration or importation of such persons as any of the states now existing shall think proper to admit." Section 2 of Article 4 deemed that "no person held to service or labour in one state . . . [and] escaping into another, shall, in consequences of any law . . . therein, be discharged from such service, but shall be delivered up on claim of the party to whom such service or labour may be due." These few words came to be known as "the Fugitive Slave Clause." One of the few who protested the measure was Gouverneur Morris, a New Yorker who represented Pennsylvania at the Constitution Convention in 1787. He had graduated from King's College (later Columbia) in New York in 1768 so he no doubt came under the influence of the moral philosophers. The author of large sections of the Constitution, he declared on August 7 that he would "never . . . concur in upholding domestic slavery," which brought "the curse of heaven on the states where it prevailed."[74] But then again, Morris of Pennsylvania could make such an attack on the slave-ocracy. The abolitionists of Pennsylvania were there to defend him.

The rewly reconstituted PAS also revised its constitution and increased its membership. As the society rejuvenated itself from its decline during the revolutionary period, its new mission included both its previous goal of preventing free blacks from being taken into slavery and the nationwide goal of abolishing slavery and bettering the condition of blacks once freed.[75] Using his organizational skills, Franklin proposed establishing a committee of twenty-four along with a number of subcommittees.[76]

A year later, in 1788, the Philadelphia Yearly Meeting urged that Friends promote "the spiritual and temporal welfare of such Negroe's and their children who have been restored to freedom." Further the meeting voted to follow the Benezet tradition to continue to provide a "pious education for black Children."[77] Benezet's *Observations on Slavery*, was also published in 1778.[78] The Quakers continued their work in assisting free black Pennsylvanians, and the PAS lobbied state and national legislatures for abolition as well as for laws preventing the return of fugitive slaves to their masters.

An Address to the Public was issued on November 8, 1789, by the PAS and was signed by Franklin. The group was incorporated that same year.[79] *An Address* was an appeal for the emancipation of slaves, the employment of freed blacks, and the education of their children. Franklin wrote, "Slavery is such an atrocious debasement of human nature, that its very extirpations, if not performed with solicitous care, may sometimes open a source of serious evils." He continued: "The unhappy man, who has long been treated as a brute animal too frequently sinks beneath the common standard of the human species. The galling chains that bind his body do also fetter his intellectual faculties, and impair the social affections of his heart."[80]

In 1790 the PAS appealed through a memorial to the Federal House of Representatives to end slavery and the slave trade, asking that the body "devise means for removing this Inconsistency from the Character of the American People." However, the southern planters prevented any movement in that direction. Then in 1794 the Convention of Philadelphia issued an address "To the Citizens of the United States," declaring of slavery that "it is inconsistent with the safety of the liberties of the United States. Freedom and Slavery Cannot long live together."[81]

Many members of the society were prominent lawyers, such as William Rawle, the president of the Pennsylvania Bar in the early nineteenth century, and David Paul Brown, who worked on determining the constitutional rights of blacks. The members of the PAS "never transcended the limits of the law" but instead used legal reasoning to support their clients' petitions for freedom.[82] They also asked local newspapers to stop printing advertisements for the sale of slaves.[83] Continuing Benezet's lifelong mission, the PAS worked to build schools and to support preexisting schools for blacks. Members of the PAS also worked to establish systems of employment for recently manumitted blacks, to find employment for free blacks, and to aid in finding work for hundreds of illegally transported slaves from ships that had docked in Philadelphia.[84] Around the same time that the PAS was undergoing constitutional revisions, members of Philadelphia's "Free People of Color" began to mobilize and eventually founded the Free African Society.

When he received a letter from the secretary to Lord Howe, Benezet realized that his was a voice listened to by the highest of authorities. In one of the last letters before his death Benezet addressed Queen Charlotte of Britain, following earlier letters to the queens of France and Portugal. Benezet hoped that slavery would come to an end with the coming of peace after the Revolutionary War. To his dismay it increased, especially in the south.

He had addressed Queen Charlotte on August 25, 1783: "I take the liberty, very respectfully, to offer to thy perusal some tracts which I believe faithfully describe the suffering conditions of many hundred thousands of our fellow creatures of the African race." In addition to sending her the letter, he included in the package some of his "Tracts the subject to which I have thus ventured to crave particular attention." He wrote to the queen, "I hope thou will kindly excuse the Freedom used on this Occasion by an ancient Man, whose Mind for more than forty years past, has been much separated from the common course of the World, & long painfully exercised in the Consideration of the Miseries under which so large a Part of Mankind."[85] The "large part of mankind" he sought to free were those with black skin. For Benezet the curse was not on them but on those of the white race that had held them in bondage.

In 1783 Benezet published *Notes on the Slave Trade.*[86] Much of the pamphlet was taken verbatim from *Observations,* without the first five-and a-half pages, which were devoted to a discussion of war and the American Revolution. *Observations* was, along with *Short Observations,* the only pamphlet in which Benezet linked the American Revolution with the fight against slavery. He challenged the American revolutionaries by writing that "the observation which the Apostle makes on War, may well be applied to those who compelled their fellow men to become their slaves, they lusted for wealth and power and desired to have, that they might consume it upon their lusts."[87] Going further, he quoted from the Declaration of Independence: "We hold these truths to be self evident." Benezet then confronted the ideas of the revolutionaries and pointed out their contradictions. He asked "that after these, and other declarations of the same kind, have been so publicly made to the world, Slavery should continue in its full force in the Colonies; and even in some cases, its band should, by Law, be further established, is a great aggravations of that guild which has for so long lain upon America." He then exclaimed to an anonymous person, a "Friend in the south," "perhaps nothing will so sensibly teach us to feel for the afflictions of the oppressed Africans, as that ourselves partake of the same cup of distress, we have so long been instrumental in causing them to drink."[88]

The Death of Friend Anthony Benezet

In *Short Observations on Slavery,* Benezet began to reflect on his life. He contemplated "the HOUR of REFLECTION that awful hour which will come upon all," when people are called on "impartially to review the transactions of their past life."[89] When Anthony Benezet died on May 3, 1784, the antislavery movement had gone from literally one man in Philadelphia to the beginning of a network with antislavery societies and manumission laws being established in America, England, and France. Black and white organizations that both sought to win equality for those newly freed and fight for the freedom of those still enslaved would soon be created.

Benjamin Rush summed up the totality of Benezet's life and the founding of the abolition movements in America—and in Britain and France. He wrote, "Great events have been brought about by small beginnings. Anthony Benezet stood alone a few years ago in opposing Negro slavery in Philadelphia and now 3/4ths of the province as well as the city cry out against it. I sometimes please myself with the hopes of living to see it abolished or put upon another footing in America."[90] It was Benezet's dream to leave the mortal world knowing that the antislavery "footing" was firmly grounded. His dream was coming true.

In Benezet's will, even before he provided for his wife, the first line read, "Be it remembered That I, Anthony Benezet, a teacher of the Free School for the Black People in Philadelphia, being of a Sound and well disposed Mind and memory, do make this my last Will and Testament." Upon the death of his wife his estate would be left to the "overseers of the Publick School of Philadelphia." He left provisions to "hire and employ a religious minded person or persons to teach a number of Negroe, Mulatto, or Indian Children to read and write, Arithmetic, plain Accounts, Needle-work, &c." He then left James Starr and Thomas Harrison fifty pounds to put in the trust "for the use of a certain Society who are forming them-selves for the relief of such black People & other who apprehend them-selves illegally detained in Slavery to enable them to employ lawyers," to aid enslaved blacks to secure their freedom. In the last line of his will he left Margaret Till "an oppress & much afflicted black woman now in John Dickinson's service the sum of five pounds."[91] Even on his deathbed the plight of the oppressed blacks remained in his thoughts and his deeds.

Long after Benezet's death, antislavery advocates continued to invoke his name. Antislavery newspapers and periodicals of the early nineteenth cen-tury time and again resurrected the legacy of Benezet. In 1784 J. Woods wrote *Thoughts on the Slavery of Negroes* in London. He paid tribute to Benezet, who in his studies of Africa "bears ample testimony to the ingenu-ity of these unhappy people in the mechanical arts, and to their capacity for the administration of civil government."[92] After Benezet's death several other important pamphlets revealed Benezet's influence. Among them were Thomas Cooper's *Letters on the Slave Trade* (1787), Africanus [Rev. Wil-liam Leigh], *Remarks on the Slave Trade, and the Slavery of the Negroes, in a Series of Letters* (1788), and James Field Stanfield's *Observations on a Guinea Voyage, in a series of Letters Addressed to the Rev. Thomas Clarkson* (1788).[93] Stan-field had worked on slave ships during the Middle Passage and was, accord-ing to Marcus Rediker, "the first to write about the slave trade from the perspective of the common sailor."[94]

Another participant in the slave trade testified to Benezet's accuracy, and this statement was included in the 1788 edition of *Some Historical Account of Guinea*. On July 7, 1783 a few months before Benezet's death, a former slave-ship captain from Bristol, Henry Gandy, wrote to William Dillwyn in London of his three voyages to Africa. On the first, in 1740, Gandy witnessed a ship-board slave revolt near Barbados. On the second voyage he then wrote: "I have carefully perused Anthony Benezet's Tracts on that subject" and had "never had such reflections arise, as I never experienced before doubtless owing to my formerly being less convinced of the iniquity of such traffic than I am now," after he had read Benezet's *Some Historical Account of Guinea*. He told Dillwyn that "a six and twenty years residence in the West-Indies gave me a full opportunity of knowing the cruelties exercised there on the slaves, hav-ing in the ways of the trade frequented almost all of the English Islands, and some of the Dutch, French and Spanish." He added, "I can therefore confi-dently affirm that Anthony Benezet, and others writers quoted by him, are by no means exaggerated."[95] Such praise for Benezet's work continued for the rest of the eighteenth century and well into the nineteenth century.

Benezet probably would have agreed with the nineteenth-century Cuban patriot José Martí, who once said, "All the glory in the world can be put in a kernel of corn." Nonetheless, the Society of Friends held a memorial for him on May 2, 1785, a year after his death. The memorial recounted his life and deeds and his work among blacks and whites. It noted that he "was buried in our Grave Yard in this city, on which solemn occasion a great concourse of Inhabitants of all ranks and professions attended, manifesting the universal esteem in which he was held." He would not have wanted crowds to gather or the masses to mourn his passing and praise his glory. But he would have been deeply moved that among the mourners were "several hundred Black people [who] in like manner testified the grateful sense they had of the benefits derived to them, through his acts of Friendship and pious Labours on their behalf."[96]

On July 15, 1798, Rush wrote, "Few men, since the days of the apostles, ever lived a more disinterested life. And yet, upon his death bed, he said he wished to live a bit longer, that he might bring down SELF." He added, "The last time he ever walked across his room, was to take from his desk six dollars, which he gave to a poor widow whom he had long assisted to maintain."[97] Joseph Redman wrote to Rush on November 14, 1798: "Anthony Benezet was undoubtedly a most worthy man, and I have little doubt that his universal philanthropy will be rewarded by his divine Master."[98]

The *Evening Fireside* of Philadelphia in 1805 noted "the language of Benezet now issues from the tomb. It speaks intelligibly to you, ye giddy and ye gay! Its precepts cannot be mistaken, may you hear them, therefore with attention. If they should prove ineffectual, proceeding, as they do, from the dead, thus will the voice of the Songster in Jerusalem be heard no more, and her 'mourners will go about the streets.' "[99]

The *Philanthropist* of Mt. Pleasant, Ohio, on June 4, 1818, reprinted the letter sent to Benezet by Patrick Henry on January 18, 1773, thanking him for a copy of his *Some Historical Account of Guinea.* The *Philanthropist* also reprinted in its September 1817 edition Benezet's letter of August 25, 1783, addressed to Charlotte, queen of Britain, pleading with her to help end the slave trade. *The Genius of Universal Emancipation,* edited by Benjamin Bundy, reprinted in its January 1831 edition Benezet's letter to the Abbé Raynal of July 16, 1781, just as the debate over slavery waxed in the U.S. Congress.

African American leaders also continued to pay homage to the gentle Quaker years after his death. On April 14, 1836, James Forten, Jr., the eldest son of the famed black abolitionist who had been deeply influenced by Benezet spoke before the Philadelphia Female Anti-Slavery Society. He told the gathering: "You are called fanatics. Well, what if you are? Ought you to shrink from this name? God forbid. There is eloquence in such fanaticism, for it whispers hope to the slave; there is sanctity in it, for it contains the consecrated spirit of religion; it is the fanaticism of a Benezet, a Rush, a Franklin, a Jay."[100] The fact that the descendant of a slave invoked the name Benezet as first among equals in the antislavery crusade showed the depth of black admiration for a man who dedicated his life to this cause. In the British parliamentary debates of the late eighteenth and early nineteenth centuries no less a figure than Wilberforce quoted the words of Benezet.

The newspaper of the Eastern Pennsylvania Anti-Slavery Society, the *Pennsylvania Freeman,* on January 10, 1839, and the *National Enquirer* a year before, on January 11, 1838, printed articles condemning colonization of the oppressed African. Both articles were signed "BENEZET," the name taken by the unidentified author in Anthony Benezet's memory over fifty years after his death.

The delegates to the Pennsylvania Black State Convention of 1848 issued an "Appeal to the Voters of the Commonwealth of Pennsylvania." After presenting their case to the enfranchised whites, the black delegates noted that "when the last scroll of the time shall be wound up on the great windlass of eternity it will present the indestructible names of your Penn's, Franklin's, Rushes, Wistar's, Benezet's, Woolman's, Morrises', Wilson's, Taylor's, and a host of others whose highest aim was justice to mankind."[101]

In 1857 John Watson, editor of the *Annual Journal,* paid tribute to the Benezet legacy with pride and to the fact that hundreds of blacks followed his coffin in the streets. "Anthony Benezet, as I have been told by eyewitnesses, had the largest funeral that had ever been seen in Philadelphia. One third-of the number were blacks, who walked in the rear."[102] Watson did not see the irony in Benezet's goals and present-day reality.

By 1859 the Board of Education of the Pennsylvania Society for the Promoting of the Abolition of Slavery (the body with overall responsibility for black education in the city) published a report, *Statistics of the Colored People of Philadelphia,* which described a large network of day and evening, charity, benevolent, orphan, and reform schools that existed in Philadelphia. The models established by Benezet had inspired them all.[103] That same year Wilson Armistead quoted from "the author of the *History of the Friends in America*," who justly observed, "had Sandiford and Lay, and Benezet and Woolman, allowed their convictions to have been silenced by the prevailing public opinion, or even by the views of [some] of there own brethren in religious profession, it is doubtful whether at this day a Free State would be found throughout the widely extended limits of the great American republic."[104] Armistead wrote in the same year that John Brown led the attack on the garrison at Harper's Ferry. Two years later Confederate forces attacked Fort Sumter and the Civil War began. The peaceful words of men like Benezet could not solve the dilemma that men should have confronted during the American Revolution seventy-five years before. By then, as Frederick Douglass would say, "The time had come to make war upon . . . the savage barbarism of slavery."

Near death, Benezet told a friend, "I am dying and feel shamed to meet the face of my maker, I have done so little in his cause." The blacks who followed his funeral procession felt differently. The enslaved African men, women, and children who Benezet fought to free viewed him as a saint among sinners, a healer amid pain, and a godsend among infidels. That is why when he died, there was the largest gathering of blacks in Philadelphia up until that time, and a companion number of whites followed his casket along the streets of Philadelphia to the burial grounds of the Society of Friends.[105]

In *Biographical Anecdotes of Anthony Benezet,* written by Rush on July 15, 1788, he told the story of "Colonel J—N, who has served in the American army, during the late war in returning from the funeral" that "pronounced an eulogium upon him. It consisted only of the following words: 'I would rather' said he 'be Anthony Benezet in that coffin, than George Washington with all his fame.'"[106] Such was the esteem held for the gentle man who with quiet dignity went about "God's work."

It is often said that sometimes the greatest tributes come from an adversary. On December 24, 1787, the proslavery *State Gazette of South-Carolina* reprinted Benjamin Rush's *"Paradise of Negro Slaves—a Dream,"* which had first been published in the *Columbian Magazine.*[107] In his *Dream* Rush paid tribute to a simple man with a grand plan to free the Atlantic world of slavery and oppression. He paid tribute to a man whose work laid the fundamental basis for future generations to gather courage in the face of often ruthless opposition.

Rush dreamed through the words and deeds of Anthony Benezet. Through Benezet the Africans told Rush about the horrors of slavery and the brutality of the slave trade where they were "once dragged by the men of your colour from their native country, and consigned by them to labour—punishment—and death."[108] Rush's dream envisioned a paradise where they would realize their freedom in death if not in life—something akin to the African concept of the transmigration of the soul. Rush's dream envisioned a paradise where they would realize their freedom in death if not in life.[109]

Benezet's dream was to create a transatlantic antislavery movement to free the enslaved Africans from their misery and to establish a network to support and educate blacks once freed. His dream was to educate whites both about their complicity with slavery and about their obligations to blacks and their duty to humankind. Rush's dream ended in a remarkable fashion:

All at once, the eyes of the whole assembly were turned from me directed to a little white man who advanced towards them, on the opposite side of the grove in which we were seated. His face was grave, placid, and full of benignity. In one hand he carried a subscription paper and a petition; in the other he carried a small pamphlet on the unlawfulness of the African Slave Trade, and a letter directed to the King of Prussia, upon the unlawfulness of war. While I was employed in contemplating this venerable figure—suddenly I beheld the whole assembly running to meet him—the air resounded with the clapping of hands—and I was awakened from my dream by the noise of a loud and general acclamation of—ANTHONY BENEZET![110]

Chronology of Atlantic Abolitionism

This chronology includes international efforts to abolish slavery in the years 1514–1808 and in particular Quaker antislavery activities during the period 1657–1804.

1514   Pope Leo X issues a papal bull condemning the slave trade and slavery.

1521–1572   In 1521 forty slaves on the Hispaniola estate of Christopher Columbus's son revolt. There are more uprisings in Hispaniola in 1533, 1537, and 1548. Revolts follow in Mexico (1523, 1527, and 1537), Puerto Rico (1527), Cuba (1533 and 1538), Colombia (1545), Honduras (1548), Panama (1555 and 1572), and Ecuador (1570).

1562–1567   Englishman John Hawkins trades and plunders in Spanish America and carries three hundred slaves from West Africa to Hispaniola.

1595   In Brazil, Amador leads slaves to devastate sugar plantations and capture the city of São Paulo.

1598   In Colombia, following a series of small slave uprisings, thousands of slaves revolt in the gold mines near Zaragoza.

1619   The first Africans arrive in Virginia.

The first representative assembly meets.

A Dutch ship delivers "twenty and odd" Africans to the English settlement of Jamestown, Virginia, where they are sold by bid as indentured servants.

1639   During a revolt on St. Kitts, five hundred whites mobilize and kill sixty rebellious slaves.

1656   Angolan and Senegambian slaves rebel in Guadeloupe.

1657   George Fox issues an epistle "To Friends Beyond the Sea That Have Black and Indian Slaves," the first work on slavery written by a Quaker.

1663   Black slaves and white servants plan a rebellion in Gloucester County, Virginia, but they are betrayed by another servant. This marks the first major slavery rebellion in British North America.

1671   George Fox and William Edmundson, an Irishman, come to the New World (Barbados). Fox preaches to the black slaves and says to the masters "that after certain years of servitude they would make them free."

1672   The Virginia colony forbids Society of Friends from taking blacks to their religious meetings.

1673   Richard Baxter publishes *A Christian Directory, or, a Summ of Practical Theologie, Conscience, in London, Which Condemned the Practice of Slavery*. The section on slavery is written in 1664–65. In it he writes "directions to those masters in foreign plantations who have Negroes and other slaves" and that "to his mind, African slavers were 'pirates,'" engaged in the "worst kinds of thievery in the world." He refers to them as beasts for their mere commodity, and betray, or destroy, or neglect their souls."

The British colony of Jamaica has its first major slave uprising.

1674   In Sandwich, Massachusetts, the Friends set aside part "of the burying place, next to the swamp" to bury blacks. Since the Quakers do not use headstones, it is impossible to identify black grave sites by name.

1675   Governor Atkins of Barbados honors the Quaker request to be relieved from patrol duty. He requires them to report all signs of insubordination among the blacks on the island.

William Edmundson is brought before Governor Atkins and is accused of preaching and stirring up rebellion among the blacks. Edmundson denies the charges and asserts that by giving the blacks religious teaching it will prevent rebellion and help maintain slavery. He believes that bad treatment and ignorance will lead to rebellion among the enslaved Africans.

A slave rebellion occurs in Barbados. The first anti-Quaker laws are passed there. Governor Atkins passes a law prohibiting "the people called Quakers from bringing Negroes to those meetings." He also forbids them from sending blacks to their schools.

1676   Members of the Society of Friends are forbidden to take slaves to Quaker meetings. The penalty for violating the law is the confiscation of one-half of the value of every slave at the meeting. A law is passed requiring all Quakers to take an oath of allegiance to the Crown. Since Quaker doctrine forbids oath taking, they would not comply. Because of the oath many Quakers leave the teaching profession, and consequently they and many others leave the island for the continent.

George Fox writes *Gospel, Family-Order*. In the work he challenges Quakers to be kind to their slaves and to bring them up as Christians. He also calls for giving freed Africans the same treatment as indentured servants are given on their freedom.

William Edmundson travels to the colonies. At the Newport Quaker center, on September 19, 1676, he sends a general letter of advice to the Quakers in America. In the letter he writes, "And Friends that have Negroes is [sic] to take great care to restrain one another. They are to be restrained and watched over, and diligently admonished in the fear of God and all men, and those things the Lord requires." He also writes that "perpetual slavery is an aggravation, and oppression upon the mind, and hath a ground; and Truth is that which works the remedy, and breaks the yoke, and removes the ground. So it would do well to consider that they [the slaves] may feel, see, and partake of your liberty in the Gospel of Christ [that] they may see and know the difference between you and the other people, and your self-denial may be known to all." In the postscript he asks the question, "And many of you count it unlawful to make slaves of the Indians: and if so, then why not the Negroes?"

1677	The Quaker Richard Sutton is arrested in Barbados "for allowing thirty Negroes to be present at their meeting."

1678   Virginia forbids Quakers to serve as schoolteachers because of their desire to teach blacks. Barbados reenacts the law against Quakers bringing blacks to meetings and in 1680 forbids Quakers from having any meetings.

Women Friends in Maryland resolve to show "strict justice" toward Africans regarding education, religious benefits, and personal treatment. They also decide that on returning to local meetings they should "impress on the minds of our brethren and Sisters a close consideration of what may be called for at our hands in regard to this People, in consequence of our high profession of Justice and Equity."

1682   William Penn grants the articles of the "Free Society of Traders." The articles state that enslaved Africans after a service of fourteen years will be bound to one place of soil and are no longer to be indiscriminately bought, sold, and transported. The articles also curtail the separation of families.

1684   The ship *Isabella* arrives in Philadelphia with 150 African slaves.

The Maryland colony forbids manumission, but a slave of a Quaker named William Dix of the Third Haven Monthly Meeting had already accumulated enough funds to purchase his freedom.

1688   Quakers of Germantown issue the first resolution condemning slavery.

Protest submitted by Germantown Quakers to Quarterly Meeting of May 4, 1688. The letter read, "These are the reasons why we are against the traffic of men-body or handled at this manner? viz., to be sold or made a slave for all the time of his life?" They were referring to the slave trading of the early Turks.

At the Quarterly Meeting in Philadelphia the members write that slavery is "a thing of too great a weight" to determine and therefore assign three members to inquire into the matter and present their findings to the Yearly Meeting. The records do not show the committee findings or what they presented to the Yearly Meeting. There is a record of "a paper . . . by some German Friends concerning the lawfulness and unlawfulness of buying and keeping Negroes." The meeting concludes that "it was adjudged not to be so proper for this meeting to give a positive judgment in the case, it having so general a relation to many other parts; and therefore at present they forbear it." The meeting does not make a decision because too many members own slaves themselves.

1690   In Jamaica three hundred slaves take control of their master's house and weapons and kill onlookers from the neighboring estate. The militia kills two hundred of the slaves and hangs the survivors, while a few manage to escape into the mountains.

1692   In Barbados, Ben, Sambo, and others lead an Afro-Creole plot.

1693   A law is enacted requiring all black slaves to carry passes from their masters.

William Bradford, a follower of George Keith, prints a pamphlet to be signed by Keith's "Christian Quakers." It is called *An Exhortation & Caution to Friends Concerning Buying and Keeping of Negroes.* He writes, "Negroes, blacks and tawnies are a real part of mankind." Because slavery violates the Golden Rule, as William Edmundson and the Germantown Quakers had said before them, the Keithians maintain that Christians have the duty and obligation to assist the enslaved Africans to escape. They reason that because God had commanded his people not to return an escaped servant to bondage, Christians could not possibly hold slaves. They also insist that the Bible says that servants should not be oppressed and that no oppression could possibly equal slavery.

1696   Philadelphia Quakers advise members to "be careful" of their Negroes. The Quakers are urged to either bring blacks to meetings or have special meetings with them and to "restrain them from loose and lewd living, as much as in them lies, and from rambling abroad on First-day or other times."

Robert Pyles of the Concord, Pennsylvania, Meeting writes of his objections to slavery, citing the dangers of slave uprisings. He believes that it is the lust for money that brought about the rise of slavery. This view is also held by the prominent Welsh-born Quaker Cadwalder Morgan. Morgan does not condemn slavery or call for its end, but after having gotten a call from God, he asserts that "I should not be concerned with them, that is the slaves."

1697   Philadelphia Monthly Meeting records show that "a paper of Pentecost Teague's is read, relating to the selling of Negroes at the public market place, and outcry, and it is the sense of this meeting that Friends ought not to sell them after that manner." . . . "It is further agreed," the records show, "that Friends do meet together this day week at this house about the first hour, to consider and write Friends of the monthly meetings in Barbados, to desire to acquaint Friends that they forbear sending any Negroes to this place, because they are too numerous here."

1698   The Philadelphia Monthly Meeting is held on October 30, where they wrote to the Barbados General Meeting to seek cooperation in suppressing shipment of slaves to Pennsylvania. The letter begins, "Dear Friend and Brethren, It having been the sense of our Yearly Meeting that many Negroes in these parts may prove prejudicial several ways to us and our posterity, it was agreed that endeavors should be used to put a stop to the importing of them; and in order there unto, that those Friends that have correspondents in the West Indies should discourage the sending any more hither."

1700   At the urging of William Penn the March 1700 Meeting begins to hold meetings for blacks and encourages all members to send their slaves.

Chief Justice Samuel Sewall of Massachusetts writes *The Selling of Joseph*. He writes that the "Ethiopians as black as they are," are "sons and daughters of the first Adam, . . . brethren and sisters of the last Adam, and the offspring of God." Sewall pays wages to his own slave Scipio. He believes slavery is only justified as punishment for a person convicted of a crime.

The Pennsylvania assembly levies a small duty on blacks. Pennsylvania enacts a law that provides legal sanction to the holding of slaves for life.

William Penn writes in his will, "I will give my blacks their freedom as is under my hand already, and to old Sam, 100 acres, to his children after he and his wife are dead forever, on common rent of one bushel of wheat yearly, forever." His widow asks the prominent Philadelphian James Logan to see to the selling of her small slave children and their parents to good people.

The first act of manumission is recorded in the colony.

The New York Yearly Meeting instructs its members to "bring their children and servants [i.e., slaves] to meeting as much as may be."

1702   Slaves attempt to commandeer the slave ship *Tiger* off the coast of Gambia. Forty slaves and two whites are killed.

1703   Friends in the Middletown Meeting in Bucks County, Pennsylvania, decide that they are not "satisfied having Negroes buried in Friends' burying ground." They appoint two members to "Fence off a portion for such use."

1710   The duty on slaves increases in Pennsylvania.

1711   In 1711 and every year after, the Chester, Pennsylvania, Meeting brings up the issue of slavery. However, the slave-owning Quakers and their Quaker friends always defeat the antislavery Quakers. The proslavery Quakers write, "Friends in many other places are concerned in it" as much or more as in Pennsylvania. The meeting held to the 1686 decision that slave trading and the importation of blacks is wrong but that it was not wrong to buy slaves for private use.

Pennsylvania increases the duty on slaves. The assembly votes to prohibit the importation of slaves.

Penn's will of 1711 supersedes that of 1701, and there is no mention of the freedom of his slaves.

A Quaker woman near New Bedford, Massachusetts, is disowned from the meeting for having a slave beaten so badly that he died. Seven months later she applies for reinstatement, and her request is denied. However, after public repentance she is later readmitted.

1712   The Privy Council votes to ban the Pennsylvania duty on slaves and the assembly gives in.

Friends in Philadelphia write to London seeking advice. In their 1712 epistle they write, "And now dear Friends, we impart unto you a concern that hath wrested the minds of some of our brethren for many years, touching the importing and having Negro slaves, and detaining them and their property as such without any limitation or time of redemption from that condition." The Philadelphia Quakers also write of their previous attempts to stop the trade in Barbados.

They also write that "other traders have flocked amongst us, over whom we have no gospel authority; and such have increased and multiplied Negroes amongst us, to the grief of diverse friends." The London body disapproves of the letter, citing that the Philadelphia Friends should have consulted with other bodies in the colonies. The London body knew that the Philadelphia group was still in the minority.

William Sotheby becomes even more vocal in his call to end the importation of slaves and condemns the owning of slaves by Quakers.

Slaves in New York rebel, killing nine whites.

1715   The Pennsylvania Yearly Meeting of Quakers shows a growing chasm between the Meeting of Chester, which had an advanced position against slavery, and other societies. The Yearly Meeting appoints Isaac Norris, Nicolas Waln, and Richard Hill to give an answer to the Chester Meeting. However, the conservative members of the Philadelphia Meeting win out, and it becomes clear that they want an end to the discussions concerning slavery.

Some Newport, Rhode Island, Friends inquire of the Monthly Meeting "whether it is agreeable to Truth for Friends to brand or burn their servants or slaves on the cheek with a letter?" The answer from the meeting is "unanimous of the mind that no Friend ought to do it, but [be] cautioned to forebear doing it in the future."

John Hepburn, one of the Quaker moderates, publishes *The American Defense of the Christian Golden Rule*. He writes that slavery is "anti-Christian, a vile . . . contradiction of the gospel of the blessed messiah." Although he had lived in America for thirty years, he never owned slaves and protested that he would not "for all the riches and honors of this world . . . be found in this anti-Christian life and practice." He also writes that a slave has committed suicide "within a few miles of the place where I write this lamentable story." In his *American Defense* he wrote,

> And so, the Negro-masters may here see,
> Some of their Dangers in Eternity.
>   For there is no Repentance in the Graves,
> Of the Wrongs done unto [t]heir Negro-Slaves.
> The present time is their Repentant-Day;
> When that is done, I have no more to say.
>   If they persist in their ungodly Gains
> I'm like to get my Labor for my Pains
>   I'll come to a close, hoping they'll amend,
> In giving God the praise, and so I End.
>   J. H.

1716   The Dartmouth Meeting (the same one that disciplined a woman five years earlier for beating her slave) put a query before the Quarterly Meeting of Rhode Island. The query was "whether it be agreeable to Truth, to purchase and keep them term of life?" The Quarterly Meeting refers the query to subordinate meetings for their opinions. All the meetings are acrimonious and have great differences. The Friends in Nantucket, where few slaves existed, quickly agreed that the buying and selling of slaves was "not agreeable to Truth." However, the Dartmouth Meeting condemns slave trading but not slavery. The Greenwich Monthly Meeting, which is made up of planters in the "Southern County" on the western shore of Narragansett Bay, takes a position in the middle. They believe that the slave trade is wrong but do not reveal their position on slavery itself.

The Philadelphia Monthly Meeting of June condemns Sotheby and demands that he both refrain from his criticism and apologize. Sotheby does as they ask and writes an apology. But he does not refrain. However, when the 1716 meeting refuses to answer the Chester Meeting's request to condemn slaveholding, Sotheby again writes a paper against slavery. He is warned that he will be disowned. Records do not show what action was taken, and when he died on September 7, 1722, it appears that he died a member in good standing.

1717   At the Quarterly Meeting in Flushing, New York, Horsman Mullenix (or Molineaux) brings up the question of slavery, and it is referred to the Yearly Meeting, which defers action for a year.

In January, Newport Friends agree to wait and see what their "brethren in their parts do." They also advise members who were concerned about slavery to "exercise Christian charity toward each other."

In April, John Farmer delivers his "Epistle Concerning Negroes" to the Nantucket Friends. He is well received. He has read the epistle to other meetings before. However, when he attempts to read it to the June Yearly Rhode Island Meeting of Ministers and Elders, he is rebuffed. They disapprove of his remarks and advise him "to forebear publishing any paper here presented until Friends be further satisfied." In Quaker jargon, some twenty Friends "labored with him." Since he will not comply with the elders' order to desist, he is disowned until he agrees to retract his words. He later gives them his papers and apologizes for speaking without their permission.

The Yearly Meeting gives the following advice: "A weighty concern being on the Meeting concerning the importing and keeping slaves, this Meeting therefore refers it to the consideration of Friends everywhere, to wait for the wisdom of God how to discharge themselves in that weighty affair; and desires it may be brought up from our monthly and quarterly meetings to our next Yearly Meeting, and also that merchants do write their correspondents in the islands [i.e., the West Indies] and elsewhere, to discourage their sending any more [slaves] in order to be sold by any Friends here. This action allows the Elders to rid themselves both of Farmer and the query of the Dartmouth Friends." The Yearly Meeting further issued the following statement: "This Yearly Meeting having had further consideration relating to Friends buying and selling slaves, does conclude that the minute made at the last yearly Meeting in their case is sufficient for the present." With this statement the New England Quakers do not deal with the issue of slavery for the next ten years.

1718   The Philadelphia Yearly Meeting endorses again the disownment of John Farmer for "certain practices . . . in the reading and publishing papers tending to division and contrary to good order used among Friends." Like George Keith, William Sotheby, and Benjamin Lay, Farmer disappears after this defeat.

William Burling of Flushing, New York, writes an appeal to the Quakers, asking that they recognize the holding of slaves as a "sin": "Oh That I could prevail so far with all my dear brethren . . . that none would any more plead for or endeavor to defend [slavery] . . . neither endeavor to shield it from the judgment of Truth. We may do well to remember, the devil is the author of all sin, and sin is the transgression of the law."

After many years of persecution, Quakers want unity above all. Therefore, they allow those who hold slaves to keep them.

Philadelphia Yearly Meeting Minutes show that the meeting believed that the "selling and keeping Negroes, men or women slaves, for term of life hath been tenderly spoken to in much love and condescension for the Truth['s] sake" and that several Friends have declared that "they were fully satisfied in their consciences that the said practice was not right."

1719   The New York Friends consult with London, as London has instructed Philadelphia to do. London gives Philadelphia the same advice that it gave to New York.

1722   The Virginia Yearly Meeting "warned its members against engaging in slave trading as a business" and had urged them to treat their Negroes kindly.

1725–26   Pennsylvania enacts comprehensive black codes, regulating the lives of both free and enslaved blacks. Owners are held legally liable for their slaves' offenses.

1726   Pennsylvania raises the duty of slaves to £10, a rather large and prohibitive sum.

1727   The London Yearly Meeting strongly condemns slave trading.

1729   Duty on slaves is lowered to 40 shillings, and an increase of slaves occurs in Philadelphia.

            Ralph Sandiford, a Quaker immigrant from England and a merchant whose shop overlooks the slave-trading market (as Benezet's house did), witnesses slave trading. In 1729 Benjamin Franklin publishes Sandiford's *A Brief Examination of the Practice of the Times*. He is particularly concerned with members of the Friends and writes that had they "stood clear . . . it might have been answered to the traders in slaves that there is a people called Quakers in Pennsylvania, that will not own this practice in word or deed. Then would they have a burning and a shining to those poor heathen, and a precedent to the nations through out the universe; which might have brought them to have seen the evil of it in themselves, and glorified the Lord in our behalf." He continues, "But I have not so learned Christ . . . that the eternal love of the Father . . . should allow his followers in their most arbitrary and tyrannical oppression that hell has invented on this globe." Sandiford has observed that the English Friends had in their 1727 Yearly Meeting voted against the "importation of Negroes from their native country and relations." Sandiford, upon hearing of the decision, hoped that "we as a community may clear ourselves and the Truth." In *A Brief Examination*, Sandiford reveals that the chief judge of the province has threatened him with "commitment" if he publishes the volume. Sandiford regrets having to publish it without approval, but he does anyway. He writes, "The sense of it [had burdened his] life night and day." Sandiford becomes ill, and only after publishing the text does he feel better.

            Of course, a text published in Philadelphia would have far greater weight and reverberate farther than one published in Nantucket. Sandiford listens to the report of the Philadelphia Quarterly and Yearly meetings and is dismayed by their conservative approach to the slave question. The meeting has stated that since the question has been debated in 1715 and 1716, no other actions are needed. Bucks County comes to no decision and refers the matter to the Yearly Meeting to make a decision. The Burlington, New Jersey, Meeting believes that the buying of slaves is wrong and that it has caused a great number of slaves to be imported.

Two other New Jersey groups line up with the more reform-minded Chester Friends.

The Quarterly Meeting of Gloucester and Salem, Massachusetts, come to believe that Friends ought not buy slaves, just as they had been urged not to import them. The Shrewsbury, Massachusetts, Friends reply that the buying of slaves is wrong and should be prohibited.

1730   Elihu Coleman, a carpenter from Nantucket, and Ralph Sandiford, a Philadelphia merchant, both Quakers, take up the cause. Coleman writes that on the "20th of the Eleventh month [January], 1729/30," while not wanting to criticize the Quakers publicly about slaveholding . . . "which had been carried on so long pretty much in silence." He fears that the "ferment or stir that such a discourse . . . may make among some, who (Demetrius of old) may say, by this craft we have our wealth." Coleman believes "it may be in some of them [i.e., some Friends]." He then writes a pamphlet titled *A Testimony Against That Antichristian Practice of Making Slaves of Men*, and as the subtitle quoted Matthew 7:12, which cites slavery as unchristian and a violation of the Golden Rule. Coleman further writes that "Many sober men . . . both in writing and in their public [i.e., Quaker] assemblies whom I could name" have spoken against slavery. He continues, "I can truly say that this practice of making slaves of men appears to be so great an evil . . . that for all the riches and glory of this world, I would not be guilty of so great a sin as this seems to be." The Nantucket Meeting approves Coleman's manuscript and sends it with him to the Quarterly Meeting held in Newport, which is full of slaves. The meeting gives him permission to print the work, and it is finally published in 1733.

The Philadelphia Yearly Meeting issues a statement, which is rather weak. It reads, "Friends sought to be very cautious of making such purchases [of Negroes] for the future, it being disagreeable to the sense of the meeting."

The Yearly Meeting also directs the Monthly Meeting "to admonish and caution any members who persisted in buying slaves."

In 1735 and 1736 the meeting repeats the advice of 1730, and in 1737 it asks the Quarterly Meeting to report on the matter. In 1743 the Pennsylvania and New Jersey Friends draw up a set of "queries" on church discipline, which will be answered annually by the local meetings. The eleventh query asks whether Friends have been observing the past advices of the Yearly Meeting that calls for an end to the importation of slaves.

1730–1740   In Jamaica the first Maroon War takes place, involving Cudjoe the Younger, Nanny, and many other leaders.

1730   A slave revolt is discovered in the Norfolk and Princess Anne counties of Virginia.

1731   Anthony Benezet and his family move to Philadelphia from London, by way of Holland and France.

Benjamin and Sarah Lay come to Philadelphia by way of Barbados and Colchester, England, where Benjamin was born in 1681.

1732   Saddened by Quaker inaction against slavery in Philadelphia, the Lays move to Abington, six miles away. He lives in a cave, eats no meat, and wears nothing made from slave labor.

            In Venezuela between 30,000 and 40,000 slaves periodically rebel.

1733   Ralph Sandiford dies. He had retired in 1731 after being cast out by the Friends. His tombstone reads, "In Memory of Ralph Sandiford, son of John Sandiford of Liverpool, he bore a testimony against Negro trade 7 Dyed the 28th. Of the 3d. Month 1733. Aged 40 years."

            While Sandiford is sick, Benjamin Lay visits him. Lay believes that Sandiford's illness and death were caused by the ill treatment that slaveholding Friends gave him. It is believed that Sandiford's death sparked Lay to write his work later mentioned.

            Coleman's pamphlet titled *A Testimony Against That Antichristian Practice of Making Slaves of Men* is published, but like Keith and others he ends his antislavery activities.

1734   In Barbados, Thomas Chalkey, a Quaker minister from Philadelphia, is shot with buckshot for trying to "persuade the planters from treating their Negroes with tyranny and cruelty."

1735   The Philadelphia Meeting repeats the advice of 1730.

            The British North American colony of Georgia bans slavery but restores it afterward.

1735–1736 In Antigua, Tackey and Tomboy lead an island-wide Afro-Creole plot. Over ninety slaves are executed.

1736   The Philadelphia Meeting repeats the advice of 1730 and 1735.

1737   Benjamin Lay's *All Slave Keepers That Keep the Innocent in Bondage* is published. Benjamin Franklin prints the book. Just as Sandiford did with his own book, Lay does not place his name on the title page. Lay writes, "I know no worse or greater stumbling blocks the devil has to lay in the way of honest inquirers than our ministers and elders keeping slaves; and by the straining and perverting Holy Scriptures, preach more to hell than ever they will bring to heaven by their feigned humility." Later he writes, "How many profuse, profligate creatures have come in servants to this country, which have been stated [i.e., designated] not only as members, but as ministers in full unity, in less time than I have been here?" He asked if it was acceptable "that three or four men that has the mark of the beast, and number of his name, slave keepers, upon them in their foreheads should have the whole rule of discipline and govern contrary to all justice and equity? Time for such old rusty candlesticks to be moved out of their places, who have disowned many less innocent than themselves!"

In *All Slave Keepers,* Lay writes about whipping his own slaves in Barbados when he caught them stealing from his store. He develops a hatred of slavery. The conditions in Barbados were too harsh for the hunchback and his hunchback wife, Sarah.

In a mass suicide attempt thirty slaves die when a hundred of them jump from the *Prince of Orange* on the British Caribbean island of St. Kitts.

1738   At the Burlington Yearly Meeting of the Friends the hunchbacked Lay comes dressed in a military uniform with a sword hidden under his coat and a Bible that has been fitted with a bladder-like container filled with blood-colored pokeberry juice. During the debate Lay rises from his seat and exclaims, "Oh all you Negro masters who are contentedly holding your fellow creatures in a state of slavery during life, well knowing the cruel sufferings those innocent captives undergo in their state of bondage, both in these North America colonies, and in the West India islands; you know they are not made slaves by any direct law, but are held by an arbitrary and self-interested custom, in which you participate. And especially you who profess to do unto all men as ye would they say do unto you and yet, in direct opposition to every principle of reason, humanity, and religion, you are forcibly retaining your fellow man, from one generation to another, in a state of unconditional servitude." He then proclaims, "You might as well throw off the plain coat as I do. It would be as justifiable in the sight of the Almighty . . . if you should thrust a sword through their hearts as I do this book."

The Philadelphia Meeting records that "pursuant to the motion from the Philadelphia County, a doorkeeper is called and gives his attendance especially on account of one Benjamin Lay, a disorderly person."

Middletown Friends write that "deceased Negroes [are] forbidden to be buried within the bounds of the graveyard belonging to the meeting."

1739   Virginia Quakers "inquired of their brethren in North Carolina whether they too treated their slaves with care."

During the Stono Uprising in South Carolina eighty slaves seize weapons and revolt with hopes of escaping to Florida and gaining freedom. Twenty-five whites are killed and thirty slaves executed.

1740   The Virginia Meeting decides that Quakers should not serve on patrols that keep the slaves from meeting or escaping at night. This act again shows the Quaker friction within society and especially southern society. The Quakers find this an easy decision to arrive at since the patrols had to travel armed, which was against the Quakers' pacifist beliefs.

1741   The English Quaker John Bell writes an open letter to colonial Friends. He writes, "Pity, mercy, and compassion in Christian tenderness" were the necessary virtues of Quakers. He goes on to demand that Quaker masters not oppress their "bond slaves, and fellow creatures . . . whether white or black." He continues that ill treatment to servants was "contrary to Truth and altogether inconsistent with the gospel of peace."

"The Great Negro Plot" of New York occurs. Rumors of revolt bring New York City to a standstill. Thirty slaves are executed (thirteen quartered and burned at the stake, seventeen hung), and four whites are hung.

1742   The New England Yearly Meeting recommends Bell's epistle to all members. This is their first major action since Coleman's 1733 testimony and is influenced by it.

1743   The Rhode Island Quarterly Meeting reports that "the practice of keeping slaves is a matter of uneasiness to many concerned Friends." Here the Yearly Meeting discusses the issue of slavery for the first time since John Farmer had broached the subject twenty-six years earlier. He had been roundly defeated in his efforts.

1744   New England Quakers strengthen their 1717 advice against Quakers importing slaves from the West Indies. Here they include a warning against buying blacks who were also imported by non-Quakers.

In the American colonies, law is passed to allow blacks to serve as witnesses in criminal or civil suits.

1745   Joseph Arnold of Rhode Island, from the Smithfield Monthly Meeting, refuses to stay in homes owned by Quaker slaveholders when he goes to the Yearly Meeting at Newport, Rhode Island, in 1745.

"College" Tom Hazzard, from South County, Rhode Island, has heard a Puritan deacon in Connecticut exclaim that Quakers are not Christians because they own slaves. He becomes so distressed that he refuses to accept any slaves from his wealthy planter father as part of his marriage dowry. He pays no attention to his non-Quaker father and disregards the loss of income. His sacrifice is considered greater because he is from a farming area that uses slaves. He nevertheless becomes quite wealthy in an area where wealthy Quaker slave traders live and flourish.

1746   John Woolman takes a three-month trip to Virginia and observes southern slavery firsthand. In the 1740s Woolman also visits Quaker meetings in Long Island, New England, New Jersey, the Maryland Eastern Shore, and other places. However, Woolman waits several years to publish his observations. During this period Woolman meets Anthony Benezet and their collaboration begins.

1748   Peter Kalm, the Swedish traveler visits. In Philadelphia, Kalm talks with Benjamin Franklin, the Quaker botanist John Bartram, and many others and finds that Quakers are as active in slavery as others. He has at first thought that enslaved Africans "had been bought by almost everyone who could afford it, the Quakers alone being an exception." But he finds that he is wrong.

Montesquieu publishes *The Spirit of the Laws*. He declares "that the state of slavery is in its own nature bad. It is neither useful to the master nor to the slave."

1749   The Scottish philosopher James Foster publishes *Discourses on All the Principal Branches of Natural Religion and Social Virtue*. He proclaims that chattel slavery "is much more criminal, and more an outrageous violation of natural rights than preceding forms of slavery."

1750   On Curacao thirty plantation slaves, including thirteen women, are killed following an uprising.

In Philadelphia Anthony Benezet, along with his Quaker brethren, establishes a school for free blacks.

1751   Rebellion begins in St. Domingue that lasts until 1757. Up to six thousand people die.

Benjamin Franklin asserts that slavery retarded the growth of the population and industries in the colonies. In *Observations Concerning the Increase in Mankind* (1751) he writes that almost "every slave [is] by nature a thief."

1753   Woolman decides to put his views in print. His father had urged him to do so from his deathbed in 1750. Woolman sends his much-revised essay to the Overseers of the Press of the Philadelphia Yearly Meeting. Benezet is a member of the committee.

Woolman writes the Philadelphia *Epistle to the Friends of Virginia*, devoting it entirely to slavery.

Slaves seize, take ashore, and destroy the *Adventure*, a British slave-trading vessel, off the coast of West Africa.

1754   Woolman issues his *Some Considerations on the Keeping of Negroes: Recommended to the Professors of Christianity of Every Denomination*, printed by James Chattin. It receives the most extensive publication of any such work up until that time.

Philadelphia's "Epistle of 1754" is a monumental moment in the fight against slavery. Benezet urges the Philadelphia Meeting to adopt the *Epistle to the Friends of Virginia* as its own. Additions from Woolman's *Some Consideration on the Keeping of Negroe's* are added.

1755   The Yearly Meeting orders that any Friends who have imported slaves or purchased them locally will be censored. Some meetings refuse to abide by the Advice of 1754–55. Woolman takes another tour of the New Jersey and Long Island areas.

University of Glasgow professor Frances Hutcheson publishes his *System of Moral Philosophy*, proclaiming "no endowments, natural or acquitted, can give a perfect right to assume power over others, without their consent . . . the subject must have a right of resistance, as the truest is broken, beside the manifest plea of necessity."

1757   Woolman tours Maryland, Virginia, and North Carolina. He goes to the Virginia Yearly Meeting at West Branch. He protests the Virginia decision to accept all the Pennsylvania queries except the query dealing with slavery, which they modify. The Virginia members listen to Woolman's protest but do not modify their decision, which does not condemn the personal use of slaves.

A slave owner, after hearing College Tom's pleas, frees his slaves.

1758   The Philadelphia Yearly Meeting votes to require all members to withdraw completely from public office. Many Quakers continue to violate the rule against owning slaves. The meeting reminds its members of the "desolating calamities of war and bloodshed." Many have hoped that Quakers will set all their slaves free. The meeting decides to send John Woolman, John Churchman, John Scarborough, John Sykes, and Daniel Stanton to visit all Quaker slaveholders under the province of the Philadelphia Meeting. The purpose of the visits is to weed out all Quakers who have bought or sold slaves from any participation in the business affairs of the church.

Woolman writes that among members of the Philadelphia Yearly Meeting "many Friends said . . . they believed liberty was the Negroes' right to which at length no opposition was made publicly. Several expressed a desire that a visit might be made to such Friends who kept slaves, to inquire into the righteousness of their motives."
Woolman visits meetings in Pennsylvania and New Jersey in December. John Sykes of Bordentown, New Jersey, and Daniel Stanton of Philadelphia travel with him.

1759   Benezet publishes *Observations on the Inslaving, Importing and Purchasing of Negroes, with Some Advice Thereon, Extracted from the Epistle of the Yearly Meeting of the People Called Quakers, Held at London in the Year 1758.* It was reprinted in Germantown, Pennsylvania, in 1759 and 1760. This tract is the first published by Benezet, and it establishes him as an antislavery propagandist and activist.

Woolman travels to Long Island, New York, where slavery is under discussion. In May 1759 the New York Yearly Meeting is held in Flushing, and it makes a reply to the London "Epistle of 1758." The members write that "we particularly observe your concern to discourage and warn against the practice of dealing in Negroes and other slaves, which is a confirmation and strengthening to many amongst us who are engaged in the same concern; and we earnestly desire that this concern may continue and increase until it shall please Divine Wisdom to direct us to some full and effectual remedy."

Maryland's Quakers at West River on the western shore adopt a decision following those of the London and Philadelphia disciplines. However, because they lost too much money, the slave-owning forces mount an appeal, and the rule against buying and selling slaves is again repealed.

1760   Maryland Quakers rescind their decision against slavery.

Sometime between 1755 and 1760 Franklin changes the words in his *Observations Concerning the Increase in Mankind*. Where it once read "almost every slave being by nature a thief," it now reads "almost every slave being a thief from the nature of slavery."

John Woolman goes back to New England to try and convince Newport ship owners (Quakers) of their evil ways. Newport is a fixture in the triangular slave-trade route. Woolman visits Narragansett Bay and later writes of the conditions: "The great number of slaves in these parts . . . and the continuance of a trade from there to Guinea, made deep impression on me, and my cries were often put up to my Father in secret, that he would enable me to discharge my duty faithfully in such ways as He might be pleased to point out to me." Woolman makes his plea to the Rhode Island Meeting. Most simply ignore him. One Quaker merchant leaves the session and meets his ship that has just come in full of slaves. Woolman writes on being told of the ship's cargo, "When I heard my belly trembled, my lips quivered, my appetite failed and I grew outwardly weak, and I trembled in myself that I might rest in the day of trouble." The next day Woolman draws up a petition to the Rhode Island Assembly and prays for the prohibition of slavery. The assembly recesses before Woolman gets there, and so he turns his petition over to the Rhode Island Yearly Meeting. The petition addresses his unhappiness at the "great number of slaves which are imported into this colony."

The New England Meeting produces a "Book of Discipline" and adopts the London and Philadelphia revisions. They also reproduce the Rhode Island minutes of 1717 and 1744. Ten years later, in 1770, they "strengthened their query to discourage selling, as well as the importing and buying of slaves."

In Jamaica, Tacky's revolt, dominated by Coromantee slaves, originates in St. Mary's parish at Easter but spreads widely through the island by Whitsun. Sixty whites are killed, four hundred blacks are executed, and six hundred others are sent to Honduras.

The Scottish jurist George Wallace publishes *A System of the Principles of the Law of Scotland*. He writes that "men and their liberty are not in commerce; they are not either salable or purchasable . . . for everyone of those unfortunate men are pretended to be slaves, has a right to be declared free, for he never lost his liberty; he could not lose it; his Prince had no power to dispose of him."

1761   The English Quakers make the decision to make disownment the penalty for anyone in the London Yearly Meeting who engages in the slave trade. The Philadelphia Yearly Meeting follows the decision and is quickly followed by meetings in New England to North Carolina.

1762   On June 3 Maryland Quakers make the buying or selling of slaves without the consent of the Quarterly or Monthly Meeting a disownable offense.

Ben Franklin and his partner David Hall publish Part Two of John Woolman's *Considerations on the Keeping of Negroes*. The Friends had volunteered to pay for the printing, but Woolman decided to publish it himself. Woolman felt that publishing it independently of the meeting would avoid antagonizing those Quakers who still owned slaves and might repent. He also felt that he could reach a wider audience with independent printing.

Benezet publishes *A Short Account of That Part of Africa Inhabited by the Negroes, and the Manner by Which the Slave-Trade Is Carried On*. It is reprinted in London in 1762, 1763, and 1768; in Dublin in 1768; and in Paris in 1767 and 1788. Benezet's pamphlets have a great impact on men and women in Britain, the mainland colonies, and France. He offers a new look at Africa and Africans and declares that they lived in peace and abundance "before the arrival of the white man."

1763   The New York Friends let the 1762 advice stand, and it is not until 1774 that they make the prohibition of "buying or selling" slaves mandatory.

Over three thousand participate in Cuffee's rebellion in Dutch Berbice (Guyana). Preceding revolts in 1733, 1749, 1752, and 1762. Many of the slaves are executed.

1765   Slave rebellions take place in Jamaica and Grenada. The antislavery article "Traite des Nègres" by Louis de Jaucourt is published in Denis Diderot's *Encyclopédie*.

1766   Benezet publishes *A Caution and a Warning to Great Britain and Her Colonies in a Short Representation of the Calamitous State of the Enslaved Negroes in the British Dominions Collected from Various Authors and Submitted to the Serious Considerations of All, More Especially Those in Power*. It is reprinted in 1767, 1768, 1785, and 1788.

In Jamaica there is a Coromantee uprising in Westmoreland parish. In July an Afro-Creole plot led by Sam, Charles, Caesar, and others surfaces in Hanover parish.

1767   Maryland Quakers issue an *Epistle of Caution and Tender Advice*, "for the discouraging of that heretofore prevailing practice of dealing in or detaining in bondage our fellow creatures."

Pennsylvania bans importation of slaves.

1768   Maryland Quakers agree to disown any members who persist in the buying and selling of slaves. Monthly meetings to "disown such persons as disorderly walkers, until they so far come to a sight or sense of their misconduct as to condemn the same the satisfaction of the said monthly meeting."

Virginia Friends debate slavery.

Slave revolt in Montserrat.

1769   Granville Sharp publishes *A Representation of the Injustice and Dangerous Tendencies of Tolerating Slavery in England.*

1769–1773   On St. Vincent the First Carib War is waged, begun by Black Caribs led by Chatoyer.

1770   Rhode Island Friends strengthen their query to "discourage the selling, as well as importing and buying slaves."

             In France, Abbé Raynal publishes *Histoire philosophique et politique des ètablissements et du commerce des Européens dans les deux Indes.*

1771   Benezet publishes *Some Historical Observations of Guinea, Its Situation, Produce, and General Disposition of Its Inhabitants. With and Inquiry into the Rise and Progress of the Slave Trade, Its Nature and Lamentable Effects.* It is reprinted in 1784, 1788, 1815, and 1968.

1772   North Carolina Friends, after years of debate, vote to demand that their members buy no more slaves except for reasons approved by the Monthly Meeting, such as preventing the breakup of families.

             In the Somerset case Lord Chief Justice Mansfield decides English law does not allow for the slave James Somerset to be returned to his "master slavery" once he entered Britain. The Somerset decision is popularly interpreted as outlawing slavery in England.

             Slaves in North America begin to petition the court in "freedom suits." Correspondence between Granville Sharp and Anthony Benezet begins, opening the way for continuing communication between Anglo-American abolitionists.

1773   Stephen Hopkins, who is elected governor of Rhode Island nine times, soon becomes one of two Quaker signers of the Declaration of Independence. He is disowned for refusing to manumit his slaves.

1774   During the period of revolutionary ferment and discussion of the rights of man, slavery issues are also discussed. Meetings in Pennsylvania, New Jersey, and elsewhere ask for a revision of the 1758 *Epistle* so as to strengthen it. Quaker assemblies where the abolitionists are in control vote for disownment, the penalty for any selling or transferring of slaves for any reason, any member "suitable for liberty" themselves. Friends are warned against hiring slaves for wages or to act as executioners and administrators of estates that include slaves.

             New York Friends vote to make the prohibition of buying or selling slaves mandatory.

             John Wesley, the founder of Methodism, publishes *Thoughts upon Slavery.*

1775   Pennsylvania Quakers help to organize the Society for the Relief of Free Negroes Unlawfully Held in Bondage, which is led by Benezet and others.

             In Madeira slavery is abolished.

In the American colonies, Lord Dunmore, the royal governor of Virginia, promises freedom to any slave who deserts and serves in the king's forces. Eight hundred blacks join the British Ethiopian Regiment. Blacks serve in colonial militia in the battles around Boston.

Philadelphia Quakers help organize the Society for the Relief of Free Negroes Unlawfully Held in Bondage. It was the first secular antislavery society in the American colonies.

The American Revolutionary War begins when shots are fired at Lexington and Concord, Massachusetts. Free blacks are among those who take part in the battles.

1775–1804   Gradual abolition laws are passed in the northern states of Vermont, Massachusetts, New Hampshire, Pennsylvania, Rhode Island, Connecticut, New York, and New Jersey.

1776   The Declaration of Independence is signed. The Yearly Meeting hears a committee report on slavery: "Many there are in membership with us who notwithstanding the labor bestowed, still continue to hold these people [our fellow men of the African race] as slaves."

The Philadelphia "Query of 1776" is adopted. Visits by Quaker manumission committees to Quaker slaveowners intensify.

U.S.-British troops evacuate Boston; Battle of Long Island, Battle of Trenton.

In Williamsburg, Virginia, a group of free blacks organizes the African Baptist Church.

Africans, enslaved and free, fight for both sides in the war.

In Jamaica an Afro-Creole plot in Hanover parish is led by Sam, Charles, Caesar, and others.

Adam Smith publishes *The Wealth of Nations,* declaring chattel slavery unprofitable and harmful to whites.

A Dutch slave ship is captured off the Gold Coast by enslaved Africans. The ship explodes and four hundred are killed.

1777   The Vermont Constitutional Convention prohibits slavery.

1778   Benezet publishes *Observations on Slavery, Treatise Bound with Serious Considerations on Several Important Subjects viz., On War and Its Inconsistency with the Gospel and the Bad Effects of Spirituous Liquors* (2nd edition).

Benezet publishes *Serious Considerations on Several Important Subjects, viz on War and Its Inconsistency with the Gospel; Observations on Slavery and Remarks on the Nature and Bad Effects of Spirituous Liquors* (2nd edition).

1779   North Carolina Quakers go to court to abolish the slave trade. The legislature rejects their case.

1780   Pennsylvania passes a gradual emancipation law, substituting indentured servitude for slavery. The constitution of Massachusetts outlaws slavery.

1781   Benezet publishes *Short Observations on Slavery, Introductory to Some Extracts from the Writing of the Abbé Raynal on That Important Subject* (reprinted 1781 and 1782).

1782   Virginia enacts a law allowing private manumissions.

1783   Benezet publishes *The Case of Our Fellow Creatures the Oppressed Africans* (reprinted in London and Philadelphia, 1783 and 1784).

The Massachusetts Supreme Court abolishes slavery.

1783   In Great Britain, Quakers form committees to work against the slave trade. A Quaker petition to end the slave trade is presented to Parliament, and Quakers print over ten thousand copies of *The Case of Our Fellow Creatures, the Oppressed Africans* and distribute them to public figures.

Granville Sharp helps publicize the facts of the *Zong* affair, in which 133 blacks had been thrown overboard at sea. The ship captain, claiming insufficient provisions to feed the white crewmen, let alone the blacks, throws the blacks overboard and then seeks insurance compensation for the slaves. Judge Mansfield rules in favor of the ship owners who, claiming the lost blacks as private property, are compensated for their loss.

1784   Benezet publishes *Notes on the Slave Trade*.

Pennsylvania Quakers revive the Society for the Relief of Negroes Unlawfully Held in Bondage. The reconstituted society is renamed the Pennsylvania Society for Promoting the Abolition of Slavery, the Relief of Free Negroes Unlawfully Held in Bondage, and for Improving the Condition of the African Race. Thomas Meredith was chosen President. James Pemberton becomes the vice president (he actually presides at the meetings). The multidenominational group also has Benjamin Rush, a Presbyterian; Tom Paine, the son of an English Quaker, but not one himself; and Tench Coxe, who also was not a Quaker. Other members include Thomas Harrison, John Todd as secretary, and James Starr as treasurer.

The standing "Negro Committee" of the Pennsylvania Monthly Meeting reprints the London Quakers' appeal to the British Parliament titled *The Case of Fellow Creatures, the Oppressed Africans* and sends it to all members of Congress in Pennsylvania and New Jersey. The original title and contacts are from Anthony Benezet's *The Case of Our Fellow Creatures the Oppressed Africans* (1783 and 1784).

Benezet dies in May. By the time of his death he has made the fight against slavery an international campaign. In America this includes revolutionaries, religious folk, and reform-minded people. The forces include Benjamin Franklin and Benjamin Rush in Pennsylvania, Thomas Jefferson and Patrick Henry in Virginia, James Otis in Massachusetts, Moses Brown and Sam Hopkins in Rhode Island, Elias Boudinot in New Jersey, and William Pinkney and Henry Laurens in South Carolina.

Gradual abolition laws are passed in Rhode Island and Connecticut.

1785   Quakers again try and bring to the attention of Congress their petition of 1783.

The legislatures of New York and New Jersey defeat gradual abolition plans.

The American Quaker Patience Brayton, traveling in England in the ministry, petitions King George to end the slave trade.

1785–1790   The first Maroon War in Dominica is waged under the leadership of Balla, Pharcell, and others.

1786   In Great Britain, Thomas Clarkson, a British abolitionist, publishes *An Essay on the Slavery and Commerce of the Human Species,* a pamphlet influenced by the work of Anthony Benezet.

Quobna Ottobah Cugoano publishes his *Thoughts and Sentiments on the Evil of Slavery.*

1787   Benjamin Franklin becomes honorary chair of the newly reorganized antislavery society, renamed the Pennsylvania Society for Relief of Free Negroes.

Richard Allen and Absalom Jones found the Free African Society.

1788   Thomas Clarkson publishes *An Essay on the Impolicy of the African Slave Trade* to show the negative effects of the slave trade on whites.

In France the Société des Amis des Noirs is established and initiates contact with abolition societies in London, Philadelphia, and New York.

Connecticut, New York, Massachusetts, and Pennsylvania forbid their citizens to participate in the slave trade.

1789   Revision of Pennsylvania Act for gradual abolition of slavery.

Providence, Rhode Island, Society for Abolishing the Slave Trade is formed in February.

In France the Société des Amis des Noirs, upon convening at the Estates General, calls for freedom for all slaves in the colonies and for the universal abolition of the slave trade. Thomas Clarkson visits France and works with the Société. At the assembly white colonists and merchants prevent debate on the slave trade.

Delaware bans its citizens from engaging in the slave trade.

Olaudah Equiano publishes *The Interesting Narrative of Olaudah Equiano or Gustavus Vassa, the African: Written by Himself.*

1791   The British House of Commons debates the slave trade. William Wilberforce's motion to introduce an abolition bill is defeated.

1792   Dutch royalty bans slave imports in its colonies by 1803.

The British House of Commons votes to terminate the slave trade by 1796. The House of Lords votes the measure down.

The Sierra Leone Company sends black refugees from the American Revolution to Africa. Many had first been sent to Nova Scotia.

1793   The Fugitive Slave Act is enacted by Congress, making it a crime to harbor fugitive slaves.

Upper Canada enacts a gradual emancipation law.

1794   Richard Allen founds the Bethel African Methodist Episcopal Church, and Absalom Jones founds the African Church, St. Thomas.

William Wilberforce's motion on abolition bill is defeated.

The French Convention outlaws slavery in all the French colonies and extends the rights of citizenship to all men.

The U.S. Congress prohibits American citizens from engaging in the slave trade with foreign countries.

1795   In Guyana there is a slave revolt in Dutch Demerara in conjunction with maroons.

On St. Vincent the Second Carib War takes place under the leadership of Chatoyer and Duvalle.

On Grenada, Julien Fédon's rebellion involves a majority of the island's slaves.

In the Dutch colony of Curacao the slaves revolt.

1796   On St. Lucia the Brigands' War begins, involving many slaves.

In England William Wilberforce's bill for abolition of the slave trade is defeated.

1797   Black Philadelphians petition the federal government to end slavery and repeal the 1793 Fugitive Slave Act. Congress rejects blacks' petition against the North Carolina state law requiring slaves manumitted by Quakers to be returned to slavery.

Delaware passes a bill for the gradual abolition of slavery. In 1789 Delaware prohibited the international slave trade and decreed that slaves living in the state could not be sold, to the south, without a licensee obtained by the owner.

1798   In Salvador, Brazil, the "Tailors Revolt" is discovered.

British forces begin withdrawal from St. Dominigue after a treaty is made with Toussaint; the struggle between mulattoes and blacks (led by Toussaint) begins.

1799   The New York Legislature adopts gradual abolition plans.

1800   Toussaint's forces take control of French St. Domingue.

Gabriel Prosser's Rebellion in Virginia occurs.

1801   Toussaint captures Spanish Santo Domingo, unifies the island, and publishes a constitution prohibiting slavery.

1802   Toussaint is betrayed and sent to France.

Blacks resist the re-establishment of slavery in Guadeloupe, which had been abolished in 1794. Thousands are killed.

1804   New Jersey becomes the last state in the north to adopt gradual abolition plans.

Haiti is declared independent and abolishes slavery.

A bill for abolition, proposed by Wilberforce, is passed by the House of Commons but tabled by William Pitt's cabinet.

1805   The House of Commons defeats a bill proposed by Wilberforce for abolishing the slave trade.

1806   The British Parliament passes a law to ban British slave trade with foreign countries.

The Haitian leader Dessalines is assassinated and succeeded by Henri Christophe.

1807   The United States and Great Britain pass laws prohibiting slave importation after January 1.

1808   In Great Britain, Thomas Clarkson publishes his two-volume *History of the Rise, Progress and Accomplishment of the Abolition of the African Slave Trade by the British Parliament.*

Sources: Various Quaker archives, epistles and Meeting records; George S. Brookes, *Friend Anthony Benezet;* Ira Brown, *The Negro in Pennsylvania History;* Roger Bruns, ed., *Am I Not a Man and a Brother;* Michael Craton, *Testing the Chains: Resistance to Slavery in the British West Indies;* David Brion Davis *The Problem of Slavery in the Age of the American Revolution;* Thomas Drake, *Quakers and Slavery in America;* W.E.B. Du Bois, *The Philadelphia Negro* and *The Suppression of the African Slave-Trade to the United States of America, 1638–1870;* Dwight Lowell Dumond, *Antislavery: The Crusade for Freedom in America* and *A Bibliography of Antislavery in America;* J. William Frost, ed., *The Quaker Origins of Antislavery;* Harry Harmer, *The Longman Companion to Slavery, Emancipation and Civil Rights;* Maurice Jackson "The Rise of Abolition," in Toyin Falola and Kevin D. Roberts, eds., *The Atlantic World, 1450–2000;* Jean R. Soderlund, *Quakers & Slavery: A Divided Spirit* . Also useful were Nancy Slacom Hornick, "Anthony Benezet: Eighteenth-Century Social Critic, Educator, and Abolitionist," *DAI* 1975; the full complement of *Quaker Biographies, The Friend*; and the many articles and writings of Henry J. Cadbury.

Notes

Introduction

Extended italics were removed from quotations of eighteenth-century works throughout this book for ease of reading when the meaning was unaffected.

1. W. E. B. Du Bois, *The Philadelphia Negro: A Social Study* (New York, 1899; 1st Schocken edition, 1967), 83.

2. Carter G. Woodson, "Anthony Benezet," *Journal of Negro History* 2 (January 1917): 47–48.

3. Brissot de Warville gave a speech to the French National Constituent Assembly in 1791, proposing to end the slave trade, but widespread opposition in that body meant that no motion reached a floor vote.

4. George Wallace, *A System of the Principle Laws of Scotland* (Edinburgh, 1760), 95.

5. Frances Hutcheson, *A System of Moral Philosophy in Three Books: To Which is Prefixed Some Accounts of the Life, Writings, and Character of the Author* (Edinburgh, 1755), vol. 2, chap. 5, sec. 2, p. 301.

6. David Brion Davis, "New Sidelights on Early Antislavery Radicalism," *William and Mary Quarterly*, 3rd series, 28, no. 4 (October 1971): 592.

7. Thomas Clarkson, *The History of the Rise, Progress and Accomplishment of the Abolition of the African Slave-Trade by the British Parliament* (1808; repr., London: Frank Cass, 1968), vol. 1, 167–68, 207.

8. Anthony Benezet, *A Short Account of That Part of Africa Inhabited by the Negroes: With Respect to the Fertility of the Country, the Good Disposition of Many of the Natives, and the Manner by Which the Slave-Trade Is Carried On* (Philadelphia, 1762), 68. Dickson D. Bruce, Jr., has written, "As Anthony Benezet said, it was a story that could be heard many times by those who took the time to listen, and made a powerful case against the institution of slavery. Benezet acknowledged its influence on him, and some later abolitionist figures also acknowledged the influence that such tales heard in childhood had upon their own adult antislavery convictions." Dickson D. Bruce, Jr., *The Origins of African American Literature, 1680–1865* (Charlottesville: University Press of Virginia, 2001), 19. See also William D. Piersen, *Black Yankees: The Development of an Afro-American Subculture in Eighteenth-Century New England* (Amherst: University of Massachusetts Press, 1988), parts 3–4.

9. Garry Wills, *Head and Heart: American Christianities* (New York: Penguin Press, 2006). The dedication page reads "To Anthony Benezet, American Saint."

Chapter 1. A Life of Conscience

1. Anthony Benezet, *A Short Account of That Part of Africa Inhabited by the Negroes, and the Manner by Which the Slave-Trade is Carried on* (Philadelphia: W. Dunlap), 3 eds. in 1762, one in 1763 and 1768. London: 1768. Dublin: 1768. Paris: 1767, 1788.

2. Anthony Benezet to Samuel Fothergill, November 27, 1758, Haverford College Quaker Collection. George Crosfield, "Memoirs of the Life and Gospel Labours of Samuel Fothergill, with selections from his correspondence also an account of The life and Travels of His Father, John Fothergill; and notices of some of his descendents," in *The Friend's Library comprising Journals, Doctrinal Treatises, and Other Writings of Members of the Religious Society of Friends,* edited by William Evans and Thomas Evans, vol. 9 (Philadelphia: William and Thomas Evans, 1845), 206–22.

3. Anthony Benezet to Benjamin Franklin, April 27, 1772, Haverford College Quaker Collection.

4. Benjamin Rush to Granville Sharpe, April 27, 1784, John A. Woods, ed. "The Correspondence of Benjamin Rush and Granville Sharp, 1773–1809," *Journal of American Studies* 1 (1967), 22–23.

5. Anthony Benezet to Guillaume-François Raynal, July 16, 1781, Haverford College Quaker Collection.

6. Roberts Vaux, *Memoirs of the Life of Anthony Benezet* (New York: Burt Franklin, 1817), 134.

7. To the six of their thirteen children then still living—Anthony, James, Daniel, Judith, Mariana, and Susanna—he left "one shilling a piece no more," believing that "I have done for each of them according to my ability to the best of my judgment." Samuel Small, Jr., *Genealogical Records of George Small . . . Daniel Benezet . . .* (Philadelphia, 1905), 195–97.

8. Quoted in Nancy Slocom Hornick, "Anthony Benezet: Eighteenth Century Social Critic, Educator and Abolitionist" (Ph.D. diss., University of Maryland, 1974), 12–13.

9. George S. Brookes, *Friend Anthony Benezet* (London: Oxford University Press, 1937), 5. Brookes interpolates part of the letter to Chastellux in his version of the one sent to Barbé-Marbois.

10. François, Marquis de Barbé-Marbois, *Our Revolutionary Forefathers: The Letters of François, Marquis de Barbé-Marbois: During His Residency in the United States as Secretary of the French Legation,* trans. and ed. Eugene Parker Chase (1969; repr., Freeport, N.Y.: Books for Library Press, 1990), 139.

11. Ibid., 139.

12. Francois Jean Chastellux, *Travels in North America in the Years 1780, 1781 and 1782,* trans. Howard C. Rice, Jr. (Chapel Hill: University of North Carolina Press, 1963), 1:165–166.

13. Carter G. Woodson rightly made this connection: "Benezet was for several reasons interested in the man far down. In the first place being Huguenot, he himself knew what it was to be persecuted." "Anthony Benezet," *Journal of Negro History* 2 (1917): 41. The Huguenot minority in France had received official recognition and tolerance from Henry IV's Edict of Nantes (1598), but Henry's grandson, Louis XIV, revoked the edict in 1685, offering Calvinists the choice between death and conversion. The government singled out Huguenot pastors for persecution but gave them alone a third option, emigration; all others who left France faced the same fate as Jean-Étienne Benezet: civil death and loss of property. The Huguenots who remained had to convert to Catholicism and to have their children baptized as Catholics.

14. William Comfort notes, "Stephen Grellet . . . around 1800 found numerous members of the [Benezet] clan" near Congénies. William Comfort, "Anthony Benezet: Huguenot and Quaker," *Proceedings of the Huguenot Society of Pennsylvania* 24 (Philadelphia, 1953): 36. William Comfort, "French and German Quakers in the Early Nineteenth Century," in *Byways in Quaker History,* ed. Howard H. Brniton (Wallingford, Pa., 1969), 99–105. Charles W. Baird, D.D., *History of the Huguenot Emi-*

gration to America. 2 vols. (New York: 1885, reprinted in 1 vol., Baltimore: Genealogical Publishing Company, 1985), 1: 148–149, 2:142–143. Henry M. Baird, *The Huguenots and the Revocation of the Edict of Nantes.* 2 vols. (New York, 1895), 2: 419–421.

15. Subdelegates were the local assistants personally appointed by the intendant, the chief royal official of a regional financial district. In the language of Old Regime France intendants were *commissaires,* that is, they held their position by commission, which could be revoked at any time. Subdelegates, too, held a simple commission, not a royal office (officers owned their positions). Most subdelegates, however, also owned a royal office. For one brief period (1704–15) Louis XIV made the subdelegates into officers for purely financial reasons. Since the baptism took place in 1713 Antoine Benezet presumably owned the position as an office. On subdelegates see B. Barbiche, *Les institutions de la monarchie française à l'époque moderne* (Paris: PUF, 1999), 399–404. Many thanks to my colleague Jim Collins for this reference.

16. Wilson Armistead, *Anthony Benezet: From the Original Memoir* (London: A. W. Bennett, 1859; revised repr. with additions, Freeport, N.Y.: Books for Library Press, 1971), 2. Web sites on Protestant genealogy contain relevant details.

17. André Ducasse, *La Guerre des Camisards* (Paris: Librairie Hachette, 1946); Jean Cavalier, *Mémoires sur la guerre des camisards: La résistance huguenote sous Louis XIV* (Paris: Payot, 1973); Hippolyte Blanc, *De l'Inspiration des Camisards* (Paris, 1859); Anna Eliza Bray, *The Revolt of the Protestants of the Cevennes: Some Account of the Huguenots in the Seventeenth Century* (London: John Murray, 1870).

18. David S. Lovejoy, *Religious Enthusiasm in the New World: Heresy to Revolution* (Cambridge, Mass.: Harvard University Press, 1985), 168.

19. Henry Van Etten, "Quakerism in France," *Bureau Friends Historical Association* 26 (1937): 35. They were also called the "Quakers of Congéniès." *The Friend,* 67, no. 26, Seventh Day, First Month 20, 1894 p. 202.

20. *The Friend,* 67, no. 26 (May 20, 1894): 202.

21. Clarke Garrett adds that the Prophets often added the dramatic and bizarre, "quite unlike the liturgies of hope and repentance that had been one of the continuities of the Huguenot prophetic movement." Clarke Garrett, *Spirit Possession: From the Camisards to the Shakers* (Baltimore: Johns Hopkins University Press, 1987), 32.

22. Ibid., 50–51.

23. Armistead, *Anthony Benezet,* 3.

24. Small, *Genealogical Records,* 194.

25. The founder of the Irish linen industry, Louis Samuel Crommelin, was the son of another Samuel, who stood as a witness for the marriage of Pierre Testart and Rachel Crommelin, Jean-Étienne's maternal grandmother. G. Lee, *The Huguenot Settlements in Ireland* (London, 1936), contains details on the Crommelin family in Ireland. The family also has a convenient genealogical Web site, tracing their heritage back to a Jean Crommelin in the fifteenth century: crommelin.org. See also the extensive genealogies of French Huguenot families at the Roelly family genealogy Web site, currently http://www.roelly.org/~pro_picards/prop/pag50 .html. The latter contains some contradictions about Rachel Crommelin, but evidence of her marriage to Pierre Testart is compelling.

26. Voltaire's complete correspondence, letter from 1728. Voltaire, *Correspondance,* vol. 1 (décembre 1704–décembre 1738) Édition Theodore Besterman (Gallimard: Paris, 1977), 223. *Les Oeuvres Completes de Voltaire,* 85, Theodore Besterman, ed. Institut et Musée Voltaire, Geneve, (University of Toronto Press, 1968) 336. Voltaire wrote: "Adresse à l'avenir toutes vos lettres chez MM. Simon et Bénezet, négo-

ciants, rue Nicolas, Londres." ("You must direct for the future all yr letters to Messrs. Simon and Benezet marchands, Nicolas street, London.")

27. Citations from the family "Memorial" show that Jean-Étienne Benezet and his wife baptized children at the "French church of Wandsworth" starting in 1717. In 1722 they baptized a child (Philippe) at the French Church of the Carré. In 1724, Gertrude Benezet was baptized. Her godfather, who was also her uncle, Pierre Benezet, was known as "the merchant of Amsterdam." She died less than a month later. Starting in 1728, the baptisms took place at St. Leonard, Shoreditch. In Hornick, "Anthony Benezet."

28. Quoted in Edith Philips, *The Good Quaker in French Legend* (Philadelphia: University of Pennsylvania Press, 1932), 49.

29. Wilson Frescoln, trans. and ed., *Voltaire's Letters on the Quakers, A Critical Translation* (Philadelphia: William H. Allen, 1953), 4. See also Ernest Dilworth, trans. and with an introduction, *Voltaire, Philosophical Letters* (New York: Bobbs Merrill, 1961); and *Voltaire: Letters on England* (London: Penguin, 1980); *Philosophical Letters: Letters Concerning the English Nation, by Voltaire (Francois Marie Arouet)*, ed. and trans. Ernest Dilworth (Mineola, N.Y.: Dover Publications, 2003). Archibald Ballantyne, *Voltaire's Visit to England, 1726–1729* (Lourdes, 1893; reprint, Geneva: Slatkin Reprints, 1970).

30. Charles Whilby, ed., *Voltaire Letters Concerning the English Nation* (New York: Burt Franklin Reprints, 1974), ix–x.

31. Frescoln, *Voltaire's Letters on the Quakers,* 7.

32. Ibid., 13.

33. Ibid.

34. Ibid., 15.

35. Ibid., 4, quoting from the article on Quakers in Voltaire's *Dictionnaire philosophique.*

36. Barbé-Marbois, *Letters,* 140.

37. R. Gwynn, *The Huguenots of London* (Brighton, U.K.: Alpha Press, 1984), 4. See his article in the *Journal of Historical Geography* (1983) for greater detail "The Distribution of Huguenot Refugees in England." *Huguenot Society of London, Proceedings,* 21 (1966), 404–436. Includes maps (1), and "The Arrival of Huguenot Refugees in England." *Huguenot Society of London, Proceedings,* 21 (1966), 366–373. (1) *Publications of the Huguenot Society of London,* xxv–xxxvi, (London, 1921–1933) documents French churches in London. It also list baptisms, marriages, occupations, and burials.

38. Vaux, in *Memoirs of the Life of Anthony Benezet* (p. 5), says London, while Brookes, in *Friend Anthony Benezet* (p. 16), opts for Philadelphia, following Anthony Benezet, in *Some Historical Account of Guinea* (London, 1788, p. 10). This question has generated considerable debate; see also Joseph Sanson, *Poetical Epistle to the Enslaved Africans* (Philadelphia, 1790), 18; Comfort, "Anthony Benezet: Huguenot and Quaker," 36; Hugh Barbour and J. William Frost, *The Quakers* (Richmond, Ind.: Friends United Press, 1994), 293; Roberts Vaux, *Life of Anthony Benezet* (Philadelphia: Sherman, 1867), 9 (many later scholars simply copied Vaux's conclusion; Armistead, *Anthony Benezet,* 4; Henry Hipsley, "Anthony Benezet," in *Friends Quarterly Examiner,* 1883, p. 397; Joseph Elkinton, *Anthony Benezet and His Times* (Philadelphia, 1898). An anonymous article in *Quaker Biographies* (1909) on Benezet suggests he was unsuccessfully apprenticed to a Quaker merchant in London (*Quaker Biographies,* series 1, vol. 3 [1909]: 88).

39. Henry J. Cadbury, "Anthony Benezet as Friend," *The Friend: A Religious and Literary Journal* 107, no. 22, Fourth Month 26, 1934, p. 359. Cadbury adds concerning Benezet's membership the Society that "Anthony was so regarded in 1736

when, according to minutes of Philadelphia Monthly Meeting, he appeared with his parents to declare his intentions of marriage" (359).

40. Hornick, "Anthony Benezet," 23.

41. Brookes, *Friend Anthony Benezet*, 18. While in England, the Benezets had nine more children, five of whom survived infancy. For an account of Huguenot settlers in America see Jon Butler, *The Huguenots in America: A Refugee People in New World Society* (Cambridge, Mass.: Harvard University Press, 1983).

42. Garrett, *Spirit Possession*, 25.

43. David Waldstreicher, *Runaway America: Benjamin Franklin, Slavery and the American Revolution* (New York: Hill and Wang, 2004), 60.

44. Ibid., 62–63.

45. Brookes, *Friend Anthony Benezet*, 19.

46. Hillel Schwartz, *The French Prophets: The History of a Millenarian Group in Eighteenth-Century England* (Berkeley: University of California Press, 1980), 203.

47. *Pennsylvania Gazette*, September 12, 1751.

48. Evarts B. Greene and Virginia D. Harrington, *American Population Before the Federal Census of 1790* (New York: Columbia University Press, 1932), 114–15. Ira Brown, "Pennsylvania's Antislavery Pioneers, 1688–1776," *Pennsylvania History* 55, no. 2 (1988): 59–60.

49. Merle Gerald Brouwer, "The Negro as Slave and as a Free Black in Colonial Pennsylvania" (Ph.D. diss., Wayne State University, 1972), 17.

50. *Pennsylvania Journal*, May 27, 1762; *Pennsylvania Gazette*, May 6, 1762.

51. This paragraph draws on Carl and Jessica Bridenbaugh, *Rebels and Gentlemen: Philadelphia in the Age of Franklin* (1942; New York: Raynal and Hitchcock, 1962), as well as Sidney and Emma Nogrady Kaplan, *The Black Presence in the Era of the American Revolution* (Amherst: University of Massachusetts Press, 1989).

52. Marcus Rediker, *Between the Devil and the Deep Blue Sea: Merchant Seamen, Pirates, and the Anglo-American Maritime World, 1700–1750* (Cambridge: Cambridge University Press, 1987), 70.

53. Billy G. Smith, *The "Lower Sort": Philadelphia's Laboring People, 1750–1800* (Ithaca, N.Y.: Cornell University Press, 1992), 4.

54. *Pennsylvania Gazette*, July 28, 1743, and May 19, 1768; see also Darold D. Wax, "The Demand for Slave Labor in Colonial Pennsylvania," *Pennsylvania History* 43 (1967): 335.

55. Julie Winch, *A Gentleman of Color: The Life of James Forten* (Oxford: Oxford University Press, 2002), 19; see also W. Jeffrey Bolster, *Black Jacks: African American Seamen in the Age of Sail* (Cambridge, Mass.: Harvard University Press, 1997).

56. Billy G. Smith and Richard Wojtowicz, *Blacks Who Stole Themselves: Advertisements for Runaways in the Pennsylvania Gazette, 1728–1790* (Philadelphia: University of Pennsylvania Press, 1989), 7; see also Allan Tully "Patterns of Slaveholding in Colonial Pennsylvania: Chester and Lancaster Counties, 1729–1758," *Journal of Social History*, 6 (spring 1973): 284–305.

57. Gary B. Nash and Jean R. Soderlund, *Freedom by Degrees: Emancipation in Pennsylvania and Its Aftermath.* (New York: Oxford University Press, 1991), 10. James Oliver Horton and Lois E. Horton, *In Hope of Liberty: Culture, Community and Protest Among Northern Free Blacks, 1700–1860* (New York: Oxford University Press, 1997), 6.

58. Winch, *Gentleman of Color*, 9.

59. Darold D. Wax, "Quaker Merchants and the Slave Trade in Colonial Pennsylvania," *Pennsylvania Magazine of History and Biography* 76, no. 2 (April 1962): 146.

60. Gary B. Nash, "Slaves and Slaveowners in Colonial Philadelphia," *William and Mary Quarterly*, 3rd series, 30, no. 2 (April 1973): 225–26.

61. Hazard, comp., "Minutes of the Provincial Council of Philadelphia"; Darold

Wax, "Africans in the Delaware: The Pennsylvania Slave Trade, 1759–1765," *Pennsylvania History* 50 (January 1983): 45.

62. Ira V. Brown, "Pennsylvania's Antislavery Pioneers, 1688–1776," *Pennsylvania History* 55, no. 2 (April 1988): 60; Allan Tully, *William Penn's Legacy: Politics and Social Structure in Provincial Pennsylvania, 1726–1755* (Baltimore: Johns Hopkins University Press, 1977), 20–21, 95.

63. Edward Raymond Turner, *The Negro in Pennsylvania: Slavery-Servitude-Freedom, 1639–1861* (1911; repr., New York: Arno Press/New York Times, 1969), 3.

64. Jill Lepore, *New York Burning: Liberty, Slavery and Conspiracy in Eighteenth Century Manhattan* (New York: Knopf, 2005); Kenneth Scott, "The Slave Insurrection in New York in 1712," *New York Historical Society Quarterly* 45 (1961): 43–74; T. J. Davis, *A Rumor of Revolt: The "Great Negro Plot in Colonial New York* (New York: Free Press, 1985); Peter Linebaugh and Marcus Rediker, *The Many-Headed Hydra: Sailors, Slaves, Commoners, and the Hidden History of the Revolutionary Atlantic* (Boston: Beacon Press, 2000), chap. 6.

65. Quoted in Gary B. Nash and Jean R. Soderlund, *Freedom by Degrees: Emancipation in Pennsylvania and Its Aftermath* (New York: Oxford University Press, 1991), 16; Winch, *Gentleman of Color*, 42.

66. Turner, *The Negro in Pennsylvania*, 23–37; Brouwer, "The Negro as Slave," 167–85; Ira V. Brown, "Pennsylvania's Antislavery Pioneers, 1688–1776," *Pennsylvania History* 55, no. 2 (April 1988): 59–77.

67. Brouwer, "The Negro as Slave," 178–79; Gary B. Nash, *Forging Freedom: The Formation of Philadelphia's Black Community, 1720–1840* (Cambridge, Mass.: Harvard University Press 1988), 4. Such ordinances were passed in 1693, 1701, 1717, 1726, 1738, 1741, 1750, and 1751. See also Gary Nash, *The Urban Crucible: Social Change, Political Consciousness and the Origins of the American Revolution* (Cambridge, Mass.: Harvard University Press, 1979), 107–11.

68. Ralph Sandiford, *The Mystery of Iniquity; In a Brief Examination of the Times . . .* , 2nd ed. (Philadelphia, 1730), 5.

69. W. E. B. Du Bois, *The Suppression of the African Slave Trade to the United States of America, 1638–1870* (New York: Russell & Russell, 1898), 222 and chaps. 3–6.

70. Darold D. Wax, "Negro Import Duties in Colonial Pennsylvania," *Pennsylvania Magazine of History and Biography* 97 (1973): 22–26.

71. *Pennsylvania Gazette,* July 8, 1731; *The Papers of Benjamin Franklin*, ed. Leonard W. Labaree (New Haven, Conn.: Yale University Press, 1959), vol. 1, 217.

72. Wax, "The Demand for Slave Labor in Colonial Pennsylvania," 335.

73. Turner, *The Negro in Pennsylvania*, 38.

74. Olaudah Equiano, *The Interesting Narrative of the Life of Olaudah Equiano, Written by Himself*, ed. Robert J. Allison (Boston: Bedford/St. Martin's, 2007), 134; Vincent Carretta, *Equiano the African: Biography of a Self-Made Man* (Athens: University of Georgia Press, 2006), 111, 113–114.

75. Jean R. Soderlund, "Black Women in Colonial Pennsylvania," *Pennsylvania Magazine of History and Biography: Women's History Issue* 107, no. 1 (January 1983): 60.

76. Smith and Wojtowicz, *Blacks Who Stole Themselves*, 9.

77. Nash, "Slaves and Slaveowners in Colonial Philadelphia," 238.

78. Anthony Benezet to Granville Sharp, May 20, 1773, Granville Sharp Letter Book, Library Company of Philadelphia; see also Brouwer, "The Negro as Slave," 132.

79. Wax, "Quaker Merchants and the Slave Trade in Colonial Pennsylvania," 144.

80. Jean R. Soderlund, *Quakers and Slavery: A Divided Spirit* (Princeton, N.J.: Princeton University Press, 1985), 153, table 6.1.

81. Nash, "Slaves and Slaveowners in Colonial Philadelphia," 226.

82. Nash, *Forging Freedom*, 9.

83. Quoted in Nash, "Slaves and Slaveowners in Colonial Philadelphia," 229.

84. Ibid., 231–32; Nash, *Forging Freedom*, 10.

85. Nash, "Slaves and Slaveowners in Colonial Philadelphia," 233.

86. Ibid., 231. From 1738 to 1755 slave burials ranged from an average of sixty-four a year from 1743–48 to between fifty-one and fifty-five in other years.

87. Nash and Soderlund, Freedom by Degrees, 75. Following Smith and Wojtowicz (*Blacks Who Stole Themselves*), I have added runaways to the four categories listed by Nash and Soderlund.

88. Nash and Soderlund, Freedom by Degrees, 76, 95.

89. Anthony Benezet to Granville Sharp, February 18, 1772 (1773), Granville Sharp Letter Book, Library Company of Philadelphia. Darold Wax quotes Thomas Riche, a leading Philadelphia merchant of the time, as saying in 1764 that the "time is over for the sale of Negroes here." Darold D. Wax, "Negro Imports into Pennsylvania," *Pennsylvania History* 32 (1965): 255.

90. Nash, *Forging Freedom*, 14, 33.

91. Ibid., 14.

92. Smith and Wojtowicz, *Blacks Who Stole Themselves*, 8.

93. Papers of Manumission 1772–1790, C27 and C28, Philadelphia Quarterly Meeting, Haverford College Quaker Collection, Manumission Book A. Papers of Pennsylvania Abolition Society, Historical Society of Pennsylvania, Manumission Book for Three Philadelphia Monthly Meetings (1772–1796, Arch Street Meeting House, Philadelphia); Nash and Soderlund, Freedom by Degrees, 57–75, 89; Soderlund, *Quakers and Slavery*, 106.

94. Soderlund, *Quakers and Slavery*, 104.

95. Nash and Soderlund, Freedom by Degrees, 91.

96. Soderlund, *Quakers and Slavery*, 106.

97. *A Brief Statement of the Rise and Progress of the Testimony of the Society of Friends Against Slavery and the Slave Trade* (Philadelphia, 1843), 24–27.

98. Quoted in Jack D. Marietta, *The Reformation of American Quakerism, 1748–1783* (Philadelphia: University of Pennsylvania Press, 1984), 275.

99. Minutes of Philadelphia Monthly Meeting, August 29, 1731, Friends Meeting House, Philadelphia.

100. Quoted in Brookes, Friend Anthony Benezet, 24.

101. Ibid.

102. Small, *Genealogical Records*, 201.

103. Albert Cook Myers, ed., *The Courtship of Hannah Logan: The Diary of John Smith* (Philadelphia, 1904), 102, 104, 114, 200; Rebecca Larson, *Daughters of Light: Quaker Women Preaching and Prophesying in the Colonies and Abroad, 1770–1775* (New York: Alfred Knopf, 1999).

104. Cadbury writes that "the minutes of the Philadelphia Monthly Meeting for Eight Month, 1731 speaks of 'Joyce Marriot, who for some time appeared in public testimony amongst us,'" as "'admitted to sit in the meetings for ministers and elders.'" Cadbury, "Anthony Benezet as a Friend," 359.

105. Myers, *Courtship of Hannah Logan*, 200.

106. Sydney V. James, *A People Among Peoples: Quaker Benevolence in Eighteenth Century America* (Cambridge, Mass.: Harvard University Press, 1963), 13–14.

107. Anthony Benezet to Jonah Thompson, April 24, 1756, Quaker Archives, Haverford College Library.

108. Barbé-Marbois, *Letters*, 153. One gets a sense of Benezet's concern about having children from a passage he underlined in his copy of George Cheyne's *The*

Natural Method of Curing Diseases of the Body and the Disorders of the Mind (London, 1753) that read, "I am fully persuaded that if anything in nature can prevent infertility, and bring fine healthy children it is a milk and seed diet, continued by Father and Mother till the effect be produced." This passage explains, in part, Benezet's vegetarianism. Henry J. Cadbury, "Anthony Benezet's Library," *Bureau of Friends Historical Society* 23 (1934): 63–75.

109. John Watson wrote in 1857 that "the ancient house of Anthony Benezet, lately taken down, stood on the site of the house now 115, Chestnut Street. It was built in the first settlement of the city for a Friend of the name of David Breintnall." Watson adds that "the very estimable character of Anthony Benezet confers an interest on every thing connected with his name; it therefore attaches to the house which he owned and dwelt in for fifty years of his life, keeping school there for children of both sexes." Watson notes without comment that "before the house came into the hands of Anthony Benezet, it was known as a public house, having the sign of 'the Hen and Chickens.'" John Watson, *Annals of Philadelphia and Pennsylvania, in the olden time, Being a Collection of Memoirs, Anecdote, and Incidents, and of the City and its Inhabitants and of the Earliest Settlements of the Inland Part of Pennsylvania, from the Days of the Founders*, 2 vols. (Philadelphia: Elijah Thomas, 1857) vol. 1, 371, 373. Roberts Vaux writes that "his House on Chestnut Street, one of the first brick dwellings erected in Philadelphia, was the resort of some of the worthiest characters in the country and his hospitable table was spread for their entertainment." Roberts Vaux, *Life of Anthony Benezet* (Philadelphia: Sherman Co., Printers, 1867), 21. Another source list that "the first outright antiquarian record by an architect may well have been William Strickland's drawing of Anthony Benezet's house on Chestnut Street commissioned by Roberts Vaux just before it was pulled down in March 1818." Richard J. Webster, *Philadelphia Preserved: Catalog of the Historic American Buildings Survey* (Philadelphia: Temple University Press, 1976), xxiv. Webster cites the *Port Folio* of Philadelphia of 1818 which, quoting an anonymous source, says of the house that "it is but a few months since one of the oldest, if not the first brick house erected in Philadelphia was torn down, to give space to a more spacious structure, and we believe that edifice to have been the last specimen in this city, toward which the curious inquirer in these matters, might have been directed" (xxiv).

110. Irv A. Bredlinger says succinctly that Anthony and Joyce Benezet "throughout their married life . . . lived in Philadelphia or within a 25-mile radius of it; Wilmington, Delaware (about 25 miles southwest of Philadelphia), Germantown(then a separate town about 13 miles from Philadelphia, now a part of the Philadelphia metropolitan area), and Burlington, New Jersey (about 25 miles east of Philadelphia). Irv A. Brendlinger, *To Be Silent Would Be Criminal: The Antislavery Influence and Writings of Anthony Benezet* (Lanham: Scarecrow Press, 2007), 12.

111. Deborah Logan to Roberts Vaux, *The Friend* 11 (1838): 169–70.

112. Anonymous, "Antidote of Mr. Anthony Benezet," *The Friend* 4 (March 16, 1831), 187. See also Nathan Kite, *A Brief Statement of the Rise and Progress of the Religious Society of Friends Against Slavery and the Slave Trade* (Philadelphia, 1843).

113. Benjamin Rush, *Essays, Literary, Moral and Philosophical* (Philadelphia: Thomas and William Bradford, 1806), 302–303.

114. Armistead, *Anthony Benezet,*105.

115. Quoted in Small, *Genealogical Records*, 202–203.

116. Brookes, *Friend Anthony Benezet*, 19.

117. "Anthony Benezet," in *Quaker Biographies: A Series of Sketches*, vol. 3 (1909), 88.

118. Small, *Genealogical Records*, 197.

119. Henry J. Bartlett, "Benezet's Contribution to Education," *The Friend* 107, no. 22 (Philadelphia: April 26, 1934), 357.

120. Vaux, *Life of Anthony Benezet*, 8; Thomas Woody, *Early Quaker Education in Pennsylvania* (New York: Arno Press, 1969), 57; Howard Haines Brinton, "The Quaker Contribution to Higher Education in Colonial America," *Pennsylvania History* 25 (1958): 234–50.

121. J. Henry Bartlett, "Benezet's Contribution to Education," *The Friend: A Religious and Literary Journal*, vol. 107, no. 26 (1934), 357–58. As Bartlett describes the "'Overseers' [committee] undertook to provide schools for the whole city, but gradually Friends' families appropriated to themselves the faculties provided at the 'Academy' and 'Primary School' at Forth and Chestnut and the general populace might find accommodations in one of the others. There were eleven schools under the Overseers, it is said. Benezet's choice was for the school attended by the poorest children. Doubtless he recognized their need as the greatest; doubtless he discovered that their response was the most encouraging." *The Friend*, 107, no. 22 (April 26, 1934), 357–358

122. Brookes, *Friend Anthony Benezet*, 28–59.

123. Anonymous, "Anecdote of Mr. Anthony Benezet," 187. This story is also reproduced in Vaux, *Memoirs of the Life of Anthony Benezet* but not in his *Life of Anthony Benezet*.

124. John F. Watson, *Annals of Philadelphia and Pennsylvania in the Olden Time; Being a Collection of Memoirs, Anecdotes, and Incidents of the City and Its Inhabitants and of the Earliest Settlements of the Inland Part of Pennsylvania from the Days of the Founders* (Philadelphia: Elijah Thomas, 1857), 373.

125. J. P. Wickersham, *A History of Education in Pennsylvania* (New York: Arno Press, 1969), 217.

126. *Pennsylvania Gazette*, October 3, 1751.

127. Woodson, "Anthony Benezet," p. 49. Woodson added that "When he discovered, however, that he could not direct the colored school and at the same time continue his female academy which he had conducted for three generations, he abandoned his own interests and devoted himself exclusively to the uplift of the colored people." Woodson, p. 49.

128. C. and J. Bridenbaugh, *Rebels and Gentlemen*, 254–55; Wickersham, *A History of Education in Pennsylvania*, 216; Woody, *Early Quaker Education in Pennsylvania*, 216. Woody erroneously wrote the year 1842 instead of 1742.

129. Anthony Benezet, *A Short Account of the People Called Quakers, Their Rise, Religious Principles and Settlement in America, Mostly Collected from Different Authors, for the Information of All Serious Inquiries, Particularly Foreigners* (Philadelphia: 1780, 1814, 1866; Paris: 1780, 1788), 1780 ed., 2–3.

130. Nancy Slocom Hornick, "Anthony Benezet and the Africans' School: Toward a Theory of Full Equality," *Pennsylvania Magazine of History and Biography* 99, no. 4 (1975): 404.

131. "Minutes of the Committee's appointed by the Three Monthly Meetings of Friends of Philadelphia to the Oversight and care of the School for Educating Africans and their descendants Commencing the 28th of the 5th Month 1770." The first history of the school, *A Brief Sketch of the Schools for Black People and Their Descendents Established by the Society of Friends in 1770* (Philadelphia: Friends Books Store, 1867), surmises that it must have been Benezet, because he was "known to have been a zealous promoter of every undertaking to benefit the people of color." W. E. B. Du Bois, in *The Philadelphia Negro: A Social Study* (Philadelphia: University of Pennsylvania Press, 1899, 83), makes the same claim. Du Bois in "Reconstruction

and Its Benefits" (*American Historical Review* 15, no. 4 [July 1910]: 781–99), noted that Benezet had laid much of the groundwork almost a century earlier. Although no records remain, African American oral tradition has it that Benezet's *Some Historical Account of Guinea* was used in the Reconstruction schools and in the first black institutions of higher learning as the first source book on African history in the United States. Margaret Hope Bacon also credits Benezet with the motion in "The Heritage of Anthony Benezet: Philadelphia Quakers and Black Education" (in Harrison, *For Emancipation and Education*, 26).

132. Minutes of the African Free School, I, 1770–1811, 53, 54, Department of Records, Arch Street Meeting House, Philadelphia; *A Brief Sketch of the Schools for Black People*, 12, 130; DuBois, *The Philadelphia Negro*, 84. DuBois writes that "in the early part of the century sixty to eight scholars attend the school. And a night school was opened. In 1844 a lot on Raspberry Street was purchased, and a schoolhouse erected. Here from 1844 to 1866, eight thousand pupils in all were instructed." Hornick ("Anthony Benezet and the Africans' School," 415). The article's author believes that the school "set the pattern, also, for many other African Schools organized in the United States."

133. Forten's biographer Julie Winch writes of James Forten's father, Thomas, that "it might well have been in Benezet's night classes that he mastered his letters and numbers." She adds that "at the friends African School James Forten's instructor was Jacob Lehre," who taught at the school before Benezet took over formal duties (in Winch, *Gentleman of Color*, 24–25). See also Hornick, "Anthony Benezet and the Africans' School," 415; William J. Simmons, *Men of Mark: Eminent, Progressive and Rising* (Chicago: Johnson Publishing Company, 1970; 1st ed., 1887), 491–92. The lack of formal roll books for the African School makes it very difficult to determine the names of the students who attended the school. The future black abolitionist Absalom Jones "was quite lucky, for his master allowed him to attain literacy and attend Anthony Benezet's Quaker School." Richard S. Newman, *Freedom's Prophet: Richard Allen, the AME Church, and the Black Founding Fathers* (New York: New York University Press, 2008), 32.

134. Minutes of the Africans' Free School, 3, 4; William C. Kashatus, III, "A Reappraisal of Anthony Benezet's Activities in Educational Reform, 1754–1784," *Quaker History* 78 (1999): 36; Carl Kaestle, *Pillars of the Republic, Common Schools and American Society, 1780–1860* (New York: Hill and Wang, 1983), 38–40.

135. Thomas Woody, *A History of Women's Education in the United States,* 2 vols. (1929; New York: Octagon, 1966).

136. *A Brief Sketch of the Schools for Black People*, 3, 16; Thomas Woody, *Early Quaker Education in Pennsylvania* (New York: Columbia Teachers College, 1920; repr. New York: AMS Press, 1972), 239–246.

137. Anthony Benezet and Isaac Zane, *Some Observations Relating to the Establishment of Schools: Agreed to by the Committee, to Be Laid for the Considerations Before the Yearly-Meeting* (Philadelphia, 1778).

138. Emma Jones Lapansky, "Philadelphia Friends and African Americans, 1680–1900: An Introduction," in *For Emancipation and Education: Some Black and Quaker Efforts, 1680–1900*, ed. Eliza Cope Harrison (Germantown, Pa.: Awbury Arboretum Association, 1997), 10.

139. Carter G. Woodson, *The Education of the Negro Prior to 1861* (Washington, D.C.: Associated Publishers, 1919). W. E. B. Du Bois, *The Philadelphia Negro* (Philadelphia: University of Pennsylvania Press, 1899), 22–23, 83–84, and George Washington Williams, *History of the Negro Race in American, 1619–1880* (1883; repr. New York: Arno Pres, 1968), 172–174. *For Emancipation and Education: Some Black and Quaker Efforts 1680–1900*, essays by Margaret Hope Bacon, Charles L. Blockson,

Roger Lane, Emma Jones Lapsansky, and Jean R. Soderlund, ed. Eliza Cope Harrison (Philadelphia: Awbury Arboretum Association, 1997).

140. Poor pay and rigorous demands led to rapid turnover. Minutes of the African School, I, 1770–811, 25–37; *A Brief Sketch of the Schools for Black People*, 3–29; Hornick, "Anthony Benezet and the African Free School," 406–13.

141. Anthony Benezet to Robert Pleasants, March 17, 1781, Haverford College Quaker Collection.

142. Anthony Benezet to Benjamin Franklin, March 5, 1783, Haverford College Quaker Collection See also Comfort, "Anthony Benezet: Huguenot and Quaker."

143. *A Brief Sketch of the Schools for Black People*, 5.

144. Minutes of the Committees appointed by the Three Monthly Meetings of Friends of Philadelphia to the Oversight and Care of the School for Educating Africans and Their Descendants, May 1782, 4.

145. "The Will of Anthony Benezet," Pemberton Papers, Historical Society of Pennsylvania.

146. *Pennsylvania Packet*, May 6, 1784.

147. *Pennsylvania Gazette*, May 12, 1784.

148. *A Brief Sketch of the Schools for Black People*, 18.

149. Hornick, "Anthony Benezet and the Africans' School," 411.

150. Anthony Benezet, *A Short Account of the People Called Quakers, Their Rise, Religious Principles and Settlement in America, Mostly Collected from Different Authors, for the Information of All Serious Inquiries, Particularly Foreigners* (Philadelphia: 1780, 1814, 1866; Paris: 1780, 1788).

151. *The Autobiography of Benjamin Franklin*, ed. Louis P. Masur (Boston: Bedford Books, 1993), 121.

152. Sydney P. Clark, *Pennsylvania Hospital—Since May 11, 1751: Two Hundred Years in Philadelphia* (New York: Newcomen Society in North America, 1951), 10.

153. *Pennsylvania Gazette*, February 6, 1752.

154. Anthony Benezet to John Smith, January 2, 1758, *The Friend* (1832), 297.

155. Thomas G. Morton, M.D., *The History of the Pennsylvania Hospital, 1751–1895* (Philadelphia: Times Printing House, 1895), 414.

156. Anthony Benezet, *The Mighty Destroyer Displayed, in Some of the Dreadful Havoc Made by the Mistaken Use as Well as Abuse of Distilled Spirituous Liquors, By a Lover of Mankind* (Philadelphia, 1774), 78, 88.

157. *Colonial Records*, VI (Harrisburg, Pa., 1851); Brookes, *Friend Anthony Benezet*, 64.

158. Carl A. Brasseaux, *Scattered to the Wind: Dispersal and Wandering of the Acadians, 1755–1809* (Lafayette: Center for Louisiana Studies, 1991), 1.

159. Quoted in Brookes, *Friend Anthony Benezet*, 63.

160. Ibid., 63.

161. *Colonial Records*, VI, 711, f. see original quoted in Brookes, *Friend Anthony Benezet*, 63.

162. *Votes and Proceedings of the House of Representatives of the Province of Pennsylvania*, IV, 524 (Brookes, *Friend Anthony Benezet*, 64).

163. *Votes of the Assembly*, IV, 622, in Brookes, *Friend Anthony Benezet*, 67. The record read "to Anthony Benezet for maintenance of French neutrals pounds 27:19:9."

164. *Votes of the Assembly*, V, 504, in Brookes, *Friend Anthony Benezet*, 74. Benezet also appeared before the assembly on August 16, 1757, where "the case of the French Neutrals was set forth by Anthony Benezet." The Acadians were "found worthy of commiserations, it was sent and strongly recommended to the commisioners to do all in their powers for them." On December 9,10, and 20, 1758, he

also appeared before the body, making pleas for the Acadians. The record of January 9, 1767, read "A Petition from Anthony Benezet of the City of Philadelphia was presented to the House and read, praying the allowance and payment of his account of money advanced for the Relief of divers of the aged and infirm French Neutrals."

165. *Votes of the Assembly,* V, 6 quoted in Brookes, *Friend Anthony Benezet;* "The Petition of Anthony Benezet was presented to the House, and read, setting forth the extreme Poverty and Distress of the many aged and sick Persons amongst the late Inhabitants of Nova Scotia, now in this city, and praying that the House would be pleased to revise and amend the Law some time ago enacted for the Relief and support of the said people, the same having been found, upon experience, unsufficient to answer the good purposes thereby intended."

166. William Reed, "The French Neutral in Pennsylvania," *Pennsylvania Historical Society Memoirs* 6 (1858): 298; *Colonial Records,* VI, 55–58.

167. D. Logan, "Anthony Benezet," *The Friend* 11 (1838): 169–70.

168. C. and J. Bridenbaugh, *Rebels and Gentlemen,* 231–32.

169. It was also called the Seven Years' War, as some date the war years from 1756 to 1763. Fighting had begun in earnest with General Edward Braddock's defeat by the French in 1754. That same year hostilities in Europe started. Combat was essentially over in North America by 1761, but the peace treaty in Europe took place in 1763, hence the Seven Years' War, dating from Britain's formal declaration of war in 1756.

170. Anthony Benezet to John Smith, June 14, 1758, Haverford College Quaker Collection.

171. Sydney James also observed that it was "Benezet who like Woolman, thought Friends in general had become too much attached to property and wanted to keep political power to preserve it." In James, *A People Among Peoples,* 169, 170.

172. Comfort, "Anthony Benezet: Huguenot and Quaker," 41.

173. Anthony Benezet to Jonah Thompson, April 24, 1756, Haverford College Quaker Collection.

174. F. Nwabueze Okoye, "Chattel Slavery as the Nightmare of the American Revolutionaries," *William and Mary Quarterly,* 3rd series, 37, no. 1 (January 1980): 12–13.

175. Anthony Benezet, *A Caution and a Warning to Great Britain and Her Colonies in a Short Representation of the Calamitous State of the Enslaved Negroes in the British Dominions, Collected from Various Authors and Submitted to the Seriousness Considerations of All, More Especially Those in Power* (Philadelphia: Henry Miller, 1766), 3.

176. Quoted in David Brion Davis, *The Problem of Slavery in the Age of the American Revolution* (Ithaca, N.Y.: Cornell University Press, 1975), 274.

177. Anthony Benezet, *Serious Considerations on Several Important Subjects, viz on War and Its Inconsistency with the Gospel: Observations on Slavery, and Remarks on the Nature and Bad Effects of Spirituous Liquors,* 2nd ed. (Philadelphia: 1778); Benezet, *Serious Reflections Affectionately Recommended to the Well-Disposed of Every Religious Denomination, Particularity Those Who Mourn and Lament on Account of the Calamities Which Attend Us and the Insensibility That So Generally Prevails* (Philadelphia, 1778).

178. Sydney James also observed that it was "Benezet who like Woolman, thought Friends in general had become too much attached to property and wanted to keep political power to preserve it." In James, *A People Among Peoples,* 170.

179. Rush, *Essays, Literary, Moral and Philosophical,* 303.

180. Benjamin Rush to Granville Sharp, May 1, 1773, in *Letters of Benjamin Rush,* ed. L. H. Butterfield (Princeton, N.J.: Princeton University Press, 1951), 80–81.

181. Anthony Benezet to John Pemberton, August 10, 1783, Haverford College Quaker Collection.

182. Jeffrey Nordlinger Bumbrey, prep., *A Guide to the Microfilm Publication of the Papers of the Pennsylvania Abolition Society at the Historical Society of Pennsylvania* (Philadelphia: Pennsylvania Abolition Society and Historical Society of Pennsylvania, 1976), 9.

183. Anthony Benezet to John Pemberton, August 10, 1783, Haverford College Quaker Collection.

184. Benezet to John Pemberton, August 10, 1783, Haverford College Quaker Collection.

185. David Cooper. *A Serious Address to the Rulers of America on the Inconsistency of Their Conduct Respecting Slavery* (Trenton, N.J., 1783).

186. C. and J. Bridenbaugh, *Rebels and Gentlemen*, 260.

Chapter 2. The Early Quaker Antislavery Movement

1. *A Poetic Epistle to the Enslaved Africans in the Character of an Ancient Negro Born a Slave in Pennsylvania* (Philadelphia, 1790). The poem is now attributed to Joseph Swanson. In the poem he invokes the names of many white Christian opponents of slavery, including George Fox, Richard Baxter, Morgan Godwyn, William Burling, Samuel Sewall, John Woolman, the bishop of Gloucester, Granville Sharp, William Wilberforce, Thomas Clarkson, Benjamin Franklin, Jacques-Pierre Brissot de Warville, the Abbé Raynal, the marquis de Lafayette, and Anthony Benezet. James Basker, ed., *Amazing Grace: An Anthology of Poems About Slavery, 1660–1810* (New Haven: Yale University Press, 2002), 414–18. See an introduction to the poem by Raphael B. Moreen, in Basker, ed., *Early American Abolitionist: A Collection of Anti-Slavery Writings, 1760–1820* (New York: Gilder Lehrman Institute, 2006), 105–10.

2. Anthony Benezet to Samuel Fothergill, October 17, 1757, Haverford College Quaker Collection.

3. William C. Braithwaite, *The Beginnings of Quakerism*, 2nd ed., rev. Henry J. Cadbury (Cambridge: Cambridge University Press, 1961); *The Second Period of Quakerism*, 2nd ed. (Cambridge: Cambridge University Press, 1961); Howard Haines Brinton, *The Religious Philosophy of Quakerism: The Beliefs of Fox, Barclay, and Penn* (Wallingford, Pa.: Pendle Hill, 1973).

4. William Penn, *Fruits of a Father's Love: Being the Advice of William Penn to His Children*, 3rd ed. (London, 1760); William Penn, *Some Fruits of Solitude in Reflections and Maxims* (New York, 1901); *William Penn on Religion and Ethics: The Emergence of Liberal Quakerism*, ed. Hugh S. Barbour (Queenston, Ontario: Edwin Mellen Press, 1991); Mary Maples Dunn, *William Penn, Politics and Conscience* (Princeton, N.J.: Princeton University Press, 1986); Alan Tully, *William Penn's Legacy: Politics and Social Structure in Provincial Pennsylvania, 1725–1755* (Baltimore: Johns Hopkins University Press, 1977). Penn married Gulielma Springett, the daughter of prominent Quakers, on April 4, 1672. Unable to force change in England, he secured land in the New World in partial repayment of money the Crown owed his father. King Charles II granted him a royal charter in 1681, and he settled in an area between New York and Maryland colonies in 1682, where he worked with the Quaker leader George Fox to create the Pennsylvania colony, the "holy experiment." Penn negotiated with the Susquehannock and Delaware (Lenni Lenape) tribes hoping to establish his "peaceable kingdom" and personally named the colony's leading city Philadelphia, "the City of Brotherly Love." There are abundant references to Sir William Penn in the *Diary of Samuel Pepys*.

5. Jean Soderlund, *Quakers and Slavery*, 17.

6. Benezet, *A Caution and a Warning*, 16.

7. Anthony Benezet to Samuel Fothergill, November 27, 1758, Haverford College Quaker Collection.

8. Benezet, *Short Account of That Part of Africa,* 64.

9. David. L. Crosby, "Anthony Benezet's Transformation of Anti-Slavery Rhetoric," *Slavery and Abolition* 23, no. 3 (December 2002): 43.

10. For example, "by 1710 there were sixteen Monthly Meetings, sixty five Particular Meetings and three Quarterly Meetings in Pennsylvania. In New Jersey there were also three Quarterly Meetings and by 1745 twenty-nine Monthly Meetings." Hugh Barbour and J. William Frost, *The Quakers* (Richmond, Ind.: Friends United Press, 1988), 77.

11. Alan Brinkley, *The Unfinished Nation: A Concise History of the American People* (New York: McGraw-Hill, 1997), 51.

12. Barbour and Frost, *The Quakers,* 77. J. William Frost, "The Dry Bones of Quaker Theology," *Church History,* 39, no. 4 (December 1970), 503–23. Henry J. Cadbury, *The Character of a Quaker* (Wallingford, Pa.: Pendle Hill, 1959).

13. Benezet, *A Caution and a Warning,* 30, 29.

14. Ibid., 29, 30.

15. George Fox, *Gospel, Family, Order, in Two Volumes,* ed. Norman Petty (Cambridge: Cambridge University Press, 1911), 354.

16. Ibid., 13–14, 15,16–17, 23.

17. Edwin B. Bronner, "An Early Antislavery Statement: 1676," *Quaker History* 67, no. 1 (1973): 50.

18. Henry Cadbury, "Glimpses of Barbados Quakerism, 1676–9," *Journal of the Barbados Museum and Historical Society* 20, no. 2 (February 1953): 67–70; quoted from Bronner, "An Early Antislavery Statement," 50.

19. William Edmundson, *A Journal of the Life, Travels, Sufferings and Labour of Love in the Work of the Ministry, of . . . William Edmundson* (Dublin, 1715), 3. See also *The Journal (Abridged) of Wm. Edmundson: Quaker Apostle to Ireland and the Americas,* ed. Caroline N. Jacob (Philadelphia: Philadelphia Yearly Meeting, Religious Society of Friends, 1968).

20. Christopher Hill, *The Experience of Defeat: Milton and Some Contemporaries* (New York: Viking Penguin, 1984), 130.

21. Braithwaite, *Second Period of Quakerism,* 626.

22. *The Papers of William Penn,* ed. Richard S. and Mary Maples Dunn (Philadelphia: University of Pennsylvania Press, 1987), 1:105.

23. William Edmundson, *A Journal of William Edmundson* (Dublin, 1715), 74–75.

24. Edmundson later visited Virginia. He is said to have been the first Friend to hold services "on record in North Carolina, and first Friends meeting in Ireland, in Pennsylvania and in New York City." He witnessed Bacon's Rebellion in Virginia and wrote about Bacon's death and the mass executions meted out by William Berkeley, the Virginia governor. He quoted King Charles as saying "that old fool has killed more people in that naked land than I did over the execution of my father." Edmundson, *Quaker Apostle to Ireland,* vi, 79.

25. Thomas Drake, *Quakers and Slavery in America* (Gloucester, Mass.: Peter Smith, 1965), 9–10.

26. Ibid., 10. Sydney James writes that he "was the first Quaker to take a stand against slavery" as a "primary theorist of charity and the self-consciousness of his sect . . . he approached the needs of the Africans much as Fox had." Sydney V. James, *A People Among Peoples: Quaker Benevolence in Eighteenth-Century America* (Cambridge, Mass.: Harvard University Press, 1963), 104. Henry Cadbury argues that "alone he deserves the memory of pre-eminence in comparison with the feeble and

slow emergence of antislavery conscience among other Christians, including Friends, throughout the British Empire." Cadbury also wrote that "like other Friends from the British Isles who visited the American colonies he was confronted unprepared with the phenomenon of Negro slavery. None of these visitors spoke out against it any earlier or stronger than Edmondson [*sic*] did." Edmundson, *Quaker Apostle to Ireland*, vi.

27. Edmundson, *Quaker Apostle to Ireland.*

28. Stephen B. Weeks, *Southern Quakers and Slavery: A Study in Institutional History* (Baltimore: Johns Hopkins University Press, 1896), 198–99; Rev. James H. McNeilly, D.D., *Religion and Slavery: A Vindication of Southern Churches* (Nashville: Publishing House of the M.E. Church, 1911); and Jennifer A. Glancy, *Slavery in Early Christianity* (Oxford: Oxford University Press, 2002).

29. "Articles of the Free Society of Traders," *Pennsylvania Magazine of History and Biography* 5 (1881): 37–50, Article 18.

30. Edward Raymond Turner, *The Negro in Pennsylvania: Slavery-Servitude-Freedom, 1639–1861* (1911; repr., New York: Arno Press and *New York Times,* 1969), 20.

31. Edward Bettle, "Notices of Negro Slavery as Connected with Pennsylvania. Read Before the Historical Society of Pennsylvania, 8th mo., 7th, 1826," *Pennsylvania Historical Society Memorials,* 1, 380–81.

32. Rev. H. P. Thompson, *Into All Lands: The History of the Society for the Propagation of the Gospel in Foreign Parts, 1701–1950* (London: SPCK, 1951); Richard B. Schlatter, *The Social Ideas of Religious Leaders* (New York: Octagon Books, 1971).

33. Lawrence E. Tise, *Proslavery: A History of the Defense of Slavery in America, 1701–1840* (Athens: University of Georgia Press, 1987), 19–20.

34. Morgan Godwyn, *The Negro's and Indians Advocate, Suing for Their Admission to the Church* (London, 1680), 4.

35. Ibid., 7, 9.

36. Ibid., 3.

37. For an excellent discussion of the work of Godwyn see Alden T. Vaughn, "Slaveholder's 'Hellish Principles': A Seventeenth-Century Critique," in Alden T. Vaughn, *Roots of American Racism: Essays on the Colonial Experience* (New York: Oxford University Press, 1995), 55–81. Robin Blackburn, *The Making of New World Slavery: From the Baroque to the Modern* (London: Verso, 1997), 74–75, 259–60.

38. Ibid., 3.

39. Benezet, *Some Historical Account of Guinea* (1788), 63–64.

40. Godwyn, *The Negro's and Indians Advocate,* 19.

41. Ibid. 3.

42. Ibid., 19, 9, 11, 13, 40, 13, 23, 35, 36.

43. Ibid., 27–33. David Brion Davis asserts that "about 1680 Godwyn had heard of good authority that the late Lord Chancellor had once declared he knew of no law of England whereby baptism would release a slave from service." Davis, *The Problem of Slavery in Western Culture* (Ithaca, N.Y.: Cornell University Press, 1966), 205.

44. Davis, *Problem of Slavery in Western Culture,* 205.

45. Morgan Godwyn, *Trade Preferr'd Before Religion, and Christ Made to Give Place to Mammon: Represented in a Sermon Relating to the Plantations* (London, 1685).

46. Comparing him with later abolitionists in the nineteenth century, David Brion Davis concluded, "It is curious that a man who actually *upheld* the institution of slavery and who demanded no more than the baptism and religious instruction of Negroes should have fallen into so many of the patterns of later antislavery thought." Davis, *Problem of Slavery in Western Culture,* 341.

47. Godwyn's writing was also packaged in Francis Brokesby's *Some Proposals Toward Propogation of the Gospel in Our American Plantations,* including *Represented by*

Morgan Godwyn, A Brief Account of Religion in the Plantations, with the Causes of the Neglect and Decay Thereof in These Parts, 2nd ed. (London: George Sawbridge, 1718), 3. The New England that Godwyn had on his mind was that of Increase and his son Cotton Mather. Increase Mather (1639–1723) and Cotton Mather (1663–1728) were the most prominent of New England's Puritan ministers. Increase, son of Richard, succeeded his father as leader of the Massachusetts Bay Colony, representing the colony before the courts of James II and later William III. His *First Principles of New England* was the first of nearly one hundred books and tracts that he wrote and made him the keeper of the orthodox Calvinist tradition. His son Cotton published nearly five hundred works. He was influenced by some Enlightenment ideas and accepted and disseminated scientific knowledge within his community.

48. Benezet knew of Godwyn's contradictions and he understood them. But then again he also know of the contradictions and inconsistencies among the Quakers. Vaughn, "Slaveholder's "Hellish Principles." Blackburn, *The Making of New World Slavery,* 73.

49. Barbour and Frost, *The Quakers,* 77; Edwin Bronner, *William Penn's Holy Experiment* (New York: Columbia University Press for Temple University Press, 1962); and Gary Nash, *Quakers and Politics: Pennsylvania, 1681–1726* (Boston: Northeastern University, 1993). By 1684 there were eight hundred Friends who "attended first-day and midweek meetings for worship in Philadelphia." Barbour and Frost, *The Quakers,* 77.

50. *Germantown Friends' Protest Against Slavery,* 1688, Haverford College Quaker Collection; see also Germantown Protest, in J. William Frost, ed., *The Quaker Origins of Antislavery* (Norwood, Pa.: Norwood Editions, 1980), 69, Document 3.

51. Ira V. Brown, "Pennsylvania's Antislavery Pioneers, 1688–1776," *Pennsylvania History* 55, no. 2 (April 1988): 63.

52. Minutes of Philadelphia Yearly Meeting, Vol. A2, 18, Burlington, July 5, 1688, Haverford College Quaker Collection.

53. Brown, "Pennsylvania's Antislavery Pioneers," 63.

54. Thomas Clarkson, *The History of the Rise, Progress and Accomplishment of the Abolition of the African Slave-Trade by the British Parliament* (1808; repr., London: Frank Cass, 1968), 1:136.

55. Cadwalder Morgan, May 28, 1696, quoted in Frost, *Quaker Origins of Antislavery,* 70. see also "Friends Intelligencer," 98 (September 6, 1941), 576. See also quoted with omissions in Drake, *Quakers and Slavery in America,* 9.

56. Quoted in Drake, *Quakers and Slavery in America,* 20.

57. Minutes of Philadelphia Yearly Meeting, Sept. 23, 1696. Quoted in Drake, *Quakers and Slavery in America,* 20.

58. Peter Kolchin, *American Slavery: 1619–1877* (New York: Hill and Wang, 1993), 64.

59. Samuel Sewall, *The Selling of Joseph: A Memorial* (Boston, 1700), 6.

60. *The Diary of Samuel Sewall, Volume 1, 1674–1729,* ed. M. Halsley Thomas (New York: Farrar, Straus and Giroux, 1973), 432–33.

61. *The Diary and Life of Samuel Sewall,* edited and with an introduction by Mel Yazawa (Boston: Bedford Books, 1998), 3.

62. Sewall, *Selling of Joseph,* 4–5.

63. Benezet would come back over seventy years later. In a letter to a "Beloved Friend" he wrote that "the passage we were seeking for is Psalms 68.31, 'Princes shall come out of Egypt, Ethiopia shall soon stretch our her hands unto God' which under name all that part of Africa inhabited by Negroes may be comprehended, and that these are the people here intended is clear from Jer. 13, 23, 'Can the Ethiopian change his skin?'" Anthony Benezet to a Beloved Friend, December 14, 1773, Haverford College Quaker Collection.

64. Sewall, *Selling of Joseph*, 2.

65. John Hepburn, *The American Defense of the Christian Rule, or an Essay to Prove the Unlawfulness of Making Slaves of Men: By Him Who Loves the Freedom of the Souls and Bodies of All Men* (New York, 1715). Reprinted and with an introduction by Henry J. Cadbury as *John Hepburn and His Book Against Slavery, 1715* (Worcester, Mass.: Davis Press, for the American Antiquarian Society, 1950).

66. Cadbury, *John Hepburn and His Book Against Slavery*.

67. Mary Stoughton Locke would narrowly assert, "Among the Quaker anti-slavery writers there were no such scholars as Cotton Mather and John Eliot, Chief Justice Sewall and Nathaniel Appleton." Locke, *Anti-Slavery in America: From the Introduction to the Prohibition of the Slave Trade (1619–1808)* (Gloucester, Mass.: Peter Smith, 1965), 23.

68. *The Athenian Oracle: Being an Entire collection of All the Valuable questions and answers in the Old Athenian Mercuries . . .* 3rd ed. (London: J. London and J. Knapton et al., 1728).

69. Roger Bruns, ed., *Am I Not a Man and a Brother: The Antislavery Crusade of Revolutionary America, 1688–1788* (New York: Chelsea House, 1983), 16.

70. Hepburn, *American Defense of the Christian Rule*.

71. W. E. B. Du Bois, *The Philadelphia Negro: A Social Study* (Philadelphia: University of Pennsylvania Press, 1899), 12.

72. Soderlund, *Quakers and Slavery*, 23.

73. Ralph Sandiford, *A Brief Examination of the Practices of the Times, by the Forgoing and the Present Dispensation: Whereby Is Manifested, How the Devil Works in the Mystery* (1729; repr., New York: Arno Press, 1969), 9.

74. Sandiford, *A Brief Examination*, 4.

75. Frost, *Quaker Origins of Antislavery*, 5.

76. *The Holy Bible; Containing the Old and New Testaments; Newly Translated out of the Original Tongues; and with Former Translations Diligently Compared and Revised . . .* (Philadelphia: R. Aitken, 1782), 1 Gen. 9:25.

77. *The Holy Bible, Containing the Old and New Testaments: New Revised Standard Version* (Grand Rapids, Mich.: World Publishing, 1997).

78. Goldenberg also argues that "some used biblical interpretation where those with Black skin had become identified as slave, a genealogy that linked Canaan (the biblical slave) with the Black would well serve that society's interests." David M. Goldenberg, *The Curse of Ham: Race and Slavery in Early Judaism, Christianity and Islam* (Princeton, N.J.: Princeton University Press, 2003), 175. See also Gene Rice, "The Curse That Never Was (Genesis 9:18–27)," *Journal of Religious Thought* 29 (1972); Ephraim Isaac, "Genesis, Judaism and the 'Sons of Ham,'" *Slavery and Abolition: A Journal of Comparative Studies* 1, no. 1 (May 1980): 7; Cain Hope Felder, "Racial Motifs in the Biblical Narratives," in *Troubling Biblical Waters: Race, Class, and Family* (Maryknoll, N.Y.: Orbis, 1989), 42.

79. Sandiford, *A Brief Examination*, v.

80. Among the arguments in the tract was that through the "Negro Trade the company yearly, at a very reasonable Rates, furnish with vast Number of Servants all His Majesties American Plantations." Anonymous, *Certain Considerations Relating to the Royal African Company*, reprinted in *Slavery, Abolition and Emancipation: Black Slaves and the British Empire*, ed. Michael Craton, James Walvin, and David Wright (London: Longman, 1976), 16.

81. *Systema Africanum: or a Treatise, Discovering the Intrigues . . . of the Guiney Company*, in Craton et al., *Slavery, Abolition, and Emancipation*, 20.

82. K. G. Davies, *The Royal African Company* (London: Longmans, Green, 1957), 213, 227.

83. W. R. Scott, "The Constitution and Finances of the Royal African Company of England till 1720," *American Historical Review* 8 (1903): 244. Quoted from the Treasury records of the Royal African Company, No. 1390, ff. 2 and 15.

84. Sandiford, *A Brief Examination*, 6–7.

85. Soderlund, *Quakers and Slavery*, 23.

86. Bruns, *Am I Not a Man and a Brother*, 46.

87. Quoted in Drake, *Quakers and Slavery in America*, 39–40.

88. Soderlund, *Quakers and Slavery*, 23.

89. Benjamin Lay, *All Slave-Keepers That Keep the Innocent in Bondage, Apostates. Pretending to Lay Claim to the Pure and Holy Christian Religion, of What Congregations Soever, but Especially in Their Ministers, by Whose Example the Filthy Leprosy and Apostasy Is Spread Far and Near* (Philadelphia: Printed for the Author, 1737).

90. Benjamin Franklin to John Wright, November 4, 1789, in *The Writings of Benjamin Franklin*, ed. Albert H. Smyth (New York: Macmillan, 1905–7), vol. 10, 62. In 1789 Franklin described his earlier support for Sandiford and Lay as evidence of his antislavery stance, and he took credit for participating with them in this antislavery activity.

91. David Waldstreicher, *Runaway America: Benjamin Franklin, Slavery and the American Revolution* (New York: Hill and Wang, 2004), 82.

92. Benjamin Lay, *All Slave-Keepers*; Roberts Vaux, *Memoirs of the Lives of Benjamin Lay and Ralph Sandiford* (Philadelphia: Solomon W. Conrad, 1815), 26–27; Soderlund, *Quakers and Slavery*, 16–17; Bruns, *Am I Not a Man and a Brother*, 46–64.

93. Vaux, *Memoirs of the Lives of Benjamin Lay and Ralph Sandiford*, 28.

94. Bruns, *Am I Not a Man and a Brother*, 46.

95. Eugene Genovese, *From Rebellion to Revolution: Afro-American Slave Revolts in the Making of the New World* (Baton Rouge: Louisiana State University Press, 1979); Peter Wood, *Black Majority: Negroes in Colonial South Carolina from 1670 Through the Stono Rebellion* (New York: W. W. Norton, 1972), 152. The Stono Rebellion of 1739 in South Carolina was the largest slave revolt in colonial North America. With a South Carolina population of 56,000, blacks outnumbered whites by almost two to one. Just as the British leader Lord Dunmore offered freedom to slaves in 1774 during the American Revolutionary war, the Spanish in Florida offered "liberty" to slaves in British possession. Enslaved Africans hearing of this offer conspired to run away to Spanish lands. On Sunday, September 9, 1739, twenty slaves seized a store, executed its owners, and burned several plantations. Led by an African slave, Jemmy, and proclaiming "liberty," they gathered at St. Paul's Parish and moved south, picking up recruits as they marched and burning plantations, killing more than twenty-five whites. Outnumbered by the heavily armed militia, they were soon captured. In the end forty-four of the insurgents were killed or hung, and many of their heads were placed on a pike at the entrance to the city's port, as was later done in New York. John Thornton points out that many of these slaves came from Angola and spoke the same language, which enabled them to communicate in secret. Some of the slaves were believed to have been trained in the use of firearms and military regimen by the Portuguese. Some had been taught the tenets of Catholicism by their Portuguese captors. They were also proficient in rice production, the South Carolina staple, just as they had been in Angola. Thornton, "African Dimensions of the Stono Rebellion," *American Historical Review* 96, no. 4 (October 1991): 1101–13.

96. Daniel Horsmanden, *The New York Slave Conspiracy* (1744; repr., New York: Beacon Press, 1971), 265–66; Thomas J. Davis, *A Rumor of Revolt: "The Great Negro Plot" in Colonial New York* (Amherst: University of Massachusetts Press, 1985); Serena R. Zabin, ed., *The New York Conspiracy Trials of 1741: Daniel Horsmanden's Journal of*

the *Proceedings and Related Documents* (Boston: Bedford/St. Martin's, 2004); Peter Linebaugh and Marcus Rediker, *Many-Headed Hydra* (Boston: Beacon Press, 2000).

97. Davis, *Problem of Slavery in Western Culture*, 321. David S. Reynolds's new work is the latest to look at John Brown: *John Brown, Abolitionist: The Man Who Killed Slavery, Sparked the Civil War, and Seeded Civil Rights* (New York: Alfred A. Knopf, 2005).

98. John Bell, *An Epistle to Friends in Virginia, Barbados, and Other Colonies and Islands in the West Indies Where Any Friends Are* (Bromley near London, 1741), 1–3.

99. Roger Anstey, *The Atlantic Slave Trade and British Abolition: 1760–1810* (Atlantic Highlands, N.J.: Humanities Press, 1975), 205.

100. Robin Blackburn, *The Overthrow of Colonial Slavery* (London: Verso Press, 1988), 80.

101. Weeks, *Southern Quakers and Slavery*, 200–201.

102. Minutes of Philadelphia Yearly Meeting 1754, Haverford College Quaker Collection.

103. Drake, *Quakers and Slavery in America*, 56; Janet Whitney, *John Woolman: American Quaker* (Boston: Little, Brown, 1942), 180–82.

104. Here following Brookes, *Friend Anthony Benezet*, 80.

105. "A proposal of making that Rule of our Discipline respecting the Importation of Negroes or the Purchasing of them after imported, more publick, together with some reasons to discourage that practice being laid before this Meeting by Anthony Benezet, it was read, and Michael Lightfoot, and others together with Anthony Benezet are desired to consider it, and prepare it, to be laid before our next Meeting, in order for Publication." Copy of the Records in Brookes, *Friend Anthony Benezet*, 80–81.

106. "From Our Yearly Meeting for the Provinces of Pennsylvania and New-Jersey held at Burlington by Adjournments for the 15th Day of the ninth month, 1754, to the 19th of the same inclusive," *Epistle*, Philadelphia Yearly Meeting Minutes 1754, Haverford College Quaker Collection.

107. Benezet, *A Short Account of the People Called Quakers*, 88.

108. *An Epistle of Caution and Advice Concerning the Buying and Selling of Slaves: Epistle of the 1754 Philadelphia Yearly Meeting*, Haverford College Quaker Collection.

109. *An Epistle of Caution and Advice Concerning the Buying and Selling of Slaves: Epistle of the 1754 Philadelphia Yearly Meeting*, "From our Yearly Meeting for the Province of Pennsylvania and New Jersey held at Burlington by Adjournments for the 15th Day of the ninth month, 1754, to the 19th of the same inclusive." Haverford College Quaker Collection.

110. Phillips P. Moulton, ed., *The Journal and Major Essays of John Woolman* (Richmond, Ind.: Friends United Press, 1989), 195.

111. Frost, *Quaker Origins of Antislavery*, 171.

112. Philadelphia Yearly Meeting of 1758, *Epistle of Caution and Advice*, Haverford College Quaker Collection.

113. Moulton, *Journal and Major Essays of John Woolman*, 95 (quoted from the *Pemberton Papers*, 15, 3, Historical Society of Pennsylvania). John Woolman, *Considerations on Pure Wisdom, and Human Policy, on Labour; on Schools* (Philadelphia, 1768). *Some Considerations on the Keeping of Negroes; Recommended to the Professors of Christianity, of Every Denomination*, 2 vols. (Philadelphia, 1754, 1762). Reprinted in Amelia Mott Gummere, ed., *The Journal and Essays of John Woolman* (New York, 1922), 334–81. G. David Houston, "John Woolman's Efforts in Behalf of Freedom," *Journal of Negro History* 2, no. 2 (April 1917): 126–38. *Friends Library* 4: "Life of John Woolman" (Philadelphia, 1840).

114. Benezet had already published *Observations on the Inslaving, Importing and Purchasing of Negroes, with Some Advice Thereon, Extracted from the Epistle of the Yearly*

Meeting of the People Called Quakers, Held at London in the Year 1758 (Philadelphia: Christopher Sower, 1759). The second edition was printed in 1760, and he was working on *A Short Account of That Part of Africa* published in 1762.

115. *The Journal and Major Essays of John Woolman,* ed. Phillips P. Moulton (Richmond, Indiana: Friends United Press, 1989), p. 157.

116. Anstey, *Atlantic Slave Trade and British Abolition,* 217.

Chapter 3. An Antislavery Intellect Develops

1. Albert Cook Myers, ed., *The Courtship of Hannah Logan: The Diary of John Smith* (Philadelphia, 1904).

2. Davis, *Problem of Slavery in Western Culture,* 391.

3. Robin Blackburn observed "philosophical attacks on New World slavery—that is to say on the institution itself rather than on the cruel excesses of particular masters—were extremely rare prior to the middle of the eighteenth century." Jean Bodin (1530–96), the French absolutist theorist, was educated at the University of Toulouse. His *Les Six Livres de la Republique* (1576) offered one of the first critical essays denouncing slavery. Jean Bodin, *The Six Books of a Commonweale: A Facsimile reprint of the English Translations of 1606 Corrected and supplemented in the light of a new comparison with the French and Latin texts,* edited and with an Introduction by Kenneth Douglas McRae (Cambridge, Mass.: Harvard University Press, 1962). Blackburn has written that Bodin made a "pointed critique in 1576 after which there was a prolonged silence until the appearance of Montesquieu's *Espirit des Lois,* in 1748; with its critical passage on the enslavement of Blacks." Blackburn, *Overthrow of Colonial Slavery,* 36.

4. In *A Short Account of That Part of Africa,* Benezet first used Foster who "shews his just, Indignation at this wicked Practice, which he declares to be 'a criminal and outrageous Violation of the natural Right of Mankind.'" *A Short Account of That Part of Africa . . . with Quotations from the Writings of Several Persons of Note, viz, George Wallace, Francis Hutcheson and James Foster* (Philadelphia, 1762), 30. *Extracts from the Writings of Several Noted Authors, on the subjects of the Slavery of the Negroes, . . . viz George Wallace, Francis Hutcheson, James Foster* (London: Library of the Society of Friends, 1978; repr. from appendix of Benezet, *Some Historical Account of Guinea*).

5. Garry Wills, *Inventing America: Jefferson's Declaration of Independence* (New York: Doubleday, 1978), 177. Wills adds that "at the college of Philadelphia, that tempestuous Scot William Smith aimed his curriculum toward the culminating study of the same philosopher, and Francis Alison drilled five future signers of the Declaration of Independence in Hutcheson's text" (177). Benjamin Franklin also had ties to Scottish thinkers like Ezra Stiles, and Thomas Jefferson studied the works of Hutcheson and Adam Smith with William Small, the Scottish-born mathematician and philosopher who also earned his medical degree in Aberdeen. See also Douglas Sloan, *The Scottish Enlightenment and the American College Ideal* (New York: Teacher's College Press, Columbia University, 1971), 122–25.

6. James Foster, D.D., *Discourses on All the Principal Branches of Natural Religion and Social Virtue,* vol. 1 (London, 1749; repr. 1750).

7. Ibid., 154. For Foster there were two "very different degrees" of servitude. He wrote "the first in what, some of the best writers on the law of nature and nations, have titled, perfect; the other incomplete free and voluntary servitude." Next were "those, who are referred to the last class, are hired and contracted servants; and those, under the first, slaves. These were generally captives of war or the descendants of such, as were esteemed a part of the conquerors property, or those, who had sold themselves, to a perpetual servitude" (154–55).

8. Ibid., 156.

9. Ibid., 159.

10. Davis, *Problem of Slavery in Age of Revolution*, 530. Few authors have explored the ideas or works of Foster.

11. Foster, *Discourses,* 17–18.

12. Ibid., 152–158.

13. Francis Hutcheson, *Alterations and Additions Made in the Second Edition of the Inquiry into Beauty and Virtue* (London, 1726), 9. Hutcheson wrote *An Essay on the Nature and Conduct of the Passions and Affections with Illustrations on the Moral Sense,* published in 1728 in Dublin. He argued that morality and virtue were at the center of man's existence. He believed that "many are really virtuous who cannot explain what Virtue is. Some act a most disinterested part in Life, who have been taught to account for all their Actions by Self Love, as the sole Spring" (3). Hutcheson by then had begun to question the purpose of life and of man's ability to comprehend both nature and society. Just as he would use his natural senses to perceive, recognize, understand, and appreciate his surroundings, he used his moral senses to determine man's morality and his benevolence. He then wrote *Considerations on Patronages Addressed to the Gentlemen of Scotland* (London: J. Robert, 1735). He saw patronage as "the unbridled authority of the Clergy in the settlement of Parish-Churches," which could possibly lead to the absolute rule of the church, as it impinged on the rights "which the Gentlemen of Scotland have lost by these laws" (4). In the second edition (1726), subtitled "Alterations and Additions," he contemplated the nature of equality in society. Writing about the "enjoyment of the greatest Pleasures" in life, he concluded "the Poor and the Low may have as free a use of these Objects, in this way as the Wealthy or Powerful."

14. Francis Hutcheson, *A System of Moral Philosophy in Three Books: To Which Is Prefixed Some Accounts of the Life, Writings, and Character of the Author* (Edinburgh, 1755; repr. New York: Augustus M. Kelly, 1968), vol. 1, chap. 1, sec. 1. In *A Short Account of That Part of Africa,* Benezet wrote that the intention of moral philosophy was to guide men and women into action that would "promote their greatest happiness and perfection." To gain that they would have to come to the aid of the less fortunate, the oppressed and the enslaved. In other words, following the theoretical lines et by Wallace and Hutcheson, he believed that freer were those who strove to make the most human beings free.

15. Benezet, *Short Account of That Part of Africa,* 34.

16. Hutcheson, *System of Moral Philosophy,* vol. 1, chap. 1, sec. 1. Hutcheson agreed with Hume that the races of peoples were different, writing that "men differ from each other in wisdom, virtue, beauty and strength," but, unlike Hume, he believed that even the "lowest of them," in this case, the enslaved, were capable of happiness and a productive life.

17. Benezet, *Short Account of That Part of Africa,* 34.

18. Hutcheson, *System of Moral Philosophy,* vol. 3, sec. 5, p. 210.

19. Hutcheson, *System of Moral Philosophy,* vol. 2, chap. 14, sec. 3. See also Anstey, *Atlantic Slave Trade and British Abolition,* 102. In essence, although Hutcheson abhorred slavery, he felt the master had a right to receive his monetary return before the slave could achieve his freedom. The captured slaves could work off their terms in ten to twelve years, which was a considerably longer period than for white indentured servants. Hutcheson differed from Benezet in that his economic attack on slavery guaranteed that the traders would get their profits. He knew that arguments against injustice were secondary. One could allow for the slave trade without supporting it. As long as slavery was profitable, the traders could ride out the opposition. But when the trade lost economic dominance, the master would have to fortify his arguments.

20. Wylie Sypher, "Hutcheson, and the 'Classical Theory of Slavery,'" *Journal of Negro History* 24 (July 1939): 263. Sypher believed that "Aristotle based his theory on two separate assumptions: first, that a man may be a slave 'by nature,' one created inferior to other men, one of the barbaroi; second, that a man may be a slave by the right of 'conquest'" (264).

21. Hutcheson, *System of Moral Philosophy,* vol. 1, 299. Aristotle's clearest ideas on slavery came in *The Politics.* He asked, "Is there any one condition one thus intended by nature to be a slave and for whom such a condition is expedient and right, or rather is not all slavery a violation of nature?" He answered, "There is no difficulty in answering this question, on grounds both of reason and fact. For that some should rule and others be ruled is a thing not only necessary, but expedient; from the hour of their birth, some are marked out for subjection, others for rule." He gave order to all levels of society: husband to wife; father to children; master to slave; Greek to barbarian; free man to slave. The slave had no rights other than as an extension of his master. He had no ability to feel or to do good. The less humanity left in the slave, the better slave he would be. In this sense Aristotle distinguished between the natural slave and the slave who was held by force and had no interest in common with his master. Aristotle, *Politics,* vol. 1, chap. 5, 1254A, 18–24.

22. Hutcheson, *System of Moral Philosophy,* vol. 2, chap. 5, sec. 2, p. 301. Anstey, *Atlantic Slave Trade and British Abolition,* 100–101. Almost twenty years after *A System of Moral Philosophy* was published, Hutcheson wrote *Letters Concerning the True Foundation of Virtue or Moral Goodness.* The question of man's responsibility to others went to the center of the discussion: "We never call that man benevolent, who is in fact useful to others, but at the same time only intends his own interest, without any desire of, or delight, in the good of others." He "loses all appearance of benevolence, as soon as we discern that it is only flowed from self-love or interest." Gilbert Burnet and Francis Hutcheson, *Letters Concerning the True Foundation of Virtue or Moral Goodness, Wrote in Correspondence Between Mr. Gilbert Burnet and Mr. Francis Hutcheson* (Glasgow, 1772), 2.

23. Hutcheson, *System of Moral Philosophy,* vol. 2, chap. 5, sec. 2, p. 301.

24. Davis, *Problem of Slavery in Western Culture,* 378.

25. Hutcheson, *System of Moral Philosophy,* vol. 3, chap. 7, sec. 3, pp. 270–71.

26. Benezet, *Short Account of That Part of Africa,* 31

27. Benezet, *A Caution and a Warning,* 23. We do not know how Benezet came to the works of Wallace, Foster, and Hutcheson. The Library Company of Philadelphia founded by Benjamin Franklin houses the libraries of James Logan and many others of Philadelphia's elite reading circle. The Quaker Library at Haverford College contains the Library of Benezet, documented by Henry Cadbury, indicating the books that were in Benezet's possession that were given to the library. See Cadbury, "Anthony Benezet's Library." There were few if any documented editions of their work in Philadelphia at the time and none today at the Library Company of Philadelphia or at Haverford College. Henry J. Cadbury, "More on Benezet's Library," *Bulletin of Friends Historical Association* 25, no. 2 (Autumn 1936), 83–85.

28. Wallace, *System of the Laws of Scotland,* 90, 89.

29. As Davis observed, "Benezet, unlike de Jaucourt, identified Wallace as the author of the doctrine that 'everyone of those unfortunate men, who are pretended to be slaves, has a right to be declared free, for he never lost his liberty.'" David Brion Davis, "New Sidelights on Early Antislavery Radicalism," *William and Mary Quarterly,* 3rd series, 28, no. 4 (October 1971), 586.

30. Benezet, *A Short Account of That Part of Africa,* 31. See also Anthony Benezet to Joseph Phipps, May 28, 1763, Haverford College Quaker Collection. "Freedom

suits" were efforts by blacks in the colonies to seek legal redress to the question of slavery. In the aftermath of the Somerset decision in England, many blacks in the mainland colonies thought they could sue and petition for their freedom. In the aftermath of the American Revolution hundreds brought these cases. Leon Higginbotham, Jr., cites the first such case heard: "A black man, John Phillip was reportedly 'baptized' in 1612 in England. As a result, in 1624, the General Court of Virginia ruled that 'John Philip, A Negro was qualified as a free man and Christian to give testimony, because he had been 'Christened in England, 12 years since.'" Leon Higginbotham, Jr., *In Matter of Color: Race and the American Legal Process. The Colonial Period* (Oxford: Oxford University Press, 1978), 21.

31. Wallace, *System of the Laws of Scotland*, 95–96. Benezet used this quote in *A Short Account of That Part of Africa*. Davis, *Problem of Slavery in the Age of Revolution;* Davis, "New Sidelights on Antislavery Radicalism."

32. Wallace, *System of the Laws of Scotland*, 95–96.

33. Anthony Benezet, *Notes on the Slave Trade* (Philadelphia: 1781), 8. Benezet did not accept the Aristotelian notion that some men were born to be slaves. He did not accept Hobbes's view that the powerful had the right to enslave the weak.

34. J. Philmore [pseud.], *Two Dialogues on the Man-Trade* (London, 1760), 54.

35. Davis, "New Sidelights on Antislavery Radicalism," 594; Philmore, *Two Dialogues*, 57.

36. Anthony Benezet to Samuel Fothergill, October 17, 1757, Haverford College Quaker Collection. Benezet included with the letter "a new Edition of John Everard's writings." The book, *Some Gospel Treasures*, is in Benezet's library at Haverford College. A copy (with Benezet's markings) is in the British Museum.

37. Anthony Benezet, *Observations on the Inslaving of Negroes*. Benezet to John Smith, December 30, 1757, Haverford College Quaker Collection.

38. Anthony Benezet to Samuel Fothergill, October 17, 1757, Haverford College Quaker Collection. Benezet to John Smith, December 30, 1757, Haverford College Quaker Collection.

39. Anthony Benezet to John Smith, December 30, 1757, Haverford College Quaker Collection; Brookes, *Friend Anthony Benezet*, 225.

40. Benezet, *Observations on the Inslaving of Negroes*, 4.

41. Vaux, *Memoirs of the Life of Anthony Benezet*, 24–25, 26; Brookes, *Friend Anthony Benezet*, contains copies of Benezet's letters on many subjects. See also "Documents: Letters of Anthony Benezet," *Journal of Negro History* 2, no. 1 (1917): 83–95. This article includes about twenty letters written by Benezet from 1772 to 1783. The letter to the Archbishop of Canterbury was written in 1758 and is the only letter included before 1772. Unless otherwise noted, all letters cited are located in the Haverford College Quaker Collection.

42. Benezet, *Observations on the Inslaving of Negroes*, 6.

43. *The Uncertainty of Death-Bed Repentance*, anonymous pamphlet attached to *Observations on the Inslaving of Negroes*, 12.

44. *Uncertainty of Death-Bed Repentance*, 13.

45. "Speak truth to power" has been adopted as a slogan by modern peace activist. The theme "taken from a charge given to Eighteenth Century Friends suggests the effort that is made from the deepest insight of the Quaker faith" ("Speak Truth to Power: A Quaker Search for an Alternative to Violence," American Friends Service Committee, Philadelphia).

46. Benezet, *A Short Account of That Part of Africa*, 6.

47. Ibid., 6, 45

48. For a useful discussion of the reasons and justifications for the enslavement of Africans, see *The Atlantic Slave Trade*, ed. David Northrup (Boston: Houghton,

2003). In this useful compilation the ideas of Eric Williams, Winthrop D. Jordan, David Brion Davis, and others are presented on the origins of New World slavery.

49. Cited in James Pope-Hennessy, *Sins of the Fathers: A Study of the Atlantic Slave Traders 1407–1807* (New York: Alfred A. Knopf, 1968), 230.

50. Bruns, introduction to letter of Anthony Benezet to Joseph Phipps May 28, 1763, in *Am I Not a Man and a Brother*, 97.

51. Anthony Benezet to Joseph Phipps May 28, 1763, Haverford College Quaker Collection. See also Bruns, *Am I Not a Man and a Brother*, 97.

52. Benezet cited "an account of part of North-America published by Thomas Jeffery, printed in 1761, speaking of the usage of the Negroes in the West India Islands." He quoted Jeffery: "It's impossible for a human heart to reflect upon the servitude of these dregs of mankind, without in some measure feeling for their misery, which ends but with their lives." Jeffery added that "[the whites] whip them mercifully on small occasions. They beat them with clubs, and you will see their bodies all a whaled and scared." Benezet, *A Caution and a Warning*, 6–7.

53. At another point Benezet used Jeffery to attack the profit motive. Jeffery wrote the whites were "not restrained form killing them, when angry, by a worthier consideration than that they lose so much." Benezet, *A Caution and a Warning*, 6–7. In other words, if the whites were compensated if they killed "their" slaves, they would beat and torture them to death. If they were not compensated, they would be more lenient in their punishments.

54. The September 18, 1766, Meeting for Sufferings approved Benezet's plea for the Overseers "carefully to revise and examine where the quotations are exactly copies, and what else relating therto as they deem necessary," regarding *A Caution and a Warning*. The first London edition of *A Caution and a Warning* appeared in 1767, with other editions following in 1768, 1785, and 1788. The London edition of *A Short Account of That Part of Africa* appeared in 1768.

55. Anthony Benezet to John Smith, March 27, 1767. Haverford College Quaker Collection.

56. Anthony Benezet to George Dillwyn, April 1767, Haverford College Quaker Collection. Judith Jennings writes "George Dillwyn, a ministering friend from America . . . was the brother of William and dearly beloved by many British Friends." Judith, Jennings, *The Business of Abolishing the British Slave Trade: 1783–1807* (London: Frank Cass, 1997), 24. see also "The American Revolution and the Testimony of the British Quakers Against the Slave Trade." *Quaker History* 2 (1981), 99–103. Nathan Kites, "George Dillwyn," in *Biographical Sketches and Anecdotes of the Members of the Religious Society of Friends* (Philadelphia: Tract Association of Friends, 1871), 182–226.

57. Anthony Benezet to Parmenas Horton, June 12, 1767, *The Friend* 41, July 9, 1867.

58. Hornick, "Anthony Benezet," 362.

59. Benezet, *A Caution and a Warning*, 3.

60. One could only imagine what Benezet would have thought had he known that "on the roll of Captain David Humphrey's black Connecticut company [one of the 14 brigades of the Continental Army] in 1781–3, among the forty-eight surnames, ten are Freedom, Freeman, or Liberty." Sidney Kaplan and Emma Nogrady Kaplan, *The Black Presence in the Era of the American Revolution* (Amherst: University of Massachusetts Press, 1999), 34.

61. Benezet, *A Caution and a Warning*, 21.

62. Ibid., 27.

63. Benezet, *Some Historical Account of Guinea* (xxxx), ii.

64. Benezet, *A Caution and a Warning*, 22.

65. Davis, *Problem of Slavery in Age of Revolution*, 251–52, n. 56.

66. Anthony Benezet to Samuel Fothergill, November 27, 1758, Haverford College Quaker Collection. George Crosfield, "Memoirs of the Life and Gospel Labours of Samuel Fothergill, with selections from his correspondence also an account of the life and travels of his father John Fothergill and notices by his descendants." In *The Friends Library: Compromising Journals, Doctrinal Treatises and other writings of members of the Religious Society of Friends*, ed. William Evans and Thomas Evans (Philadelphia: William and Thomas Evans, 1845), vol. 9, 206–22.

67. Anthony Benezet to Samuel Allinson, October 23, 1774, Haverford College Quaker Collection.

68. Benezet had read the account of Captain John Snelgrave, who paid attention to the life and death patterns of the Africans, "knowing the Kormantines to be desperate Fellows, who despised Punishment and even Death itself: For it has often happened at Barbados and other Islands, that, on their being any Ways hardly dealt with, to break them from their Stubbornness in refusing to work, twenty, or more, have hanged themselves, at a time, in one Plantation." Captain William Snelgrave, *A New Account of Some Parts of Guinea and the Slave Trade, in 1730*, in Thomas Astley, *A New General Collection of Voyages and Travels*, 4 vols. (1745–47; repr., London: Frank Cass, 1968), vol. 2, 507.

69. Benezet, *Short Account of That Part of Africa*, 47.

70. Snelgrave, *New Account of Some Parts of Guinea*, in Astley, *New General Collection*, vol. 2, 508.

71. The best accounts of the history of the maroon tradition are Richard Price, ed., *Maroon Societies: Rebel Slave Communities in the Americas* (Baltimore: Johns Hopkins University Press, 1979), and Mavis C. Campbell, *The Maroons of Jamaica* (Trenton, N.J.: Africa World Press, 1990). General patterns of slave revolts are outlined in Eugene D. Genovese, *From Rebellion to Revolution: Afro-American Slave Revolts in the Making of the New World* (New York: Vantage, 1979), chaps. 1 and 2. Gerald W. Mullin, *Flight and Resistance: Slave Resistance in Eighteenth-Century Virginia* (London: Oxford University Press, 1972).

72. Bruns, *Am I Not a Man and a Brother*, 97.

73. Anthony Benezet to Joseph Phipps, May 28, 1763, Haverford College Quaker Collection.

74. Ibid.

75. Peter Wood, *Black Majority: Negroes in Colonial South Carolina from 1670 Through the Stono Rebellion* (New York: W. W. Norton, 1974), 219.

76. For the 1720 figures see Wood, Black Majority; 1750 and 1770 figures are from Ira Berlin, *Many Thousand Gone: The First Two Centuries of Slavery in North America* (Cambridge, Mass.: Harvard University Press, 1998), 370; see also *Historical Statistics of the United States, Colonial Times to 1970*, 2 vols. (Washington, D.C.: Bureau of the Census, 1975), vol. 2, 1,168; see "Map of Slave Distribution in South Carolina," in Philip D. Morgan, *Slave Counterpoint: Black Culture in the Eighteenth Century Chesapeake and Lowcountry* (Chapel Hill: University of North Carolina, 1998), 96 (in 1770 the slave population was 65,178, which was still 61 percent of the state's total).

77. Anthony Benezet to Joseph Phipps, May 28, 1763, Haverford College Quaker Collection. See also Bruns, *Am I Not a Man and a Brother*, 98.

78. Richard Price records that in Surinam an average sugar estate had 228 slaves, over seventeen times more than plantations in Maryland and Virginia. Price, *The Guiana Maroons: A Historical and Bibliographical Introduction* (Baltimore: Johns Hopkins University Press, 1976), 16. Sally and Richard Price show that in Surinam "the slave population, which came from a variety of West and Central African societies, contained an unusually high ratio of African to Creoles, and of recently arrived

Africans to seasoned slaves," noting that "the colony's ratio of Africans to Europeans was also extreme—more than 25:1, and as high as 65:1 in the plantation districts." Richard and Sally Price, eds. *Stedman's Surinam: Life in an Eighteenth-Century Slave Society,* abridged, modernized edition of *Narrative of a Five Years Expedition Against the Revolted Negroes of Surinam,* by John Gabriel Stedman (Baltimore: Johns Hopkins University Press, 1992), xii.

79. Price and Price, *Stedman's Surinam.* Anthropologists Richard and Sally Price documented that "during the early years of the colony, Indian and Africans toiled side by side as plantation slaves; in some cases Indians facilitated Africans' escapes and harbored them in the forest; and settled groups of maroons." They have also shown that "likewise," groups of maroons "assimilated small groups of Indians." Stedman also observed how the Dutch secured the aid of the Indians to suppress the maroons. Stedman also relied on Thomas Clarkson's essays much as Clarkson had used Benezet's to understand the nature of the slave trade (xii, 327). William Lauren Katz, *Breaking the Chains: African American Slave Resistance* (New York: Atheneum, 1990), 15. Michael Craton, *Testing the Chains: Resistance to Slavery in the British West Indies* (Ithaca, N.Y.: Cornell University Press, 1982), 270–72. Craton chronicled the events at Barbice, then Dutch Guyana, in 1763. Benezet referred to Barbice as Barbie. There were slave revolts in Barbice, the Dutch colony in 1733, 1749, 1752, and 1762, and a smaller one in 1768. In 1768 there was also a revolt in the French colony of Montserrat. See Harry Harmer, *The Longman Companion to Slavery, Emancipation, and Civil Rights* (London: Longman, 2001).

80. Anthony Benezet to David Barclay, April 29, 1767, Haverford College Quaker Collection. As mentioned earlier, Barclay's family owned stock in the Royal African Company. Eric Williams, *Capitalism and Slavery.* (Chapel Hill: University of North Carolina, 1944; repr. New York: Capricorn Books, 1966), 43. Michael Craton, *Testing the Chains: Resistance to Slavery in the British West Indies* (Ithaca, N.Y.: Cornell University Press, 1982), 21, 147, 191. The Caribs were the indigenous Indian people of the Lesser Antilles, the Caribbean, and parts of South America. Culturally they were more Amerindian than African. They lived under a confederation of groupings and combined Native American customs with African traditions, bringing together the Indian skills with bow and arrows and the African knowledge of guerrilla warfare. Led by their chief, Joseph Chatoyer, they refused the offer, and in 1769 the first skirmishes occurred near the Yambou River, where soldiers and road builders were captured. For three years the situation remained at an impasse until the British secretary of state, Lord Hillsborough, sent in troops in April 1772. By May 1773 Governor Leybourne acknowledged losses of "72 men killed and 80 wounded in the fighting, with 110 dead from disease and 428 sick. In white lives this had become one of the most costly of Britain's servile wars in the Caribbean." Michael Craton, *Testing the Chains: Resistance to Slavery in the British West Indies* (Ithaca: Cornell University Press, 1982), 151.

81. From the 1670s revolts were continuous. The first Maroon War, with its origins in 1663, lasted through seventy years of irregular skirmishes, with the main battles from 1730 to 1740. In 1739 the British offered peace to the Cockpit County maroons if they agreed to help recapture runaway slaves, and a treaty was signed. Kenneth Bilby and Diane Baird N'Diaye, "Creativity and Resistance: Maroon Culture in the America," *Smithsonian Institution: 1992 Festival of Folklife Booklet* (Washington, D.C.: Smithsonian Institution, 1992), 54. The British also conceded to other maroon communities where "free towns" were established. The Second Maroon War of 1795 saw 300 maroons battle over 1,500 British soldiers. Although the maroons eventually surrendered, they still maintained control of their territory, existing as a "nation within a nation." As was the case in South Carolina and Geor-

gia during the French and Indian Wars, slaves used the conflict to escape, knowing that the colonists would have problems fighting on two fronts, just as the leaders of Tacky's Revolt in Jamaica had predicted. As Bilgy and N'Diaye observed, "Those that the British made peace treaties with were neither European generals nor Native American chieftains. . . . They were rather enslaved Africans who had managed to escape plantations and form new societies in the wilderness" (54). After almost a hundred years of being unable to defeat the maroons, the British were forced to propose treaties recognizing the freedom that their former slaves had already seized and granting them land and political autonomy.

82. The goal of maroons was to establish their own "nation," their own independent communities. They were most common in the Caribbean, Latin America, and Brazil, where there were both higher proportions of blacks to whites, as well as land conditions (mountains, swamps, and forests) that were easier to defend and where their former masters would have difficulty navigating the terrain. Maroons in Jamaica, Surinam, and St. Vincent paid special attention to intracolonial conflicts and to conflict among imperialist nations, and often ran away at the peak of those events.

83. Slaves in Jamaica and elsewhere also wanted to overthrow slavery, just as badly as the colonialists wanted the overthrow of British tyranny. Akans, or Coramantees, led Tacky's Rebellion in 1760, an event that Benezet knew about. Starting on Easter Sunday, 150 blacks, led by the slave Tacky, attacked the main fort at Port Maria, just as Akans and other slaves had done in New York in 1741. Occurring at the height of the French and Indian War (1757–63), the slaves no doubt felt that the British could not wage full battle on both fronts, on the mainland and in the Caribbean. The center of the revolt was in St. Mary's parish, which had a high concentration of Akan slaves. The rebellion was not suppressed until October 1761. In the end almost four hundred slaves, sixty whites, and sixty free blacks were killed. As was the pattern, those participating slaves who were not hung or shot were "transported" out of the colony.

84. Benjamin Franklin to Anthony Benezet, February 10, 1773, in Smyth, *Writings of Benjamin Franklin*, vol. 6, 9. Benezet, it seems, confused the rebellion on St. Vincent with Surinam in 1772, as there was no reported mention of a slave rebellion in Surinam that year. The event in St. Vincent that Benezet referred to must have been the First Carib War (1769–73) with the Black Caribs. By the end of the French and Indian War in 1763, Britain had captured St. Vincent, Dominica, Tobago, and Grenada from France. The British soon sent in land surveyors, settlers, and troops. As was always the case, the British began to encroach on the land of the indigenous peoples. Indicating a new closeness, Franklin thanked Benezet "for the 4 copies you sent of your Translations of the French book, I have given two of them to friends here, who I thought the subject might suit" (9). The work was *The Path of Christian Perfection, Translated from the French by Anthony Benezet in the Year 1758.*

85. Richard Price, "Maroons: Rebel Slaves in the Americas," *Smithsonian Institution: 1992 Festival of American Folklife Booklet* (Washington, D.C.: Smithsonian Institution, 1992): 62. Price says "the English word 'maroon' derives from the Spanish word *Cimarron*—itself based on an Arawakan (Taino) Indian root. *Cinmarron* originally referred to domestic cattle that had taken to the hills in Hispaniola, and soon after it was applied to the American Indian slaves." For detailed descriptions of the maroons of Surinam see Sidney W. Mintz and Richard Price, *The Birth of African American Culture,* (Boston: Beacon Press, 1992); Price, *First Time: The Historical Vision of an Afro-American People* (Baltimore: John Hopkins University Press, 1983); and Price, *Alabi's World,* (Baltimore: Johns Hopkins University Press, 1991).

86. Anthony Benezet to Granville Sharp, March 29, 1773, Haverford College Quaker Collection.

87. Anthony Benezet to Robert Pleasants, April 8, 1773, Haverford College Quaker Collection.

88. Ibid. Surinam, in the Dutch West Indies, was used as a "staging point" by the Dutch for the slave trade in the early 1700s. In 1693 many slaves escaped from Surinam, and in 1757 a slave rebellion occurred on the Dutch colony at the logging camps along the Tempati River. By 1770 there were fifty thousand slaves in Surinam, and between the other Dutch colonies in Demerara, Essequilbo, and Barbice, there were another fourteen thousand.

89. Benjamin Franklin to Anthony Benezet, February 10, 1773, in Smyth, *Writings of Benjamin Franklin*, vol. 6, 9.

90. Benezet may have confused the rebellion on St. Vincent's with the events in Surinam in 1772, as no known documented rebellion occurred in Surinam in 1772.

91. Eric Foner, *The Story of American Freedom* (New York: W. W. Norton, 1998), 33.

Chapter 4. Visions of Africa

1. A detailed list of all the narratives appears in J. D. Fage, *A Guide to Original Sources for Pre-Colonial Western Africa Published in European Languages* (Madison: University of Wisconsin African Studies Department, 1994), and proved invaluable as a source of cross-references. See also Peter Hogg, *The African Slave Trade and Its Suppression* (London: Frank Cass, 1973); and *The Antislavery Collection 18th–19th Century*, from the Friends' Library, London, available on microfilm at Yale University and the Library of Congress.

2. Jonathan Sassi, "Africans in the Quaker Image: Anthony Benezet, African Travel Narratives, and Revolutionary-Era Antislavery," *Journal of Early Modern History* 10, nos. 1–2 (2006), 102; *The Charter, Laws, and Catalogue of Books, of the Library Company of Philadelphia: With a Short Account of the Library Prefixed* (Philadelphia, 1770); Cadbury, "Anthony Benezet's Library," 63–75; Edwin Wolf II, *The Library of James Logan of Philadelphia, 1624–1751* (Philadelphia: Library Company of Philadelphia, 1971); Edwin Wolf, "The Library of James Logan" *A.B. Bookman's Weekly* 52 (1973), 1380–87, 1523–27; Edwin Wolf, "James Logan Bookman Extradaordinary," *Proceedings of the Historical Society of Massachusetts* 79 (1967), 31–46

3. Benezet, *Some Historical Account of Guinea* (1772), 98.

4. Ibid., 3.

5. C. Duncan Rice, *The Rise and Fall of Black Slavery* (New York: Harper and Row, 1975), 17, 200. Historians discussing Benezet's use of travel narratives have typically followed Rice's superficial assessment of Benezet's writings. That assessment ignores the complex calculus Benezet applied to his selective use of these works.

6. Anthony Benezet, *The Plainness and Innocent Simplicity of the Christian Religion. With Its Salutary Effects, Compared to the Corrupting Nature, and Dreadful Effects of War. With Some Account of the Blessing Which Attends on a Spirit Influenced by Divine Love, Producing Peace and Good Will to Men. Collected by A. Benezet* (Philadelphia, 1782; London, 1800); Anthony Benezet, trans., *The Plain Path to Christian Perfection* (Philadelphia, 1772), 80.

7. Anthony Benezet, *The Potent Enemies of America Laid Open: Being Some Account of the Baneful Effects Attending the Use of Distilled Spirituous Liquors, and the Slavery of the Negroes* (Philadelphia, 1774); *The Mighty Destroyer Displayed, in Some Account of the Dreadful Havoc Made by the Mistaken Use as Well as Abuse of Distilled Spirituous Liquors. By a Lover of Mankind* (Philadelphia, 1774), 78, 88; *An Extract from a Treatise on the Spirit of Prayer, or the Soul Rising out of the Vanity of Time into the Riches of Eternity. With Some Thoughts on War; Remarks on the Nature and Bad Effects of Spirituous Liquor; and Considerations on Slavery* (Philadelphia, 1778, 1780).

8. Anthony Benezet, *Serious Reflections Affectionately Recommended to the Well-Disposed of Every Religious Denomination, Particularly Those Who Mourn and Lament on Account of the Calamities Which Attend Us and the Insensibility That So Generally Prevails* (Philadelphia, 1778). Reprinted in Brookes, *Friend Anthony Benezet*, 495.

9. Benezet, *Some Historical Account of Guinea* , 2.

10. Richard Hakluyt, The Original Writings and Correspondence of the Two Richard Hakluyts, ed. E. G. R. Taylor (London, 1935), 2:368.

11. Irwin R. Blacker, introduction to Richard Hakluyt, *Hakluyt's Voyages: The Principal Navigation, Voyages, Traffiques & Discoveries of the English Nation* (New York: Viking, 1965), 3.

12. William Dampier, *A New Voyage Around the World Describing Particularly the Isthmus of America, Several Coasts and Islands of Cape Verde, the Passage by Terra del Fuego, the South Sea Coast of Chili, Peru, and Mexico; the Isle of Guam, One of the Ladrones, Mindanao, and Other Philippine and East India Islands, near Cambodia, China, Formosa, Luconia, Celebes&c. New Holland, Sumatra, Nichobar Isles; the Cape of Good Hope, and Santa Hellena* (London: Printed for James Knapton at the Crown in St. Paul's Churchyard). Excerpted in Astley, *New General Collection*, vol. 1, repr. ed. (London: Argonaut Press, 1927; repr. New York: Dover Productions, 1968).

13. Richard Nisbet, *Slavery Not Forbidden by Scripture* (Philadelphia, 1773) (housed at the Library Company of Philadelphia).

14. Benjamin Rush, *A Vindication of the Address, to the Inhabitations of the British Settlements . . . in Answer to a Pamphlet Entitled "Slavery Not Forbidden by Scripture"* (Philadelphia, 1773), 197–223.

15. Richard Ligon, *A True & Exact History of the Island of Barbados . . .* (London, 1657), 47.

16. Winthrop D. Jordan, *White over Black: American Attitudes Toward the Negro, 1550–1812* (New York: W. W. Norton, 1968), chap. 1. Other sources are Martin Bernal, *Black Athena*, vols. 1 and 2 (New Brunswick, N.J.: Rutgers University Press, 1987, 1991); Thomas F. Gossett, *Race: The History of an Idea in America* (Oxford: Oxford University Press, 1963); Ivan Hannaford, *Race: The History of an Idea in the West* (Baltimore: Johns Hopkins University Press, 1996); Frank M. Snowden, Jr., *Blacks in Antiquity: Ethiopians in the Greco-Roman Experience* (Cambridge, Mass.: Harvard University Press, 1970).

17. According to Philip Curtin, "the period 1741–1810 marks the summit of the plateau, when the long-term annual rates of delivery hung just above 60,000 a year. . . . Thus about 60 percent of all slaves delivered to the New World were transported during the century 1721–1820." Philip D. Curtin, *The Atlantic Slave Trade* (Madison: University of Wisconsin Press, 1969), 265; Joseph E. Inikori and Stanley L. Engerman, eds., *The Atlantic Slave Trade* (Durham, N.C.: Duke University Press, 1992). Inikori and Engerman have challenged Curtin's figure of 9.57 million slaves brought to the Americas; they believe that the ultimate figure is unlikely to be less than 12 million or more than 20 million captives exported from Africa in the transatlantic slave trade. Inikori believes that the "total figure of slaves imported globally to be 15.4 million" (5–6). Joseph Inikori, "Measuring the Atlantic Slave Trade: An Assessment of Curtin and Anstey," *Journal of African History* 17 (1976), 197–223. Somewhere in the middle of these conflicting figures are those of Paul Lovejoy, who estimates the number to be 11,698,000. Paul E. Lovejoy, "The Volume of the Atlantic Slave Trade: A Synthesis," *Journal of African History* 23 (1982), 473–500. All agree that the trade lasted from between 1518 and 1850 and the heyday of the slave trade was 1701 to 1800. Most slaves were taken to Brazil or the Caribbean. New studies on the Atlantic slave trade include David Eltis and David Richardson, *Routes to Slavery: Direction, Ethnicity and Mortality in the Transatlantic Slave Trade* (London: Frank Cass,

1997); and David Eltis, *The Rise of African Slavery in the Americas* (Cambridge: Cambridge University Press, 2000).

18. David Brion Davis and Steven Mintz, *The Boisterous Sea of Liberty: A Documentary History of America from Discovery Through the Civil War* (New York: Oxford University Press, 1998), 57. During the seventeenth century the number of slaves in the mainland colonies grew exponentially. For example, in 1650 there were only 150 blacks in Virginia, but by 1704 that number had risen to 10,000.

19. Ira Berlin, *Generations of Captivity; A History of African-American Slaves* (Cambridge, Mass.: Harvard University Press, 2003), Table 1.

20. Richard Hofstadter, *America at 1750* (New York: Vintage, 1973), chap. 1.

21. Peter Fryer, *Staying Power: The History of Black People in Britain* (London: Pluto, 1984), 7; Philip D. Curtin, *The Image of Africa: British Ideas and Actions, 1780–1850* (Madison: University of Wisconsin Press, 1964), 10. There is a rich body of literature on images of blacks in Britain. See also Eva Beatrice Drake, *The English in Romantic Thought* (Washington, D.C: Associated Publishers, 1842); and *Slavery, Abolition and Emancipation: Writings in the British Romantic Period*, ed. Sukhdev Sandhu et al. (London: Pickering and Chatto, 1999). There were only 14,000 blacks in Britain in the mid-eighteenth century, and many were referred to as "body servants" rather than slaves. For a good summary of Africa during the independence movements of the 1950s and 1970s, see also Vincent Bakpetu Thompson, *Africa and Unity: The Evolution of Pan-Africanism* (London: Longman, 1969), 377–78. Kwame Anthony Appiah and Henry Louis Gates, Jr., eds., *Encyclopedia Africana* (New York: Basic Civitas Books, 1999).

21. Paul Edwards and James Walvin, *Black Personalities in the Era of the Slave Trade* (Baton Rouge: Louisiana State University Press, 1983), 22.

22. Bernard Romans, *A Concise Natural History of East and West Florida* (New York: Printed for the Author, 1775), quoted in Jordan, *White over Black*, 305. See also Lester B. Scherer, "A New Look at Personal Slavery Established," *William and Mary Quarterly*, 3rd series, 30, no. 4 (October 1973), 645–52.

23. Jordan, *White over Black*, 96.

24. Paul Edwards and James Walvin, *Black Personalities in the Era of the Slave Trade* (Baton Rouge: Louisiana State University Press, 1983).

25. Edmund S. Morgan, *American Slavery, American Freedom: The Ordeal of Colonial Virginia* (New York: Norton, 1975). See also Morgan, "Slavery and Freedom: The American Paradox," *Journal of American History* 59 (June 1972): 5–29; Linebaugh and Rediker, *Many-Headed Hydra*, 247; Peter Linebaugh and Marcus Rediker, "'The Many-Headed Hydra': Sailors, Slaves, and the Atlantic Working Class in the Eighteenth Century," *Journal of Historical Sociology* 3, no. 3 (September 1990), 225–52; Allan Kulikoff, "The Progress of Inequality in Revolutionary Boston," *William and Mary Quarterly*, 3rd series, 28, no. 3 (1971): 375–412; James T. Lemon and Gary B. Nash, "The Distribution of Wealth in Eighteenth-Century America: A Century of Change in Chester County Pennsylvania, 1693–1802," *Journal of Social History* 2 (1968): 1–24.

26. Jordan, *White over Black*, 97. For a fascinating new study on the middle passage, slave conditions, and slave resistance aboard ship, see Marcus Rediker, *The Slave Ship: A Human History* (New York: Viking Press, 2007).

27. Curtin, *Image of Africa*, 30.

28. Edwards and Walvin, *Black Personalities in the Era of the Slave Trade*, 40.

29. Milton Cantor, "The Image of the Negro in Colonial Literature," *New England Quarterly* 36 (December 1963): 457.

30. Sue Peabody, *"There Are No Slaves in France": The Political Culture of Race and Slavery in the Ancien Regime* (New York: Oxford University Press, 1996), chaps. 1 and 2.

31. Peter C. Mancall, ed., *Travel Narratives from the Age of Discovery: An Anthology* (New York: Oxford University Press, 2007), 24.

32. Curtin, *Image of Africa*; Lawrence E. Tise, *Proslavery: A History of the Defense of Slavery in America* (Athens: University of Georgia, 1987); Davis, *Problem of Slavery in Western Culture*; Alden T. Vaughn, *Roots of American Racism: Essays on the Colonial Experience* (New York: Oxford University Press, 1995); Anthony J. Barker, *The African Link: British Attitudes to the Negro in the Era of the African Slave Trade, 1550–1807* (London: Frank Cass, 1978); Jordan, *White over Black*.

33. John Locke, John Locke, *Two Treatises of Government, a Critical Edition with an Introduction and Apparatus Criticus,* ed. Peter Laslett (Cambridge: Cambridge University Press, 1967), book 2, 159.

34. Statutes at Large of South Carolina, vol. 1, p. 55. See also A. Leon Higgenbotham Jr., *In Matter of Color: Race and the American Legal Process: The Colonial Period* (New York: Oxford University Press, 1978), 163.

35. Edwards and Walvin, *Black Personalities in the Era of the Slave Trade*, 41.

36. Wylie Sypher, *Guinea's Captive Kings: British Anti-Slavery Literature of the XVIII Century* (New York: Octagon, 1969), 67.

37. David Humphries, *An Account of the Endeavors Used by the Society for the Propagation of the Gospel in Foreign Parts* (London, 1730), 5.

38. John Woolman, *Considerations on Keeping Negroes* (Philadelphia, 1762), 32.

39. Arthur Lee, *An Essay on the Vindication of the Continental Colonies of America* (London, 1764), 30.

40. Granville Sharp to J. Bryant, quoted in Sharp, *Just Limitation of Slavery in the Laws of God* (London, 1776), 44–46.

41. *Virginia Gazette*, August 20, 1772, quoted in Jordan, *White over Black*, 255.

42. Eric Williams, *Capitalism and Slavery* (Chapel Hill: University of North Carolina Press, 1944); David Brion Davis, *Slavery and Human Progress* (London: Oxford University Press, 1984); Jordan, *White over Black*.

43. Anthony Benezet, *Short Observations on Slavery* (Philadelphia, 1781), 5.

44. Olaudah Equiano, *The Interesting Narrative Written by Himself,* ed. Robert J. Allison (New York: Bedford St. Martin's, 2006), 47; "The Life of Olaudah Equiano or Gustavus Vassa, The African, Written by Himself," in *Great Slave Narratives*, ed. Arna Bontemps (Boston: Beacon Press, 1969), 19–20.

45. Benezet, *Observations on the Inslaving of Negroes* .

46. Benezet, *Short Account of That Part of Africa*, 2nd ed., 5.

47. Ibid.

48. Benezet, *Some Historical Account of Guinea*, 84, 88.

49. Benezet, *Observations on the Inslaving of Negroes*, 8.

50. Benezet, *Some Historical Account of Guinea*, 65.

51. Barker, *African Link*, 22.

52. *Universal Modern History* (London, 1747, 1st ed.). A yearly edition is produced. Volume 1 contains sections on ancient Africa and was also referred to as the *Universal Ancient History*. Anthony Barker also points out in *The African Link* that "from the late seventeenth century such detailed surveys were supplemented by a second category of more succinct reference materials," such as "Edmund Bohun's Geographical Dictionary, which reached six editions between 1688–1710," 22.

53. *Universal Modern History* (1760), xvii, 90, quoted in P. J. Marshall and Glyndwr Williams, *The Great Map of Mankind* (Cambridge, Mass.: Harvard University Press, 1982), 238. Marshall and Williams point out that "the *History* itself supplied an appropriate example of this confusion."

54. Benezet, *Some Historical Account of Guinea*, ii–iii, 1.

55. Ibid., 2–3.

56. Among the volumes Benezet consulted, maps appeared in many editions: Willem Bosman, *A New and Accurate Description of the Coast of Guinea: Divided into the Gold, the Slave, and the Ivory Coasts* (London: Frank Cass,1967), between the introduction and author's preface and between the table of contents and page 1; and Snelgrave, *New Account of Some Parts of Guinea*, between the introduction (xxii) and page 1. Maps appear throughout Astley, *New General Collection*: Brüe excerpts, vol. 2, between 144 and 145; Barbot excerpts, vol. 2 between 528 and 529 and 564–565; Lope Gonsalvo excerpts, vol. 3, between index and 1. For pictures depicting forts and factories see note 99.

57. Benezet, *Short Account of That Part of Africa*, 5.

58. Benezet, *Some Historical Account of Guinea*, 2.

59. Benezet, *Potent Enemies of America*; Benezet, *Mighty Destroyer Displayed*, 78, 88; Benezet, *Extract from Treatise on Spirit of Prayer*.

60. Benezet, *Some Historical Account of Guinea*, 4.

61. Wilson Armistead wrote that Benezet "did not indulge in any superfluity in dress, his clothing being made in the most simple manner, and some of the material selected for the durability of its texture." Armistead, *Anthony Benezet*, 131. Benezet like Lay was roundly criticized by upper-echelon Quakers for wearing clothes until they literally fell off his back. Like Lay, he refused to wear any clothing made by slave labor.

62. Benezet, *Some Historical Account of Guinea*, 5–6. In his later years Lay and his wife lived in a cave near Philadelphia. Benezet did not fall prey to the notion of African as caveman and did not make that claim relative to Lay. See Chapter 3 for further details.

63. The homes and lifestyle of the Quaker elite are superbly documented and described in Frederick B. Tolles, *Meeting House and Counting House: The Quaker Merchants of Colonial Philadelphia, 1682–1763* (New York: Norton, 1948); and Carl and Jessica Bridenbaugh, *Rebels and Gentlemen: Philadelphia in the Age of Franklin* (New York: Reynal and Hitchcock, 1942).

64. Benezet, *Some Historical Account of Guinea*, 98.

65. Robin Law, *Slave Coast of West Africa, 1550–1750* (Oxford: Clarendon Press, 1991). The narratives provide, as Curtin writes, "an admission that African states had a history." Curtin, *Image of Africa*, 24; see William Heffernan, "The Slave Trade and Abolition in Travel Literature," *Journal of the History of Ideas* 34, no. 2 (April–June 1973): 185–208; Peter C. Mancall offers an extensive look at travel narratives in the sixteenth and early seventeenth centuries in *Travel Narratives from the Age of Discovery*.

66. Patrick Manning, *Slavery and African Life: Occidental, Oriental, and African Slave Trades* (New York: Cambridge University Press, 1990).

67. Robin Law, "Early European Sources Relating to the Kingdom of Ijebu (1500–1700): A Critical Survey," *History of Africa* 9 (1982): 253. Most of these records date from the late seventeenth and early eighteenth centuries. See also Robin Law and Kristin Mann, "West Africa in the Atlantic Community: The Case of the Slave Coast," *William and Mary Quarterly*, 3rd series, 56, no. 2 (April 1999): 307–34. Law argues that these sources supplement the occasional dispatches from the travelers sent to the royal authorities in *Slave Coast of Africa*, p. 22. He adds "the value of these records is limited, of course, by their concentration upon matters of commerce, though since local political conditions and events crucially affected the operation of commerce this limitation is less restrictive than might be supposed." Law, *The Slave Coast of West Africa, 1550–1750: The Impact of the Atlantic Slave Trade on an African Society* (Oxford: Clarendon Press, 1991), 8. As with the work of U. B. Phil-

ips and his disciples, years later the financial records reveal a good deal about the slave masters and the economic aspect of slavery but offer little about the slaves or their families, community, religion, or culture. Ulrich Bonnell Philips, *American Negro Slavery: A Survey of the Supply, Employment and Control of Negro Labor as Determined by the Plantation Regime* (1918; repr., Baton Rouge: Louisiana State University Press, 1966). Curtin, *Atlantic Slave Trade.* While giving some insights into the methodological problems involved with using such sources, the knowledgeable researcher can use descriptions of records from the European trade and the principal chartered companies: the English Royal African Company, the French Guinea and Indies Companies, the South Sea Company, and the Dutch West India Company.

68. Robin Law, "History and Legitimacy: Aspects of the Use of the Past in Pre-Colonial Dahomey," *History in Africa* 15 (1988), 432. Law does warn, however, that the "European reports were more often based upon what Europeans were told than on what they themselves had witnessed, [and] they should be regarded rather as preserving contemporary *African* perceptions and interpretations of events, which can be compared with the retrospective presentations of the same events in later traditions." Robin Law, ed., *The English in West Africa: The Local Correspondence to the Royal African Company of England, 1691–1699, Part 2* (Oxford: Printed for the British Academy by Oxford University Press, 2001), 302.

69. Additionally Benezet read Gothard Athus's collection of voyages, "A True Historical Description of the Gold Coast," Latin translations from original languages compiled in Theodor de Bry, *India Orientalis,* Part 5 (Frankfurt am Main: M. Becker, 1599). Benezet quoted Artus: "They are a sincere inoffensive People, and do no Injustice either to one another or Strangers . . . it is a capital crime to injure a Foreigner . . . which is severely punished." *Benezet, Short Account of That Part of Africa,* 14. In his later *Some Historical Account of Guinea* (p. 36), Benezet omitted the words "which is severely punished." This omission may represent his distaste for the violence whites dealt to blacks. Excerpted in Astley, *New General Collection,* vol. 3.

70. Anthony J. Barker carefully observed, "In the first hand accounts of Africa there is a meaningful division between the 17th and 18th centuries. For most of the 17th century the primary sources were the largely ephemeral contacts by early slave traders and voyagers recorded in Hakluyt; the more extensive descriptions by Leo Africanus; and Richard Jobson's *Golden Trade* (1623)" (*The Golden Trade, in the Discovery of the River Gambia* [1623 ed.], with additional material, David Gamble and P. E. H. Hair [London: Hakluyt Society, 1999]). Barker, *African Link,* 17.

71. In her new study, *Trickster Travels: A Sixteenth-Century Muslim Between Worlds* (New York: Hill and Wang, 2006), Natalie Zemon Davis takes a unique approach, using the tale of an imaginary bird to uncover the complexities of Leo Africanus. See also Amin Maalouf, *Leo Africanus* (New York: New Amsterdam, 1986); and Mancall, *Travel Narratives from the Age of Discovery,* Part I, Document 6, 96–112.

72. "Al-Hasan ibn Muhammad al-Wizaz al Fasi was an Andulusian Moor born in 1493 of wealthy parents. The family was driven from Spain and settled in Fez, from which Al-Hassan made numerous journeys throughout North Africa and the Western Sudan as judge, clerk, merchant and diplomat. In 1518 he was captured by Christian corsairs off Tunisia, taken to Rome, and baptized Giovanni Lioni, from which the more popular Leo Africanus was derived. His famous *The History and Description of Africa and the Notable Things Therein Contained,* which he wrote in Italian, was completed in 1526. The manuscript was published in 1550 in Ramausio's collection entitled *Voyages and Travels.* An English translation was published in London in 1600." Robert O. Collins, ed., *Documents from the African Past* (Princeton, N.J.: Markus Wiener, 2001), 32.

73. Benezet, *Some Historical Account of Guinea,* 41–42. Benezet had also read Leo

Africanus extracts attached in Francis Moore's *Travels into the Inland Parts of Africa* (London: Printed by E. Cave for the author, 1738).

74. Benezet, *Some Historical Account of Guinea* (1772 ed.), 43; (London, 1788 ed.), 36–37.

75. Awnsham and John Churchill, eds., *A Collection of Voyages and Travels* (London: A. and J. Churchill, 1704). Thomas Phillips and Jean Barbot were included in vols. 5 and 6.

76. Astley, *New General Collection*. While Benezet may have read some of the original French sources or the Dutch ones (which he could also read, as he lived in Holland for a brief period after fleeing England), he always cited the English editions in his own works. Fage, *Guide to Original Sources*, 52. Fage notes that the Astley version of Barbot's journal is not complete: a full English translation appeared only in 1992.

77. Barker noted that "while the 18th century was to see many collections, none appeared at all in the period between 1625 and 1704; yet in the last 40 years of the 17th century there were at least 18 new works containing significant descriptions of Africa and, frequently, of the slave systems in the West Indies. Of these, many were reissued and six achieved at least four editions each. The 18th century produced well over 50 new works of synthesis; and again most were reissued, some as many as 20 times." Barker, *African Link*, 22.

78. In *Slave Coast of West Africa*, Law divided the narratives into three broad categories: the writer's personal experiences and recollections, ethnographic work, and customs and institutions and "explicitly historical work." Included in his study are men like the Englishman William Snelgrave; the Frenchman Jean Barbot; the Dutchman Willem Bosman; and the French naval officer Chevalier des Marchais (1–25). Marchais's four-volume *Voyage du Chevalier des Marchais en Guinée, isles voisines et à Cayenne*, edited by Jean-Baptiste Labat, was published in Paris in 1730. Labat, a Dominican who had lived in the West Indies, later published his own work on the New World, the *Histoire d'Amerique* (Paris, 1772). Labat relied on many of the same sources used by Benezet, such as André Brüe and Bosman. Law includes works like Snelgrave's *New Account of Some Parts of Guinea*. See also Law, *The Oyo Empire c. 1600–c. 1836: A West African Imperialism in the Era of the Atlantic Slave Trade* (Oxford: Clarendon Press, 1977); Law, "Jean Barbot as a Source for the Slave Coast of West Africa," *History of Africa* 9 (1982), 155–73; Law, "Early European Sources Relating to the Kingdom of Ijebu," *History of Africa* 13 (1986), 245–60; Law, "Problems of Plagiarism, Harmonization and Misunderstanding in Contemporary European Sources: Early (Pre-1680s) Sources for the 'Slave Coast' of West Africa," *Paideuma* 33 (1987): 337–58; Law, "The Slave Trader as Historian: Robert Norris and the History of Dahomey," *History of Africa* 16 (1989): 219–35; Law, "The Gold Trade of Whydah in the Seventeenth and Eighteenth Centuries," in David Hence and T. C. McCaskie, eds., West African Economic and Social History: Studies in Memory of Marion Johnson (Madison: University of Wisconsin Press, 1990), 105–18; Phillip Curtin, *The Image of Africa: British Ideas and Action, 1780–1850* (Madison: University of Wisconsin Press, 1964). Curtin also observes that ever since Hakluyt's *Principal Voyages Traffiques & Discoveries of the English Nations* was published in 1599, the literate English public had access to travel literature in quite a few European languages. According to Curtin, "from the mid-15th to the mid-18th century, several hundred different travellers left some account of their voyage to Guinea." He further notes, "Many of these journals and reports had dropped from sight by the 1780s, but about 20 different works had come to be accepted as a canon of West African knowledge" (11).

79. John Atkins, *A Voyage to Guinea, Brazil and the West Indies: In His Majesty's Ships,*

the Swallow *and* Weymouth (1705; repr., Northbrook, Ill.: Metro Books, 1972); Bosman, *New and Accurate Description*; A. Dalzell, *History of Dahomey* (London, 1793).

80. James Walvin, *Black and White: The Negro and English Society, 1555–1945* (London: Penguin, 1973), 28. These volumes included the first English translations of some older texts, but volumes 4 and 5, published in 1732, drew special attention because they first published the accounts of two former slave traders Thomas Phillips and Jean Barbot.

81. André Brüe, *Voyages and Travels Along the Western Coasts of Africa, on Account of the French Commerce, by the Sieur Andre Brue, Many Years Director-General of the French Sanaga Company at Fort St. Louis* (first published in Jean-Baptiste Labat, *Nouvelle relation de l'Afrique Occidentale contenant une description exacte du Sénégal . . .* [Paris, 1728]; first translated and excerpted in English in Astley, *New General Collection*, vol. 2).

82. Benezet, *Short Account of That Part of Africa*, 8.

83. Brüe had been the director-general of the Senegal Company at Fort St. Louis in Senegambia and stayed in Senegal from 1697 to 1723, where he played a major role in expanding and consolidating the colony. He traveled to nearby countries; made deals with the local chiefs; sought territorial concessions in order to establish new settlements, factories, and forts; and played an important role in the establishment of the French slave trade in Senegambia. Brüe's narrative was first published in Labat's *Nouvelle Voyage* (which was based on Brüe's papers), thereby guaranteeing it an immediate audience (extracts and translations in Astley, *New General Collection*, vol. 2). See also *The Memoirs of Jean-Baptiste Labat*, trans. and abridged by John Eaden (London: Constable, 1931). See also anonymous *Voyages aux Cotes de Guinée dans l'Amérique faits en 1702* (Amsterdam, 1719); A. Biet, *Voyages de la France Equinoxiale en l'isle de Cavenne . . .* (Paris, 1654); J. Bouton, *Relation de l'établissement des Français depuis l'an 1635 en l'île de la Martinique, l'une des Antilles* (Cramoisy, 1640); P.F.X. de Charlevoix, *Histoire de l'isle Espagnole ou de Saint Dominique* (Amsterdam, 1733); J. Clodore, *Relation de ce qui c'est passé dans les isles et terre ferme de l'Amérique pendant la dernière guerre* (Paris, 1671); Draise de Grandpierre, *Relation de divers voyages faits dans l'Afrique, dans l'Amérique et aux Indes Occidentales* (Paris, 1718).

84. Brüe then demanded goods shipped from the interior to the coast while Lut Sukaabe Faal wanted free trade with all European nations, especially the British, who paid double the prices offered by the French. Faal successfully carried out a blockade of the French and convinced French authorities to arrest Brüe for his seizure of the English ship *William and Jane*. Eventually Brüe got out of prison and resumed his activities. Boubacar Barry, *Senegambia and the Atlantic Slave Trade* (London: Cambridge University Press, 1998), 83–85.

85. Benezet, *Some Historical Account of Guinea*, 83.

86. Benezet, *Short Account of That Part of Africa*, 16. This shows long-standing ties to the New World.

87. Barry, *Senegambia and the Atlantic Slave Trade*, 73.

88. Stephanie E. Smallwood, *Saltwater Slavery: A Middle Passage from Africa to the American Diaspora* (Cambridge, Mass.: Harvard University Press, 2007), chap. 6.

89. Law, "Problems of Plagiarism," 337–58; Law, "Early European Sources Relating to the Kingdom of Ijebu," 245–60; Law, "Gold Trade of Whydah," 105–18.

90. Brüe, *Voyages and Travels Along the Western Coasts of Africa*, 73, quoted in Astley, *New General Collection*, vol. 2, 27–158.

91. Anthony Benezet, *A Short Account of the People Called Quakers* (Philadelphia, 1780, 1814, 1866; Paris, 1780, 1788); Benezet, *Plain Path to Christian Perfection*; Benezet, *Plainness of the Christian Religion*.

92. Benezet, *A Caution and a Warning*, 20.

93. Benezet, *Observations on the Inslaving of Negroes*, 5–6.

94. Benezet, *Short Account of That Part of Africa*, 4, *Some Historical Account of Guinea* (1771), 19. Willem Bosman was the chief factor for the Dutch West India Company at Elmina Castle on the coast of the present Republic of Ghana. His *A New and Accurate Description of the Coast of Guinea* consists of twenty letters written around 1700. Bosman "may have borrowed some material from the Amsterdam geographer Olfert Dapper, whose *Descriptions of Africa* had been published nearly twenty years earlier. Axim was one of the important trading towns of the Gold Coasts." "William Bosman: Justice and Warfare art Axim. 1700," in *Documents of the African Past,* ed. Robert O. Collins (Princeton: Markus Wiener Publishers), 121.

95. Benezet, *Short Account of That Part of Africa*, 9.

Seale's eighteenth-century map of the Coast of Africa from Cape Blanco, Lat. 20, 40' N to the Coast of Angola Lat. 11' S. with explanatory Notes of All Forts and Settlements belonging to the Several, European Powers, list 34 forts with "Elmina, or St. George Del Mina, the principal Fort on the Gold Coast belonging to the Dutch Company. Carrington Bowles's 1771 map, A New Account and Correct Map of the Coast of Africa from Sta. Cruz Lat 30 North to the Coast of Angola Lat 11 S. With Explanatory Notes of all the Forts and Settlements belonging to the Several European Powers, list 34 Forts and Settlements as well as Elmina or St. George Del Mina, the principal Fort on the Gold Coast belonging to the Dutch West Indian Company.

96. Bosman, *New and Accurate Description*, xviii; and Astley, *New General Collection*, vol. 2, 3. Benezet appears to have had independent access to the 1721 Bosman narrative as well as the 1732 edition first published in Churchill and Churchill, *Collection of Voyages and Travels*.

97. Benezet, *Observations on the Inslaving of Negroes*, 3.

98. In several of the volumes there are detailed illustrations of these forts, see Astley, *New General Collection*, vol. 2, between 14 and 15 and between 298 and 299, and vol. 3, between 38 and 39.

99. W. O. Blake, *The History of Slavery and the Slave Trade, Ancient and Modern* (Columbus, Ohio: J. and H. Miller, 1858), 99.

100. T. Jeffery's 1768 map *The Western Coast of Africa from Cape Blanco to Cape Virga* cites Francis Moore, *Account of the English Settlement on the River Gambia in 1730*. Jeffery wrote "James Fort. The Principal settlement stands on and Island of the same name which commands the Trade of the River." Carrington Bowles's 1771 map *A New Account and Corrects Map of the Coast of Africa from Sta. Cruz, Lat. 30 North to the Coast of Angola Lat 11 S.* lists thirty-four forts, including illustrations of "Forts at Elmina or St. George Del Mina," at "Cape Coast Castle, the principal Fort Factory, belonging to the English African Company" of "Accra, a Fort belonging to the English Company," and many others.

101. Jean Barbot, "A Description of the Coasts of North and South-Guinea," in Churchill and Churchill, *Collection of Voyages and Travels*, vol. 5, 12. Barbot was an employee of English and French trading companies who made at least two voyages to West Africa between 1678 and 1682.

102. Collins, *Documents from the African Past*, 115.

103. Rediker, *Slave Ship*, 284–301.

104. Benezet, *Observations on the Inslaving of Negroes*, 4.

105. Jean Barbot, *Barbot on Guinea: The Writings of Jean Barbot on West Africa 1678–1712* (London: Hakluyt Society, 1992), vol. 2, 549. Originally published as Jean Barbot, *A Description of the Coasts of North and South-Guinea . . . . With an appendix being a general account of the first discoveries of America . . . By John Barbot . . . Now first printed from his original manuscript.* Volume 5 of Churchill's *Collection*, 1732, reprinted 1744–46 and 1752. Excerpted in Astley's *Collection*, vols. 2, 3.

106. Benezet, *Observations on the Inslaving of Negroes*, 5.

107. Ibid., 3.

108. Letter 9 in Barbot, *Barbot on Guinea*, vol. 1, 106. While quoting extensively from Barbot, Benezet seldom, and this mainly in his later works, footnoted or indicated page numbers for his sources, and so we have no way of noting whether he read the original French manuscript, the English edition of 1688, or later editions. A comparison of the first edition of Barbot and Benezet shows that Benezet usually stayed very close to the original. However, in this paragraph Benezet chose not to cite Barbot to the effect that these savages treat their slaves like dogs, and often leave them to die of hunger; but then it is not true that these people sell each other, only that they sell themselves, when driven to it by famine or some other desperate need" (106–7).

109. Law, "Jean Barbot as a Source for the *Slave Coast of West Africa*," 155–73.

110. Benezet, *Some Historical Account of Guinea*, 33–34.

111. Letter 2 in Barbot, *Barbot on Guinea*, vol. 2, 335.

112. Benezet, *Short Account of That Part of Africa*, 9–10.

113. William Smith, *A New Voyage to Guinea* (London: Printed for John Nourse, opposite Katherine-Street in the Strand, 1744); also excerpted in Astley, *New General Collection*, vol. 2, 266; Benezet, *Short Account of That Part of Africa*, 9–10.

114. Smith, *New Voyage to Guinea*, 33.

115. Benezet, *Some Historical Account of Guinea*, 65.

116. Ibid., 19.

117. John Atkins, *A Voyage to Guinea, and the West-Indies in His Majesty's Ships, the* Swallow *and the* Weymouth . . . *by John Atkins, Surgeon in the Royal Navy* (London: Printed for Ceasdar Ward and Richard Chandler, at the Ship between the Temple Gates in Fleet-Street; and sold at their shop in Scarborough, 1735; 2nd ed., 1737); also excerpted in Astley, *New General Collection*, vol. 2, 177–78.

118. Atkins, *Voyage to Guinea*, 178–179.

119. Benezet, *A Caution and a Warning*, 21. On two occasions Benezet quoted Atkins accounts of ship captians who forced enslaved Africans to eat parts of severed body parts of their fellow captives. "The reader," says Atkins, "may be curious to know their punishments: Why, Captain Harding, wishing the Stoutness and Worth of the two Slaves, did, as in other Countries they do by Rogues of Dignity, whip and scarify them only; while three other Abettors but not actors, nor of Strength for it, he sentenced to cruel Deaths, making them first eat the Heart and Liver of one of them killed." Benezet, *A Short Account of that Part of Africa* (1762), pp.49–50. He also uses this quote in *Some Historical Account of Guinea*, p. 124. He is quoting Atkins from Astley's *New Collections of Voyages [etc.]* 1745–47. Vol. II, p. 449. In his *A Caution and a Warning*, Benezet quotes a "serious person of undoubted credit, who had it from the captain's own mouth, the master of a vessel, who brought a cargo of slaves to Barbados." This person serves as evidence that Benezet gained evidence using oral sources that he encountered on the docks and throughout the Philadelphia area. The slaves on board ship refused to eat and the captain forced them. Benezet writes that the captain "obliged all the Negroes to come upon deck, where they persisting in their resolution of not taking food, he caused his sailors to lay hold upon one of the most obstinate. And chopt the poor creature into small pieces, forcing some of the other to eat a part of the mangled body; withal swearing to the survivors, that he would use them all, one after the other, in the same manner, if they did not consent to eat." *A Caution and a Warning*, 20–21. In both instances Benezet makes clear that it was the whites and not the Africans who initiated the events and that neither black nor white was accused of cannibalizing the other.

120. Atkins had written an earlier work, *The Naval Surgeon*, in 1732. There he observed that "the black color, and wooly teguments of these Guineans, is what first obtrudes itself on our observations, and distinguishes them from the rest of mankind." While this is a purely empirical observation, similar to saying that Northern Europeans have white skin, that Atkins did not give the black skin negative characteristics is noteworthy. John Atkins, *The Naval Surgeon: Or a Practical System of Surgery* (London, 1732), 20–21.

121. Atkins, *Voyage to Guinea*, 129.

122. Ibid., 150.

123. While Benezet often used excerpts from the Astley volumes, when he had the original version of a work, he used that. For example, in the footnotes on page 7 of the 1788 edition of *Some Historical Account of Guinea*, he cited Astley, *New General Collection*, vol. 2, p. 86. He then cites William Smith's *Voyage to Guinea*, pages 31, 34. On page 8 he cites the Astley *New General Collection*, as well as "Moor's Travels into distant parts of Africa, page 198." On page 14 he cites "Adanson, 253, ibid," and on page 17 he refers to "Astley's Collection, vol 2, page 475" and later to "W. Bosman's Description of Guinea, page 440."

124. P. J. Marshall and Glendwr Williams argue that in works like Smith's and others "there is more of this: a defense of African polygamy as being similar to the European practice of one wife and several mistresses." P. J. Marshall and Glendwr Williams, *The Great Map of Mankind: Perceptions of New Worlds in the Age of Enlightenment* (Cambridge, Mass.: Harvard University Press, 1982), 235.

125. Sassi argues that Benezet "chose to ignore" the section on the Africans' sexual practices, but he then rightly notes that the "editor of the Astley *Collection* John Green, did not include it in the large selection from Smith's travel narrative that he reprinted, judging—on what grounds we do not know." Jonathan Sassi, "Africans in the Quaker Image: Anthony Benezet, African Travel Narratives, and Revolutionary-Era Antislavery," *Journal of Early Modern History* 10, nos. 1–2 (2007): 117.

126. Smith, *New Voyage to Guinea*, 200.

127. Ibid., 267.

128. Sassi, "Africans in the Quaker Image," 116. For an interesting comparison of the exploits of the king, see *Beneath the Underdog* by the legendary jazz bassist and composer Charles Mingus (New York: Penguin, 1971).

129. Benezet, *Some Historical Account of Guinea* (1788), 18. Benezet cited Smith's *New Voyage to Guinea*, 112.

130. Benezet described the Africans in the southern region as belonging to "a country settled by Caffres and Hottentots, who have never been concerned in the making or selling of slaves." *Some Historical Account of Guinea* (1772), 6.

131. Barbot, "Description of the Coasts of North and South-Guinea," vol. 5, 12. Barbot was an employee of English and French trading companies, and he made at least two voyages to West Africa between 1678 and 1682.

132. Felix N. Okoye, *The American Image of Africa: Myth and Reality* (Buffalo: Black Academy Press, 1971), 5. Okoye cites as references the works of William Smith, William Snelgrave, Robert Norris, and Jean Barbot.

133. Adam Potkay and Sandra Burr offer a good geographical description of the region: "In the eighteenth century, the name 'Guinea' referred to the vast stretch of the West African coast from the river Senegal down to the kingdom of Angola." Ukawsaw "Gronniosaw calls the Gold Coast a 'city' in Guinea, perhaps to correct the common notion that 'Guinea' and the 'Gold Coast' denoted the same area. The Gold Coast, however, is a diverse area within Guinea, named for the rich deposits of gold that Portuguese traders found there in the fifteenth century. It encom-

passes the coastal strip between Benyori and the Volta River, as well as the groins immediately north of that area, in what is now modern Ghana." Adam Portay and Sandra Butt, eds., *Black Atlantic Writers of the Eighteenth Century: Living the New Exodus in England and America* (New York: St. Martin's Press, 1995), 53, n. 4.

134. Benezet, *Some Historical Account of Guinea* (1788), 6.

135. Benezet, *Some Historical Account of Guinea* (1772), 6; Thomas Kitchen, 1772 map, *A Chart of the Gold Coast, Wherein Are Distingish'd All the Forts and Factories Belonging to the Several European Powers*. On the map Kitchen writes that "Guinea takes its name from a Town call'd Guiney which the Portuguese touched at when they first visited this Coast In its largest extent, it Comprehends Slave Coast, Gold Coast, Ivory Coast & Grain Coast."

136. Atkins, *Voyage to Guinea*, 38.

137. Benezet, *Some Historical Account of Guinea* (1772), 5.

138. Ibid., 8. Smith's exact words were "provisions of all Kinds are very plenty, and exceedingly cheap here." Smith, *New Voyage to Guinea*, 31. Benezet in most cases quoted exactly. He lists the pages of Smith's voyage in his footnotes as "William Smith's voyage, page 31, 34." In fact the quote is from pages 33–34.

139. Benezet, *Some Historical Account of Guinea* (1772), 9.

140. Ibid., 8–9. Thomas Kitchen gives a good description in his 1772 *Map of Western Coast of Africa*.

141. Walter Rodney, "The Guinea Coast," in *The Cambridge History of Africa*, ed. Richard Gray (London: Cambridge University Press, 1975), vol. 4, 223. See also Walter Rodney, *The History of the Upper Guinea Gold Coast: 1546–1800* (New York: Monthly Review Press, 1970); J. D. Fage, *A History of West Africa* (London: Cambridge University Press, 1969).

142. J. D. Fage, *An Atlas of African History* (Bungay, Suffolk: Edward Arnold Publishers, 1958), 30–31.

143. Willem Bosman and T. Edward Bowdich, like Barbot, also used the term. Barbot, *Barbot on Guinea*, and T. Edward Bowdich, *Mission from Cape Coast to Ashantee* (London, 1819).

144. Law, *Slave Coast of West Africa*, 13, 14.

145. Benezet, *Some Historical Account of Guinea*, 17, 18.

146. The actual words of Snelgrave, as printed in the collection, are "they are usually averse to drinking *to* Excess, and when they see any one drunk, they inform against him, and he is severely punished by the King, attended by the Priests, according to the laws of the Country." Astley, *New General Collection*, 560.

147. William Snelgrave, *A New Account of Some Parts of Guinea, and the Slave Trade* (1734; repr., London: Frank Cass, 1971) (excerpted in Astley, *New General Collection*, vol. 2). Benezet also used Snelgrave when he published the anonymous *Two Dialogues on the Man-Trade* (London, 1760; map inserted between introduction p. xxii and p. 1).

148. Benezet, *Some Historical Account of Guinea* (1772), 22.

149. Ibid., 35.

150. Benezet, *Short Account of That Part of Africa*, 17. Law suggests that the people of this region have been credited with "the introduction of important cultural innovations, including the technique of the manufacture of salt by evaporation of seawater and the improved form of the canoe." Law, *Slave Coast of West Africa*, 25.

151. Quoted in Benezet, *Some Historical Account of Guinea*, 39.

152. Thomas Kitchen, 1772 "Map of Congo," Library of Congress, Geography and Maps Division.

153. Benezet, *Some Historical Account of Guinea*, 34.

154. John Thornton, *The Kingdom of Kongo: Civil War and Transition 1642–1728*

(Madison: University of Wisconsin Press, 1983), 6. See also Thornton, *Africa and the Making of the Atlantic World, 1400–1800,* 2nd ed. (New York: Cambridge University Press, 1998).

155. Benezet, *Some Historical Account of Guinea,* 37.

156. *The Oxford English Dictionary* defines *profit* in many ways. The most standard of definitions would define *profit* in the twelfth century as "to make progress, to advance to go forward" or in the sixteenth and seventeenth centuries as " to be of advantage, use or benefit to: to do good to benefit further, advance, promote." *Gain* is defined as "to be suitable, useful, or advantageous." *The Oxford English Dictionary,* 2nd ed. (Oxford; Clarendon Press, 1989), s.v. "Profit."

157. Quoted in Adam Hochschild, *Bury the Chains: Prophets and Rebels in the Fight to Free an Empire's Slaves* (Boston: Houghton Mifflin, 2005), 87.

158. Benezet, *Some Historical Account of Guinea* (1772), 1.

159. Endre Sìk, *The History of Black Africa,* 7th ed. (Budapest: Akadèmiai Kiadò, 1970), vol. 1, 125.

160. Michel Adanson, *A Voyage to Senegal, the Isle of Gorée, and the River Gambia* (Dublin: G. And A. Ewing, 1759).

161. Barker, *African Link,* 103.

162. Adanson, *Voyage to Senegal.*

163. Michel Adanson, *Voyage au Sénégal,* présenté par Denis Reynaud et Jean Schmidt (Paris: Publications de l'Université de Saint-Étienne, 1996), 17.

164. Adanson, *Voyage to Senegal,* 54.

165. Ibid., 162; T. Jeffery's 1768 *Map of Western Coast of Africa* describes "the Marcadores or Mandingos inhabiting Galam and the Serakoles, trade with those of Bambouk disposing of their Gold to the Europeans, these people not chusing to have any partners in this Trade would give no information of this Country, so that it was a difficult matter to get any for the Natives being extreamly Jealous of Strangers who they knew coveted their Ore."

166. Benezet, *Some Historical Account of Guinea* (1772), 13–14; Adanson, *Voyage to Senegal,* 253–54.

167. Law, "Slave Trader as Historian," 219–35.

168. Archibald Dalzel, *The History of Dahomy, and Inland Kingdom of Africa, compiled from Authentic Memoirs* (London, 1793; reprinted with a new introduction by J. D. Fage, 1967); Robert Norris, *Memoirs of the Reign of Bossa Ahades of Dahomy, an Inland Country of Guiney, to Which Are Added the Author's Journey to Abomey, the Capital, and a Short Account of the African Slave Trade* (1789; repr. London: University of London, 1968); Law, "Slave Trader as Historian," 219–35.

169. Atkins, *Voyage to Guinea,* 60.

170. Moore, *Travels into the Inland Parts of Africa,* 179, iii.

171. Benezet, *Some Historical Account of Guinea* (1772), 143–44.

172. Ibid., 13–14; Adanson, *Voyage to Senegal,* 253–54.

173. Benezet, *Some Historical Account of Guinea* (1772), 83.

174. Hornick, "Anthony Benezet and the African's School," ; Roger Bruns, "Anthony Benezet's Assertion of Negro Equality," *Journal of Negro History* 56 (1972): 230–38; Roger Bruns, "A Quaker's Antislavery Crusade : Anthony Benezet," *Quaker History* 652 (1976), 81–92.

175. T. Jeffery's 1768 *Map of Western Coast of Africa.*

176. Benezet, *Some Historical Account of Guinea* (1772), 11–12. At another point he wrote that "Jobson takes notice of several good qualities of the Negro priests, particularly their great sobriety" (11–12).

177. Ibid., 83.

178. Richard Jobson, *Golden Trade,* 9, 126–27.

179. Benezet, *Some Historical Account of Guinea* (1772), 27, 29.

180. Ibid., 27–28, 28–29.

181. Samuel Purchas, *Purchas His Pilgrim* (London, 1613, 1614, 1617, 1626—*Purchas his Pilgrimes* . . . 4 vols., London, 1625; reprinted 20 vols., Glasgow, 1905–1907, original pagination shown). It was printed in 1623 and chronicled his 1620–21 voyage up the Gambia River. In 1625 it was included in Purchas's *Purchas His Pilgrim.*

182. Samuel Purchas, *Hakluytus Posthumus, or Purchase His Pilgrimess* (Glasgow: repr., 1906), vol. 5, 303. It was also excerpted in Astley, *New General Collection*, vol. 2.

183. Jobson, *Golden Trade*, 140, 83, 136.

184. Astley, *New General Collection*, vol. 2, 268.

185. Benezet, *Short Account of That Part of Africa*, 24–25.

186. Francis Moore, *Travels into the Inland Parts of Africa*, title page; also excerpted in Astley, *New General Collection*, vol. 2. Benezet mistakenly wrote the title as *Travels into Distant Parts of Africa* and cited Francis Moor instead of Francis Moore.

187. Ibid., 30.

188. Ibid.

189. Ibid., 179, iii. Moore used similar words, which he did not attribute to Africanus but no doubt were taken in part from Africanus: "They lived in common having no property in lands nor goods, no tyrants, nor superior lords; but supported themselves in an equal state upon the natural produce of the country" (iii).

190. Benezet, *Some Historical Account of Guinea* (1772), 9.

191. Astley, *New General Collection*, vol. 2, 268.

192. Benezet, *Some Historical Account of Guinea* (1772), 83.

193. *Gentlemen's Magazine* 7 (1738), 473.

194. Michael A. Gomez, *Exchanging Our County Marks: The Transformation of African Identities in the Colonial and Antebellum South* (Chapel Hill: University of North Carolina Press, 1998); Gomez, "Ladinos, Gelofes and Mandingos" in *Black Crescent: The Experience and Legacy of African Muslims in the Americas* (Cambridge: Cambridge University Press, 2005); Sylviane A. Diouf, *Servants of Allah: African Muslims Enslaved in the Americas* (New York: New York University Press, 1998).

195. Captain William Snelgrave, *New Account of Some Parts of Guinea*, in Astley, *New General Collection*, 2:507.

196. Richard Dunn described travelers' accounts, which mention the elaborately staged and mournful funeral rites at African burials. West Africans believed that their ancestors would protect them from the other world; hence it was essential to honor the dead in the best way possible. Richard Dunn, *Sugar and Slaves: The Rise of the Planter Class in the English West Indies, 1624–1713* (New York: W. W. Norton, 1973), 250–51.

197. Godfrey Loyer, *A Jacobite, Abstract of a Voyage to Iffini on the Gold Coast in 1701 With a Description of the Country and Its Inhabitants*, in Astley, *New General Collection*, 1st ed.), 2:441–42.

198. In March 1688 Sir Hans Sloane also observed the African tradition: "The Negroes from some countries think they return to their own country when they die in Jamaica and therefore regard death but little, imagining they shall change their condition, by that means, from servile to free, and so for this reason often cut their own Throats. Whether they do thus, or naturally, their country people make great lamentations, mourning and howlings about them expiring. and at their Funeral throw Rum and Victuals into their Graves, to serve them in the other World. Sometimes they bury it in the ground, at other times spill it on the Graves." Sloane, *A Voyage to the Islands Madera, Barbados, Nieves, S. Christophers and Jamaica* (London: Printed by B. M. for the Author, 1707), xlviii.

199. Peter Kolb, *The Present State of the Cape of Good-Hope or a Particular Account of the Several Nations of the Hottentots,* introduction by W. Peter Carstens (1731; repr., New York: Johnson Reprint, 1968). The work was published in German in 1719 as *Caput Bonae Spei Hodiernum.* The first English edition appeared in 1731. It was also translated into Dutch where it was read in South Africa shortly before he died in 1726. In 1746 the work appeared in volume 3 of the Astley Collection printed in London. Carstens writes that "the origin of the term 'Hottentots' is uncertain but it has become a term of abuse in contemporary South Africa. The word *Khoikhoin* was used by all these people when referring to themselves collectively." I am grateful to Meredith McKittrick of Georgetown University and Timothy L. Scarnecchia of Kent State University for information on the Khoi peoples. Excerpts in Astley, *New General Collection,* vol. 3. For an informative discussion of Kolb and his account the Khoikhoi see, Anne Good, "The Construction of an Authoritative Text : Peter Kolb's Description of the Khoikhoi at the Cape of Good Hope in the Eighteenth Century," in Peter Mancall, ed., *Bringing the World to Europe: Travel Accounts and Their Audiences* (Leiden: Brill, 2007), 61–94, and M. Van Wyk Smith, " 'The Most Wretched of the Human Race': The Iconography of the Khoikhoin (Hottentots) 1500–1800," *History and Anthropology* 5 (1992), 285–330.

200. Benezet, *Some Historical Account of Guinea* (1772), 101. Benezet also calls attention to his use of the works of Kolb in a footnote and writes, "See Kolben's account of the Cape of Good Hope." At times he calls him Peter Holben.

201. Benezet, *Short Account of That Part of Africa,* 20.

202. Ibid., 21–22. For examples of enslaved Africans' resistance, including refusing to eat and jumping overboard, see Rediker, *The Slave Ship,* 284–302.

203. Benezet, *Some Historical Account of Guinea* (1772), 101–2.

204. Kolb, *Present State of the Cape of Good-Hope,* 47, 48.

205. Benezet, *Some Historical Account of Guinea* (1772), 102.

206. Kolb, *Present State of the Cape of Good-Hope,* 70–73.

207. Benezet, *Short Account of That Part of Africa,* 19–20. In a few cases he makes errors, as he copies by candlelight after teaching at the Quaker Schools, but he is by and large meticulous in his copying and editing.

208. He quoted "A Brue, speaking of the Fuli, whose country joints to the Falofs, says 'that being curious to see the Method by which they administer Justice, he was carried to a place where he could observe what passed incognito.' " Benezet, *Short Account of That Part of Africa,* 19–20.

209. Kolb, *Present State of the Cape of Good-Hope,* 297.

210. Benezet, *Short Account of That Part of Africa,* 25.

211. Michel de Montaigne, *Four Essays,* trans. M. A. Screech (New York: Penguin, 1995), 1. The full title of Girolamo Benzoni's work is *Historia del Mondo, A New History of the New World Containing All That Spaniards Have Done up to the Present in the West Indies, and of the Harsh Treatment Which They Have Meted to Those People Yonder . . . Together with a Short History of a Massacre Committed by the Spaniards on Some Frenchmen in Florida* (1759, 1st and 2nd eds.). These included Girolamo Benzoni's *Historia del mondo novo* in French.

212. Montaigne, "Of the Cannibals," in *Four Essays,* 7–8.

213. Anthony Pagden, *Lords of All the World* (New Haven: Yale University Press, 1995).

214. "Remarks Concerning the Savages of North America" (1784), in Smyth, *Writings of Benjamin Franklin,* 97.

215. Donald M. Frame, trans., *The Complete Essays of Montaigne* (Stanford, Calif.: Stanford University Press, 1965), 153.

216. Montaigne, "Of the Cannibals," in *Four Essays,* 9–10.

217. Frame, *Complete Essays of Montaigne*, 12.

218. Benezet, *Short Account of That Part of Africa*, 13. Benezet seemed to have used various excerpts from Bosman here. Bosman wrote that "the Negro Inhabitants are generally very rich, driving a great Trade with the Europeans." Bosman, *New and Accurate Description*, 5.

219. Frame, *Complete Essays of Montaigne*, 154.

220. Equiano, *Interesting Narrative of Olaudah Equiano* (Allison ed.), 7.

221. Moore, *Travels into the Inland Parts of Africa*, 30–31. On one occasion Benezet improperly attributed this statement to Captain Bartholomew Stubbs, who he said was "mentioned by Fr. Moor in his account." Benezet, *Some Historical Account of Guinea* (1772), 10–11.

222. Moore, *Travels into the Inland Parts of Africa*, 30–31.

223. Cited in James Pope-Hennessy, *Sins of the Fathers: A Study of the Atlantic Slave Traders, 1407–1807* (New York: Alfred A. Knopf, 1968), 230.

224. Sloane, *Voyage to the Islands* (also known as *The Natural History of Jamaica*).Benezet makes use of it when he publishes an extract from the anonymous *Two Dialogues on the Man-Trade* (London, 1760), which quotes from Sloane. Sloane left his native Ireland to study medicine in England. Taking a special interest in botany and pharmacy coupled with his penchant for collecting plants, artifacts, and assorted specimens, he finished his medical studies in 1683. He was elected to the Royal Society in 1685 and became its secretary in 1693. He was elected to full membership in the Royal College of Physicians in 1687. From 1687 to 1688 Sloane served as the personal physician to the governor of Jamaica, the second duke of Albemarle. Sloane returned to England in 1689 when the duke died; he then served the duke's widow as her personal physician for the next five years. He became a promoter of public health initiatives, such as inoculation against smallpox, at the time an unpopular practice in Britain. He went on to serve as personal physician to Queen Anne, King George I, and King George II, and served as the president of the Royal College of Physicians from 1719 to 1735. After Sir Isaac Newton died in 1727, he was elected president of the Royal Society, a post he held until 1741 when he retired. He lived to the ripe age of ninety-three, collecting and writing until his death.

225. By the time Sloane reached Jamaica, England had since 1660 "acquired the basis of what later became the British Empire" through the use of slave labor in St. Kitts, Barbados, Jamaica, Maryland, and Virginia. At the time "the Royal Society was part of the social and economic order which chose slavery as the most viable means for generating wealth via commodity production, and thus was in varying degrees interconnected with slavery." Mark Govier, "The Royal Society, Slavery and the Island of Jamaica: 1600–1700," *Notes and Records of the Royal Society of London* 53, no. 2 (May 1999): 203–4; Robert Worthington Smith, "The Legal Status of Jamaican Slaves Before the Anti-slavery Movement," *Journal of Negro History* 30, no. 3 (July 1945): 293–303; Frank Wesley Pitman, "The Organization of Slave Labor," *Journal of Negro History* 11, no. 4 (October 1926): 595–609; Pitman, "The Treatment of the British West Indian Slaves in Law and Custom, *Journal of Negro History* 11, no. 4 (October 1926): 610–28; Pitman, "The Breeding and Mortality of Eighteenth Century Slaves in the British West Indies," *Journal of Negro History* 11, no. 4 (October 1926): 629–49.

226. Although Benezet refers to Sloane's *Natural History of Jamaica*, it is not to be confused with Edward Long's *History of Jamaica or , General survey of the antient and modern state of that island with reflections on its situation, settlements, inhabitants, climate, products, commerce, laws, and government; in three volumes, illustrated with copper plates* (London: T. Lowndes, 1774); reprinted as *The History of Jamaica: reflections on its situ-*

ation, settlements, inhabitants, climate, products, commerce, laws, and government (Montreal: McGill-Queen's University Press, 2002). Sloane wrote the book primarily to document the flora, fauna, natural history, and beauty of Jamaica. As a practicing physician he also paid close attention to the medical and healing practices of the blacks and their folkways, music, customs, religious beliefs, and social relations. Two years before, Sloane wrote *A Letter from a Merchant at Jamaica to A Member of Parliament in London, Touching the African Trade; To Which Is Added, a Speech Made by a Black of Guadeloupe at the Funeral of a Fellow-Negro* (London, 1710). Jack Greene has analyzed many early antislavery tracts and calls this one "a scathing indictment of Jamaican slave society that anticipates most of the objections antislavery writers would make later in the century." *A Letter* "challenges the legality of purchasing the enslaved, and questions the humanity, civility, and English-ness of free Jamaican settlers." Jack Greene, "A Plain and Natural Right to Life and Liberty: An Early Natural Rights Attack on the Excesses of the Slave System in Colonial British America," *William and Mary Quarterly*, 3rd series, 57, no. 4 (October 2000), 793–94. Richard D. Sheridan, *Doctors and Slaves: A Medical and Demographic History of Slavery in the British West Indies, 1680–1834* (Cambridge: Cambridge University Press, 1985); Eric St. John Brooks, *Sir Hans Sloane: The Great Collector and His Circle* (London: Batchworth, 1954); G. R. de Beer, *Hans Sloane and the British Museum* (London: Oxford University Press, 1953); Wendy D. Churchill, "Bodily Differences? Gender, Race and Class in Hans Sloane's Jamaican Medical Practice, 1687–1688," *Journal of the History of Medicine and Allied Sciences* 60, no. 4 (2005): 391–444; Dunn, *Sugar and Slaves.*

227. As one of Sloane's biographers, Eric St. John Brooks, observed long ago, "It may be remarked that, in common with the men of his time, Sloane felt no more horror of slavery than he had squeamishness about experiments on living animals." St. John Brooks added that Sloane "mentions, without any sign of disgust, the revolting punishment which Jamaican planters meted out to obdurate slaves. He regarded such treatment as necessary in the case of so stubborn a race." St. John Brooks, *Sir Hans Sloane*, 70. We might add that these lines, save one, were the sum of St. John Brooks's observations about Sloane's own observations about blacks. Here St. John Brooks quoted Sloane's observation of places where "serpents and other venomous creatures . . . fly from men" and find places where "they are thought to make fierce and dangerous attacks when surprised." Sloane concluded that "the same places remote, remote from settlement, are very often full of runaway negros, who lye in ambush to kill the whites who come within their reach" (70).

228. Benezet, *Short Account of That Part of Africa*, 53–54. Sloane's exact words were, "The Punishment for crimes of Slaves are usually for Rebellions, burning them, by nailing them down on the ground with crooked Sticks on every Limb, and them applying the Fire by Degrees from the Feet and Hands, burning them gradually up to the Head, whereby their pains are extravagant. For Crimes of a lesser nature, Gelding or chopping off half of the Foot with an Ax. These punishments are suffered by them with great constancy. For running away they put Iron Rings of great weight on the Ankles, or Pottocks abut their Necks, which are Iron Rings with two long Necks riveted to them, or a Spur in the mouth. For Negligence, they are usually whipt by the Overseers with Lance-Wood Switches, till they be bloody, and several of the Switches broken, being first tied up by their Hands in the Mill Houses. Beating with Manati Straps is thought too Cruel, and therefore prohibited by the Customs of the Country. The Cica-trices are visible on their Skins, for ever after and a slave the more he have of those, is the less valu'd. After they are whip'd till they are Raw, some put on their Skins, Pepper, and Salt to make them Smart. At other

times their Masters, will drop melted Wax on their Skins, and use several very exqui-site Torments. These punishments are sometimes merited by the Blacks who are a very perverse Generation of People, and though they appear harsh, yet are scarce equal to some of their Crimes, and inferior to what Punishments other European nations inflict on their Slaves in the East-Indies as may be seen by Moquet, and other Travellers." Sloane, *Voyage to the Islands*, lvi.

229. Benezet, *Short Account of That Part of Africa*, 58. Sloane's work ended, how-ever, in 1725, ten years before the Antiguan uprising, so either Philmore had another source or he used Sloane's words about a past revolt. Benezet seemed to copy Philmore's chronological error. The kings and generals described by Phil-more were the titles given to the plot leaders who gave orders to kill whites, just as they would in New York four years later where whites were to be the kings and the blacks were the generals. The Antiguan blacks, living closely together on a small island, had retained their "Africanisms" longer than many of the slaves in the colo-nies and had used their links with their African past to plot their freedom. Benezet read of these conspirators, who were Coromantees or Akans from the west coast of Africa. West Indian authorities, writing of Tackey, said he was "of considerable Fam-ily in his own country, but not as was commonly thought of Royal Blood; and yet it was fully proved that he had for many Years covertly assumed among his Country-men, the Title of King, and had been by them addressed and treated as such." *Gen-uine Narrative of the Intended Conspiracy of the Negroes at Antigua* (London, 1737), quoted in Craton, *Testing the Chains*, 120. Benezet miscopied the words Philmore quoted from what he termed "an account of those plots laid by the blacks in Anti-gua." Philmore quoted from the author: "The king 'that is, who was to have been king of the blacks, had the plot succeeded,' and his two generals, with two others were all broke on the wheel. Four more of the principal conspirators were burnt the same day; as were seven on the next day. Six were hung alive in chains on gib-lets, and starved to death: after which their heads were cut off, and their bodies burnt; and fifty eight others were at several times, chained to stakes and burnt alive." Philmore, *Two Dialogues*, 52–53.

230. Benezet, *Short Account of That Part of Africa*, 57.

231. Michael Craton, "Jamaican Slavery," in *Race and Slavery in the Western Hemi-sphere: Quantitative Studies*, ed. Stanley L. Engerman and Eugene D. Genovese (Princeton, N.J.: Princeton University Press, 1975), 254; David Barry Gaspar, *Bond-men and Rebels: A Story of Master Slave Relations in Antigua, with Implications for Colo-nial British America* (Baltimore: Johns Hopkins University Press, 1985), 5.

232. Benezet, *A Caution and a Warning*, 6. William Burke, *An Account of the Euro-pean Settlements in America. In Six Parts* (London, 1757).

233. Benezet, *A Caution and a Warning*, 5.

234. Ibid., 6–7. For a fascinating account of the slavemaster brutality in the Atlantic world, especially Jamaica, and the enslaved blacks' use of death and its sur-rounding rituals as tools for resistance, see Vincent Brown, *The Reaper's Garden: Death and Power in the World of Atlantic Slavery* (Cambridge, Mass.: Harvard University Press, 2008).

235. Tise, *Proslavery*, 16.

236. Thomas Thompson, *The African Trade for Negro Slaves, Shewn to Be Consistent with the Principles of Humanity, and with the Laws of Revealed Religion* (Canterbury: Simons and Kirby, 1772). Benezet's copy of the Thompson pamphlet is housed at the Rutgers University Library, New Brunswick, New Jersey. Another copy is at the Haverford College Library, Quaker Collection. Major excerpts containing the mar-ginal notes of Benezet are in Tise, *Proslavery*, 26–27, and in Bruns, *Am I Not a Man and a Brother*, 217–20.

237. Thompson, *Into All Lands*, 38, 40, 69–73.

238. Quoted in Tise, *Proslavery*, 25.

239. Anthony Benezet to Granville Sharp, March 29, 1773, *Granville Sharp Letter Book* (Philadelphia: Library Company of Philadelphia). To bolster his religious appeal Thompson wrote that "the Jewish constitution" did not view selling slaves as a violation of natural law. Benezet underlined this point and wrote in the margins, "This is a false foundation! For the Jewish Constitutions were *not* strictly consistent" on slavery as not being a violation of natural law. Benezet wrote this on page 15 of his copy of Thompson's book, housed at Rutgers University; see also Bruns, *Am I Not a Man and a Brother*, 219.

240. Emmanuel Chukwudi Eze, *Race and the Enlightenment: A Reader* (Cambridge: Blackwell, 1977), 34. According to John Immerwahr, Beattie was "primarily known because he was a source for some of Kant's knowledge of Hume" and "had a clear understanding of Hume's racism." John Immerwahr, "Hume's Revised Racism," *Journal of the History of Ideas* 53, no. 3 (July–September 1992): 483; see Sir William Forbes, *Life, and Writings of James Beattie, LL.D* (London: Roper, 1824).

241. James Beattie, *An Essay on the Nature and Immutability of Truth: In Opposition to Sophistry and Skepticism*, ed. Lewis White Beck (1770; repr., New York: Garland, 1983), 477–84. Beattie was a professor of moral philosophy and logic at the University of Aberdeen.

242. Ibid., 480. Emmanuel Chukwudi Eke makes special note that "Beattie's specific objections to Hume are directed against Hume's suggestion that 'all other species of men . . . [are] naturally inferior to the whites.'" Eke, *Race and the Enlightenment*, 34.

243. Three years after Beattie's pamphlet *Personal Slavery Established* came out, an examination of previous arguments concerning the innate inequality of humans was published. Using Hume's idea, the "anonymous author" wrote that "there never was a civilized nation of any other complexion than white; nor ever any individual eminent either in action of speculation that was not rather inclining to the fair. Africa, except a small part of it, inhabited by those of our own colour, is totally overrun with Barbarism." He told his readers that unlike Africans "the Europeans are blessed with reason, and therefore capable of improvement," and placed whites in one category and nonwhites in another. *Personal Slavery Established, by the Suffrages of Custom and Right Reason. Being a Full Answer to the Gloomy and Visionary Reveries, of All the Fanatical and Enthusiastically Writers on the Subject* (Philadelphia, 1773), 18–19. In a provocative essay Lester B. Scherer argues that *Personal Slavery Established* on "comparative examination, however, shows that it was actually an antislavery satire on Nisbet's *Slavery Not Forbidden*." Scherer, "A New Look at *Personal Slavery Established*," *William and Mary Quarterly*, 3rd series, 30, no. 4 (October 1973), 646; Jordan argues that the pamphlet "plagiarized David Hume in order to combat the environmentalist contentions of Benjamin Rush." Jordan, *White over Black*, 305–6.

244. Benezet, *Some Historical Account of Guinea*, introductory page. The revised editions of Benezet's *Some Historical Account of Guinea*, which appeared regularly until his death in 1784, and *Notes on Slavery* and *Short Observations on Slavery*, were other direct replies to men like Nisbet and Thompson.

245. Robin Blackburn, *Overthrow of Colonial Slavery*, 155. He added, "In different ways abolitionism, democratic politics and Enlightenment philosophy all contained within them a potential to develop a secular doctrine of universal human rights" (155). Beattie may have developed his antislavery ideas because of his association with the antislavery scientist Joseph Priestley (whom we have discussed elsewhere); Joseph Priestley, *Autobiography of Joseph Priestley* (Guildford: Billing & Sons, 1970), 113; Robert E. Schofield, *The Enlightened Joseph Priestley: Study of His Life and Work from 1773 to 1804* (University Park: Pennsylvania State University Press, 2004), 44.

246. Hume made the changes in the 1776 revised edition. David Hume, *Essays, Moral, Political and Literary* (1776; repr., London: Oxford University Press, 1966), 213. Hume then wrote, "I am apt to suspect the negroes to be naturally inferior to the whites. There scarcely ever was a civilized nation of that complexion, nor even of individual eminent in action or speculation." Beattie, *Essay on the Nature and Immutability of Truth.* Beattie also wrote *Dissertation Moral and Critical* (London: Strahan, 1783). Eze, *Race and the Enlightenment,* 37. For a discussion of the debates between Hume and Beattie, see James Somerville, *The Enigmatic Parting Shot: What Was Hume's "Compleat Answer to Dr. Reid and to That Bigoted Silly Fellow, Beattie"?* (Aldershot, U.K.: Avebury, 1995). In this sense Hume differed little from Sharp or Woolman, who also wrote unflattering things about blacks. Beattie succeeded in partially changing Hume's position about other races of mankind, but Hume's racism toward the blacks remained as firm as ever. While never quite upholding the full humanity of the African, Beattie affirmed that people of European stock were at times "savages." He believed that there was a natural progression of all human races and peoples. To bolster his argument he added, "The Africans and Americans are known to have many ingenious manufacturers and arts among them, which even Europeans, would find it no easy matter to imitate." Beattie added that "the condition of a slave is not favorable to genius of any kind," but neither was the condition of an oppressed white. *An Essay on the Nature and Immutability of Truth,* 481–82. Beattie wrote, "A man defective in common sense may acquire learning, may even possess genius to a certain degree, but the defect of nature he never can supply." Quoted in John Ruskin Clark, *Joseph Priestley: A Comet in the System* (San Diego: Torch, 1990), 96; Immerwahr, "Hume's Revised Racism," 481–86.

247. Prince Hoare, *Memoirs of Granville Sharp, Esq. Composed from His Own Manuscripts and Other Authentic Documents in the Possession of His Family and of the African Institution with an Observation on Mr. Sharp's Biblical Character by the Right Rev. the Lord Bishop of Salisbury* (London: Henry Colborn, 1820), 158.

248. John Wesley to Anthony Benezet, quoted in Vaux, *Memoirs of the Life of Anthony Benezet,* 53.

249. See Bosman, *New and Accurate Description.*

250. Eric Foner, *The Story of American Freedom* (New York: W. W. Norton, 1998), 33.

251. Keith A. Sandiford, *Measuring the Moment: Strategies of Protest in Eighteenth-Century Afro-English Writing* (London: Associated University Press, 1988), 51.

252. Benezet, *Some Historical Account of Guinea* (1772), 63–65.

253. Benezet, *Short Account of That Part of Africa,* 25.

254. Bodin, *Six Bookes of a Commonweale.*

255. Benezet, *Short Observations on Slavery,* 33.

256. Benezet, *Some Historical Account of Guinea* (1772), 2.

257. Ibid., 16; Adanson, *Voyage to Senegal,* 54.

258. Benezet, *Short Account of That Part of Africa,* 25.

259. Benezet, *Some Historical Account of Guinea* (1772), 64–65.

Chapter 5. Building an Antislavery Consensus in North America

Note to epigraph: Benjamin Rush to Granville Sharp, May 13, 1774, quoted in John A. Woods, ed., "The Correspondence of Benjamin Rush and Granville Sharp, 1773–1809," *Journal of American Studies* 1, no. 1 (1967): 3.

1. Anthony Benezet to Samuel Fothergill, October 17, 1757, Haverford College Quaker Collection. Benezet included with the letter "a new Edition of John Everard's writings." The book, *Some Gospel Treasures,* is in Benezet's library at Haverford.

A copy (with Benezet's markings) is in the British Museum. "The Fothergills," in *Quaker Biographies: A Series of Sketches, Chiefly Biographical, Concerning Members of he Society of Friends, From the Seventeenth Century to More Recent Times,* vol. 4 (1914), 29–66.

2. See Maurice Jackson, "The Rise of Abolition," in *The Atlantic World, 1450–2000,* ed. Toyin Falola and Kevin Roberts (Bloomington: Indiana University Press, 2008), 211–48; and Chapter 6 below.

3. The August 3, 1713, *Boston New-Letter* advertised "Three Negro Men and two women to be sold and seen at the House of Mr. Josiah Franklin at the Sign of the blue Ball in Union Street Boston." J. A. Leo Lemay, *The Life of Benjamin Franklin,* vol. 1, *Journalist* (Philadelphia: University of Pennsylvania Press, 2006), 22. Franklin's father also had indentured servants, and in the *Boston Gazette* of December 22, 1719, he advertised his own "servant." On July 9, 1722, he placed an ad in the *New-England Courant*: "Ran away from his Master Mr. Josiah Franklin of Boston . . . an Irish Servant, named William Tinsley, about 20 years of Age." For apprehending and returning Mr. Tinsley there awaited "Forty Shillings Reward, and all necessary Charges paid" (vol. 1, 23).

4. Walter Isaacson, *Benjamin Franklin, An American Life* (New York: Simon & Schuster, 2003), 66.

5. *Pennsylvania Gazette,* November 11–18, 1731, and May 4–11, 1732, in William E. Juhnke, "Benjamin Franklin's View of the Negro and Slavery," *Pennsylvania History* 41, no. 44 (October 1974), 377; Carl Van Doren, *Benjamin Franklin* (New York: Penguin, 1991), 128–29. Over a decade later Franklin still owned blacks. On March 10, 1743, he ran another ad in the *Pennsylvania Gazette*: "A Negro Man twenty-two Year of Age, of uncommon Strength and Activity . . . and is very faithful in Employment; Any Person that wants such a one, may see him by inquiring of the Printer hereof" (*Pennsylvania Gazette,* March 10, 1743). According to David Waldstreicher, "Between one-fifth and one-quarter of the paper's advertisements directly concerned unfree labor. The profit generated was considerable, not to mention essential to the life of Franklin's entire printing business, for ad revenue was far more dependable than subscriptions, which so often remained uncollected." Waldstreicher, *Runaway America,* 24.

6. Smith and Wojtowicz, *Blacks Who Stole Themselves*; Jonathan Prude, "To Look upon the 'Lower Sort': Runaway Ads and the Appearance of Unfree Laborers in America," *Journal of American History* 78, no. 1 (June 1991): 124–57. Waldstreicher suggests that Franklin "participated directly as well as indirectly in the local slave and servant trade, selling goods and persons alike and acting as a true middleman—not just as a provider of information in their exchange." *Runaway America,* 24.

7. Peter Kalm, *Travels in North America* (1770; repr., New York: Dover, 1974), 206.

8. Quoted in Jack D. Marietta, The Reformation of American Quakerism, 1748–1783 (Philadelphia: University of Pennsylvania Press, 1984), 100; Gary B. Nash, The Unknown American Revolution: The Unruly Birth of Democracy and the Struggle to Create America (New York: Viking, 2005), 42; Nash, Forging Freedom, 31; Nash and Soderlund, Freedom by Degrees, 52.

9. H. W. Brands, *The First American* (New York: Harper and Row, 2000), 700.

10. Among these were the economic theories of Adam Smith, Lord Kames, Richard Price, David Hume, Anne-Robert-Jacques Turgot, and Thomas Malthus's *Essay on Population.*

11. Benjamin Franklin, "Observations Concerning the Increase of Mankind," in *The Writings of Benjamin Franklin,* ed. Albert Henry Smyth (1905; repr., New York: Haskell House, 1970), vol. 3, 65.

12. Franklin, "Observations Concerning the Increase of Mankind," in Smyth, *Writings of Benjamin Franklin*, vol. 3, 66; Franklin, "Observations Concerning the Increase of Mankind," in Lawrence W. Labaree et al., eds., *The Papers of Benjamin Franklin* (New Haven, Conn.: Yale University Press, 1958–84), vol. 4, 229–34.

13. Franklin, "Observations Concerning the Increase of Mankind," in Smyth, *Writings of Benjamin Franklin*, vol. 3, 66, 67 . Franklin revealed something that would later be discussed by Adam Smith, Benezet, and Thomas Clarkson. Franklin raised in 1755 the same economic arguments against slavery that Smith would make in *An Inquiry into the Nature and Causes of the Wealth of Nations* (1776). Franklin, like Adam Smith and Thomas Clarkson a generation later, thus focused on the negative effects of slavery on whites.

14. Franklin, "Observations Concerning the Increase in Mankind Written in Pennsylvania 1751," in *The Interest of Great Britain Considered with Regards to the Colonies and the Acquisition of Canada & Guadalupe* (London: T. Becket, 1760), 50–56; and 2nd ed. (London and Boston, 1761), 52–57. Franklin, "Observations Concerning the Increase of Mankind," in Labaree, *Papers of Benjamin Franklin*, vol. 4, 229–34.

15. Juhnke, "Benjamin Franklin's View of the Negro and Slavery," 377. Juhnke incorrectly listed this change as taking place in the 1769 edition, eighteen years after the original printing, but the change seems to have been made years before, sometime between 1755 and 1760. Studying multiple copies in the Library of Congress Rare Book room clearly shows that the changes were made between the 1755 and 1760 printings. They appear first in the 1760 London edition. For example, *Observations* was attached to William Clarke, *Observations on the late and present conduct of the French, with regard to her encroachments upon the British colonies in North America* (Boston: 1755) to which is appended *Observations Concerning the Increase in Mankind.* The changes are not reflected in this edition. Nor are the changes reflected in Hazards Collection, "Observations on the Late and Present Conducts of the French with regard, 1755 which means that they were made between this and the 1760 London and Boston editions. In an attached edition to the Hazard Collection, Isaac Grey "A Serious address to such people called Quakers, on the continent of North America, as profess scruples relative to the present government: exhibiting the ancient real testimony of that people, concerning obedience to civil authority" (Philadelphia, 1788), the changes are not reflected. See also Francis Brokesby, *Some Proposals towards propagating of the gospel in our Amercing Plantations*, 2nd ed. (London: Strawbridge, 1708); *Observations* (Boston: S. Kneeland, 1755); Benjamin Franklin, *The Interest of Great Britain Considered: with regard to her colonies, and the acquisitions of Canada and Guadeloupe; to which are added, Observations concerning the increase of mankind, peopling and countries* (London: William Bradford, 1760; 2nd ed. London: T. Becket, 1761). Editions also are included in Hazards edition, Isaac Grey, *A serious address to such of the peoples called Quakers, on the continent of North American, as profess scruples relative to the present government exhibiting the ancient and real testimony of that people, concerning obedience to civil authority* (Philadelphia: R. Bell, 1778) in *A Collection of memorials concerning divers deceased ministers and pothers of the people called Quakers in Pennsylvania, New Jersey, and parts adjacent* (Philadelphia: J. Crukshank, 1787). None of these reflected the changes. The changes to point 12 and the deletion of point 24 are reflected in Benjamin Franklin, "Observations Concerning the Increase of Mankind," in Smyth, *Writings of Benjamin Franklin*, vol. 3, 67, 72–73.

16. Franklin, "Observations Concerning the Increase of Mankind," in Smyth, *Writings of Benjamin Franklin*, vol. 3, 68. Economic concern for whites, not humanitarian concern for blacks, initially inspired Franklin's changes in his *Observations*.

As Lemay noted in his biography of Franklin, "In 1751 . . . Franklin attacked slavery for economic reasons, but it was not until he was convinced by the moral arguments against slavery, especially in the writings of his friend Anthony Benezet, a Philadelphia Quaker, that he became an abolitionist." Lemay, *Life of Benjamin Franklin,* vol. 1, *Journalist,* 23. Franklin argued before the Pennsylvania Assembly in 1756 against the policy of recruiting white indentured servants into the king's army. He believed that taking whites away from work would cause the colonists to rely more on slave labor. He insisted that "the People will be driven to the Necessity of providing themselves with Negro Slaves," and this would prove dangerous as "the Growth of the Country by Increase of white Inhabitants will be prevented," making the "Province weakened rather than strengthened (as every Slave may be reckoned a domestic enemy)." Franklin, speech before the Pennsylvania Assembly, February 11, 1756, in Labaree, *Papers of Benjamin Franklin,* vol. 6, 398.

17. In the 1760 English edition Franklin deleted point 24, just as he modified point 12, but the original wording on point 12 and the whole of point 24 can be found in all American printings, including the version published in Smyth's 1905 edition of the *Writings of Benjamin Franklin.* At that point Franklin argued that whites should act "where we have so fair an Opportunity, by excluding all blacks and Tawneys, of increasing the lovely white and Red." Franklin, "Observations Concerning the Increase of Mankind," in Smyth, *Writings of Benjamin Franklin,* vol. 3, 72–73; Labaree, *Papers of Benjamin Franklin,* vol. 3, 474. The changes to point 12 and the deletion of point 24 are reflected in Benjamin Franklin, "Observations Concerning the Increase in Mankind Written in Pennsylvania 1751," in *The Interest of Great Britain Considered with Regards to the Colonies and the Acquisition of Canada & Guadalupe* (2nd Boston ed.), 52–57. The original point 12 and the entire point 24 is left in "Observations," in Smyth, *Writings of Benjamin Franklin,* vol. 3, 63–73.

18. John Waring to Benjamin Franklin, January 25, 1757, in Labaree, *Papers of Benjamin Franklin,* vol. 7, 101.

19. Benjamin Franklin to John Waring, January 3, 1758, in Labaree, *Papers of Benjamin Franklin,* vol. 7, 356.

20. Benjamin Franklin to John Waring, December 12, 1763, in Labaree, *Papers of Benjamin Franklin,* vol. 10, 395–96. The Bray Associates was a society founded by Thomas Bray, an English philanthropist. Bray had met M. D'Allone, a Dutchman living in The Hague, who shared with Bray an interest in converting Africans to Christianity. D'Allone gave Bray a good deal of money to convert blacks in the West Indian plantations, and on his death he left Bray £900 to continue the work. When Bray died in 1730, Bray Associates was formed to instruct black children to read and to teach them about Christianity, with the goal of converting them at a young age. During these years Franklin read the early pamphlets of Anthony Benezet. Early copies of Benezet's works were donated to the Library Company of Philadelphia, the nation's first public library, founded by Franklin.

21. Benjamin Franklin to Deborah Franklin, London, June 27, 1760, in Smyth, *Writings of Benjamin Franklin,* vol. 4, 23.

22. Franklin had also read Benezet. Early copies of Benezet's works were donated to the Library Company of Philadelphia.

23. Jack Fruchtman, Jr., *Atlantic Cousins: Benjamin Franklin and His Visionary Friends* (New York: Thunder's Mouth Press, 2005), 36–39.

24. Benjamin Franklin to Abiah Franklin, April 12, 1750, in Labaree, *Papers of Benjamin Franklin,* vol. 3, 474; see Juhnke, "Franklin's View of the Negro and Slavery," 377.

25. Labaree, Papers of Benjamin Franklin, vol. 4, 231.

26. Juhnke, "Franklin's View of the Negro and Slavery," 378–89; Mathew T. Mellon, *Early American Views on Negro Slavery* (New York: Mentor Books, 1969).

27. Nash, *Unknown American Revolution*, 123.

28. Namely, Benezet's *Observations on the Inslaving, Importing and Purchasing of Negroes* (1758); *A Short Account of That Part of Africa Inhabited by the Negroes* (1762). Early copies of Benezet's works were donated to the Library Company of Philadelphia. Franklin wrote, "I find in Capt. Seagraves's Account of his Voyage to Guinea" that "a Dutch Ship came into the Road and some of the blacks going on Board her were treacherously seized and carried off as Slaves." Benjamin Franklin, *A Narrative of the Late Massacres in Lancaster County, I* (Philadelphia, 1764), 306. It seems Franklin simply misspelled the captain's name and was referring to Captain William Snelgrave, who in 1734 published *A New Account of Some Parts of Guinea, and the Slave Trade*. Benezet had made use of Snelgrave's *New Account* many times, and Franklin, it seems, discovered him by way of Benezet.

29. Brookes, *Friend Anthony Benezet*, 27, 28–29. The title of the paper was "Der Hoch Deutsch Pennsylvanische Geschicht Schreiber, oder Sammlung Wichjtiger Nachrichten aud der Natur und Kirchen-Reich" [The High German Pennsylvania Recorder of Events, or Collection of Important News from the Realm of Nature and the Church] (27, n. 21). Benezet, working as a proofreader for the German newspaper, apparently was familiar with this form of German, which is not of modern usage.

30. Benjamin Franklin to Anthony Benezet, August 22, 1772, in Smyth, *Writings of Benjamin Franklin*, vol. 5, 431–32; Brookes, *Friend Anthony Benezet*, 422.

31. Benjamin Franklin, "The Somerset Case and the Slave Trade," in Verner W. Crane, ed., *Letters to the Press, 1758–1775* (Chapel Hill: University of North Carolina Press, 1950), 222. Benezet had written, "By a late compilation there is now eight hundred & fifty thousand negroes in the English Islands & Colonies; and an hundred thousand more yearly imported by our Nation; about a third of this number is said to perish in the passage & seasoning, before they are set to labour." Anthony Benezet to Benjamin Franklin, April 27, 1772, Haverford College Quaker Collection. Some of the letters printed in Brookes omit several important lines or paragraphs, therefore distorting their original meaning.

32. Franklin, "The Somerset Case and the Slave Trade," in Verner W. Crane, *Letters to the Press, 1758–1775* (Chapel Hill: University of North Carolina Press, 1950), 222. Franklin speaks of the British love of tea, and later rum, which was dependent on slave labor in the West Indian and American sugar cane plantations.

33. Ibid., 199.

34. Benjamin Franklin to Anthony Benezet, August 22, 1772, in Smyth, *Writings of Benjamin Franklin*, vol. 5, 432.

35. Anthony Benezet to Benjamin Franklin, April 27, 1772, Haverford College Quaker Collection.

36. Benjamin Franklin to Anthony Benezet, February 10, 1773, in Smyth, *Writings of Benjamin Franklin*, vol. 6, 9.

37. Anthony Benezet to Granville Sharp, April 4, 1773, Haverford College Quaker Collection.

38. Benjamin Franklin to Dean Woodward, April 10, 1773, in Smyth, *Writings of Benjamin Franklin*, vol. 5, 10. Woodward (1726–84) was dean of Clogher from 1726 to 1781, chancellor of St. Patrick's in 1772, and bishop of Cloyne from 1781 to 1794.

39. Benjamin Franklin to Anthony Benezet, July 14, 1773, in Smyth, *Writings of Benjamin Franklin*, vol. 6, 102.

40. Benjamin Franklin to marquis de Condorcet, March 20, 1774, in Smyth, *Writings of Benjamin Franklin*, vol. 6, 221.

41. Brands, *First American*, 701.

42. Anthony Benezet, *Short Observations on Slavery*, 11–12.

43. Anthony Benezet to Benjamin Franklin, March 5, 1783, Haverford College Quaker Collection.

44. Waldstreicher writes that Franklin "declined to bring the matter of slavery to the Constitutional Convention of 1787 when asked to do so by the abolition society that he served as president. There are enough smoking guns, to be sure, to condemn Franklin as a hypocrite, Jefferson-style, if one wishes to do so." *Runaway America*, xiii. However, it is clear that Franklin's actions against slavery extended beyond the Constitutional Convention.

45. Jared Sparks, ed., *The Works of Benjamin Franklin*, containing several political and historical tracts not included in any former ed. (Boston: Hilliard, Gray, and Company, 1836–40), vol. 10, 320–21; Juhnke, "Franklin's View of the Negro and Slavery," 386.

46. Sparks, *Works of Benjamin Franklin*, vol. 10, 513–14.

47. Of the eighty-four years of Franklin's life he spent twenty-seven in European capitals and was in America for about ten of his last forty years.

48. Arthur Stuart Pitt, "Franklin and the Quaker Movement Against Slavery," *Friends Historical Association Bulletin* 32 (1943): 13–31.

49. Sparks, *Works of Benjamin Franklin*, vol. 10, 403.

50. Benjamin Franklin, "Memorial to Congress, February 3, 1790," in Sparks, *Works of Benjamin Franklin*, vol. 10, 403.

51. Ibid.

52. Anthony Benezet to Benjamin Franklin, July 12, 1781, Haverford College Quaker Collection.

53. Benjamin Rush to Granville Sharp, May 13, 1774, in Woods, "Correspondence of Benjamin Rush and Granville Sharp," 3.

54. His many scientific articles and books included the five-volume Medical Inquires and Observations (1794–98) and Medical Inquires and Observations upon Diseases of the Mind (1812).

55. Lamin Sanneh, *Abolitionist Abroad: American Blacks and the Making of Modern West Africa* (Cambridge, Mass.: Harvard University Press, 1999), 96.

56. David Brion Davis writes that "in Paris, thanks to Franklin's introductions, he became acquainted with the Physiocrats, the elder Mirabeau and Diderot, the latter entrusting him with correspondence to deliver to Hume." Davis, *Problem of Slavery in Western Culture*, 486.

57. Joseph Priestley, *Autobiography of Joseph Priestley* (London: Billing Sons, 1970), 89. Franklin had sent to Rush "Observations on Different Kinds of Air" by Joseph Priestley, a paper read at the Royal Society and published in its *Philosophical Transactions*, the journal of the Royal Society. Joseph Priestley, the Unitarian clergyman, multilinguist, and scientist is credited with helping lay the foundations of chemistry as a science. Priestley was also a friend of John Fothergill, who may have first introduced him to the discussions about slavery. Like the Presbyterian Rush, the agnostic Franklin, and the Quaker Benezet, the Unitarian Priestley took a rational and studied approach to develop his antislavery thinking, yet he at times turned to spiritual verse.

58. John Ruskin Clark, *Joseph Priestley: A Comet in the System* (San Diego: Torch, 1990), 40.

59. Quoted from Clark, *A Comet in the System*, 40. Indeed according to David Brion Davis, "abolitionist agitation was still on the rise when loyalist mobs were attacking the premises of men like Joseph Priestley and Thomas Walker, and when other dissidents were being tried for treason and sedition." Davis, *Problem of Slavery in Age of Revolution*, 364.

60. Garry Wills writes that "to be like a Quaker was an Enlightenment boast." Wills, *Head and Heart: American Christianities* (New York: Penguin, 2007), 136.

61. Peter Linebaugh, *The London Hanged: Crime and Civil Society in the Eighteenth Century* (London: Penguin, 1991), 310, 316.

62. Friends Society of Philadelphia, *Quaker Biographies: A Series of Sketches* (Philadelphia: Friends Society of Philadelphia, Yearly Meeting, Books Committee, 1914), 26. John Fothergill later welcomed John Woolman to London and would become a contributor to Benezet's School for Black People, also known as the African Free School.

63. Rush also supported the death sentence. David Brion Davis wrote that "the 'strain for consistency' did not prevent Rush from being a crusader for freedom and a personal tyrant who imprisoned his own son for life in his own mental hospital and who tortured alcoholics and mental deviants for the supposed good of society." Davis, *Problem of Slavery in Age of Revolution*, 274.

64. Cadbury, "Anthony Benezet's Library," 64.

65. Benjamin Rush, *A Warning Voice to the Intemperate* (Philadelphia, 1817), 10.

66. Winch, *Gentleman of Color*, 25. According to Winch, Forten's biographer, Rush apparently helped the young James find work.

67. Absalom Jones, and Richard Allen, *A Narrative of the Proceedings of the Black People, During the Late and Awful Calamity in Philadelphia, in the Year 1793* (Philadelphia: William W. Woodward, 1795), 5. See Mathew Carey, *A Short Account of the Malignant Fever, Lately Prevalent in Philadelphia* (Philadelphia: Mathew Carey, 1793). Richard S. Newman, *Freedom's Prophet: Bishop Richard Allen the AME Church and the Blacks Founding Fathers* (New York: New York University Press), chaps. 2, 3. Jones and Allen also wrote that Rush "told us we could increase our utility, by attending to his instruction, and accordingly directed us where to procure medicine duly prepared, with proper directions, how to administer them, and at what stages of the disorder to bleed, and when we found ourselves incapable of judging what was proper to be done, to apply to him" (p. 5). I am grateful to John R. McNeill for help in understanding this process. See also Roy Porter, *Greatest Benefit to Mankind* (New York: W. W. Norton, 1998), 313–14.

68. Sidney Kaplan and Emma Nogrady Kaplan, *The Black Presence in the Era of the American Revolution*, rev. ed. (Amherst: University of Massachusetts Press, 1989), 102.

69. Winch, *Gentleman of Color*, 188.

70. The society was led by Robert Finley, a white minister from Princeton, New Jersey, who believed that resettlement to Africa would bring about an end to slavery. Supporters of the American Colonization Society included former American presidents James Monroe and James Madison and Supreme Court Justice John Marshall. However, the most ardent supporter was Henry Clay, the Kentucky senator and slaveholder. Finley left his home in New Jersey and traveled to Washington to meet with Clay, who was to give the keynote address at the founding meeting of the society. However, on his way he met with James Forten and other Philadelphia black leaders. To his dismay they opposed his plan. The humanitarian Finley wrote that the society's mission had three basic goals: "We would be cleared of them; we would send to Africa a population partially civilized and Christianized . . . [and] blacks would be put in a better condition." Philip Foner, *History of Black Americans* (Westport, Conn.: Greenwood Press, 1975), 585–86. See also Sanneh, *Abolitionist Abroad*.

In January 1817 Forten, Allen, and Jones organized a convention in Philadelphia, attended by three thousand blacks, to express their opposition to colonization. Forten wrote Paul Cuffee, who supported colonization, that "I must mention to you that the whole continent seems to be agitated concerning Colonising the People of

Colour." He further told Cuffee that just as the American Colonization Society was meeting a month before, "the People of Colour here was very much fritened at first." He later added that "they were afraid that all the free people would be Compelled to go, particularly in the southern States." The Philadelphia blacks knew that the chief aim of the society was to deport all blacks who had won their freedom or could read and write. These blacks, mostly former slaves, would most likely come to aid their enslaved brethren, and the whites knew this. Winch, *Gentleman of Color*, 190.

71. Winch, *Gentleman of Color*, 63; Hornick, "Anthony Benezet," 430–31, 435. *The Case of Our Fellow-Creatures The Oppressed Africans, respectfully recommended to the Serious Considerations of the Legislature of Great-Britain, by the People called Quakers* (London: James Phillips, 1784).

72. L. H. Butterfield, ed., *Letters of Benjamin Rush* (Princeton, N.J.: Princeton University Press, 1951), vol. 1, 80–81.

73. Benjamin Rush to Benjamin Franklin, May 1, 1773, in Butterfield, *Letters*, vol. 1, 78–79.

74. Benjamin Rush to Granville Sharp, May 1, 1773, in Butterfield, *Letters*, vol. 1, 81. The letter is also in Prince Hoare, *Memoirs of Granville Sharp* (London: 1820), 119.

75. Benjamin Rush, *An Address to the Inhabitants of the British Settlements in America, upon Slave-Keeping* (Philadelphia, 1773).

76. Ibid., 1–2.

77. Benjamin Rush, *An Address to the Inhabitants*, 20, in Butterfield, *Letters*, vol. 1, 78–79.

78. Benjamin Rush to Jacques Barbeu Dubourg, April 29, 1773, in Butterfield, *Letters*, vol. 1, 76. The law was titled "An Act for making perpetual the Act entitled, An Act for laying a Duty on Negroes and Mulatto Slaves imported into this Province, and laying an additional Duty on the said Slaves." The law was passed on January 26, 1773. *Pennsylvania Archives*, 8th series, viii, 6965–66.

79. Benjamin Rush to Jacques Barbeu Dubourg, April 29, 1773, in Butterfield, *Letters*, vol. 1, 76.

80. Rush, *An Address to Inhabitants*, 26.

81. W. E. B. Du Bois first chronicled the impact of the Pennsylvania laws in his Harvard University doctoral thesis. Du Bois, "The Suppression of the African Slave Trade 1638–1870" (Ph.D. diss., Harvard University, 1898), 222.

82. Ira Vernon Brown, *The Negro in Pennsylvania History* (University Park: Pennsylvania Historical Association, 1970), 6.

83. Du Bois described many such laws that were passed. Du Bois, "Suppression of the African Slave Trade," 201–29.

84. Woods, "Correspondence of Benjamin Rush and Granville Sharp," vol. 1, 3. Rush had first written to Sharp on May 1, 1773. He wrote " from the amiable character which I have received of you form my worth friend Mr. Anth. Benezet, I have taken the liberty of introducing myself to your correspondence by sending you a pamphlet entitled *An Address to the Inhabitants of the British Settlements in America*." *Letters of Benjamin Rush*, 80–81. The letter is also in Hoare, *Memoirs of Granville Sharp*, 118–19.

85. *Vermont State Papers, 1779–86*, 244. Vermont Constitution, 1777, Preamble and Chapter One, in Bruns, ed., *Am I Not a Man and a Brother*, 429–32. Following Vermont in 1777 was Pennsylvania (1780), Massachusetts (1783), New Hampshire (1783), Rhode Island (1784), New York (1799), and New Jersey (1804).

86. Nisbet, *Slavery Not Forbidden by Scripture*, 21–23.

87. Jordan, *White over Black*, 307.

88. Nisbet, *Slavery Not Forbidden by Scripture*, 21–23.

89. *The Poems of Phillis Wheatley,* revised, ed. Julian D. Mason, Jr. (Chapel Hill: University of North Carolina Press, 1966), 53.

90. See also the Schomburg Library of Nineteenth-Century Black Women Writers, *The Collected Poems of Phillis Wheatley*, ed. John Shields (New York: Oxford University Press, 1988).

91. Wheatley had also written Washington, congratulating him on his appointment as head of the Continental Army. Washington later wrote to Colonel Joseph Reed that "at first, with a view of doing justice to her great poetical genius, I had a great mind to publish the poem; but not knowing whether it might not be considered rather as a mark of my own vanity, than as a compliment to her, I laid it aside." George Washington to Colonel Joseph Reid, quoted in *Poems of Wheatley*, ed. Mason, 164–165. Fritz Hirschfeld, *George Washington and Slavery: A Documentary Portrayal* (Columbia: University of Missouri Press, 1997), 88. He later wrote to "Miss Phillis" to thank her for the poem and to apologize for the delay in responding owing to the many duties he had during the Revolutionary War. For an excellent discussion of Wheatley see Henry Louis Gates, Jr., *The Trials of Phillis Wheatley: America's First Black Poet and Her Encounters with the Founding Fathers* (New York: Basic Civitas, 2003). Like Benezet, Miss Phillis, as she was called, also wrote to Selena, the Countess of Huntingdon, a follower of Whitefield and an associate of the English Methodist antislavery minister John Wesley. Richard Nisbet referred to her work as "a few silly poems." Thomas Jefferson also dismissed her work. Franklin told his nephew Jonathan Williams Franklin, Sr., that "upon your recommendations I went to see the black Poetess and off'd her any service I could do for her. . . . And I have heard nothing of her." Quotations in Gates, *Trials of Phillis Wheatley*, 34.

92. Benjamin Rush, "A Vindication of the Address to the Inhabitants of the British Sentiments, on the Slavery of the Negroe's in America, in Answer to a Pamphlet Entitled, 'Slavery Not Forbidden by Scripture: Or a Defense of the West-India Planters from the Aspersions Thrown out Against Them by the Author of the Address'" (Philadelphia, 1773); "An Answer to Richard Nisbet" (1773), quoted in Bruns, *Am I Not a Man and a Brother*, 232. Rush also wrote that in Boston "there was a Negro girl about 18 years of age, who has been but 9 years in the country, whose singular genius and accomplishments are such as not only do honor to her sex, but to human nature." Rush, *An Address to the Inhabitants*, 2n. *Poems of Phyllis Wheatley*, ed. Mason, 29.

93. Bruns, *Am I Not a Man and a Brother*, 236.

94. Anthony Benezet to Samuel Allinson, November 30, 1772, Haverford College Quaker Collection.

95. Anthony Benezet to William Dillwyn, August 20, 1783, Haverford College Quaker Collection.

96. Included were Benezet's Observations on the Inslaving of Negroes, A Short Account of That Part of Africa, and Some Historical Account of Guinea.

97. *The Selected Writings of Benjamin Rush*, ed. Dagobert D. Runes (New York: Philosophical Library, 1947), 15; Phillip Gould, *Barbaric Traffic: Commerce and Antislavery in the 18th Century Atlantic World* (Cambridge, Mass.: Harvard University Press, 2003), 85, offers an interesting interpretation of this passage.

98. Benjamin Rush to Granville Sharp, in Woods, "Correspondence of Benjamin Rush and Granville Sharp," 4.

99. Granville Sharp to Benjamin Rush, February 21, 1774, in Brookes, *Friend Anthony Benezet*, 447.

100. Granville Sharp to Benjamin Rush, February 1774, in Brookes, *Friend Anthony Benezet*, 446.

101. Ibid.

102. "Paradise of Negro Slaves a Dream," in Benjamin Rush, *Essays, Literary, Moral and Philosophical*, ed. Michael Meranze (1806; repr., Schenectady: Union College Press, 1988), 187, 188.

103. Historians have as varied opinions of Lee and his motives as slaveholders had of his writings. Roger Bruns observes: "A man who once characterized Africans as brutes with a 'savage appetite for blood' and referred to the Negro race 'as the most detestable that ever the earth produced' wrote one of the most significant antislavery articles of the eighteenth century." He added, "Lee's racist notions did not lead him to a defense of slavery. He saw the institution as abominable, retarding the growth of commerce and learning, violating justice, and exposing the community to a looming horror of black insurrection." Bruns, *Am I Not a Man and a Brother*, 107. Gary Nash took a more positive view of Lee, describing him as a man who was "infected by the antislavery ideas beginning to blossom on both sides of the Atlantic." Gary Nash, *Race and Revolution* (Madison, Wis.: Madison House, 1990), 91. Louis W. Potts spent only two pages on Lee's antislavery work and does not view it as a current in his revolutionary stream. Lee's "Address on Slavery," the work that shook the foundations of slaveholding in Virginia, merited no mention in Potts's biography of Lee. He did note, however, that in his *Essay in Vindication of the Continental Colonies of America, from a Censure of Mr. Adam Smith, in His Theory of Moral Sentiments, with Some Reflections on Slavery in General* that Lee "set out first to catalogue the depravity and barbarism of Negroes in Africa, then to prove that Negroes slaves in America shared the same characteristics." Louis W. Potts, *Arthur Lee: A Virtuous Revolutionary* (Baton Rouge: Louisiana State University Press, 1981), 28. Christopher L. Brown seems closer to true understanding of Lee and his motives. Lee, as Brown argues, "took up his pen not because he objected to slavery, but because he despised black people and disliked seeing them described as 'heroes' by Adam Smith." Christopher L. Brown, *Moral Capital: Foundations of British Abolitionism* (Chapel Hill: University of North Carolina Press, 2006), 116.

104. Arthur Lee, *An Essay on the Vindication of the Continental Colonies of America, from a Censure of Mr. Adam Smith, in his Theory of Moral Sentiments, with Some Reflection on Slavery in General* (London, 1764), 11–13, 37–38, 42.

105. Ibid., 11–13, 37–38, 42.

106. Arthur Lee, "Address on Slavery," *Rind's Virginia Gazette*, March 19, 1767. Reprinted also in Nash, *Race and Revolution*, 91–96, and Anthony Benezet and John Wesley, *Views of American Slavery, Taken a Century Ago* (Philadelphia: Association for the Diffusion of Religious and Useful Knowledge, 1858), 109–12.

107. Roger Bruns, introduction to "Arthur Lee, Address on Slavery, March 19, 1767," in *Am I Not a Man and a Brother*, 107. Lee, "Address on Slavery."

108. Lee, "Address on Slavery."

109. David Brion Davis notes that Lee's 1767 *Virginia Gazette* article was "later widely publicized by Robert Pleasants and Benezet; but when Benezet reprinted it, he removed the strongest passages, which warned that the slaves might with justice rise in mass insurrection." Davis, *Problem of Slavery in Age of Revolution*, 231, n. 27. Benezet deleted sections related to violence and slave revolts in Philmore's *Two-Dialogues on the Man Trade*.

110. Lee, "Address on Slavery."

111. Lee, "Address on Slavery."

112. Jonathan Boucher, *Causes and Consequences of the American Revolution in Thirteen Discourses Preached in North America, Between the Years of 1763 and 1775* (1797; repr., New York: Russell & Russell, 1967), 39.

113. Anne Y. Zimmer, *Jonathan Boucher: Loyalist in Exile* (Detroit: Wayne State University Press, 1978), 298.

114. Jonathan Boucher, *Reminiscences, of an American Loyalist, 1738–1789, being the autobiography of the Revd. Jonathan Boucher, Rector of Annapolis in Maryland and afterwards Vicar of Epsom, Surrey, England, edited by his grandson* (1925; repr. Port Washington, N.Y.: Kennikat Press, 1967), 58, 98. In fact, Boucher wrote of seeing "thousands of slaves as well-informed, as well-clad, as well-fed, and in every respect as well-off as nine out of ten of the poor in every kingdom of Europe" (98).

115. Boucher, *Causes and Consequences of the American Revolution*, 41. Boucher called Lee "a mere rhetorician," unqualified to lecture his fellow Virginians. He used what would become a standard practice, quoting Montesquieu, "an ingenious French writer who well observes, that 'the state of slavery is, in its own nature bad; it is neither useful to the master, nor to the slave.'" Boucher continued the Montesquieu quote: "'Not to the slave, because he can do nothing through a motive, of virtue; nor to the master, because, by having an unlimited authority over his slaves, he insensibly accustoms himself to the want of all moral values, and from thence grows fierce, hasty, severe, voluptuous, and cruel'" (41). Boucher also became one of the first proslavery advocates to quote Locke. In a footnote he wrote, "It is, however, remarkable, that the great champion of liberty, and advocate of humanity, Mr. Locke, by the 10th article, or item, of the Constitution which he drew up for the government of Carolina, gives every freeman of Carolina absolute power and property over his slaves of what opinion or religion forever" (41).

116. A few days after Robert was born in 1723, the Henrico County sheriff came into his parents' home and took away their possessions as punishment for refusing "to b[e]ar arms." The sheriff was Thomas Jefferson, whose "grandson and namesake was none other than Thomas Jefferson of Monticello." Jay Worrall, Jr., *The Friendly Virginians: America's First Quakers* (Athens, Ga.: Iberian, 1994), 111.

117. Nash, *Unknown American Revolution*, 117. Gary B. Nash and Graham Russell Hodges, *Friends of Liberty, Thomas Jefferson, Thadeusz Kosciuszko, and Agrippa Hull: A Tale of Three Patriots, Two Revolutions and a Tragic Betrayal of Freedom in the New Nation* (New York: Basic Books, 2008), 40.

118. Worrall, *Friendly Virginians*, 243.

119. Andrew Levy offers an interesting look at the debates over slavery and emancipation in *The First Emancipator: The Forgotten Story of Robert Carter, the Founding Father Who Freed His Slaves* (New York: Random House, 2005).

120. Patrick Henry to Robert Pleasants, January 18, 1773, Haverford College Quaker Collection.

121. Roger Atkinson, Pleasants's brother-in-law, wrote a letter to Samuel Pleasants, Robert's brother, on October 7, 1774. A non-Quaker, Atkinson shared information about his observations concerning the seven Virginia delegates to the Continental Congress's proceedings in Philadelphia. He wrote, "The 4th a real half Quaker, Patrick Henry, your brother's man. Moderate and mild and in religious matters a saint, but the very devil in politics—a son of thunder." Worrall, *Friendly Virginians*, 174; "Letters of Robert Pleasants of Curles," *William and Mary Quarterly*, 2nd series, 1 (1921): 108.

122. Robert Pleasants to Anthony Benizette [*sic*], quoted in Worrall, *Friendly Virginians*, 177; "Letters of Robert Pleasants of Curles," 108.

123. Anthony Benezet to Samuel Allinson, October 23, 1774, Haverford College Quaker Collection. A copy of the letter was sent to Robert Pleasants the same day.

124. Robert Pleasants to Anthony Benezet, February 1781, cited in Brookes, *Friend Anthony Benezet*, 437.

125. Roger Wilkins, *Jefferson's Pillow: The Founding Fathers and the Dilemma of Black Patriots* (Boston: Beacon, 2001), chaps. 1–2; Paul Finkleman, *Slavery and the Founders: Race and Liberty in the Age of Jefferson* (New York: M. E. Sharpe, 1996), 109–10; A.

Leon Higgenbotham, Jr., *In Matter of Color: Race and the American Legal Process, The Colonial Period* (New York: Oxford University Press, 1978), 19–61.

126. Anthony Benezet, *Thoughts on the Nature of War and Its Repugnancy to the Christian Life. Extracted from a Sermon on the 29th Nov. 1759* (Philadelphia, 1766, 1776, 1778). The ten-page tract was published in Philadelphia in 1766, 1776, and 1778. Benezet distributed it to members of the Congress as well as his *Serious Reflections Affectionately Recommended* in 1778. Of the latter work Governor Livingston of New Jersey wrote, "The piece on slave keeping is excellent, but the arguments against the unlawfulness of war, have been answered a thousand times." Vaux, *Memoirs of the Life of Anthony Benezet*, 51; Brookes, *Friend Anthony Benezet*, 128–29. Perhaps the African American historian Carter G. Woodson explains Benezet's anguish during the period best. Wrote Woodson, "His sympathetic nature too impelled him to speak in behalf of the suffering soldiers of the American Revolution. Adhering to the faith of the Quakers, he could not help but to shudder at the horrors of that war. He was interested in not only soldiers but also the unfortunate Americans on whom they were imposed. He saw in the whole course of war nothing but bold iniquity and crass inconsistency of nations, which professed Christianity." Woodson added, "To set forth the distress, which such a state of the country caused him, Benezet wrote a dissertation entitled 'Thoughts on the Nature of War,' and distributed it among persons of distinction in America and Europe." Linking the war with slavery, Woodson noted, "In 1778 when the struggle for independence had reached a crisis he issued in the interest of peace with the enemy a work entitled, 'Serious Reflections on the Times addressed to the Well-disposed of every Religious Denomination.'" Woodson may have gotten the complete title of the work wrong, but he, like Du Bois, was one of the first historians to get the message of Benezet right. Carter G. Woodson, "Anthony Benezet," *Journal of Negro History* 2 (1917): 43.

127. Anthony Benezet to Henry Laurens, December 1776, Haverford College Quaker Collection. For an analysis of the Quakers and the revolution see Arthur J. Mekeel, *The Relation of the Quakers to the American Revolution* (Washington, D.C.: University of America Press, 1979).

128. Marcus Rediker, *The Slave Ship: A Human History* (New York: Viking, 2007), 133, 385 note 22.

129. Gregory D. Massey, *John Laurens and the American Revolution* (Columbia: University of South Carolina Press, 2000), 14. See also Daniel L. McDonough, *Christopher Gadsden and Henry Laurens: The Parallel Lives of Two American Patriots* (London: Associated University Presses, 2000), 18–21.

130. David Duncan Wallace, *The Life of Henry Laurens with a Sketch of the Life of Lieutenant-Colonel John Laurens* (1915; repr., New York: Russell & Russell, 1967), 445. As early as May 1755 Laurens had written letters to friends about the number and quality of enslaved Africans he had begun to import. He distinguished between the Gambian slaves, whom he favored; the Angolan slaves, who brought great profits; and the Calabar slaves, who, he observed, committed frequent suicides, thus causing him to lose money (76).

131. A few years later, in March 1779, Commander George Washington decided after recent British successes to muster black troops. By May 2,400 British soldiers under the command of General Augustine Prevost marched from Georgia to South Carolina. Seeing this, the Congress in Philadelphia finally advised the South Carolinians to consider the arming of their slaves. The South Carolina leaders summarily rejected the proposal. John Laurens, now back in South Carolina and a member of the state's legislature, put forth the proposal, which failed miserably. In his father's words the proposed legislation was "blown up with contemptuous huzzas." Yet his father was surprised that John's proposal got any votes at all. In 1782 he again

brought the proposal legislation before the state legislature and again it failed. The surprise was that he got twice as many votes as he had two-and-a-half years earlier. McDonough, *Christopher Gadsden and Henry Laurens*, 242.

132. Wallace, Life of Henry Laurens, 445.

133. Henry Laurens to John Laurens, August 14, 1776, quoted in Wallace, *Life of Henry Laurens*, 446.

134. John Laurens to Henry Laurens, October 26, 1776, quoted in Wallace, *Life of Henry Laurens*, 447.

135. Massey, *John Laurens and the American Revolution*, 227.

136. Anthony Benezet to Henry Laurens, December 1776, Haverford College Quaker Collection.

137. Peter H. Wood, "'Liberty Is Sweet': African-American Freedom Struggles in the Years Before Independence," in *Beyond the American Revolution: Explorations in the History of American Radicalism*, ed. Alfred E. Young (DeKalb: Northern Illinois University Press, 1993), 149–94; Wood, "'Taking Care Of Business' in Revolutionary South Carolina: Republicanism and the Slave Society," in *The Southern Experience in the American Revolution*, ed. Jeffrey J. Crow and Larry B. Tise (Chapel Hill: University of North Carolina Press, 1978), 268–93; Wood, *Black Majority*. Another Laurens biographer, Daniel J. McDonough, rightly noted, "The large number of slaves forced most South Carolinians to adopt a more cautious tone than their northern counterparts in their exclamations concerning liberty and their denunciations of British efforts to 'enslave' America." McDonough, *Christopher Gadsden and Henry Laurens*, 162.

138. Anthony Benezet, *Serious Reflections Affectionately Recommended to the Well-Disposed of Every Religious Denomination, Particularly Those Who Mourn and Lament on Accounts of the Calamities Which Attend Us and the Insensibility That So Generally Prevails* (Philadelphia, 1778), quoted in Brookes, *Friend Anthony Benezet*, 495.

139. Theodore Parsons and Eliphalet Pearson, *A Forensic Dispute on the Legality of Enslaving the Africans Held at the Public Commencement* (Boston: John Botle, 1773). Tise also discussed this work in *Proslavery: A History of the Defense of Slavery*, 30–32, 378–79.

140. Jonathan Sassi, *"The whole country have their hands full of Blood this day," Transcription and Introduction of an Antislavery Sermon Manuscript Attributed to the Reverend Samuel Hopkins* (Worcester, Mass.: Worcester American Antiquarian Society, 2004), 55. Sassi found that Samuel Hopkins had taken his own information about Africa from Pearson, just as Pearson had from Benezet.

141. Benjamin Quarles, *The Negro in the American Revolution* (New York: W. W. Norton, 1973), 35.

142. John Allen, *The Watchman's Alarm to Lord N—th; or, the British Parliamentary Boston Port-Bill Unwrapped* [*sic*] (Salem, Mass., 1774), 27.

143. Bruns, *Am I Not a Man and a Brother*, 328; Nash, *Race and Revolution*, 117; Linebaugh and Rediker, *Many-Headed Hydra*, 227.

144. Quoted in Mack Thompson, *Moses Brown, Reluctant Reformer* (Chapel Hill: University of North Carolina Press, 1962), 176. Brown consulted with Benezet on the value of foreign languages and the publication of a primer and school curriculum. He also became a member of a committee that opened a school on November 8, 1784 (162–63).

145. His father died in his early youth, and Moses was raised by an uncle, Obadiah, a rum distiller, shipper, and merchant. He and his three brothers, Nicolas, John, and Joseph, became known as the "Four Brown Brothers of Providence," specializing in candle making and iron works. Moses's first wife died in 1773, and after a period of withdrawal from the family business he remarried. His second and third

wives were Quakers, and he joined the Friends. Robert Morton Hazelton, *Let Freedom Ring! A Biography of Moses Brown* (New York: New Voices, 1957).

146. Anthony Benezet to Moses Brown, May 8, 1774, Haverford College Quaker Collection.

147. Charles Rappleye, *Sons of Providence: The Brown Brothers, the Slave Trade and the American Revolution* (New York: Simon & Schuster, 2006), 169.

148. Walter Stahr, *John Jay: Founding Father* (New York: Continuum, 2005), 2–3, 8.

149. The reference seems to be to Benezet's *Serious Considerations on Several Important Subjects* (Philadelphia, 1778).

150. Anthony Benezet to John Jay, president of the Congress, February 7, 1779, Haverford College Quaker Collection. See Richard B. Morris, ed., *John Jay: The Making of a Revolutionary, Unpublished Papers, 1745–1780* (New York: Harper & Row, 1975), 544–45. This letter was also printed in *The Friend* 7, 1833.

151. John Jay to Anthony Benezet, March 5, 1779, *The Friend* 7, 1833. A reprint of the letter in Morris, *John Jay: The Making of a Revolutionary*, incorrectly lists Jay as responding to Benezet's letter of February 2 instead of the correct date of February 7 (p. 572).

152. Morris, *John Jay: The Making of a Revolutionary*, 544–45.

153. Landa M. Freeman, Louise V. North, and Janet M. Wedge, comps., *Selected Letters of John Jay and Sarah Livingston Jay* (Jefferson, N.C.: McFarland, 2005), 297.

154. Cassandra Pybus, *Epic Journeys of Freedom: Runaway Slaves of the American Revolution and Their Global Quest for Liberty* (Boston: Beacon Press, 2006), 28.

155. Peter Jay to John and James Jay, September 1, 1779, in *The Papers of John Jay* (Columbia University, Book of Negroes, PRO 30/55/100). I am grateful to Cassandra Pybus for bringing this to my attention.

156. Freeman, North, and Wedge, *Selected Letters of John Jay and Sarah Livingston Jay*, 299; Morris, *John Jay: The Making of a Revolutionary*, 471.

157. Quoted from the exhibit *Slavery in New York* (New York: New-York Historical Society, 2006).

158. Benezet, *A Caution and a Warning*, 16.

159. Benezet, *Observations on the Inslaving of Negroes*.

160. Benezet, *Short Account of That Part of Africa*, 64.

161. Moncure D. Conway, ed., The *Writings of Thomas Paine, 1774–1779* (New York: AMS Press, 1967), 4. Reprinted from *Postscript to the Pennsylvania Journal and Weekly Advertiser*, March 8, 1775; see also Thomas Paine, *Common Sense and Related Writings*, ed. Thomas P. Slaughter (Boston: Bedford/St. Martin's, 2001), 14.

162. Linebaugh and Rediker, *Many-Headed Hydra*, 227.

163. Rappleye, *Sons of Providence*, 225.

164. David Cooper, *A Serious Address to the Rulers of America, on the Inconsistency of Their Conduct Respecting Slavery: Forming a Contract Between the Encroachment of England on American Liberty and American Injustice in Tolerating Slavery* (Trenton, N.J., 1783), microfilm, pp. 12–13, in Anti-Slavery Collection, London Society of Friends, British Museum.

165. Cooper, *Serious Address*, 6, 11, 15.

166. Anthony Benezet to John Pemberton, September 10, 1783, Haverford College Quaker Collection.

167. David Cooper to Samuel Allinson, *Friends' Review* 15, 1861–62.

168. George Washington's signed copy is held at the Boston Athenaeum.

169. John P. Kaminski and Gaspare J. Saladino, eds., *The Documentary History of the Ratification of the Constitution*, gen. ed. Merrill Jensen, *Commentaries on the Constitution*, vol. 15, *18 December 1787 to 31 January 1788* (Madison: State Historical Society of Wisconsin, 1981), 433.

170. Nash, *Race and Revolution*, 20; Nash, *Forgotten Fifth: African Americans in the Age of Revolution* (Cambridge, Mass.: Harvard University Press, 2006), 71–75.

171. F. Nwabueze Okoye, "Chattel Slavery," 12–13.

172. Samuel Johnson, *No Taxation No Tyranny*, 3rd ed. (London, 1775), 89; Nash, *Unknown American Revolution*, 212; Waldstreicher, *Runaway America*, 211–12.

173. Conway, *Writings of Thomas Paine*, 1:7–8; Eric Foner, *Tom Paine and Revolutionary America* (London: Oxford University Press, 1976), 73.

174. Quoted in François Furstenberg, *In the Name of the Father: Washington's Legacy, Slavery and the Making of the Nation* (New York: Penguin, 2006), 193. Washington's last will freed his 124 slaves on the death of his wife, Martha. Fritz Hirscheld, *George Washington and Slavery: A Documentary Portrayal* (Columbia: University of Missouri Press, 1997), 211–12, 56–62.

175. Linebaugh and Rediker, *Many-Headed Hydra*, chap. 7.

176. Anthony Benezet, *Notes on the Slave Trade* (Philadelphia, 1781), 8. Benezet did not accept the Aristotelian notion that some men were born to be slaves. He did not accept Hobbes's view that the powerful had the right to enslave the weak.

Chapter 6. Transatlantic Beginnings and the British Antislavery Movement

1. As Ruth Fisher has noted, "It became quite the fashion for rich ladies and gentlemen to be attended by young Black boys as evidenced by the paintings and literature of that age." Ruth Ana Fisher, "Granville Sharp and Lord Mansfield," *Journal of Negro History* 28 (1943), 381. In portraits of the time blacks can be seen fanning and attending to the rich whites. On black England see Anstey, *Atlantic Slave Trade and British Abolition*; Gretchen Gerzina, *Black England: Life Before Emancipation* (London: John Murray, 1995); James Walvin, *Black Ivory: A History of British Slavery* (Washington, D.C.: Howard University Press, 1994); Peter Fryer, *Staying Power: The History of Black People in Britain* (London: Pluto Classic Press, 1984); F. O. Shyllon, *Black People in Britain, 1555–1833* (London: Oxford University Press, 1977), and *Black Slaves in Britain* (London: Oxford University Press, 1974).

2. Anthony Benezet to Thomas Seeker, the archbishop of Canterbury, undated letter of 1758, cited in Vaux, *Memoirs of the Life of Anthony Benezet*, 25.

3. Anthony Benezet, *A Caution and a Warning* (Philadelphia, 1766, 1767, 1784, 1785), and (London, 1767, 1768, 1785, 1788.) He used many sources, including "an account in *Hill's* Naval History, page 293" and accounts of "when Captain Hawkins returned from his first voyage to Africa." Benezet, *Caution*, 36, 41. See below for more details on Benezet's calculations and his source, which provided exact figures for Liverpool: 101 ships transporting over 30,000 Africans.

4. Anthony Benezet to the Society for the Propagating of the Gospel, April 26, 1767, quoted in Brookes, *Friend Anthony Benezet*, 272.

5. Clarkson, *History of the Abolition of the African Slave-Trade*, vol. 1, 256.

6. C. Duncan Rice rightly calls their relationship "fundamental to the history of the Atlantic anti-slavery movement." *Rise and Fall of Black Slavery*, 199.

7. Julius Sherrard Scott, III "The Common Wind: Currents of Afro-American Communication in the Era of the Haitian Revolution," Ph.D. diss., Duke University, 1986. Scott uses the term "the Common Wind" to document the many forms and networks of communication that blacks used in Haiti to express their desire for freedom.

8. Granville Sharp to Anthony Benezet, July 7, 1773, Haverford College Quaker Collection, cited in Steven M. Wise, *Though the Heavens May Fall: The Landmark Trial That Led to the End of Human Slavery* (New York: DeCapo Press, 2005), 23, from

Hoare, *Memoirs of Granville Sharp* (1828 ed.), 193. For most of my references from Hoare's *Memoirs of Granville Sharp,* I use the 1820 first edition.

9. One of Granville Sharp's older brothers, William, became a surgeon, who came to Granville's aid in his campaign against slavery; two other brothers became ministers. When it came time to educate young Granville, there was no money left, so he received little by the way of formal education. Early in life Sharp came to believe that he was unworthy of ministering God's grace, so he decided against a career in the ministry.

10. Hoare, *Memoirs of Granville Sharp,* 27–29.

11. Fryer, *Staying Power,* 115.

12. Jonathan Strong, quoted in Walvin, *Black Ivory,* 13.

13. Fryer, *Staying Power,* 115–16.

14. William Blackstone, *Commentaries on the Laws of England* (Oxford: Clarendon Press, 1765–69), vol. 1, 127, quoted in Fryer, *Staying Power,* 116.

15. Quoted in Hoare, *Memoirs of Granville Sharp,* 35.

16. Walvin, *Black and White,* 118.

17. James Oldham, *English Common Law in the Age of Mansfield* (Chapel Hill: University of North Carolina Press, 2004). Oldham notes that "Attorney General Philip Yorke (later to become Lord Hardwicke) and Solicitor General Talbot gave an opinion in 1729 in favor of the rights of a master over his slave in Great Britain," 310.

18. Fisher, "Granville Sharp and Lord Mansfield," 381–89.

19. Hoare, *Memoirs of Granville Sharp,* 36. He adds a note that "the Opinion of Yorke and Talbot [was] quoted (many years afterwards) in Bowyer's 'Poems on the Abolition of the Slave Trade.' The Earl of Hardwicke, with feelings which honour to his heart, but under the influence of less accurate information than was his due, addressed a note to Mr. Bowyer, questioning the influence of the statement."

20. *Dictionary of National Biography,* vol. 18, 1339–40, s.v. "Yorke and Talbot Opinion of 1729."

21. Wise, Though the Heavens May Fall, 25. On Mansfield's views see Davis, *Problem of Slavery in Age of Revolution,* 392.

22. Hoare, *Memoirs of Granville Sharp* (1820 ed.), 43. In the second edition (1828) Hoare wrote, "In 1767, he accidentally met with a copy of this book on a stall, and, without any knowledge whatever of the author, caused this edition to be printed and published having added thereto an account of the endeavors of the Society for the Propagation of the Gospel" (145).

23. Wise, *Though The Heavens May Fall,* 35.

24. Cited in Shyllon, *Black People in Britain,* 199–200.

25. Blackstone vacillated over his opinions. At first he wrote in 1765 "and this spirit of liberty is so implanted in our constitution, and rooted even in our very soil, that a slave or a negro, the moment he lands in England falls under the protection of the laws and becomes *eo instanto* a freeman." In 1767 after being informed that the Yorke and Talbot decision differed from his own reasoning, he changed his formulation. He then wrote, "a slave or negro, the moment he lands in England, falls under the protection of the laws, and so far becomes a freeman; though the master's right to his service may probably still continue." Quoted in Robin Blackburn, *The Overthrow of Colonial Slavery, 1776–1848* (London: Verso, 1988), 81. See also Hugh Thomas, *The Slave Trade: The Story of the Atlantic Slave Trade, 1440–1870* (New York: Simon and Schuster, 1997), 471–73. After discussing Blackstone, Thomas praises Benezet (using Sharp's words) as a "worthy old Quaker." Actually, Sharp had written to Lord North in 1772 that one of his antislavery tracts (presumably one that he had sent to North) had been "reprinted in America, by Anthony

Benezet, a worthy old Quaker at Philadelphia, whose other publications had already begun to awaken the attention of the Americans to injustice and danger of tolerating slavery." Hoare, *Memoirs of Granville Sharp*, 116. Thomas also writes that "in the history of abolition, Benezet like Aphra Behn and the half forgotten Tomás de Mercado should have a place of honor. He was not only a link between the writings of the moral philosophers, such as Montesquieu and the Quakers, but also one between American and Britain; and indeed the Anglo-Saxons and the French." Unfortunately Thomas falls victim to his own words when he writes of Benezet, as "a tiny ugly man with no presence." Yet this man did have the presence in Thomas's own words to serve as "the most vital link" in the growing Atlantic antislavery community.

26. Hoare, *Memoirs of Granville Sharp*, 83.

27. Quoted in Bruns, *Am I Not a Man and a Brother*, 197.

28. Granville Sharp, *The Law of Liberty or Royal Law, By Which All Mankind Will Certainly Be Judged! Earnestly Recommended to the Serious Considerations of All Slaveholders and Slavedealers* (London: B. White, 1776), 23.

29. Hoare, *Memoirs of Granville Sharp*, 34. The transcriptions of this and many other letters as transcribed in Brookes, *Friend Anthony Benezet*, prove inadequate, as many are improperly copied, at times are incorrectly documented, and leave out important texts. Nonetheless, the work serves as a very important source in reviewing the body of work left by Benezet.

30. Anthony Benezet to Granville Sharp, May 14, 1772, Haverford College Quaker Collection. Charles Stuart, *A Memoir of Granville Sharp to Which Is Added Sharp's "Law of Passive Obedience," and an Extract from His "Law of Retribution"* (New York: Anti-Slavery Society, 1836), 20.

31. Granville Sharp, manuscript notes of letter to Lord North, February 18, 1772, in Hoare, *Memoirs of Granville Sharp*, 80.

32. Ibid.

33. Rice, *Rise and Fall of Black Slavery*, 199.

34. Granville Sharp to Frederick North, Eighth Baron North, February 18, 1772, in Hoare, *Memoirs of Granville Sharp*, 78–79. Sharp also wrote to Benezet on November 8, 1772, and February 18, 1773, on this matter.

35. Anthony Benezet to Granville Sharp, May 14, 1772, Haverford College Quaker Collection. See also E. C. P. Lascelles, *Granville Sharp and the Freedom of Slaves in England* (New York: Negro Universities Press, 1968), 36–38 (originally published in 1928).

36. Granville Sharp to Anthony Benezet, August 21, 1772, Haverford College Quaker Collection.

37. Anthony Benezet to John Fothergill, April 28, 1773, cited in Judith Jennings, *The Business of Abolishing the British Slave Trade, 1783–1807* (London: Frank Cass, 1997), 22.

38. Brown, *Moral Capital*, 99.

39. Hoare, *Memoirs of Granville Sharp*, 144. Hoare notes that a "congeniality of spirit had singularly united these two philanthropists before any correspondence was opened between them." Simon Schama, *Rough Crossings: Britain, the Slaves, and the American Revolution* (New York: Harper Collins, 2006), 57, makes note of the coincidence but makes no mention of the role of Benezet's writings in Sharp's activities.

40. Clarkson, in *History of the Abolition of the African Slave-Trade*, vol. 1, 170, wrongly asserts that when Benezet "heard that Mr. Granville Sharp had obtained in the year 1772, the noble verdict in the cause of Somerset the slave, he opened a correspondence with him, which he kept up, that there might be an union of action

between them for the future, as far as it could be effected, and that they might each give encouragements to the other to proceed." In fact, Benezet had written to Sharp during the case and had received word of the decision from Sharp himself in response to his own letter.

41. Granville Shape to Anthony Benezet, August 21, 1772, Haverford College Quaker Collection.

42. Granville Sharp to John Fothergill, February 1772, in Hoare, *Memoirs of Granville Sharp*, 81.

43. Hoare, *Memoirs of Granville Sharp*, 81 (see letter). Here and in many other cases antislavery writers initially published a work anonymously, a widespread eighteenth-century practice.

44. Somerset's ruling read, "The only question before us is whether the cause on the return is sufficient. If it is, the Negro must be remanded; if it is not he must be discharged. Accordingly, the return states that the slave departed and refused to serve; whereupon he was kept, to be sold abroad. So high an act of dominion must be recognized by the law of the country where it is used. The power of a master over his slave has been extremely different in different countries. The state of slavery is of such a nature that it is incapable of being introduced on any reason, moral or political, but only by positive law, which preserves its force long after the reasons, occasion, and time itself from whence it was created is erased from memory. It is so odious that nothing can be suffered to support it but positive law. Whatever inconveniences, therefore, may follow from the decision, cannot say this case is allowed or approved by the law of England and therefore the black must be discharged." Carl Stephenson, *English Constitutional History* (New York: Harper and Row 1937), quoted from T. B. Howell, ed., *A Complete Collection of State Trials to 1783,* 2nd ed. (London, 1816–1826). *State Trials,* Somerset Case 20, 82. *Somerset v. Stewart,* in W. Cobbett, T. B. Howell, et al., eds., *State Trials,* 34 vols. (London, 1809–1828), vol. 20, 1–82.

45. For a full legal discussion of the case see James Oldham, "New Light of Mansfield and Slavery," *Journal of British Studies* 27, no. 1 (January 1988), 45–68; and William M. Wiecek, "Somerset, Lord Mansfield and the Legitimacy of Slavery in the Anglo American World," *University of Chicago Law Review* 42 (1974–75), 86–146. Hoare, *Memoirs of Granville Sharp* (1820) , 80.

46. George Wallace, *A System of the Principles of the Laws of Scotland* (Edinburgh: W. Milar, 1760), 95–96.

47. Granville Sharp to Anthony Benezet, August 21, 1772, Haverford College Quaker Collection. Sharp also sent along with Benezet's pamphlet "copies of my former book, to obviate some false prejudices relating to the doctrines of *Property in Slaves.*"

48. Granville Sharp to John Fothergill, October 27, 1772, in Hoare, *Memoirs of Granville Sharp,* 105.

49. Granville Sharp, *The Just Limitation of Slavery in the Laws of God* (London, 1776; repr., Westport, Conn.: Negro Universities Press, 1969), 1.

50. Clarkson, *History of the Abolition of the African Slave-Trade,* vol. 1, 62–68. As Benjamin Quarles noted, "Negroes in New England had followed the case with deep interest." Quarles, *The Negro in the American Revolution* (New York: W. W. Norton, 1961), 37.

51. Quoted from Shyllon, *Black People in Britain,* 165. "In 1773 an advertisement in the *Virginia Gazette,* for runaway slaves asserted that a couple fled to Britain 'where Negroe's imagine they will be free (a Notion now to prevalent among the Negroe's greatly to the vexations and Prejudice of their master's.'" Maurice Jackson, "The Rise of Abolition," in Toyin Falola and Kevin D. Roberts, eds., *The Atlantic World, 1450–2000* (Bloomington: Indiana University Press, 2008), 235.

52. Kaplan and Kaplan, *Black Presence in the American Revolution,* 72. Later, "A fugitive Baccus has fled his master in frontier Georgia and would attempt 'to board a vessel for Great Britain . . . from the knowledge he has of the late Determination of Somerset's Case'" (72).

53. Herbert Aptheker, ed., *A Documentary History of the Negro People in the United States: From Colonial Times Through the Civil War,* vol. 1 (New York: Citadel Press, 1951), 7–8.

54. Aptheker, *Documentary History of the Negro People,* vol. 1, 69; Mary Stoughton Locke, *Antislavery in America: From the Introduction of African Slaves to the Prohibition of the Slave Trade, 1609–1808* (Boston: Ginn, 1901), 69.

55. James Oliver Horton and Lois E. Horton, *Hard Road to Freedom: The Story of African America* (New Brunswick, N.J.: Rutgers University Press, 2001), 62–64.

56. Anthony Benezet to Samuel Allinson, October 30, 1772, Haverford College Quaker Collection.

57. J. Bigelow, *The Works of Benjamin Franklin* (Philadelphia: J. B. Lippincott, 1887), vol. 2, 507. *Franklin's Letters to the Press,* ed. Crane, 221–23. David Waldstreicher, *Runaway America: Benjamin Franklin, Slavery, and the American Revolution* (New York: Hill and Wang, 2004), 199–200.

58. Horton and Horton, *Hard Road to Freedom,* 62.

59. Collections of the Massachusetts Historical Society, 5th series, III (Boston, 1877), 432, in Aptheker, *Documentary History,* vol. 1, 8–9.

60. Eric Williams, *Capitalism and Slavery,* with a new introduction by Colin A. Palmer (Chapel Hill: University of North Carolina Press, 1994), 45. Shyllon, *Black People in Britain,* 24–25, rightly emphasizes this narrow point about forcible removal.

61. James Oldham, *English Common Law in the Age of Mansfield* (Chapel Hill: University of North Carolina Press, 2004), 308.

62. Eric Metaxas, *Amazing Grace: William Wilberforce and the Heroic Campaign to End Slavery* (San Francisco: Harper San Francisco, 2007), 95.

63. Oldham, *English Common Law,* 308. Oldham, *The Mansfield Manuscripts and the Growth of English Law in the Eighteen Century,* vol. 2, "Slavery" (Chapel Hill: University of North Carolina, 1992), chap. 21, 1221–44.

64. The phrase comes from Williams (*Capitalism and Slavery,* 45), who shared this assessment.

65. Oldham, *English Common Law,* 308.

66. Shyllon, *Black People in Britain,* again rightly emphasizes this element of Mansfield's reasoning. Oldham (*English Common Law,* 308) remarks in this context that "Mansfield did, apparently state his opinion of the absurdity of the idea of an enforceable contract between slave and master, but the opinion was given only in passing during an intermediate phase of the case and received only fleeting mention in the press." Here again one can see the influence of Wallace on Mansfield.

67. Walvin, *Black Ivory,* 15.

68. Granville Sharp to Anthony Benezet, August 21, 1772, Haverford College Quaker Collection.

69. Clarkson, *History of the Abolition of the African Slave-Trade,* 170.

70. Walvin, *Black Ivory,* 15.

71. Granville Sharp to Anthony Benezet, August 21, 1772, Haverford College Quaker Collection. See also Brookes, *Friend Anthony Benezet,* 418–22; Hoare, *Memoirs of Granville Sharp,* 100–101; Bruns, *Am I Not a Man and a Brother,* 196–99.

72. Sharp wrote this in his personal copy of Benezet, *A Caution and a Warning to Great Britain* that was found in his library after his death in 1813. Quoted in Brookes, *Friend Anthony Benezet,* 89. Brown, *Moral Capital,* 198

73. Sharp, *Just Limitation of Slavery in the Laws of God.* Unlike Sharp's earlier works, this tract is made up mainly of biblical references and arguments.

74. Granville Sharpe to Anthony Benezet, August 21, 1772, Haverford College Quaker Collection. Sharp added "Respect must be had to the rights of the Colonies; and a petition from thence if addressed to Parliament, ought to relate to the slave trade (with its bad effects and consequences) in general, and not merely to the importation of slaves into the colonies, because the colonies have a right themselves to prohibit such importation respectively in their own Assemblies, with the King's concurrence; which they will be sure to obtain in this matter, if asked for by a majority." Nowhere in his plan does Sharp advocate the immediate and complete freedom of the slaves. He added, "a petition also to the King, from a small number (if a larger, or a majority, cannot be obtained) against the toleration of slavery in the colonies, might have very good effects." Sharp to Benezet August 21, 1772. Haverford College Quaker Collection; Hoare, *Memoirs of Granville Sharp,* 102.

75. "The Correspondence of Benjamin Rush and Granville Sharp," 5. Christopher Brown writes that "in later letters to Benezet and Pennsylvanian Benjamin Rush, Sharp insisted that colonies address abolition petitions to the king, as a petition to the king and Parliament would seem to legitimate unconstitutional authority and compromise the dignity of their legislatures." *Moral Capital,* 164–65. David Brion Davis goes one step further. Sharp he argues "regarded the colonial slave codes 'null and void' . . . believing that 'since the invalid laws had long been in force and had won the assent of kings, they had to be formally repealed by the colonial assemblies, in order to preserve 'in each branch of the legislature, that reciprocal faith that is due to all solemn compacts.'" For Sharp, "imperial conflict would be advantageous to the abolition cause." Davis, *The Problem of Slavery in the Age of Revolution,* 396–97.

76. "The Correspondence of Benjamin Rush and Granville Sharp," 5; Hoare, *Memoirs of Granville Sharp,* 102.

77. Anthony Benezet to Granville Sharp, April 4, 1773, Haverford College Quaker Collection.

78. Anthony Benezet to Granville Sharp, November 8, 1772, February 18, 1773, in Hoare, *Memoirs of Granville Sharp,* 113.

79. Anthony Benezet to Granville Sharp, March 29, 1773, in Hoare, *Memoirs of Granville Sharp,* 169–70.

80. Anthony Benezet to Granville Sharp, April 5, 1773, in Hoare, *Memoirs of Granville Sharp,* 113–14.

81. A. Leon Higginbotham, Jr., *In Matter of Color: Race and the American Legal Process: The Colonial Period* (New York: Oxford University Press, 1978), 94–96.

82. Anthony Benezet to Granville Sharp, 1773 (no exact date appears on the letter), in Hoare, *Memoirs of Granville Sharp,* 114.

83. Hoare, *Memoirs of Granville Sharp,* 114.

84. Anthony Benezet to Granville Sharp, May 16, 1774, in Hoare, *Memoirs of Granville Sharp,* 171–72.

85. Hoare, *Memoirs of Granville Sharp,* 173.

86. Quoted in Charles Stuart, *A Memoir of Granville Sharp: To Which Is Added Sharp's "Law of Passive Obedience," and an Extract from His "Law of Retribution"* (New York: American Antislavery Society, 1836), 21.

87. Hoare, *Memoirs of Granville Sharp,* 235. Schama (*Rough Crossings,* 57) notes that Sharp resigned from his job at the Ordnance Office because of the war.

88. James St. David to Granville Sharp, March 14, 1779, in Hoare, *Memoirs of Granville Sharp,* 278.

89. Hoare, *Memoirs of Granville Sharp,* 236

90. Brookes, *Friend Anthony Benezet*, 87.

91. Hoare, *Memoirs of Granville Sharp*, 173.

92. Warren Thomas Smith, *John Wesley and Slavery* (Nashville: Abingdon Press, 1986), 30–34.

93. Anstey, *Atlantic Slave Trade and British Abolition*, 240.

94. Nehemiah Curnock, ed., *The Journal of John Wesley* (London, 1840), vol. 5; Smith, *John Wesley and Slavery*, 78; Brookes, *Friend Anthony Benezet*, 84.

95. Curnock, *Journal of John Wesley*, February 12, 1772 .

96. Smith (*John Wesley and Slavery*, 91) gives a figure of 30 percent.

97. Benezet, *Some Historical Account of Guinea* (1771), 75.

98. John Wesley, *Thoughts upon Slavery* (London: R. Hawes, 1774), 7. Reprinted in Anthony Benezet and John Wesley, *Views of American Slavery: Taken a Century Ago* (Philadelphia: Association of Friends for the Diffusion of Religious and Useful Knowledge, 1858), 74–75. Wesley's *Thoughts* went through thirteen editions, not counting its bindings with many of Benezet's works. Wesley, a prolific writer of hymns, ended *Thoughts* with the third of four verses found in his "Hymn 432," originally written in 1758 but published as part of a collection of 525 hymns in 1779. In 1781 he gave it the title *For the Heathens*: "The servile progeny of Ham, Seize as the purchase of thy blood; Let all the heathens know thy name; From idol to the living God, The dark Americans convert, And shine in every pagan heart." John Wesley, *The Works of John Wesley*, vol. 7, *A Collection of Hymns,* ed. Franz Hildebrandt and Oliver A. Beckerlegge (Oxford: Clarendon Press, 1983), 609.

99. Olaudah Equiano, *The Interesting Narrative of the Life of Olaudah Equiano or Gustavus Vassa, the African, Written by Himself,* ed. Werner Sollors (New York: Norton, 2001), quoted on p. 20, discussion of Benezet in the introduction, pp. xvi–xix.

100. Wesley, *Thoughts upon Slavery,* 12. For example, Benezet calls Brüe "the principal factor to the French African Company, who lived 16 years in that country"; Wesley simply says Brüe "lived sixteen years in that country."

101. Benezet, *A Caution and a Warning* , 22; Wesley, *Thoughts upon Slavery*, 11–12.

102. Granville Sharp to Anthony Benezet, January 7, 1774, Haverford College Quaker Collection. See also Anstey, *Atlantic Slave Trade and British Abolition,* 240, and Smith, *John Wesley and Slavery,* 98.

103. Benezet to Wesley, May 23, 1774, Haverford College Quaker Collection. See also Brookes, *Friend Anthony Benezet,* 318.

104. Wesley's biographer Warren Thomas Smith summed up Benezet's intentions quite nicely. He wrote, "It is interesting that Benezet rushed to get *Thoughts upon Slavery* into print in America. It appears he had few qualms about adding his own notes and other materials." Smith concluded, "Of course, he might have said the same about Wesley's use of his material." Smith, *John Wesley and Slavery,* 99.

105. Wesley, *Thoughts upon Slavery* (reprinted in Philadelphia, with notes, and sold by Joseph Crukshank, 1774); Wesley, *Works of John Wesley,* vol. 11, "Thoughts upon Slavery."

106. Anonymous, *A Supplement to Mr. Wesley's Pamphlet Entitled* Thoughts upon Slavery (London: H. Reynell, 1774), 2, 107.

107. An African Merchant, *A Treatise upon the Trade from Great-Britain to Africa* (London, 1772).

108. Sollors, *Interesting Narrative of Olaudah Equiano,* 90. John Wesley, letter to William Wilberforce, February 24, 1791, in *Letters of John Wesley,* ed. John Teoford (London: Epworth Press, 1931), vol. 7, 264–65.

109. Olaudah Equiano, *The Interesting Narrative of the Life of Olaudah Equiano Written by Himself,* edited with an introduction by Robert J. Allison (Boston: Bedford Books of St. Martin's Press, 1995), 152.

110. Anthony Benezet to John Wesley, May 23, 1774, Haverford College Quaker Collection. Benezet had had an earlier public confrontation with another SPG member, William Knox. See Tise, *Proslavery*, 22.

111. Smith, *John Wesley and Slavery*, 66; *Journal of John Wesley*, vol.7, 7; Vaux, *Memoirs of the Life of Anthony Benezet*, 45; Anthony Benezet to John Wesley, May 5, 1774, and Anthony Benezet to John Wesley, May 23, 1774, Haverford College Quaker Collection. See also reprint of letter in *Arminian Magazine* 10 (1787), in Brookes, *Friend Anthony Benezet*, 318, 321.

112. In one of the North Carolina papers an ad read, "Run away last November from the subscriber, Kent River, a Negro-fellow, named Zeb, aged 36 years. As he is outlawed; I will pay £20 out of what the Act of Assembly allows in such cases, to any person who shall produce his head severed from his body, and £5, if brought home alive." Benezet makes the reader aware that as long as the master would get reimbursed for mistreated and murdered slaves, he would continue to treat them as disposable property. Anthony Benezet to John Wesley, May 5, 1774, Haverford College Quaker Collection.

113. Anthony Benezet to George Dillwyn, August 5, 1773.

114. Benezet, *Observations on Slavery*, 32; *Notes on the Slave Trade*, 1.

115. Wesley, *Thoughts upon the Slave Trade*, 2nd ed. (London, 1774), 24; Benezet, *Notes on the Slave Trade*, 4.

116. Wesley, *Thoughts upon the Slave Trade* (Philadelphia, 1774), 10–14, 52.

117. Wesley, *Thoughts upon the Slave Trade*, 23; Benezet, Observations on Slavery, 32–33; Benezet, *Notes on the Slave Trade*, 1–2.

118. Wesley, *Thoughts upon the Slave Trade*, 25–26; Benezet, *Observations on Slavery*, 37; Benezet, *Notes on the Slave Trade*, 6.

119. Wesley, *Thoughts upon the Slave Trade*, 26; Benezet, *Observations on Slavery*, 38; Benezet, *Notes on the Slave Trade*, 7.

120. Wesley, *Thoughts upon the Slave Trade*, 27; Benezet, *Observations on Slavery*, 38–39; Benezet, *Notes on the Slave Trade*, 7–8.

121. Irv A. Brendlinger has written extensively about John Wesley and slavery. See Brendlinger, "A Study of the Views of the Major Eighteenth Century Evangelicals on Slavery and Race, with Special Reference to John Wesley" (Ph.D. diss., University of Edinburgh, 1982); Brendlinger, "John Wesley and Slavery: Myth and Reality," unpublished. "Anthony Benezet, the True Champion of the Slave," in Paul N. Anderson and Howard R. Macy, eds., *Truth's Bright Embrace: Essays in Honor of Arthur O. Roberts* (Newberg, Ore.: George Fox University Press, 1996), 81–99; Brendlinger, *To Be Silent Would Be Criminal* (Lanham, Md.: Scarecrow Press, 2007).

122. Wesley, *Thoughts upon the Slave Trade*, 27; Benezet, *Observations on Slavery*, 39; Benezet, *Notes on the Slave Trade*, 8.

123. Benezet, *A Caution and a Warning*, 41; *Some Historical Account of Guinea* (Philadelphia, 1772), 129–30, and (London, 1788), 108–109). Quobna Ottobah Cugoano, *Thoughts and Sentiments on the Evils of Slavery*, edited and with an introduction and notes by Vincent Carretta (New York: Penguin Classics, 1999), 75–76 (original publication, London, 1787).

124. Gomer Williams, *History of Liverpool Privateers, and the Letters of Marquee, with an Account of the Liverpool Slave Trade* (London: William Heinemann, 1897), 674.

125. Ibid., 473–74. Based on his compilations, Williams drew up the chart on p. 678, which appears in the appendix to Chapter 5. In one of the few references to the *Liverpool Memorandum Book* by another writer, Gomer Williams noted, "We find, for instance, in the returns, that 58 vessels cleared for Africa in the year 1752, but from *Williamson's Memorandum Book*, published in 1753, we know that in 1752, Liverpool possessed no less than 88 vessels employed in the African trade, all of which,

with one exception, carried slaves. . . . From the same *Memorandum Book,* we learn that there were in Liverpool, in the year 1752, 1,901 merchants, who were members of the Company trading to Africa, established by an Act of Parliament in 1750. . . . In the same year there were in London, 135 African merchants, and in Bristol 157, though the African trade of the latter was less extensive than that of Liverpool." Williams, *History of Liverpool Privateers,* 472–73.

126. Elizabeth Donnan, *Documents Illustrative of the History of the Slave Trade: Volume II The Eighteenth Century* (Washington, D.C.: Carnegie Institute of Washington, 1931), vol. 2 (for the years 1752–53), 488–507. One document that examined the Liverpool slave trade was a petition of Matthew and John Stronge. The petition is directed "To the Right Honorable William Pitt, Esq., His Majesty's Principal Secretary of State. The letter shows that Matthew and John Stronge had fitted out a Snow called *Clayton* of Liverpool for the African Trade which sailed from the River Bonny in Africa on the 22nd of February 1752 having on Board 324 Slaves bound to the West Indies. There was mutiny aboard ship, and the chief mate was forced to steer it towards Pernambuco in Brazil. When the ship reached port, the Portuguese took Possession of the Ship and Secured the Nine Pirates. The captain of the ship then sold the slaves who now numbered only about 200 because of sickness and death. The Stronges, who also represented other merchants of Liverpool, petitioned Pitt so that the said Pirates might be Delivered up to him to be sent to England and Tried and Punished and that the Balance of the Sale of the Slaves might be Paid to him for the Benefit of your Petitioners."

127. By a Geniune "Dicky Sam," *Liverpool and Slavery* (Liverpool: A. Bowker and Son, 1884), 119. See "The Company of Merchants Trading in Africa: June 24, 1752," in Donnan, *Documents Illustrative of the History of the Slave Trade: Volume II,* 492–93.

128. Gail Cameron and Stan Cooke, *Liverpool, Capital of the Slave Trade* (Liverpool: Birkenhead Press, 1992), 1. One of the early historians of the port city, J. Wallace wrote in 1795 in *A General and Descriptive History of the Ancient and Present State of the Town of Liverpool* that "so early as the year 1744 she (Liverpool) employed more than one half of the vessels engaged in that branch of commerce (the slave trade) and imported annually from Africa more than one half of the slaves purchased by all the vessels of Great Britain." Wallace also gave a very apt summary to the role of Liverpool in the slave trade, one that Benezet would have agreed with: "Almost every man in Liverpool is a merchant, and he who cannot send a bale will send a bandbox. . . . Almost every order of people is interested in a Guinea cargo. It is well known that many of the small vessels that import about a hundred slaves are fitted out by attorneys, drapers, ropers, grocers, tallow-chandlers, barbers, tailors, etc. Some have one eighth, some a fifteenth, and some a thirty-second" (1, 11).

129. Benezet, *Some Historical Account of Guinea,* 108. The *Liverpool Memorandum Book* does not turn up in any of the listings of early libraries in Philadelphia nor in the present Library of Congress or the British Museum, so I have not been able to consult the original.

130. Benezet, *Some Historical Account of Guinea* (1772), chap. 13, 130.

131. Comparing Benezet's, Cugoano's, Snelgrave's, and Philmore's figures with those of Philip Curtin and earlier ones by Elizabeth Donnan, we find a quite similar estimation. Philip D. Curtin, *The Atlantic Slave Trade: A Census* (Madison: University of Wisconsin Press, 1969), 158 and throughout. Curtin has been praised for his prodigious methodological approach and criticized because of what many have seen as low estimates of those taken into slavery. Ira Berlin, *New Generations of Captivity: A History of African-American Slaves* (Cambridge, Mass.: Harvard University Press,

2003), 271–79; Davis, "New Sidelights on Early Antislavery Radicalism," 593; Donnan, *Documents Illustrative of the History of the Slave Trade*, 4 vols; Wood, *Black Majority*. J. Philmore, *Two Dialogues on the Man-Trade* (London: J. Waugh, 1760) and extracts attached at end of Benezet, *A Short Account of That Part of Africa Inhabited by the Negroes*, 2nd ed., with Large Additions and Amendments (Philadelphia: W. Dunlap, 1762). 3 eds. in 1762, one in 1763 and 1768. London: 1768. Dublin: 1768. Paris: 1767, 1788.

132. Clarkson, *History of the Abolition of the African Slave-Trade*, vol. 1, 167–68, 207.

133. Thomas Clarkson, *An Essay on the Slavery and Commerce of the Human Species, Particularity the African*, translated from a (Prize) Latin dissertation (London, 1786).

134. Thomas Clarkson, *An Essay on the Impolicy of the Slave Trade, in Two Parts* (London, 1786), p. x.

135. Clarkson, *History of the Abolition of the African Slave-Trade*, vol. 1, 207–208. Papers of Thomas Clarkson from the British Library, London, Fair Minute Books of the Committee for the Abolition of the Slave Trade, 22 May 1787–9 July 1819.

136. James Walvin, "Abolishing the Slave Trade: Anti-Slavery and Popular Radicalism, 1776–1807," in *Artisans, Peasants and Proletarians, 1760–1860*, ed. Clive Emsley and James Walvin (London: Dawson Press, 1980), 152.

137. Clarkson, *Essay on the Impolicy of the African Slave Trade*, 53.

138. Rediker, *The Slave Ship*, chapter 10.

139. Jennings, *Business of Abolishing the British Slave Trade*, 22.

140. Davis, *Problem of Slavery in Age of Revolution*, 224. Drescher attributed the pamphlet to Benezet. Another Quaker Joseph Woods has also been credited with helping to write the pamphlet. He had written opposing Hume's ideas on slavery and blacks.

141. *The Case of Our Fellow-Creatures, the Oppressed Africans, Respectfully Recommended to the Serious Consideration of the Legislature of Great-Britain, Buy the People Called Quakers* (London: James Phillips, 1784), 15, 16.

142. Brown, *Moral Capital*, 266. Both Drescher (*Capitalism and Antislavery*, 63) and Brown write that the pamphlet drew no response.

143. Clarkson, *History of the Abolition of the African Slave-Trade*, vol. 1, chap. 10, 243–58.

144. Ibid., vol. 1, 256. The members were Granville Sharp, William Dillwyn, Samuel Hoare, George Harrison, John Lloyd, Joseph Woods, Thomas Clarkson, Richard Phillips, John Barton, Joseph Hooper, James Philips, and Philip Sampson.

145. Ibid., vol. 1, 249.

146. Brown, *Moral Capital*, 24.

147. "To William Wilberforce," London, February 24, 1791, in Eayrs, *Letters of John Wesley*, 489–90.

148. Irv A. Brendlinger has added to the study of Wesley and his antislavery views. In his compilations of a few of Benezet's letters and writings he included a letter that Wesley wrote to Samuel Hoare on August 18, 1787. Brendlinger correctly notes that Benezet had a profound influence on Wesley and that the letter to Hoare bore Benezet's stamp as did Wesley's 1791 letter to Wilberforce. John Wesley to Samuel Hoare, quoted from *The Letters of John Wesley, A.M*, ed. John Telford, standard edition (London: Epworth Press, 1872), vol. 8, 275, in Irv A. Brendlinger, *To Be Silent Would Be Criminal: The Antislavery Influence and Writings of Anthony Benezet* (Lanham, Md.: Scarecrow Press, 2007), 113–114. Wesley's letter to Wilberforce is also published in *Letters of John Wesley*, vol. 8, 264–265, February 24–25; see also Irv A. Brendlinger, "A Study of the Views of Major Eighteenth Century Evangelicals on Slavery and Race," Ph.D. dissertation (Edinburgh, 1982). The thesis offers a look at the ideas of William Wilberforce, John Newton, Thomas Clarkson, James Ramsey, Granville Sharp, Anthony Benezet, and John Wesley.

149. George Eayrs, ed., *Letters of John Wesley: A Selection of Important and New Letters* (London: Hodder and Stoughton, 1915), 489.

150. *The Annual Register or a View of the History, Politics, and Literature for the Year 1791*(London: Dodsley's Annual Register,) 243–46.

151. *The Debate on a Motion for the Abolition of the Slave Trade, 2nd April 1792 in the House of Commons, Wilberforce and Pitt Present*, 4–5 (Parliamentary Debates, British Library, London). See also for 1791 debates, Hazard Pamphlets, Debate, vol. 70, no. 1, *Speech of William Wilberforce,* and Hazard Pamphlets, vol. 70, no. 7, *Debate on a Motion for the Abolition of the Slave-Trade* (Great Britain, Parliament, Library of Congress, Rare Book Collection, Washington, D.C.).

152. Parliamentary Debates, 12.

153. The reference is to Frances Moore, cited by Benezet on p. 24 of *A Short Account of That Part of Africa.*

154. Parliamentary Debates, 18; Benezet's *Some Historical Account of Guinea*, 112–13.

155. Parliamentary Debates, 33; Benezet's *A Caution and a Warning*, 18.

156. Parliamentary Debates, 40.

157. Ibid., 14. Charles Stuart, *A Memoir of Granville Sharp: To Which is added Sharp's "Law of Passive Resistance," and an Extract from His "Law of Retribution"* (New York: American Anti-Slavery Society, 1836), 53.

158. Ibid., 40. In 1792 the U.S. Congress passed a law that only "free able-bodied white male citizens" could enlist in the militias in peacetime. This ruling included those who had fought in the Revolutionary War and their descendants. Gail Buckley, *American Patriots: The Story of Blacks in the Military from the Revolution to Desert Storm* (New York: Random House, 2001), 48.

159. Parliamentary Debates, 40.

160. Dresher writes that "the Privy Council and Parliamentary hearings on the slave trade between 1788 and 1792, like public out of doors, represented a paradigmatic leap in the relationship between the British metropolis and the Atlantic Slave System." Dresher, *Capitalism and Antislavery*, 88.

161. Metaxas, *Amazing Grace*. David Crystal, ed., *The Cambridge Biographical Encyclopedia*, 2nd ed. (Cambridge: Cambridge University Press, 1999).

Chapter 7. Benezet and the Development of the Antislavery Movement in France

1. Henri Grégoire, *An Enquiry Concerning the Intellectual and Moral Facilities, and Literature of Negroes*, new edition with an introduction by Graham Russell Hodges, trans. David Bailie Warden (1810; repr., Armonk, N.Y.: M. E. Sharpe, 1997), xxv. Among the Englishmen, in addition to Sharp and Wesley, we find those we would associate with America, such as Benjamin Lay and John Woolman.

2. Ibid., 111–12.

3. Edward Seeber offers a full description of such sources in chapter 2 of *Anti-Slavery Opinion in France During the Second Half of the Eighteenth Century* (Baltimore: Johns Hopkins University Press, 1937), 87. *Oroonoko* was first translated into French in 1745, with later editions in 1751 and 1756 and a fourth, illustrated edition in 1769. Three later editions appeared in 1779, 1788, and 1799.

4. *Avertissement à La Grande-Bretagne et à ses colonies, ou Tableau abrégé de l'état misérable des Nègres esclaves dans les dominations anglaise*, in Edward Seeber, *Anti-Slavery Opinion in France*, 85; Benezet, *Short Account of That Part of Africa.*

5. William B. Cohen argues Benezet was "an American Quaker of French origin, who was closely read in France." Cohen, *The French Encounter with Africans: White Response to Blacks, 1530–1880* (Bloomington: Indiana University Press, 1980), 152.

6. Guillaume-Thomas Raynal, *Histoire philosophique et politique, des establissemens &*

du commerce des Européens dans les deux Indes (Paris, 1772, 1774, 1780, 1781, 1783, 1784); *A Philosophical and Political History of the Settlements and Trade of the Europeans in the East and West Indies* (London: W. Strahan, 1783); Hans-Jürgen Lüsebrink and Manfred Tietz, introduction to *Lectures de Raynal,* vol. 286 of *Studies on Voltaire and the Eighteenth Century* (Oxford: Oxford University Press, 1991), 3. Lüsebrink and Tietz write that Raynal's associates and contemporaries referred to him as *l'apôtre de la liberté. Apôtre* can be translated as apostle, advocate, or leader.

7. Sue Peabody, *"There Are No Slaves in France": The Political Culture of Race and Slavery in the Ancien Régime* (New York: Oxford University Press, 1996), 101.

8. *Voltaire's Letters on the Quakers: A Critical Translation,* trans. and ed. Wilson Frescoln (Philadelphia: William A. Allen, 1953), 18; Seeber, *Anti-Slavery Opinion in France,* 85; Edith Phillips, *The Good Quaker in French Legend* (Philadelphia: University of Pennsylvania Press, 1932), 43ff.

9. Seeber, *Anti-Slavery Opinion in France,* 87. The letter incorrectly stated that the Quakers had voted in the assembly for general emancipation. This historical inaccuracy became the basis for many French writers' notations of 1769 as a turning point in antislavery activism in America.

10. Peabody, *"There Are No Slaves in France,"* 4.

11. Edoardo Tortarolo, "La réception de *l'Histoire des deux Indes* aux Etats-Unis," *Lectures de Raynal,* vol. 333 of *Studies on Voltaire and the Eighteenth Century,* 305.

12. Grégoire, *An Enquiry,* 16.

13. Tortarolo, "La réception de *l'Histoire des deux Indes,*" 316.

14. Guillaume-Thomas Raynal, *A Philosophical and Political History of the Settlements,* vol. 2 (London: W. Strahan, 1783). Raynal also published *Révolution d'Amérique* in 1781. In the 1760s Raynal began collecting sources and compiling what would become his most famous work, *L'Histoire des deux Indes.* The first edition appeared as a seven-volume work in 1770, followed by a second edition in 1774; the third addition appeared as a ten-volume work in 1780. Raynal published the first two editions anonymously in order to avoid personal repercussions by the French government's condemnation of the book. By the third edition Raynal took the bold step of publishing the work under his name and included a portrait of himself on the front cover. To escape an inevitable arrest, Raynal went into exile and spent his time traveling, passing through Liège and the court of Frederick II in Berlin. In 1785 Raynal gained permission to return to France on the condition that he not leave the regions of Languedoc and Provence.

15. Raynal, *Philosophical and Political History of the Settlements,* vol. 2, 314–15.

16. Anthony Benezet, *Short Observations on Slavery, Introductory Remarks to Some Extracts from the Writing of the Abbé Raynal on That Important Subject* (Philadelphia: John Crukshank, 1781, 1782).

17. Benezet, *Short Observations on Slavery,* 7. Just as Raynal laid out in a brief paragraph the intent of each chapter, so did Benezet in *Some Historical Account of Guinea.* While Benezet did not organize most of his other works like this, the format was quite common in the narratives that both he and Raynal used as source materials.

18. Paul Benhamou, "La diffusion de *l'Histoire des deux Indes* en Amérique (1770–1820)," in *Raynal, de la polémique à l'histoire,* ed. Gilles Bancarel and Gianluigi Goggi, *Studies on Voltaire and the Eighteenth Century* (Oxford: Voltaire Foundation, 2000), 301–7.

19. Bancarel and Goggi, *Raynal, de la polémique à l'histoire,* 11–14. Notably, Raynal maintained contacts and acquaintances in the offices of the royal administration, the office of the Minister of Foreign Affairs, and in the colonial bureau. Specifically, his relationships with Pierre Malouet, commissaire of Saint-Domingue, and Jean Dubuc, head clerk of the colonial bureau, granted Raynal access to unedited

administrative documents concerning the gradual abolition of slavery. Near the end of his life Raynal prepared an additional set of questions, which he had intended to send through the French diplomatic corps to gather statistics for the revision of his book.

20. Michèle Duchet, "L'Histoire des deux Indes: Sources et structure d'un texte polyphonique," *Lectures de Raynal*, 10.

21. Hans-Jürgen Lüsebrink and Anthony Strugnell, introduction to *L'Histoire des deux Indes: récriture et polygraphie*, vol. 333 of *Studies on Voltaire and the Eighteenth Century* (Oxford: Oxford University Press, 1995), 2. Lüsebrink draws a distinction between these "transversal" sources and the "vertical" sources, contributing mainly to the descriptions of geography, botany, and the economy. The "transversal" sources may have included Abbé Prévost, author of *Histoire générale des voyages*; A. L. de Jussieu, author of *Universal History, from the Earliest Account of Time*; and above all Denis Diderot. *L'Histoire des deux Indes* reflected the style of Diderot's *L'Encyclopédie* in that it functioned as a compilation of contemporary information and thinking.

22. Lüsebrink and Strugnell, introduction to *L'Histoire des deux Indes*, 15.

23. Gianluigi Goggi, "Quelques remarques sur la collaboration de Diderot à la première édition de *L'Histoire des deux Indes*," in *Lectures de Raynal*, 17–51. While Diderot's contributions to the third edition are not debated, his contributions to the first edition are.

24. Seeber, *Anti-Slavery Opinion in France*, 62. While such passages show clearly that Raynal drew on Diderot, it is not known whether Diderot was personally involved in the writing of the first and second editions or whether he first contributed in the drafting of the third edition. Historian Jean-Claude Halpren suggests that Diderot may have been the cause of essential changes in the depiction of Africans between the first and third editions. To offer descriptions of Africa and Africans, Raynal relied first on the travel writings of Abbé Prévost, Abbé Demanet, and Abbé Proyart, who wrote his *Histoire de Loango* in 1776.

25. Raynal, *Philosophical and Political History of the Settlements*, 238.

26. Goggi, "Quelques remarques," 35; Blackburn, *Overthrow of Colonial Slavery*, 53. The revolutionary content of the passages on slavery in *L'Histoire* have led to speculation that Jean de Pechméja, an early utopian socialist, wrote them. In fact, some of the more inflammatory remarks attributed to Pechméja in the extreme antislavery message were eventually removed. He wrote that "whoever justifies so odious a system deserves scornful silence from the philosopher and a stab with the poniard from the Negro." Quoted in Davis, *Problem of Slavery in Western Culture*, 418. Blackburn notes that the 1781 edition of *L'Histoire* offered the possibility of gradual independence: "Pechmeja's extreme anti-slavery passages were retained as a warning of what might happen if moderate reform was not adopted" (Blackburn, *Overthrow of Colonial Slavery*, 170). Diderot is attributed with having revised some passages on slavery for the third edition.

27. Hans-Jürgen Lüsebrink, "La réception de l'Adresse à l'Assemblée nationale," in Bancarel and Goggi, *Raynal, de la polémique à l'histoire*, 337. For example, on June 4, 1791, only days after the delivery of Raynal's letter, the journal *Le Patriote français* attributed "le fameux morceau sur l'esclavage" to Pechméja. Likewise, the journal *Nouvelles extraordinaires* wrote on June 14 that the true authorship of *L'Histoire* had already come into question and that Raynal's letter only served to reenforce and legitimize these doubts.

28. Blackburn, *Overthrow of Colonial Slavery*, 54, quoting Raynal, *A Philosophical and Political History of the Settlements and Trade of the Europeans in the East and West Indies*, 2nd ed. (London, 1776), vol. 3, 466–67. This passage derives from the sec-

ond French edition of 1774. The historian Hans Wolpe extensively studied the changes made between the various editions of *L'Histoire* and argued that the omission of Pechméja's volatile writing grew out of stylistic changes. For the third edition of *L'Histoire*, Raynal also employed the help of de Jussieu and Diderot to elaborate his typology of Africans. Diderot's insistence on this point reflected the endeavor, first pursued by eighteenth-century philosophers to—according to T. Carlos Jacques—"develop a science of Man which aspired to be fully inclusive of all peoples, including foreigners." See T. Carlos Jacques, "From Savages and Barbarians to Primitives: Africa, Social Typologies, and History in Eighteenth-Century French Philosophy," *History and Theory* 36, no. 2 (May 1997): 197. Jacques shows, however, that a belief in the common humanity of man that is shaped by circumstance easily gave rise to a belief in the power of Europeans to transform African societies. Ironically, the same ideas that gave abolitionism a new theoretical foundation would pave the way for colonialism.

Black leaders in the nineteenth and early twentieth centuries also came to respect Raynal. Maria Stewart, the black abolitionist, feminist, and orator whose works were reported in William Lloyd Garrison's *Liberator,* borrowed the words of Raynal in an address given at the African Masonic Hall in Boston on February 27, 1833. She echoed Raynal's words in speaking of the departed David Walker and indirectly of Toussaint: "but where is the man that has distinguished himself in the modern days by acting wholly in the defense of African rights and liberty. There was one, although he sleeps, his memory lives." Maria Stewart, "Address at the African Mason Hall," February 27, 1833, in *Productions of Mrs. Maria W. Stewart, Presented to the First African Baptist Church and Society, of the City of Boston* (Boston: Friends of Freedom and Virtue, 1835).

A generation later, William J. Simmons, the son of slaves, a graduate of Howard University, and a Civil War veteran published *Men of Mark: Eminent, Progressive and Rising* in 1887 (rept., Chicago: Johnson Publishing, 1970). Simmons was also a black writer, educator, and biographer. His was the first biographical dictionary of blacks, the majority of whom were born under slavery. He noted that "there was a French author called Abbé Raynal who was much opposed to slavery. One of his books fell into the hands of Toussaint and made a deep impression upon him. . . . the question was discussed in that book, what should be done to overthrow slavery" (666).

Anna Julia Cooper wrote her University of Paris doctoral thesis on slavery in France and Haiti in 1925. She was a rarity in the field because she was not only a black woman, but also sixty-six years old at the time. In her subsequent book, *Slavery and the French Revolutionists (1788–1805)*, she wrote that "Montesquieu, Rousseau, Voltaire, Filangieri and Raynal thundered against slavery," and she praised Condorcet, Grégoire, and the "Friends of the Blacks." *Slavery and the French Revolutionists (1788–1805)*, translated with a foreword and introductory essay by Frances Richardson Keller (Lewiston, N.Y.: Edwin Mellen Press, 1988), 35, 62–66.

29. Seeber, *Anti-Slavery Opinion in France,* 72. Raynal also added a radical commentary on the Code Noir, the edict of Louis XIV issued in 1685, which was subsequently revised in 1745, 1767, and 1788: "Then the Code Noir will disappear; and then the Code Blanc will be terrible if the victor relies only on the law of revenge." Taking examples from Raynal's other writings, Seeber shows that not only did Raynal believe that black labor was needed in the French colonies but also that Africans came closer to the life of reasoned men by going to the colonies than by staying in their native lands. Seeber concludes that considering these pragmatic complexities, Raynal's opposition to slavery was fundamentally philosophical and he conceived of the practice as a violation of the natural rights of man.

30. Daniel P. Resnick, "The Société des Amis des Noirs and the Abolition of Slavery," *French Historical Studies* 7, no. 4 (Autumn 1972): 566.

31. Resnick, "Société des Amis des Noirs," 565–66. Resnick writes that "when Mirabeau wanted a model of a slave ship, he had it made to specifications of the English ship *Brooks,* instead of finding a French example to dramatize France's own complicity." He cites that "in the twelve-volume collection of pamphlets of the Amis des Noirs . . . no cross-section or plan of a French slave ship appeared in the collection, nor was one ever produced by the society" (566, n. 25, and 563, n. 14); Curtin, *Atlantic Slave Trade,* 282–86; Perry Viles, "The Slaving Interest in the Atlantic Ports, 1763–1792," *French Historical Studies* 7, no. 4 (Autumn 1972): 529–43. Marcus Rediker gives a wonderful history of the *Brooks* in *The Slave Ship,* chap. 10.

32. Tortarolo, "La réception de l'Histoire des deux Indes," 305.

33. Davis, "New Sidelights on Early Antislavery Radicalism," 590. Davis often minimizes the work of Benezet, preferring to emphasize the impact of Woolman. See, for example, his epilogue, "John Woolman's Prophecy," in *Problem of Slavery in Western Culture,* 483–93.

34. Davis, "New Sidelights on Early Antislavery Radicalism," 590.

35. Ibid., 590–91. Davis does note of Benezet's *A Caution and a Warning* that "in 1767 this pamphlet was reprinted in England and translated into French" (591).

36. Ibid., 591.

37. Alfred Owen Aldridge, *Franklin and His French Contemporaries* (Westport, Conn.: Greenwood Press, 1976), 23.

38. Franklin shared with Benezet his ideas concerning philosophical concepts. He sent Benezet a packet that included "a little System of Morals that may give distinct Ideas on that Subject of Youth." He then told Benezet that if he agreed with the general concepts in the book, "I will send you more if you desire it." Benjamin Franklin to Anthony Benezet, February 10, 1773, in Smyth, *Writings of Benjamin Franklin* (1906), vol. 6, 9; Franklin was referring to Jacques Barbeu Dubourg's "Petit Code de l'Humanite." Benjamin Franklin to Barbeu Dubourg, London, June 1, 1772, in Aldridge, *Franklin and His French Contemporaries,* 25–26.

39. Tortarolo, "La réception de *l'Histoire des deux Indes,*" 315.

40. Anthony Benezet to Abbé Raynal, July 16, 1781, Haverford College Quaker Collection.

41. Richard Baxter, *Baxter's Directions to Slave-holders, revived: first printed in London, in the year 1673. To which is subjoined, a letter from the worthy Anthony Benezet, late of this city, deceased, to the celebrated abbe Raynal, with his answer, which were first published in the Brussels gazette, March 7, 1782* (Philadelphia: Francis Bailey, 1785), 9–10.

42. Abbé Raynal to Anthony Benezet, December 26, 1781, Haverford College Quaker Collection.

43. Davis, "New Sidelights on Early Antislavery Radicalism," 591.

44. Seeber, *Anti-Slavery Opinion in France,* 123.

45. Resnick, "Société des Amis des Noirs and the Abolition of Slavery," 560. See also Eloise Ellery, *Brissot de Warville: A Study in the History of the French Revolution* (Boston, 1915), 442–47; C. Perroud, "La Société française des Amis des Noirs," *Révolution française* 79 (1916): 122–47; "La Société française des Amis des Noirs et Condorcet," *Révolution française* 50 (1906): 481–511. The rules and preamble are all included in Jean-Antoine-Nicolas de Caritat, marquis de Condorcet, *Condorcet, Foundations of Social Choice and Political Theory,* trans. and ed. Ian McLean and Fiona Hewitt (Brookfield, Vt.: Edward Elgar, 1994), 341–59. Étienne Clavière (1735–93), the Swiss-born financier, on March 8, 1788, read a lengthy statement outlining the purpose of the newly founded Société. He had developed a close friendship with Mirabeau and often helped him prepare his speeches. Clavière was also a close

confidant of Brissot, whom he had first met in London. In his statement he delineated the role and nature of universal reason and praised the founding members on their work and emulation of the Quakers. He said that "in order that Liberty be given to the Blacks in the French possessions; not by slavish imitation [of the Quakers] but by a reasoned conviction which will make of that liberty a present given with as much joy as it is received." Quoted in Marcel Dorigny and Bernard Gainot, *La Société des Amis des Noirs* (Paris: UNESCO, 1998), 129. Clavière wrote to the Pennsylvania Abolition Society in 1788 that the French had again followed their lead and founded a society to end slavery in the colonies. Continuing his work with Brissot, Clavière coauthored with him *De la France et des Etats-Unis* in 1787. Clavière who prepared the final drafts of one of the last publications of the Société titled *Adresse de la Société des Amis des Noirs à l'Assemblée nationale . . . dans laquelle on approfondit les relations politiques et commerciales entre la Métropole et les Colonies.*

Honoré Gabriel Riqueti, comte de Mirabeau (1749–1791), was born into a family that had been ennobled in 1685. As a member of the newly formed Constituent Assembly he had raised questions about the denial and lack of black representation and asked why the whites in St. Domingue had such a large number of seats. He found that slaves were counted as humans for representational purposes (of course without a vote). This state of affairs no doubt satisfied not only the colonists in the Antilles but also those in North America some years before the Dred Scott decision. Lafayette, Grégoire, and several others joined Mirabeau in his mission demanding mulatto representation. He proclaimed in language that C. L. R. James admired and that Robin Blackburn believes echoed the debates of the U.S. Constitutional Convention: "You claim representation proportionate to the number of inhabitants. The free Blacks are proprietors and tax payers, and yet they have not been allowed to vote. And as for the slaves, either they are men or they are not; if the colonists consider them men, let them free them and make them electors and eligible for seats; if the contrary is the case, have we, in apportioning deputies according to the populating of France, taken into consideration the number of our horses and mules." Quoted in C. L. R. James, *The Black Jacobins: Toussaint L'Ouverture and the San Domingo Revolution* (New York: Vintage, 1962), 60; quoted also in Blackburn, *Overthrow of Colonial Slavery,* 174.

46. J. P. Brissot de Warville, *An Oration upon the Necessity of Establishing at Paris, a Society to Promote the Abolition of the Slave Trade and Slavery of the Negroes* (Philadelphia, 1788), 140–41, 154. See also Davis, *Problem of Slavery in Age of Revolution,* 95.

47. Jean-Pierre Brissot de Warville, *New Travels in the U.S.A., 1788,* trans. Mara Soceanu Vamos and ed. Durand Echeverria (Cambridge, Mass.: Harvard University Press, 1964), 239.

48. Seeber, *Anti-Slavery Opinion in France,* 165.

49. Brissot, *New Travels,* 218 ("Letter 21, The School for Negroes in Philadelphia—American Authors Who Have Written in Defense of Negroes").

50. Ibid.

51. Ibid.

52. Brissot, *New Travels,* 203. Chastellux had praised George Fox but had little to say in a positive light about Quakers. Fox, he wrote, went to "Barbados in 1671, not to preach against the slave trade or against slavery, but to bring Negroes to the knowledge of God and to urge their masters to treat them more kindly." Brissot noted that "in those days, however, men's minds were not yet ready for reform" (219).

53. Ibid., 230. General Thomas Mifflin was the speaker of the Pennsylvania assembly.

54. The Society for the Relief of Free Negroes Unlawfully Held in Bondage was

first founded in Philadelphia in 1775 by Benezet and others. It was revised in 1784, the year of Benezet's death. In 1787 it was reorganized into the Pennsylvania Society for Promoting the Abolition of Slavery, the Relief of Free Negroes Unlawfully Held in Bondage and for Improving the Condition of the African Race. The London Society for the Abolition of the Slave Trade was organized in 1787. Its president was Granville Sharp.

55. Benezet, *Short Observations on Slavery*, 3.

56. Brissot, *New Travels*, 217–18.

57. Marquis de Chastellux, *Travels in North America in the Years 1780, 1781 and 1782*, revised translation with introduction and notes by Howard C. Rice, Jr. (1786; repr., Chapel Hill: University of North Carolina Press, 1963), vol. 1, 235–43.

58. Ibid., vol. 1, 165.

59. Benezet's *A Short Account of the People Called Quakers: Their Rise, Religious Principles and Settlements in America, Mostly Collected from Different Authors for the Information of All Serious Inquirers, Particularly Foreigners* was published in France as *Observations sur l'orgine, les principles et l'etablissment en Amérique de la Société connue sous la denomination de Quakers ou Trembleurs*.

60. Chastellux, *Travels in North America*, vol. 1, 166; Phillips, *The Good Quaker in French Legend*. Benezet later informed the marquis of the dangers and costs of war and of the toll it took in human lives. Linking war with imprisonment and impoverishment, he cried that the war and its aftermath take "a hundred thousand livres a year. But that is enough to build his hospitals and establish manufactures; this doubtless is the use thy make of their riches." In the December 10, 1780, entry to his journal, a day after praising Benezet, Chastellux visited both Anglican and Quaker churches. He attacked the Quakers for their simple meeting places and for pedestrian services. He "arrived just after women had stopped talking. She was followed by a man who talked a great deal of nonsense about inner grace, the illumination of the spirit, and other dogma of his sect, which he kept repeating but avoided explaining." Describing the members as "inattentive and bored," it was obvious that Chastellux opposed the very principles the Quakers held so dear. By contrast he described an Anglican service that he attended describing it as a "sort of Opera, both became of the music and the scenery: a handsome pulpit placed before a handsome organ, a handsome minister in that pulpit, reading and speaking with truly theatrical grace."

61. In 1777 an anonymous Frenchman wrote a journal subsequently titled *On the Threshold of Liberty: Journal of a Frenchman's Tour of the American Colonies in 1777*, trans. Edward D. Seeber (Bloomington: Indiana University Press, 1959). It was originally published in 1918 by Eugène Griselle as *Revue du dix-huitième siècle* (Paris, 1918), 52–73. The narrator offers some interesting formulations about the blacks in the mainland colonies. At one point he writes that "only the Negroes do not enjoy this good fortune so deserved and so well earned by those who make the land fruitful and enrich their masters. Sold by those who snatched them from their homelands, they did not become slaves conditionally or for fixed terms like the whites sent over from Europe as punishment: they had no more help of becoming free then did their fellow blacks who cultivated the Antilles" (123).

62. J. Hector St. John Crèvecoeur, *Letters from an American Farmer*, ed. Susan Manning (Oxford: Oxford University Press, 1997), 153–54. Crèvecoeur was born Michel Guillaume Saint-Jean de Crèvecoeur in Caen, France, in 1735. He had lived in America since 1759. Sent to New France (Canada) in 1755 as a cadet in the French military contingent, he saw action in the French and Indian Wars and was promoted to lieutenant. After the war he stayed in America and worked as a cartographer. He became a citizen of the colony of New York in 1765 and spent the next

few years traveling, from Nova Scotia to Virginia and on the Mississippi, Appalachia, and Ohio rivers. As a naturalized New Yorker he purchased a large plot of land in Orange County and settled down to farm and later write. By now a married father of three, he saw his peaceful existence come to a halt with the events of 1776. Although some thought he was of Tory sentiment, the British arrested and imprisoned him in 1778, and the few possessions he had, including some of his first letters, were confiscated. He was finally released and allowed to board a ship to Europe, ending up in London in 1781. There, in 1782 he began arranging for the publication of his English edition of *Letters from an American Farmer*. Going to France the next year, he spent time in Caen to regain his health and found his way to Paris and a circle of intellectuals, among them Benjamin Franklin; the Physiocrats leader, Etienne-Francois Turgot; and Georges-Louis Leclerc de Buffon. He returned to New York in 1783 as the official representative of Louis XVI. *Letters* was dedicated to Abbé Raynal, whose *L' Histoire des deux Indes* he had greatly admired. French editions of his *Letters* were published in 1784. The French edition *Lettres d'un cultivateur américain* was expanded primarily because of Crèvecoeur's later discussion with other like-minded men.

63. Crèvecoeur, *Letters from an American Farmer*, 156.

64. Ibid., 157. Christopher Iannini, "'The Itinerant Man': Crèvecoeur's Caribbean, Raynal's Revolution, and the Fate of Atlantic Cosmopolitanism," *William and Mary Quarterly,* 3rd series, 61, no. 2 (April 2004): 201–34.

65. Crèvecoeur, *Letters from an American Farmer*, 156.

66. Benjamin Franklin to the marquis de Condorcet, London, March 20, 1774, in Smyth, *Writings of Benjamin Franklin*, vol. 6, 221–22.

67. Marie Jean Caritat, marquis de Condorcet, "Reflections on Negro Slavery," Lynn Hunt, ed. *The French Revolution and Human Rights, A Brief Documentary History* (Boston: Bedford, 1996), 55. See also Louis Sala-Molins, *Dark Side of the Light: Slavery and the French Enlightenment,* translated and with an introduction by John Conteh-Morgan (Minneapolis: University of Minnesota Press, 2006), chapter 1; Blackburn, *The Overthrow of Colonial Slavery,* 170–71.

68. Condorcet, "Rules for the Society of the Friends of Negroes (1788)," in Condorcet, *Foundations of Social Choice and Political Theory*, 341.

69. Ibid., 343. See also Richard Popkin, "Condorcet Abolitionists," in Lenora Cohen Rosenfield, ed., *Condorcet Studies*, 2 vols. (Atlantic Highlands, N.J.: Humanities Press, 1984–87) 1:35–48.

70. Ibid., 342–43.

71. Condorcet, "Part Five: Equality," in Condorcet, *Foundations of Social Choice and Political Theory*, 267. When the National Assembly met in 1789 and began to debate representation, the planters who lived in France but owned plantations in Saint-Domingue claimed representation based on the slave population. Using his prior arguments concerning proportional representation, Condorcet countered the planters' demand for twenty-one seats, telling them they were only entitled to two. The French lobby won the seat and organized themselves into the Club Massiac, the most vigilant adversaries of the Société.

72. Grégoire, *An Enquiry*, xi.

73. Ibid., xxv–xxvi. While the blacks are listed separately, there is no indication that Grégoire saw them as anything but equal to the others, who are listed not by race but by nationality, although in the eighteenth century people would often have considered the French and the British to be "races."

74. Benezet, *Short Account of That Part of Africa*, 12.

75. Grégoire, *An Enquiry*, 47.

76. James Albert Ukawsaw Gronniosaw, *A Narrative of the Most Remarkable Particu-*

lars in the Life of James Albert Ukawsaw Gronniosaw, an African Prince, As Related by Himself (1774).

77. Grégoire criticized the lack of mention of a large number of men, "in Suhm, the Puffendorf of the last century, not that of many national writers who merit distinction, such as Persini, Blarn, Jehan de Brie, John de Lois." Grégoire, *An Enquiry*, 111–12.

78. Grégoire, *An Enquiry*, 92. In the final parts of Grégoire's *Enquiry* he has three chapters, titled "Talents of the Negroe's for the arts and trades," "Literature of Negroes," and "Of Negroes' and Mulattoes distinguished by their talents and their works."

79. Thomas Jefferson, *Notes on the State of Virginia*, ed. William Peden (New York: Norton, 1954), xii, n. 1. An unauthorized edition of *Notes* was published privately in Paris in 1785, while the Jefferson-authorized edition appeared in London in 1787. There has been speculation that the questions may have in fact been drawn up by the French naturalist Buffon; François Barbé-Marbois, *Our Revolutionary Forefathers*, trans. and ed. Eugene Parker Chase (Freeport, N.Y.: Books for Libraries Press, 1969). Barbé-Marbois, who was the secretary of the French delegation at Philadelphia and was later to become French consul-general to the United States in 1781, had asked Jefferson in the form of several queries for information on various states. Barbé-Marbois had also written about Wheatley.

80. Henry Louis Gates, Jr., *The Trials of Phillis Wheatley: America's First Black Poet and Her Encounters with the Founding Fathers* (New York: Basic Books, 2003), 41, 42.

81. Jefferson, *Notes on the State of Virginia*, 139, 140.

82. Jefferson to Grégoire, February 25, 1809, *Writings*; Grégoire, *An Enquiry*, ix.

83. In their recent study Gary Nash and Graham Russell Gao Hodges write that while living in Paris and serving as the United States minister to France, Jefferson often met and visited with Lafayette in the French leader's home. There and in other places he also met with French intellectuals. Among them were "François Jean de Beauvoir, Marquis de Chastellux; Marie Jean Antoine Nicolas de Caritat, Marquis de Condorcet; George-Louis Leclerc, Comte de Buffon; François Alexander Frédéric, Duc de la Rochefoucauld-Liamcourt; Constantin François Chasseboeuf, Comte de Volney; Abbé Raynal and Abbé Grégoire." They describe "Abbé Raynal a fierce campaigner against slavery, and the Marquis de Condorcet, a founder of the antislavery Société des Amis des Noirs. They also note that "five years among abolitionist friends of the Enlightenment seemed to have made little impact on the repatriated Jefferson," who continued to own slaves in America and brought several with him to Paris, including Sally Hemings, who bore him several children. Gary B. Nash and Graham Russell Gao Hodges, *Friends of Liberty: Thomas Jefferson, Tadeusz Kosciuszko, and Agrippa Hull* (New York: Basic Books, 2008), 119–120, 131.

84. Dorigny and Gainot, *La Société des Amis des Noirs*, 19.

85. Hans Wolpe, *Raynal et sa Machine de Guerre* (Palo Alto, Calif.: Stanford University Press, 1957).

86. Dorigny and Gainot, *La Société des Amis des Noirs*, 26.

87. Ibid., 91.

88. Thomas Clarkson, *History of the Abolition of the African Slave-Trade*, 1:219–55.

89. Lafayette had not been invited to become a charter member of the Société because it had decided not to enlist great nobles as charter members. However, when he found out about the society, he asked to be considered as a charter member, and it seems he was successful. From 1777 to 1834 he exchanged letters with Thomas Clarkson and Granville Sharp concerning slavery and the slave trade. Melvin Kennedy, *Lafayette and Slavery: From His Letters to Thomas Clarkson and Granville Sharp* (Easton, Pa.: American Friends of Lafayette, 1950), 5–6.

90. Dorigny and Gainot, *La Société des Amis des Noirs*, 187. The members of the Société were products of the upper classes. They were nobles, intellectuals, priests, and financiers. Women were allowed to join, an unusual situation for the period, most likely owing to the influence of Condorcet, but they were not permitted to attend the debates and only were allowed to attend the twice-yearly general assembly, which was open to all.

91. The research centered on the following points: the trade in black slaves, sugar-cane production in the French colonies, the trade of the Compagnie du Sénégal, individual ship owners, the French situation on the African coasts, the number of Africans exported on the coast, what that exportation costs in sailors, merchandise that was the basis of the trade, the number of blacks on the islands, the product of the labor of the blacks per capita, the ratio and numbers of the two sexes, the variability in the number of new slaves necessary for different plantations caused by the difference in treatments, and the number of black matrons, their lifestyles, and customs.

92. Resnick, "Société des Amis des Noirs and the Abolition of Slavery," 563.

93. Davis, *Problem of Slavery in the Age of Revolution*, 95.

94. Lynn Hunt, ed. and trans., *The French Revolution and Human Rights: A Documentary History* (Boston: Bedford Books, 1996), 101–18. See also Sala-Molins, *Dark Side of the Light*, 125–29, 131.

95. Davis, *Problem of Slavery in the Age of Revolution*, 223.

96. Jeremy Popkin, "The Pre-Revolutionary Origins of Political Journalism," in Jack R. Censer, ed., *The French Revolution and Intellectual History* (Chicago: Dorsey Press, 1989), 110–33. For a good description of events in France plus a chronology of events in 1789, see Chapter 12, "The Death of the Ancién Regime, 1787–1789," in James B. Collins, *From Tribes to Nations: The Making of France 500–1799* (Toronto: Wadsworth, 2002), 517–59.

97. Seeber, *Anti-Slavery Opinion in France*, 161.

98. Napoleon reversed the decision on July 6, 1802.

99. Dorigny and Gainot, *La Société des Amis des Noirs*, 243, n. 443.

100. Ibid., 94.

101. Charles Porset, "Société des amis des Noirs," in *Encyclopédie de la France-Maconneire*, ed. Eric Sauiner (Paris: Librairie générale française, 2000), 819. The *fermiers généraux* leased the general tax farm, which collected many of the duties levied on the commerce related to the slave trade.

102. Alyssa Sepinwall pointed out, "Grégoire was also invited as the only honorary member to join the patrician members of the Société des Amis des Noirs. . . . , even though he could not afford the high membership fee." Alyssa Goldstein Sepinwall, *The Abbé Grégoire and the French Revolution: The Making of Modern Universalism* (Berkeley: University of California Press, 2005), 86. Edna Hindie Lemay, *La vie quotidienne des députés aux états généraux, 1789* (Paris: Hachette, 1989), Mercier to Grégoire, January 8, 1790, and Cabinis to Grégoire, March 19, 1790, both in Archives Nationales, France, 510 AP 2, dossiers M and C/D; and Dorigny, "The Abbé Grégoire and the Société des Amis des Noirs," in Jeremy D. Popkin and Richard Popkin, eds., *Abbé Grégoire and His World* (Boston: Kluwer Academic Press, 2000), 27–39. The first mention of his actual association with the Société comes in the December 4, 1789, minutes of the organization where "M. de Warville [Brissot] reported that MM the Abbè Grégoire, Pétion de Villeneuve and Charles de Lameth had said in favor of the citizens of color and the black slaves in the colonies in the National Assembly" (Popkin and Popkin, 29). Graham Hodges has written in the introduction to Grégoire's *Enquiry*, "Grégoire's initial involvement in the abolitionist movement dated back to 1787, when he joined the Société des Amis des Noirs, which

was modeled after the English Slave Trade Committee." Gorigny and Gainot's discovery of recent Société records show that Grégoire did not in fact join on his own accord but was instead given an honorary membership and took part in four debates and meetings of the Société between January 3 and April 30, 1790. Thus, while Grégoire was never a truly active member of the Société, he nonetheless saw his main role as a spokesman against slavery in the National Assembly. Yet given the fact that the Société was never a group of antislavery activists with the singular zeal of those led by Benezet or by Sharp, the role of Grégoire among the French should not be minimized. Dorigny believes he may not have felt comfortable in the Société because of his "very evident difference in social standing separating him from other members" (xii).

103. Dorigny and Gainot, *La Société des Amis des Noirs*, 294–95.

104. Ibid., 275, n. 552.

105. Resnick, "Société des Amis des Noirs and the Abolition of Slavery," 562, n. 10.

106. Sepinwall, *Abbé Grégoire and the French Revolution*, 151.

107. Quoted from the unpublished manuscript of Brissot de Warville entitled *Sur les Têtes exaltées* (circa late 1790) quoted from sales catalogue *Against the Tide: Commentaries on a Collection of African Americana, 1711–1987*, ed. Randy F. Weinstein (New York: Glenn Horowitz Bookseller, 1986), 19. The letter was written a short time after he wrote his *Lettre à M. Barnave*, in the fall of 1790. The letter criticized Antoine-Pierre Barnave who convinced the National Assembly to deny rights to the mulattos in the French West Indian colonies.

108. Jacques-Pierre Brissot, "Letter Addressed to the Marquis," Paris, July 1, 1786, in *Extracts from a Critical Examination of the Marquis de Chastellux's Travels in North America in a Letter Addressed to the Marquis*, Trinity College, Atkinson Library, Hartford, Connecticut.

109. Ibid.

110. See Christopher L. Miller, *The French Atlantic Triangle: Literature and Culture of the Slave Trade* (Durham: Duke University Press, 2007). Clarence Mumford, *The Black Ordeal of Slavery and the Slave Trading in the French West Indies, 1625–1715*, 3 vols. (Lewiston, N.Y.: Edwin Mellen, 1991).

111. "Lettre de la Convention pour l'abolition de l'esclavage aux Etats-Unis, réunie à Philadelphie à la Société des Amis des Noirs à Paris," in Dorigny and Gainot, *La Société des Amis des Noirs*, 370.

112. Dorigny and Gainot, *La Société des Amis des Noirs*, 396.

Chapter 8. African Voices

Note to epigraph: Joseph Jekyll, Esq., M.P., "Letter LVII to Mr. F[isher], Charles Street, January 27, 1778," in *Letters of the Late Ignatius Sancho, An African, to Which Are Prefixed, Memoirs of His Life* (London: Printed for William Sancho [Wilkes and Taylor, Printers, Chancery-lane], 1803), 125–27. In the quote "the author" refers to Anthony Benezet, "the book" to *Some Historical Account of Guinea*, and "the sect" to the Quakers.

1. Frederick Douglass, *Narrative of the Life of Frederick Douglass: An American Slave, Written by Himself* (New York: Signet, 1968), 92.

2. W. E. B. Du Bois, *The Souls of Black Folk* (1903, repr., New York: Fawcett, 1961), 17.

3. James Albert Ukawsaw Gronniosaw, *A Narrative of the Most Remarkable Particulars in the Life of James Albert Ukawsaw Gronniosaw, an African Prince, As Related by Himself*, in Henry Louis Gates, Jr., and William L. Andrews, *Pioneers of the Black Atlantic:*

Five Slave Narratives from the Enlightenment, 1772–1826 (Washington, D.C.: Civitas Counterpoint, 1998), 30–59; Adam Potkay and Sandra Burr, *Black Atlantic Writers of the Eighteenth Century: Living the New Exodus in England and the Americas* (New York: St. Martin's Press, 1995), 22–63; Yuval Taylor, *I Was Born a Slave: An Anthology of Classic Slave Narratives* (Chicago: Lawrence Hill, 1999), 2–28.

4. Gates and Andrews, *Pioneers of the Black Atlantic*, 5.

5. Ukawsaw Gronniosaw, *A Narrative of the Most Remarkable Particulars in the Life of James Albert Ukawsaw Gronniosaw, an African Prince, As Related by Himself* (Bath, [1772]), in Sukhdev Sandhu and David Dabydeen, eds., *Slavery, Abolition and Emancipation: Writings in the British Romantic Period*, vol. 1, *Black Writers* (London: Pickering & Chatto, 1999), 1.

6. Cadbury, "Anthony Benezet's Library," 63–75.

7. Benezet's original copy of the narrative is contained in Benezet's library, which he donated to the Society of Friends and is housed in the Haverford College Quaker Collection.

8. Gronniosaw, *A Narrative of the Life of James Albert Ukawsaw Gronniosaw*, in Gates and Andrews, *Pioneers of the Black Atlantic*, 45.

9. Of the best-known tracts written by Africans, Gronniosaw's was the most moderate. Although he was a convert to Calvinism, Gronniosaw, like Equiano and Cugoano, also admired the evangelical style of George Whitefield and wrote about seeing him speak. As Adam Potkay and Sandra Burr explained, "The basic drama we find in the lives of Gronniosaw, [John] Marrant, and [Olaudah] Equiano—uncertainty, despair, quickening, and regeneration—reflects not only Whitefield's influence, but that of the Puritan world of letters that Whitefield inherited, [including Richard] Baxter's *A Call to the Unconverted* (1658) [and John] Bunyan's *Holy War* (1682) of which Gronniosaw's read." Walter Shirley, who was a cousin of the countess of Huntingdon, a close associate of Whitefield, wrote the preface to his narrative. The countess had inherited Whitefield's slaves and the rest of his property when he died in 1770. Like Equiano, Gronniosaw developed a style of the "talking book," where in certain scenes the book "speaks to him." Potkay and Burr, *Black Atlantic Writers of the Eighteenth Century*, 8. Vincent Carretta points out that "when the countess inherited Whitefield's Georgia holdings in 1770, she too became a slave owner. Like most evangelicals during the period, neither Whitefield nor the countess saw slavery and Christianity as incompatible. Nowhere in the New Testament is slavery specifically prohibited." Vincent Carretta, *Equiano, the African* (Athens: University of Georgia Press, 2005), 168.

10. Potkay and Burr, *Black Atlantic Writers of the Eighteenth Century*, 23–26, 54, n. 11.

11. Gates and Andrews, *Pioneers of the Black Atlantic*, 9. Benezet, who lived in Holland for a few years after his family fled France, may also have spoken Dutch.

12. Quobna Ottobah Cugoano, *Thoughts and Sentiments on the Evil of Slavery*, edited and with an introduction and notes by Vincent Carretta (New York: Penguin Classics, 1999; original publication, London, 1787), 12, 39. See also Francis Adams and Barry Sanders, eds., *Three Black Writers in Eighteenth-Century England* (Belmont, Calif.: Wadsworth, 1971).

13. Cugoano, *Thoughts and Sentiments on the Evil of Slavery*, 75.

14. Gates and Andrews, *Pioneers of the Black Atlantic*, 14. Gates and Andrews also list Patrick Gordon, *Geography Anatomized* (London, 1693), and the *Geography of England* (London, 1744); James Tobin, *Cursory Remarks upon the Reverend Mr. Ramsay's Essay* (London, 1785); and Gordon Turnbult, *Apology for Slavery* (London, 1786). Gates and Andrews offer no explanation that some of the works that they "wrestled with" were published after Gronniosaw's narrative.

15. Brown, *Moral Capital*, 297. Cugoano, *Thoughts and Sentiments on the Evil of Slavery*, 164. Carretta writes in the introduction that Cugoano relies without acknowledgment on William Robertson's (1721–93) *The History of America* (London, 1777) for his account of the new world.

16. Cugoano, *Thoughts and Sentiments on the Evil of Slavery*, 75–76.

17. Benezet, *A Caution and a Warning*, 41; *Some Historical Account of Guinea* (Philadelphia, 1772), 129–30, and (London, 1788), 108–109.

18. Benezet, *Some Historical Account of Guinea* (1772), chap. 13 , 128–30, 131, and (London, 1788), 108–10; *A Caution and a Warning* (1766), 40–42.

19. Cugoano, *Thoughts and Sentiments on the Evil of Slavery*, 29.

20. Brown, *Moral Capital*, 297. Henri Grégoire listed Cugoano along with Othello, Phillis Wheatley, Julien Raymond, Ignatius Sancho, and Gustavus Vasa under the category "Negro and Mulattoes." While the blacks are listed separately, there is no indication that Grégoire saw them as anything but equal to the others, who are listed not by race but by nationality. Grégoire, *An Enquiry*, xxv–xxvi.

21. Cugoano, *Thoughts and Sentiments on the Evils of Slavery*, 41.

22. Roxann Wheeler, "'Betrayed by Some of My Own Complexion': Cugoano, Abolition, and the Contemporary Language of Racialism," in Vincent Carretta and Philip Gould, eds., *Genius in Bondage: Literature of the Black Atlantic* (Lexington: University of Kentucky Press, 2001), 17–38; 25. Vincent Carretta, ed., *Unchained Voices: An Anthology of Black Authors in the English Speaking World of the Eighteenth Century* (Lexington: University of Kentucky Press, 1996).

23. For other examples of blacks who wrote in the language of Cugoano, see Dorothy Porter, ed., *Early Negro Writings, 1760–1837* (Baltimore: Black Classic Press, 1995); Benjamin Brawley, ed., *Early Negro American Writers* (Chapel Hill: University of North Carolina Press, 1935); and John Ernest, *Liberation Historiography: African American Writers and the Challenge of History, 1794–1861* (Chapel Hill: University of North Carolina Press, 2004).

24. Vincent Carretta called Cugoano "the most radical African British voice in the Eighteenth Century" and noted that in the 1791 edition of *Thoughts and Sentiments on the Evils of Slavery* Cugoano gave a positive assessment of the Somerset ruling and called Sharp "the indefatigable friend of mankind . . . whose name we should always mention with the greatest reverence and honor." *Equiano, the African*, 209.

25. Quobna Ottobah Cugoano, *Thoughts and Sentiments of the Evil and Wicked Traffic of the Slavery and Human Commerce of the Human Species, Humble Submitted to the Inhabitants of Great Britain* (London, 1789); Thomas Clarkson, *An Essay on the Slavery and Commerce of the Human Species, Particularly the African* (London, 1786); Anthony Benezet, *A Caution and a Warning to Great Britain and Her Colonies in a Short Representation of the Calamitous State of the Enslaved Negroes in the British Dominions: Collected from Various Authors and Submitted to the Serious Consideration of All, More Especially Those in Power* (Philadelphia, 1766; London, 1767, 1768, 1785, 1788).

26. Cugoano, *Thoughts and Sentiments of the Evil and Wicked Traffic*, 76.

27. Ibid.

28. In addition to Carretta's introduction to Cugoano's *Thoughts and Sentiments on the Evil of Slavery*, see the introduction to Paul Edwards, ed., *Thoughts and Sentiments on the Evils of Slavery* (New York: Humanities Press, 1969); John Saillant, "Antiguan Methodism and Antislavery Activity," *Church History* 69 (1999): 108–109; and Keith Sandiford, *Measuring the Moment: Strategies of Protest in Eighteenth-Century Afro-English Writing* (Selinsgrove, England: Susquehanna University Press, 1998).

29. Cugoano, *Thoughts and Sentiments of the Evil and Wicked Traffic*, 98–99.

30. Ibid.

31. Cugoano, *Thoughts and Sentiments on the Evil of Slavery*, appendix, letters, and petitions of Cugoano, 194.

32. Ibid., see intro. by Vincent Carretta p. xx.

33. Ibid., 145. The editor of this edition, Vincent Carretta, writes "I have found no record of Cugoano's having opened a school" (181, n. 4).

34. Equiano, *Interesting Narrative of Olaudah Equiano*, ed. and with an introduction by Robert J. Allison (Boston: Bedford, 1995), 145. Originally published in 1789.

35. Adanson, *Voyage to Senegal*, was published after Astley's *New General Collection* and cited independently by Benezet in 1762; Barbot, *Description of the Coasts of North and South-Guinea* (vol. 5 of Churchill and Churchill's *Collection*, and excerpted in Astley's *New General Collection*); Bosman, *New and Accurate Description of the Coast of Guinea* (excerpted in Astley, *New General Collection*).

36. Benezet, *Some Historical Account of Guinea* (1772), 6. While Edwards uses the 1788 London edition, I use the earlier 1772 first London edition, as well as the 1788 edition. This work was Benezet's most substantial on Africa. His first study was *A Short Account of That Part of Africa Inhabited by Negroes* (Philadelphia, 1762).

37. Olaudah Equiano, *The Life of Olaudah Equiano*, ed. Paul Edwards (London: Longman African Writers, 1998), 1. In referring to his 1967 abridgments of Equiano's *Narrative*, Edwards admits to having made an error in "having cut a number of passages which ought not to have been excluded" and of rectifying that error in this edition. In this instance Edwards has shown "as a consequence of misreading a jotted note—'3–4,000 miles' for instance—Equiano appears to have come up with the figure, 3,400 instead of Benezet's 'three or four thousand' miles." Edwards, *The Life of Olaudah Equiano*, xxi. Edwards also writes that Equiano had made a note of reading *Some Historical Account of Guinea* and "subsequently made a slight error in reading it" (xxi). Carretta, *Equiano, the African*, 313. Edwards has also shown the influence on English writers on Equiano, most notably Milton and his *Paradise Lost*, Alexander Pope, and Thomas Day.

38. Potkay and Burr, *Black Atlantic Writers of the Eighteenth Century*, 53, n. 4.

39. Equiano, *Interesting Narrative of Olaudah Equiano* (Allison edition), 18.

40. For a discussion concerning his age and birthplace see Carretta, *Equiano, the African*, especially chaps. 1, 13, and 14. Response to Paul Lovejoy's "Autobiography and Memory: Gustavus Vassa, alias Olaudah Equiano, the African," *Slavery and Abolition* 28, no. 1 (2007): 115–19. Carretta, "Olaudah Equiano or Gustavus Vasa? New Light on an Eighteenth-Century Question of Identity," *Slavery and Abolition* 20, no. 3 (December 1999): 96–105; and "Questioning the Identity of Olaudah Equiano, or Gustavus Vassa, the African," in Felicity Nussbaum, ed., *The Global Eighteenth Century* (Baltimore: Johns Hopkins University Press, 2003), 226–35.

41. Paul Lovejoy, "Autobiography and Memory: Gustavus Vassa, alias Olaudah Equiano, the African," *Slavery and Abolition* 27, no. 3 (2006): 317–47. Lovejoy concludes that "the reflections and memories used in autobiography are always filtered, but despite this caveat, I would conclude that Vassa was born in Africa and not in South Carolina." Paul Lovejoy, "Construction of Identity: Olaudah Equiano or Gustavus Vassa?" *Historical Speaking: The Bulletin of the Historical Society* 7, no. 3 (January–February 2006): 5.

42. Catherine O. Acholonu, "The Home of Olaudah Equiano—A Linguistic and Anthropological Survey," *Journal of Commonwealth Literature* 12, no. 1 (1987): 40; Catherine Obianju, *The Igbo Roots of Olaudah Equiano* (Owerri, Nigeria: Afa Publications, 1989).

43. Carretta, *Equiano, the African*, 319. George E. Boulukos, "Olaudah Equiano and the Eighteenth-Century Debate on Africa," *Eighteenth-Century Studies* 40, no. 2 (Winter 2007): 241–57.

44. James Green, "The Publishing History of Olaudah Equiano's *Interesting Narrative,*" *Slavery and Abolition* 16, no. 3 (1995): 362–75.

45. Edwards, *The Life of Olaudah Equiano,* 3.

46. Benezet, *Some Historical Account of Guinea* (Philadelphia, 1772), 17, 36. Benezet, the Quaker, found particularly disturbing some sections of the travel narratives that he felt were sexually suggestive.

47. Bosman, *New and Accurate Description of the Coast of Guinea,* 357.

48. Barbot, *Barbot on Guinea.* According to the editors, "Barbot does not, however, accept the view that adultery with wives of the king or great men of Whydah was punished by death as stated in Bosman" (pp. 357–58, 650).

49. Equiano, *Interesting Narrative of Olaudah Equiano* (Allison ed.), 40. On page 144 of the 1772 edition of *Some Historical Account of Guinea,* Benezet had written that "except in the above instance, and some others, where the power if the Negroe King is unlawfully exerted over their subjects, the slave-trade is carried on in Guinea with some regard to the laws of the country, which allows of none to be sold, but prisoners of war, or people adjudged to slavery in punishments for crimes." The asterisk at the bottom of the page read "see note page 109." The note on page 109 refers to Benezet's reference to an African king who traded with the Europeans. Benezet wrote, "Note, This Negroe King thus refusing to comply with the factor's wicked proposals, shews, he was sensible to his own conduct was not justifiable; and it likewise appears the factor's only concern was to procure the greatest number of slaves, without any regard to the injustice of the method by which they were procured. This, Andrew Brue, was for a long time, principal director of the French African factory in those parts; in the management of which, he is in the collection said to have extraordinary success." See also Philadelphia edition (1771), 73.

50. Benezet, *Some Historical Account of Guinea* (1772), 46, 96.

51. Olaudah Equiano, *Interesting Narrative of Olaudah Equiano* (Allison, ed.), 39.

52. Ibid., 95 (p. 16 in original Equiano edition). Not all editions of the original narrative or later reprints contain the Equiano footnotes.

53. Benezet, *A Caution and a Warning* (1762), 48. As will be later shown, Equiano was also familiar with this work.

54. James Walvin, *An African's Life: The Life and Times of Olaudah Equiano, 1745–1797* (London/New York: Cassell, 1998), 178–79. Walvin also noted that "Quakers distributed Benezet's tracts to all of England's major schools (Charterhouse, St. Paul's, Merchant Taylor's, Eton, Winchester, Harrow and Westminster) and spread them, via Friends, across the face of Britain" (180).

55. Benezet, *Some Historical Account of Guinea,* 143–44.

56. Equiano, *Interesting Narrative of Olaudah Equiano* (Allison ed.), 193–94. Benezet had written that "Africa has about ten thousand miles of sea coast, and extends in depth near three thousand miles from east to west, and as much from north to south, stored with vast treasures of materials, necessary for trade and manufactures of Great-Britain; and from its climate, and the fruitfulness of its soil, capable, under proper management, of producing in the greatest plenty, most of the commodities which are imported into Europe from those parts of America subject to the English government; and as, in return, they would take our manufacturers, the advantages of this trade would soon become so great, that it is evident this subject merits the regard and attention of the government." Benezet, *Some Historical Account of Guinea* (1772), 144. Equiano also read Edmund Burke's *An Account of the European Settlements in America* first published in six parts (London: R. and J. Dodsley, 1758), after he read about it in Benezet's work. See also Edmund Burke, "Sketch of a Negro Code." In Paul Langford, ed., *The Writings and Speeches of Edmund Burke* (Oxford: Clarendon Press, 1981). *Essays, Commercial and Political, on*

the *Real and Relative Interests of the Imperial and Dependent States, Particularly Those of Great Britain, and Their Dependencies; Displaying the Probable Causes of, and a Mode of Compromising the Present Disputes between This County and her American Colonies; to Which Is Added and Appendix, on the Means of Emancipating Slaves without Loss to Their Properties* (Newcastle, England, 1777).

57. Carretta, *Equiano, the African,* 98.

58. Ibid., 179, 242.

59. Sloane, *Voyage to the Islands,* lvii.

60. Anthony Benezet, *Some Historical Account of Guinea* (1772), 170–71.

61. Equiano, *Interesting Narrative of Olaudah Equiano* (Allison ed.), 97.

62. Ibid. 193. Walvin, *An African's Life,* 181.

63. Benezet, *Some Historical Account of Guinea* (1772), 1. Walvin, *An African's Life,* 181.

64. For an excellent discussion of Adam Smith and his views on slavery see Davis, *Problem of Slavery in Age of Revolution,* chaps. 7 and 8. Seymour Drescher, *The Mighty Experiment: Free Labor Versus Slavery in British Emancipation* (New York: Oxford University Press, 2002), chap. 2. James Oakes, "The Peculiar Fate of the Bourgeois Critique of Slavery," in Winthrop D. Jordan, ed., *Slavery and the American South* (Jackson: University of Mississippi Press, 2003), 29–48.

65. Adam Smith, *An Inquiry into the Nature and Causes of the Wealth of Nations* (London, 1776), bk. 1, chap. 8; bk. 3, chap. 2; bk. 4., chap. 7. Equiano learned to appreciate the enlightened thinkers; among them were Jean-Jacques Rousseau and Montesquieu, whom Benezet quoted extensively in *Some Historical Account of Guinea* and other of his works. Equiano, *Interesting Narrative of Olaudah Equiano* (Sollors ed.), xvi.

66. Equiano, *Interesting Narrative of Olaudah Equiano* (Allison ed.), 194.

67. Ibid. Eric Williams argued (and the debate continues) long ago that it was only when "the expenses of slavery, in the form of the cost and maintenance of slaves, productive and unproductive, exceed the cost of hired laborers" and cut deeply into profits would the ending of slavery be in the interest of certain economic classes of the whites. Eric Williams, *Capitalism and Slavery* (Chapel Hill: University of North Carolina Press, 1944), 7. For a succinct discussion of the reviews of the work at its publication among black and white scholars, see the introduction by Colin A. Palmer to the 1994 edition published on its fiftieth anniversary (Chapel Hill: University of North Carolina Press, 1994), xi–xxii.

68. Equiano, *Interesting Narrative of Olaudah Equiano* (Allison ed.), 194–95. Equiano may not have realized that man, once tied to the land, would now be chained to the machine. Production relations would not follow the path he had hoped for. It would not be the person who worked the machine who would control production any more than the peasant who worked the land, whether in the Americas or Europe, controlled the land. Production relations would change, but ownership relations would not. Those tied to the land changed the way they worked, but that did not mean that they worked less or were any less exploited or oppressed.

69. Equiano, *Interesting Narrative of Olaudah Equiano* (Allison ed.), 186.

70. Walvin, *An African's Life,* 129.

71. Equiano, *Interesting Narrative of Olaudah Equiano* (Allison ed.), 186. In some of the versions this section is not presented in Chapter 12 as it was in the original but as Appendix B.

72. Walvin, *An African's Life,* 130.

73. John Wesley to William Wilberforce, February 24, 1791, in Telford, *Letters of John Wesley,* vol. 7, 264–65.

74. Wise, *Though the Heavens May Fall,* 205–207; Shyllon, *Black People in Britain,* 222–40; Shyllon, *Black Slaves in Britain,* 184–99.

75. Hoare, *Memoirs of Granville Sharp*, 236 (March 19, 1783, Extracts from Diary, 1783–1798). Carretta, *Equiano, the African*, 237.

76. Hoare, *Memoirs of Granville Sharp*, 352.

77. Shyllon, *Black People in Britain*, 228.

78. Metaxas, *Amazing Grace*, 103–13. Equiano's account (and Cugoano's) also moved Wesley, just as Benezet had been moved by Gronniosaw's. As Werner Sollors noted, "John Wesley (whose antislavery position was aroused earlier when he read Benezet's *Account of Guinea*) reacted with particular empathy when he learned in Equiano's *Narrative* of the curtailment of the rights of free blacks." Equiano, *Interesting Narrative of Olaudah Equiano* (Sollors ed.), xxv; Potkay and Burr, *Black Atlantic Writers of the Eighteenth Century*, 10.

79. Jekyll, *Letters of the Late Ignatius Sancho*, i.

80. He was born in the same year that the Yorke-Talbot decision occurred, which years later Lord Hardwicke said gave proof positive that blacks were "like stock on a farm," . . ."was passed down from White man to White man." Helen Tunnicliff Catterall, ed., *Judicial Cases Concerning American Slavery and the Negro*, 5 vols. (Washington, D.C.: Carnegie Institution of Washington, 1926–37), vol. 1, 9–12.

81. Jekyll, *Letters of the Late Ignatius Sancho*, i.

82. Ibid., i.

83. Vincent Carretta, ed. *Ignatius Sancho, Letters of the Late Ignatius Sancho, An African* (New York: Penguin Books, 1998), xi–xii.

84. Sandhu and Dabydeen, *Slavery, Abolition and Emancipation*, vol. 1, 65.

85. Paul Edwards and Polly Rewt, eds., *The Letters of Ignatius Sancho* (Edinburgh: Edinburgh University Press, 1994).

86. Sancho, *Letters of the Late Ignatius Sancho*. See also Carretta, *Letters of the Late Ignatius Sancho*.

87. Jekyll, "Letter LVII to Mr. F[isher] Charles Street, January 27, 1778," in Carretta, *Letters of the Late Ignatius Sancho*, 125–27. See also Carretta, *Letters of the Late Ignatius Sancho*, 111–12. (1) Carretta writes that Mr. Fisher "was probably Jabez Fisher (1717–1806) of Philadelphia," who subscribed to Sancho's *Letters*. (2) Here "Sancho refers to recent antislavery works such as Benezet's *Short Account of That Part of Africa*." (3) The sect referred to the Quakers, which according to Carretta, "Mr. F—was probably a Quaker." (4) "Turban . . . lawn sleeves: the dress respectively, of the Muslims and Anglican clergy." (5) p. 288. Fisher was Jabez Fisher, a Philadelphian who sent Sancho the works of Benezet and the poems of Phillis Wheatley. Sancho wrote at length praising Benezet. The poems most likely were Phillis Wheatley, *Poems on Various Subjects, Religious and Moral* (London, 1773). Carretta lists Sancho "as the first literary critic of African descent to comment on Wheatley's poetry." (6) Luke 10:30–37. Carretta, *Unchained Voices*, 77–109.

88. Carretta, *Unchained Voices*. Carretta concludes, "Thus one could be (after the Union of 1707) a Scots-Briton, a Welsh-Briton, and (in the nineteenth century) an Irish-Briton, as well as an English Briton. Or an Afro-Briton" (p. 7). Carretta wrote that Phillis Wheatley, Francis Williams, and "Sancho rarely address the issues of the abolition of the slave trade or of slavery itself" (p. 12). Sancho's letters seem to prove otherwise.

89. Jekyll, *Letters of the Late Ignatius Sancho*, 34.

90. Carretta, *Letters of the Late Sancho*, letter 1, p. 130.

91. Ibid., 149–50.

92. Edwards and Rewt, *Letters of Ignatius Sancho*, 13.

93. Jekyll, *Letters of the Late Ignatius Sancho*, vii–viii.

94. Roxann Wheeler wonderfully summed up the role of men like Cugoano, Equiano, Gronniosaw, Sancho, and the early African writers, comparing them to

"what motivational speakers today call 'retail therapy.' Olaudah Equiano and, to a lesser extent, Cugoano, following the early Quaker abolitionist Anthony Benezet, took their cases to the public." Wheeler, " 'Betrayed by Some of My Own Complexion,' " 25.

95. Ruth Bogin, "Liberty Further Extended: A 1776 Antislavery Manuscript by Lemuel Haynes," *William and Mary Quarterly*, 3rd series, 40, no. 1 (January 1983), 94.

96. John Saillant, *Black Puritan, Black Republican: The Life and Thought of Lemuel Haynes, 1753–1833* (New York: Oxford University Press, 2006), 10. Saillant believes that "had the young Haynes been adopted into a New England free black or slave family, or placed into one by the white people who witnessed his first days, he would probably have been absorbed into . . . a school of miseducation. . . . Although New England free blacks and slaves included many skilled laborers, and some literate men and women, rarely did white society offer them any opportunities that would have helped them move beyond domestic service and common labor" (p. 11).

97. "The Battle of Lexington," in Richard Newman, ed., *Black Preacher to White America: The Collected Writings of Lemuel Haynes, 1774–1833* (Brooklyn, N.Y.: Carlson 1990), 12, stanza 16. See also Gary Nash, *Landmarks of the American Revolution* (New York: Oxford University Press, 2003), 16–17. This poem was first discovered and published by Ruth Bogin in the *William and Mary Quarterly* in 1985.

98. F. Nwabueze Okoye, "Chattel Slavery as the Nightmare of the American Revolutionaries," *William and Mary Quarterly*, 3rd series, 37, no. 1 (January 1980): 3–28.

99. William B. Sprague, *Sketches of the Life and Character of the Rev Lemuel Haynes, A. M.* (New York: Negro Universities Press, 1969; first published by Harper & Brothers, 1837). This work makes no mention of Haynes's role in the American Revolution or his writing on slavery. Joseph R. Washington, Jr., *The First Afro-American Honorary Degree Recipient: The Critical Civil Conflict of Interest of Class Calvinists and Competing Religious and Secular Puritans: Patriot Lemuel Haynes Portrayed (as the Initial Colored Congregational Clergyman)* (Lewiston, N.Y.: Edwin Mellen Press, 1990).

100. Bogin, "Liberty Further Extended," 87. Newman, *Black Preacher to White America*, xxv–xxxiii.

101. Frederick Douglass, "The Meaning of the Fourth of July to the American Negro," speech at Rochester, New York, July 5, 1852, in Philip Foner, ed., *The Life and Times of Frederick Douglass,* 4 volumes (New York: International Publishers, 1950), vol. 2, "Pre-Civil War Years," 192. In this speech Douglass, while acknowledging the importance of American independence, questions its importance to enslaved blacks.

102. *Liberty Further Extended: or Free Thoughts on the Illegality of Slave-Keeping; Wherein Those Arguments That Are Used in Its Vindications Are Plainly Confuted. Together with an Humble Address to Such as Are Concearrned in the Practise.* Ruth Bogin found this document at Harvard University and first published it in the *William and Mary Quarterly* in 1983. She ascertained that it was written in 1776. A full text is published in Richard Newman, ed., *Black Preacher to White America*, 17–30, and in the *William and Mary Quarterly*, 3rd series, 40, no. 1 (January 1983), 94–105.

103. Bogin, "Liberty Further Extended," 94; Newman, *Black Preacher to White America*, 17–30.

104. Newman, *Black Preacher to White America*, 20 (see also Bogin, "Liberty Further Extended," 96).

105. Ibid., 25 (see also Bogin, "Liberty Further Extended," 100–101).

106. Ibid., 20 (see also Bogin, "Liberty Further Extended," 96).

107. Ibid., 21. Haynes wrote, "N. Brue, Directory of the French factory at Senegal, who Lived twenty-seven years in that country says, 'that the Europeans are far

from being desiring to act as peacemakers among the Negros which would Be acting contrary to their interest, since the greater the wars, the more are the slaves procured." Haynes then cites Willem Bosman, although he incorrectly writes the name as "William Boseman, factor of the Dutch at Delmina, where he resided sixteen years." Borrowing word for word from Benezet, like Wesley and Equiano, he then cited "William Smith, who was sent By the African company, to visit the settlements in the year 1726." Like Benezet, he used the same famous passage from Smith: "that the Discerning Natives accounted it their greatest unhapyness that they were Ever visited by the Europeans" and that "Wherever Christianity comes, there comes with it a Sword, a gun, powder, and Ball" (p. 21).

108. Bogin, "Liberty Further Extended," 88.

109. Newman, *Black Preacher to White America,* 27 (see also Bogin, "Liberty Further Extended," 102).

110. Anthony Benezet, *Some Historical Account of Guinea* (London, 1772), 85–86.

111. Newman, *Black Preacher to White America,* 29–30 (see also Bogin, "Liberty Further Extended," 104).

112. Benezet, *Some Historical Account of Guinea* (London, 1772), 94–95.

113. Dickson D. Bruce, Jr., *The Origins of African American Literature, 1680–1865* (Charlottesville: University of Virginia Press, 2001), 100. See also Porter, *Early Negro Writings,* and John Ernest, *Liberation Historiography: African American Writers and the Challenge of History, 1794–1861* (Chapel Hill: University of North Carolina Press, 2004).

114. Newman, *Black Preacher to White America,* 19.

115. Saillant, *Black Puritan, Black Republican,* 46. See also Joanna Brooks and John Saillant, eds., *"Face Zion Forward": First Writers of the Black Atlantic, 1785–1798* (Boston: Northeastern University Press, 2002).

116. Rev. Wm. Douglass, *Annals of the First African Church in the United States of American Now Styled the African Episcopal Church of St. Thomas* (Philadelphia: King & Baird, 1861), 18; Winch *Gentleman of Color,* chap. 6.

117. W. E. B. Du Bois, *The Philadelphia Negro* (Philadelphia: University of Pennsylvania Press, 1899), 19.

118. Nash, *Forging Freedom,* 98.

119. Douglass, *Annals of the First African Church,* 19; Leroy Hopkins and Eric Ledell Smith, *African Americans in Pennsylvania,* Pennsylvania Historical and Museum Commission Web site, http://www.phmc.state.pa.us/ppet/africanamericans (accessed May 21, 2008).

120. Richard Allen and Absalom Jones, *A Narrative of the Proceedings of the Black People, During the Late Awful Calamity in Philadelphia in the Year 1793 and a Refutation of Some Censures Thrown Upon Them in Some Late Publications* (Philadelphia: William W. Woodward, at Franklin's head, 1794; repr. ed. Independence National Historical Park, 1993). See also Richard Newman, Patrick Rael, and Philip Lapsansky, *Pamphlets of Protest: An Anthology of Early African-American Protest Literature, 1790–1860* (New York: Routledge, 2001); Milton C. Sernett, ed., *African American Religious History: Documentary Witness* (Durham: Duke University Press, 1999).

121. Leslie J. Pollard, "Black Beneficial Societies, and the Home for the Aged and Infirm Colored Persons: A Research Note," *Phylon (1960)* 41, no. 3 (1980): 230–34.

122. Du Bois, *Philadelphia Negro,* 20.

123. Nash, *Forging Freedom,* 100–101; Margaret Hope Bacon, *But One Race: The Life of Robert Purvis* (Albany: State University of New York Press, 2007), 19.

124. Nash, *Forging Freedom,* 193.

125. Douglass, *Annals of the First African Church,* 24.

126. Drake, *Quakers and Slavery,* 16.

127. Henry Cadbury, "Negro Membership in the Society of Friends," *Journal of Negro History* 21, no. (1936): 167.

128. Cadbury, "Negro Membership in the Society of Friends," 168. (That scene seems eerily reminiscent of the Jim Crow South of the twentieth century, where blacks who wanted to attend movies or shows were required to sit in the balcony or the rear.)

129. Nash, *Forging Freedom,* 191.

130. Richard Allen, *The Life, Experience, and Gospel Labors of the Rt. Rev. Richard Allen: To Which Is Annexed the Rise and Progress of the African Methodist Episcopal Church in the United States of America: Containing a Narrative of the Yellow Fever in the Year of Our Lord of 1793: With an Address to the People of Color in the United States/Written by Himself* (Philadelphia: Lee and Yeocum, 1888), 25.

131. Nash, *Forging Freedom,* 112–13.

132. Milton C. Sernett, *Black Religion and American Evangelicalism: White Protestants, Plantation Missions, and the Flowering of Negro Christianity, 1787–1865* (Metuchen, N.J.: Scarecrow Press, 1975), 117–18, 219–20. Sernett gives clarity as to the date of the St. George's event, which has often been portrayed as occurring in 1787 instead of the actual date of 1792. For example, Carol V. R. George writes that the final "withdrawal from St. George's came in November 1787, seven months after the Preamble for the Free African Society was first composed." Carol V. R. George, *Segregated Sabbaths: Richard Allen and the Rise of Independent Black Churches, 1760–1840* (New York: Oxford University Press, 1973), 55.

133. Allen, *The Life, Experience, and Gospel Labors of the Rt. Rev. Richard Allen,* 25.

134. Brown, *Negro in Pennsylvania History,* 13.

135. Nash, *Forging Freedom,* 123.

136. Nash, *Forging Freedom,* 123, 124–25. Nash has also shown how racism rose in Philadelphia, as in Carey's account: "The city's saviors . . . were the rising immigrant merchant Stephen Girard and other whites who organized an emergency hospital just outside the city, where they selfishly tended the sick and dying. For the black Philadelphians who drove the death carts, buried the dead, and nursed the sick in the back streets and alleys of the city Carey had few good words" (124–25). For an insightful new study on Allen, see Richard S. Newman, *Freedom's Prophet: Bishop Richard Allen, the AME Church, and the Black Founding Fathers* (New York: New York University Press, 2008).

137. Winch, *Gentleman of Color,* 152–53. Nash, *Forging Freedom,* 186. See also Winch, "The Making and Meaning of James Forten's Letters from Man of Colour," *William and Mary Quarterly,* 3rd series, 64, no. 1 (January 2007): 129–138. Du Bois had the highest of praise for Forten. In the *Philadelphia Negro,* he wrote, "Born in 1766 and educated by Benezet, he 'was a gentlemen, by nature, easy in many and able in intercourse; popular as a man or trade or gentleman of the pave, and well received by the gentry of the lighter shade'" (quoted by W. C. Bolivar in the *Philadelphia Tribune*).

138. Hoare, *Memoirs of Granville Sharp,* 255.

139. Gayraud S. Wilmore, *Black Religion and Black Radicalism: An Interpretation of the Religious History of African Americans,* 3rd ed. (Maryknoll, N.Y.: Orbis Books, 1998), 271.

140. The work of Allen and Jones and the establishment of the FAS led to the formation of many African American religious denominated bodies. Among them were the African Methodist Episcopal Church, the African Methodist Episcopal Zion Church, the Christian Methodist Episcopal Church, the National Baptist Convention USA Incorporated, the National Baptist Convention of America Unincor-

porated, the Progressive National Baptist Convention, and the Church of God in Christ. See Robert J. Batastini and J. Alfred Smith, Sr., eds., *African American Heritage Hymnal* (Chicago: GIA Publications, 2001).

141. Wilmore, *Black Religion and Black Radicalism*, 108.

142. Du Bois, *The Philadelphia Negro*, 197.

143. Richard R. Wright, *The Negro in Pennsylvania: A Study in Economic History* (New York: Arno Press, 1969), 37.

144. Bacon, *But One Race: The Life of Robert Purvis*, 19.

145. *William and Mary Quarterly* has published the proceedings of a forum, "Black Founders in the New Republic," sponsored by the journal and the Black Antislavery Writings Project 1760–1829. The talks by the six panelists appear on the *William and Mary Quarterly* 64, no. 1, January 2007 and on its Web site, at http://www.historycooperative.org. The collection of the Black Antislavery Writings Project (pre-1830) (http://www.liberalarts.udmercy.edu/history/ba_archives), joined with C. Peter Ripley et al., eds., *The Black Abolitionist Papers*, 5 vols. (Chapel Hill: University of North Carolina Press, 1985–1992), provide a compilation of the works and writings of African American leaders in the abolitionist movement. See also Peter Hinks, *David Walker and the Problem of Antebellum Slave Resistance* (University Park: Pennsylvania State University Press, 1997); Patrick Rael, *Black Identity and Black Protest in the Antebellum North* (Chapel Hill: University of North Carolina Press, 2003); John Stauffer, *The Black Hearts of Men: Radical Abolitionist and the Transformation of Race* (Cambridge, Mass.: Harvard University Press, 2003); and Newman, Rael, and Lapsansky, *Pamphlets of Protest*.

Epilogue: Benezet's Dream

1. Tom Paine, "African Slavery in America," in Conway, ed., The *Writings of Thomas Paine*, 8.

2. "The Correspondence of Benjamin Franklin and Granville Sharp, 1773–1809," 15–16.

3. Lamin Sanneh, *Abolitionist Abroad: American Blacks and the Making of West Africa* (Cambridge, Mass.: Harvard University Press, 2000), 42.

4. Gary B. Nash and Graham Russell Gao Hodges, *Friends of Liberty: Thomas Jefferson, Thadeusz Kosciuszko, and Agrippa Hull: A Tale of Three Patriots, Two Revolutions, and a Tragic Betrayal of Freedom in the New Nation* (New York: Basic Books, 2008), 121. See also Pybus, *Epic Journeys of Freedom*, chapters 5–9; Schama, *Rough Crossings*, 189–220, and Graham Russell Gao Hodges, ed., *The Black Loyalists Directory: African American Exiles After the American Revolution* (New York: Garland, 1996).

5. Locke, *Antislavery in America*, 31.

6. Benezet, *Short Account of That Part of Africa* (1762, 1st ed.), 27–28.

7. Benezet, *Short Account of That Part of Africa* (1762, 2nd ed.), 69. Benezet, *Some Historical Account of Guinea* (1772), 138.

8. Benezet, *Short Account of That Part of Africa* (1762, 2nd ed.), 69.

9. Ibid., 70.

10. Benezet, *Some Historical Account of Guinea* (1772), 139.

11. Benezet, *Short Account of That Part of Africa* (1762, 2nd ed.), 69–70.

12. Ibid., 70.

13. Benezet, *Some Historical Account of Guinea* (1772), 140.

14. Benezet, *A Short Account of That Part of Africa* (1762, 2nd ed.), 71.

15. Ibid., 72.

16. Benezet, *Some Historical Account of Guinea* (1772), 140–41. Benezet added as a footnote, "The hard usage the Negroes meet with in the plantations, and the

great disproportions between them and the white people, will always be just cause of terror. In Jamaica, and some parts of South Carolina, it is supposed that there are fifteen blacks to one white." *Short Account of That Part of Africa,* 72; *Some Historical Account of Guinea* (1771 ed.), 70–71, and (1772 ed.), 140.

17. Benezet, *Some Historical Account of Guinea* (1772), 141.

18. Benezet, *Short Account of That Part of Africa* (1762, 2nd ed.), 69–70; Benezet, *Some Historical Account of Guinea* (1772), 138–39.

19. Benezet, *A Short Account of That Part of Africa* (1762, 2nd ed.), 70; Benezet, *Some Historical Account of Guinea* (1772), 139.

20. Anthony Benezet to Joseph Phipps, May 28, 1763, Haverford College Quaker Collection. Also reprinted in Bruns, *Am I Not a Man and a Brother,* 98.

21. Anthony Benezet, *Short Account of That Part of Africa* (1762, 2nd ed.), 72. Benezet did not include this section in his longer *Some Historical Account of Guinea.* The exclusion may be because he also said that the Africans did not "live to in the same wild unsettled manner as the American Indians do" (72). Benezet later worked among the Native Americans, which no doubt led him to understand their culture, their heritage, and their treatment by the whites.

22. Anthony Benezet to John Fothergill, April 28, 1773, Haverford College Quaker Collection.

23. Du Bois, *Souls of Black Folk,* 21.

24. Benezet, *Short Account of That Part of Africa.*

25. W. E. B. Du Bois, "Of the Dawn of Freedom," in *Souls of Black Folk,* 23.

26. Wayne J. Eberly, "The Pennsylvania Abolition Society: 1775–1830" (Ph.D. diss., Pennsylvania State University, 1973), 22–23.

27. Bumbrey, *Microfilm Publication of the Papers of the Pennsylvania Abolition Society.* Nevil's protests were denied in court, but the Pennsylvania Abolition Society secretary, Thomas Harrison, later purchased her freedom in 1781.

28. Nash, *Landmarks of the American Revolution,* 17. Bogin, "Liberty Further Extended," 93–103; Newman, *Black Preacher to White America,* 17–30.

29. Hoare, *Memoirs of Granville Sharp,* 183.

30. Edward Needles, *An Historical Memoir of the Pennsylvania Society for Promoting the Abolition of Slavery; The Relief of Free Negroes Unlawfully Held in Bondage, and for Improving the Condition of the African Race Compiles from the Minutes of the Society and Other Official Documents* (Philadelphia: Marrihew and Thompson, 1848), 26. It also formed a Standing Committee, later renamed the Acting Committee.

31. Eberly, "Pennsylvania Abolition Society," 22.

32. Margaret H. Bacon, *History of the Pennsylvania Society for Promoting the Abolition of Slavery: The Relief of Negroes Unlawfully Held in Bondage; and for Improving the Condition of the African Race* (Philadelphia: Pennsylvania Abolition Society, 1959), ii–3.

33. Bumbrey, *Microfilm Publication of the Papers of the Pennsylvania Abolition Society),* 7. Ira Brown believes there were seventeen original members. Ira V. Brown, "The Negro in Pennsylvania History", *Pennsylvania History Studies,* no. 11 (University Park: Pennsylvania History Studies, 1970), 5.

34. Bacon, *History of the Pennsylvania Society for Promoting the Abolition of Slavery,* 3. Jeffrey Bumbrey assesses the work of the Abolition Society, writing that "between 1775 and 1784, some programs initiated by the Abolition Society were continued by a few members acting as individuals. Although most historians note that the Abolition Society had no part in securing passage of the Pennsylvania Gradual Emancipation Law in 1780, Anthony Benezet waged a strong campaign in its' favor'" (8). It is a mistake, however, to separate Benezet from the work of the society, as he served as an inspiration and catalyst for every aspect of abolitionism. Although Franklin and Paine worked closely with the Pennsylvania legislature, there was little

doubt that Benezet pushed them. Bumbrey admitted that because of the war and the Quaker withdrawal from the assembly, Benezet simply was the Pennsylvania Abolition Society. Bumbrey does show that "the aging Benezet tried several times to revitalize the Society between and 1783 but to no avail" (8).

35. Brookes, *Friend Anthony Benezet*, 97.

36. Quoted in Bruns, *Am I Not a Man and a Brother*, 379.

37. Anthony Benezet to Selina, countess of Huntingdon, March 4, 1775, Haverford College Quaker Collection

38. Hoare, *Memoirs of Granville Sharp*, 183.

39. Philadelphia Yearly Meeting Minutes, 1776.

40. "Report of Committee to Visit Slaveholders in Philadelphia," in J. William Frost, ed., *The Quaker Origins of Antislavery* (Norwood, Pa.: Norwood Editions, 1980), 243.

41. Du Bois, *Philadelphia Negro*, 12.

42. Roll 53A Monthly Meeting of Friends of Philadelphia, Manumission Book, "A Record of Manumission for Slaves Released from Bondage Within the Limits of the Three Monthly Meetings of Friends of the City of the City & Liberties of Philadelphia" [1774–1796], October 36, 1776, p. 15.

43. Monthly Meeting of Friends of Philadelphia, Manumissions Book, "A Record of Manumissions for Slaves Released from Bondage Within the Limits of the Three Monthly Meetings of Friends of the City & Liberties of Philadelphia [1774–1796]." Arch Street Meeting House.

44. Roll 53A Monthly Meeting of Friends of Philadelphia, Manumission Book, "A Record of Manumission for Slaves Released from Bondage Within the Limits of the Three Monthly Meetings of Friends of the City of the City & Liberties of Philadelphia" [1774–1796], May 5, 1780, p. 41. Arch Street Meeting House.

45. Monthly Meeting of Friends of Philadelphia, Manumissions Book, "A Record of Manumissions for Slaves Released from Bondage Within the Limits of the Three Monthly Meetings of Friends of the City & Liberties of Philadelphia" [1774–1796]. In June 1780 the records show that "our friend Anthony Benezet reported, that he hath had an . . . pretty full conference with Thomas Maybury in our last meeting, in which he discovered much the same Disposition as heretofore." Maybury refused to part with his slaves, "pursuant to the direction the Meeting in the 2nd month last."

46. *A Brief Statement of the Rise and Progress of the Testimony of the Society of Friends Against Slavery and the Slave Trade* (Philadelphia, 1843), 24–27.

47. Quoted in Jack D. Marietta, *The Reformation of American Quakerism 1748–1783* (Philadelphia: University of Pennsylvania Press, 1984), 275.

48. Committee to Inquire into the Conditions of Freed Slaves, "Minute Book," 1781–1785, Historical Society of Pennsylvania, Minutes of Philadelphia Yearly Meeting 1776.

49. Committee to Inquire into the Conditions of Freed Slaves, "Minute Book," 1781–1785, Historical Society of Pennsylvania, July 30, 1785, and Historical Society of Pennsylvania, Minutes 55 of Philadelphia Yearly Meeting 1776.

50. Nash and Soderlund, *Freedom by Degrees*, 4.

51. Emma Lapsansky, *The Black Presence in Pennsylvania: "Making it Home"* (University Park: Pennsylvania Historical Association, 2001), 7.

52. Nash and Soderlund, *Freedom by Degrees*, 4

53. Anthony Benezet to George Dillwyn, anno. 1783, Haverford College Quaker Collection. Cadbury, "Anthony Benezet as a Friend," p. 360.

54. Anthony Benezet to George Dillwyn, (not dated by Anthony Benezet, on back of sheet in another hand: Philadelphia, Anno 1783), Haverford College Quaker Collection.

55. Dates of emancipation in the northern states were 1771, Vermont; 1780, Pennsylvania (gradually instituted); 1783, Massachusetts; 1783, New Hampshire; 1784, Rhode Island; 1799, New York (gradually instituted); and 1804, New Jersey (gradually instituted; abolition completed by statute in 1846). Jessie Carney Smith, ed., *Black Firsts: 2,000 years of Extraordinary Black Achievement,* in *Chronology of African American History,* 8 (Detroit: Visible Ink, 1994), 68.

56. Needles, *Historical Memoir of the Pennsylvania Society for Promoting the Abolition of Slavery,* 26.

57. Ibid., 26.

58. Nash and Soderlund, *Freedom by Degrees,* 124.

59. Ibid., 125.

60. Margaret H. Bacon lists Benjamin Franklin as its president, with James Pemberton, secretary, Jonathan Penrose, second vice president, and Benjamin Rush and Tench Coxe as secretaries. *History of the Pennsylvania Society for Promoting the Abolition of Slavery,* 3

61. For a full list of officers throughout the years see *The Oldest Abolition Society: Being a Short Story of the Labors of the Pennsylvania Society for the Promoting the Abolitions of Slavery, the Relief of Free Negroes Unlawfully Held in Bondage, and for Improving the Condition of the African Race* (Philadelphia: Published for the Society, 1911), 13–14.

62. Drake, *Quakers and Slavery in America,* 94.

63. Needles, *Historical Memoir of the Pennsylvania Society for Promoting the Abolition of Slavery,* 30.

64. Price, "Observations on the Importance of American Liberty" (London, 1787).

65. Needles, *Historical Memoir of the Pennsylvania Society for Promoting the Abolition of Slavery,* 30.

66. Ibid., 31.

67. Ibid., 31.

68. Hoare, *Memoirs of Granville Sharp,* 252–53, Stuart, *A Memoir of Granville Sharp,* 32–33.

69. Benjamin Rush to Jeremy Belknap, August 19, 1788, in Rush, *Letters of Benjamin Rush,* vol. 1, 481.

70. Locke, *Antislavery in America,* 89.

71. Richard S. Newman, *The Transformation of American Abolitionism: Fighting Slavery in the Early Republic* (Chapel Hill: University of North Carolina Press, 2002), 47, 41–42, 23.

72. Donald L. Robinson, *Slavery, and the Structure of American Politics, 1765–1820* (New York: Harcourt Brace Jovanovich, 1971); Duncan J. MacLeod, *Slavery, Race and the American Revolution* (London: Cambridge University Press, 1974).

73. Adam Rothman, *Slave Country: American Expansion and the Origins of the Deep South* (Cambridge, Mass.: Harvard University Press, 2005), 4, 33–34. Rothman adds "thus, the Federal Constitution protected slavery without ever using the word. The three-fifths clause (Article 1, Section 2) gave an advantage in the House of Representatives to states with large slave populations. The slave-trade clause (Article 1, Section 9) prevented the national government from prohibiting the importation of slaves for twenty years. As the fugitive clause (Article 4, Section 2) prevented runaway slaves from finding any legal refuge in 'free' states" (4).

74. Quoted in Rappleye, *Sons of Providence,* 243.

75. Bumbrey, *Microfilm Publication of the Papers of the Pennsylvania Abolition Society.*

76. Sparks, *Works of Benjamin Franklin,* vol. 10, 513–14. See also *The Oldest Abolition Society,* 4–5.

77. *The Oldest Abolition Society,* 4–5.

78. Anthony Benezet, *Observations on Slavery* (Philadelphia, 1788). It was bound with *Serious Considerations on Several Important Subjects, viz., On War and Its Inconsistency with the Gospel and the Bad Effects of Spirituous Liquors*, also written in 1788.

79. Newman, *Transformation of American Abolitionism*, 22.

80. Sparks, *Works of Benjamin Franklin*, vol. 10, 513–14.

81. In Edward Raymond Turner, *The Negro in Pennsylvania: Slavery—Servitude—Freedom, 1639–1861* (Washington, D.C.: American Historical Association, 1911), 215.

82. Newman, *Transformation of American Abolitionism*, 28–30.

83. Needles, *Historical Memoir of the Pennsylvania Society for the Promoting the Abolition of Slavery*, 28.

84. Bumbrey, *Microfilm Publication of the Papers of the Pennsylvania Abolition Society*.

85. Anthony Benezet to Queen Charlotte, August 25, 1783, Haverford College Quaker Collection.

86. Benezet, *Notes on the Slave Trade* (1783).

87. Benezet, *Observations on Slavery*, 27.

88. Benezet, *Observations on Slavery*, 28. Benezet noted at the bottom of the page, "By a law of the Province of North-Carolina, May 1777. All Slaves who have been set free, except by license first obtained form the County court, for what said court shall judge to be a meritorious service, shall be seized and sold by the sheriff to the highest bidder."

89. Benezet, *Short Observations on Slavery: "Introduction to Some Extracts from the Writing of the Abbe Raynal, on That Important Subject"* (Philadelphia, 1781), 12.

90. Benjamin Rush to Granville Sharp, May 1, 1773, in Butterfield, *Letters of Benjamin Rush*, 80–81.

91. The will of Anthony Benezet. Pemberton Papers, Historical Society of Pennsylvania.

92. J. Woods, *Thoughts on the Slavery of the Negroes* (London, 1784), 15. Like Equiano and Cugoano, Woods wrote at the bottom of the page, "Ch. 7—Benezet on the Slave Trade."

93. Thomas Cooper's *Letters on the Slave Trade: First Published in Wheeler's Manchester Chronicle and since re-printed with Additions and Alterations* (Manchester, 1787), Africanus [Rev. William Leigh], *Remarks on the Slave Trade, and the Slavery of the Negroes, in a Series of Letters* (London: J. Phillips and Norwich: Chase and Co., 1788) James Field Stanfield, *Observations on a Guinea Voyage, in a series of Letters Addressed to the Rev. Thomas Clarkson* (London: James Phillips, 1788).

94. Marcus Rediker, *The Slave Ship: A Human History* (New York: Viking, 2007), 133, 385 note 22.

95. "EXTRACT of a Letter from Henry Gandy of Bristol, formerly Captain in the African Trade, to William Dillwyn of Walthamstow dated 26th of 7th Month 1783." Appendix X in the 1788 London edition of *Some Historical Account of Guinea*.

96. Philadelphia Monthly Meeting the 29th of the 4th month, 1785, in Brookes, *Friend Anthony Benezet*, 175.

97. Rush, *Essays Literary, Moral and Philosophical*, 186.

98. Joseph Redman to Benjamin Rush, November 14, 1798, in Brookes, *Friend Anthony Benezet*, 59 (original letter in Ridgeway Library, Philadelphia).

99. *Evening Fireside* 1 (1805), 169.

100. Philip S. Foner and George E. Walker, eds., *Proceedings of the Black State Conventions, 1840–1865*, vol. 1, *New York, Pennsylvania, Indiana, Michigan, Ohio* (Philadelphia: Temple University Press, 1979), 125.

101. Ibid.

102. John F. Watson, *Annals of Philadelphia and Pennsylvania in the Olden Time*

Being a Collection of Memoirs, Anecdote, and Incidents of the City and Its Inhabitants and of the Earliest Settlement of the Inland Part of Pennsylvania, from the Days of the Founders (Philadelphia: Elijah Thomas, 1857), 373.

103. Benjamin C. Bacon, *Statistics of the Colored People of Philadelphia*, 2nd ed. (Philadelphia: Board of Education, 1859).

104. Armistead, *Anthony Benezet*, 74. *Brief Statement of the Rise and Progress of Antislavery in the Society of Friends*, 58, 59.

105. Benezet is buried in the graveyard on which the Arch Street Meeting House was later built.

106. Rush, *Essays Literary, Moral and Philosophical* (Philadelphia, 1806). Reprint editions, ed. and with introduction by Michael Meranze, *Essays, Literary and Philosophical* (Schenectady, N.Y.: Union College Press, 1988), 186.

107. Rush's work was first published in the *Columbian Magazine; or Monthly Miscellany* (Philadelphia: Sedden, Spotswood, Cist and Trenchard, 1787), 235–38. The South Carolina editors added only one line: "SIR, I seldom dream, and when I do, seldom dream of any thing worthy of the attention of the public." "To the EDITOR of the COLUMBIAN MAGAZINE in *State Gazette of South-Carolina*," December 12, 1787, vol. 46, issue 3573, page [1].

108. For an excellent literary analysis of Rush's *Dream* and the language of other eighteenth-century antislavery advocates, see Philip Gould, *Barbaric Traffic: Commerce and Antislavery in the Eighteenth-Century Atlantic World* (Cambridge, Mass.: Harvard University Press, 2003).

109. Godfrey Loyer (a French monk), on the Gold Coast of Africa in 1711, wonderfully described this aspect of the religious doctrines of the Africans: "The doctrine of the Transformation of the Souls is believed by the Negros; so that hoping for nothing real or permanent, they are only concentrated to gather riches and enjoy the Pleasures of this Life as long as they can. When you talk to them of heaven or hell, they burst-out laughing. They believe the World to be eternal, and the Soul immortal; that after their death their Soul will go to the other World, which they place in the Centre of the Earth; that there it will animate a new Body in the Womb of a Woman; and that the Souls from thence, would do the same. So that according to this doctrine, there is a constant Intercourse or Exchange of inhabitants between these two worlds." Godfrey Loyer, a Jacobite, *Abstract of a Voyage to Iffini on the Gold Coast in 1701 with a Description of the Country and Its Inhabitants*, in Astley, *New General Collection*, vol. 2, 441–42.

110. Rush, "Paradise of Negro Slaves—A Dream," in *Essays Literary, Moral and Philosophical*, 188–89.

Primary Sources

Antislavery Collection: Eighteenth and Nineteenth Centuries, Library of the Society of Friends, London, England (37 volumes on 25 microfilm reels)
Arch Street Meeting House, Department of Records, Philadelphia:
    Minutes of the Africans' School, 1770–1784, 2 volumes
    Papers of the Friendly Association, 1756–1760, 2 volumes
    Minutes of the African Free School
    Manumission records
Bibliothèque nationale de France, François Mitterrand, Paris, Anthony Benezet materials
Black Abolitionist Papers Microfilm, 17 reels, Ann Arbor, Michigan: University Microfilms, 1981–1983
British Library:
    Thomas Clarkson Collection
    "Minute Book of the Committee for the Society for the Effecting the Abolition of the Slave Trade"
    Granville Sharp Collection
    Hans Sloane Caribbean Manuscripts
    Papers of William Wilberforce
    Parliamentary Debates, 1792
Folger Shakespeare Library
Georgetown University, Lauinger Special Collections, Petition of Belinda, a slave, February 4, 1783, *American Museum or Universal Magazine,* vol. 1, 1787
Haverford College Library, Quaker Collection, Haverford, Pennsylvania:
    Papers and Letters of Anthony Benezet, ms. coll. 853 (includes letters Benezet wrote and those written to him)
    Allinson Family Papers 1702–1939 (ms. coll. 968)
    Dillwyn Family Papers
    Fothergill Family Papers
    George Vaux Collection of correspondence and documents, 1659–1914 (ms. coll. 1167)
    Letters of Moses Brown, 1774, 1776, 1783, 1787
    London Yearly Meeting, Epistles sent and received, 1713–1714
    London Yearly Meeting, Extracts of Minutes, 1757–1783
    New England Yearly Meeting, Minutes, 1717–1774
    Marginal notes in personal library of Anthony Benezet
    Manumission Certificates, Philadelphia Yearly Meetings
    Minutes and records of Penn Charter School, 2 volumes
    Minutes and records of Philadelphia Yearly Meeting, 1740–1784, microfilm of originals
    Minutes of Philadelphia Yearly Meeting, M. for S., 1755–1784, microfilm of originals.
    Philadelphia Yearly Meeting, Minutes, PYM, 1688–1716

Minutes of PYM, M. for S., 1755–1784, microfilm of originals
Minutes of PYM, M. for S., 1755–1784, microfilm of originals
Philadelphia Yearly Meeting, Minutes, 1688–1716
Philadelphia Yearly Meeting, Minutes, 1796
Philadelphia Yearly Meeting, Minutes, PYM, 1723–1743
Philadelphia Yearly Meeting, Minutes, 1754–1758, and *An Epistle of Caution and Advice*
Philadelphia Yearly Meeting, Minutes, 1760–1776
Philadelphia Monthly Meeting Minutes, PMM, 1698–1700
Philadelphia Monthly Meeting, Minutes, PMM, 1757–1778
North Carolina Yearly Meeting, Minutes, 1755–1780
Philadelphia Yearly Meeting, 1779–1783
Statutes at Large of Pennsylvania, 1700, 1712
The Constitution of the Pennsylvania Society for Promoting the Abolition of Slavery
Historical Society of Pennsylvania, Philadelphia:
American miscellaneous, Case 8, Box 6
Benezet Papers, Yi 2, 7291–7193
Benjamin Lay, *All Slave-Keepers That Keep the Innocents in Bondage, Apostates Pretending to Lay Claim to the Pure & Holy Christian Religion*
Dr. Benjamin Rush, Manuscript correspondence
Pemberton Papers, vol. 32, 106, the Will of Anthony Benezet
Vaux Papers
Pennsylvania Abolition Society Manuscripts
Preamble of the Free African Society
Library Company of Philadelphia:
Letter books of Granville Sharp, Benjamin Rush, and Thomas Clarkson
Autographed Manuscript Will Signed, Anthony Benezet
Benjamin Franklin, *An Address to the Public,* from the Pennsylvania Society for the Promoting of the Abolition of Slavery
Library of Congress, Marian S. Carson Collection, William Thornton Papers:
Manuscript Division, Hazards Collection: Rare Book Collection
Liverpool Central Public Library, *The Liverpool Memorandum Book; or, gentleman's, merchant's and tradesman's daily pocket-journal, for the year M,DCC,LIII: so contrived as to be useful and convenient for all sorts of people, particularly, with regard to their expensed and occasional*
National Archives, Washington, D.C., Quaker Petition to Congress, Record Group 360
Rutgers University Libraries, Special Collections.
Smithsonian Institution Libraries, National Museum of American History, Antislavery Collection
Swarthmore College, Pennsylvania Friends' Historical Collection, "Minutes of the Committee's appointed by the Three Monthly Meetings of Friends of Philadelphia to the Oversight and Care for Educating Africans and Their Descendants Commencing on the 28th of the 5th month 1770"
Trinity College, Hartford, Conn., Watkinson Library Rare Book Collection, Letter of Jean Pierre Brissot, July 1, 1786
University of Pennsylvania Archives, Philadelphia:
Caspar Wistar Papers
Timothy Matlack Papers
William Penn Charter School Archives, 1666–1981 (ms. coll. 1115)

Index

Acknowledgments

I have been fortunate at Georgetown University. There I have been a student, a worker, an alumnus, a professor, and most recently the proud father of a Georgetown graduate. Along the way I found support and kindness from many souls. Late-night talks with the security guards, especially Patricia Watkins, and early-morning talks with the janitorial crews have kept my feet on the ground. Elizabeth English, Djuana Shields, and Kathy Gallagher of the history department have given helping hands along the way. The librarians at Lauinger Library have always answered my queries and aided me in my research. Special thanks go to Professor Emeritus Dorothy Brown. She is one grand lady. The president of Georgetown University, Jack DeGioia, offered me meaningful employment, which helped me provide for my family when I was in graduate school. Darryl E. Christmon, vice president and chief financial officer for the Georgetown main campus, has been a kind and supportive colleague. I am indebted to Carole Sargent and Andrew Rolfson of Georgetown's Office of Scholarly Publications.

My mentor, Marcus Rediker, formerly of Georgetown and now at the University of Pittsburgh, first steered me to Anthony Benezet. Often times I have thanked him for that and often times I have not. His profound knowledge of early American and Atlantic history and his penetrating studies of "history from below" have inspired me.

Many members of the faculty at Georgetown have offered their kind words and insights. They have treated me with dignity and respect, and that is all a person could ask for in this sometimes-unkind world. I am especially grateful to Adam Rothman, Joe McCartin, and Michael Kazin, who read key sections and complicated formulations. My faculty chair, John Tutino, along with Gabor Agoston, Chandra Manning, David Goldfrank, Osama Abi-Mershed, Catherine Evtuhov, Andrzej Kaminski, and Judith Tucker always inquired of my work, which lifted my spirits. Richard Stites, who shares my love for the cultures of the world and the American popular song, showed me that a serious scholar can also have serious fun. Without the support of Jim Collins this project could not have been completed. Although he has been in the midst of finishing several important books on early modern French history, he always took the time to discuss my ideas and to assure me that there was really a light at the end of the tunnel. He has been my teacher, my colleague, and my friend, made more special by our common love for our children, for the study of history, the game of basketball, and the music of Thelonious Monk. Former Georgetown student Amy Byers was essential in the final editing of this project and Lena Jackson, also a recent Georgetown graduate, aided me in countless ways, especially in locating and analyzing maps and along with Miles Jackson, the ways of computers. I am indebted to Denise Benskin and Sarah Cook, two outstanding students, who did research and translations related to the debates over slavery in France and the development of the Société des Amis des Noirs, and to Jim Collins and Alyssa Goldstein Sepinwall, two leading scholars of early modern France, for their insights. Former dean Jane Dammen McAuliffe, the new president of Bryn Mawr, supported my efforts, as did Rosemary Kilkenny, Georgetown's Vice President for Institutional Diversity, Equity and Affirmative Action, and Angelyn Mitchell, director of the African American Studies Program.

Robin Blackburn of Verso Press and Yale Professor Emeritus David Brion Davis gave me precious time whenever I visited with them. I am equally indebted to James Miller of George Washington University, Lou Outlaw of Vanderbilt University, Father Joseph Brown S.J. of Southern Illinois University, David Schwartzman and Ethelbert Miller of Howard University, Clarence Lusane at the American University, Charles Behling of the University of Michigan, and James Early at the Smithsonian Institution. Although they come from different scholarly disciplines they always showed that great scholars could also be great human beings.

I have visited many libraries and research facilities. I thank all of those who I have burdened with my queries and demands. I thank the librarians, especially those at the rare book collections and archives at Howard University, Yale University, Bryn Mawr College, the University of Pennsylvania, Swarthmore College, Trinity College, the Library of Congress, Haverford College, and Georgetown University. Roger Bruns at the National Archives showed me the way to invaluable materials. Bonita Grant of the Rutgers University Special Collections and Harold Batie of the Folger Shakespeare Library offered kind assistance.

Stephanie Thomas and Jim Roan of the Smithsonian Institution's American History Library provided key assistance in helping me locate articles and borrow books and microfilm from all over the country and England. I owe special thanks to the good people at Special Collections Haverford College: Ann Upton, the Quaker bibliographer and special collections librarian; Diana Franzusoff Peterson, manuscripts librarian; and Emma Lapsansky-Werner, professor of Quaker history and curator of the Quaker Collection. A special appreciation is given to the Society of Friends in Philadelphia but especially to Margaret Bacon, historian of the Quakers, and William Spawn, keeper of the records. Mr. Spawn paved the way for my work among the voluminous records at the Quaker archives in the Philadelphia area. The Friends Historical Association in London, England, also aided me in locating valuable Quaker records, statements, and correspondence. Phil Lapsansky at the Library Company of Philadelphia; Adrienne Petrisko at the Public Library in Ardmore, Pennsylvania; and Peter Hogg of the British Museum offered invaluable help in the searching of Scottish philosophical works and African travel narratives. The staff at the Liverpool Central Library, in Liverpool, England, helped me locate very important commercial records concerning the slave trade in the eighteenth century. At the University of Pennsylvania, Michael Zuckerman and Richard Dunn, former director of the McNeil Center for Early American Studies, always gave me their time and insight into complicated topics, as did other members of the center's weekly seminars. My gratitude goes to Robert Lockhart, senior editor at the University of Pennsylvania Press, who realized the need for a study on Benezet, and to Noreen O'Connor-Abel, project editor, who skillfully and with great patience helped me ready this work for publication.

A fellowship at the Kluge Center for Scholarly Studies at the Library of Congress allowed me to complete the research and much of the final writing for this study. Special thanks go to James Billington, Secretary of the Library of Congress, to Kluge Center director, Carolyn Brown, to Mary Lou Reeker, and to the entire Kluge staff. A special thanks goes to Meg McAleer of the manuscript division. Reference librarians Sybil Moses, Tony Mullan, Bruce Martin, Betty Culpepper, and Mike Klein, at the Geography and Map Division, went beyond the call of duty in assisting me.

I have been fortunate to receive research grants from Georgetown University, the Carnegie Mellon Foundation, Haverford College, and the Library Company of Philadelphia. I have also served as a fellow at the Smithsonian Institution and the McNeil Center for Early American Studies at the University of Pennsylvania, and as the Ann Plato Fellow at Trinity College, which allowed me to do initial research.

A special thanks goes to the members of my jazz fraternity, the brothers of the Listening Group, especially Tom Porter, Ron Clark, Medaris Banks, Tony Rankin, and Lou Marshall. We African American men have gotten together once a month for years to share fine food, lively conversation, and great jazz music. My best buddies have always been there for me in thought and deed. James Steele of Brooklyn, New York, always called at just the right time to give support. James Bennett provided good information on Washington, D.C., politics. Hank Hucles of Gloucester, Virginia, always encouraged me to "loosen up." He and his family allowed me to take my family down to Gloucester, a wonderful place on the water and in the country. It is the site of Bacon's Rebellion and of Jackson's retreat. My godparents, Esther and the late James Jackson, of Brooklyn, New York, by way of Virginia, heroes of the movement for social justice, checked on me constantly to offer support.

My greatest debt goes to my family. Laura Ginsburg, my wife, is my anchor and my heart. One often hears people talk about their better halves, but when you put both halves together many times you get only 40 percent. But with Laura I start with 150 percent, and anything I bring to the table is just gravy—for it was she who kept the family together, as I for years traveled the city, country, and the globe trying to make the world a better place, and when I did not succeed, turned to my dream of becoming a college professor. My daughter, Lena, has been my savior and my redeemer. I wish I had her spirit and her ability to take life in stride. My son, Miles, has been my courage and my humor, my inspiration and my spirit. On way too many nights they have been awakened as I yelled at the computer, and they rushed to my study to help me find what I had lost. My mother, Zeola D. Ballard, has been my kindness and my forgiveness. She encouraged me to give up work in the Newport News Shipyard years ago to complete undergraduate school. My grandmother, the late Pearl L. Dickinson, the woman who helped raise me in the Piney Woods of Alabama and Newport News, would be proud. She only finished the third grade and never made more than a few dollars a week, washing the clothes of the rich white people, but her dignity always prevailed. She will forever be my hero and my shero. To all, I can only offer the words of Kahlil Gibran: "Your kindness touched my silent heart and made it sing."

LaVergne, TN USA
02 October 2009
159673LV00004B/1/P